**Great inland hi...
east–west**

Page 206

The east–west highways link Highway One
with Australia's vast interior. Discover historic
mining towns and a sunburnt landscape of
wheat and sunflowers. Welcome to rural
Australia.

g Tasmania

4

Spirit of Tasmania across Bass
explore the highways and byways
nd State. Fascinating historical
exquisite national parks are
to this small landmass.

Dear Dad,
We hope you get
many happy travels,
Love Steve, Kelly
& Eli bump
(Happy Birthday)
(2003

Explore
Australia by
Caravan

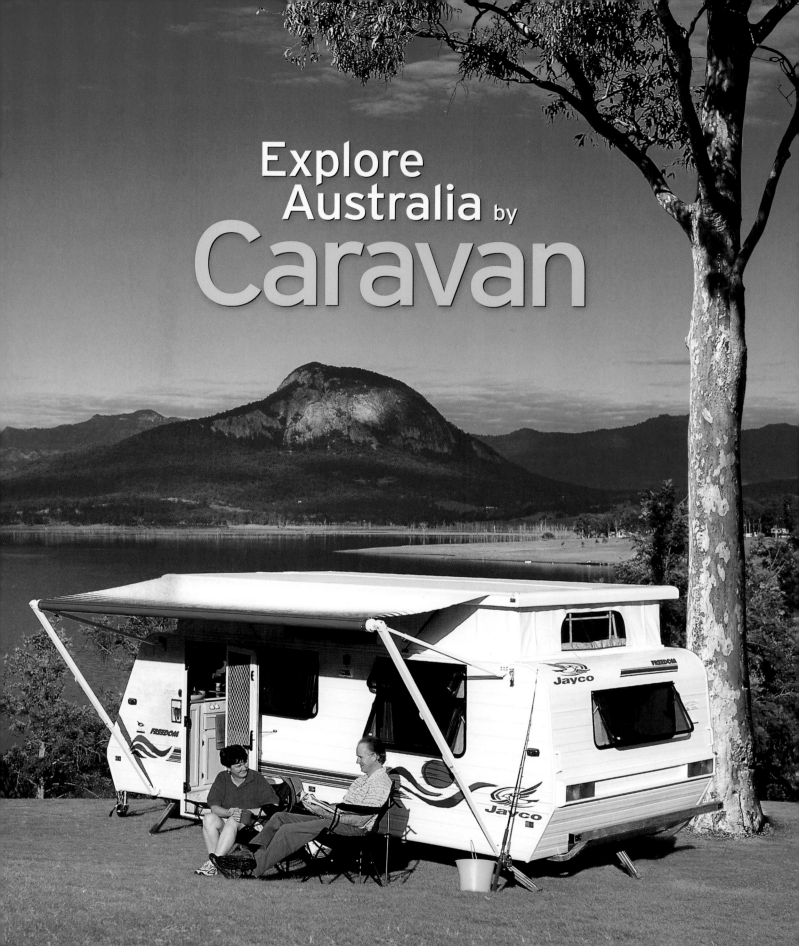

Explore
Australia by
Caravan

EXPLORE AUSTRALIA

Explore Australia Publishing Pty Ltd
12 Claremont Street
South Yarra, Victoria 3141, Australia

First edition published by Explore Australia Publishing Pty Ltd, 2003

10 9 8 7 6 5 4 3 2 1

Printed and bound in China by Everbest Printing Co. Ltd

National Library of Australia
Cataloguing-in-Publication data

Tait, John, 1948– .
    Explore Australia.

    Includes index.
    ISBN 1 74117 000 1.

    1. Automobile travel – Australia – Guidebooks. 2. Trailer
    camps – Australia – Guidebooks. 3. Australia – Guidebooks.
    I. Tait, Jan, 1949– . II. Title.

919.4047

Publisher's note: Every effort has been made to ensure that the information in this book is accurate at the time of going to press. The publisher welcomes information and suggestions for correction or improvement. Write to the Publications Manager, Explore Australia Publishing, 12 Claremont Street, South Yarra, Victoria 3141, Australia or email explore@hardiegrant.com.au

Disclaimers: The publisher cannot accept responsibility for any errors or omissions. The representation on the maps of any road or track is not necessarily evidence of public right of way. Prices and opening hours of attractions and fees and facilities at caravan parks are subject to change; remember to phone ahead and confirm details.

Photographs:
Front cover: Travelling along David Low Way near Noosa. 4WD courtesy of Nissan and caravan courtesy of Jayco.
    Explore Australia Publishing/Nick Rains
Back cover: Road through the Boranup Forest, Western Australia.
    Andrew Gregory
Back cover inset images from top to bottom: Cabin/Image courtesy of Ellis Beach Oceanfront Bungalows and Leisure Park, Queensland; Camper trailer/Image courtesy of Heaslip Camper Trailers; Motorhome/Image courtesy of Swagman
Half-title page: Driving along the beach at Fraser Island.
    Nick Rains
Title page: Phil and Jillian Parker in front of caravan at Moogerah Dam, near Ipswich. Caravan courtesy of Jayco.
    Explore Australia Publishing/Nick Rains

CONTENTS

HOW TO USE THIS BOOK

Explore Australia by Caravan is divided into five main sections.

Our favourite parks

A list of all 'Authors' choice' caravan parks from around Australia – the top recommendations. Contains a description of each park and a reference to the relevant map and page number in full caravan park directory.

Chapters 1, 2, 3 and 4

Chapter 1 takes you around Australia on Highway One. It is divided into segments of the journey, like Melbourne to Sydney, with each segment then divided into smaller parts, like Bega to Batemans Bay. Bega to Batemans Bay and all other legs of the trip have a double-page spread that includes a map, details on major towns on or near the tour route, photographs and descriptions of attractions in the area, travel tips, local festival information, and details of Authors' choice caravan parks in the region. Chapter 2, 3 and 4 follow the same format. Chapter 2 covers the great inland highways – south–north, Chapter 3 great inland highways east–west, and Chapter 4 Tasmania.

Making the most of your trip

The essential information on choosing and preparing a rig, trip timing and planning, permits, finances, packing and road rules.

Australian road atlas

Provides map coverage of each state.

Caravan park directory

A directory of 600 caravan parks on or near the tour routes, and recommended by the authors. Each entry has contact details, a brief description of the park, and details on sites, facilities and payment.

Roads, highways and freeways covered in the trip, and total number of kilometres.

TOUR OPENING

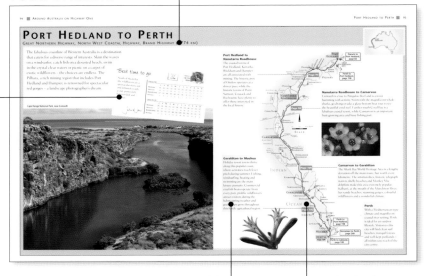

Weather details for the region, to give you an idea of the best time of year to visit.

Brief overview of each section of the trip; information on the landscape and towns, cities and attractions.

Map showing the whole trip from start to finish.

Caravan park recommended in directory.

Authors' choice caravan park.

Travel tip on how to make the most of your time in the area.

Practical notes on the roads, highways and freeways you will travel on.

TOUR SECTION

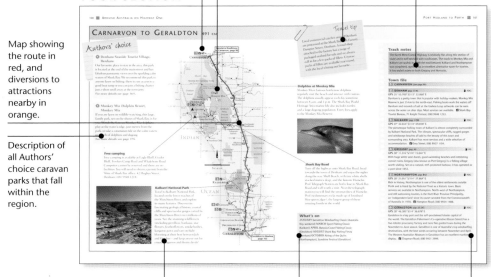

Map showing the route in red, and diversions to attractions nearby in orange.

Description of all Authors' choice caravan parks that fall within the region.

Descriptions and photographs on attractions in the area, with relevant contact details.

List of local events and festivals throughout the year that may coincide with your trip.

Brief overview of the major towns on or near the route, with details of town population, geographical position and visitor information centres.

Details on attractions in and around the city.

CITY FEATURE

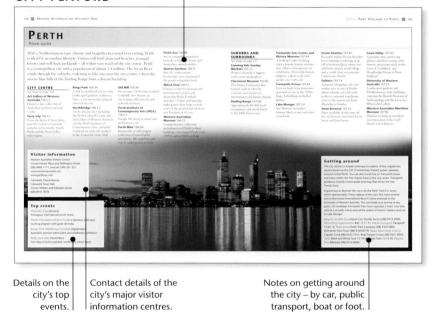

Details on the city's top events.

Contact details of the city's major visitor information centres.

Notes on getting around the city – by car, public transport, boat or foot.

AUSTRALIAN ROAD ATLAS

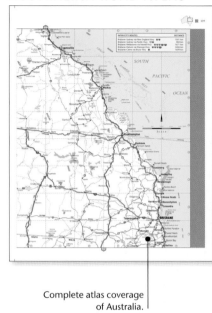

Complete atlas coverage of Australia.

CITY MAPS

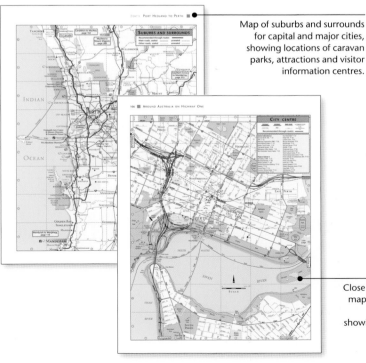

Map of suburbs and surrounds for capital and major cities, showing locations of caravan parks, attractions and visitor information centres.

Close up city-centre map of capital and major cities, showing attractions in the area.

CARAVAN PARK DIRECTORY

Directory containing 600 caravan parks on or near the tour routes; each listing with contact details, a brief description, and information on sites, facilities and payment.

Alphabetical by location, with references to the page/map it appears on within the relevant chapter.

MAP LEGEND

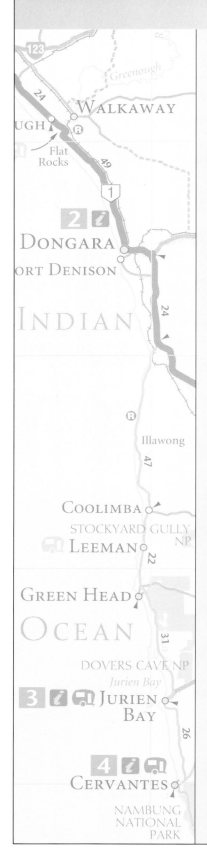

TOURING INFORMATION

🚐 Recommended caravan park (listed in directory)
◉ Authors' choice caravan park (listed in directory)
🚐 Other caravan park
ℹ Visitor information centre
RH Roadhouse
▲ Camping area
⊙ Rest area without toilets
🅃 Rest area with toilets
🅖 Rest area with toilets – camping permitted
O'Sullivans Gap ● Place of interest
Clark Dam ● Landmark
✈ Commercial airport
Sugarloaf Point Lighthouse ★ Lighthouse
McArthur River Mine ✕ Mine site
⛽ PDG Petrol Diesel Gas (in Town file)
1 Information in Town file (Highway One)
2 Information in Town file (north–south routes)
3 Information in Town file (east–west routes)
4 Information in Town file (Tasmanian routes)
HEXHAM Beginning/end of trip (Highway One)
MOREE Beginning/end of trip (north–south)
ORANGE Beginning/end of trip (east–west)
ROSEBERY Beginning/end of trip (Tasmanian routes)

ROADS AND RELATED SYMBOLS

	Tour route	Diversions	Other roads
Freeway/highway/main road, sealed			
Highway/main road, unsealed			
Other road, sealed			
Other road, unsealed			
Vehicular track			
Other linear features	Ferry	Walking Track	RAILWAY
	Dog Fence	STATE BORDER	Fruit Fly Exclusion Zone

National highway route marker   M31 A87 1
National route marker   1 A1
State route marker   5
Metroad route marker   4
Toll   ▯ Toll
Toll gantry, Melbourne only   ▯ Toll (e-TAG)
Agricultural check point   △ Agricultural Check Point
Kilometres between two points   ▸ 25 ▸

CITIES, TOWNS AND LOCALITIES

State capital	◉ BRISBANE
Town over 50 000	◉ NEWCASTLE
Town 10 000–50 000	◉ BROOME
Town 5000–10 000	◉ KATHERINE
Town 1000–5000	◎ TOCUMWAL
Town 200–1000	◎ BURKETOWN
Town under 200	○ PAYNES FIND
Suburb	○ HORNSBY
Aboriginal community	◎ DOOMADGEE
Homestead	□ Theda
Locality	○ Bombah Point

WATER FEATURES

Permanent Lake

Intermittent Lake

River — Waterfall

River — Lock

Island
Reef

MARINE RESERVES

LAND FEATURES

NATIONAL PARKS

OTHER RESERVES

ABORIGINAL LANDS

PROHIBITED AREAS

INTRODUCTION

ABOUT THE AUTHORS

Born in New South Wales and now based in Queensland's Gold Coast hinterland, John and Jan Tait have spent many years travelling around Australia and leading tour groups to its remotest corners. John and Jan have an extensive knowledge of and passion for Australia, and get enormous satisfaction from encouraging others to travel.

For us, many of our years have been spent camping in tents. Then came the camper-trailer, then the four-wheel drive camper, and then the Winnebago motorhome. Our Winnebago motorhome has celebrated more than 12 birthdays, and we carried out much of the research for this book in it.

We have experienced all facets of touring and thoroughly enjoy every part of it. We have been lucky, having had the opportunity to write touring books during our travels, and could see that there was the need for a friendly touring guide to assist all those adventurers, both new and experienced, who enjoy travelling in their caravans, campervans or motorhomes, or simply packing a tent and heading off.

The format of this book has been designed to make travelling as enjoyable and uncomplicated as possible. We felt that it was logical to structure the book around this country's great web of highways, and that it would have to include good quality, up-to-date maps. After lengthy planning it was agreed that these maps would be specially drawn for the book, aided by the extensive data we would collect in the field.

As well as specific details of different tour routes to take, we wanted to include friendly and usable information on towns and attractions to visit near the routes, and places to stay along the way.

There is really only one way to find out about many things – get out there, go and visit places, and draw your own conclusions. And that's what we did. We drove in excess of 70 000 km on the mainland and crossed Bass Strait to include Tasmania. Australia is a big country and if it is space you're looking for, then this is the right place. Australia's wonderful attractions – the rugged coastal ranges draped in rainforest, the wide treeless plains, the golden crops stretching across several States, the magnificent, sweeping sandy beaches – are all linked by kilometres of highways. Each of these highways is punctuated by cities, towns and small communities offering a wealth of different experiences.

Our vehicle was fitted with a Garmin GPS unit, which accurately recorded our movements everywhere we went. Jan also used the GPS (Global Positioning System) to record a host of other information including the specific location of roadside stops, accurate plots of town centres, and the exact locations of caravan parks and major intersections. This information was stored on a laptop computer before being whisked off to the cartographic team at *Explore Australia*, who have miraculously turned the data into a collection of wonderful maps. We spent more than a year collecting the detailed road information and the cartographic team have spent equally as long or longer meticulously drawing the maps.

We visited every one of the 600 caravan parks that we have recommended in this book, speaking with owners or managers and soaking up a little of the mood and ambience. Based on our findings and feelings we made a personal choice on whether to include these parks in this book, and have awarded an 'Authors' choice' logo to those that we felt offered something extra special.

We have thoroughly enjoyed writing this book and hope that you will enjoy using it. Australia is a great place, and if this book inspires you to get out there and see some of it, you will be greatly rewarded.

John & Jan

OUR FAVOURITE PARKS

Australia has a wealth of caravan parks. They are fantastic alternatives to motel rooms – they are cheaper and therefore perfect for big trips, they give you a taste of outdoor living, and, well, they accommodate caravans. To us, travelling in a caravan or motorhome, or simply exploring by car with a tent, is *the* best way to see Australia. If we were staying in motel rooms we would be missing out on half the fun.

Here is a list of our favourite parks – almost ninety of the best parks on or near the tour routes described in this book. These parks are the ones that we drop into whenever we have a chance, the ones we really look forward to staying at. They are located on the touring maps and are marked with this symbol ☺ 🚐 for easy reference.

We believe that good accommodation is important, which is why each time we have found a good caravan park we have made a note of it. It can be exciting, like finding a good meal in an unexpected place or meeting a friendly person full of information. It can be the making of a trip – that final thing that turns a good trip into a great one.

Many caravan parks have fabulous locations, great recreational facilities and activities, and unique features that can make your stay all the more interesting. They also offer you a great chance to meet other travellers over, say, a barbecue. Caravan parks are outdoor living at its finest, and you may decide that you never want to go home!

What makes a good caravan park can be any number of things, and usually a combination of them. A scenic location, good facilities, excellent service – normally we consider their price as well, but we do believe that excellent parks are worth paying for.

Our favourites range from urban parks to those in regional towns, to parks in the outback and just about in the middle of nowhere. While it is probably not possible to organise your trip so that you stay at one of these parks every night, it is usually possible to stay in at least a few of these parks during your travels. For the other nights, you should be able to find the details of other recommended parks in our more comprehensive directory beginning on page 350.

We hope you will enjoy the Authors' choice parks as much as we have.

The lake at White Ibis Holiday Village in Sutton, New South Wales, is complete with ducks and all – a perfect place to unwind

John & Jan

New South Wales

Pick any river or beach in New South Wales and more times than not you will find a caravan park set up somewhere nearby. Caravan parks are in prime locations, like the caravan park right next to the Kiama Blowhole. As well as beaches, rivers and well known coastal towns, New South Wales has many other features, like the gorgeous Blue Mountains, and that desert outpost, Broken Hill. You will find good caravan parks in most holiday areas.

Blowhole Point Holiday Park, Kiama

With an outlook over the town and harbour, this park occupies a fabulous piece of real estate adjoining the lighthouse and the famous blowhole. Mostly protected from the south-easterly wind, the park has basic amenities, a restaurant, tennis courts and two rock pools for swimming in, but it is the spectacular views that make it so good.

For more details and map location see pages 16 and 372.

Blue Dolphin Holiday Resort, Yamba

This riverfront, award-winning park is on the Clarence River estuary. It is an excellent park, with everything you would expect of a five-star establishment, including a cafe. Yamba is a popular holiday town.

For more details and map location see pages 32 and 394.

Blue Lagoon Beach Resort, Bateau Bay

Tucked away at the water's edge, this beach-front park has a pool, spa and even its own restaurant. It is an ideal place for a quiet break, although it is busy at the height of the Christmas and Easter holidays.

For more details and map location see pages 26 and 354.

Boomerang Way Tourist Park, Tocumwal

This well-cared-for, owner-operated park is 500 m from the centre of Tocumwal and away from the highway's noise. The park has a large swimming pool as well as a covered barbecue area and is ideal both for an overnight stay or an entire holiday. Minimum bookings apply during the Christmas, January and Easter holiday periods.

For more details and map location see pages 154 and 390.

Broken Hill Caravan Park, Broken Hill

With its heated pool, covered barbecues and well-stocked kiosk, this large park is our pick of the Broken Hill parks and we regularly stay here. It is easily accessible from the Barrier Highway and is a good base in Broken Hill.

For more details and map location see pages 244 and 357.

Caves Caravan Park, Wellington

Relax and let a few days slip by at this spacious park, located 6 km south of the town centre alongside the Wellington Caves, a popular tourist attraction. It is a quality park and makes an ideal stopover.

For more details and map location see pages 240 and 393.

Dubbo City Caravan Park, Dubbo

Enjoy the sights of Dubbo from this quality park. Conveniently located on the Newell Highway about 2 km from the city centre and just a short drive from the Western Plains Zoo, this park has a selection of accommodation, plush lawns and good facilities, including a handy car-washing bay.

For more details and map location see pages 156, 240 and 364.

East's Bathurst Holiday Park, Kelso

This park is owned by one of the East brothers, well known in the caravan park industry. It is a quality park on the Great Western Highway, 5 km east of the centre of Bathurst, and offers a range of accommodation and great facilities. Minimum bookings apply during the Easter holidays, the October long weekend and Mount Panorama race weekends.

For more details and map location see pages 238 and 372.

Forbes River Meadows Caravan Park, Forbes

Located about 1.5 km south of Forbes, alongside the highway, this owner-operated park is a convenient and ideal overnight stop. It has shady trees, large expanses of lawn, spotless amenities and a pool. We like staying here.

For more details and map location see pages 156 and 366.

Garden of Eden Caravan Park, Eden

Enjoy the excellent amenities, tennis court and swimming pool at this well-appointed, reasonably priced park, just 2 km from the town centre. Things are always going on at this park, like the recent construction of a new laundry block and the installation of TV cables. This is a great place for an overnight stay or for a longer holiday. Pets are allowed at the owners' discretion.

For more details and map location see pages 10 and 365.

Griffith Tourist Caravan Park, Griffith

This owner-operated caravan park stands out because of its excellent facilities and the fact that it is a great base from which to explore the interesting Griffith area. It has a large number of ensuite sites, a pool, a spa and a tennis court. We always enjoy staying at Griffith.

For more details and map location see pages 166 and 369.

Holiday Hub Beach Resort, Pambula Beach

This beachside park is one of our favourite parks in the popular family holiday region of the south coast of New South Wales. It has a new pool complex, a licensed restaurant and spotless amenities, and is a great family park. The resident kangaroos will be

You will find kangaroos, rainbow lorikeets and gorgeous views at Holiday Hub Beach Resort

a hit with the children. A beach and a national park form the park's boundaries.

For more details and map location see pages 10 and 382.

Island View Beach Resort, Narooma

Stroll to the beach or picnic on green lawns under shady trees at this quality park, located on the Princes Highway 5 km south of Narooma. With very good amenities and lots of appeal, it is ideal for a family holiday and conveniently located for an overnight stay.

For more details and map location see pages 12 and 380.

Nelligen Park, Nelligen

What makes this park so appealing is its lovely setting on a grassy bend of the Clyde River. The township of Nelligen, just 10 km from Batemans Bay, is a great place to stay for a few days or even just overnight. The park is only a short walk from the town centre and the local hotel, which is well known for its meals. The park has good facilities and great expanses of green grass, spacious enough for a game of cricket.

For more details and map location see pages 14, 211 and 380.

North Star Holiday Resort, Hastings Point

This award-winning park has an impressive range of facilities, including a fully licensed restaurant. This park is a cut above most: the amenities are excellent, the beach is a short walk across the road and the town centre is just 500 m away – we highly recommend it.

For more details and map location see pages 34 and 369.

Ocean Beach Holiday Park, Umina

Just 2 km from the centre of Umina and set in a fabulous beachfront position, this

It is a tough choice between the beach and the pool at Ocean Beach Holiday Park, Umina

quality park is a favourite of ours. There is a wide range of facilities, and kids' activities are held most weekends and during the school holidays. It is only about an hour from Sydney. Minimum bookings sometimes apply.

For more details and map location see pages 26 and 392.

One Mile Beach Holiday Park is set on a fabulous curve of Anna Bay

One Mile Beach Holiday Park, Anna Bay

This quality, award-winning caravan park is located in the popular Port Stephens region, just a few kilometres south of Nelson Bay. Set alongside a popular patrolled surf beach, it has excellent amenities and great recreational facilities including mini-golf, a tennis court and a resort-style swimming pool. A real favourite with us – we always enjoy staying here.

For more details and map location see pages 28 and 352.

Racecourse Beach Tourist Park, Bawley Point

It is hard to resist staying at a wonderful, award-winning beachside park such as this. Just 9 km from the Princes Highway, it has good facilities including mini-golf, a heated pool, a sauna and a tennis court. Minimum bookings apply in peak holiday periods.

For more details and map location see pages 14 and 355.

Riverside Caravan Park, Croki

Set on the banks of the Manning River in a quiet off-highway location, this small, well-designed owner-operated park is a perfect base from which to explore the attractions of Ellenborough Falls and Crowdy Bay National Park. The park has

drive-through sites ideally suited for an overnight stop; however, if there is time, stay two nights so you can have a chance to see the local area.

For more details and map location see pages 28 and 362.

Riverside Caravan Park, Nyngan

We really like it when a lot of effort has gone into a park and this is the case with Riverside. The park is set in a quiet riverfront location on the western side of Nyngan and strategically located near the junction of the Mitchell and Barrier highways. It has most of the normal park facilities and, while it has highway frontage, it is set well back in large spacious grounds.

For more details and map location see pages 242 and 381.

Rose Gardens Tourist Park, Narromine

Within the grounds of this quality owner-operated park you will find a historic church, built in 1872. Along with this unusual feature the park offers a range of accommodation, including an ensuite railway carriage, and bicycles for hire. It is set alongside the Mitchell Highway on the eastern approach to Narromine and, in our opinion, is a great park at a very competitive price.

For more details and map location see pages 156, 242 and 380.

Seven Mile Beach Holiday Park, Gerroa

Swim at the beach or sit back, relax and watch TV at this large, fabulous beachside park. It has great facilities, including ensuite sites with full Austar TV hook-up. It also has excellent amenities and is in a wonderful location. The park is divided into two units by the main road.

For more details and map location see pages 16 and 367.

Sydney Lakeside Narabeen, Sydney

This is our pick of Sydney's caravan parks. It is a large, well-grassed park on the banks of Narrabeen Lake and just a short stroll from the beach. It is located in a quiet area, away from the city humdrum on the north shore. The excellent amenities complete the picture. This is a good base for exploring Sydney.

For more details and map location see pages 23 and 388.

In spring White Ibis Holiday Village comes alive with blossom

White Ibis Holiday Village, Sutton

Take the time to sit by the lake, relax and feed the ducks at White Ibis, one of our favourite parks. Located in a spacious rural setting around a lake, it is just 14 km north of Canberra and easily accessible from the Federal Highway. This is a good base for exploring Canberra and the park's facilities include a range of accommodation, a well-stocked shop and a tennis court. We enjoy staying here.

For more details and map location see pages 210, 215 and 389.

Northern Territory

There are some truly stunning places to visit in the Northern Territory, and many people return from a trip around Australia with some of their best memories, and photographs, from their time there. The Territory's attractions are too many to list: Uluru, Kakadu, Kings Canyon, Rainbow Valley, Darwin, Mataranka . . . In more recent years the Northern Territory has realised the commercial potential of its beauty, which means that there are now many first-class accommodation establishments, including a handful of excellent caravan parks.

Douglas Daly Tourist Park, Douglas Daly

This is a picturesque park on the banks of the Douglas River. Each Thursday they serve free coffee and scones for morning tea and on Wednesday and Sunday evenings they have buffalo roasts. The park is about 40 km along a sealed road from the Stuart Highway (turn off the highway 6 km north of the Hayes Creek Roadhouse). It has good facilities, including a licensed restaurant, and is close to the Douglas Hot Springs.

For more details and map location see pages 74 and 364.

Kings Creek Station, Kings Canyon

This large camping area on a cattle station is our choice of places to stay when we visit the Kings Canyon area. It caters solely for tourists and has numerous sites in bush settings. The facilities include a pool, barbecues, a restaurant and a shop. The station also offers several fabulous activities including camel rides, helicopter flights and quad (four-wheel motorbike) rides. Kings Canyon is 39 km away along a sealed road.

For more details and map location see pages 186 and 373.

Low Level Caravan Park, Katherine

This is one of the more appealing parks in Australia and we really enjoy staying here. Owner-operated, it has excellent facilities, including a relaxed licensed bistro and kiosk that operate during the winter tourist season. Bookings are absolutely essential at peak times.

For more details and map location see pages 75 and 372.

MacDonnell Range Holiday Park, Alice Springs

Enjoy a delicious, free pancake breakfast every Sunday morning at this large, quality park – one of the Alice Springs parks we choose to stay at. It has numerous activities during the tourist season (April to October), including nightly talks on the stars, bush tucker and other subjects, and has a great range of tourist park facilities. Located 4.5 km south of the city centre, it is a great base for exploring the region. Bookings are essential in the tourist season.

For more details and map location see pages 189, 193 and 352.

Outback Caravan Park, Tennant Creek

This large, well-appointed park is just 1 km from the town centre and off the highway. We find it an ideal base for a few days exploring this interesting area. Facilities include a pool, spa and a new entertainment area, for bush cooking and poetry recitals.

For more details and map location see pages 194, 260 and 390.

Kings Creek Station offers camel rides, quad rides and helicopter flights

Palms Village Resort, Darwin

Located on the Stuart Highway 19 km from Darwin, this is a large park with good facilities and a quality licensed restaurant. We find it a good base for exploring Darwin and the surrounding areas.

For more details and map location see pages 74, 79 and 363.

MacDonnell Range Holiday Park is in a stunning setting near the MacDonnell Ranges

Queensland

Many people have heard of or been to the Gold Coast, yet it is certainly not all Queensland has to offer. There are great places to visit both inland and north of that famous strip of coast and hopefully you will find time to travel in both directions. As you travel north above Brisbane the scenery and climate become quite tropical, with mangrove swamps, rainforest and magnificent beaches. Inland there are some rich agricultural and industrial areas, like the Darling Downs in the south, and the mining country in the north. Great caravan parks are incredibly plentiful; there is almost *too* much choice.

Bailey Bar Caravan Park, Charleville

We regularly stay at this very good owner-operated park. Set in a quiet, off-highway location about 1.5 km from the town centre, the park has great lawns, clean amenities and good facilities. It offers a range of accommodation and runs bush poetry events during the middle months of the year.

For more details and map location see pages 170 and 360.

Beachcomber Coconut Caravan Village, South Mission Beach

Mission Beach is a dream holiday destination and this park is a perfect place to stay. It is set in a fabulous location just across the road from the beach. Walk to the shops, play on the half-size tennis court or enjoy a barbecue. The park also has a resort-style swimming pool.

For more details and map location see pages 56 and 388.

Blue Gem Caravan and Tourist Park, Sapphire

For those interested in trying their luck in the gemfields, this award-winning park is a good base. It forms part of a shop and service-station complex and is centrally located in Sapphire on the banks of Retreat Creek, where sapphires were first discovered in 1875. Facilities at this park are excellent for the price.

For more details and map location see pages 258 and 387.

Broadwater Tourist Park, Gold Coast

Position is everything, and this spacious council-owned park fronts the Gold Coast broadwater. It has very good facilities and outstanding views across the water to Marina Mirage. The park has several restaurants within walking distance and is about 1.5 km from the Southport business and shopping centre.

For more details and map location see pages 36 and 368.

Cairns Coconut Caravan Resort, Cairns

Enjoy the excellent facilities of this five-star park, on the southern approach to Cairns 7 km from the centre. There is a cafe, a kids club in school holidays, free mini-golf, tennis and aqua aerobics, and the list continues. Yes, we have stayed here often and we like it a lot.

For more details and map location see pages 56, 60 and 359.

Exchange Hotel Van and Camping Park, Torrens Creek

This park has an unusual appeal and we like it. It is small, well maintained and conveniently located next to the Exchange Hotel. It is good value, being budget priced but with plenty of green grass, although there are only a small number of powered sites.

For more details and map location see pages 264 and 391.

Flying Fish Point Caravan Park, Flying Fish Point

This quality owner-operated park is opposite the water in this small town about 7 km from Innisfail. The park provides patrons with a free fish barbecue for lunch each Wednesday during the tourist season and there are a limited number of fishing dinghies available for use. The park has very good facilities.

For more details and map location see pages 56 and 366.

Fraser Lodge, Hervey Bay

Explore Hervey Bay, go whale-watching or relax and enjoy the pool, the barbecues and the tennis court at Fraser Lodge, a quality tourist park in Torquay, a quiet area of Hervey Bay. The park is just a short walk from the beach and close to many local restaurants.

For more details and map location see pages 46 and 370.

Gilbert Park Tourist Village, Cloncurry

We regularly stay at this quality family-operated park, located on the main highway 2 km east of the town centre. Relax in the pool and spa or enjoy a meal in the covered barbecue area. With clean amenities and a range of facilities, the park also adjoins a small rocky hill known as Sunset Hill, the perfect place to sit and enjoy the sunset.

For more details and map location see pages 176, 266 and 361.

Glebe Weir, via Taroom

Fishing is the main attraction at this popular, out-of-the-way camping area, 52 km north-east of Taroom. The weir is a renowned spot for yellow-belly and saratoga. The camping ground is reached along a narrow bitumen road from the highway. Amenities are basic and the showers are cold water only, but there are a number of powered sites. This is a great park for the budget conscious and is suitable for larger motorhomes.

For more details and map location see pages 162 and 367.

Karumba Point Tourist Park, Karumba

We like this popular, quality park, located 7.5 km from Karumba. It has a unique attraction: a free fish barbecue for guests each Wednesday and Saturday night during the winter tourist season. The park is always busy during the tourist season so booking is necessary.

For more details and map location see pages 178 and 372.

Kingfisher Camp, via Doomadgee

This is a great place to spend a few quiet days under shady trees on lush lawns beside a large waterhole on the Nicholson River. There are dinghies for hire. The camp is open between April and October and is reached along unsealed roads from Savannah Way to the west of Doomadgee. It is part of Bowthorn station.

For more details and map location see pages 68 and 373.

Major Mitchell Caravan Park, Mitchell

Soak away your aches at the artesian spa pools or wander into the centre of town for a bit of sightseeing, both just a short walk from this, modern popular park. Its greatest attraction, however, is the unique offer of the first two nights free, on all sites. This park gets very busy during the tourist season and space is often scarce. Check in at the Great Artesian Spa complex just over the river from the park.

For more details and map location see pages 254 and 378.

Mooloolaba Beach Caravan Park, Mooloolaba

This park is split into two sites. The main section is in Parkyn Parade, while the smaller section is at Mooloolaba Beach. We think the beachside section has the best outlook of any park in Australia: it overlooks the fabulous beach and is just across the road from the resort-style main street of this popular holiday town. The beachside section has sites for motorhomes, campervans and caravans but there are no tent sites. Registration is at Parkyn Parade.

For more details and map location see pages 44 and 378.

Myall Creek Caravan Park, Dalby

Enjoy dinner at one of the local bistros, pop into the RSL club for a drink or walk to the centre of town – all possible from this conveniently located park. Owner-operated, it is a good quality park with clean, modern amenities and easy access to the highway.

For more details and map location see pages 250 and 363.

Possum Park Caravan and Camping Park, Miles

We always enjoy staying at this unique caravan park. Once a World War II munitions dump, the underground bunkers have been

Some great caravan parks are tucked in amongst the high-rise buildings along Queensland's Gold Coast

converted to cabins. Owner-operated, it is a great park set in a quiet location alongside the Leichhardt Highway, 20 km north of Miles. It has clean amenities and good facilities.

For more details and map location see pages 160, 252 and 378.

Seventeen Seventy Camping Ground, Seventeen Seventy

It is hard to resist the excellent, absolute beachfront location of this council-owned park. At this subtropical hideaway it is almost possible to tie the dinghy up to the caravan. The park has good basic amenities, with a playground nextdoor. Beachfront sites are unpowered, though still very popular. Minimum bookings apply in holiday season.

For more details and map location see pages 48 and 387.

Sunset Caravan Park, Mount Isa

Relax by the pool or enjoy a meal in the pleasant barbecue area at this popular owner-operated park, situated 1.6 km from the centre of town and away from highway traffic. We feel that this is the best caravan park in Mount Isa and it may be necessary to book during the peak winter months.

For more details and map location see pages 261 and 379.

Tallebudgera Creek Tourist Park, Gold Coast

A favourite of ours, this popular holiday caravan park is about 5 km north of Palm Beach, towards Burleigh Heads. It fronts onto the Tallebudgera Creek and is just a short walk to the beach. This park is among the Gold Coast's best parks, centrally located with very good amenities and a wide range of facilities, including a tennis court and a heated pool.

For more details and map location see pages 37 and 368.

Travellers Rest Caravan and Camping Park, Midge Point

There are no more sandflies or midges at Midge Point than elsewhere, but there is a wonderful out-of-the-way beachside caravan park with lovely manicured lawns, large shady trees and a host of great features. We really enjoy staying here.

For more details and map location see pages 53 and 377.

Villa Holiday Park, Roma

This is our choice of places to stay in Roma. A winery and shop adjoin the park, and there are large grassed areas, modern facilities and a large selection of cabins. The park is well maintained and located about 2 km from the town centre. The quality of this park means it gets very busy during the tourist season and space is often scarce. We recommend you to book.

For more details and map location see pages 252 and 386.

Woodlands Holiday Village, Townsville

This is an interesting park located about 15 km north of the city alongside the Bruce Highway. The park has a good range of facilities and each site has private ensuite amenities. We find it a convenient place to stop overnight and often stay here.

For more details and map location see pages 52, 265 and 391.

South Australia

South Australia is a State with a rich and varied geography and a well-preserved history. A 3700-kilometre coastline curves around the south of the State offering a diversity of scenery, from the rugged coastline beneath the Nullarbor to the lush wetlands of the Coorong. Above Adelaide is a pocket of hills, valleys and lakes containing some of Australia's best known farming regions, and a short way north begins a vast tract of desert, the underground mining town of Coober Pedy at its centre. Travelling around South Australia will keep you on your toes, and there is a small but good selection of caravan parks here that will ensure you are well rested.

Burra Caravan and Camping Park, Burra

This picturesque park is situated along a creek just two minutes walk from the centre of Burra – a historic mining town. The park has good basic facilities and plenty of large shady trees. It is an excellent base from which to explore the town. Minimum bookings are required at Easter and on long weekends.

For more details and map location see pages 246 and 358.

Hahndorf Resort, Hahndorf

This is a budget-priced park with good amenities and a great location. In a rural setting, the park is just 1.5 km from the centre of Hahndorf, a very popular tourist destination. It has small lakes with ducks and other birdlife, a range of accommodation and an appealing restaurant. We regularly stop off here for a night or two.

For more details and map location see pages 132 and 369.

Levi Park Caravan Park, Adelaide

The Levi Park is just 6 km from the city and a very good base for exploring central Adelaide. It has shady caravan sites and pleasant grassed tent sites, all located in a magnificent historic garden. The River Torrens flows by the park.

For more details and map location see pages 129 and 351.

Renmark Riverfront Caravan Park, Renmark

This park makes a perfect holiday destination and we have stayed here many times. It is an ideal base from which to explore the area. Set on the Murray River about 2 km from the town centre, it has shady grassed areas – great for relaxing picnics – and good facilities. Minimum bookings are required during long weekends and holiday periods.

For more details and map location see pages 222 and 385.

Stuart Range Caravan Park, Coober Pedy

Located close to the Stuart Highway, this park has good facilities including an extensive range of accommodation, a pool and barbecues. Stop for dinner at the park's very popular pizza shop. There are no water hook-ups in the Coober Pedy parks due to the shortage of water; most parks have coin-in-the-slot water points for filling tanks.

For more details and map location see pages 182 and 361.

In winter Cradle Mountain Tourist Park is often covered in snow

Tanunda Caravan and Tourist Park, Tanunda

Enjoy the Barossa Valley experience from this popular park. Situated right in the heart of the Barossa Valley, it is a great base for exploring this fabulous wine-producing region. Located 1.5 km from the town centre, with easy access, it offers patrons a good range of accommodation and facilities, including bicycle hire.

For more details and map location see pages 224, 246 and 389.

Tasmania

Tasmania is in many ways Australia's ultimate holiday destination. An island state so green and idyllic – you could be forgiven for thinking that it was put there with the purpose of holidays alone, as if all the beautiful farmland exists just to set the scene. But Tasmania is a very real place, from rugged forest and mountain regions, to tall cliffs and wild seas, to colourful flower farms, to famous colonial sites like Port Arthur. There is so much to see in such a small landmass, and accommodation is of high quality.

Cradle Mountain Tourist Park, Cradle Mountain

Set in bushland just outside the World Heritage-listed Tasmanian wilderness area, this quality park has good facilities including a large recreational building with open fireplaces. It is a popular camping site for walkers from around the world who come to walk the renowned Overland Track in the Cradle Mountain–Lake St Clair National Park.

For more details and map location see pages 290 and 362.

Port Arthur Caravan and Cabin Park, Port Arthur

Explore the historic Port Arthur area from this popular, quality caravan park, only 1 km from the Port Arthur Historic Site and high above sheltered waters. It offers a good range of facilities and lots of shady trees. Bookings are recommended during busy holiday periods.

For more details and map location see pages 300 and 383.

Port Sorell Lions Caravan Park, Port Sorell

This popular beachfront park is owned and operated by the Lions Club. It is close to the centre of town, adjacent to the boat ramp and ideal for family holidays. It is an easy drive to the Devonport ferry terminal from here. Bookings are required in holiday periods.

For more details and map location see pages 278 and 384.

Scamander Forest Campground, Scamander

Enjoy the peace and quiet at this Forestry Tasmania camping area, set in a forested area on the banks of the upper Scamander River. Access is along 10 km of unsealed roads; just follow the signs. It is ideal for motorhomes and camper-trailers and camping is free.

For more details and map location see pages 303 and 387.

Stanley Cabin and Tourist Park, Stanley

This park, on the water's edge, is a 200-m stroll from the centre of town – a perfect base for exploring historic Stanley. A spectacular geological feature, The Nut, which is the remains of an old volcano, forms a towering backdrop behind the town. The park has very good amenities and nicely grassed sites, and booking is necessary in holiday periods.

For more details and map location see pages 288 and 388.

Strahan Caravan and Tourist Park, Strahan

Explore the fabulous western coastal region from this popular resort-style park, only 1.5 km west of the centre of Strahan. It has basic but good amenities. We stay here when we visit Strahan.

For more details and map location see pages 292 and 388.

Treasure Island Caravan Park, Hobart

Located about 9 km north-west of the city this is a quiet, off-highway park on the banks of the Derwent River. The park is close to the Cadbury Factory, a popular tourist attraction, and close to shops. The park has good basic amenities and is ideal as a base to explore the Hobart region. We prefer to use this park although both the recommended parks in Hobart are of similar quality.

For more details and map location see pages 285 and 370.

Victoria

Victoria has some truly classic destinations. Old goldmining towns like Ballarat and Castlemaine exist to the north of Melbourne. To the east is the aptly named Great Ocean Road – lush rainforests and amazing vistas of sea and sandstone. To the east of Melbourne are fishing villages like Lakes Entrance, and to the north is the Murray River. The tourist industry in Victoria is well established and most towns have very good accommodation on offer.

Ballarat Goldfields Holiday Park, Ballarat

Centrally located (only 2 km from the city centre) and easily accessible, this quality tourist park has a wide range of accommodation and very good facilities, including a heated pool and spa, free barbecues, bathrooms for children and families, and recreation rooms. We especially like it because it is just a short distance from Sovereign Hill, one of Ballarat's major tourist attractions and our favourite place to visit in the area.

For more details and map location see pages 228 and 353.

Beacon Resort, Queenscliff

This is one of Victoria's few five-star caravan parks. The award-winning establishment has all the trimmings you would expect from a five-star park, including very good recreational facilities: an indoor heated swimming pool and tennis courts. In addition to all this, it is just a short walk to the beach.

For more details and map location see pages 141 and 385.

Boathaven Holiday Park, Ebden

Located about 12 km east of Wodonga, this park is one of Australia's few five-star rated caravan parks. Set on 4 ha of landscaped grounds on the shores of Lake Hume, Boathaven offers a range of recreational facilities including a pool, spa, tennis court, volleyball court and canoe and bicycle hire. There is a large kiosk and a number of pleasant,

shaded sites. Minimum bookings apply during Christmas, January and Easter holiday periods.

For more details and map location see pages 216 and 364.

Frankston Holiday Village, Melbourne

Catering specifically for tourists, this is a good quality park in the south-eastern suburbs. It is ideal for those exploring the Mornington Peninsula or connecting with the Sorrento–Queenscliff ferry. The park offers a very good range of facilities including a heated pool, tennis court and barbecues. Minimum bookings apply during holiday periods.

For more details and map location see pages 147 and 377.

Set up the tent or park the caravan in the shadow of the ranges at Halls Gap Caravan and Tourist Park

Halls Gap Caravan and Tourist Park, Halls Gap

We find this large park ideal for a holiday at any time of the year and regularly stay here. Located in the centre of town, it is within

The owners of Boathaven Holiday Park have created a tropical setting on the banks of Lake Hume

easy reach of most of the area's attractions and makes a good base for exploring the Grampians. A playground and pool are nearby. Minimum bookings apply during all holiday periods.

For more details and map location see pages 230 and 369.

Lake King Waterfront Caravan Park, Eagle Point

Ideal for a family holiday or as a relaxing retreat, this neat and tidy park fronts onto a lake and has its own jetties and boat ramp. It is a popular recreation area and the park has good holiday camping facilities.

For more details and map location see pages 6 and 364.

Mallacoota Foreshore Camp Park, Mallacoota

This picturesque caravan park sprawls along the water's edge. There are over 600 sites in the park and the reception building is just 150 m from the town centre. Some waterfront sites even have their own moorings.

For more details and map location see pages 9 and 376.

Narrawong Holiday Park, Narrawong

This pretty park is in a fabulous, quiet beachside and riverfront position off the main highway. Offering a range of accommodation, it is close to Portland and has good fishing and swimming, and a range of facilities including tennis courts. Campfires are permitted. Just a short walk to the centre of the small community, this park is in a great position and is reasonably priced.

For more details and map location see pages 134 and 380.

Ocean Beach Holiday Village, Warrnambool

Across the road from the beach, this well-kept, owner-operated park is ideal for a holiday or just a few days away. With its excellent facilities, including popular undercover camp kitchen and new movie room, the park can be busy; it is a good idea to book in holiday periods. (Minimum bookings apply during the Christmas and Easter holidays.) We always enjoy staying here.

For more details and map location see pages 136 and 393.

River Beach Camping Ground, Mildura

The beautiful setting of this park – shady trees, green lawns and the river winding by –

makes it a favourite of ours. Large and spacious, the park is located 4 km west of Mildura opposite a popular swimming beach. Sit back and enjoy the scenery with a fresh lunch from the park's takeaway shop.

For more details and map location see pages 220 and 378.

Victoria Lake Holiday Park, Shepparton

Set on the shores of Victoria Park Lake, this picturesque park is centrally located on the main highway 1 km south of the city centre (although there are long-term plans to construct a bypass around Shepparton). With good facilities and great waterfront sites, it is the park we like to stay at when in Shepparton.

For more details and map location see pages 152 and 387.

Zeally Bay Caravan Park, Torquay

Great for a family holiday and just across the road from the beach, this quality caravan park caters especially for tourists and families. Facilities include a tennis court and a cafe, and the park is only 1.2 km north of the town centre.

For more details and map location see pages 139 and 391.

Western Australia

Western Australia is a long way from the eastern seaboard, where most of Australia's population lives. That journey across the Nullabor Plain, by car especially, can feel like you're on a slow road to nowhere, but once you arrive the west coast seems like paradise. The Margaret River region is world famous for surf beaches and wine. In the north, the Pilbara and the Kimberley region draws you into an ancient landscape of magnificent gorges, wildflowers and deserts, and Monkey Mia just below them is a famous dolphin feeding ground. The more time you have in Western Australia the better. Accommodation options are definitely not thin on the ground.

The sites at Denham Seaside Tourist Village offer magnificent views of Shark Bay

Denham Seaside Tourist Village, Denham

Our favourite place to stay in the area, this well-managed park is located at the end of the main street and has a fabulous panoramic view over the sparkling calm waters of Shark Bay. We recommend this park to anyone keen on fishing: there is easy access to a good boat ramp or you can join a fishing charter just a short stroll away at the town jetty. The park is uniquely paved with local shell grit, Monkey Mia Reserve is just a 20-minute drive away and the rugged Francois Peron National Park is nearby.

For more details and map location see pages 100 and 363.

Eighty Mile Beach Caravan Park, Eighty Mile Beach

We often stay at this quality beachside park, located 9 km off the Great Northern Highway and 45 km west of Sandfire Roadhouse. The owners have spent a lot of time developing it and we like what they have done. It is a popular fishing spot and a great place to rest and read a good book.

For more details and map location see pages 92 and 365.

Esperance Seafront Caravan Park, Esperance

This large park is just 2 km from the town centre and across the road from the beach – in fact, it is possible to walk to town along the beach. The park has good amenities and a lovely grassed playground area that seems to host a serious 'beach' cricket

Esperance Seafront Caravan Park is all green grass, Norfolk pines and aquamarine waters in summer

match most summer afternoons. We enjoy spending a few days here.

For more details and map location see pages 117 and 366.

Greenough Rivermouth Caravan Park, Greenough

Set at the mouth of the Greenough River just 10 km south of Geraldton, this large, well-shaded park is protected from the onshore winds and has very good facilities. Cook in the camp kitchen or buy takeaway food from the park's well-stocked shop. This is an enjoyable place to stay, especially for a family holiday, and we like to stay here and commute to Geraldton.

For more details and map location see pages 102 and 368.

Kalgoorlie Accommodation Village, Kalgoorlie–Boulder

Excellent quality and convenience make this a stand-out park in our opinion, and it is a great base from which to explore the gold-mining history of Kalgoorlie. Located off the main road, close to the airport and about 2 km from the centre of Boulder, it has a wide range of facilities to suit both overnight travellers or those staying longer. There is a pool, a camp kitchen and a range of accommodation. We always stay here when we pass through Kalgoorlie.

For more details and map location see pages 271 and 371.

Mandalay Holiday Resort, Busselton

This is an excellent-quality caravan park for tourists, one of the best in Australia. It is just across the road from the beach and about 4 km from the town centre. There is a popular resort-style pool, large grassed playing areas and a convenient boat park. Holiday periods are extremely busy, when booking is essential.

For more details and map location see pages 112 and 359.

Merredin Caravan Park and Av-a-Rest Village, Merredin

This park is of a quality that is rarely found in an inland town the size of Merredin and we highly recommend it. From here it is a comfortable 260 km to Perth or 335 km to Kalgoorlie; Merredin is an excellent choice for an overnight stop. The park facilities include a pool and camp kitchen, and the adjoining road-house serves meals.

For more details and map location see pages 272 and 377.

Middleton Beach Caravan Park, Albany

A great place for a holiday, this quality park has a fabulous position and fronts onto 500 m of a popular swimming beach. Just 3 km from the Albany post office, it has good amenities and a range of facilities including a new TV room. Albany is a premier holiday destination and bookings are necessary in peak periods.

For more details and map location see pages 115 and 351.

Monkey Mia Dolphin Resort, Monkey Mia

If you are keen on wildlife watching, this large, family park, set on the shores of Shark Bay, is for you. Watch the famous Monkey Mia dolphins play at the water's edge, just metres from the park, or take a catamaran ride on the calm waters in search of dolphins and dugong. Some people come to see the dolphins while others come to soak up the balmy winter climate and perhaps catch a few fish. Along with very good facilities and a wide range of accommodation options, the park has a fully licensed restaurant, a well-stocked general store and a cafe.

For more details and map location see pages 100 and 378.

Peoples Park Caravan Village, Coral Bay

This is a great holiday park, set in a wonderful location across the road from the fabulous beach and close to the coral reef. Diving and fishing are very popular along with coral viewing in glass-bottom boats. Coral Bay is very busy during holidays and booking is essential. The park adjoins a cafe and a well-stocked general store.

For more details and map location see pages 98 and 362.

Perth International Tourist Park has lovely leafy surrounds even though it is only 17 km from the city centre

Perth International Tourist Park, Perth

This is a magnificent park with excellent amenities, located in the eastern suburbs 17 km from the centre of Perth. In the high season, the park runs children's activities and walking tours for people staying in the park. It has a secure van-storage area.

For more details and map location see pages 107 and 383.

Taunton Farm Caravan Park, Cowaramup

We think this is possibly the best base for exploring the wonderful Margaret River region and its many wineries. It is a quality park in a great farm setting and we always enjoy our stays here.

For more details and map location see pages 112 and 362.

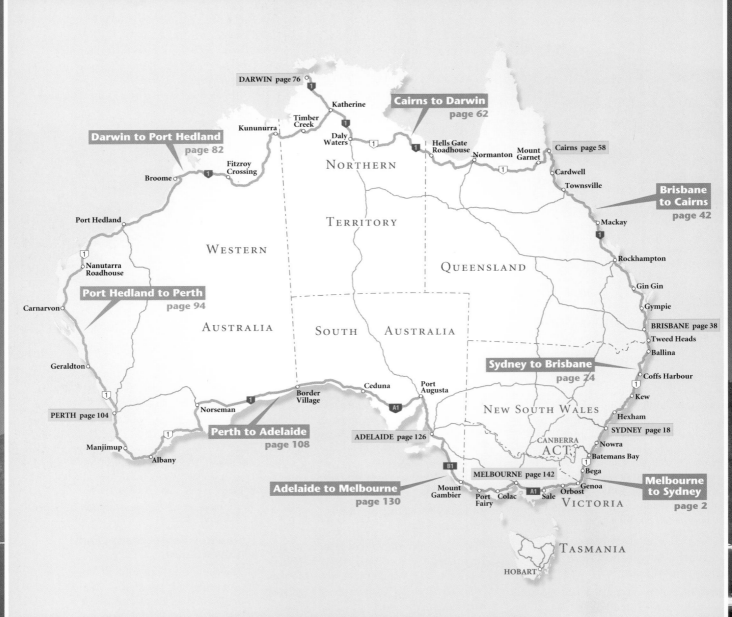

DARWIN page 76

Katherine

Kununurra

Timber
Creek

Cairns to Darwin
page 62

Daly
Waters

Hells Gate
Roadhouse

Darwin to Port Hedland
page 82

Fitzroy
Crossing

NORTHERN

Normanton

Mount
Garnet

Cairns page 58

Broome

Cardwell

Townsville

Port Hedland

TERRITORY

QUEENSLAND

**Brisbane
to Cairns**
page 42

Nanutarra
Roadhouse

WESTERN

Mackay

Rockhampton

Port Hedland to Perth
page 94

Gin Gin

Carnarvon

AUSTRALIA

SOUTH

AUSTRALIA

Gympie

BRISBANE page 38

Geraldton

Tweed Heads

Ballina

Sydney to Brisbane
page 24

Coffs Harbour

Ceduna

Port
Augusta

Kew

PERTH page 104

Border
Village

NEW SOUTH WALES

Hexham

Norseman

SYDNEY page 18

ADELAIDE page 126

CANBERRA
ACT

Nowra

Manjimup

Batemans Bay

Albany

Bega

MELBOURNE page 142

Genoa

**Melbourne
to Sydney**
page 2

Adelaide to Melbourne
page 130

Mount
Gambier

Port
Fairy

Colac

Sale

Orbost

VICTORIA

TASMANIA

HOBART

Chapter 1

Around Australia on Highway One

HIGHWAY ONE is a great tourist experience and often the chosen route of those embarking on that great adventure – travelling around Australia. The 14 000-km highway links capital cities and provincial centres in the five mainland States and the Northern Territory. You can start your journey at any point along the highway, and make a detour on the connecting inland highways as well. There are plenty of interesting towns, national parks and other attractions to see.

Although the highway is a major road for most of its length, conditions vary greatly. It ranges from a two-lane country road to an eight-lane super highway. One 635-km section between Normanton in north Queensland and Borroloola in Northern Territory is unsealed, mostly restricted to four-wheel drives and open only in the drier months.

Highway One will take you through the densely populated east coast, over the long and lonely Nullarbor Plain, and through mining country, farming country and fishing towns. You will see forests, deserts, cities and sea. Whether you have a month or a year, travelling around Australia on Highway One is an unforgettable experience.

MELBOURNE TO SYDNEY

PRINCES FREEWAY, PRINCES HIGHWAY (1037 KM)

This scenic coastal section of the Princes Highway links the major cities of Melbourne and Sydney. The route travels through the Latrobe Valley coalfields, numerous coastal holiday resorts, excellent fishing towns, quiet villages and the busy industrial city of Wollongong. Along the way there are many good art and craft shops to browse through, coffee shops to enjoy a quiet cappuccino in, and places to hire a canoe from and enjoy a paddle in a still lagoon.

Croajingolong National Park, near Mallacoota

Best time to go

This is a great year-round tourist route and the many coastal resorts, always popular during school holiday periods, reach fever pitch at the height of summer.

John & Jan

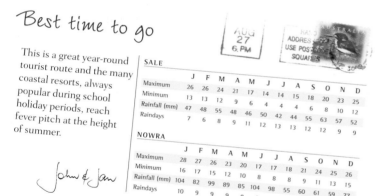

SALE	J	F	M	A	M	J	J	A	S	O	N	D
Maximum	26	26	24	21	17	14	14	15	18	20	23	25
Minimum	13	13	12	9	6	4	4	4	6	8	10	12
Rainfall (mm)	47	48	55	48	46	50	42	44	55	63	57	52
Raindays	7	6	8	9	11	12	13	13	12	12	9	9

NOWRA	J	F	M	A	M	J	J	A	S	O	N	D
Maximum	28	27	26	23	20	17	17	18	21	24	25	26
Minimum	16	17	15	12	10	8	8	8	9	11	13	15
Rainfall (mm)	104	82	99	89	85	104	98	55	60	61	59	77
Raindays	10	9	9	8	9	9	9	8	8	8	9	10

Pakenham to Sale

After the highway escapes Melbourne's outer suburban sprawl it bypasses most of the towns that it once linked. Worth the detour, though, is the remarkable old mining township of Walhalla.

Sale to Orbost

The highway winds through the magnificent Gippsland Lakes region, a popular holiday destination. The area becomes very busy during holiday periods, especially in mid-summer when tourists flock to the beach and lakes.

Melbourne

Melbourne is a vibrant and multicultural metropolis offering great restaurants, excellent shopping, tree-lined boulevards and magnificent gardens.

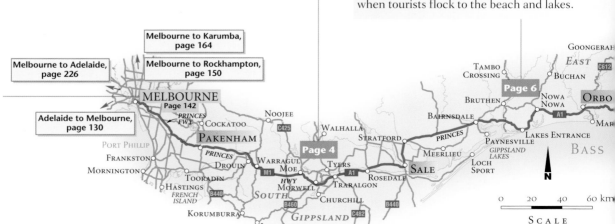

Melbourne to Karumba, page 164

Melbourne to Adelaide, page 226

Melbourne to Rockhampton, page 150

Melbourne Page 142

Adelaide to Melbourne, page 130

Page 4

Page 6

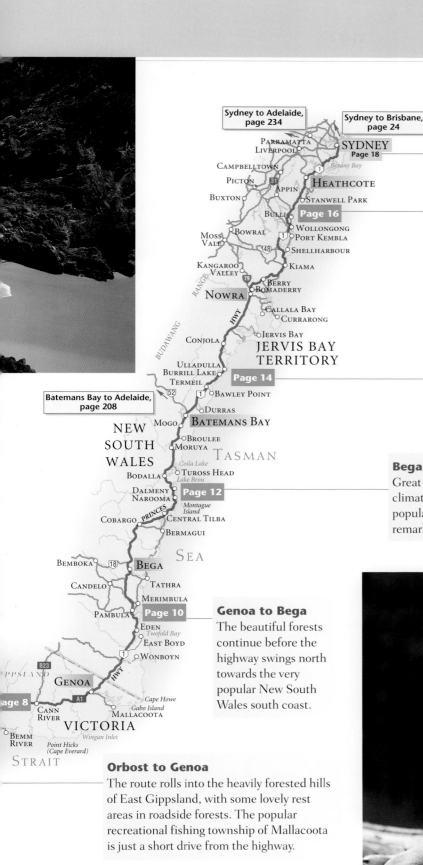

Sydney to Adelaide,
page 234

Sydney to Brisbane,
page 24

PARRAMATTA
LIVERPOOL
SYDNEY
Page 18
CAMPBELLTOWN
Botany Bay
PICTON
HEATHCOTE
BUXTON
APPIN
STANWELL PARK
BULLI
Page 16
BOWRAL
WOLLONGONG
PORT KEMBLA
MOSS
VALE
SHELLHARBOUR
KANGAROO
VALLEY
KIAMA
BERRY
BOMADERRY
NOWRA
CALLALA BAY
CURRARONG
CONJOLA
JERVIS BAY
JERVIS BAY
TERRITORY
ULLADULLA
BURRILL LAKE
TERMEIL
Page 14
BAWLEY POINT
DURRAS
MOGO
BATEMANS BAY
BROULEE
NEW
SOUTH
WALES
MORUYA
TASMAN
BODALLA
Coila Lake
TUROSS HEAD
Lake Brou
DALMENY
NAROOMA
Page 12
*Montague
Island*
COBARGO
CENTRAL TILBA
BERMAGUI
SEA
BEMBOKA
BEGA
CANDELO
TATHRA
MERIMBULA
PAMBULA
Page 10
EDEN
Twofold Bay
EAST BOYD
WONBOYN
Genoa to Bega
GENOA
The beautiful forests
continue before the
highway swings north
towards the very
popular New South
Wales south coast.
age 8
CANN
RIVER
*Cape Howe
Gabo Island*
MALLACOOTA
VICTORIA
BEMM
RIVER
*Point Hicks
(Cape Everard)*
Wingan Inlet
STRAIT

BUDAWANG RANGE
HWY
PRINCES
HWY

Sydney

Sydney is one of the world's most beautiful
cities, with its sweeping surf beaches, soaring
cliffs and the glittering waters of Sydney
Harbour. Combined with great restaurants,
superb architecture and interesting historic
sites, this city is an irresistible destination.

Nowra to Heathcote

Winding through the countryside, the
highway passes two of our favourite towns,
the charming Berry and Kiama, and the
rolling sea before reaching Heathcote.

Batemans Bay to Nowra

Holiday-makers enjoy this region's white sandy
beaches, picturesque holiday resorts, rolling
green hills and pretty lakes and streams.

Bega to Batemans Bay

Great fishing, excellent holiday resorts and a good
climate ensure this picturesque coastal region is always
popular. The historic village of Central Tilba and the
remarkable Mogo Zoo are two great attractions.

Batemans Bay to Adelaide,
page 208

Orbost to Genoa

The route rolls into the heavily forested hills
of East Gippsland, with some lovely rest
areas in roadside forests. The popular
recreational fishing township of Mallacoota
is just a short drive from the highway.

PAKENHAM TO SALE 153 KM

Historic Windsor House

Picturesque Windsor House, Walhalla's only brick dwelling, was built in 1878 by J. Gloz using 90000 handmade bricks. It is classified by the National Trust, and also listed as being of national significance. Used for many years as a boarding house, the building has been restored and is now a luxury B&B. Right Hand Branch Road; (03) 5165 6237.

Explore a goldmine

Experience part of our colourful mining history on a tour of the Long Tunnel Extended Gold Mine at historic Walhalla. The richest single mine in Victoria, it operated between 1865 and 1914. Tours are conducted from Wednesday to Friday at 1.30 p.m. and additional tours operate at 2 p.m. and 3 p.m. on weekends, public holidays and school holidays. Main Road; (03) 5165 6259; entry fee applies.

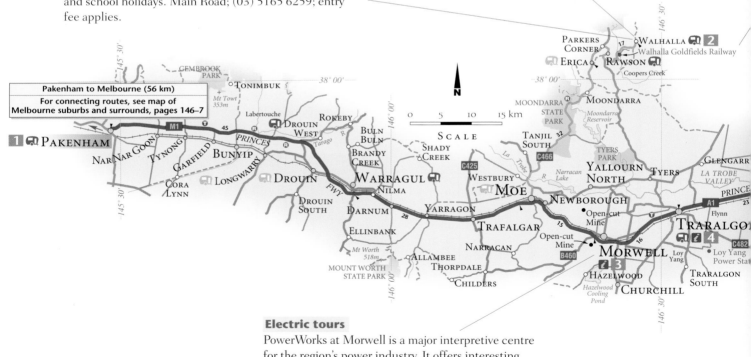

Electric tours

PowerWorks at Morwell is a major interpretive centre for the region's power industry. It offers interesting guided tours of the coal-mining and power-generating facilities for individuals and groups; bookings are essential. Ridge Road; (03) 5135 3415; entry fee applies; open 9 a.m. to 5 p.m. daily.

Scenic railway

The spectacular Walhalla Goldfields Railway operates between the Thomson Station (adjoining the Thomson River Bridge) and Walhalla along several kilometres of restored track, which winds through the picturesque Stringers Creek Gorge. The railway operates every weekend, on public holidays and during school holidays. Thomson Station; (03) 5126 4201; fare applies.

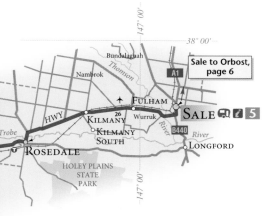

What's on

Sale to Orbost, page 6

FEBRUARY Bunyip Country Music Festival
MARCH Gippsland Field Days (Warragul)
OCTOBER Sale Agricultural Show
NOVEMBER Traralgon Agricultural Show

Track notes

The M1 heads east from Melbourne, bypassing many towns. The highway to Sale is a wide, well-signposted, excellent road. There are ample opportunities to pull off the highway and adequate roadside service centres. During holiday periods traffic can increase dramatically.

Town file

1 PAKENHAM pop. 9512   🛢 PDG
GPS 38° 04.701' S/145° 28.947' E
Pakenham has traditionally been a farming area that, in more recent years, has been increasingly absorbed by Melbourne's outer suburban sprawl. The town has a good shopping centre and a number of fast food outlets and service stations alongside the highway.

2 WALHALLA pop. 15   🛢 None
GPS 37° 56.485' S/146° 26.971' E
Set in a steep-sided valley, the beautifully located goldmining town of Walhalla attracts large numbers of tourists with its historic attractions and buildings and its period shops. The Long Tunnel Extended Gold Mine is open to visitors. There are also excellent local heritage walks that trace this town's golden history.

3 MORWELL pop. 13 823   🛢 PDG
GPS 38° 13.969' S/146° 22.399' E
Morwell was settled in 1861 and during its early history it supplied provisions to diggers heading to the Walhalla and Tanjil goldfields. At the centre of the Latrobe Valley coalfields, Morwell today has grown into a major regional city servicing the coalfields and associated power-generating facilities. The town has good shopping and all services. Markets are held at Latrobe Road each Sunday. Morwell is bypassed by the M1.
🛈 PowerWorks Visitor Centre, Ridge Road; (03) 5135 3415.

4 TRARALGON pop. 18 993   🛢 PDG
GPS 38° 11.892' S/146° 32.279' E
Traralgon is a busy commercial centre. The nearby Loy Yang Power Station sources coal from an enormous deposit representing half of the known brown coal reserves in the Latrobe Valley. The town has good country-town shopping and most services. 🛈 Latrobe Visitor Information Centre, 'The Old Church', Princes Highway; (03) 5174 3199 or 1800 621 409; www.latrobe.vic.gov.au

5 SALE pop. 13 366   🛢 PDG
GPS 38° 06.701' S/147° 03.940' E
Sale is the main administrative centre in Gippsland and offers excellent shopping and all services. In 1888 the completion of the Sale Canal linked the town with the Thomson River, establishing a busy port for steamers working the Gippsland Lakes. Today the city has strong links with the rich offshore oil and gas fields. The East Sale airbase is the home of the awesome RAAF Roulettes. 🛈 Central Gippsland Information Centre, Princes Highway; (03) 5144 1108; www.gippslandinfo.com.au

SALE TO ORBOST 164 KM

Authors' choice

⊛ Lake King Waterfront Caravan Park, Eagle Point

Ideal for a family holiday or as a relaxing retreat, this neat and tidy park fronts onto a lake and has its own jetty. It is a popular recreation area and the park has good holiday camping facilities.
For more details see page 364.

Travel tip

The beautiful town of Lakes Entrance is one of the most popular tourist destinations in Victoria and, even though there are a large number of caravan parks in and near town, bookings are essential during holiday periods. This town can become extremely busy!

A scenic route at high altitude

The Great Alpine Road joins the Princes Highway just east of Bairnsdale. This road winds over the rooftop of Victoria through Omeo, the State's highest town, and climbs through Mount Hotham Alpine Village before descending into the lovely town of Bright in north-east Victoria.

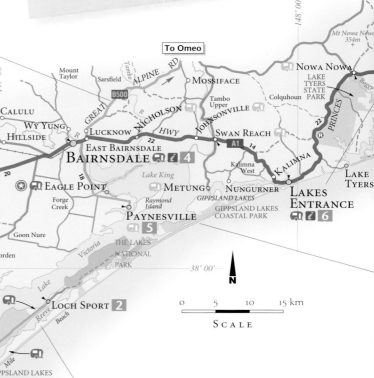

What's on

FEBRUARY/MARCH Jazz Festival (Paynesville) **EASTER** Loch Sport Easter Festival **APRIL** East Gippsland Field Day (Bairnsdale) **APRIL/MAY** Shakespeare on the River Festival (Stratford) **DECEMBER** Larger than Lakes Festival (Lakes Entrance)

Beautiful beach

Ninety Mile Beach stretches from Paradise Beach to Marlo. The pounding surf rolls in from Bass Strait and holiday-makers flock to the area, which has great fishing. The Bass Strait offshore oil and gas facilities are serviced from points along this section of coast.

Woodwork worth a look

The amazing carved stumps along the Lakes Entrance foreshore are a spectacular attraction for tourists and worth stopping for. Each piece has been carved from a tree stump.

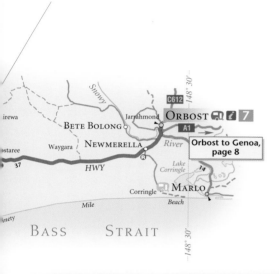

Lake activities

The Gippsland Lakes are an extensive lake system separated from Bass Strait by the dunes forming Ninety Mile Beach. The lakes include many small islands and an endless choice of waterways that are navigable by small craft. Fishing, boating, water-skiing, sailing, swimming and canoeing are all popular recreational activities. Eagle Point and Paynesville are both good bases from which to explore the lakes.

Track notes

The Princes Highway travels around the Gippsland Lakes and through numerous popular holiday towns. The road surface is good, although during busy holiday periods traffic can build dramatically.

Town file

1 SALE (see page 5)

2 LOCH SPORT pop. 800   ⛽ PDG
GPS 38° 02.750' S/147° 35.013' E
Loch Sport is set on a long spit between Lake Reeve and Lake Victoria. Fishing and water sports are the main attractions. Loch Sport has limited shopping and services but can be very busy in the holiday periods.

3 STRATFORD pop. 1350   ⛽ PDG
GPS 37° 57.911' S/147° 04.793' E
On the banks of the Avon River, Stratford is the site of the first permanent settlement in Gippsland. At the centre of a lush dairying area, the town has limited shopping and services but is a popular rest stop.

4 BAIRNSDALE pop. 10 890   ⛽ PDG
GPS 37° 49.551' S/147° 37.985' E
The old lakes port of Bairnsdale is an excellent and popular base for exploring the Gippsland Lakes region. The town has good shopping and a wide range of services. Markets are held on the fourth Sunday of each month at Howitt Park. ℹ 240 Main Street; (03) 5152 3444.

5 PAYNESVILLE pop. 2661   ⛽ PDG
GPS 37° 55.165' S/147° 43.207' E
A popular resort town, Paynesville is almost surrounded by water. The town has a strong history in shipbuilding, and today retains much of the region's boating repair and maintenance industry. Water sports and fishing are the main recreational pursuits. The town has basic shopping and services. Nearby Raymond Island is a wildlife sanctuary.

6 LAKES ENTRANCE pop. 5248   ⛽ PDG
GPS 37° 52.896' S/147° 59.131' E
This popular resort town lies at the eastern extremity of the extensive Gippsland Lakes system and is a year-round holiday destination. There are approximately 25 caravan parks in town and many have a large number of permanent holiday vans. There is a good shopping centre and most services. ℹ Corner Marine Parade and the Esplanade; (03) 5155 1966 or 1800 637 060; www.lakes-entrance.com

7 ORBOST pop. 2150   ⛽ PDG
GPS 37° 42.567' S/148° 27.201' E
Located on the fertile river flats of the Snowy River, Orbost has a selection of shops and a small range of services. There is a nice park in the main street that is ideal for a picnic lunch. The town is just off the highway and the small diversion is worthwhile. ℹ 13 Lochiel Street; (03) 5154 2424; www.lakesandwilderness.com.au

ORBOST TO GENOA 122 KM

What's on
NEW YEAR'S DAY Marlo Races
EASTER Festival of the Southern Ocean (Mallacoota)

Sale to Orbost, page 6

Coastal camping and fishing
Cape Conran Coastal Park is located 19 km east of Marlo. There is a range of camping options and beachside cabins along East Cape Beach. Operated by Parks Victoria, this is a popular holiday destination with lovely beaches and good coastal fishing.

Historic first sightings
Captain Cook's journals on his ship *Endeavour* record the crew's first sighting of the Australian coast on 19 April 1770. They named the place Point Hicks after Lieutenant Hicks who made the sighting. Accommodation is available at the lighthouse on this remote stretch of coast.

Refreshing rainforest walk

Alongside the Princes Highway where it crosses the Thurra River is a walking track that meanders through the beautiful Drummer Rainforest. A stroll through this temperate rainforest is a relaxing break and a great idea if you need to stretch your legs after a long drive.

Genoa to Bega, page 10

A special national park

The 86000-ha Croajingolong National Park conserves a large expanse of undisturbed habitat along 100 km of coastline. It is classified as a UNESCO World Biosphere Reserve. The park boasts over 300 bird species, including glossy-black cockatoos, king parrots and lyrebirds. There are walking trails, camping areas and magnificent views from Genoa Peak. There is also excellent surf-fishing. The park can be reached from Mallacoota.

Track notes

The undulating, forested ranges of East Gippsland embrace the highway as it winds inland away from the coast. Forest roadside rest areas are ideal for a short break.

Town file

1 ORBOST (see page 7)

2 MARLO pop. 322   🅿 P
GPS 36° 53.421' S/149° 54.649' E
The Snowy River rises on the slopes of Mount Kosciuszko and travels through the rugged, isolated ranges of East Gippsland before flowing from a quiet lagoon into Bass Strait. Marlo is a small tourist town at the mouth of the river. Sailing boats and paddle-steamers once ferried produce and passengers to and from the port. At Cape Conran Coastal Park, 19 km east of town, you will find good fishing and lovely beaches.

3 CANN RIVER pop. 246   🅿 PDG
GPS 36° 23.324' S/149° 53.241' E
The small township of Cann River services the local timber and dairying industries. The town is strategically located at the junction of the Princes and Cann River highways, which link with the Monaro Highway, forming a direct, fully sealed route to Canberra. The township has limited services but is well situated for tourists passing through the area.

4 MALLACOOTA pop. 982   🅿 PDG
GPS 36° 19.445' S/150° 03.801' E
At the mouth of the Mallacoota Inlet, this resort town has a lot of appeal for tourists and outdoors-loving people. The town is surrounded by great bushwalking tracks, lovely beaches and protected waterways. There is good fishing, boating and easy access to Croajingolong National Park. Mallacoota's temperature is about five degrees warmer than Melbourne, making it a popular year-round resort. The Mallacoota Foreshore Camp Park sprawls along the waterfront and has an amazing 600 sites. There is a limited range of shops and services in town.

5 GENOA pop. 120   🅿 PD
GPS 36° 22.118' S/150° 04.315' E
Genoa is a small village at the intersection of the Princes Highway and the Mallacoota turn-off. The town has basic services for travellers.

GENOA TO BEGA 111 KM

Authors' choice

✪ Garden of Eden Caravan Park, Eden

Enjoy the excellent amenities, tennis court and swimming pool at this well-appointed, reasonably priced park, just 2 km from the town centre. Things are always going on at this park, like the recent construction of a new laundry block and the installation of TV cables. This is a great place either for an overnight stay or for a long holiday. Pets are allowed at the owners' discretion.

For more details see page 365.

✪ Holiday Hub Beach Resort, Pambula Beach

This beachside park is one of our favourite parks in the popular family holiday region of the south coast of New South Wales. It has a new pool complex, a licensed restaurant and spotless amenities, and is a great family park. The resident kangaroos will be a hit with children.

For more details see page 382.

The Candelo Markets

The small, historic village of Candelo, with its delightful old-world charm, draws a large crowd when it hosts the largest markets on the south coast on the first Sunday of each month. With over 150 stallholders, these busy markets are definitely worth a visit – you never know what you might find.

What's on

FEBRUARY Far South Coast National Show (Bega) **JUNE** Merimbula Jazz Festival **SEPTEMBER/OCTOBER** Bega Festival **OCTOBER** Eden Whale Festival, Country Music Festival by the Sea (Merimbula) **OCTOBER/NOVEMBER** Spring Festival (Merimbula)

Bega to Batemans Bay, page 12

Orbost to Genoa, page 8

Whale-watching mecca

During the winter months, humpback whales migrate north from Antarctic waters to the east coast of Australia. Eden has become a popular whale-watching port, and cruises to view these majestic giants operate between October and November as the whales return south.

Spot a killer whale

Established in 1931, the Eden Killer Whale Museum houses much of the history of early Eden and the skeleton of 'Old Tom', a killer whale renowned for his amazing antics. We find this a fascinating place to visit. 94 Imlay Street; (02) 6496 2094; entry fee applies; open 9.15 a.m. to 3.45 p.m. Monday to Saturday, 11.15 a.m. to 3.45 p.m. Sunday.

Boyd's Tower

Built at Red Point to serve as a lighthouse during the 1840s, Boyd's Tower was never used as intended. Instead, it became a whale-spotting tower for the strong local whaling industry. The tower is now conserved within the Ben Boyd National Park. A park entry fee applies.

Track notes

The Princes Highway carries local and tourist traffic and the volume increases during holiday periods. The highway skirts the coastline around Eden before sweeping inland through the dairy farming regions of the Bega River valley. There are numerous rest areas along the roadside, many in peaceful forested areas.

Town file

1 GENOA (see page 9)

2 EDEN pop. 3106   ⛽ PDG
GPS 37° 04.114' S/149° 54.502' E
On the shores of Twofold Bay (one of the world's deepest natural harbours) and surrounded by lush, rugged forests, Eden was once a major whaling port. In more recent times, however, the town's focus has turned to whale-watching, which attracts large numbers of tourists during October and November. 🚹 Princes Highway; (02) 6496 1953.

3 PAMBULA pop. 765   ⛽ PDG
GPS 36° 55.703' S/149° 52.476' E
George Bass, on his epic voyage in an open whale boat from Sydney Cove to Victoria, sailed up the Pambula River in 1797. Graziers soon followed, establishing a thriving rural industry. Today visitors are attracted to the beauty of the area. A walking and cycling trail links Pambula with Merimbula. Markets are held on the second Sunday of each month.

4 MERIMBULA pop. 4383   ⛽ PDG
GPS 36° 53.421' S/149° 54.649' E
Merimbula is a major holiday centre. The beaches, lakes, bushland and year-round pleasant climate attract visitors to this region dubbed the 'Sapphire Coast'. The town boasts a resort-style shopping centre with a good selection of cafes and restaurants. There is excellent local swimming, surfing and fishing, and the local wharf is a popular spot to wet a line. 🚹 Beach Street; (02) 6495 1129; www.sapphirecoast.com.au

5 TATHRA pop. 1684   ⛽ PD
GPS 36° 43.458' S/149° 58.743' E
Tathra is a popular beachside resort town just south of Mogareeka Inlet and the mouth of the Bega River (which is sometimes closed to the sea). The historic Tathra Wharf, classified by the National Trust, is a renowned fishing spot. The town has safe, patrolled surf beaches popular with holidaying families, and fishing is a major attraction throughout the region. 🚹 Tathra Wharf; (02) 6494 4062; www.sapphirecoast.com.au

6 BEGA pop. 4190   ⛽ PDG
GPS 36° 40.598' S/149° 50.568' E
Bega is the commercial centre for this region. It services a strong dairy industry and is famous for its locally produced cheeses. The town is close to the junction of the Princes and Snowy Mountains highways.
🚹 Princes Highway; (02) 6492 2045; www.sapphirecoast.com.au

BEGA TO BATEMANS BAY 146 KM

Authors' choice

⊛ Island View Beach Resort, Narooma

Stroll to the beach or picnic on green lawns
under shady trees at this quality park, located
on the Princes Highway 5 km south of Narooma.
With very good amenities and lots of appeal,
it is ideal for a family holiday and conveniently
located for an overnight stay.

For more details see page 380.

Historic Central Tilba

Step back into the past and visit the village of
Central Tilba, classified by the National Trust.
Browse through the period shops along the main
street and see the craftwork of talented local
artisans. The town is just a short drive off the
Princes Highway.

What's on

MARCH Bermagui Seaside Fair EASTER Easter Rodeo
(Moruya) MAY Eurobodalla Cycle Classic (Batemans
Bay to Moruya) JUNE Deua River Bush Races
(Moruya) OCTOBER Great Southern International
Blues Festival (Narooma) NOVEMBER Bayfest
Carnival (Batemans Bay)

Batemans Bay to Nowrah, page 14

Batemans Bay to Canberra, page 210

Genoa to Bega, page 10

KINGS HWY

Cullendulla
LONG BEACH
MURRAMARANG NP
7 BATEMANS BAY
BATEHAVEN
Batemans Bay
6 MOGO
Mogo Zoo
MALUA BAY
TOMAKIN
MOSSY POINT
BROULEE
5 MORUYA
MORUYA HEADS
EUROBODALLA
CONGO
Bergalia
NATIONAL
Meringo
PARK
Coila Lake
TUROSS HEAD
BODALLA
Tuross Lake
EUROBODALLA
Lake Brou
NATIONAL
Eurobodalla
PARK
TASMAN
DALMENY
Wagonga
Wagonga Inlet
BODALLA
NAROOMA **4**
Montague Island
STATE
MONTAGUE ISLAND NATURE RESERVE
FOREST
Corunna Lake
EUROBODALLA NATIONAL PARK
SEA
CENTRAL TILBA
TILBA TILBA
Wallaga Lake
2 COBARGO
PRINCES
WALLAGA LAKE NP
BERMAGUI **3**
BERMAGUI SOUTH
BIAMANGA
QUAAMA
NATIONAL
Murrah Lagoon
Brogo
PARK
Bunga
MIMOSA
Wapengo
ROCKS
TANJA
NATIONAL
Grevillea Estate Winery
BEGA **1**
PARK

N

SCALE
0 5 10 15 km

Meet an endangered species

Mogo Zoo is a privately owned zoo dedicated to the survival of endangered species. There are several exhibits but the red pandas, snow leopards and golden lion tamarins are our favourites. Tomakin Road; (02) 4474 4930; entry fee applies; open 9 a.m. to 5 p.m. daily.

Alternative scenic route

The coastal drive between Moruya and Batemans Bay is a great scenic diversion along this picturesque coast. Along the way are several small communities, secluded beaches and a selection of caravan parks.

Exceptional fishing opportunities

Fishing is a great tourist attraction throughout this coastal region. Those who are keen will find jetties and rocky points to cast from, along with quiet lagoons and endless numbers of bays, lakes and rivers. Big-game anglers flock to the region between November and June in search of a substantial catch. Fishing charters operate from most ports along the coast.

Travel tip

We always enjoy stopping for lunch at Cobargo and browsing through the shops on the main street. Lake Leather is one of our favourite shops in town; it showcases a wide range of quality outdoor clothing, boots, accessories and leather craft.

Track notes

This section of the Princes Highway is a major route and carries a diverse range of traffic that intensifies greatly during holiday periods. The road has several overtaking lanes and numerous roadside rest spots.

Town file

1 **BEGA** (see page 11)

2 **COBARGO** pop. 397   PDG
GPS 36° 23.324' S/149° 53.241' E
Cobargo is a small country town that still retains its character. It has interesting buildings, cafes, art and craft shops and a fabulous leather shop where we often cannot resist buying something.

3 **BERMAGUI** pop. 1196   PDG
GPS 36° 25.619' S/150° 04.565' E
Bermagui is an excellent fishing destination. There are many great spots for coastal angling but during summer big-game fishing is the major attraction, when numerous charter boats operate from the port. Bermagui has basic shopping and services. Craft markets are held on the last Sunday of each month. 🛈 Lamont Street; (02) 6493 3054.

4 **NAROOMA** pop. 3389   PDG
GPS 36° 13.115' S/150° 07.939' E
Narooma is a popular fishing resort town at the mouth of the Wagonga Inlet. The town has a challenging cliff-top golf course and offers numerous fishing charters. Boat cruises operate to the famous penguin and seal colonies of Montague Island Nature Reserve. 🛈 Princes Highway; (02) 4476 2881 or 1800 240 003; www.naturecoast-tourism.com.au

5 **MORUYA** pop. 2602   PDG
GPS 35° 54.556' S/150° 04.934' E
Moruya is at the heart of a strong dairy-farming region and close to lush forest-covered ranges. Many of the town's buildings were built with the same locally quarried granite used in the construction of the Sydney Harbour Bridge. Moruya has good shopping and all basic services. Markets are held in Main Street each Saturday.

6 **MOGO** pop. 230   PD
GPS 35° 46.976' S/150° 08.532' E
Rich in history, Mogo is home to the Mogo Zoo. The specialty shops, galleries and art and craft shops make this an interesting place to visit.

7 **BATEMANS BAY** pop. 9568   PDG
GPS 35° 42.401' S/150° 10.681' E
Situated on the sweeping estuary of the magnificent Clyde River, this resort town is located at the junction of the Kings and Princes highways. Batemans Bay has beautiful beaches and great restaurants and is a popular fishing spot. Markets are held at the high school on the third Sunday of each month. 🛈 Corner Princes Highway and Beach Road; (02) 4472 6900 or 1800 802 528; www.naturecoast-tourism.com.au

BATEMANS BAY TO NOWRA 116 KM

Nowra to Heathcote, page 16

Authors' choice

⊛ Racecourse Beach Tourist Park, Bawley Point

It is hard to resist staying at a wonderful, award-winning beachside park such as this. Just 9 km from the Princes Highway, it has good facilities including mini-golf, a heated pool, a sauna and a tennis court. Minimum bookings apply in peak holiday periods.

For more details see page 355.

Something for aviation enthusiasts

Australia's Museum of Flight is located just outside the gates of the Naval Air Station, HMAS *Albatross*. The museum has a fine collection of military aircraft, memorabilia, weapons and aviation equipment. Fly-in days and airshows are held regularly. Albatross Road, Nowra; (02) 4424 1920; entry fee applies; open 10 a.m. to 4 p.m. daily.

Historic Milton

Classified as a historic village by the National Trust, Milton features many distinguished buildings dating back to 1860. Art and craft shops, antique shops and cafes line the main street. The Milton Settlers Fair is staged each year on the October long weekend. Poet Henry Kendall was born here in 1839.

A mountain climb

Morton National Park's Pigeon House mountain was recorded by Captain Cook in 1770 as he sailed up the east coast. At 719 m the mountain dominates the countryside. The rewarding climb to the top, including a series of steel ladders, takes about 4 hours (return) from the carpark. The carpark can be reached in a conventional car along an unsealed road.

Map labels

BOMADERRY
Comerong Island
Crookhaven Heads
NOWRA
Shoalhaven River
GREENWELL POINT
Australia's Museum of Flight
Nowra Hill
CULBURRA
FALLS CREEK
HMAS Albatross
NEW SOUTH WALES JERVIS BAY NATIONAL PARK
CALLALA BAY
35° 00'
CURRARONG
Jervis Bay
Bewong
HUSKISSON
Hyams Beach
Point Perpendicular
WANDANDIAN
VINCENTIA
JERVIS BAY TERRITORY
ST GEORGES BASIN
SANCTUARY POINT
St Georges Basin
JERVIS BAY
CUDMIRRAH
NATIONAL
Swan Lake
SUSSEX INLET
BOODEREE NP
SCALE
0 5 10 15 km
PARK
SWANHAVEN
JERVIS BAY TERRITORY
Conjola
CUDMIRRAH
TASMAN
CONJOLA NP
Lake Conjola
BENDALONG
MORTON
Pointer Gap Lookout
YATTE YATTAH
LAKE CONJOLA
NATIONAL
MOLLYMOOK
SEA
MILTON
PARK
Pigeon House 719m
Burrill Lake
ULLADULLA
KINGS POINT
BURRILL LAKE
Dolphin Point
Wairo Beach
TABOURIE LAKE
TERMEIL
BAWLEY POINT
35° 30'
PRINCES
KIOLOA
MURRAMARANG NP
Pebbly Beach
EAST LYNNE
Durras Lake
DEPOT BEACH
NELLIGEN
KINGS HWY
Cullendulla
DURRAS
LONG BEACH
MURRAMARANG NP
BATEMANS BAY
BATEHAVEN
Batemans Bay

Batemans Bay to Canberra, page 210

(see page 210)

Bega to Batemans Bay, page 12

Captivating bay

Jervis Bay is a water wonderland renowned for its white sand and crystal clear water. The spectacular Point Perpendicular protects the northern entrance to the harbour and Hyams Beach inside the bay is reputed to have the whitest sand in the world. Water sports and scuba-diving are popular recreational pursuits.

What's on

JANUARY, MAY, AUGUST, NOVEMBER Australia's Museum of Flight fly-in days (Nowra) EASTER White Sands Carnival (Huskisson) APRIL Milton Scarecrow Festival AUGUST Food and Wine Festival by the Sea (Ulladulla) OCTOBER Spring Festival (Nowra)

Travel tip

Finding good eateries to stop at along the road is not always easy. We recommend the Bewong Roadhouse, just south of the St Georges Basin turn-off. It is an older roadhouse where we have enjoyed meals or sometimes just a coffee. There is plenty of parking for cars and caravans.

Track notes

The Princes Highway between Batemans Bay and Nowra is a major route carrying large volumes of traffic including heavy transports. The road follows the coastal plain and from time to time the sea comes into view. For a diversion, there are numerous roads winding to the sea; some are sealed while others are not. The highway has a number of overtaking lanes and the traffic normally flows well.

Town file

1 BATEMANS BAY (see page 13)

2 ULLADULLA pop. 8384   PDG
GPS 35° 21.440' S/150° 28.454' E
Located on the Princes Highway, Ulladulla is a busy fishing port and a popular beachside holiday resort. The town has a busy main street with good shopping and most services. Markets are held on the second Sunday of each month at the wharf. *i* Civic Centre, Princes Highway; (02) 4455 1269; www.shoalhaven.nsw.gov.au

3 SUSSEX INLET pop. 2651   PD
GPS 35° 09.403' S/150° 36.141' E
Sussex Inlet is a resort town located on the shores of the channel connecting St Georges Basin with the sea. Its population is largely made up of retirees and holiday-makers, and fishing and boating enthusiasts are particularly attracted to the area. The town has a small shopping strip and limited services.

4 HUSKISSON pop. 3350   PDG
GPS 35° 02.334' S/150° 40.298' E
Huskisson overlooks the protected waters of Jervis Bay. The bay is a wide, natural harbour renowned for its wonderful clear water, where scuba-diving and other water sports are the main pursuits. The Lady Denman Maritime Museum on Dent Street chronicles the area's early shipbuilding history. The town has a small shopping centre and basic services are available. Markets are held on the second Sunday of each month at White Sands Park.

5 NOWRA pop. 23 823   PDG
GPS 34° 52.483' S/150° 36.182' E
Nowra is a key regional centre located on the banks of the Shoalhaven River. The bustling town services numerous small communities dotted along the adjacent coast, as well as the nearby naval airbase and a strong farming community. Nowra has a good shopping centre and all services are available. Markets are held on the third Sunday of each month.
i Shoalhaven Visitors Centre, corner Princes Highway and Pleasant Way; (02) 4421 0778 or 1800 024 261; www.shoalhaven.nsw.gov.au

NOWRA TO HEATHCOTE 128 KM

Authors' choice

⊛ Seven Mile Beach Holiday Park, Gerroa

Swim at the beach or sit back, relax and watch TV at this large, fabulous beachside park. It has great facilities, including ensuite sites with full Austar TV hook-up. It also has excellent amenities and is in a wonderful location. The park is divided into two sections by the main road.

For more details see page 367.

⊛ Blowhole Point Holiday Park, Kiama

With an outlook over the town and harbour, this park occupies a fabulous piece of real estate adjoining the lighthouse and the famous blowhole. Mostly protected from the south-easterly wind, the park has basic amenities, but it is the spectacular views that make it so good.

For more details see page 372.

Heathcote to Sydney (41 km)
For connecting routes, see map of Sydney suburbs and surrounds, pages 22–3

Rare rainforest experience

Beautiful Minnamurra Rainforest in the Budderoo National Park is a rare tract of subtropical rainforest adjoining Minnamurra Falls. There are elevated timber boardwalks (some with disabled access), an excellent visitor information centre and the Lyrebird Cafe. (02) 4236 0469; park fee applies; open 9 a.m. to 5 p.m. daily.

Picturesque highlands route

The fully sealed road linking Nowra and Moss Vale through Kangaroo Valley is a short route across the Southern Highlands from the Hume Highway. It is narrow and winding in places as it climbs over the ranges and there are steep climbs and descents, but the picturesque scenery makes it worthwhile. It is suitable for caravans but care is needed.

Scenic diversion

North of the Shoalhaven River, this alternative route takes in several resort towns including Shoalhaven Heads and Gerringong. The scenic drive, along a fully sealed road, follows the river estuary and panoramic coastline.

Map labels

HEATHCOTE
MILITARY RESERVE
HEATHCOTE NATIONAL PARK
WATERFALL
ROYAL NATIONAL PARK
Woronora Reservoir
HELENSBURGH
DHARAWAL STATE RECREATION AREA
STANWELL PARK
COALCLIFF
SCARBOROUGH
DHARAWAL NR
Lake Cataract
COLEDALE
THIRROUL
BULLI
TASMAN
Cordeaux Reservoir
CORRIMAL
FAIRY MEADOW
ILLAWARRA ESCARPMENT STATE RECREATION AREA
FIGTREE
WOLLONGONG
SEA
PORT KEMBLA
34° 30'
PRIMBEE
Lake Illawarra
WINDANG
WARILLA
SHELLHARBOUR
Bass Point
SCALE
0 5 10 15 km
N
Minnamurra Rainforest Centre
Minnamurra Falls
DUNMORE
JAMBEROO
BUDDEROO NATIONAL PARK
BARREN GROUNDS NATURE RESERVE
Blowhole
KIAMA
To Moss Vale
150° 30'
KANGAROO VALLEY
RED ROCKS NR
Fox Ground
WERRI BEACH
GERRINGONG
GEROA
CAMBEWARRA
BERRY
SEVEN MILE BEACH NATIONAL PARK
BOMADERRY
Coolangatta
SHOALHAVEN HEADS
COMERONG ISLAND NR
Comerong Island
Crookhaven Heads
NOWRA
GREENWELL POINT
Shoalhaven River

Batemans Bay to Nowra, page 14

Travel tip

The township of Berry is a tourist destination in its own right. Numerous cafes, restaurants and a great range of shops draw many visitors to the town. We like stopping in Berry so we can stroll through the craft shops and linger over lunch, enjoying the relaxed atmosphere.

What's on

FEBRUARY Kiama Jazz Festival
EASTER Easter Jazz Festival
(Wollongong) APRIL Berry Country Fair
JUNE Australian Folk Festival (Kiama)
SEPTEMBER Spring and Corrimal
Festival (Wollongong) NOVEMBER
Harbourfest (Wollongong)

Kiama Blowhole

The dramatic Kiama Blowhole, discovered by explorer George Bass in 1797, is only a short distance from the town centre. When the seas are running from the south-east, spectacular plumes of water spray up, reaching as high as 60 m. The blowhole is floodlit at night until 1 a.m.

Track notes

The highway passes through spectacular countryside along the coastal plain between Nowra and Wollongong. The journey can be a little slow in places and there are not a lot of overtaking opportunities. Wollongong and Sydney are linked by a major freeway. This section of the route carries large volumes of traffic including commuters and numerous coal trucks. The freeway can also be affected by thick fog.

Town file

1 NOWRA (see page 15)

2 BERRY pop. 1604 　　　　　　　　　　⛽ PDG
GPS 34° 46.538' S/150° 41.817' E
Berry first developed as a private town to service the interests of the original landowner, Alexander Berry. With its quaint main street of craft shops, restaurants and cafes, the town has become a popular tourist destination. It also has many fine old buildings classified by the National Trust. Markets are held on the first Sunday of each month at the showgrounds.

3 KIAMA pop. 11 711 　　　　　　　　⛽ PDG
GPS 34° 40.308' S/150° 51.388' E
Located on a spectacular coastline, picturesque Kiama services the local fishing, farming and dairying industries. The famous blowhole on the headland is the town's major attraction. Kiama's setting, the harbour and the caravan parks combine to make this one of our favourite stops. There is a good shopping strip and most services are available. Markets are held on the third Sunday of each month. 🛈 Blowhole Point; (02) 4232 3322 or 1300 654 262; www.kiama.com.au

4 SHELLHARBOUR pop. 3697 　　　　⛽ PDG
GPS 34° 34.771' S/150° 51.999' E
Until the railway reached Shellharbour in the 1880s, the town was a notable shipping port. Today this beachside holiday resort at the southern end of Lake Illawarra has almost been absorbed in the Wollongong urban sprawl. Shellharbour has a small shopping centre and limited services. 🛈 Ground floor, Lamerton House, Lamerton Cresent; (02) 4221 6169.

5 WOLLONGONG pop. 219 761 　　　⛽ PDG
GPS 34° 25.524' S/150° 53.845' E
One of Australia's major industrial cities and the third largest city in New South Wales, Wollongong lies on the coast at the foot of a sandstone escarpment. The city provides services to a large section of the south coast and has excellent shopping and a wide range of services. Large iron and steel plants are located nearby at Port Kembla and coal mining continues throughout the region. Markets are held every Thursday and Saturday in Harbour Street. 🛈 93 Crown Street; (02) 4227 5545 or 1800 240 737.

6 HEATHCOTE 　　　　　　　　　　⛽ PDG
GPS 34° 05.188' S/151° 00.547' E
An outer suburb of Sydney, Heathcote is at the southern gateway to the greater metropolitan area.

SYDNEY
YOUR GUIDE

With a population of 4 million and over 2 million international visitors each year, Sydney is widely regarded as one of the world's most beautiful cities. It is Australia's largest city and boasts great restaurants, superb architecture, cultural diversity and interesting historic sites. All this, set within a landscape of sweeping surf beaches, bushland, soaring cliffs and the glittering waters of Sydney Harbour, makes this city an irresistible destination.

CITY CENTRE
See map on page 21.

Art Gallery of New South Wales 21 E5
One of the most comprehensive collections in the country, including the largest permanent collection of Aboriginal art in the world.

Australian Museum 21 D6
Australia's oldest; housing natural history displays and one of the world's best indigenous exhibitions.

Australian National Maritime Museum 21 B5
The maritime adventures of an island continent, from the seagoing ways of the Aboriginal people to today's beach culture.

Cadmans Cottage 21 C2
The oldest existing residence in Australia, built in 1816; also the National Parks and Wildlife Service Information Centre.

Chinese Garden 21 B7
Lakes, waterfalls, pavilions and rare exotic species.

Customs House 21 D3
An 1885 Classical Revival building, home to a display of contemporary and indigenous art and culture.

Darling Harbour 21 B6
Leisure precinct containing some of the city's major cultural and entertainment institutions.

Government House 21 E3
Set within the lush surrounds of the Royal Botanic Gardens; the magnificent state rooms, with period furnishings, may be seen on guided tours.

Hyde Park Barracks Museum 21 D5
Fine example of Georgian Colonial architecture, completed in 1819; contains a fascinating museum of social and architectural history; opposite is Hyde Park, home to some interesting civic memorials.

Visitor information

Sydney Visitor Centre The Rocks
106 George Street
(02) 9255 1788

Sydney Visitor Centre Darling Harbour
Palm Grove
(02) 9281 0788

Circular Quay Information Kiosk
Corner Alfred and Pitt streets

Martin Place Information Kiosk
Corner Elizabeth Street and Martin Place

Town Hall Information Kiosk
George Street

Manly Visitor Information Centre
Manly Wharf Forecourt
(02) 9977 1088

Justice and Police Museum 21 D3
Displays the history of crime and punishment in Sydney.

Museum of Sydney 21 D4
A thought-provoking survey of what has made Sydney the city it is.

Oxford Street 21 F8
Heartland of gay Sydney.

Powerhouse Museum 21 B7
Former power station that now houses fascinating scientific, social and technological displays.

The Rocks 21 D2
Historic waterside area with weekend market, galleries, cafes and craft shops.

Royal Botanic Gardens 21 E4
On the site of Sydney's first farm, these magnificent gardens contain some 17 000 native and exotic species.

State Library of New South Wales 21 D4
Includes the Mitchell Library, and its priceless collection of Australiana.

Sydney Aquarium 21 B5
An amazing array of sea life swims through underwater tunnels; also a living replica of the Great Barrier Reef.

Sydney Harbour Bridge 21 D1
The second longest single-span bridge in the world. The south-east Pylon Lookout contains the Harbour Bridge Exhibition and a viewing platform; there is a 3-hour guided climb to the top.

Sydney Observatory 21 C3
Features night viewing and an astronomy museum.

Sydney Opera House 21 E2
An architectural giant of the 20th century; guided tours are available.

Sydney Tower 21 D5
The highest observation deck in the Southern Hemisphere; for a bird's eye view of the city.

Victoria Barracks 21 F8
Considered one of the best examples of Imperial military architecture in the world.

Top events

Sydney Festival (January)
Arts, culture and summer fun.

Gay and Lesbian Mardi Gras (February)
Sydney's biggest party.

Archibald Prize Exhibition (March–April)
National portrait prize – and the best gossip in Sydney.

Australian Fashion Week (May)
The latest in Australian and international delights.

Sydney Film Festival (June)
A winter retreat for film lovers.

City to Surf (July)
Challenging road-race taking in Heartbreak Hill.

Australian International Motor Show (November)
Latest and futuristic models in a 10-day showcase.

SYDNEY (CONTINUED)
YOUR GUIDE

SUBURBS AND SURROUNDS

See map on pages 22–3.

Bondi Beach 23 J5
Excellent for swimming and strolling.

Centennial Park 23 I5
Beautiful 220 ha of woodland, lakes, trails and gardens.

Elizabeth Bay House 23 I5
Built in 1839; a museum charting the life of the upper classes in 19th-century Sydney.

Elizabeth Farm 23 G4
Incorporates the oldest European building in Australia (1793).

Homebush Bay 23 H5
Focus of the Sydney 2000 Olympic Games.

Ku-ring-gai Chase National Park 23 I1
A magnificent stretch of bush set around the Hawkesbury River; fishing, bushwalking and river cruises are popular.

Manly 23 J4
Seaside holiday village; its beach is one of Sydney's best.

North Head 23 J4
The best coastal views in Sydney.

Old Government House 23 G4
Australia's oldest public building, with the country's best collection of Colonial furniture.

Old Quarantine Station 23 J4
Used to house afflicted convicts; take an evening ghost tour and enjoy the billy tea and damper afterwards.

Royal National Park 23 H8
A landscape of sandstone outcrops, woodland, rainforest, cliffs and beaches.

Sydney Tramway Museum 23 H7
The largest collection of trams in the Southern Hemisphere; runs novelty tram trips.

Taronga Zoo 23 I4
First opened in 1916, of particular interest is the Free Flight Birdshow.

Vaucluse House 23 J5
Once the home of Blue Mountains explorer W. C. Wentworth, the house is fully furnished, with a beautiful 19th-century landscaped garden.

Getting around

Travelling through Sydney can be a daunting thought for those from out of town. The traffic is dense, the peak 'hour' lasts for several hours and some of the traffic lanes are narrow. However, with some planning, Sydney is not a difficult city to negotiate. Carefully choose a main through-route and then navigate using the route signs. Main routes are generally clearly signposted. If you are travelling in a motorhome or towing a van we feel it is easier to keep to the centre lane and flow with the traffic. We avoid left-hand lanes wherever possible as these regularly end with little warning. Keep an eye on the lane width as they do vary and try not to wander from your lane. The South Western Motorway (Route 5),the Western Motorway (Route 4), the Eastern Distributor (Route 1) and the Hills Motorway (Route 2) are all toll roads with attended toll gates. Beware of using parking meters as they are very expensive. All the major attractions within the city can be reached easily on foot. However, the red Explorer Buses do circuits of the city attractions, and the blue buses cover the bay and beaches. For the outlying attractions and the harbourside eastern suburbs, take a ferry ride and enjoy the harbour experience.

Airport shuttle bus Airport Express 13 15 00; Motoring organisation NRMA 13 21 32; Public transport Bus, Train and Ferry Information Line 13 15 00; Bus tours and speciality trips Explorer Buses (red for city sights, blue for Bondi and eastern suburbs, yellow for airport) 13 15 00, Metro Monorail and Light Rail (02) 8584 5288; Taxis ABC Taxis 13 25 22, Legion Cabs 13 14 51, Manly Cabs 13 16 68, Premier Cabs 13 10 17; Water Taxis Water Taxis Combined (02) 9555 8888; Cruises Bounty Cruises (02) 9247 1789, Captain Cook Cruises (02) 9206 1111, Matilda Cruises (02) 9264 7377, Blue Line Cruises (02) 8296 7296.

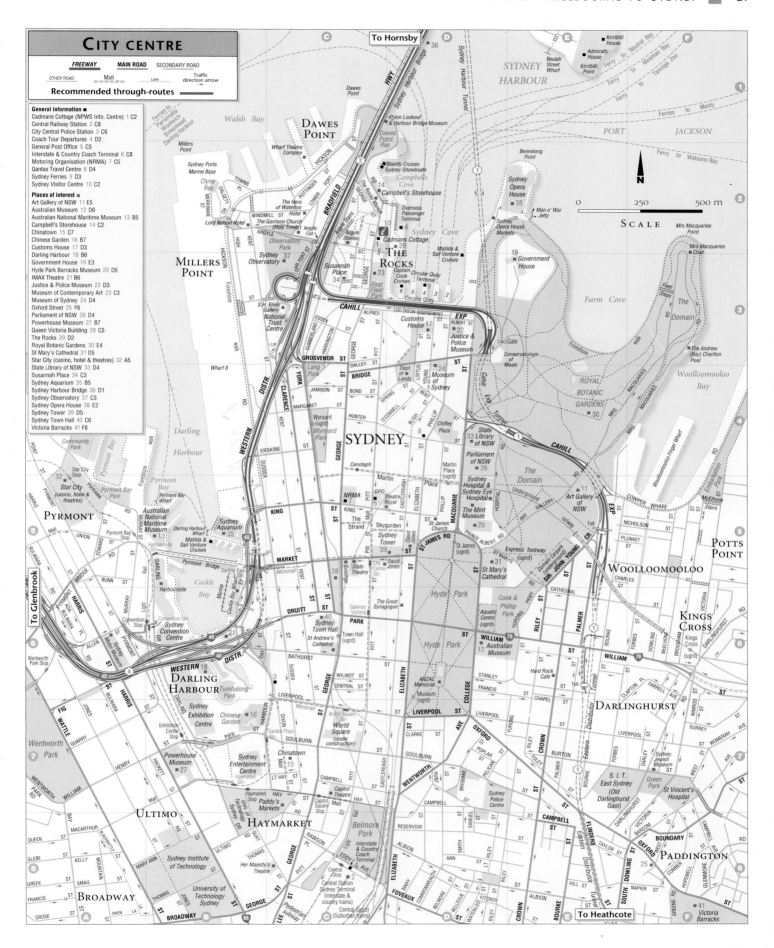

CITY CENTRE

FREEWAY	MAIN ROAD	SECONDARY ROAD
OTHER ROAD	Mall	Lane
		Traffic direction arrow

Recommended through-routes

General information ■
- Cadmans Cottage (NPWS Info. Centre) 1 C2
- Central Railway Station 2 C8
- City Central Police Station 3 C6
- Coach Tour Departures 4 D2
- General Post Office 5 C5
- Interstate & Country Coach Terminal 6 C8
- Motoring Organisation (NRMA) 7 C5
- Qantas Travel Centre 8 D4
- Sydney Ferries 9 D3
- Sydney Visitor Centre 10 C2

Places of interest
- Art Gallery of NSW 11 E5
- Australian Museum 12 D6
- Australian National Maritime Museum 13 B5
- Campbell's Storehouse 14 C2
- Chinatown 15 C7
- Chinese Garden 16 B7
- Customs House 17 D3
- Darling Harbour 18 B6
- Government House 19 E3
- Hyde Park Barracks Museum 20 D5
- IMAX Theatre 21 B6
- Justice & Police Museum 22 D3
- Museum of Contemporary Art 23 C3
- Museum of Sydney 24 D4
- Oxford Street 25 F8
- Parliament of NSW 26 D4
- Powerhouse Museum 27 B7
- Queen Victoria Building 28 C5
- The Rocks 29 D2
- Royal Botanic Gardens 30 E4
- St Mary's Cathedral 31 D5
- Star City (casino, hotel & theatres) 32 A5
- State Library of NSW 33 D4
- Susannah Place 34 C3
- Sydney Aquarium 35 B5
- Sydney Harbour Bridge 36 D1
- Sydney Observatory 37 C3
- Sydney Opera House 38 E2
- Sydney Tower 39 D5
- Sydney Town Hall 40 C6
- Victoria Barracks 41 F8

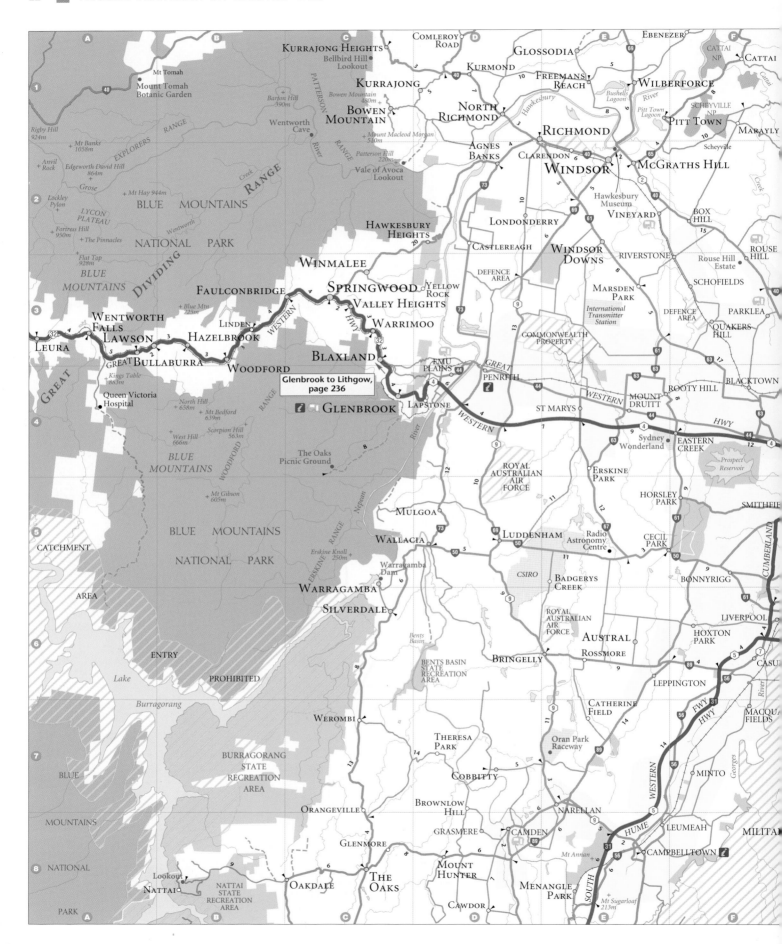

Glenbrook to Lithgow,
page 236

SUBURBS AND SURROUNDS

Recommended through-routes
Main roads, sealed   unsealed
Other roads, sealed   unsealed

SOUTH PACIFIC

OCEAN

TASMAN SEA

Hornsby to Hexham,
page 26

Nowra
to Heathcote,
page 16

0   5 km

SCALE

N

SYDNEY TO BRISBANE

PACIFIC HIGHWAY (966 KM)

The rambling Pacific Highway is a major coastal route
linking New South Wales and sunny Queensland.
Squeezed between the Great Dividing Range and the
sea, the entire coastal strip is a popular year-round
tourist destination. The golden beaches of the central
New South Wales coast, the subtropical resorts of
northern New South Wales and the world-class
Gold Coast are all exciting destinations for
holiday-makers.

Smoke Cape Lighthouse, Hat Head National Park

Best time to go

The constant mild climate
means holiday-makers can
make use of the area's
natural coastal features
practically all year round.
October to April is ideal
swimming weather on this
beautiful section of coast.

John & Jan

NEWCASTLE

	J	F	M	A	M	J	J	A	S	O	N	D
Maximum	26	25	25	23	20	17	17	18	20	22	24	25
Minimum	19	19	18	15	12	10	8	9	11	14	16	18
Rainfall (mm)	91	106	122	116	116	118	97	76	74	74	70	82
Raindays	11	11	12	12	12	12	11	10	10	11	11	11

MURWILLUMBAH

	J	F	M	A	M	J	J	A	S	O	N	D
Maximum	29	29	28	26	24	21	21	22	25	26	28	29
Minimum	19	19	18	15	13	10	9	9	11	14	16	18
Rainfall (mm)	198	231	228	176	160	90	75	52	43	86	130	164
Raindays	16	17	17	15	14	11	9	8	11	14	14	14

Brisbane

Brisbane's subtropical climate and river-setting are very appealing. Buy a ferry pass and criss-cross the river to explore the city's many highlights.

Ballina to Tweed Heads

The highway climbs across a rich volcanic range between coffee and macadamia nut plantations before sweeping down towards the fabulous alternative-lifestyle town of Byron Bay. The beautiful beaches south of the Tweed River are popular holiday destinations.

Coffs Harbour to Ballina

Winding its way through forest, the highway also passes lush dairy farms and runs alongside the Clarence River for long stretches. Take time out to explore Grafton's gorgeous parks.

Hexham to Kew

From Hexham you will journey through the hills and forests near Bulahdelah. The coast is a holiday playground with pristine beaches, still lakes and numerous caravan parks.

Tweed Heads to Beenleigh

The route sweeps inland through the Gold Coast hinterland. The glamorous Gold Coast is renowned for great beaches, excellent weather and a resort lifestyle. Its many theme parks are popular and colourful tourist attractions.

Kew to Coffs Harbour

The coastal towns south of Port Macquarie are popular holiday spots, while further north the highway skirts the Dorrigo Plateau, an area of outstanding natural beauty.

Hornsby to Hexham

The route winds its way north across the Hawkesbury River and sweeps inland to the Hunter River. The coastal road north of the Hawkesbury is a popular alternative, with access to Lake Macquarie and a good selection of caravan parks.

Sydney

Sydney is one of the world's most beautiful cities, with its sweeping surf beaches, soaring cliffs and the glittering waters of Sydney Harbour. Combined with great restaurants, superb architecture and interesting historic sites, this city is an irresistible destination.

Brisbane to Augathella, page 248

Brisbane to Cairns, page 42

Sydney to Adelaide, page 234

Melbourne to Sydney, page 2

BRISBANE
Page 38

BEENLEIGH

Page 36

IPSWICH
LOGAN

NERANG
SURFERS PARADISE

QUEENSLAND
TWEED HEADS

MURWILLUMBAH
BOGANGAR
POTTSVILLE

Page 34
BRUNSWICK HEADS
Cape Byron
KYOGLE
BYRON BAY
LISMORE
LENNOX HEAD
CASINO
BALLINA

EVANS HEAD

CORAL

MACLEAN
YAMBA

Page 32
SEA
GRAFTON

NYMBOIDA
WOOLI

DORRIGO
PLATEAU
SANDY BEACH

DORRIGO
COFFS HARBOUR
BELLINGEN
SAWTELL
URUNGA
NAMBUCCA HEADS
MACKSVILLE
Page 30

TASMAN
KEMPSEY
NEW SOUTH
WALES
CRESCENT HEAD
Point Plomer
WAUCHOPE
PORT MACQUARIE
KEW
LAKE CATHIE
NORTH HAVEN

Crowdy Head
GLOUCESTER
TAREE
HARRINGTON
NABIAC
SEA
FORSTER–TUNCURRY
Page 28
PACIFIC PALMS
DUNGOG
BULAHDELAH
BRANXTON
HAWKS NEST
NELSON BAY
HEXHAM
RAYMOND TERRACE
WOLLOMBI
NEWCASTLE
SWANSEA
Page 26

WISEMANS
FERRY
THE ENTRANCE
WINDSOR
GOSFORD
HORNSBY
PALM BEACH
SYDNEY
Page 18

N

0   25   50   75   100 km
SCALE

BRISBANE
SYDNEY

HORNSBY TO HEXHAM 140 KM

Authors' choice

⊛ Ocean Beach Holiday Park, Umina

Just 2 km from the centre of Umina and set in a fabulous beachfront position, this quality park is a favourite of ours. Kids' activities are held most weekends and during the school holidays. It is only about an hour from Sydney. Minimum bookings sometimes apply.

For more details see page 392.

⊛ Blue Lagoon Beach Resort, Bateau Bay

Tucked away at the water's edge, this beachfront park has a pool, spa and even its own restaurant. It is an ideal place for a quiet break, although it is busy at the height of the Christmas and Easter holidays, when we recommend that you book.

For more details see page 354.

Old Sydney revisited

Old Sydney Town is a classic tourist attraction, a re-creation of the harsh realities of the early settlement as it was in 1788. Pacific Highway, Somersby; (02) 4340 1104; entry fee applies; open 10 a.m. to 4 p.m. Wednesday to Sunday, daily during school holidays.

Hexham to Kew, page 28

SCALE
0   5   10   15 km

Sydney to Hornsby (21 km)
For connecting routes, see map of
Sydney suburbs and surrounds, pages 22–3

Scenic coast diversion

An alternative route to Hexham, via Newcastle, is to follow the coast more closely, taking in Gosford, Terrigal and several small waterfront communities. The road skirts Tuggerah Lake and Lake Macquarie, and passes numerous excellent surfing and swimming beaches. There are many caravan parks close to the route and shopping centres are never far away.

A wildlife adventure

The award-winning Australian Reptile Park has a fascinating display of snakes and an incredible range of other wildlife, including everyone's cuddly favourites. Pacific Highway, Somersby; (02) 4340 1022; entry fee applies; open 9 a.m. to 5 p.m. daily.

Travel tip

The alternative route through Gosford and Newcastle to Hexham is a must for those with the time. Great beaches, some incredible vistas and a never-ending selection of restaurants and eateries make this a pleasurable trip. The route is clearly signposted; however, during the peak holiday periods the area becomes very busy.

Fort Scratchley

Newcastle's Fort Scratchley, perched high above the entrance to the harbour, houses an interesting maritime and military museum. The site also has a number of historic buildings and a network of underground tunnels. Fort Drive; (02) 4929 3066; open 10.30 a.m. to 4 p.m. on weekends and public holidays.

What's on

MARCH Newcastle Regional Show, Terrigal Beach Food, Wine and Chocolate Festival APRIL Lake Macquarie Heritage Afloat Festival (Toronto) SEPTEMBER Springtime Flora Festival (Gosford) OCTOBER Gosford City Arts Festival DECEMBER Tuggerah Lakes Mardi Gras Festival (The Entrance)

Track notes

The Pacific Highway between Hornsby and Hexham is a spectacular freeway, winding through rugged sandstone escarpments and crossing the picturesque Hawkesbury River. Traffic can increase greatly on holiday weekends. Several freeway exits allow access to many coastal towns. Service centres on the freeway provide fuel and food.

Town file

1 HORNSBY PDG
GPS 33° 42.229' S/151° 05.939' E
Located on the northern outskirts of Sydney, the suburb of Hornsby is easily accessible from the freeway. Hornsby has a large shopping centre and a quality caravan park. ℹ 28–44 George Street; (02) 9847 6683.

2 GOSFORD pop. 25 690 PDG
GPS 33° 25.243' S/151° 20.292' E
Gosford is a key regional city servicing the central coast. The region has grown significantly and many residents commute daily to Sydney. Gosford has excellent shopping and all services. ℹ 200 Mann Street; 1300 130 708; www.cctourism.com.au

3 THE ENTRANCE pop. 5348 PDG
GPS 33° 20.450' S/151° 29.841' E
Located on a narrow isthmus, this town is squeezed between the ocean and Tuggerah Lake. Fishing, sailing, windsurfing, swimming and surfing are all popular pursuits. ℹ Marine Parade; 1300 130 708; www.cctourism.com.au

4 SWANSEA pop. 7959 PDG
GPS 33° 05.371' S/151° 38.261' E
Swansea lies between the shores of Lake Macquarie and the ocean. It has excellent access to the lake and is close to great surfing beaches. Swansea has good shopping and is just 29 km south of Newcastle. A visitor information centre is at the nearby town of Blacksmiths. ℹ Lake Macquarie Visitor Information Centre, 72 Pacific Highway, Blacksmiths; (02) 4972 1172 or 1800 802 044; www.lakemac.com.au

5 NEWCASTLE pop. 270 324 PDG
GPS 32° 55.583' S/151°46.886' E
The Pacific Highway now bypasses the major industrial city of Newcastle. Excellent surfing and swimming beaches close to town draw many holiday-makers to the region. Newcastle has excellent shopping and all services. The nearby Hunter Valley is one of Australia's best wine-producing regions, and many wineries welcome visitors. ℹ Wheeler Place, Hunter Street; (02) 4974 2999 or 1800 654 558.

6 HEXHAM pop. 150 PDG
GPS 32° 49.468' S/151° 41.031' E
Hexham is a small highway service centre set at the strategic junction of the New England and Pacific highways, on the south banks of the Hunter River. A roadhouse complex provides services to motorists.

HEXHAM TO KEW 202 KM

Authors' choice

⊛ One Mile Beach Holiday Park, Anna Bay

This quality, award-winning caravan park is located in the popular Port Stephens region, just a few kilometres south of Nelson Bay. Set alongside a popular patrolled surf beach, it has excellent amenities and great recreational facilities including mini-golf, a tennis court and a resort-style swimming pool. A real favourite with us – we always enjoy staying here.
For more details see page 352.

⊛ Riverside Caravan Park, Croki

Set on the banks of the Manning River in a quiet off-highway location, this small, well-designed owner-operated park is a perfect base from which to explore the attractions of Ellenborough Falls and Crowdy Bay National Park. The park has drive-through sites ideally suited for an overnight stop; however, if there is time, stay two nights so you have a chance to see the local area.
For more details see page 362.

O'Sullivans Gap

The old Pacific Highway once climbed over O'Sullivans Gap. This picturesque drive through lush forests is a pleasant alternative to the bypass built in 1999.

Kew to Coffs Harbour, page 30

Hornsby to Hexham, page 26

What's on

JANUARY Craftathon (Taree), Summer Rodeo (Wingham)
MARCH Agricultural Show (Wingham) **EASTER** Aquatic Festival (Taree) **APRIL** Australian Ironman Triathlon (Forster–Tuncurry)
MAY Manning Valley Beef Week (Wingham) **OCTOBER** Oyster Festival (Forster–Tuncurry) **NOVEMBER** Show and Rodeo (Bulahdelah), Show and Rodeo (Wingham)

Map place names: Ellenborough Falls, Comboyne, Kew, Kendall, North Haven, Elands, Dunbogan, BULGA PLATEAU, COORABAKH NP, YOORIGAN NATIONAL PARK, LAURIETON, Bobin, Killabakh, Johns River, CROWDY BAY, Marlee, Lansdowne, Moorland, Coopernook, Coralville, NATIONAL PARK, WINGHAM, Crowdy Head, HARRINGTON, Cedar Party Creek, Croki, MANNING POINT, TAREE, Tinonee, Purfleet, OLD BAR, TASMAN, Burrell Creek, WALLABI POINT, Rainbow Flat, DIAMOND BEACH, Krambach, HALLIDAYS POINT, NABIAC, SEA, Wang Wauk, FORSTER–TUNCURRY, Willina, Coolongolook, BOOTI BOOTI NATIONAL PARK, Coomba, GREEN POINT, Wootton, O'Sullivans Gap, WALLINGAT NATIONAL PARK, Wallis Lake, Tiona, Elizabeth Bay, Markwell, Elizabeth Beach, Boomerang Beach, Rosenthal, BLUEYS BEACH, PACIFIC PALMS, BULAHDELAH, Bungwahl, Sandbar, SMITHS LAKE, Myall Lake, SEAL ROCKS, Sugarloaf Point Lighthouse, MYALL LAKES NATIONAL PARK, Bombah Point, MYALL LAKES NATIONAL PARK, PACIFIC, Bombah Broadwater, Tamboy, Myall River, Broughton Island, LIMEBURNERS CREEK, Karuah, Seaham, TEA GARDENS, HAWKS NEST, Williams, Port Stephens, SHOAL BAY, RAYMOND TERRACE, LEMON TREE PASSAGE, NELSON BAY, Grahamstown Lake, Fighter World, TOMAREE NP, BERESFIELD, Hunter River, ANNA BAY, BOAT HARBOUR, HEXHAM, WILLIAMTOWN

SCALE 0 5 10 15 20 km

N

Spectacular falls

The Bulga Plateau, north of Wingham, makes an interesting diversion. The 160-m Ellenborough Falls are reputed to be the longest single-drop waterfall in the Southern Hemisphere.

The Lakes Way

This magnificent scenic drive winds past three lake systems, over 20 beaches, three national parks and several State forests. The route is dotted with pretty picnic spots and lookouts overlooking stunning water-filled vistas. Paddle in the shallows, throw a line into the surf, scramble along the rocky coastline while keeping an eye out for migrating whales (June to August), or explore the area surrounding the Sugarloaf Point Lighthouse – this tour can be as active or relaxing as you want to make it.

Track notes

This section of the Pacific Highway is one of Australia's busiest, carrying large volumes of interstate east-coast traffic in addition to substantial local traffic. The traffic can also be extremely heavy in the key holiday periods. The road surface has been greatly improved over recent years and there is an ongoing effort to complete the upgrade and lane duplication.

Town file

1 HEXHAM (see page 27)

2 BULAHDELAH pop. 1113　　PDG
GPS 32° 24.815' S/152° 12.463' E
Situated at the foot of the Great Dividing Range, this small town has good shopping and licensed clubs, and is surrounded by bush reserves. The beautiful Myall River is a feature of Bulahdelah with riverside parks, boat ramps and houseboats. Corner Pacific Highway and Crawford Street; (02) 4997 4981; www.greatlakes.org.au

3 FORSTER–TUNCURRY pop. 15 943　　PDG
GPS 32° 11.082' S/152° 30.472' E
The popular family and fishing holiday centre of Forster–Tuncurry graces the entrance of picturesque Wallis Lake. This shallow tidal waterway is a boating and recreational playground. Galleries, cinemas, fun parks, restaurants, cruises and magnificent coastal scenery provide interest and entertainment for holiday-makers of all ages. Little Street; (02) 6554 8799 or 1800 802 692; www.greatlakes.org.au

4 TAREE pop. 16 702　　PDG
GPS 31° 53.941' S/152° 27.474' E
This culturally diverse town is the hub of the Manning River valley and features excellent sporting and shopping facilities with roads leading to quaint craft villages, seaside beauty spots and mountain national parks. Riverfront parklands right in the centre of town provide space to relax. Manning Valley Visitor Information Centre; 21 Manning River Drive; (02) 6552 1900 or 1800 801 522; www.retreat-to-nature.com

5 WINGHAM pop. 4446　　PD
GPS 31° 51.513' S/152° 22.052' E
Wingham offers visitors a step back in time. National Trust buildings and manicured gardens give this town character. Wingham Brush, close to the town centre, has giant Moreton Bay figs and interesting wildlife and is the largest remaining riverine rainforest in New South Wales.

6 KEW pop. 180　　PDG
GPS 31° 37.512' S/152° 43.185' E
Kew is a small, tidy town on the Pacific Highway. The visitor information centre offers free tea and coffee and has an interesting display on Nancy Bird Walton, who was born in Kew and was one of Australia's pioneer aviators. It also houses a painting illustrating the impact of the timber industry on the town – just look for the big axe out the front! Pacific Highway; (02) 6559 4400 or 1300 303 154.

KEW TO COFFS HARBOUR 191 KM

Go bananas

The Big Banana was one of Australia's earliest 'big' attractions. Today visitors can take a train around the plantation, see the bananas growing and visit the packing sheds, then try a chocolate-coated banana or banana split at the cafe. For the more energetic, there is a toboggan ride and ice-skating rink. Pacific Highway north of Coffs Harbour; (02) 6652 4355; entry free but fee applies for attractions; open 9 a.m. to 4 p.m. daily.

Historic gaol

The historic Trial Bay Gaol was first occupied in 1886, by 'good conduct' prisoners; it then became an alien internment camp for Germans during World War I. Today you can wander through re-created cells. The gaol and attached museum are maintained by the National Parks and Wildlife Service, and located in the Arakoon State Recreation Area, east of South West Rocks. (02) 6566 6168; entry fee applies; open 9 a.m. to 4.30 p.m. daily.

Timbertown

At the Timbertown Heritage Theme Park many buildings delightfully re-create a timber town of the 1880s: features include a blacksmith, leather-worker, sawmill and steam train. Take a Cobb & Co. coach to bush camps for demonstrations of sleeper cutting and shingle splitting, then eat damper and roast meat at the hotel. Oxley Highway, Wauchope; (02) 6585 2322; entry free but fee applies for attractions; open 9.30 a.m. to 3.30 p.m. daily.

Coffs Harbour to Ballina, page 32

Hexham to Kew, page 28

Track notes

Drifting through forests and passing through coastal towns, this section of the highway is a comfortable drive with great stretches of divided road and several popular roadside rest areas.

Town file

1 KEW (see page 29)

2 PORT MACQUARIE pop. 33 709 ⛽ PDG
GPS 31° 25.734' S/152° 54.763' E
Port Macquarie is a regional centre at the mouth of the Hastings River. Founded as a convict settlement in 1821, it is one of the State's oldest towns and now a popular holiday spot. There is very good shopping and all services. 🄲 Clarence Street; (02) 6581 8000 or 1300 303 155; www.portmacquarieinfo.com.au

3 KEMPSEY pop. 8630 ⛽ PDG
GPS 31° 04.871' S/152° 50.591' E
Kempsey is the centre for a diverse agricultural area. Among the town's industries is the Akubra hat factory. 🄲 Pacific Highway, South Kempsey; (02) 6563 1555 or 1800 642 480; www.kempsey.midcoast.com.au

4 SOUTH WEST ROCKS pop. 3514 ⛽ PDG
GPS 30° 53.219' S/153° 02.498' E
South West Rocks is a popular destination for camping, bushwalking, fishing and boating. It has a small shopping centre and basic services. 🄲 1 Ocean Drive; (02) 6566 7099.

5 NAMBUCCA HEADS pop. 6253 ⛽ PDG
GPS 30° 38.545' S/153° 00.212' E
Nambucca Heads, at the picturesque mouth of the Nambucca River, is a holiday destination, and fishing, surfing and windsurfing are popular. It has good country-town shopping and all services. 🄲 Corner Pacific Highway and Riverside Drive; (02) 6568 6954 or 1800 646 587; www.nambuccatourism.com

6 URUNGA pop. 2716 ⛽ PDG
GPS 30° 30.106' S/153° 00.724' E
Founded by cedar cutters, Urunga boasts pristine waterways and good beaches. Windsurfing, fishing and water-skiing are popular on the rivers. Urunga has a small shopping centre and basic services. 🄲 Pacific Highway; (02) 6655 5711 or 1800 808 611.

7 COFFS HARBOUR pop. 22 177 ⛽ PDG
GPS 30° 17.912' S/153° 06.747' E
Beginning as a port for cedar cutters in the 1840s, Coffs Harbour developed into a key regional town and holiday destination. A fishing fleet operates from the harbour and bananas flourish on nearby hillsides. There is very good regional shopping and all services. 🄲 Corner Pacific Highway and McLean Street; (02) 6652 1522 or 1300 369 070; www.coffscoast.com.au

Watch dolphins and sea-lions perform
The Pet Porpoise Pool at Coffs Harbour is terrific entertainment for the whole family. The pool is home to rescued dolphins, seals and penguins. There is a great sea circus display at 10.30 a.m. and 2.15 p.m. where children can play ball with the dolphins, and visitors are encouraged to touch the sea-lions. Orlando Street; (02) 6652 2164; entry fee applies; open 9 a.m. to 5 p.m. daily.

What's on

APRIL Gaol Break Festival (South West Rocks)
AUGUST Bellingen Jazz Festival SEPTEMBER All Star Country Music Festival (Kempsey)
OCTOBER Festival of Golf (Coffs Harbour)

COFFS HARBOUR TO BALLINA 211 KM

Authors' choice

✪ Blue Dolphin Holiday Resort, Yamba

This riverfront, award-winning park is on the Clarence River estuary. It is an excellent park, with everything you would expect of a five-star establishment, including a cafe. Yamba is a popular holiday town and minimum bookings apply at the park during holiday periods.
For more details see page 394.

Rainforest by the beach

The World Heritage-listed Iluka Nature Reserve contains the largest remnants of beachside (littoral) rainforest in New South Wales. Easy walking paths through the lilly pillies in this compact reserve are popular with birdwatchers, while endangered animals and birds, such as the black-necked stork, the little tern and the squirrel glider, make their home here.

Inland alternative

The Summerland Way is a picturesque, alternative route linking Brisbane and Grafton. It is about the same distance as the Pacific Highway, but cuts inland from Grafton. The fully sealed road takes in Casino, Kyogle and Beaudesert, climbing through the ranges close to the Queensland border.

What's on

JANUARY Reef to Beach Swim (Woolgoolga)
EASTER MacLean Highland Gathering
JULY Evans Head Fishing Classic
OCTOBER/NOVEMBER Jacaranda Festival (Grafton) **NOVEMBER** Yamba Seafood Expo

Ballina to Tweed Heads, page 34

To Brisbane

Kew to Coffs Harbour, page 30

Thursday Plantation

BALLINA

MEERSCHAUM VALE
EMPIRE VALE
WARDELL
CORAKI
BROADWATER
BROADWATER NATIONAL PARK
WOODBURN
EVANS HEAD
NEW ITALY
BUNGAWALBIN NP
BUNDJALUNG
TABBIMOBLE
NATIONAL
PARK
CORAL
Woombah
Browns Rocks
CHATSWORTH
ILUKA NR
HARWOOD
ILUKA
Ferry
YAMBA
MACLEAN
ANGOURIE
LAWRENCE
Dilkoon
Ferry
Wooloweyah Estuary
SUMMERLAND WAY
YURAYGIR
BRUSHGROVE
COWPER
TYNDALE
SEELANDS
Clarence
ULMARRA
BROOMS HEAD
EATONSVILLE
TUCABIA
JUNCTION HILL
NATIONAL
SEA
WATERVIEW HEIGHTS
GRAFTON
Pillar Valley
PARK
MINNIE WATER
Lake Hiawatha
YURAYGIR
COUTTS CROSSING
NATIONAL
WOOLI
Orara
PARK
North Solitary Island
Halfway Creek
Kungala
RED ROCK
SCALE
0 5 10 15 20 km
CORINDI
CORINDI BEACH
GLENREAGH
SHERWOOD NR
ARRAWARRA
MULLAWAY
SAFETY BEACH
Lower Bucca
WOOLGOOLGA
SANDY BEACH
EMERALD BEACH
Coffs Harbour Zoo
CORAMBA
MOONEE BEACH
KORORA
Big Banana
COFFS HARBOUR

N
PACIFIC HWY
Richmond

Medicinal oil

Tea-tree oil is reputed to have extraordinary medicinal effects, being antiseptic and fungicidal. Thursday Plantation pioneered the development of the tea-tree oil industry and now exports its products around the world. Visitors can see the oil being produced, walk through herb gardens and find their way through a maze constructed from tea-trees (pictured). Gallens Road, off the Pacific Highway north of Ballina; (02) 6686 7273; open 9 a.m. to 5 p.m. daily.

Rafting across the Pacific

See an unusual boat in Ballina's Naval and Maritime Museum: the famous Las Balsas raft (made from balsa wood) that successfully made the epic journey from Ecuador in South America to Ballina in 1973. Regatta Avenue; (02) 6681 1002; admission by donation; open 9 a.m. to 4 p.m. daily.

Travel tip

There are several key centres and numerous small resort towns along this coastal strip of New South Wales. The miles of sandy beaches, national parks, wide river estuaries, nearby mountain ranges and delightful subtropical climate attract many visitors, and fishing, surfing, boating, golf, bowls and just touring are all popular recreational pursuits.

Track notes

The Pacific Highway winds through towering forests and past dairy farms. There are several overtaking lanes and many popular coastal towns are off the highway, but the road still passes through small communities.

Town file

1 COFFS HARBOUR (see page 31)

2 WOOLGOOLGA pop. 3772   ⛽ PDG
GPS 30° 06.647' S/153° 11.974' E
Woolgoolga has one of Australia's largest Sikh communities and the impressive Guru Nanak Sikh temple is prominent in town. Woolgoolga, with good basic shopping and services, nestles by a patrolled beach and offers varied fishing.

3 GRAFTON pop. 16 562   ⛽ PDG
GPS 29° 41.475' S/152° 56.012' E
Grafton, on the mighty Clarence River, is famous for graceful buildings, many classified by the National Trust, and magnificent jacarandas. Grafton has good regional shopping and is home to a fine art gallery and museum. ℹ Clarence River Visitor Information Centre, Pacific Highway; (02) 6642 4677.

4 MACLEAN pop. 3157   ⛽ PD
GPS 29° 27.374' S/153° 11.816' E
Maclean is proud of its Scottish heritage – many signs carry Gaelic translations. It is the base for a prawning fleet that operates along the Clarence River. ℹ Lower Clarence Visitors Centre, Ferry Park, Pacific Highway; (02) 6645 4121.

5 YAMBA pop. 4721   ⛽ PDG
GPS 29° 26.212' S/153° 21.675' E
Picturesque Yamba overlooks the estuary of the Clarence River. There is good rock, beach and deep-sea fishing. A commercial fishing fleet operates from here. South of Yamba are legendary surfing spots. A ferry links Iluka and Yamba daily.

6 EVANS HEAD pop. 2613   ⛽ PD
GPS 29° 97.083' S/153° 25.857' E
Evans Head is a popular holiday destination, with safe swimming beaches, surf beaches and a quiet estuary. It nestles between the Broadwater and Bundjalung national parks.

7 BALLINA pop. 16 056   ⛽ PDG
GPS 28° 52.131' S/153° 33.590' E
At the mouth of the Richmond River, Ballina is an ideal base from which to explore the northern rivers region. The beaches and estuary are popular for fishing and surfers flock here. Ballina is the centre of the tea-tree industry. ℹ Las Balsas Plaza, River Street; (02) 6686 3484; www.discoverballina.com

BALLINA TO TWEED HEADS 92 KM

Authors' choice

⭐ **North Star Holiday Resort, Hastings Point**

This award-winning park has an impressive range of excellent facilities, including a fully licensed restaurant. This park is a cut above most: the amenities are excellent, the beach is a short walk across the road and the town centre is just 500 m away – we highly recommend it. **For more details see page 369.**

Mount Warning – a volcanic caldera
Mount Warning (1157 m) is the most prominent natural feature in the region. The core of an extinct volcano, it towers over Murwillumbah and its caldera landform straddles the New South Wales and Queensland border. A 4.5-km walking track through rainforest (with a steep scramble at the top) leads to the summit of Mount Warning, the first point in Australia to experience the morning sun. Allow about 5 hours for the walk.

What's on
JANUARY Festival of the Fish 'n' Chips (Brunswick Heads)
MARCH/APRIL East Coast International Blues and Roots Festival (Byron Bay) MAY Art, Food and All That Jazz (Kingscliff) JUNE Wintersun Festival (Tweed Heads) AUGUST Tweed Valley Banana Festival and Harvest Week (Murwillumbah)

Tweed Heads to Beenleigh, page 36

Coffs Harbour to Ballina, page 32

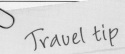

Travel tip

The Brunswick Heads Fishermen's Cooperative, located on the river's edge adjoining the marina, has a large retail outlet with a delicious selection of fresh and cooked seafood. Buy fresh fish to take away or enjoy freshly cooked fish and chips in the adjoining park. The shop is open daily.

Exceptional art and craft

Griffith Galleries at Treetops Environment Centre houses a magnificent range of paintings, ceramics, cut glass, jewellery and exquisite timber pieces. It is clearly signposted to the south-east off the Murwillumbah to Tweed Heads road. Clothiers Creek Road, Condong; (02) 6672 3068.

Beside the sea

A popular deviation from the Pacific Highway is the Tweed Coast Way, which follows the picturesque coastline between Pottsville and Chinderah, through Hastings Point and past Cabarita Beach. Several quality caravan parks are located along this route.

Cape Byron Lighthouse

Cape Byron is the easternmost point on mainland Australia and is part of the Arakwal National Park. An automated lighthouse – the most powerful in Australia – takes the prominent position atop the cape. Visitors are welcome at the lighthouse, which was built in 1901 and is an imposing structure, but there is no access inside. From the headland there are tremendous views, and in season you can see whales, dolphins, manta rays and much more.

Track notes

The Pacific Highway has undergone enormous changes recently: it now bypasses the ranges south of Murwillumbah and their accident black spots. Byron Bay to Tweed Heads is now a relaxing drive.

Town file

1 BALLINA (see page 33)

2 BANGALOW pop. 896   PD
GPS 28° 41.188' S/153° 31.461' E
Bangalow is a small town bypassed by the highway. The craft shops, eating spots and galleries attract tourists. There are basic services and limited shopping.

3 BYRON BAY pop. 6130   PDG
GPS 28° 38.658' S/153° 36.745' E
Byron Bay is a popular resort town with restaurants, accommodation, extensive resort-style shopping and most services. The town has a magnetic appeal to backpackers with its surfing, beaches, alternative lifestyle and wonderful climate. Dairy products, coffee, macadamia nuts and tropical fruits are produced (and sold) locally. 🅸 80 Jonson Street; (02) 6685 8050; www.visitbyronbay.com

4 MULLUMBIMBY pop. 2870   PD
GPS 28° 33.192' S/153° 29.985' E
Situated in lush, subtropical country, Mullumbimby is known for its fabulous woodwork. The town has good country-town shopping. Markets are held on the third Saturday of each month.

5 BRUNSWICK HEADS pop. 1835   PDG
GPS 28° 32.442' S/153° 33.102' E
Brunswick Heads is a popular resort town well known for good fishing; it is home to a fishing and prawning fleet. Brunswick Heads has limited services and a small shopping centre.

6 MURWILLUMBAH pop. 7657   PDG
GPS 28° 19.593' S/153° 23.756' E
On the banks of the Tweed River, Murwillumbah is at the centre of the rich Tweed Valley. It has restaurants, hotels, clubs and a good regional shopping centre. 🅸 World Heritage Rainforest Centre, corner Alma Street and Pacific Highway; (02) 6672 1340.

7 TWEED HEADS pop. 37 775   PDG
GPS 28° 10.370' S/153° 32.586' E
Tweed Heads lies on the New South Wales side of the border with Queensland, adjoining Coolangatta. The town occupies both banks of the Tweed River and numerous boats operate on the estuary. There are fishing and diving charters available, as well as cruises up the Tweed River. Tweed Heads is known for its great clubs and has extensive shopping and all services. 🅸 Tweed Mall Shopping Centre; (07) 5536 4244 or 1800 674 414; www.tweed-coolangatta.com

TWEED HEADS TO BEENLEIGH 71 KM

Authors' choice

✪ Tallebudgera Creek Tourist Park, Palm Beach

A favourite of ours, this popular holiday caravan park fronts onto Tallebudgera Creek and is just a short walk to the beach. It is among the Gold Coast's best parks, centrally located with very good amenities and a wide range of facilities, including a tennis court and a heated pool.
For more details see page 368.

✪ Broadwater Tourist Park, Southport

Position is everything, and this spacious park fronts the Gold Coast broadwater. It has very good facilities and outstanding views across the water to Marina Mirage. There are several restaurants within walking distance and it is 1.5 km from the Southport shopping centre.
For more details see page 368.

Travel tip

The world-famous Gold Coast has many kilometres of magnificent beaches where swimmers, families, board-riders, sunbathers and windsurfers all enjoy the sun and the surf. However, the currents can be treacherous and swimmers should always swim between the flags on the many patrolled beaches.

Dreamworld daze

Dreamworld is located alongside the Pacific Motorway at Coomera. It offers amazing rides and much wildlife, including Bengal tigers on Tiger Island. Dreamworld Parkway, off Pacific Motorway; 1800 073 300; entry fee applies; open 10 a.m. to 5 p.m. daily.

Movie magic

Warner Bros Movie World is both a theme park and a fully operational movie studio. This is a major family attraction with action-packed shows and exhilarating rides. Pacific Highway, Oxenford; (07) 5573 3999; entry fee applies; open 10 a.m. to 5 p.m. daily.

Lamington National Park

The World Heritage-listed Lamington National Park is in the Gold Coast hinterland. This area of rugged ranges and deep valleys is covered in subtropical rainforest. Try a treetop walk, gaze at the cascading waterfalls, marvel at the huge buttresses of giant figs or spot a rare regent bowerbird. Binna Burra and O'Reilly's are two popular tourist lodges in the park. (07) 5533 3584.

Sea World fun

Sea World is one of the Gold Coast's premier theme parks. There is something for everyone: thrilling rides, spectacular entertainment and exciting attractions, including polar bears. Seaworld Drive, Main Beach; (07) 5588 2205; entry fee applies; open 10 a.m. to 5 p.m. daily.

Parrot paradise

Currumbin Wildlife Sanctuary is one of the best attractions in this area. The sanctuary is home to the world's largest collection of Australian native animals, spread over 27 ha of landscaped grounds. The park is especially famous for the magnificent rainbow lorikeets that visit each day to be fed. Tomewin Street, off the Gold Coast Highway; (07) 5534 1266; entry fee applies; open 8 a.m. to 5 p.m. daily.

Map labels

SOUTH STRADBROKE ISLAND CP
rrigee
SOUTH STRADBROKE ISLAND
Nerang Head
Sea World
GOLD
153° 30'
GOLD
MAIN BEACH
28° 00'
SURFERS PARADISE 3
BROADBEACH
Conrad Jupiters Casino
CORAL
COAST
7
MIAMI
BURLEIGH HEADS
Burleigh Head
BURLEIGH HEAD NP
SEA
COAST
8
PALM BEACH
CURRUMBIN
Currumbin Wildlife Sanctuary
ELANORA
TUGUN
QUEENSLAND
BILINGA
Kirra Beach
Captain Cook Memorial & Lighthouse
North Head
Cobaki Broadwater
2 COOLANGATTA
TWEED HEADS 1
GGABEEN
COBAKI
NEW SOUTH WALES
Terranora Broadwater
1
UKEREBAGH NR
153° 30'

Ballina to Tweed Heads, page 34

Track notes

This section of the Pacific Highway is an eight-lane superhighway linking the Gold Coast and Brisbane. The Gold Coast Highway meanders along the coast; we have chosen this as the main tour route because most tourist attractions and caravan parks are easily reached from it.

Town file

1 TWEED HEADS (see page 35)

2 COOLANGATTA pop. 6618 PDG
GPS 28° 10.088' S/153° 32.134' E
Coolangatta is across the border, in Queensland, from its twin town Tweed Heads, and the two share good shopping and services. Corner Griffith and Warner streets; (07) 5536 7765; www.goldcoasttourism.com.au

3 SURFERS PARADISE PDG
GPS 27° 59.542' S/153° 25.037' E
Surfers Paradise, with world-famous beaches and a great subtropical climate, is at the heart of the Gold Coast. The area is alive day and night with busy restaurants, nightclubs and shops. The Gold Coast has excellent shopping and all services. 64 Ferny Avenue; (07) 5592 2699; www.goldcoasttourism.com.au

4 NERANG pop. 14 467 PDG
GPS 27° 58.542' S/153° 19.037' E
Nerang is a key service centre for residents living in the nearby ranges. It is also the gateway to the beautiful Lamington National Park.

5 SOUTHPORT PDG
GPS 27° 58.542' S/153° 24.037' E
Southport has extensive shopping, all services and a large commercial centre. Southport is on the Gold Coast's scenic broadwater and has an excellent caravan park, numerous restaurants and popular clubs.

6 BEENLEIGH pop. 8108 PDG
GPS 27° 42.542' S/153° 11.037' E
The Pacific Highway bypasses Beenleigh but access is clearly signposted. Beenleigh is home to a historic rum distillery.

What's on

JANUARY Summer Carnival (Surfers Paradise) JUNE Wintersun Festival (Coolangatta) AUGUST Flower Festival (Tamborine) SEPTEMBER Beenleigh Show OCTOBER Indy Carnival (Surfers Paradise)

BRISBANE

YOUR GUIDE

The city of Brisbane straddles the lazy curves of the Brisbane River, which winds its way through the suburbs to Moreton Bay. The long fingers of Moreton and Stradbroke islands create a barrier to the Pacific Ocean, providing the city with a vast body of calm water at its foreshore. Inland, a hilly subtropical terrain provides breathing space and a beautiful backdrop for the city with its population of more than 1.6 million.

CITY CENTRE

See map on page 40.

Brisbane City Hall 40 C4
Architectural landmark of the city centre; also houses the contemporary work of the Brisbane City Gallery.

Brisbane Cricket Ground ('The Gabba') 40 F8
Home to the Australian Rules football team the Brisbane Lions; hosts international and State cricket matches.

Brunswick Street Mall 40 E1
Part of a lively inner-city neighbourhood with reasonably priced cuisine from all corners of the world; fascinating markets on Sundays.

City Botanic Gardens 40 D5
Ornamental plantings, glittering ponds, a mangrove boardwalk and broad sweeps of lawn on the banks of the Brisbane River.

Customs House 40 E3
Gallery and restaurant in historic riverside setting.

Eagle Street Pier 40 D4
Popular gathering spot with restaurants, bars and cafes; on Sundays, setting for Brisbane's largest open-air market.

Queensland Art Gallery 40 B5
Renowned artists represented from Australia and abroad; features a meditative Water Mall.

Queensland Maritime Museum 40 C7
Seafaring relics charting Queensland's maritime history from the Dutch landing at Cape York in 1606; includes dry dock with World War II frigate.

Queensland Museum 40 B5
Extensive natural history collection with endangered species display and a virtual 'trip' back 220 million years.

St John's Cathedral 40 D2
Gothic-style building with the only stone-vaulted ceiling in a cathedral in the Southern Hemisphere.

Sciencentre 40 C5
Interactive science displays for all the family.

South Bank Parklands 40 C6
Beach, rainforest and butterfly house in the city; on Friday evenings, a magical setting for Lantern Village Market; Craft Village on Saturdays and Sundays.

Visitor information

Brisbane Visitor Information Centre
Queen Street Mall
(07) 3006 6290
www.brisbanetourism.com.au

Visitor Information Centre South Bank Parklands
Allgas building, Stanley Street Plaza
(07) 3867 2051

Redlands Tourism Centre
1 Passage Street, Cleveland
(07) 3821 0057

Bayside Information Centre
66 Bay Terrace, Wynnum
(07) 3893 0589

Redcliffe Tourist Information Centre
Pelican Park, Hornibrook Esplanade
(07) 3284 3500

Story Bridge 40 F2
The city's best known landmark and largest steel cantilever bridge in Australia.

SUBURBS AND SURROUNDS

See map on page 41.

Bribie Island 41 F1
Excellent for bushwalking, crabbing, fishing and boating; access from Caboolture–Bribie Island Road (via bridge).

Lone Pine Koala Sanctuary 41 C6
Visit the world's largest koala sanctuary.

Miegunyah 41 D5
Historic house with displays commemorating Queensland's pioneering women.

Mount Coot-tha Forest Park 41 C5
Take in the sensational views from the summit; wander through Mount Coot-tha Botanic Gardens and visit the Tropical Dome, Japanese Garden and Australian Plant Community area.

Mount Glorious 41 A4
Dense forests and spectacular views; visit Walk-about Creek Wildlife Centre en route.

New Farm Park 41 D5
Nestled on the river bend at the end of Brunswick Street; garden oasis of tropical and ornamental species; includes a restaurant in an attractive garden setting.

Newstead House 41 D5
A classic Australian homestead on the banks of the river at Breakfast Creek.

North Stradbroke Island 41 F6
Popular destination for fishing, surfing, swimming, horseriding and canoeing; includes national park; access by ferry from Cleveland.

Ormiston House 41 F5
Former home of the founder of Queensland's big sugar industry (open Sundays, March to November).

Redcliffe Peninsula 41 E2
Juts out into Moreton Bay, providing beautiful sandy beaches; swimming is generally safe and the fishing is excellent.

St Helena Island 41 F4
Former penal settlement, now a national park; cruises to the island depart from the Manly Boat Harbour.

Getting around

Brisbane has well-signed roads and little traffic congestion, yet it is not an easy city for the first-time visitor to negotiate. There is a criss-crossing network of major motorways and a number of one-way streets. An up-to-date road map and some careful planning are necessary. Brisbane's best through-routes are all multi-lane motorways with staffed tollgates (see Suburbs and surrounds map, page 41). The Gateway Motorway also provides excellent access to Brisbane Airport. We suggest you leave your caravan on the city outskirts and catch public transport to visit the sights. The transport system (bus, rail and ferry) is efficient, with a couple of excellent bus routes specifically for tourists. A boat trip on the Brisbane River is a must, and there is a very good commuter ferry service that stops at key destinations around the city.

Airport shuttle bus Coachtrans Skytrans Airport Service (07) 3860 6999; **Motoring organisation** RACQ 13 19 05; **Public transport** TransInfo (bus, ferry, rail) 13 12 30; **Bus tours** City Sights and City Lights tourist trips 13 12 30; **Brisbane River trips** Kookaburra River Queens (07) 3221 1300, Mirimar Cruises (07) 3221 0300; **Taxis** Black & White Cabs 13 10 08, Yellow Cabs 13 19 24.

Top events

Queensland Winter Racing Carnival (May–June)
Two months of excitement on and off the racecourse.

Brisbane International Film Festival (August)
A showcase of Australian and international cinema.

'The Ekka' – Royal Brisbane Show (August)
An ideal event for families.

Brisbane River Festival (September)
Regattas, aquatic feats and dragon boats.

Spring Hill Fair (September)
Two days of markets, performers and delicious cuisine.

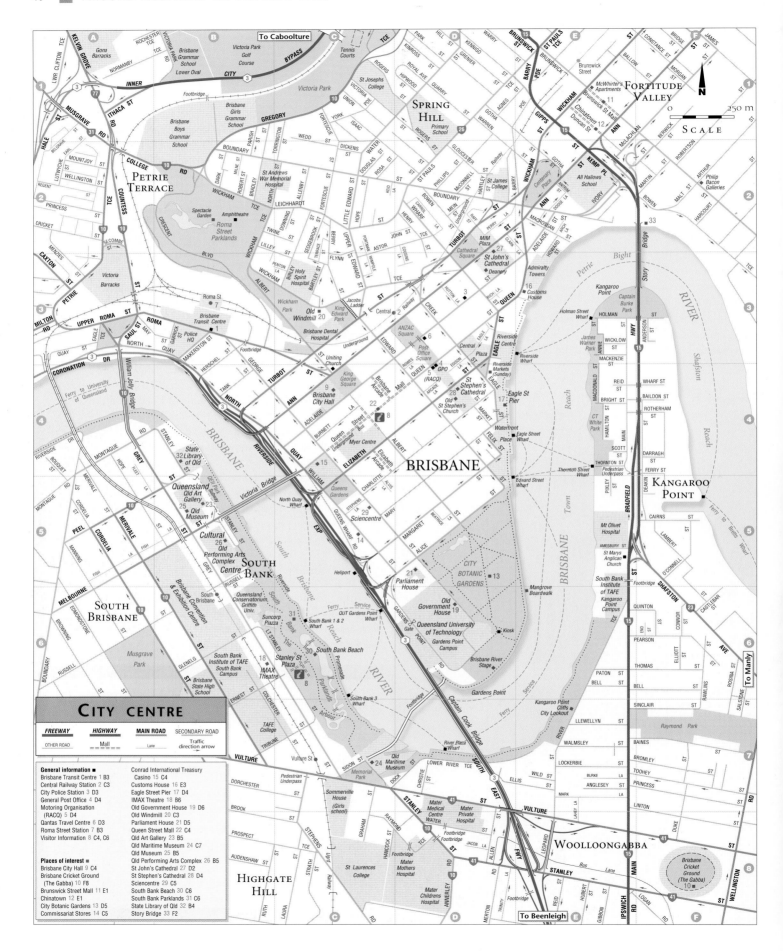

CITY CENTRE

FREEWAY	HIGHWAY	MAIN ROAD	SECONDARY ROAD
OTHER ROAD	Mall	Lane	Traffic direction arrow

General information ■
Brisbane Transit Centre 1 B3
Central Railway Station 2 C3
City Police Station 3 D3
General Post Office 4 D4
Motoring Organisation
(RACQ) 5 D4
Qantas Travel Centre 6 D3
Roma Street Station 7 B3
Visitor Information 8 C4, C6

Places of interest ■
Brisbane City Hall 9 C4
Brisbane Cricket Ground
(The Gabba) 10 F8
Brunswick Street Mall 11 E1
Chinatown 12 E1
City Botanic Gardens 13 D5
Commissariat Stores 14 C5

Conrad International Treasury
Casino 15 C4
Customs House 16 E3
Eagle Street Pier 17 D4
IMAX Theatre 18 B6
Old Government House 19 D6
Old Windmill 20 C3
Parliament House 21 D5
Queen Street Mall 22 C4
Qld Art Gallery 23 B5
Qld Maritime Museum 24 C7
Qld Museum 25 B5
Qld Performing Arts Complex 26 B5
St John's Cathedral 27 D2
St Stephen's Cathedral 28 D4
Sciencentre 29 C5
South Bank Beach 30 C6
South Bank Parklands 31 C6
State Library of Qld 32 B4
Story Bridge 33 F2

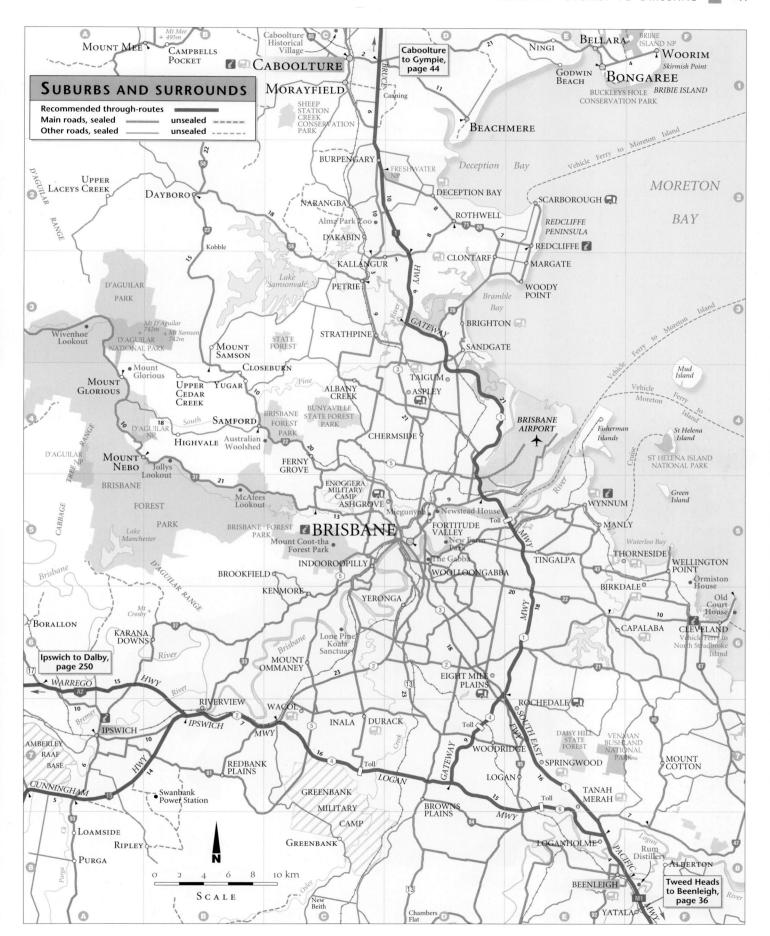

SUBURBS AND SURROUNDS

Recommended through-routes
Main roads, sealed   unsealed
Other roads, sealed   unsealed

MOUNT MEE
CAMPBELLS POCKET
Mt Mee + 495m
Caboolture Historical Village
CABOOLTURE
MORAYFIELD
BELLARA
BRIBIE ISLAND NP
WOORIM
Skirmish Point
NINGI
GODWIN BEACH
BONGAREE
BUCKLEYS HOLE CONSERVATION PARK
BRIBIE ISLAND

Caboolture to Gympie, page 44

Canning
SHEEP STATION CREEK CONSERVATION PARK
BEACHMERE
Deception Bay
MORETON BAY

UPPER LACEYS CREEK
D'AGUILAR RANGE
DAYBORO
BURPENGARY
FRESHWATER NP
DECEPTION BAY
SCARBOROUGH
REDCLIFFE PENINSULA

NARANGBA
Alma Park Zoo
DAKABIN
ROTHWELL
REDCLIFFE
MARGATE
Kobble
KALLANGUR
PETRIE
CLONTARF
WOODY POINT
Bramble Bay

D'AGUILAR PARK
Lake Samsonvale
STRATHPINE
BRIGHTON
SANDGATE

Wivenhoe Lookout
Mt D'Aguilar + 742m
Mt Samson + 742m
MOUNT SAMSON
State Forest
TAIGUM
ASPLEY

D'AGUILAR NATIONAL PARK
Mount Glorious
CLOSEBURN
Pine
ALBANY CREEK
CHERMSIDE

MOUNT GLORIOUS
UPPER CEDAR CREEK
YUGAR
SAMFORD
BUNYAVILLE STATE FOREST PARK
BRISBANE AIRPORT

D'AGUILAR NP
HIGHVALE
BRISBANE FOREST PARK
Australian Woolshed

MOUNT NEBO
Jollys Lookout
FERNY GROVE
Fisherman Islands
St Helena Island
St HELENA ISLAND NATIONAL PARK

D'AGUILAR RANGE
BRISBANE FOREST
McAfees Lookout
ENOGGERA MILITARY CAMP
ASHGROVE
Miegunyah
Newstead House
WYNNUM
Green Island

CABBAGE
Lake Manchester
BRISBANE FOREST PARK
Mount Coot-tha Forest Park
BRISBANE
FORTITUDE VALLEY
New Farm Park
MANLY

Brisbane
D'AGUILAR RANGE
INDOOROOPILLY
The Gabba
WOOLLOONGABBA
TINGALPA
THORNESIDE
Waterloo Bay

Mt Crosby +
BROOKFIELD
KENMORE
YERONGA
WELLINGTON POINT
Ormiston House

BORALLON
KARANA DOWNS
Lone Pine Koala Sanctuary
BIRKDALE
CAPALABA
CLEVELAND
Old Court House

Ipswich to Dalby, page 250

WARREGO HWY
Bremer
River
IPSWICH
RIVERVIEW
WACOL
MOUNT OMMANEY
INALA
DURACK
EIGHT MILE PLAINS
ROCHEDALE
DAISY HILL STATE FOREST
VENMAN BUSHLAND NATIONAL PARK
MOUNT COTTON

AMBERLEY RAAF BASE
IPSWICH
REDBANK PLAINS
Swanbank Power Station
WOODRIDGE
SPRINGWOOD

CUNNINGHAM
GREENBANK MILITARY CAMP
BROWNS PLAINS
LOGAN
TANAH MERAH

LOAMSIDE
RIPLEY
GREENBANK
LOGANHOLME
Rum Distillery
Logan

PURGA
New Beith
ALBERTON

N

0 2 4 6 8 10 km

SCALE

Chambers Flat
BEENLEIGH
YATALA

Tweed Heads to Beenleigh, page 36

BRISBANE TO CAIRNS
BRUCE HIGHWAY (1703 KM)

The Bruce Highway links Brisbane with Cairns in the north and several large regional cities in between. The coast is dotted with great holiday destinations, romantic island resorts, lush tropical rainforests and sparkling beaches. The popular Sunshine Coast is just an hour or so from Brisbane. Further north are the Whitsunday Islands and the colourful city of Cairns. Busy cargo ports, fields of lush sugarcane, orchards of tropical fruits, sandy beaches, mountains and great accommodation choices ensure the continuing popularity of this section of the Queensland coast.

Best time to go

The weather ranges from moderate, dry winters in the subtropical south to hot, wet summers in the north. Tourists travelling in northern areas will enjoy the more moderate conditions between April and November.

John & Jan

MARYBOROUGH

	J	F	M	A	M	J	J	A	S	O	N	D
Maximum	31	30	29	27	25	22	22	23	26	28	29	31
Minimum	21	21	19	17	13	10	9	9	12	15	18	20
Rainfall (mm)	165	174	158	90	80	67	53	40	43	75	86	127
Raindays	13	14	14	12	11	8	7	6	6	8	9	11

INGHAM

	J	F	M	A	M	J	J	A	S	O	N	D
Maximum	32	31	31	29	27	25	25	26	28	30	32	32
Minimum	23	23	22	20	18	15	14	14	16	19	21	22
Rainfall (mm)	388	466	390	209	120	44	32	42	36	50	131	214
Raindays	14	18	17	16	14	7	6	7	6	8	10	12

Lady Musgrave Island, which can be reached from Gladstone

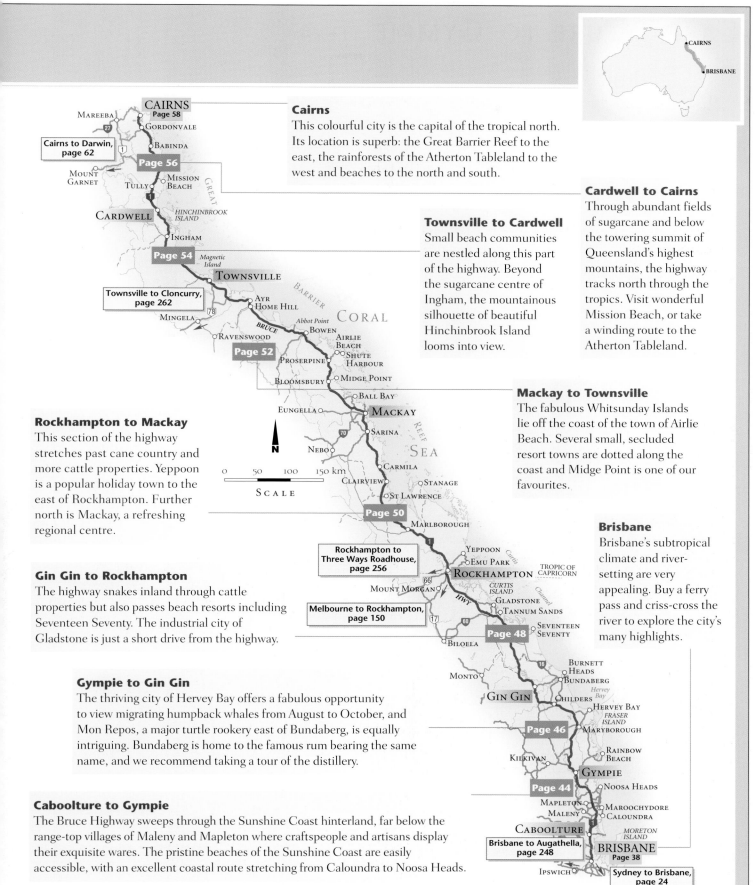

Cairns
This colourful city is the capital of the tropical north. Its location is superb: the Great Barrier Reef to the east, the rainforests of the Atherton Tableland to the west and beaches to the north and south.

Cardwell to Cairns
Through abundant fields of sugarcane and below the towering summit of Queensland's highest mountains, the highway tracks north through the tropics. Visit wonderful Mission Beach, or take a winding route to the Atherton Tableland.

Townsville to Cardwell
Small beach communities are nestled along this part of the highway. Beyond the sugarcane centre of Ingham, the mountainous silhouette of beautiful Hinchinbrook Island looms into view.

Mackay to Townsville
The fabulous Whitsunday Islands lie off the coast of the town of Airlie Beach. Several small, secluded resort towns are dotted along the coast and Midge Point is one of our favourites.

Rockhampton to Mackay
This section of the highway stretches past cane country and more cattle properties. Yeppoon is a popular holiday town to the east of Rockhampton. Further north is Mackay, a refreshing regional centre.

Brisbane
Brisbane's subtropical climate and river-setting are very appealing. Buy a ferry pass and criss-cross the river to explore the city's many highlights.

Gin Gin to Rockhampton
The highway snakes inland through cattle properties but also passes beach resorts including Seventeen Seventy. The industrial city of Gladstone is just a short drive from the highway.

Gympie to Gin Gin
The thriving city of Hervey Bay offers a fabulous opportunity to view migrating humpback whales from August to October, and Mon Repos, a major turtle rookery east of Bundaberg, is equally intriguing. Bundaberg is home to the famous rum bearing the same name, and we recommend taking a tour of the distillery.

Caboolture to Gympie
The Bruce Highway sweeps through the Sunshine Coast hinterland, far below the range-top villages of Maleny and Mapleton where craftspeople and artisans display their exquisite wares. The pristine beaches of the Sunshine Coast are easily accessible, with an excellent coastal route stretching from Caloundra to Noosa Heads.

Cairns to Darwin, page 62

Townsville to Cloncurry, page 262

Rockhampton to Three Ways Roadhouse, page 256

Melbourne to Rockhampton, page 150

Brisbane to Augathella, page 248

Sydney to Brisbane, page 24

CABOOLTURE TO GYMPIE 114 KM

Authors' choice

⊛ Mooloolaba Beach Caravan Park, Mooloolaba

This great park is split into two sites. The main section is in Parkyn Parade, while the smaller section is at Mooloolaba Beach. We think the beachside site has the best outlook of any park in Australia: it overlooks the fabulous beach and is just across the road from the resort-style main street of this popular holiday town.

For more details see page 378.

What's on

JUNE Caboolture Agricultural Show AUGUST Country Music Muster (Gympie), Sugar Festival (Nambour), Caloundra Arts and Crafts Festival SEPTEMBER Noosa Jazz Festival (Noosa Heads) OCTOBER Gold Rush Festival (Gympie) DECEMBER/JANUARY Woodford Folk Festival

A welcome for visitors

The villages dotted among the lush, green rolling hills of the Blackall Range include Maleny, Montville, Flaxton and Mapleton. Tourists and day trippers are really welcome here. We like to browse through the numerous craft shops, linger at the coffee shops, watch artists at work and take in the wonderful views over the Glass House Mountains and the coastal plain.

Jagged mountains

The Glass House Mountains were named by Captain Cook when he sailed north along the coast in 1770, as he thought they resembled glass furnaces. They rise like jagged shards from the hinterland inland from Caloundra.

Market day

Locals and tourists alike flock to the Eumundi Markets in search of craft, great gifts, fresh produce or that elusive bargain. Spend a delightful morning strolling around the hundreds of stalls. The selection is huge – leatherwork, pottery, clothing, toys, iron work, candles, soaps and much more. Open 6.30 a.m. to 1.30 p.m. Wednesdays and 8 a.m. to 1 p.m. Saturdays.

Gympie to Gin Gin, page 46

GYMPIE

GREAT SANDY NATIONAL PARK

BOREEN POINT

COORAN

POMONA

TEWANTIN NOOSAVILLE NOOSA HEADS

COOROY SUNSHINE BEACH

EUMUNDI PEREGIAN BEACH

Buderim Ginger Factory COOLUM BEACH

YANDINA MUDJIMBA

NAMBOUR BLI BLI MAROOCHYDORE

MAPLETON MOOLOOLABA

FLAXTON BUDERIM

MONTVILLE FOREST GLEN CORAL

Big Pineapple

MALENY CALOUNDRA

Mary Cairncross Park Diamond Valley

LANDSBOROUGH

Australia Zoo

SEA

BEERWAH

GLASS HOUSE MOUNTAINS

GLASS HOUSE MOUNTAINS NP

BRIBIE ISLAND NP

WOODFORD BEERBURRUM BRIBIE ISLAND

ELIMBAH DONNYBROOK

WAMURAN TOORBUL

WOORIM

CABOOLTURE BONGAREE

BEACHMERE

BURPENGARY

Caboolture to Brisbane (48 km)
For connecting routes, see map of Brisbane suburbs and surrounds, page 41

SCALE 0 10 km

Travel tip

The scenic route along the top of the range through Maleny and Montville is almost another world. Craft shops, coffee shops, restaurants, artisans at work and fabulous views to the coast make this a magnificent trip. The views over the Glass House Mountains from Mary Cairncross Park are awesome on a clear day. The route up and down the range is steep, but the road is good.

Year-round sunshine

The Sunshine Coast is one of Queensland's fastest growing residential regions and it is also a popular tourist destination. The sunshine, beaches and subtropical climate make it a very attractive coastal area. Noosa Heads, Coolum Beach and Maroochydore are the centre of this thriving holiday area.

The crocodile hunter at home

Australia Zoo, home of television's popular 'Crocodile Hunter', Steve Irwin, is one of Australia's great wildlife parks. It has a large crocodile display, as well as birds of prey, monitors, snakes and much more, but we love Harriet, a 172-year-old giant Galapagos tortoise. This is our favourite attraction in the area. Glass House Mountains Tourist Route, Beerwah; (07) 5494 1134; entry fee applies; open 8.30 a.m. to 4 p.m. daily.

Track notes

The Bruce Highway to Cooroy is multi-lane. North of Cooroy it winds through hills and, although there are overtaking lanes, progress is often slow. The alternative Caloundra–Noosa Heads route is picturesque, with great views.

Town file

1 CABOOLTURE pop. 17 571   PDG
GPS 27° 05.100' S/152° 57.073' E
Caboolture is a satellite town of Brisbane with the Glass House Mountains to the north. Caboolture has most services and country-town shopping.
55 King Street; (07) 5495 3122; www.caboolt4retourism.com.au

2 CALOUNDRA pop. 28 329   PDG
GPS 26° 48.278' S/153° 07.834' E
Caloundra has great patrolled beaches, all services and good shopping. It lies at the northern end of Pumicestone Passage, a protected waterway.
7 Caloundra Road; (07) 5491 0202 or 1800 644 969; www.caloundratourism.com.au

3 MAROOCHYDORE pop. 28 509   PDG
GPS 26° 39.242' S/153° 05.037' E
The commercial centre of the Sunshine Coast, Maroochydore has all services, excellent shopping and good restaurants. The Maroochy River is popular for fishing but the patrolled beaches are the major tourist attraction. Corner Aerodrome Road and Sixth Avenue; (07) 5479 1566; www.maroochytourism.com

4 NAMBOUR pop. 12 205   PDG
GPS 26° 36.542' S/152° 57.037' E
Nambour, the administrative centre of the Sunshine Coast, is home to a sugar mill: during harvest, cane trains roll through town. Nambour has been bypassed by the new highway, but it is worth taking the old one to visit the town and nearby attractions including the famous Big Pineapple. Nambour has all services and good shopping. 5 Coronation Avenue; (07) 5476 1933.

5 NOOSA HEADS pop. 17 776   PDG
GPS 26° 23.800' S/153° 05.297' E
Noosa's famous north-facing beach, scenic bays and great national park attract many tourists. It has lots of accommodation, numerous restaurants, fabulous resort-style shopping in Hastings Street and most services.
Hastings Street roundabout; (07) 5447 4988; www.tourismnoosa.com.au

6 GYMPIE pop. 10 813   PDG
GPS 26° 11.387' S/152° 39.678' E
Gold was discovered in Gympie in 1867 and a gold rush followed. Queensland's largest nugget, the 37 kg (975 oz) Curtis nugget, was found here. Gympie has most services and good shopping. Cooloola Regional Information Centre, Matilda's Roadhouse Complex, Bruce Highway, Kybong; (07) 5483 5554.

GYMPIE TO GIN GIN 202 KM

Authors' choice

⊛ Fraser Lodge, Hervey Bay

Explore Hervey Bay, go whale-watching or relax and enjoy the pool, the barbecues and the tennis court at Fraser Lodge, a quality tourist park in Torquay, a quiet area of Hervey Bay. The park is just a short walk from the beach and close to many local restaurants.

For more details see page 370.

Bundy rum

The famous Bundaberg Rum Distillery has a popular visitor centre and offers guided tours of its operations. The tour takes you through the process of making rum from the raw molasses through fermentation and distillation, maturation and bottling, and ends with a sample tasting. Whittred Street; (07) 4131 2900; entry fee applies; open 9.30 a.m. to 4.30 p.m. weekdays, 9.30 a.m. to 3.30 p.m. weekends.

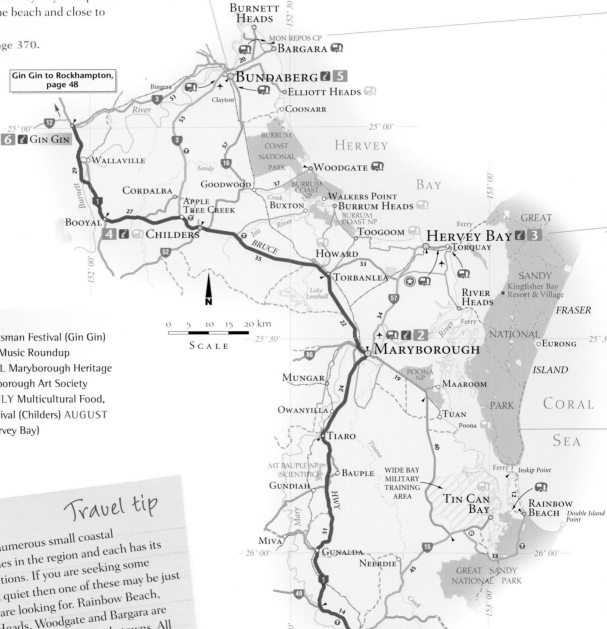

Gin Gin to Rockhampton, page 48

Caboolture to Gympie, page 44

What's on

MARCH Wild Scotsman Festival (Gin Gin) EASTER Country Music Roundup (Bundaberg) APRIL Maryborough Heritage Week JUNE Maryborough Art Society Annual Festival JULY Multicultural Food, Wine and Arts Festival (Childers) AUGUST Whale Festival (Hervey Bay)

Travel tip

There are numerous small coastal communities in the region and each has its own attractions. If you are seeking some peace and quiet then one of these may be just what you are looking for. Rainbow Beach, Burrum Heads, Woodgate and Bargara are just a few of the quiet beachside towns. All can be reached along sealed roads and most are popular fishing areas.

Turtle beach

Mon Repos Conservation Park (a beach) is an important turtle-breeding area. Flatback, green and endangered loggerhead turtles come ashore to lay eggs between November and January, and the hatchlings emerge between January and March. The National Parks and Wildlife Service offers evening tours from November to March; with luck you will see females laying their eggs or a clutch emerging. Mon Repos Road; (07) 4159 1652; entry fee applies for night viewing: 7 p.m. to 2 a.m. in season.

Humpback whales

Whale-watching is popular along the east coast of Australia, but nowhere more so than at Hervey Bay when the majestic humpback whales migrate north during the winter months. About 15 boats offer whale-watching cruises from Hervey Bay, starting in late July and drawing to a close in late October.

Fraser Island

The World Heritage-listed Fraser Island is a great holiday destination, particularly for fishing. Fraser Island is the world's largest sand island, and a four-wheel drive is necessary to explore it. It has many beautiful creeks and lakes as well as the better known ocean beaches. Regular barge services operate from Inskip Point, River Heads and Hervey Bay, while several tour companies offer day trips to the island.

Track notes

The Bruce Highway services coastal towns and regional centres and carries heavy transports. It is in good condition with some recent improvements and passes through grazing country and sugarcane fields.

Town file

1 GYMPIE (see page 45)

2 MARYBOROUGH pop. 21 286   PDG
GPS 25° 32.297' S/152° 42.033' E
Maryborough, one of the oldest cities in Queensland, has many historic buildings, including old 'Queenslander' homes. Cattle, cane farming and a large engineering works are the local industries. Maryborough has all services and very good regional shopping. Bruce Highway, Maryborough South; (07) 4121 4111.

3 HERVEY BAY pop. 32 054   PDG
GPS 25° 16.911' S/152° 50.458' E
Hervey Bay, a holiday destination, is a fast-growing centre across the bay from Fraser Island. Recent developments include a hospital. Regular barges operate to Fraser Island. Hervey Bay has all services, good shopping and numerous resort-style restaurants and cafes. Corner Urraween Road and Maryborough–Hervey Bay Road; (07) 4124 2912 or 1800 811 728; www.herveybaytourism.com.au

4 CHILDERS pop. 1483   PDG
GPS 25° 14.184' S/152° 16.707' E
Childers is in a rich volcanic farming area; itinerant labourers and backpackers flock here in search of seasonal work. Situated on the highway, the town has most services and a country-town shopping strip. Pharmaceutical Museum, 90 Churchill Street; (07) 4126 1994.

5 BUNDABERG pop. 41 025   PDG
GPS 24° 52.002' S/152° 20.780' E
Bundaberg is at the centre of a large sugarcane-growing region. Bert Hinkler, the pioneer aviator, was one of the city's favourite sons; however, Bundaberg is probably best known for its rum distillery. Bundaberg has a subtropical climate and is a major port for international yachts. It has all services and very good shopping. 271 Bourbong Street; (07) 4153 8888 or 1800 308 888; www.bundabergregion.info

6 GIN GIN pop. 958   PDG
GPS 24° 59.469' S/151° 57.377' E
Originally settled by Gregory Blaxland (one of the party that crossed the Blue Mountains in 1813), Gin Gin is at the centre of a strong pastoral industry and an embryonic wine industry. The region was home to one of Queensland's few bushrangers, James McPherson, the 'Wild Scotsman', and an annual festival bears his name. It has country-town shopping and all services. Bruce Highway; (07) 4157 3060.

GIN GIN TO ROCKHAMPTON 270 KM

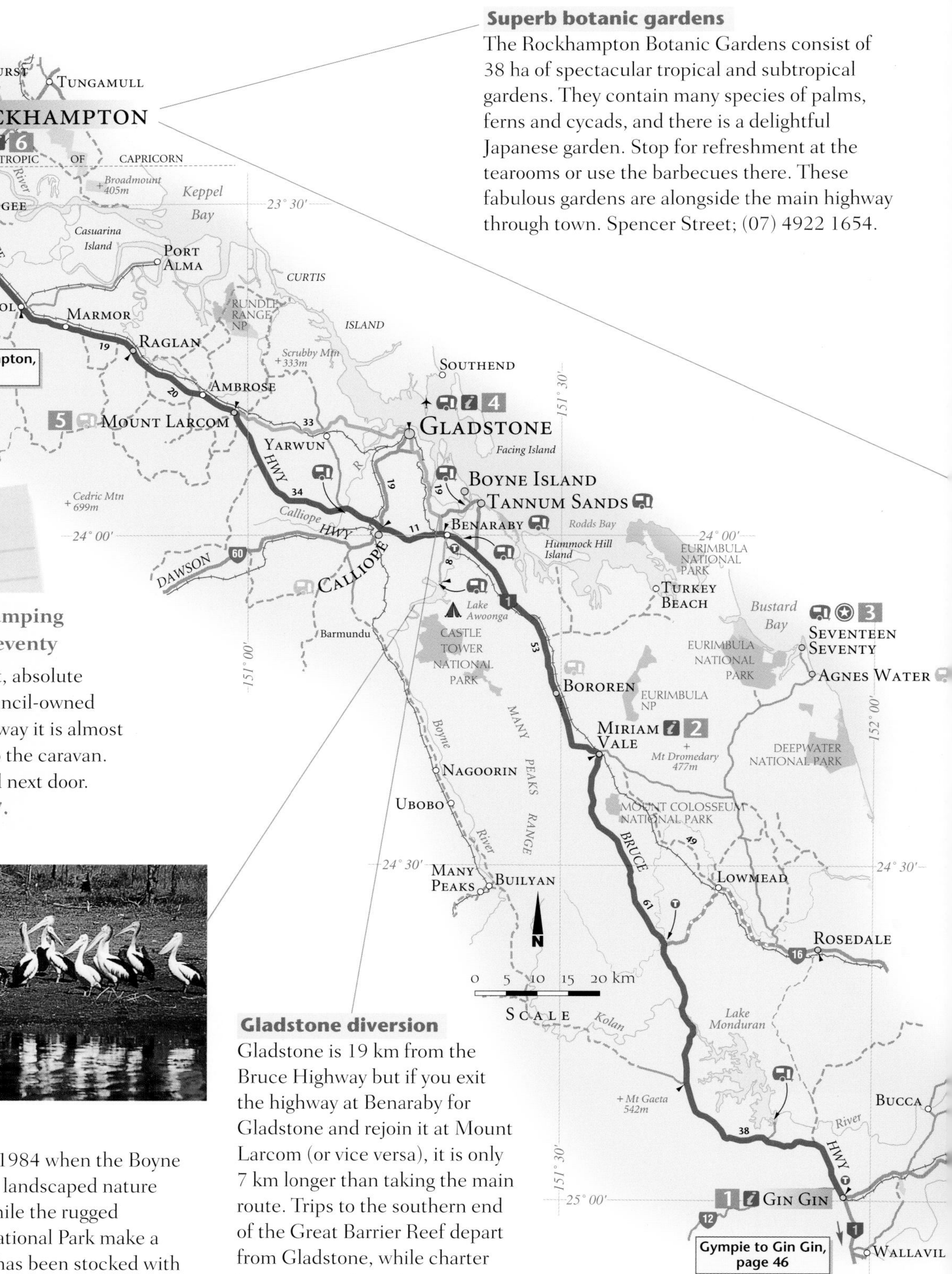

Rockhampton to Mackay,
page 50

Rockhampton to
Barcaldine,
page 258

Miles to Rockhampton,
page 162

Superb botanic gardens

The Rockhampton Botanic Gardens consist of 38 ha of spectacular tropical and subtropical gardens. They contain many species of palms, ferns and cycads, and there is a delightful Japanese garden. Stop for refreshment at the tearooms or use the barbecues there. These fabulous gardens are alongside the main highway through town. Spencer Street; (07) 4922 1654.

Authors' choice

⊛ Seventeen Seventy Camping Ground, Seventeen Seventy

It is hard to resist the excellent, absolute beachfront location of this council-owned park. At this subtropical hideaway it is almost possible to tie the dinghy up to the caravan. The park also has a playground next door.
For more details see page 387.

Catch that barramundi

Lake Awoonga was formed in 1984 when the Boyne River was dammed. There are landscaped nature trails and fabulous birdlife, while the rugged mountains of Castle Tower National Park make a beautiful backdrop. The lake has been stocked with barramundi, and it also has a camping ground.

Gladstone diversion

Gladstone is 19 km from the Bruce Highway but if you exit the highway at Benaraby for Gladstone and rejoin it at Mount Larcom (or vice versa), it is only 7 km longer than taking the main route. Trips to the southern end of the Great Barrier Reef depart from Gladstone, while charter boats set out from the marina for sportfishing.

Gympie to Gin Gin,
page 46

SCALE
0 5 10 15 20 km

Rockhampton's historic buildings

Rockhampton is situated on the banks of the Fitzroy River, and began life, in 1855, as a river port. Wander down Quay Street today and you will see many fine 19th-century buildings – Quay Street has been listed as a 'historic streetscape'. In particular, visit the sandstone Customs House (pictured) with its impressive copper dome and semi-circular Corinthian colonnade (now housing the visitor information centre), the Criterion Hotel and the ANZ Bank, which dates from 1864.

What's on

MARCH/APRIL Harbour Festival (Gladstone)
MAY Australian Bush Music Festival (Rockhampton),
Commemorative Festival (Seventeen Seventy) JUNE
Mount Larcom Agricultural Show SEPTEMBER
Gurang Gurang Festival (Miriam Vale)

Travel tip

If you are looking for a delicious lunch and a break from the road, we highly recommend the roadhouse at the northern end of Miriam Vale. You can buy freshly cut mud-crab sandwiches and also bread that has been baked on the premises. We can rarely resist calling in when we pass.

Track notes

The Bruce Highway is the main road along the east coast of Queensland and carries much traffic, although road trains are not permitted. Numerous roads wind to the coast from the highway, some unsealed. Rest areas along the highway are popular overnight stops, especially the one at Calliope River.

Town file

1 GIN GIN (see page 47)

2 MIRIAM VALE pop. 421   ⛽ PDG
GPS 24° 19.570' S/151° 33.207' E
Miriam Vale, a small town with old-style buildings and famous for its mud-crab sandwiches, is a good access point for Seventeen Seventy and Agnes Water. It has basic facilities. 🅵 Discovery Coast Information Centre, Roe Street; (07) 4974 5428.

3 SEVENTEEN SEVENTY pop. 203   ⛽ PD
GPS 24° 10.160' S/151° 52.937' E
In May 1770 Captain Cook and the crew of the *Endeavour* landed at the then-named Round Hill Inlet. Today the uniquely named Seventeen Seventy nestles close to this spot. It offers long sandy beaches, palm trees and good fishing. The road to Agnes Water and Seventeen Seventy has finally been sealed; both townships have basic services and facilities.

4 GLADSTONE pop. 26 415   ⛽ PDG
GPS 23° 50.624' S/151° 15.367' E
Gladstone is a busy industrial port with a subtropical climate. The area has the largest power station in Queensland, the world's largest alumina plant and Australia's largest cement works, and is the State's largest multi-cargo port. Gladstone has an impressive marina and a large commercial fishing fleet, plus an enviable reputation for fresh seafood, especially mud crabs. There is excellent shopping and all services are available. 🅵 Marina Ferry Terminal; (07) 4972 9000.

5 MOUNT LARCOM pop. 213   ⛽ PD
GPS 23° 48.369' S/150° 58.225' E
Mount Larcom is a small community named after a local geographical feature. Services are limited.

6 ROCKHAMPTON pop. 57 770   ⛽ PDG
GPS 23° 22.769' S/150° 30.927' E
On the Tropic of Capricorn, Rockhampton is one of Queensland's major cities. 'Rocky' is known for its beef, with more than one-third of Australia's cattle on Central Queensland properties. The Fitzroy River divides the city, and the Capricorn Coast is a 30-minute drive away. Rockhampton has all services and excellent regional shopping. 🅵 Customs House, Quay Street; (07) 4922 5339 or 1800 805 865; www.rockhamptoninfo.com

ROCKHAMPTON TO MACKAY 334 KM

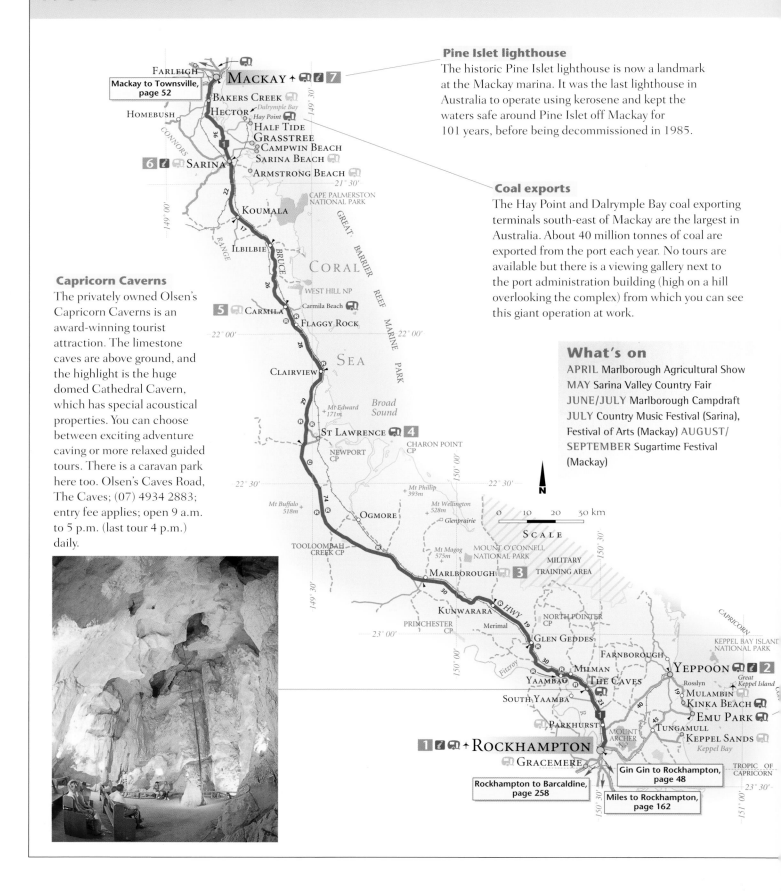

Pine Islet lighthouse

The historic Pine Islet lighthouse is now a landmark at the Mackay marina. It was the last lighthouse in Australia to operate using kerosene and kept the waters safe around Pine Islet off Mackay for 101 years, before being decommissioned in 1985.

Coal exports

The Hay Point and Dalrymple Bay coal exporting terminals south-east of Mackay are the largest in Australia. About 40 million tonnes of coal are exported from the port each year. No tours are available but there is a viewing gallery next to the port administration building (high on a hill overlooking the complex) from which you can see this giant operation at work.

Capricorn Caverns

The privately owned Olsen's Capricorn Caverns is an award-winning tourist attraction. The limestone caves are above ground, and the highlight is the huge domed Cathedral Cavern, which has special acoustical properties. You can choose between exciting adventure caving or more relaxed guided tours. There is a caravan park here too. Olsen's Caves Road, The Caves; (07) 4934 2883; entry fee applies; open 9 a.m. to 5 p.m. (last tour 4 p.m.) daily.

What's on

APRIL Marlborough Agricultural Show
MAY Sarina Valley Country Fair
JUNE/JULY Marlborough Campdraft
JULY Country Music Festival (Sarina), Festival of Arts (Mackay) AUGUST/SEPTEMBER Sugartime Festival (Mackay)

Mackay to Townsville, page 52

Rockhampton to Barcaldine, page 258

Gin Gin to Rockhampton, page 48

Miles to Rockhampton, page 162

A singing ship

On the headland at Emu Park is a fabulous sculpture – the singing ship. It was built as a bicentenary memorial to Captain Cook in 1980, which also happened to be Emu Park's centenary. It really does sing! (Sea breezes cause hidden organ pipes to make sounds.) This unique, white, ship-shaped sculpture can be heard whistling eerily in the on-shore breezes, which blow most of the time.

Track notes

The Bruce Highway is a major route carrying heavy transports and much tourist traffic; there are ample opportunities to overtake. The road passes through cane country and cattle-grazing properties. You can drive from Rockhampton to Mackay in one day, but there are many overnight stops along this route.

Town file

1 ROCKHAMPTON (see page 49)

2 YEPPOON pop. 8810   ⛽ PDG
GPS 23° 07.810' S/150° 44.953' E
Yeppoon is the largest town on the Capricorn Coast, a very popular holiday destination. Yeppoon has most services and very good resort-style shopping. ℹ Capricorn Coast Tourist Information Centre, Scenic Highway; (07) 4939 4888; www.capricorncoast.com.au

3 MARLBOROUGH pop. 150   ⛽ PD
GPS 22° 48.795' S/149° 53.299' E
Marlborough is now off the highway but was once an important stop when the old route had few services between here and Sarina. Marlborough has basic services.

4 ST LAWRENCE pop. 180   ⛽ PD
GPS 22° 21.040' S/149° 31.426' E
St Lawrence is on the north–south railway line and many trains run through it. The only services really available are at the store. St Lawrence was an important port in the 1800s but today just the remains of the wharf are left.

5 CARMILA pop. 200   ⛽ PD
GPS 21° 54.513' S/149° 24.571' E
Carmila is a small community, with cattle and sugarcane as the area's main industries. Carmila has basic services, mostly from the store and roadhouse.

6 SARINA pop. 3201   ⛽ PDG
GPS 21° 25.445' S/149° 13.052' E
Sarina is at the centre of a strong regional sugar industry. The visitor information centre has a good display of local craft, plus homemade preserves for sale. Sarina has most services and good country-town shopping. ℹ Railway Square; (07) 4956 2251.

7 MACKAY pop. 44 880   ⛽ PDG
GPS 21° 08.478' S/149° 11.151' E
Mackay, midway between Brisbane and Cairns, is a major regional centre at the mouth of the Pioneer River. The main industry is sugarcane and there are several mills nearby. The Bowen Basin coalfields are inland from Mackay and many of the city's residents work in the coal industry. Mackay has all services and excellent regional shopping. ℹ 320 Nebo Road; (07) 4952 2677 or 1300 130 001; www.mackayregion.com

MACKAY TO TOWNSVILLE 390 KM

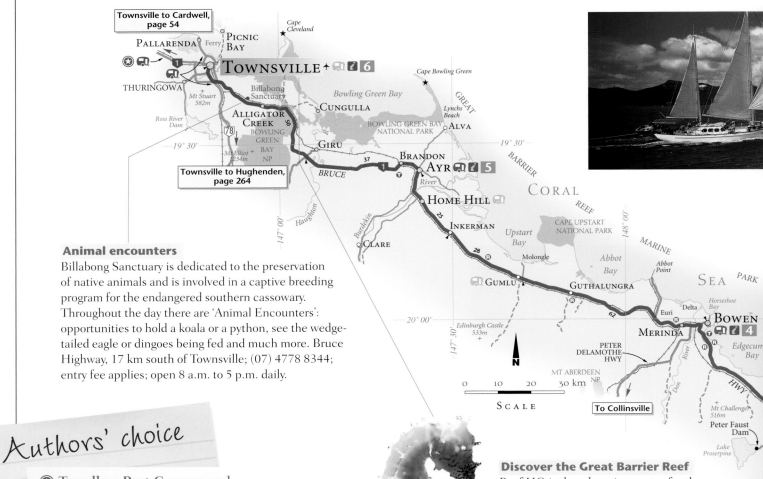

Animal encounters

Billabong Sanctuary is dedicated to the preservation of native animals and is involved in a captive breeding program for the endangered southern cassowary. Throughout the day there are 'Animal Encounters': opportunities to hold a koala or a python, see the wedge-tailed eagle or dingoes being fed and much more. Bruce Highway, 17 km south of Townsville; (07) 4778 8344; entry fee applies; open 8 a.m. to 5 p.m. daily.

Authors' choice

⊛ Travellers Rest Caravan and Camping Park, Midge Point

There are no more sandflies or midges at Midge Point than elsewhere, but there is a wonderful out-of-the-way beachside caravan park with lovely manicured lawns, large shady trees and a host of great features. We really enjoy staying here.

For more details see page 377.

⊛ Woodlands Holiday Village, Townsville

This is an interesting park located about 15 km north of the city alongside the Bruce Highway. The park has a good range of facilities and each site has private ensuite amenities. We find it a convenient place to stop overnight, and often stay here.

For more details see page 391.

Discover the Great Barrier Reef

Reef HQ is the education centre for the Great Barrier Reef Marine Park Authority. Here you can see a living coral reef in an aquarium environment, and the ecosystem that surrounds it: fish, crustaceans, shellfish, turtles, sharks and sea stars. Reef HQ is a unique attraction and we recommend a visit. Flinders Street, Townsville; (07) 4750 0800; entry fee applies; open 9 a.m. to 5 p.m. daily.

What's on

MAY Rodeo (Bowen) **JUNE** Proserpine Agricultural Show, Bowen River Races and Rodeo (Bowen River, south-east of Bowen) **JULY** Australian Festival of Chamber Music (Townsville) **SEPTEMBER** Bowen Family Fishing Classic

The wonderful Whitsundays

Forming part of the Great Barrier Reef Marine Park (a World Heritage Area), the Whitsunday Passage is a remarkable naturally protected waterway. Some 74 islands, fabulous beaches, clear blue water and a range of resorts make this an international year-round holiday destination.

Rockhampton to Mackay, page 50

Track notes

The Bruce Highway between Mackay and Townsville traverses a rich plain where sugarcane is the predominant crop. From June to November expect to meet slow-moving harvesting equipment and cane trains. The well-maintained highway has ample overtaking opportunities.

Town file

1 MACKAY (see page 51)

2 PROSERPINE pop. 3247   PDG
GPS 20° 24.100' S/148° 34.908' E
Proserpine, a sugar town on the highway, is the turn-off for Airlie Beach and Shute Harbour. It has an airport, good shopping and most services. *Whitsunday Information Centre, Bruce Highway; (07) 4945 3711 or 1800 801 252; www.whitsundaytourism.com

3 AIRLIE BEACH pop. 3029   PDG
GPS 20° 16.173' S/148° 43.223' E
Airlie Beach overlooks the Whitsunday Passage and is a great holiday destination, with an incredible sense of timelessness. The town has resort-style shopping and a wonderful tropical climate. Nearby Shute Harbour has regular boat services to several Whitsunday islands. *277 Shute Harbour Road; (07) 4946 6665 or 1800 819 366.

4 BOWEN pop. 8985   PDG
GPS 20° 00.723' S/148° 14.781' E
Bowen is the centre of a diverse region: fruit and vegetables grow in the rich river delta, cattle-grazing properties lie inland, a fishing fleet operates from the harbour, coal is mined near Collinsville and the Bowen Saltworks are situated south of town (you cannot miss the salt pans from the highway). There are beautiful beaches where snorkelling is popular. Bowen is known as the 'Mural Capital of the Mainland'; 22 murals on building walls, each by a Queensland artist, clearly depict the history of the area. Bowen has most services and good shopping. *Bruce Highway, Mount Gordon; (07) 4786 4222; www.bowentourism.com.au

5 AYR pop. 8597   PDG
GPS 19° 34.587' S/147° 24.285' E
On the northern bank of the mighty Burdekin River, Ayr has most services and good shopping. *Burdekin Visitors Information Centre, Bruce Highway, Plantation Creek; (07) 4783 5988.

6 TOWNSVILLE pop. 75 990   PDG
GPS 19° 15.494' S/146° 49.106' E
Townsville is one of Queensland's major cities. It is an administrative, commercial and educational centre with historic buildings and a fabulous redeveloped waterfront precinct. The busy port handles beef, minerals and sugar. There is a substantial military presence around Townsville, with army and airforce bases close by. The shopping is very good and the city has all services. *Bruce Highway; (07) 4778 3555 or 1800 801 902; www.townsvilleonline.com.au

TOWNSVILLE TO CARDWELL 161 KM

Picnic beside a pool

Cardwell Forest Drive is a well-signposted 9-km drive through pine plantations and native forests. The drive takes in a lookout, the Spa Creek pool, picnic areas and a range of forest information stations. There are easily accessible swimming holes at many of the stops along the way. This is a pleasant drive along a maintained gravel forestry road; it is, however, also frequented by logging trucks.

Sugar from cane

Queensland supplies much of Australia and a significant proportion of the world with sugar, and Ingham is right at the heart of the action. Ingham's Victoria Mill (pictured) opened in 1883 and is the largest sugar mill in the Southern Hemisphere. From the late 1800s to the mid 1900s many Europeans, and especially Italians, flooded in to work on the burgeoning canefields. Today over 60 per cent of Ingham's population are of Italian descent.

Travel tip

There are numerous free camping areas along this section of highway – beside the road, in beachside communities and in towns. Most have a 24-hour or 48-hour limit. During the winter they fill quickly. Bluewater Creek is one of the most popular and, while it is large, there are almost always campers in it. We often stop here, sometimes just for lunch under a shady tree.

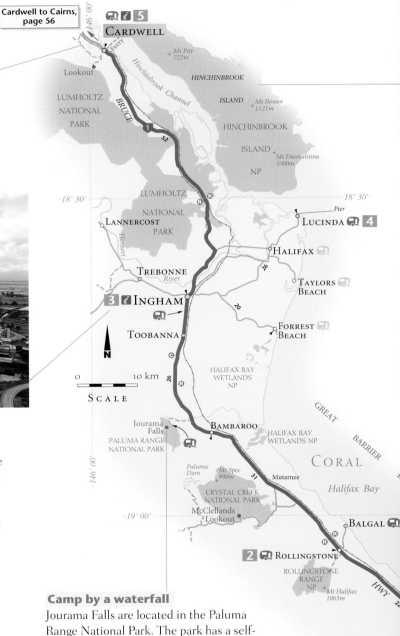

Cardwell to Cairns, page 56

Camp by a waterfall

Jourama Falls are located in the Paluma Range National Park. The park has a self-registration camping area that is accessible to caravans, reached along 2.8 km of unsealed road. The area is forested and is popular with birdwatchers: you may see beautiful azure kingfishers flitting around Waterview Creek. A 1.5-km walking track leads to the cascading falls lookout. The waterfall plunges over salmon granite, down into the crystal-clear creek, which has swimming holes.

Hinchinbrook Island National Park

Hinchinbrook Island is Australia's largest island national park. Mangrove shores, pristine beaches and dense rainforest blanket this rugged island, dominated by the towering Mount Bowen (1121 m). Bushwalking is popular, with several marked walking tracks, while the more adventurous bushwalkers take the world-renowned Thorsborne Trail across the island, which takes 4 to 7 days and requires self-sufficiency. A ferry operates from Cardwell daily between May and October, and on Sundays, Wednesdays and Fridays between November and April.

What's on

MAY Australian Italian Festival (Ingham), Coral Sea Memorial (Cardwell) JUNE Ingham Country Music Festival JULY Ingham Show SEPTEMBER Hinchinbrook Family Fishing Classic (Lucinda) OCTOBER Maraka (Ingham)

Track notes

The Bruce Highway follows the coastal plain but the mountains are larger than they were further south and the road runs closer to the foot of the range. The road winds through waving canefields and throughout the cane harvesting season (July to November) there may be slow-moving agricultural machinery and cane trains operating. The highway is generally well maintained, but the surface can break up and potholes can develop during the wet season.

Town file

1 TOWNSVILLE (see page 53)

2 ROLLINGSTONE pop. 150   ⛽ PD
GPS 19° 02.710' S/146° 23.652' E
Rollingstone is a small community on the highway. A nice, shady, free camping ground is an important feature here; limited services are available in the township.

3 INGHAM pop. 5012   ⛽ PDG
GPS 18° 39.039' S/146° 09.268' E
Ingham developed to support the local sugarcane industry: two local sugar mills crush the annual harvest. The town has a large Italian population and each year in May the town hosts the Australian Italian Festival. Ingham has most services and good country-town shopping. 🏛 Bruce Highway; (07) 4776 5211.

4 LUCINDA pop. 664   ⛽ PD
GPS 18° 31.659' S/146° 20.032' E
Lucinda is sited on the picturesque coast at the southern entrance to Hinchinbrook Channel. The surrounding waters are some of Queensland's most popular fishing spots – even the Lucinda Wharf is popular. The spectacular and rugged Hinchinbrook Island lies just to the north. Lucinda is a major sugar port with a bulk-sugar-loading jetty stretching nearly 6 km out to sea. The town has basic services and a small number of shops. Its seafood shops are extremely popular.

5 CARDWELL pop. 1421   ⛽ PDG
GPS 18° 15.275' S/146° 01.120' E
Cardwell, the oldest town in north Queensland, is on the beach overlooking Rockingham Bay (to the north-east). It is a very popular tourist centre with excellent fishing. The region supports a strong timber industry. A regular ferry service to Hinchinbrook Island operates from town. Cardwell has seen significant development in recent years with many new homes and a new marina. Most services are available and there is a good selection of shops. 🏛 Rainforest and Reef Infomation Centre, 142 Victoria Street; (07) 4066 8601.

CARDWELL TO CAIRNS 184 KM

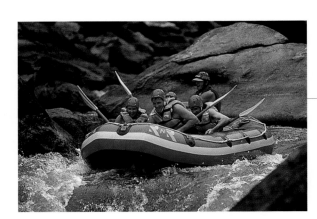

Queensland's highest peak
Mount Bartle Frere is Queensland's highest peak (1622 m). A 15-km-return walking track winds through the rainforest to the summit; it begins from Josephine Falls, reached via a turn-off from the highway 2 km south of Miriwinni. The track is suitable for fit and experienced walkers only.

Rafting rapids
Whitewater rafting is a great attraction on the Tully, Barron and North Johnstone rivers. R'n'R Rafting have a number of options to suit all, including families (minimum age is 13 years for whitewater rafting). Guided trips operate most days. 107 Draper Street, Cairns; (07) 4051 7777; fee applies.

Authors' choice

⊛ **Beachcomber Coconut Caravan Village, South Mission Beach**

Mission Beach is a dream holiday destination and this park is a perfect place to stay. It is set in a fabulous location just across the road from the beach. Walk to the shops, play on the half-size tennis court or enjoy a barbecue.
For more details see page 388.

⊛ **Flying Fish Point Caravan Park, Flying Fish Point**

This quality owner-operated park is opposite the water in this small town 7 km from Innisfail. The park provides patrons with a free fish barbecue for lunch each Wednesday during the tourist season and there are a limited number of fishing dinghies available for use.
For more details see page 366.

⊛ **Cairns Coconut Caravan Resort, Woree**

Enjoy the excellent facilities of this five-star park, on the southern approach to the city 7 km from the centre of Cairns. There is a cafe, a kids club in school holidays, free mini-golf, tennis and aqua aerobics, and the list continues. Yes, we have stayed here often and we like it a lot.
For more details see page 359.

What's on
JULY Cassowary Carnival (Mission Beach), Tully Agricultural Show AUGUST Banana Festival (Mission Beach) OCTOBER Innisfail Harvest Festival, Aquatic Carnival (Mission Beach) DECEMBER Innisfail Opera Festival

Travel tip

Some of Australia's prettiest scenery is found along this tropical and mountainous coastline: rugged mountains, lush rainforest, waterfalls, the Great Barrier Reef islands, holiday resorts and a lot more. We love this part of Australia, although be patient with the weather: it can rain often.

Sweet things

The Australian Sugar Industry Museum showcases the multicultural heritage of this strong industry and houses a permanent display of historic and innovative equipment. Bruce Highway, Mourilyan; (07) 4063 2656; entry fee applies; open 9 a.m. to 5 p.m. Monday to Saturday, 9 a.m. to 3 p.m. Sunday.

Paronella Park

Paronella Park is a privately built garden, listed by the National Trust. Begun in the early 1930s, its magnificent stairways, buildings (including a 'castle') and gardens have to be seen to be believed. Japoonvale Road (old Bruce Highway), Mena Creek; (07) 4065 3225; entry fee applies; open 8.30 a.m. to 5 p.m. daily.

Track notes

The Bruce Highway winds through sugarcane as it skirts the Bellenden Ker Range, which is often shrouded in cloud. This section of coast is one of Australia's highest rainfall areas, so expect wet conditions, although most of the rain falls between November and April.

Town file

1 CARDWELL (see page 55)

2 TULLY pop. 2509   ⛽ PDG
GPS 17° 55.994' S/145° 55.408' E
Tully has a large mill, which processes around 2 million tonnes of sugarcane annually. The mill runs tours; bookings at the tourist information centre. The area around Tully is also known for its timber and tropical fruits, and the Tully River is an exciting whitewater-rafting destination. Tully has most services and good shopping. 🛈 Bruce Highway; (07) 4068 2288.

3 MISSION BEACH pop. 1013   ⛽ PD
GPS 17° 52.031' S/146° 06.432' E
Mission Beach, one of Australia's most popular holiday destinations, has magnificent white sandy beaches, swaying palms and tropical rainforests. Day cruises to Dunk Island operate from the jetty. 🛈 Porters Promenade; (07) 4068 7099.

4 INNISFAIL pop. 8987   ⛽ PDG
GPS 17° 31.575' S/146° 01.843' E
Innisfail is in a major sugar-producing region. Fishing is also important and a large fleet operates from here. Innisfail has most services and good regional shopping. The visitor information centre is in Mourilyan.
🛈 Corner Eslick Street and Bruce Highway, Mourilyan; (07) 4061 7422; www.greatgreenway.com

5 BABINDA pop. 1228   ⛽ PD
GPS 17° 20.646' S/145° 55.495' E
Babinda is squeezed between the coast and the Bellenden Ker Range. Annual rainfall in the ranges is over 8000 mm, which is great for agriculture, and Babinda processes much of the sugarcane grown in the area. The Boulders Wildland Park, with its large water-worn granite boulders, is 6 km from town; the park has walking tracks, camping and a popular swimming hole. Babinda has limited services. 🛈 Corner Bruce Highway and Munro Street; (07) 4067 1008.

6 GORDONVALE pop. 3682   ⛽ PDG
GPS 17° 05.952' S/145° 46.819' E
Gordonvale is at the junction of the Bruce and Gillies highways, on the Musgrave River. Walshs Pyramid to the south of town, rising 922 m, is an impressive sight and a walking challenge. Gordonvale has basic services and shops.

7 CAIRNS (see page 58)

CAIRNS
YOUR GUIDE

This modern, colourful city is the capital of the tropical north. The cosmopolitan Esplanade traces the bay foreshore, and parks and gardens abound with tropical colour. Its location is superb: the Great Barrier Reef to the east, the rainforests and plains of the Atherton Tableland to the west and palm-fringed beaches to the north and south. Cairns is a great black-marlin fishing location and offers access to the Great Barrier Reef for fishing, snorkelling, scuba-diving and viewing the fabulous coral from glass-bottom boats.

CITY CENTRE
See inset map on page 60.

Cairns Museum 60 F2
Fascinating displays of Aboriginal, gold-rush, timber and sugarcane history.

Cairns Regional Gallery 60 F2
Housed in a historic building; includes work of local artists.

Esplanade 60 F1
Birdwatching opportunities and a 3-km walking trail with beautiful views.

Marlin Jetty 60 F2
Departure point for many cruises; game-fishing boats also moor here.

Rusty's Bazaar 60 F2
Vibrant weekend markets with arts and crafts, clothes and fresh produce.

Trinity Wharf 60 F2
Historic area with interesting neoclassical buildings.

SUBURBS AND SURROUNDS
See map on page 60.

Australian Butterfly Sanctuary 60 A4
Over 2000 butterflies in a forest setting; guided tours available.

Australian Woolshed 60 C5
Daily ram shows, spinning, shearing, and sheepdog demonstrations.

Barron Gorge National Park 60 B5
Contains Wrights Lookout with stunning views of Barron Falls, spectacular after heavy rain.

Birdworld Kuranda 60 A4
Spectacular tree-lined paths and endangered birds.

Flecker Botanic Gardens 60 D6
Featuring an Aboriginal plant-use area and over 200 species of palms as well as lawns, lakes and lily ponds; free guided walks on weekdays at 1 p.m.

Great Barrier Reef and islands 60 D3
Can be explored by private charters, daily cruises or by air; day-trip cruises to Fitzroy and Green islands are available, some in glass-bottom boats.

Kuranda Markets 60 A4
Held Wednesday to Friday and Sunday; wide range of stalls including arts and crafts.

Kuranda Scenic Railway 60 B5
A 100-year-old steam train travels 34 km through rainforest and up steep slopes along Barron Gorge and past Barron Falls.

Visitor information
Tourism Tropical North Queensland
51 The Esplanade, Cairns
(07) 4051 3588
www.tropicalaustralia.com.au

Royal Flying Doctor Service
60 D6
A visitor information centre with displays of the origins and history of the service; open daily.

Skyrail Rainforest Cableway 60 B5
Spectacular gondola cableway, with boardwalk stops, through rainforest to Kuranda.

NORTHERN REGION
See map on page 61.

Cairns–Port Douglas Scenic Route 61 F8–D5
One of the most spectacular coastal drives in Australia.

Cape Tribulation 61 D1
A rainforest and reef World Heritage Area within the Daintree National Park; offers a rich mix of coastal rainforest, mangroves, swamp and heath.

Cape York Peninsula (not shown on map)
Many areas of the Cape are traditional Aboriginal lands or national parks and are a sanctuary for much of Australia's unique flora and fauna. During the wet season virtually all road transport stops as there are almost no sealed roads or bridges in the area; June to November are the recommended months to visit. A reliable and well-equipped four-wheel drive is essential for this area. Permits are required to visit some areas of Aboriginal land.

Hartley's Creek Crocodile Farm 61 E7
Set in lush rainforest, home to hundreds of crocodiles as well as koalas, kangaroos, dingoes, snakes, cassowaries and more; crocodile products are available, including crocodile-foot back scratchers.

Mossman Gorge 61 B5
Take the short walk through Daintree National Park to picturesque cascades through the gorge.

Port Douglas 61 D5
International holiday destination surrounded by lush vegetation and pristine rainforests; known for its excellent cuisine.

Getting around
Cairns is fairly compact and easy to negotiate. All the main city attractions are within walking distance although guided bus tours with Cairns Discovery Tours are also on offer. Most cruises to the Great Barrier Reef and surrounding islands depart from Marlin Jetty or Trinity Wharf. There are some stunning scenic drives in the region. Most of the tropical north can be reached by conventional vehicle; however, in outback and remote wilderness areas seasonal rains can make roads impassable. Some roads are best negotiated with the use of a four-wheel drive. Check road conditions with the RACQ.

Airport shuttle bus Australia Coach (07) 4048 8355; Motoring organisation RACQ 13 19 05; Public transport Cairns–Port Douglas Transport Services (07) 4099 4850; Bus Tours Cairns Discovery Tours (07) 4053 5259; Taxis Taxis Australia 13 22 27, Black and White Cabs 13 10 08; Great Barrier Reef Tours Great Adventures (07) 4044 9944, Big Cat Green Island Reef Cruises (07) 4051 0444.

Top events
Cairns Tropical Garden Show (May)
Australia's largest tropical garden show.

Agricultural Show (July)
Huge event with an agricultural, pastoral and mining theme.

Cairns Amateurs (September)
Horseracing with off-course social events including fashions of the field.

Reef Festival and Hook, Wine and Sinker Festival (October)
Variety of entertainment centred around the Esplanade, including a Grand Parade and fireworks.

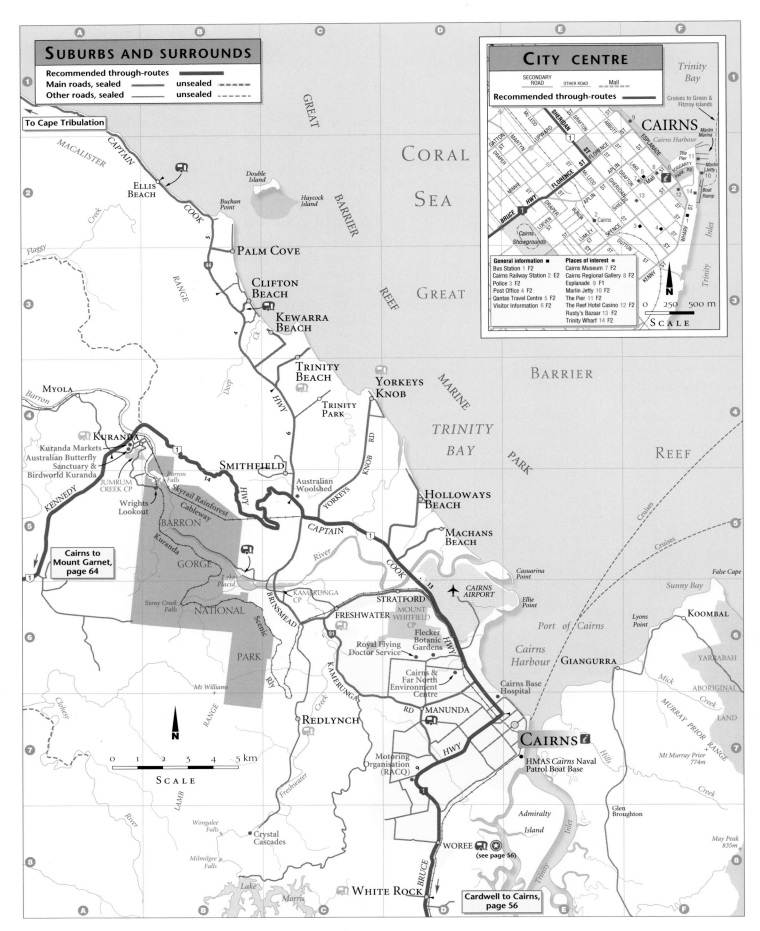

SUBURBS AND SURROUNDS

Recommended through-routes
Main roads, sealed — unsealed
Other roads, sealed — unsealed

CITY CENTRE

SECONDARY ROAD   OTHER ROAD   Mall
Recommended through-routes

CAIRNS

Cruises to Green & Fitzroy islands

General information ■
Bus Station 1 F2
Cairns Railway Station 2 E2
Police 3 F2
Post Office 4 F2
Qantas Travel Centre 5 F2
Visitor Information 6 F2

Places of interest ■
Cairns Museum 7 F2
Cairns Regional Gallery 8 F2
Esplanade 9 F1
Marlin Jetty 10 F2
The Pier 11 F2
The Reef Hotel Casino 12 F2
Rusty's Bazaar 13 F2
Trinity Wharf 14 F2

0   250   500 m
SCALE

To Cape Tribulation

CORAL SEA

GREAT BARRIER REEF

GREAT BARRIER REEF

MACALISTER RANGE

ELLIS BEACH
Double Island
Buchan Point
Haycock Island

PALM COVE

CLIFTON BEACH
KEWARRA BEACH

TRINITY BEACH

YORKEYS KNOB

TRINITY PARK

MARINE PARK

TRINITY BAY

MYOLA

KURANDA
Kuranda Markets
Australian Butterfly Sanctuary &
Birdworld Kuranda
JUMRUM CREEK CP
Wrights Lookout
Skyrail Rainforest Cableway
Barron Falls
SMITHFIELD
Australian Woolshed

HOLLOWAYS BEACH

MACHANS BEACH

Cairns to Mount Garnet, page 64

BARRON GORGE
NATIONAL PARK
Lake Placid
Stony Creek Falls

KAMERUNGA CP
BRINSMEAD
STRATFORD
FRESHWATER
MOUNT WHITFIELD CP
Flecker Botanic Gardens
Royal Flying Doctor Service
Cairns & Far North Environment Centre

CAIRNS AIRPORT
Casuarina Point
Ellie Point

Port of Cairns
Cairns Harbour

GIANGURRA
KOOMBAL
YARRABAH ABORIGINAL LAND

MURRAY PRIOR RANGE

Sunny Bay
False Cape
Lyons Point

Cairns Base Hospital

MANUNDA

REDLYNCH

Mt Williams

Motoring Organisation (RACQ)

CAIRNS
HMAS Cairns Naval Patrol Boat Base

Mt Murray Prior 774m

Admiralty Island
Glen Broughton

May Peak 835m

0 1 2 3 4 5 km
SCALE

Wongalee Falls
Crystal Cascades
Milmilgee Falls

WOREE
(see page 56)

Lake Morris

WHITE ROCK

Cardwell to Cairns, page 56

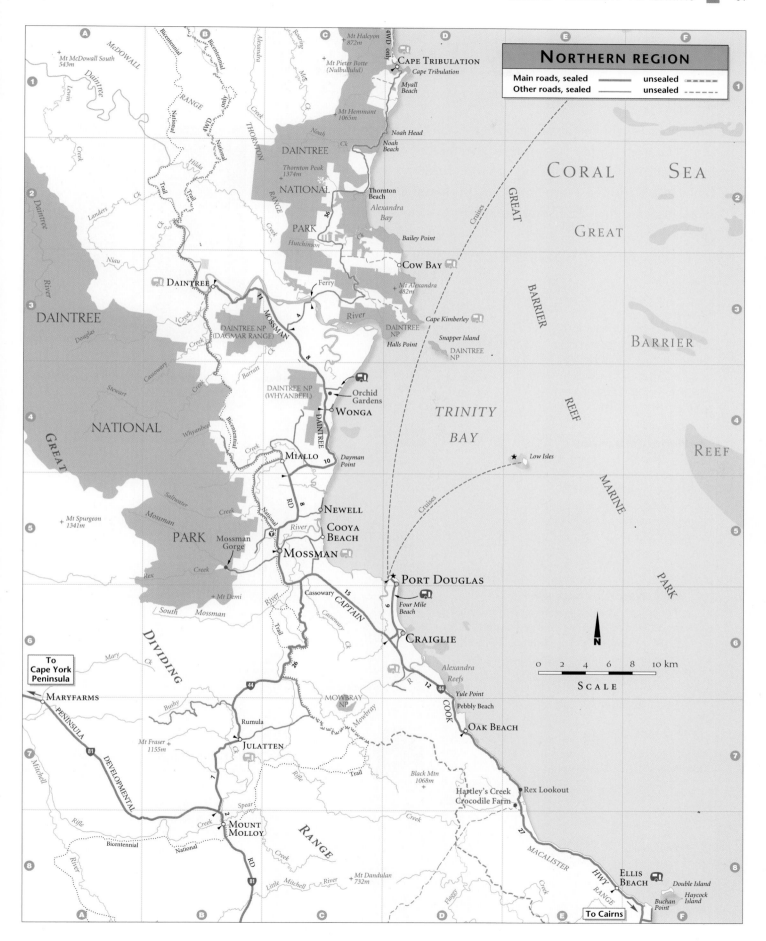

NORTHERN REGION

Main roads, sealed ——— unsealed - - - -
Other roads, sealed ——— unsealed - - - -

Mt McDowall South
543m

McDOWALL

Bicentennial

Bicentennial

Mt Halcyon
872m

4WD only

CAPE TRIBULATION

Cape Tribulation

Myall
Beach

DAINTREE

Mt Pieter Botte
(Nulbululul)

RANGE

National

Levin

Daintree

Mt Hemmant
1065m

Noah Head

Noah
Beach

THORNTON

National

NATIONAL

Thornton Peak
1374m

Thornton
Beach

Alexandra
Bay

Hutchinson

Bailey Point

COW BAY

DAINTREE

Ferry

Mt Alexandra
482m

Cape Kimberley

Snapper Island

DAINTREE
NP

Halls Point

DAINTREE
NP

DAINTREE NP
(DAGMAR RANGE)

MOSSMAN

DAINTREE NP
(WHYANBEEL)

Orchid
Gardens

WONGA

DAINTREE

NATIONAL

Mt Spurgeon
1341m

MIALLO

Dayman
Point

RD

NEWELL

**COOYA
BEACH**

Mossman
Gorge

MOSSMAN

PORT DOUGLAS

Four Mile
Beach

Cassowary

CAPTAIN

Mt Demi

CRAIGLIE

South Mossman

DIVIDING

MOWBRAY
NP

Alexandra
Reefs

**To
Cape York
Peninsula**

MARYFARMS

PENINSULA

Rumula

COOK

Yule Point

Pebbly Beach

OAK BEACH

Mt Fraser
1155m

JULATTEN

Black Mtn
1068m

DEVELOPMENTAL

Trail

Hartley's Creek
Crocodile Farm

Rex Lookout

Spear

**MOUNT
MOLLOY**

National

RANGE

MACALISTER

Mt Dandulan
732m

RD

RANGE

HWY

**ELLIS
BEACH**

Double Island

Haycock
Island

Buchan
Point

To Cairns

CORAL   SEA

GREAT

GREAT

BARRIER

BARRIER

REEF

TRINITY

BAY

Low Isles

REEF

MARINE

PARK

N

0 2 4 6 8 10 km

SCALE

CAIRNS TO DARWIN

KENNEDY HIGHWAY, GULF DEVELOPMENTAL ROAD, BURKETOWN NORMANTON ROAD, NARDO

Journey across the top of Australia in this classic section of Highway One. The route climbs steeply from the coastal plain of Cairns to the agricultural Atherton Tableland and then further west to the Barkly Tableland. Karumba, Normanton and Burketown are sun-drenched winter havens, great for fishing and perfect escapes from the chill of the southern winter. Litchfield and Kakadu national parks and the spectacular Nitmiluk Gorge are extremely popular tourist destinations.

Darwin
Darwin has great restaurants, interesting museums and a fabulous range of tourist and leisure activities. Its climate, hot and dry then hot and humid, adds to Darwin's tropical feel.

Katherine to Darwin
Stop at fabulous Litchfield National Park, the historic Pine Creek goldfields and the many historic World War II sites. Kakadu National Park is easily accessible by two fully sealed routes.

Daly Waters to Katherine
The Stuart Highway sweeps northward, passing by Mataranka Thermal Pool and Cutta Cutta Caves. The spectacular Nitmiluk Gorge is just a short drive from Katherine, a major centre.

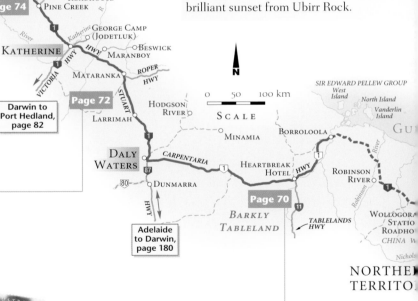

Kakadu National Park diversion
This amazing World Heritage-listed park has so much to offer, from cruising the spectacular Yellow Water Billabong to watching the brilliant sunset from Ubirr Rock.

Hells Gate Roadhouse to Daly Waters
Unsealed and subject to seasonal closures east of Borroloola, the Carpentaria Highway crosses several gulf tributaries. Borroloola is just the place to try for a barramundi.

Best time to go

Travel is popular in the cooler, dry months between April and October; the hotter, more humid wet season makes travel uncomfortable and swollen rivers can render many roads impassable.

NORMANTON

	J	F	M	A	M	J	J	A	S	O	N	D
Maximum	35	34	34	34	32	29	29	31	34	36	37	36
Minimum	25	25	24	22	19	16	15	17	20	23	25	25
Rainfall (mm)	259	249	158	30	8	9	3	2	3	11	44	144
Raindays	14	14	9	2	1	1	1	0	0	1	5	9

DARWIN

	J	F	M	A	M	J	J	A	S	O	N	D
Maximum	32	32	33	34	33	31	32	33	34	34	34	
Minimum	25	25	24	23	21	20	21	23	25	26	26	
Rainfall (mm)	393	330	258	103	14	3	1	2	13	52	124	242
Raindays	19	18	16	7	1	1	0	2	5	10	15	

URKETOWN ROAD, CARPENTARIA HIGHWAY, STUART HIGHWAY (2404 KM)

Palm Cove, Cairns

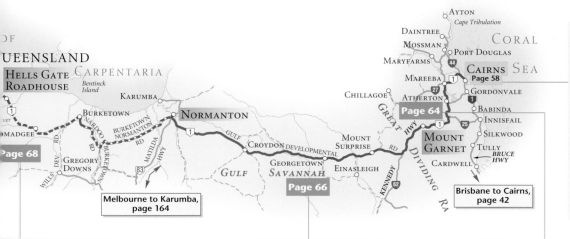

Cairns

This modern, colourful city is the capital of the tropical north. Its location is superb: the Great Barrier Reef to the east, the rainforests and plains of the Atherton Tableland to the west and palm-fringed beaches to the north and south.

Normanton to Hells Gate Roadhouse

Almost entirely unsealed, this seasonal route is best suited to four-wheel drives. Historic Burketown still retains much of its frontier character.

Mount Garnet to Normanton

On your way through this area, visit the amazing Undara Lava Tubes. Further west the *Gulflander*, linking Croydon and Normanton, is one of the world's great trains.

Cairns to Mount Garnet

Perched high above the coastal plain, the Atherton Tableland has some fabulous tourist attractions: enjoy the activities at the scenic Lake Tinaroo or spend time at one of the many excellent craft shops.

CAIRNS TO MOUNT GARNET 193 KM

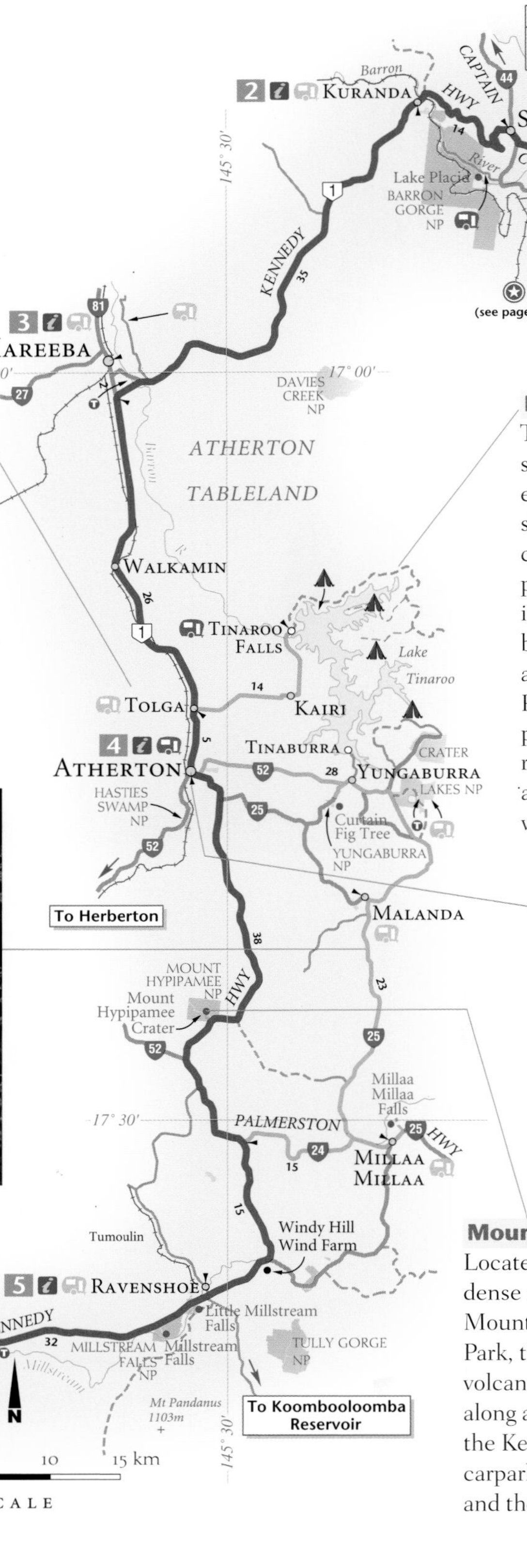

Stunning woodwork

Tolga Woodworks is renowned for high quality woodwork, much of which is handmade in the adjoining workshop. The town itself has a long history in timber, and cedar and maple still grow in the region. Kennedy Highway; (07) 4095 4488; open 9 a.m. to 5 p.m. daily.

A scenic drive

Turn east off the highway at Atherton and enjoy the sights along this alternative route. Stop at Yungaburra, a historic township with 28 heritage-listed buildings. At Peterson Creek there is a platypus-viewing platform and you can see these unique creatures in the early morning and late afternoon. Three km south-west from Yungaburra you will find the Curtain Fig, the Atherton Tableland's most famous tree. A 50-m walk brings you to this amazing strangler fig tree with its curtain of aerial roots stretching 15 m to the ground. Also worth a stop are the spectacular Millaa Millaa Falls (pictured).

Lake Tinaroo

There is plenty to do at t scenic lake. Water-sport enthusiasts can try water skiing, jet-skiing, sailing canoeing. For those who prefer fishing, barramun is in season year-round a black bream are abunda as are redclaw crayfish. Parks and picnic areas a plentiful around the reservoir, while camping areas are dotted along th water's edge.

Mount Hypipamee crater

Located in the small pocket of dense rainforest that forms Mount Hypipamee National Park, this eerie, narrow, extinc volcanic crater can be reache along a short sealed road from the Kennedy Highway. From t carpark it is an easy 250-m wa and the view is extraordinary.

Map labels:

Cairns
For more detail, see maps on pages 60–1

KURANDA
SMITHFIELD
CORAL SEA
CAIRNS
Lake Placid
BARRON GORGE NP
Barron River
CAPTAIN HWY
COOK HWY
KENNEDY

(see page 56)
Cardwell to Cairns, page 56

MAREEBA
17° 00'
DAVIES CREEK NP
17° 00'

ATHERTON TABLELAND

WALKAMIN

TINAROO FALLS
Lake Tinaroo

TOLGA
KAIRI

ATHERTON
HASTIES SWAMP NP
TINABURRA
YUNGABURRA
CRATER LAKES NP
Curtain Fig Tree
YUNGABURRA NP

To Herberton

MOUNT HYPIPAMEE NP
Mount Hypipamee Crater

MALANDA

Millaa Millaa Falls

17° 30'
PALMERSTON

MILLAA MILLAA

HWY

Tumoulin
Windy Hill Wind Farm

RAVENSHOE
Little Millstream Falls
MILLSTREAM FALLS NP
Millstream Falls
TULLY GORGE NP

MOUNT GARNET
INNOT HOT SPRINGS
KENNEDY

Mt Pandanus 1103m

To Koombooloomba Reservoir

Mount Garnet to Normanton, page 66

N

0   5   10   15 km

SCALE

Travel tip

North Queensland has numerous waterfalls and there are many on the Tableland. Our favourites include the Millstream Falls, south-west of Ravenshoe (a 300-m walk from the carpark and picnic area to the viewing platform), and the much-photographed Millaa Millaa Falls (easily reached and visible from the carpark, but also just a short walk to the base of the falls).

What's on

APRIL Mareeba Rodeo **MAY** Mount Garnet Races and Rodeo **JULY** Malanda Show **AUGUST** Warbirds Airshow (Mareeba) **OCTOBER** Atherton Food Festival

Historic steam train

Railco operates a 1927 C-17-class steam train, *Roger*, from Platypus Park in Atherton along Queensland's steepest railway line to Herberton. Platypus Park, Herberton Road; (07) 4091 4871; fee applies; departs 10.30 a.m., returns 3 p.m. Wednesdays, Sundays and public holidays.

Track notes

The highway climbs from Cairns, but it is an easy drive, with overtaking lanes. Beyond Kuranda the highway is mostly two-lane with some slow-vehicle lanes. Past Atherton some sections are single-width bitumen.

Town file

1 CAIRNS (see page 58)

2 KURANDA pop. 666   PDG
GPS 16° 49.129' S/145° 37.989' E
High above Cairns and surrounded by rainforest, Kuranda is a magnet for visitors. The Kuranda scenic train and the Skyrail Cableway both terminate in this vibrant village, populated by artists and people seeking an alternative lifestyle. The Kuranda Markets, held every Wednesday, Thursday, Friday and Sunday, are still a major attraction after 26 years. ⓘ Kuranda Village; (07) 4093 9311; www.kuranda.org

3 MAREEBA pop. 6874   PDG
GPS 16° 59.524' S/145° 25.337' E
Mareeba is a multicultural town servicing an intensive local agricultural industry. The former tobacco-growing area is now rich in tea-tree, nuts, fruit, coffee and sugarcane, all irrigated from nearby Lake Tinaroo. There is good shopping. ⓘ 345 Byrnes Street; (07) 4092 5674.

4 ATHERTON pop. 5693   PDG
GPS 17° 16.076' S/145° 28.490' E
Atherton is the hub of the Tableland and has supermarkets and all facilities. The area is home to many local artists and the gallery adjoining the visitor information centre displays their work. This is the last spot for auto gas for westbound travellers until the Burke and Wills Roadhouse (south of Normanton), 810 km away. ⓘ Corner Silo Road and Main Street; (07) 4091 4222; www.athertontableland.com

5 RAVENSHOE pop. 867   PD
GPS 17° 36.379' S/145° 28.950' E
Nestled in the Great Dividing Range, 920 m above sea level, this former timber community is Queensland's highest town. Waterfalls are close by and the barramundi-stocked Koombooloomba Reservoir is 38 km south. Ravenshoe has good shopping. ⓘ Moore Street; (07) 4097 7700.

6 INNOT HOT SPRINGS pop. 120   PD
GPS 17° 39.993' S/145° 14.350' E
Developed as a tin-mining town last century, Innot Hot Springs has a hotel, a very good mechanical repair shop and a caravan park. Enjoy a relaxing soak at the thermal spring-fed pools and spas.

7 MOUNT GARNET pop. 406   PD
GPS 17° 40.529' S/145° 06.760' E
Mount Garnet has had a rich mining history since 1881, and you can still try your luck at one of the public fossicking areas. The township has minimal facilities and the roadhouse meets travellers' needs.

MOUNT GARNET TO NORMANTON 515 KM

Travel tip

Estuarine, or saltwater, crocodiles are *extremely dangerous*. They are found throughout northern Australia, inhabiting fresh water – rivers and waterholes – as well as coastal water. Do not swim in waterways in the north and take care near water, boat ramps, fish-cleaning areas and when fishing. Observe crocodiles from a distance and camp away from water where crocodiles may be present.

A trip back in time

The *Gulflander* is one of the world's unique train trips. The railway has operated continually since 1891 and the diesel railmotor departs year-round from Normanton each Wednesday at 8.30 a.m. for the 152-km journey to Croydon, returning Thursday. Normanton Railway Station; (07) 4745 1391; fee applies.

Soak away your aches

The Tallaroo Hot Springs are a naturally occurring group of five terraced springs set among melaleuca and pandanus. Entry fee applies; open Sunday to Friday from Easter to the end of September.

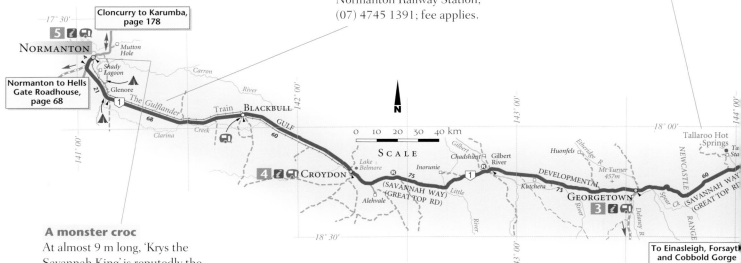

Cloncurry to Karumba, page 178

Normanton to Hells Gate Roadhouse, page 68

To Einasleigh, Forsayth and Cobbold Gorge

A monster croc

At almost 9 m long, 'Krys the Savannah King' is reputedly the largest estuarine crocodile ever caught. A lifesize replica of this monster sits in the park next door to the council offices in Haig Street, Normanton.

What's on

APRIL Barra Classic Fishing Tournament (Normanton) JUNE Normanton Rodeo and Campdraft AUGUST Croydon Campdraft SEPTEMBER Poddy Dodgers Music Festival (Croydon) OCTOBER Bushman's Ball (Georgetown)

Tracks of a volcano

The Undara Lava Tubes are huge tunnels and caves formed by lava that flowed about 200 000 years ago. This rare and fascinating geological formation can only be visited on a guided tour from Undara Lava Lodge; 1800 990 992; cost varies depending on tour; tours operate daily, booking essential.

Topaz gemfield

O'Briens Creek Gemfield near Mount Surprise is renowned for its gem-quality topaz. Obtain a fossicking licence from the BP service station in Mount Surprise or the mining registrar in Georgetown; (07) 4062 1104.

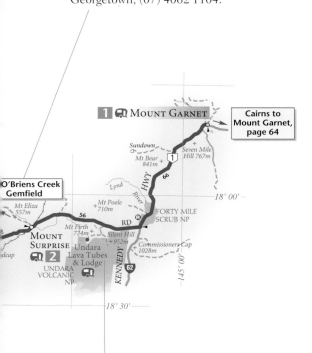

Track notes

In the late 1990s the road from Georgetown to Normanton was finally sealed, making it possible to drive and tow caravans from the Atherton Tableland in the east. From Mount Garnet to Normanton the route is now a sealed all-weather road; however, during the wet season (November to March) it may be cut by flooding.

Town file

1 MOUNT GARNET (see page 65)

2 MOUNT SURPRISE pop. 65   ⛽ PD
GPS 18° 08.816' S/144° 19.127' E
Mount Surprise is a small community on the edge of the immense Undara lava field and is a centre for gem fossicking, with topaz, quartz, spinel, aquamarine and garnet found locally. The *Savannahlander* railmotor stops overnight each week on its 3-day run between Cairns and Forsayth. Limited services are available in town.

3 GEORGETOWN pop. 298   ⛽ PD
GPS 18° 12.160' S/143° 32.977' E
Once the heart of a promising goldfield on the Etheridge River, Georgetown is now the administrative centre for the region. Einasleigh, Forsayth and Cobbold Gorge lie to the south and ghost towns are scattered around the old diggings. Fossicking is popular in this diverse geological region; obtain permits from the local mine warden's office. 🛈 St George Street; (07) 4062 1485.

4 CROYDON pop. 223   ⛽ PD
GPS 18° 12.160' S/142° 14.662' E
Croydon was once the gold capital of the north. Gold was discovered in 1885 and the town boomed, but by 1925 it was all over and the population had dwindled to 400. Today Croydon is a neat town with much of its heritage well preserved. Most basic services are available and travellers will feel welcome here. 🛈 Samwell Street; (07) 4745 6125.

5 NORMANTON pop. 1328   ⛽ PD
GPS 17° 40.179' S/141° 04.770' E
Following the discovery of rich gold deposits along the Etheridge River and copper in Cloncurry, Normanton became, for a time, an important inland river port. The railway to Croydon was completed in 1891, and many original buildings, including the railway station, Westpac Bank, Burns Philp building and the council offices, are good examples of early architecture. Possibly the most identifiable landmark in town is the famous 'Purple Pub'. Normanton has most basic services. There are two camping areas about 30 km outside of town, but these can get flooded out during the wet season. 🛈 Carpentaria Shire Council, Haig Street; (07) 4745 1268.

NORMANTON TO HELLS GATE ROADHOUSE 407 KM

Authors' choice

⭐ **Kingfisher Camp, via Doomadgee**

This is a great place to spend a few quiet days under shady trees on lush lawns beside a large waterhole on the Nicholson River. There are dinghies for hire. The camp is open between April and October and is reached along unsealed roads from Savannah Way to the west of Doomadgee. It is part of Bowthorn Station.

For more details see page 373.

Clouds of glory

The Morning Glory is a unique cloud formation that can be seen around the Gulf of Carpentaria between September and December. The spectacular tubular formations spread from horizon to horizon, stretching for hundreds of kilometres, usually rolling in from the Gulf in banks of three or four, and are accompanied by strong winds.

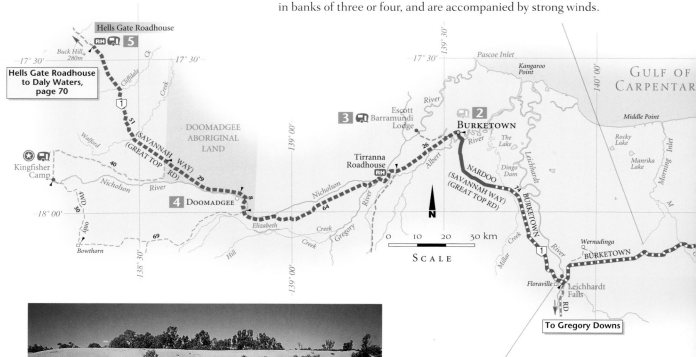

Hells Gate Roadhouse to Daly Waters, page 70

Leichhardt River

The Leichhardt River is a major Gulf tributary, winding its way north from the ranges south of Mount Isa. Between Normanton and Burketown the main road crosses the river at Floraville just above Leichhardt Falls. A short stroll takes you to the top of the falls, but during the dry season they may not be flowing.

Travel tip

We often stop at Kingfisher Camp on Bowthorn Station, owned by the McGinnis family. On Saturday nights the family often comes to Kingfisher Camp and cooks dinner for those who would like to eat out (booking necessary). The family has an interesting history, much of which is revealed by Kerry McGinnis in her books *Pieces of Blue* and *Heart Country*.

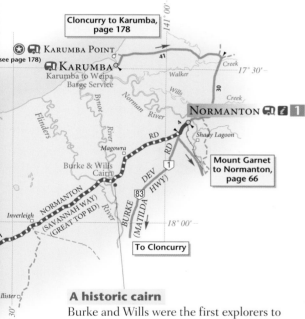

Cloncurry to Karumba, page 178

Mount Garnet to Normanton, page 66

A historic cairn

Burke and Wills were the first explorers to cross the continent from south to north, in 1860–61, reaching the coast near the mouth of the Bynoe River. Their northernmost camp on the banks of the Bynoe River is clearly signposted from the road.

What's on

APRIL World Barramundi Handline-rod Fishing Championships (Burketown) MAY Gregory River Canoe Race (Gregory Downs)

Track notes

The Savannah Way from Normanton to Borroloola (in the Northern Territory) is an unsealed, maintained road, usually only passable in the dry season. The road has improved greatly over recent years, but for those planning to complete this section we would still recommend that touring be limited to four-wheel drives and off-road camper-trailers or off-road caravans. The Savannah Way is the new name being given to the road network linking Cairns with Darwin. The section from Mount Surprise through to Cape Crawford has been known by different names, the Great Top Road being the most common, but many businesses along the route are now using the Savannah Way instead.

Town file

1 **NORMANTON** (see page 67)

2 **BURKETOWN** pop. 220   PD
GPS 17° 44.452' S/139° 32.881' E
The oldest town on the Gulf of Carpentaria, with a history dating back 140 years, is now a centre for the regional cattle industry. Burketown is about 25 km from the Gulf by boat. The town has no all-weather access road and a small amount of rain can quickly close the local black-soil roads. There is great barramundi fishing in the Gulf tributaries near Burketown. Basic services are available.

3 **ESCOTT BARRAMUNDI LODGE**   PD
GPS 17° 44.299' S/139° 24.901' E
Escott Barramundi Lodge is a working cattle property on the banks of the Nicholson River. Facilities include a comfortable caravan park, various types of accommodation and a licensed bar and dining area. Fishing is a major attraction here with good access to the river. Access to the lodge is by unsealed road only.

4 **DOOMADGEE** pop. 754   PD
GPS 17° 56.183' S/138° 49.841' E
Doomadgee is an Aboriginal community on the Nicholson River between Burketown and Hells Gate Roadhouse. The community store is open to visitors, selling fuel and basic requirements.

5 **HELLS GATE ROADHOUSE**   PD
GPS 17° 27.307' S/138° 21.361' E
This landmark roadhouse complex was established by the local station owners some years ago to service travellers on the unsealed Great Top Road. Basic stores, fuel, limited mechanical repairs, accommodation and meals are offered in addition to camping. Tours of the area are conducted from Hells Gate Roadhouse by Savannah Guides.

HELLS GATE ROADHOUSE TO DALY WATERS 704 KM

A legendary pub

The historic Daly Waters Pub, on Stuart Street, was built in the 1930s to service the crew and passengers of international aircraft. Today it still caters for travellers, with most now arriving by road to enjoy the famous nightly Beef and Barra Barbecue during the April to October tourist season.

Caranbirini Conservation Reserve

This reserve lies 500 m from the Carpentaria Highway, 46 km south-west of Borroloola. Protected within this reserve are sandstone pillars up to 25 m high, all good examples of this type of escarpment formation. Explore the maze of pillars; there is an easy 60-minute walk along a marked route. Take your camera with you as there are some great photo opportunities.

Daly Waters to Katherine, page 72

Three Ways Roadhouse to Daly Waters, page 196

Travel tip

At the border between Queensland and the Northern Territory you cross between time zones. Queensland operates on Eastern Standard Time (EST) while the Northern Territory is on Central Standard Time (CST). The difference is 30 minutes. Neither one has daylight saving. If travelling west turn clocks back 30 minutes and when travelling east turn clocks forward 30 minutes.

The lost city

Only accessible by air, these towering sandstone columns in the Abner Range form a spectacular 'lost city'. Helicopter trips available from Heartbreak Hotel; (08) 8975 9928.

A town with a riotous past

Borroloola was once a tough frontier town, filled with wild characters. However, its police station is no longer needed for its original purpose and is now a regional museum managed by the National Trust. It houses a special display dedicated to the police presence in Borroloola in the late 1800s as well as exhibits covering the Aboriginal significance of the area, Macassan visitation and early European exploration. It is clearly signposted off Robinson Road.

GULF OF
CARPENTARIA

— 16° 00' —

— 16° 30' —

0   10   20   30 km
SCALE

Normanton to
Hells Gate Roadhouse,
page 68

What's on

JUNE Borroloola Fishing Classic, Brunette Downs Races (Brunette Downs Station, 250 km south of Cape Crawford) AUGUST Borroloola Campdraft and Gymkhana SEPTEMBER Daly Waters Rodeo and Campdraft

Track notes

The road from Hells Gate Roadhouse to Borroloola is maintained gravel. Although it crosses many rivers there is just one bridge, across the McArthur River outside Borroloola. River crossings may be impassable during the wet season and some have water in them in the dry. We recommend a four-wheel drive, an off-road camper-trailer or an off-road caravan if driving through the area. The Carpentaria Highway between Borroloola and Daly Waters is a sealed all-weather road. Between Borroloola and Cape Crawford watch for very large road trains, hauling ore from the McArthur River mine to Bing Bong (54 km north of Borroloola).

Town file

1 **HELLS GATE ROADHOUSE** (see page 69)

2 **WOLLOGORANG STATION AND ROADHOUSE**   ⛽ PD
GPS 17° 12.720' S/137° 56.789' E
Wollogorang is the oldest continually settled grazing property in the Northern Territory. While it is still a working property, there is now a roadhouse complex with accommodation, meals and a caravan park. It is possible to reach the Gulf using property tracks; obtain permission from Wollogorang. Fuel and basic supplies are available.

3 **BORROLOOLA** pop. 551   ⛽ PD
GPS 16° 05.285' S/136° 18.314' E
This frontier town has had a colourful past. To the south, the giant McArthur River mine extracts a complex silver–lead–zinc ore which is road-freighted to the nearby port of Bing Bong. Fishing is the area's main attraction; there are numerous fishing camps along the coastal rivers. The Gulf of Carpentaria and the Sir Edward Pellew islands to the north are also popular fishing destinations. Most supplies and services are available.
🛈 Lot 384 Robinson Road; (08) 8975 8799.

4 **HEARTBREAK HOTEL**   ⛽ PD
GPS 16° 40.994' S/135° 43.624' E
The Heartbreak Hotel lies at the junction of the Tablelands and Carpentaria highways, in the locality of Cape Crawford. The hotel complex here provides accommodation, fuel and meals, and has a caravan park. The rich Barkly Tableland stretches to the south and there are several 'lost city' escarpment rock formations in the area; the hotel offers helicopter flights to the more remote formations.

5 **DALY WATERS** pop. 20   ⛽ PD
GPS 16° 15.215' S/133° 22.162' E
Daly Waters was a refuelling point for Qantas international flights during the 1930s. Today a few houses and the historic hotel are all that remain, but the latter has become an extremely popular and renowned stop-off for tourists. About 1 km north of Daly Waters is a tree with a barely identifiable carved letter 'S' on its trunk, believed to have been marked by explorer John McDouall Stuart as he struggled to cross the continent in the 1860s. 🛈 Daly Waters Pub, Stuart Street; (08) 8975 9927.

DALY WATERS TO KATHERINE 272 KM

Katherine to Darwin,
page 74

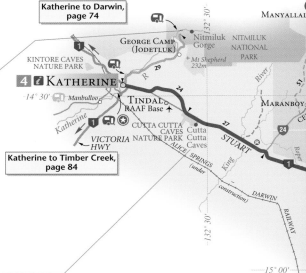

Authors' choice

⊛ Low Level Caravan Park, Katherine

This is one of the more appealing parks in Australia and we really enjoy staying here. Owner-operated, it has excellent facilities, including a relaxed licensed bistro and kiosk that operate during the winter tourist season. Booking is absolutely essential at peak times. **For more details see page 372.**

Katherine to Timber Creek,
page 84

Rare bats
The Cutta Cutta Caves are 27 km south-east of Katherine, close to the Stuart Highway, and are the only caves open to the public in the Territory. The limestone caves have spectacular stalactites and stalagmites, and are home to rare orange horseshoe-bats and ghost bats. Entry fee applies; tours of the Cutta Cutta Caves are run daily at 9, 10 and 11 a.m. and 1, 2 and 3 p.m.

Amazing gorges
Nitmiluk National Park is 29 km north-east of Katherine. The Katherine River has cut through the rocks, and you will marvel at the beauty of this national park. Boat cruises and canoeing are both popular ways to see the 13 gorges, and with more than 100 km of walking tracks bushwalkers are also catered for. A visitor information centre at the gorge is open daily and has a host of information available, along with a display centre and coffee shop.

Palms by the pool
Mataranka Thermal Pool was proclaimed as a reserve in 1967 to preserve the pool and surrounding palm forest. The water is a constant 34 degrees Celsius and flows at an amazing 30.5 million litres per day. The adjoining camping ground is very popular with travellers, who stop for a dip in the rock-paved thermal pool.

What's on
MAY Back to the Never Never Festival (Mataranka) JUNE Canoe Marathon (Katherine) JULY Katherine Agricultural Show AUGUST Mataranka Rodeo

Experience Aboriginal culture

Manyallaluk, 102 km north-east of Katherine, is an Aboriginal community that has won major tourism awards for its innovative program that allows visitors to interact with Aboriginal culture. Activities include basket weaving, collecting bush tucker, painting, spear throwing and lighting a fire with fire sticks.

A bush tucker lunch of barramundi and kangaroo is often included in the day's activities. There is also a pleasant small camping area with a limited number of powered sites. The community is an alcohol-free area. We highly recommend this experience; bookings are essential. Manyallaluk Experience; (08) 8975 4727 or 1800 644 727; fee applies for a day's activities; open daily during tourist season.

Track notes

The Stuart Highway is a wide, well-maintained road through this area. The road to Nitmiluk Gorge is also sealed and suitable for caravans, as is the short sealed road to the Cutta Cutta Caves. For those planning to visit Manyallaluk, the last 35 km are unsealed but the road is well-maintained gravel and is normally in good condition during the dry season.

Town file

1 DALY WATERS (see page 71)

2 LARRIMAH pop. 25   🅿 PDG
GPS 15° 34.492' S/133° 12.988' E
Larrimah became a town during World War II, when the historic Gorrie Airfield was built about 10 km to the north. The railway from Darwin terminated near Larrimah. Today the town has a hotel and service stations to cater for travellers. Fran, a local identity who is a mine of information, runs a tearoom from the old police station.

3 MATARANKA pop. 667   🅿 PDG
GPS 14° 55.449' S/133° 04.078' E
The historic town of Mataranka is in the heart of Never Never country, Jeannie Gunn having made this area famous in her classic *We of the Never Never*, which describes her experiences on nearby Elsey Station around 1902. The town has a range of accommodation and camping areas to cater for most budgets. Most basic services are available here. ℹ Stockyard Gallery, Stuart Highway; (08) 8975 4530.

4 KATHERINE pop. 7979   🅿 PDG
GPS 14° 18.983' S/132° 25.265' E
Katherine is a major centre in the heart of the Northern Territory at the junction of the Stuart and Victoria highways. There is a selection of caravan parks and a wide range of accommodation, and the town has most services. From a tourist's point of view, one of the most popular features in the Katherine area is the spectacular Nitmiluk Gorge. The Tick Market (like a flea market) operates on the first Saturday evening of each month, just near the tourist information centre. ℹ Corner Lindsay Street and Katherine Terrace; (08) 8972 2650.

Travel tip

Katherine caters well for tourists and has an excellent visitor information centre with plenty of parking. While in Katherine try Tommo's Bakery. It sells a range of delicious, home-baked fresh bread, cakes, pies and pastries and we rarely pass through Katherine without paying a visit. Corner Giles and Second streets (on the Gorge Road); open six days (closed Sundays).

Manyallaluk

14° 30'

BUNGA
ARNHEM RD
BESWICK
ABORIGINAL
LAND
TRUST

Creek
Mataranka Thermal Pool
MATARANKA
3 ℹ
9
ELSEY NP
JILKMINGGAN
Elsey
15° 00'
ROPER 20 HWY
River

Elsey Cemetery

MANGARRAYI
ABORIGINAL
LAND TRUST

Roper

133° 30'

WUBALAWUN
ABORIGINAL
LAND TRUST

5° 30'
15° 30'

133° 00'

LARRIMAH 2

N

0 10 20 30 km
SCALE

16° 00'
16° 00'

HWY
92

Kalala

Hells Gate Roadhouse to Daly Waters, page 70

1 ℹ DALY WATERS
CARPENTARIA HWY

Three Ways Roadhouse to Daly Waters, page 196

Hi Way Inn Roadhouse
87

KATHERINE TO DARWIN 314 KM

Authors' choice

⊛ Douglas Daly Tourist Park, Douglas Daly

This is a picturesque park on the banks of the Douglas River. Each Thursday they serve free coffee and scones for morning tea and on Wednesday and Sunday evenings they have buffalo roasts. The park is about 39 km along a sealed road from the Stuart Highway (turn off the highway 6 km north of the Hayes Creek roadhouse). It has good facilities and is close to the Douglas Hot Springs.

For more details see page 364.

⊛ Palms Village Resort, Palmerston

Located on the Stuart Highway 19 km from Darwin, this is a large park with good facilities and a quality licensed restaurant. We find it a good base for exploring Darwin and the surrounding areas.

For more details see page 363.

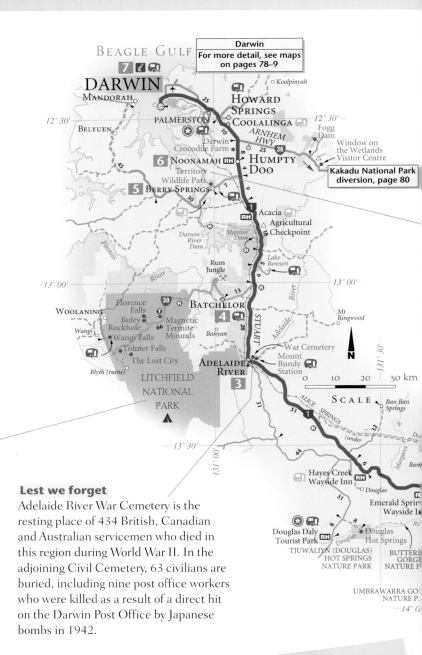

Litchfield National Park

At the spectacular Litchfield National Park you will see numerous waterfalls cascading from a sandstone plateau. There are also good examples of magnetic termite nests, a small 'lost city' formation and some relics of early pastoral interests. There are several camping areas in the park, although Wangi Falls is the only one suitable for caravans. A network of all-weather sealed roads links many of the popular sites within this beautiful national park.

Lest we forget

Adelaide River War Cemetery is the resting place of 434 British, Canadian and Australian servicemen who died in this region during World War II. In the adjoining Civil Cemetery, 63 civilians are buried, including nine post office workers who were killed as a result of a direct hit on the Darwin Post Office by Japanese bombs in 1942.

What's on

MAY Gold Rush Festival (Pine Creek) JUNE Pine Creek Rodeo

Travel tip

A visit to Litchfield National Park is a rewarding experience. Our favourite camping area is Wangi Falls, but it gets very busy in the dry (tourist) season. Arrive early if you want a campsite, especially a caravan site, as there is no reservation system. The swimming hole is a great place to relax and its kiosk serves food, drinks and ice-creams.

Wildlife of the Northern Territory

The Territory Wildlife Park at Berry Springs showcases a wide range of native flora and fauna. Set on 400 ha of bushland, the park includes a large aquarium tunnel, wetlands and a nocturnal house. Cox Peninsula Road, Berry Springs; (08) 8988 7200; entry fee applies; open 8.30 a.m. to 6 p.m. daily.

Railway memories

Pine Creek Railway Station was built in 1888 as part of the grand plan to connect South Australia and Darwin by rail. Pine Creek was the end of the line for 29 years until an extension to Katherine was constructed; the final completion of the Alice Springs to Darwin railway is planned for 2004. The station is now a National Trust museum with an 1877 steam locomotive and other railway memorabilia on display. Entry fee applies; open daily during the dry season.

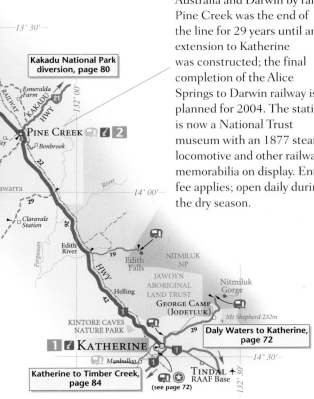

Track notes

The well-maintained Stuart Highway traverses low, undulating hills north of Pine Creek. There are a few overtaking lanes along this section. The only sealed access to Litchfield National Park is via Batchelor; the alternative route between Wangi Falls and Berry Springs has an unsealed section that can be rough for two-wheel drives towing caravans.

Town file

1 KATHERINE (see page 73)

2 PINE CREEK pop. 521 ⛽ PDG
GPS 13° 49.638' S/131° 50.487' E
Pine Creek owes its existence to a gold rush in the 1870s. The Northern Goldfields Loop tourist drive takes in the historic mining area, following the rich mineral fault-line to the north. There is a general store and basic services are available. 🛈 Diggers Rest Motel, 32 Main Terrace; (08) 8976 1442.

3 ADELAIDE RIVER pop. 279 ⛽ PDG
GPS 13° 14.308' S/131° 06.299' E
Adelaide River was a base for servicemen during World War II and in 1947 was chosen by the Commonwealth War Graves Commission as the site for the War Cemetery. The township has a hotel and service stations, and basic services are available. There are caravan parks in Adelaide River, but we prefer the facilities at Mount Bundy Station, 3 km east of town.

4 BATCHELOR pop. 645 ⛽ PD
GPS 13° 02.817' S/131° 01.653' E
Batchelor began as a town servicing Australia's first uranium mine, at Rum Jungle. Mining has long ceased and Batchelor is now best known as the entrance to the beautiful Litchfield National Park. A supermarket, service station, hotel and caravan park meet travellers' basic needs.

5 BERRY SPRINGS pop. 190 ⛽ PD
GPS 12° 42.762' S/130° 59.692' E
The small village of Berry Springs on the Cox Peninsula Road is the location of the award-winning Territory Wildlife Park. The nearby Berry Springs Nature Park is ideal for a picnic or swim, while the Lakes Resort Caravan Park is a good base from which to explore this area. Berry Springs has basic services.

6 NOONAMAH pop. 8 ⛽ PDG
GPS 12° 38.054' S/131° 04.449' E
Noonamah is a roadhouse, supermarket and hotel complex on the Stuart Highway a few kilometres south of its junction with the Arnhem Highway. The nearby Darwin Crocodile Farm has crocodile feeding daily at 2 p.m.

7 DARWIN (see page 76)

DARWIN
YOUR GUIDE

Darwin is about the size of a large provincial town, with all the facilities you would expect of a capital city. Its climate changes from hot and dry to hot and humid later in the year. Twice rebuilt, Darwin has a spacious, ordered feel thanks to the wide streets, newish low buildings and expansive manicured lawns. But it is also a city with a magnificent tropical chaos as streets give way to mangrove estuaries, brightly coloured foliage and huge ocean tides.

CITY CENTRE

See map on page 78.

Aquascene 78 B5
Hand feed Darwin's many fish species at high tide.

Australian Pearling Exhibition 78 F7
Exhibits on the history and science of this important industry.

Bicentennial Park 78 B5
Take a stroll on the Esplanade at sunset; extensive trails, memorial sites and brilliant views.

Christ Church Cathedral 78 E6
Built in 1902, hit by Japanese gunfire in 1942 and destroyed by cyclone Tracy in 1974; the new building incorporates the original porch and an incredible altar that was hewn from a jarrah log more than 400 years old.

Darwin Botanic Gardens 78 C1
Lush gardens that date back to a vegetable patch established in the 1870s; impressive tropical, orchid and palm collections, and a self-guided Aboriginal plant-use trail.

Deckchair Cinema 78 F6
Dry-season screenings of alternative films under the stars (May to October).

Lyons Cottage 78 C6
Built in 1925 to house British and Australian Telegraph Company staff; now a museum on the history of the city.

Mindil Beach Sunset Market 78 A1
Live entertainment, exotic foods, art and craft, a tropical sunset and beach fireworks; Thursday nights, May to October, and Sunday nights, June to September.

Overland Telegraph Memorial 78 D7
Marks the centenary of significant Darwin events, including the completion of the Overland Telegraph line between Adelaide and Darwin, and the laying of the overseas cable to Java.

Top events

Touring Car Championships (May)
V8 supercars in a 3-day contest.

Royal Darwin Show (July)
Darwin's premier event.

Darwin Rodeo and Country Music Concert (July or August)
Three days of 'yee-ha', Top End style.

Darwin Cup Carnival (August)
The city's premier horse race.

Festival of Darwin (September)
A feast of visual and performing arts.

Visitor information

Tourism Top End
Corner Mitchell and Knuckey streets, Darwin
(08) 8936 2499
www.nttc.com.au

Parliament House 78 D7
Darwin's most imposing modern building; free guided tours on Saturdays at 10 a.m. and 12 noon.

Stokes Hill Wharf 78 F8
Once the main port of the city, now a popular leisure area with food outlets, a pearl store, bar and restaurant.

World War II Oil Storage Tunnels 78 E7
Network of five concrete tunnels built to store oil for the navy; one tunnel is open to the public and features photographs and stories of the war years.

SUBURBS AND SURROUNDS
See map on page 79.

Australian Aviation Heritage Centre 79 B4
Impressive list of exhibits including a massive B52 bomber and the wreckage of a Zero fighter shot down over Darwin in 1942.

Casuarina Coastal Reserve 79 B2
Long, white sandy beach, dunes, and mangrove and monsoon vine thickets; walking and cycling track to Nightcliff; includes Aboriginal sacred site, Old Man Rock.

Crocodylus Park 79 C4
For a safe encounter with these prehistoric monster reptiles, among other wildlife; also a research centre and museum.

Cullen Bay Marina 79 A5
Wonderful views, waterfront dining, shops and boardwalk; departure point for sunset cruises.

Darwin Crocodile Farm 79 F8
Houses 7000 estuarine and freshwater crocodiles combined; tours and feeding displays.

Darwin Harbour Cruises 79 A5
Explore the beautiful Darwin coastline.

East Point Military Museum 79 A4
Artillery, war planes, archival footage of Japanese bombings and photographic collection.

Fannie Bay Gaol Museum 79 A4
Darwin's prison from 1883 to 1979; local history displays and remnants of prison history such as old cells and gallows.

Howard Springs 79 E5
Nature reserve with a spring-fed, crocodile-free pool for swimming.

Museum and Art Gallery of the Northern Territory 79 A4
Features one of the most significant Aboriginal collections, and a cyclone Tracy gallery.

Getting around

Darwin is very easy to negotiate either by car or on foot. The streets are well signed and traffic is light even at peak times. The Tour Tub is a service that provides a bus tour of the city's top sights. It departs daily from the north end of Smith Street Mall. The Darwin Bus Service provides a link between the city centre and outlying suburbs; the main terminal is on Harry Chan Avenue. A tour of the harbour is a must. Cullen Bay Marina is the departure point for cruises around Fannie Bay, Stokes Hill Wharf and Frances Bay, and for ferry trips to Mandorah on the Cox Peninsula.

Airport shuttle bus Darwin Airport Shuttle (08) 8981 5066; **Motoring organisation** AANT (08) 8981 3837; **Public transport** Darwin Bus Service (08) 8924 7666; **Bus tours** Tour Tub (08) 8981 5233; **Boat cruises** City of Darwin Cruises 0417 855 829, Darwin Pearl Lugger Cruises (08) 8942 3131, Spirit of Darwin (08) 8981 3711; **Taxis** Darwin Radio Taxis 13 10 08.

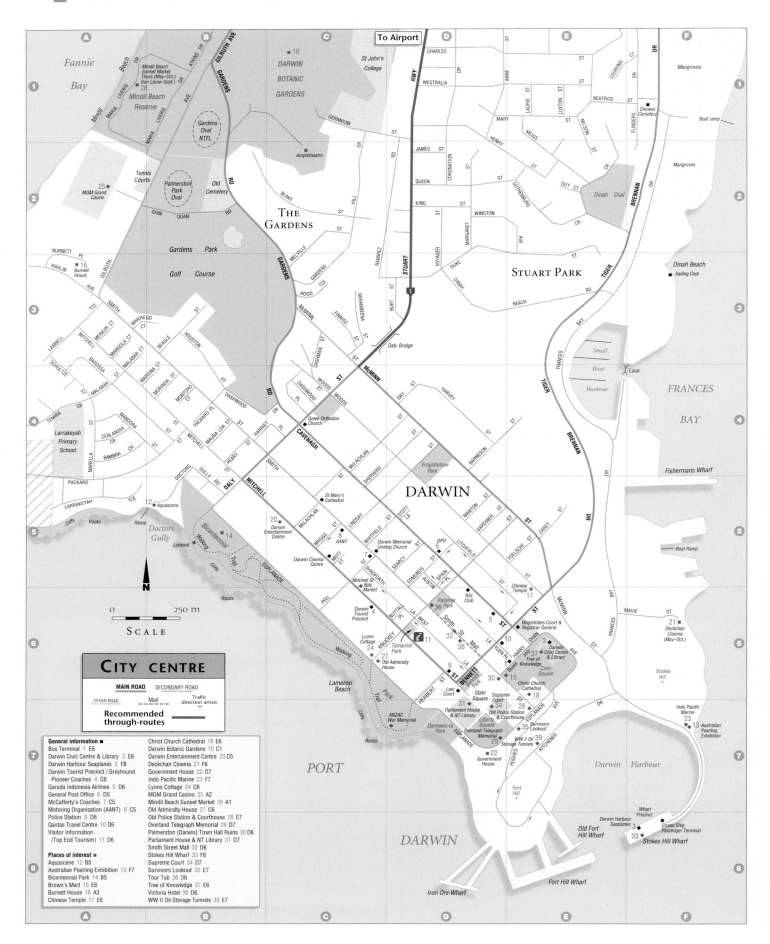

To Airport

Fannie
Bay

Mindil Beach Sunset Market Thurs (May–Oct.) Sun (June–Sept.) 26

Mindil Beach Reserve

19

DARWIN BOTANIC GARDENS

St John's College

CHARLES ST

WESTRALIA ST

Gardens Oval NTFL

Amphitheatre

Tennis Courts

25
MGM Grand Casino

Palmerston Park Oval

Old Cemetery

THE GARDENS

JAMES ST

QUEEN ST

KING ST

WINSTON

STUART PARK

Dinah Oval

Dinah Beach Sailing Club

Gardens Park

Golf   Course

16 Burnett House

Daly Bridge

McMINN ST

Frogshollow Park

DARWIN

Small Boat Harbour

Lock

FRANCES BAY

Fishermans Wharf

Larrakeyah Primary School

Greek Orthodox Church

12 Aquascene
Ramp

Doctors Gully
Lookout

14

Bicentennial   Walking   Trail

20 Darwin Entertainment Centre

St Mary's Cathedral

Darwin Cinema Centre

8 AANT

Darwin Memorial Uniting Church

GPO 6

Chinese Temple 17

RSL Club

Boat Ramp

Mitchell St Nite Market

Raintree Park 36

MAVIE ST

21 Deckchair Cinema (May–Oct.)

Darwin Tourist Precinct 4

Lyons Cottage 24

27 Old Admiralty House

11

32

38

5

10

2

Darwin Civic Centre & Library

37 Tree of Knowledge

Civic Square

15

30

Christ Church Cathedral

18

Stokes Hill

Indo Pacific Marine

23 13 Australian Pearling Exhibition

Lameroo Beach

ANZAC War Memorial

Law Court

State Square

Supreme Court 34

31 Parliament House & NT Library

Damoera-ra Park

Liberty Square

Overland Telegraph Memorial 29

Old Police Station & Courthouse 28

35 Survivors Lookout

WW II Oil Storage Tunnels 39

22 Government House

Darwin Harbour

Fort Hill

PORT

DARWIN

Iron Ore Wharf

Fort Hill Wharf

Old Fort Hill Wharf

Darwin Harbour Seaplanes 3

33

Wharf Precinct

Cruise Ship Passenger Terminal

Stokes Hill Wharf

N

0   250 m

SCALE

CITY CENTRE

MAIN ROAD   SECONDARY ROAD

OTHER ROAD   Mall   ↑ Traffic direction arrow

Recommended through-routes

General information ■
Bus Terminal 1 E6
Darwin Civic Centre & Library 2 E6
Darwin Harbour Seaplanes 3 F8
Darwin Tourist Precinct / Greyhound
   Pioneer Coaches 4 C6
Garuda Indonesia Airlines 5 D6
General Post Office 6 D5
McCafferty's Coaches 7 C5
Motoring Organisation (AANT) 8 C5
Police Station 9 D6
Qantas Travel Centre 10 D6
Visitor Information
   (Top End Tourism) 11 D6

Places of interest ■
Aquascene 12 B5
Australian Pearling Exhibition 13 F7
Bicentennial Park 14 B5
Brown's Mart 15 E6
Burnett House 16 A3
Chinese Temple 17 E6

Christ Church Cathedral 18 E6
Darwin Botanic Gardens 19 C1
Darwin Entertainment Centre 20 C5
Deckchair Cinema 21 F6
Government House 22 D7
Indo Pacific Marine 23 F7
Lyons Cottage 24 C6
MGM Grand Casino 25 A2
Mindil Beach Sunset Market 26 A1
Old Admiralty House 27 C6
Old Police Station & Courthouse 28 E7
Overland Telegraph Memorial 29 D7
Palmerston (Darwin) Town Hall Ruins 30 D6
Parliament House & NT Library 31 D7
Smith Street Mall 32 D6
Stokes Hill Wharf 33 F8
Supreme Court 34 D7
Survivors Lookout 35 E7
Tour Tub 36 D6
Tree of Knowledge 37 E6
Victoria Hotel 38 D6
WW II Oil Storage Tunnels 39 E7

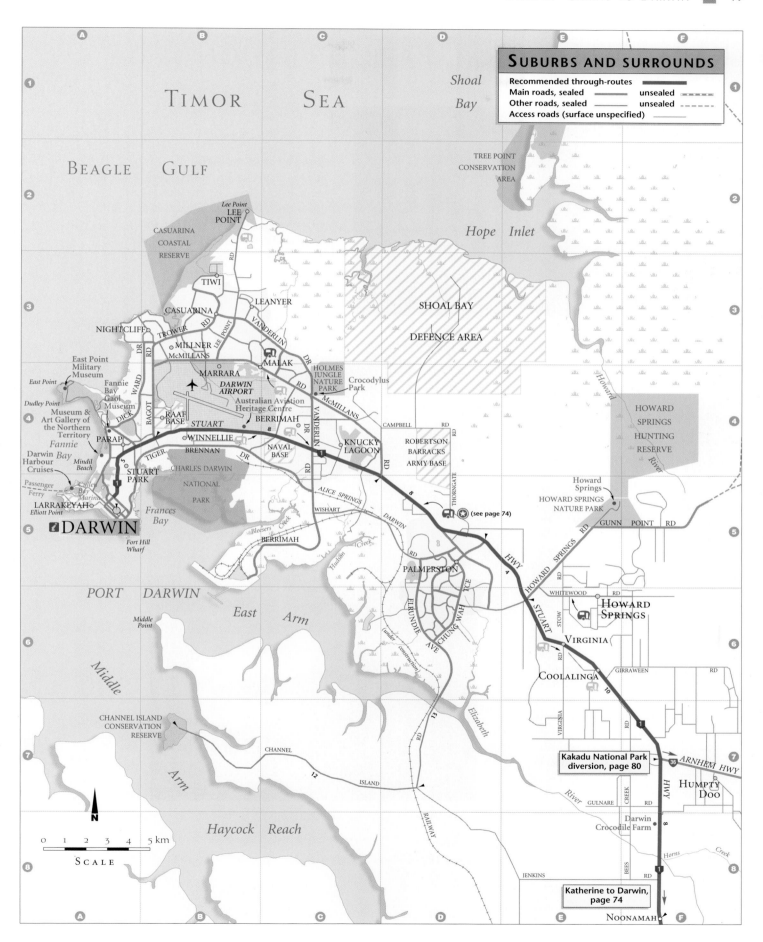

SUBURBS AND SURROUNDS

Recommended through-routes
Main roads, sealed   unsealed
Other roads, sealed   unsealed
Access roads (surface unspecified)

TIMOR SEA

Shoal
Bay

BEAGLE GULF

TREE POINT
CONSERVATION
AREA

Hope Inlet

CASUARINA
COASTAL
RESERVE

Lee Point
LEE
POINT

TIWI

LEANYER

SHOAL BAY

CASUARINA

VANDERLIN

DR

NIGHTCLIFF

TROWER

RD

LEE POINT

RD

MILLNER
McMillans

DEFENCE AREA

East Point
Military
Museum

East Point

DICK

WARD

BAGOT

DR

RD

MALAK

MARRARA

DARWIN
AIRPORT

HOLMES
JUNGLE
NATURE
PARK

Crocodylus
Park

McMILLANS

HOWARD
SPRINGS
HUNTING
RESERVE

Howard

River

Fannie
Bay Gaol
Museum

Australian Aviation
Heritage Centre

Dudley Point

Museum &
Art Gallery of
the Northern
Territory

RAAF
BASE

STUART

WINNELLIE

BERRIMAH

8

CAMPBELL

RD

ROBERTSON
BARRACKS
ARMY BASE

Howard
Springs

HOWARD SPRINGS
NATURE PARK

Fannie
Bay

PARAP

TIGER

DR

BRENNAN

NAVAL
BASE

VANDERLIN

GN

KNUCKY
LAGOON

THORNGATE

RD

8

GUNN POINT RD

Darwin
Harbour
Cruises

Mindil
Beach

STUART
PARK

CHARLES DARWIN

NATIONAL

ALICE SPRINGS

RD

DARWIN

(see page 74)

HOWARD

SPRINGS

RD

STOW

Passenger
Ferry

Cullen
Bay
Marina

5

PARK

WISHART

RD

LARRAKEYAH

DARWIN

Elliott Point

Fort Hill
Wharf

Frances
Bay

Bleesers

Creek

BERRIMAH

Creek

Hudson

PALMERSTON

HWY

4

STUART

WHITEWOOD RD

HOWARD
SPRINGS

PORT DARWIN

East Arm

Middle
Point

ELRUNDIE

AVE

CHUNG WAH

TCE

Elizabeth

STOW

RD

VIRGINIA

Girraween

RD

COOLALINGA

GIRRAWEEN RD

10

VIRGINIA

RD

CHANNEL ISLAND
CONSERVATION
RESERVE

13

Middle

CHANNEL

12

ISLAND

River

GULNARE

RD

1

Kakadu National Park
diversion, page 80

36

ARNHEM HWY

HUMPTY
DOO

Arm

Haycock Reach

RAILWAY

Darwin
Crocodile Farm

8

Horns

Creek

N

0 1 2 3 4 5 km

SCALE

JENKINS

BEES RD

1

Katherine to Darwin,
page 74

NOONAMAH

KAKADU NATIONAL PARK DIVERSION 421 KM

A haven for waterbirds

The Fogg Dam Conservation Reserve lies outside Kakadu but is an excellent place to view birds, as they congregate here to feed. Boardwalks wind around the reserve, taking you through a variety of fascinating habitats.

Jumping crocodiles

Jumping Crocodile Cruises on board the Adelaide River Queen have been popular for many years. The exciting cruise may help you understand why these awesome creatures have survived for more than 150 million years. Adelaide River Bridge, Arnhem Highway; (08) 8988 8144 or 1800 888 542; fee applies; cruises operate daily.

Window on Kakadu

Yellow Water (Ngurrungurrudjba) Billabong is one of the most accessible windows to the Kakadu wetland. There is a boardwalk but the billabong is best viewed on a boat tour. A large number of bird species, abundant wetland flora and some estuarine crocodiles are usually seen. Tours depart from Gagudju Lodge, Cooinda; (08) 8979 0145; fee applies; 1.5-hour or 2-hour cruises six times daily.

What's on

MAY Gold Rush Festival (Pine Creek) JUNE Pine Creek Rodeo AUGUST Wind Festival (Jabiru)

A fascinating rock-art gallery

For many thousands of years Aboriginal people have produced rock art, and Ubirr Art Site is a fine gallery containing red ochre, X-ray style and post-European contact painting. A 1-km circular walking track can be covered in about 45 minutes. Illustrated explanations of the styles are on display at the Bowali Visitor Centre near Jabiru. There is a camping area nearby at the East Alligator Ranger Station.

Track notes

The Arnhem and Kakadu highways are wide sealed roads with good visibility and ample opportunities for overtaking. There are numerous stops and tracks leading off the highways throughout the park and drivers need to be aware of slow-moving tourist traffic. Burning off takes place in the park during the dry season; take care if you encounter it, as the smoke can impair visibility. All vehicles entering the national park must pass through tollgates.

Town file

1 PINE CREEK (see page 75)

2 COOINDA pop. 30   PD
GPS 12° 54.787' S/132° 33.261' E
Cooinda's Gagudju Lodge resort complex is situated close by the fabulous Yellow Water (Ngurrungurrudjba) Billabong and offers most basic services including fuel, accommodation, camping and a small resort-style shop. Bus transfers to the Yellow Water cruise boats leave from the front of the resort. The Warradjan Aboriginal Cultural Centre (known as 'the turtle') is a 1-km drive or a short walk along a bush pathway.

3 JABIRU pop. 1696   PDG
GPS 12° 40.390' S/132° 49.963' E
Jabiru was constructed for workers at the area's three planned uranium mines and their families. Completed in 1982, the town has since become a major tourist centre after being surrounded by the World Heritage-listed Kakadu National Park. Jabiru offers most services; its retail outlets include a supermarket, service station and good bakery. The Bowali Visitor Centre, in Kakadu National Park, is only a short drive or 1.5-km walk from Jabiru. **i** 6 Tasman Plaza; (08) 8979 2548. Bowali Visitor Centre, Kakadu Highway; (08) 8938 1120.

4 HUMPTY DOO pop. 4798   PD
GPS 12° 34.342' S/131° 06.238' E
The site of a failed attempt to grow rice on a large scale in the 1950s, Humpty Doo has developed into an intensive market gardening area, not far from Darwin's outer suburbs. Mango and other fruit plantations are common and the town has a shopping complex and most basic services.

Traditional art and craft

The East Alligator River forms the eastern boundary of Kakadu National Park, and here Cahills Crossing links Kakadu with Arnhem Land. A permit is required to enter the area. Permits to visit the Injalak Art Centre at Oenpelli, 15 km east of the crossing on an unsealed road, can be obtained from the Northern Lands Council Office in Jabiru. At Injalak you can see locally produced ochre bark and paper paintings, as well as traditionally woven baskets and mats.

Travel tip

Kakadu National Park is a wetland where mosquitoes are usually present. Apart from being a nuisance they can also carry debilitating diseases, so pack tropical-strength personal insect repellent and cover up in long-sleeved clothing and trousers around dusk and dawn. We also use citronella candles, the type in a little bucket, to repel mosquitoes.

DARWIN TO PORT HEDLAND

STUART HIGHWAY, VICTORIA HIGHWAY, GREAT NORTHERN HIGHWAY, BROOME HIGHWAY (2167 KM)

Highway One links Darwin and Katherine before sweeping west towards Port Hedland. Across the border into Western Australia the lush Ord River region, the rugged Kimberley and the long, sweeping beaches of Broome are just a few of the attractions in this beautiful north-west region. The landscape ranges from rugged rocky hills and deep gorges to rich irrigated fields, intersected by the great Victoria, Ord and Fitzroy rivers.

Windjana Gorge, West Kimberley

Darwin to Katherine
Stop off at the fabulous Litchfield National Park, the historic Pine Creek goldfields and the numerous historic World War II sites, all on this part of the Stuart Highway. Kakadu National Park is easily accessible by two fully sealed routes.

Kununurra to Fitzroy Crossing
Once past Kununurra, visit the historic old Halls Creek townsite or the remarkable beehive-shaped outcrops of the Bungle Bungles (four-wheel drive only). Geikie Gorge is easily reached and a cruise is the best way to see its spectacular sights.

Broome to Port Hedland
This long section of the Great Northern Highway parallels the coast, although the sea is rarely in sight. Turn off towards one of the coastal camping areas, popular for fishing and ideal for a few days' rest, before heading into the busy industrial centre of Port Hedland.

Fitzroy Crossing to Broome
On the way to Broome take a diversion into Derby, a frontier port town at the head of King Sound. Further west the magnificent beaches, the relaxing charm and the comfortable cooler months make Broome a great place to stay.

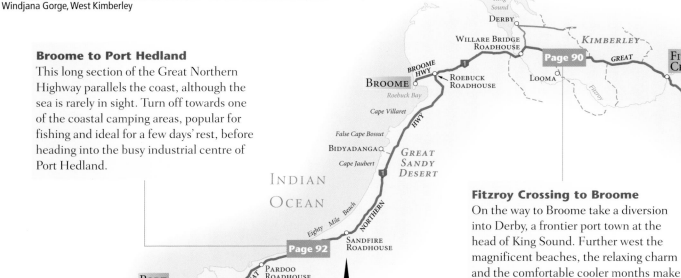

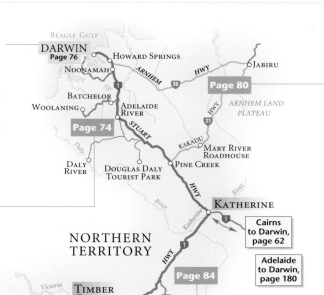

Darwin

Darwin has interesting museums, great restaurants and a fabulous range of tourist and leisure activities. Its climate – hot and dry then hot and humid – adds to Darwin's tropical feel.

DARWIN Page 76

Howard Springs

Noonamah

Batchelor

Woolaning

Adelaide River

Page 74

Daly River

Douglas Daly Tourist Park

Jabiru

Page 80

ARNHEM LAND PLATEAU

Mary River Roadhouse

Pine Creek

Kakadu

Katherine

Cairns to Darwin, page 62

Adelaide to Darwin, page 180

Page 84

NORTHERN TERRITORY

Victoria

Timber Creek

Page 86

Victoria River Roadhouse

WESTERN AUSTRALIA

Wyndham

Kununurra

Victoria

Lake Argyle

Amanbidji

Turkey Creek (Warmun)

Bungle Bungle Range

Ord

Page 88

Halls Creek

Denison Plains

Northern

Kakadu National Park diversion

This fabulous World Heritage-listed park has so much to offer, from cruising the spectacular Yellow Water Billabong with its extensive wildlife to watching the brilliant sunset from Ubirr Rock.

Katherine to Timber Creek

The Victoria Highway sweeps past a number of the Territory's legendary cattle properties and crosses the great Victoria River. The rugged Gregory National Park will appeal to those with four-wheel drives.

Timber Creek to Kununurra

Journeying by grassy plains and winding through picturesque rocky ranges, you will cross from the Northern Territory to Western Australia in this section. Turn off to the magnificent Lake Argyle, just 34 km off the highway.

Cable Beach, Broome

Best time to go

The temperate dry season, between May and November, ensures comfortable and usually dry travelling conditions. It is far less comfortable during the hot wet season.

John & Jan

KATHERINE

	J	F	M	A	M	J	J	A	S	O	N	D
Maximum	35	34	35	34	32	30	30	33	35	38	38	37
Minimum	24	24	23	20	17	14	13	16	20	24	25	24
Rainfall (mm)	235	213	161	33	6	2	1	1	6	29	87	197
Raindays	15	13	10	2	1	0	0	1	3	7	12	

BROOME

	J	F	M	A	M	J	J	A	S	O	N	D
Maximum	33	33	34	34	31	28	30	30	32	33	34	34
Minimum	26	26	25	22	18	15	14	15	18	22	25	26
Rainfall (mm)	158	144	101	30	21	23	4	3	1	1	13	77
Raindays	10	9	7	2	2	2	1	0	0	0	1	5

KATHERINE TO TIMBER CREEK 285 KM

Victoria River tours

Take a tour down Victoria River with Max's Victoria River Boat Tours. Operating from Timber Creek, they offer a 3.5-hour tour cruising 40 km of the Victoria River. This is a great opportunity to view the local wildlife, including estuarine crocodiles, birds and wallabies, along with the spectacular sunset over the river. Victoria Highway, Timber Creek; (08) 8975 0850; fee applies.

Walk on the wild side

Gregory National Park features spectacular limestone gorges, sandstone formations and rugged ranges. Follow one of the marked walking tracks in the Victoria River section such as Joe's Creek Walk, which starts alongside the Victoria Highway 10 km west of Victoria River Roadhouse. There are also several camping areas in the park, but facilities and vehicle access are limited so check with the Parks and Wildlife Office at Timber Creek; (08) 8975 0888.

Map labels

Katherine to Darwin, page 74

Daly Waters to Katherine, page 72

KINTORE CAVES NATURE PARK

STUART

1 ⓘ KATHERINE

14° 30'

Manbulloo

132° 00'

Katherine River

HWY

King

59

Limestone

Creek

15° 00'

66

VICTORIA

132° 00'

HWY

River

(see page 72)

N

5   10   15   20 km

SCALE

Track notes

The Victoria Highway between Katherine and Timber Creek is a wide sealed road with views across numerous interesting hill formations around Victoria River Roadhouse and Timber Creek (the only service points along this section). Gregory National Park is accessible from the Victoria Highway or from the unsealed Buchanan Highway. While many of the tracks are only suitable for four-wheel drives, there are some that are accessible by two-wheel drives (but towing trailers or caravans is not recommended).

Town file

To get from Darwin to Katherine, see Katherine to Darwin, page 74.

1 **KATHERINE** (see page 73)

2 **VICTORIA RIVER ROADHOUSE**   ⛽ PDG

GPS 15° 36.970' S/131° 07.672' E

The Victoria River Roadhouse complex, on the banks of the great river, is almost completely surrounded by the Victoria River section of Gregory National Park. The fully licensed roadhouse has accommodation, fuel, food and a caravan park, and is a popular stopover for travellers and an excellent base for fishing during the fishing season. Boat cruises operate during the tourist season upstream from the roadhouse.

3 **TIMBER CREEK** pop. 566   ⛽ PDG

GPS 15° 39.681' S/130° 28.817' E

Timber Creek is rich in Territory history – drovers, stockmen and early settlers all used this historic river port – and today it is a busy service centre for travellers along the Victoria Highway. The old police station is now a National Trust museum with displays of historical artefacts (open April to August). There is a historical reserve approximately 15 km north-west of town that includes Gregory's Tree, an old boab tree inscribed by the explorer Augustus Gregory in the 1850s. The Parks and Wildlife Office is at the western end of town and most facilities are available in town. Approximately 115 km south you will find one of the largest cattle stations in the country, Victoria River Downs. ⓘ Max's Victoria River Boat Tours, Victoria Highway; (08) 8975 0850.

Travel tip

About 40 km south of its intersection with the Victoria Highway, the unsealed Buchanan Highway winds through Jasper Gorge for several kilometres. The scenery is spectacular and just south of the Jasper Creek crossing there is a small, signposted bush camping area. There are no facilities but this camping area is a great base for exploring the gorge.

What's on

APRIL/MAY Fishing competitions (Timber Creek)
MAY Timber Creek Rodeo JUNE Canoe Marathon
(Katherine) JULY Katherine Agricultural Show
SEPTEMBER Timber Creek Races

TIMBER CREEK TO KUNUNURRA 227 KM

Zebra rock

Thought to be unique to a small area near Kununurra, this type of sedimentary stone has unusual contrasting striped and spotted patterns, hence its name. Local craftspeople at the Zebra Rock Gallery shape and polish the stone into items ranging from jewellery to wine racks. Zebra rock can be found in most shops in Kununurra or at the Zebra Rock Gallery in Packsaddle Road; entry fee applies; open 8 a.m. to 6 p.m. daily.

Ord River tours

Operating for more than 14 years, the award-winning Triple J Tours offers a range of Ord River tours. Our favourite is a fabulous 6-hour round trip beginning with a bus trip from Kununurra to Lake Argyle, returning the 55 km down the Ord River in one of the Triple J boats. The excellent scenery and the guides' love and knowledge of the area all contribute to this great experience. This is our pick of the things to do in this area. Coolibah Drive, Kununurra; (08) 9168 2682; fee applies; operates year-round.

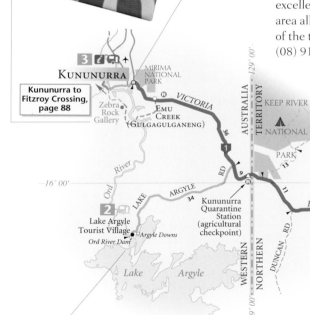

Kununurra to Fitzroy Crossing, page 88

Ord River Dam

Completed in 1971, this enormous engineering feat resulted in Lake Argyle, which encompasses an area of 2000 sq. km and can hold enough water to fill 54 Sydney Harbours (at flood level). The vast Argyle Downs Station, once owned by the pioneering Durack family, sadly lies totally submerged beneath the lake. Argyle Downs Homestead, near the dam and Lake Argyle Tourist Village, is a reconstruction of the Duracks' original homestead and is open daily during the tourist season. The lake has a fascinating array of wildlife.

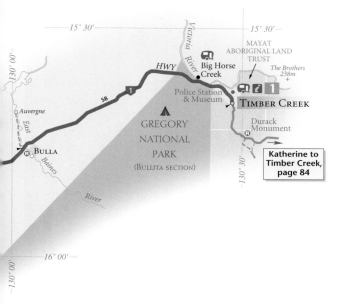

Bushwalking and camping

Keep River National Park offers visitors excellent opportunities for bushwalking, photography and camping. There are short and long walks and two camping areas within the park. Rugged sandstone formations and Aboriginal art sites are special features of the park. Access is by a gravel road suitable for two-wheel drives.

Track notes

The Victoria Highway is a wide sealed road and the section between Timber Creek and Kununurra is easy driving. Unsealed roads lead off the Victoria Highway to Gregory National Park and Keep River National Park. There are some undulating parts on the highway and the Kununurra Quarantine Station at the border breaks the trip for westbound travellers. All westbound traffic must stop here. Fresh fruit and vegetables, plants, flowers, seeds, nuts, honey and used fruit and vegetable containers must all be declared and forfeited. It is best not to have any of these on arrival and plan to re-stock with fresh produce in Kununurra. Eastbound traffic is unaffected. At the border westbound travellers should move their clocks back by 1.5 hours; eastbound travellers should move their clocks forward by 1.5 hours.

Town file

1 **TIMBER CREEK** (see page 85)

2 **LAKE ARGYLE TOURIST VILLAGE** pop. 25   🛢 PD
GPS 16° 06.772' S/128° 44.380' E
Lake Argyle Tourist Village is a small township at Ord River Dam. Mainly associated with tourism, the village is only open during the tourist season (April to October). One of the major attractions here is the Durack family's historic Argyle Downs Homestead, reconstructed from the original before the lake was flooded (the ruins of the original homestead can still be seen on the lake floor by divers). The village has basic services, accommodation, fuel and a caravan park. Outside the tourist season the dam wall and lookouts are still open but the facilities are closed.

3 **KUNUNURRA** pop. 4884   🛢 PDG
GPS 15° 46.448' S/128° 44.340' E
The damming of the mighty Ord River saw the birth of a new township, Kununurra. The town is located downstream from the Ord River Dam on the banks of Lake Kununurra, a diversion dam (completed in 1963) that channels water to an enormous irrigation area where crops of sugarcane, melons, bananas and a whole range of other produce thrive. The town has all facilities and caters well for tourists. 🗊 Coolibah Drive; (08) 9168 1177.

What's on

JUNE Dam to Dam Dinghy Race (Kununurra) JULY Kununurra Agricultural Show AUGUST East Kimberley Art Show (Kununurra) APRIL–OCTOBER Paddy's Market, Whitegum Park (Kununurra, alternate Saturdays)

KUNUNURRA TO FITZROY CROSSING 646 KM

Travel tip

The Kimberley is home to the boab tree and local Aboriginal people carve the nuts decoratively. The quality of the carving and the shape of the nuts vary but some are excellent. In the Wyndham area local craftspeople and shops sell them. Expect to pay about $25–40 for a really good sample.

Feed the crocodiles

Join in the excitement of feeding the crocodiles and komodo dragons at 11 a.m. every day at the Wyndham Zoological Gardens and Crocodile Park. Crocodile meat is on sale for adventurous cooks. Barytes Road, Wyndham Port; (08) 9161 1124; open 8.30 a.m. to 4 p.m. daily between March and November.

The spectacular Bungle Bungle Range

Horizontal bands of orange and grey colour the striking sandstone domes of the Bungle Bungle Range in Purnululu National Park. There are two camping areas (but few facilities) within the park. However, the 53-km access road from the Great Northern Highway is only suitable for four-wheel drives with good clearance and off-road camper-trailers, not for two-wheel drives or caravans. Open April to December.

Geikie Gorge National Park

The spectacular Geikie Gorge was carved by the mighty Fitzroy River through the limestone of a 350-million-year-old Devonian reef. The Department of Conservation and Land Management (CALM) runs cruises through the gorge; departure times vary so check at the Fitzroy Crossing Visitors Centre. Camping is no longer permitted at Geikie Gorge National Park. Open 6.30 a.m. to 6.30 p.m. daily between April and November; restricted access during the wet season.

What's on

JULY Rodeo (Fitzroy Crossing)
AUGUST Bastion Billy Cart Races (Wyndham), Halls Creek Cup, Wyndham Cup NOVEMBER Barra Splash fishing tournament (Fitzroy Crossing)

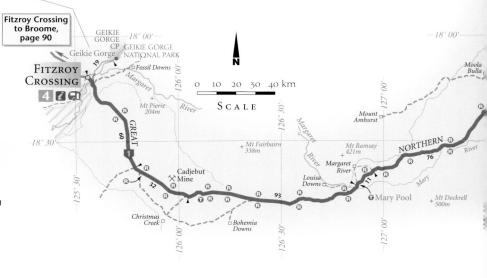

Fitzroy Crossing to Broome, page 90

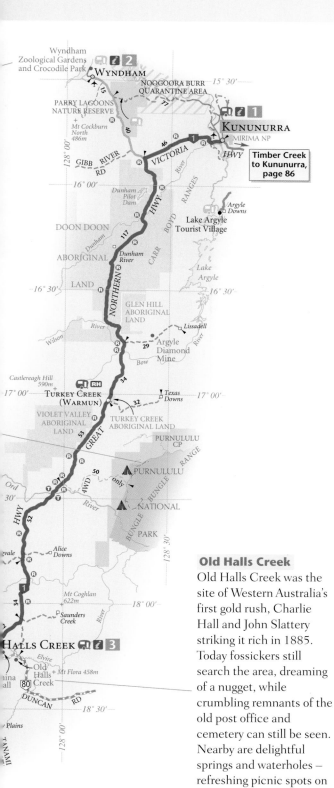

Old Halls Creek

Old Halls Creek was the site of Western Australia's first gold rush, Charlie Hall and John Slattery striking it rich in 1885. Today fossickers still search the area, dreaming of a nugget, while crumbling remnants of the old post office and cemetery can still be seen. Nearby are delightful springs and waterholes – refreshing picnic spots on hot days. There is a shop and camping area at the old town site.

Track notes

The Durack Ranges lie to the west as you drive along the Victoria and Great Northern highways between Kununurra and Halls Creek, with isolated cattle stations along the way. The road here is subject to flash flooding and can be cut for short periods following storms. Between Halls Creek and Fitzroy Crossing the highway is wide and well maintained, with numerous rest areas. The minor road to Geikie Gorge National Park is sealed.

Town file

1 KUNUNURRA (see page 87)

2 WYNDHAM pop. 868   PDG
GPS 15° 29.236' S/128° 07.397' E
The most northerly town in Western Australia, Wyndham lies on the Cambridge Gulf, into which five rivers drain; these can be clearly identified from the panoramic lookout at the top of the Bastion Range. Thousands of fortune seekers landed at Wyndham during the 1886 Halls Creek gold rush; today the port exports cattle from the Kimberley and produce from the Ord irrigation area. An excellent museum catalogues Wyndham's early history. Basic facilities are available in town.
Kimberley Motors, Great Northern Highway; (08) 9161 1281.

3 HALLS CREEK pop. 1263   PDG
GPS 18° 13.466' S/127° 40.057' E
Gold was found at the Elvire River in 1885 and thousands flocked to the new field, but the rush was short-lived, lasting just four years. In 1910 the Canning Stock Route was completed, enabling East Kimberley cattle to be driven 2000 km overland from old Halls Creek to Wiluna and the southern goldfields markets. The modern town was relocated 15 km to the west in the 1950s when the Great Northern Highway was completed. Most services are available in Halls Creek. The Argyle Diamond Mine, the largest producing diamond mine in the world and probably best known for its pink diamonds, is located 197 km north in the Pitt Range. Just east of Halls Creek you will find China Wall, a vertical quartz formation that winds its way across many kilometres, looking like a white wall made from large stones. Corner Great Northern Highway and Hall Street; (08) 9168 6262.

4 FITZROY CROSSING pop. 1147   PDG
GPS 18° 11.875' S/125° 34.033' E
The town developed to service travellers fording the mighty Fitzroy River at this point. A low bridge was constructed in 1935, but was closed for months during wet seasons. The current high-level bridge across the river was built in 1974. The Crossing Inn, located near the old ford, dates back to the 1890s. Picturesque waterholes that are a haven for wildlife and fish are found close to Fitzroy Crossing. The town has most basic services.
Flynn Drive; (08) 9191 5355.

FITZROY CROSSING TO BROOME 398 KM

National park camping

Camp at the spectacular Windjana Gorge National Park. The gorge itself is 3.5 km long and cuts through the limestone of the Napier Range, part of an ancient reef. The camping area has toilets and water. On the way to the gorge, stop at Tunnel Creek National Park, Western Australia's oldest cave system, where water has eroded a tunnel beneath the Napier Range. These parks can be reached from either direction, although Gibb River Road from Derby is the most common route.

Japanese Cemetery

You can discover a little of the multicultural heritage of Broome through a visit to the Japanese Cemetery in Port Road. Large roughly hewn headstones mark the graves of more than 900 Japanese pearl divers who died during the early days of the pearling industry.

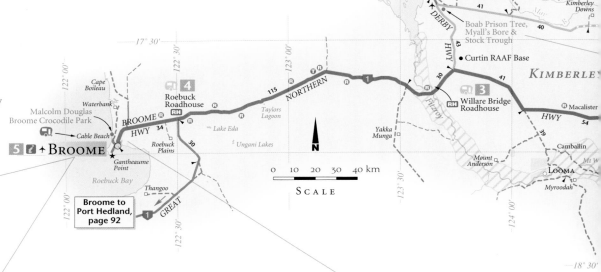

Pearling museum

Pearl Luggers Museum in Broome provides a fascinating insight into the history of the pearling industry. There are two original luggers, fully restored, and a host of memorabilia from the early pearling days (the lugger pictured is at Streeters Jetty). The museum offers guided tours. 33 Dampier Terrace; (08) 9192 2059; entry fee applies; open daily.

Crocodile feeding

Malcolm Douglas, well known for his TV documentaries, established the Malcolm Douglas Broome Crocodile Park at Cable Beach in 1983. It is a great place to see some very impressive, large crocodiles, particularly at feeding times. Cable Beach Road West; (08) 9192 1489; entry fee applies; open daily.

Travel tip

For quality food, casual atmosphere and a superb outlook over the ocean, Cable Beach Tearooms is one of our favourite Broome eateries. Open daily for breakfast, lunch and dinner, it is within easy walking distance from the Cable Beach caravan parks and is a great vantage point from which to view the fabulous sunsets.

What's on

JUNE/JULY Derby Races **JULY** Boab Festival (Derby)
AUGUST Broome Rodeo **AUGUST/SEPTEMBER**
Shinju Matsuri, or the Festival of the Pearl (Broome)

Kununurra to
Fitzroy Crossing,
page 88

Boab Prison Tree

The bulbous trunk of the Kimberley boab tree can grow to such enormous widths that police patrols during the 19th and early 20th centuries reputedly used the hollows as overnight rest points. The Boab Prison Tree, 7 km south of Derby, is the most famous of these outback 'gaols', although there are other 'prison' trees throughout the region. Alongside the Derby prison tree, Myall's Bore feeds water into a 100-m-long stock trough, the longest in Australia.

Track notes

The Great Northern Highway between Fitzroy Crossing and Roebuck Roadhouse is a wide, well-maintained sealed road. Road trains use the highway and many haul ore to the port at Derby from mines close to Fitzroy Crossing. The Derby and Broome highways are both wide sealed roads. A long one-lane bridge crosses the Fitzroy River near Willare Bridge Roadhouse and it may be necessary to give way to oncoming traffic.

Town file

1 FITZROY CROSSING (see page 89)

2 DERBY pop. 3236   ⛽ PDG
GPS 17° 18.240' S/123° 37.853' E
Located on King Sound, Derby experiences the highest tidal range in Australia (the record high tide is 11.8 m). The town's main jetty, where ships load ore from nearby mines, can be left high and dry at low tide. The main industries in the area are pastoral and mining. The port was used by pearl luggers in the 1880s (fine pearl shell was found in King Sound in 1883) and five pearl farms operate in the area today. The Gibb River Road tracks east from Derby, winding through the heart of the Kimberley. Best suited to four-wheel drives, the greatly improved road is still considered a challenge by many tourists. Two supermarkets and a selection of other shops provide most necessities. 🛈 1 Clarendon Street; (08) 9191 1426; www.derbytourism.com.au

3 WILLARE BRIDGE ROADHOUSE   ⛽ PDG
GPS 17° 43.606' S/123° 39.298' E
Just to the east of the Fitzroy River, Willare Bridge Roadhouse offers fuel, food and camping to travellers and locals. There is usually a good selection of fresh sandwiches and cakes. Souvenirs and a range of supermarket items are also available.

4 ROEBUCK ROADHOUSE   ⛽ PDG
GPS 17° 50.892' S/122° 30.048' E
This roadhouse is strategically located at the intersection of the Great Northern and Broome highways. It offers accommodation, meals and fuel and has a small adjoining caravan park.

5 BROOME pop. 11 368   ⛽ PDG
GPS 17° 57.101' S/122° 14.625' E
Broome is a fascinating town, with a tropical climate, a rich history and a distinctive style of architecture. There has been rapid growth in the past decade due to tourism, and the wonderful Cable Beach, the historic Chinatown and the tempting pearl shops are just a few of the great attractions. The town has all services, good shopping and an excellent range of accommodation. Coles supermarket is open 24 hours 7 days. 🛈 Corner Broome Road and Bagot Street; (08) 9192 2222; www.ebroome.com/tourism

BROOME TO PORT HEDLAND 611 KM

Authors' choice

⊛ Eighty Mile Beach Caravan Park, Eighty Mile Beach

We often stay at this quality beachside park, located 9 km off the Great Northern Highway and 45 km west of Sandfire Roadhouse. The owners have spent a lot of time developing it and we like what they have done. It is a popular fishing spot and a great place to rest and read a good book.

For more details see page 365.

Travel tip

The trip between Broome and Port Hedland is more than 600 km, so plan to take a break. Sandfire and Pardoo roadhouses both have basic overnight camping but if you have the time, and do not mind the unsealed access roads, break your trip with a stay at either the Eighty Mile Beach Caravan Park or the Port Smith Caravan Park.

Giant salt mounds

From the Red Bank Bridge, on the approach to Port Hedland, you will see Cargill Salt's massive stockpiles of salt, awaiting export to world markets. Salt is recovered by the natural dehydration of seawater from large evaporative ponds. The area also provides a habitat for vast numbers of beautiful birds.

Wheelbarrow races

In the 30-year-old annual Black Rock Stakes entrants participate in a light-hearted wheelbarrow marathon (loaded with iron ore), starting 118 km south-west at Whim Creek and finishing in Port Hedland. It is worth being in town in June to join in the street party.

Port Hedland to Nanutarra Roadhouse, page 96

Newman to Port Hedland, page 204

Iron-ore tour

Take the 1.5-hour tour of BHP's Nelson Point facilities for a closer investigation of the company's local operations, state-of-the-art technology and massive machinery. Tours operate each weekday departing at 9.30 a.m. from the Port Hedland Tourist Bureau in Wedge Street.

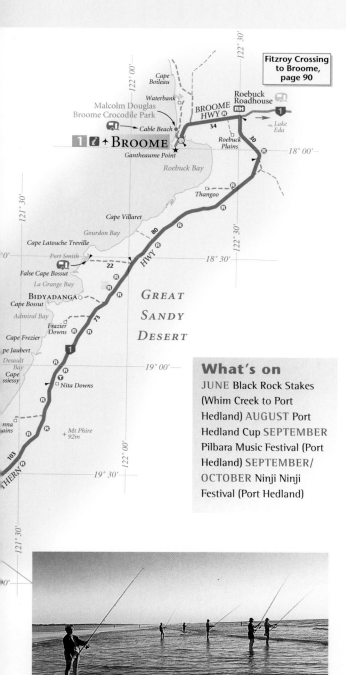

Fitzroy Crossing to Broome, page 90

What's on

JUNE Black Rock Stakes (Whim Creek to Port Hedland) AUGUST Port Hedland Cup SEPTEMBER Pilbara Music Festival (Port Hedland) SEPTEMBER/ OCTOBER Ninji Ninji Festival (Port Hedland)

Fishing

Fishing is popular along the north-west coast and people flock to the several caravan parks and resorts between Broome and Port Hedland in the cooler dry months. This coast is subject to large tidal movements so check tide charts (available from information centres) before venturing onto tidal flats. Also note that poisonous stone fish inhabit the coastal waters so wear strong footwear if walking on rocky reef areas.

Track notes

This is a long stretch of road with little to see; the road, however, is wide, sealed and well maintained. There is access to the coast from various points, with camping or accommodation at five locations. Access to the camping areas along the beach is by unsealed roads and the distance from the highway ranges from 10 to 23 km. There are ample rest areas along this section of highway.

Town file

1 BROOME (see page 91)

2 SANDFIRE ROADHOUSE   PDG
GPS 19° 46.129' S/121° 05.492' E
Sandfire Roadhouse is a complex midway between Port Hedland and Broome. Fuel, accommodation, meals and a caravan park are available at this isolated outpost. For northbound travellers this is the last refuelling point before Roebuck Roadhouse at the junction of Broome Highway.

3 PARDOO ROADHOUSE   PDG
GPS 20° 03.239' S/119° 49.654' E
Pardoo Roadhouse is located 152 km north of Port Hedland. Access is available to the beach at Cape Keraudren (a great spot for walking, shell collecting or fishing) just 10 km away. Fuel, meals, accommodation and a caravan park are available at the roadhouse complex.

4 PORT HEDLAND pop. 12 846   PDG
GPS 20° 18.772' S/118° 34.587' E
Port Hedland is home to BHP's bulk ore-loading facility and handles the largest tonnage of any of the iron-ore ports. Iron ore is delivered, by the BHP-owned railway network, to Port Hedland from mines as far afield as Newman. A recent addition, and also a large employer, is the BHP Hot Briquette Iron Plant, completed in 1999. You can discover the town's history on a self-guided walk, take a whale-watching tour between July and October or indulge in some excellent fishing, particularly for mud crabs. Fishing charter operators are based in town. Port Hedland has most facilities and services. 🛈 13 Wedge Street; (08) 9173 1711; www.porthedlandtouristbureau.com

5 SOUTH HEDLAND pop. 650   PD
GPS 20° 24.408' S/118° 35.771' E
When the iron-ore boom began in the 1960s it quickly became obvious that Port Hedland did not have sufficient land suitable to develop housing and infrastructure for the planned explosion in the population. This led to the development of South Hedland, 20 km to the south, and today this primarily residential area has a large shopping complex, education facilities and government offices. There are two caravan parks in South Hedland.

PORT HEDLAND TO PERTH

GREAT NORTHERN HIGHWAY, NORTH WEST COASTAL HIGHWAY, BRAND HIGHWAY (1774 KM)

The fabulous coastline of Western Australia is a destination that caters for a diverse range of interests. Skim the waves on a windsurfer, catch fish on a deserted beach, swim in the crystal clear waters or picnic on a carpet of exotic wildflowers – the choices are endless. The Pilbara, a rich mining region that includes Port Hedland and Dampier, is renowned for spectacular red gorges – a landscape photographer's dream.

Best time to go

South of Shark Bay the wildflowers are a spectacular drawcard and definitely worth a visit, particularly between July and October.

John & Jan

ONSLOW

	J	F	M	A	M	J	J	A	S	O	N	D
Maximum	36	36	35	33	29	25	25	27	29	32	34	35
Minimum	24	24	23	20	16	13	11	12	14	17	19	22
Rainfall (mm)	27	53	48	20	48	45	18	9	1	1	1	5
Raindays	3	4	3	2	4	4	2	2	1	0	0	1

LANCELIN

	J	F	M	A	M	J	J	A	S	O	N	D
Maximum	29	30	28	25	22	20	19	19	20	22	25	27
Minimum	17	18	17	15	12	11	10	10	10	12	14	16
Rainfall (mm)	10	12	15	31	88	131	129	93	56	31	22	7
Raindays	2	2	4	7	13	17	18	16	13	9	6	3

Cape Range National Park, near Exmouth

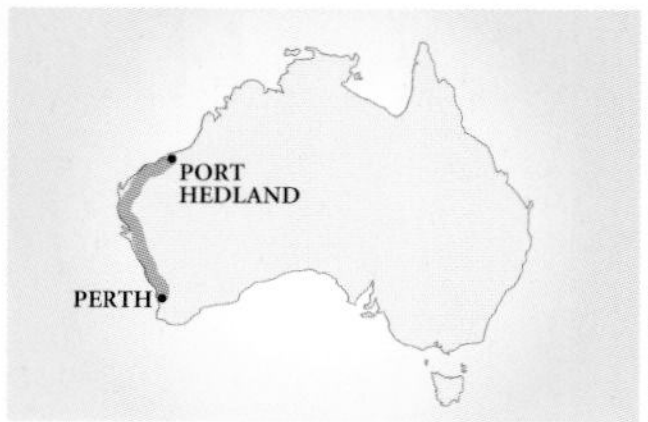

Port Hedland to Nanutarra Roadhouse

The coastal towns of Port Hedland, Karratha, Wickham and Dampier are all associated with mining. The historic port of Onslow operates at a slower pace while the historic towns of Point Samson, Cossack and Roebourne have plenty to offer those interested in the local history.

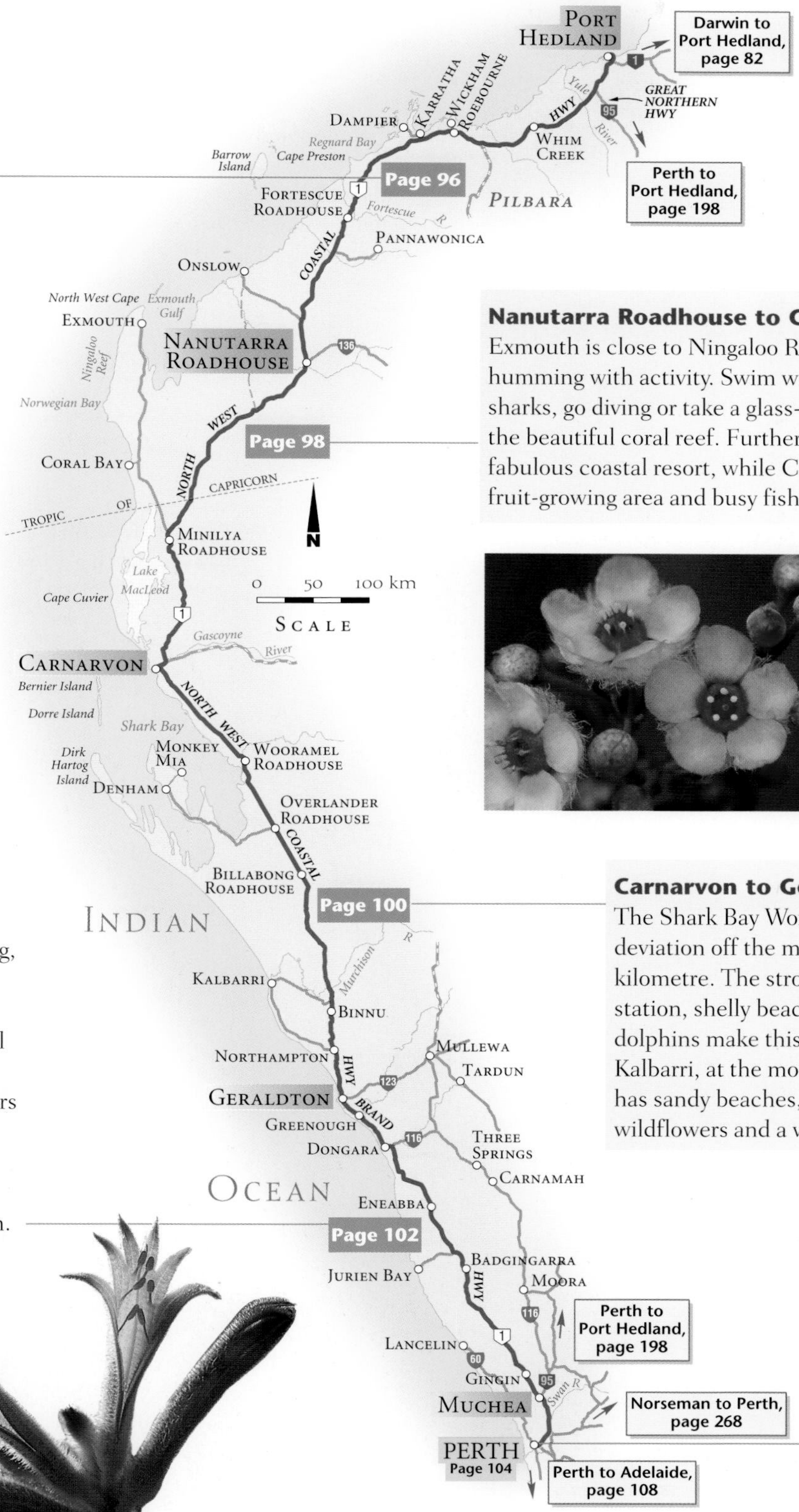

Nanutarra Roadhouse to Carnarvon

Exmouth is close to Ningaloo Reef and is a town humming with activity. Swim with the magnificent whale sharks, go diving or take a glass-bottom boat tour to see the beautiful coral reef. Further south Coral Bay is a fabulous coastal resort, while Carnarvon is an important fruit-growing area and busy fishing port.

Geraldton to Muchea

Holiday resort towns thrive along this popular coast, where activities reach fever pitch during summer. Fishing, windsurfing, boating and swimming are the main leisure pursuits. Commercial crayfish boats operate from every port, prolific wildflowers attract visitors during the balmy spring weather and grain crops grow throughout this fertile agricultural region.

Carnarvon to Geraldton

The Shark Bay World Heritage Area is a lengthy deviation off the main route, but worth every kilometre. The stromatolites, historic telegraph station, shelly beaches and Monkey Mia dolphins make this area extremely popular. Kalbarri, at the mouth of the Murchison River, has sandy beaches, stunning gorges, colourful wildflowers and a wonderful climate.

Perth

With a Mediterranean-type climate and magnificent coastal river setting, Perth is ideal for an outdoor lifestyle. Visitors to this city will find clean surf beaches, tranquil forests and well-kept parklands – all within easy reach of the city centre.

Darwin to Port Hedland, page 82

Perth to Port Hedland, page 198

Page 96

Page 98

Page 100

Page 102

Perth to Port Hedland, page 198

Norseman to Perth, page 268

Perth to Adelaide, page 108

Page 104

PORT HEDLAND TO NANUTARRA ROADHOUSE 498 KM

Termite mounds

Keep a lookout for termite mounds along the road to Onslow. These prolific features are the work and habitat of the spinifex termite, which eats grass, not wood. Many mounds are in excess of 100 years old and incorporate a network of tunnels reaching down to underground water.

Old Onslow

The original location of Onslow was at the mouth of the Ashburton River, where it was established in 1885. The town was moved 47 km north-east to its present site in 1925. Many buildings were relocated but the old brick and stone police quarters and a cemetery still remain at the old site.

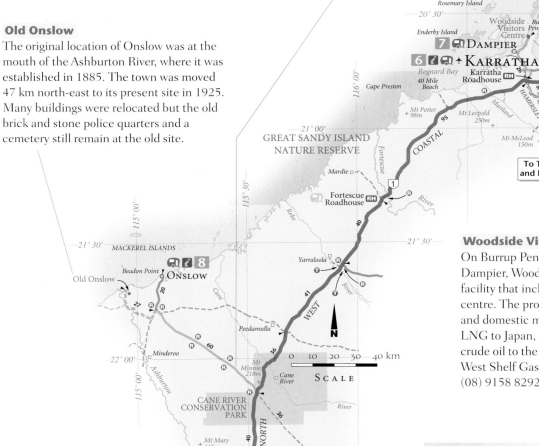

Woodside Visitors Centre

On Burrup Peninsula, 8 km north-east of Dampier, Woodside has a major onshore facility that includes an excellent visitors centre. The project supplies gas to industrial and domestic markets in Western Australia, LNG to Japan, and LPG, condensate and crude oil to the world market. North West Shelf Gas Project Visitors Centre; (08) 9158 8292; open daily.

What's on

JULY Port Walcott Regatta (near Point Samson)
JULY/AUGUST Dampier Classic Game Fishing
Competition AUGUST Ashburton Race Club Meet
(Onslow) AUGUST Roebourne Cup

Travel tip

A worthwhile detour is to follow the Hamersley Iron railway from Dampier to Tom Price. Suitable for most vehicles, this unsealed private road is the quickest link between Karratha, Millstream and Karijini national parks, and Tom Price. A permit is required (obtainable during office hours from the Hamersley Iron administrative office at Parker Point, Dampier, or from the Tom Price mine gatehouse office).

Historic town of Cossack

Cossack was the first landing point for pastoralists on Western Australia's north-west coast in 1863. The port developed rapidly, later becoming the first pearling port in the State. The town flourished in the 19th century but by World War I pearling had moved north to Broome and only a few inhabitants remained. Today the historic township, only 12 km north of Roebourne, is a tourist destination, with restored heritage buildings, a social history museum and an art gallery.

Track notes

The North West Coastal Highway is a well-maintained, wide sealed road. Many of the rest areas along this section are simply wider verges at the road's edge; the only ones shown on the map are where it is possible to exit the road corridor and stop safely away from fast-moving traffic.

Town file

1 PORT HEDLAND (see page 93)

2 SOUTH HEDLAND (see page 93)

3 ROEBOURNE pop. 958   PDG
GPS 20° 46.708' S/117° 08.676' E
Roebourne is the oldest surviving town on the north-west coast of Australia, dating back to 1864. The information centre is located in the restored Old Roebourne Gaol, which also houses a small free museum.
Queen Street; (08) 9182 1060; www.pilbara.com

4 WICKHAM pop. 1649   PD
GPS 20° 40.487' S/117° 08.593' E
This centre was established in the 1970s to service the needs of the mining industry. Large ore carriers load from one of the longest (2.7 km) and tallest (17.8 m above high water) jetties in Australia.

5 POINT SAMSON pop. 255   P
GPS 20° 37.837' S/117° 11.830' E
Point Samson is a small, appealing coastal community just 20 km north of Roebourne. The town has good beaches and a safe boat harbour. Fishing is popular and fishing boat charters operate from the harbour.

6 KARRATHA pop. 10 057   PDG
GPS 20° 44.109' S/116° 0.857' E
Karratha has all the services found in larger regional centres. On the outskirts there is an industrial estate with motor dealers, tyre retailers and mechanical workshops.   4548 Karratha Road; (08) 9144 4600.

7 DAMPIER pop. 1424   PDG
GPS 20° 39.704' S/116° 42.414' E
Established in the 1960s by Hamersley Iron, Dampier is a major export port. The nearby coastal waters and the Dampier Archipelago are popular game-fishing areas.

8 ONSLOW pop. 588   PDG
GPS 21° 38.312' S/115° 06.827' E
Onslow, 80 km north of the highway, has most basic services. History buffs should visit the Goods Shed Museum attached to the visitors centre.
Second Avenue; (08) 9184 6644; www.pilbara.com

9 NANUTARRA ROADHOUSE   PDG
GPS 22° 32.294' S/115° 29.589' E
This roadhouse is an important service centre on the highway.

NANUTARRA ROADHOUSE TO CARNARVON 362 KM

Authors' choice

⊛ Peoples Park Caravan Village, Coral Bay

This park is a great holiday spot, set in a wonderful location across the road from the fabulous beach and close to the coral reef. Diving and fishing are very popular along with coral viewing in glass-bottom boats. Coral Bay is very busy during holidays and booking is essential. The park adjoins a cafe and a well-stocked general store.

For more details see page 362.

Communication relay station

Aficionados of radio communication systems can visit some of the facilities of the Harold E. Holt US Naval Communication Station, just 15 km north of Exmouth. The base is a relay station communicating with ships and submarines in the Indian and south-western Pacific oceans. At the main antenna field, a little further north, the centre mast stands 388 m high.

Diving, fishing and whale-watching

Diving is one of the many popular activities along the coast from Coral Bay (one of our favourite places) to Exmouth, and a diversion to the Exmouth Peninsula is not to be missed. The Ningaloo Marine Park protects the State's largest fringing coral reef and divers can explore the exquisitely coloured corals and view awesome creatures such as whale sharks, migrating manta rays and humpback whales. See the sharks between March and June and the whales between August and November. The area is fast becoming a major tourist destination: charter and tour boat operators can take you big game fishing, diving (both experienced and inexperienced divers are catered for) or coral viewing in a glass-bottom boat.

What's on

JANUARY Gulf Classic (Exmouth, Australia Day weekend fishing competition) MAY Fremantle to Carnarvon Yacht Race (even-numbered years) AUGUST Carnarvon Festival OCTOBER Gamex (Exmouth, game-fishing tournament)

Carnarvon to Geraldton, page 100

Travel tip
At Carnarvon take a trip along South River Road or North River Road to sample the fresh tropical fruit available at the farm gates. Westoby, in Robinson Road, and Munro's Banana Plantation, in South River Road, are two to seek out for delicious bananas, mangoes, pineapples, tomatoes and melons.

Port Hedland to Nanutarra Roadhouse, page 96

Camp in Cape Range National Park
Experience the rugged beauty of Cape Range National Park, with its spectacular gorges and picturesque coastline. Follow one of the several walking trails, take in the panoramic views from Charles Knife Canyon or contemplate the crystal blue waters of Yardie Creek Gorge. Access to the national park is by unsealed roads suitable for a two-wheel drive, except for the Yardie Creek crossing, which requires a four-wheel drive. Campsites in the park have limited facilities (water is not available). For more information contact the Department of Conservation and Land Management district office, 22 Nimitz Street, Exmouth; (08) 9949 1676; entry fees apply to the national park.

Track notes
The North West Coastal Highway is a well-maintained wide road. The Minilya–Exmouth road, Burkett Road and the road to Coral Bay are sealed and the road around North West Cape is sealed as far as the national park. Although sealed, the Minilya–Exmouth road can be a little bouncy in places and care should be taken.

Town file
1 NANUTARRA ROADHOUSE (see page 97)

2 EXMOUTH pop. 3058   PDG
GPS 21° 55.759' S/114° 07.394' E
Exmouth was established in 1967 as a support town for the Harold E. Holt US Naval Communication Station. After being hit hard by tropical cyclone Vance in March 1999, the town has recovered and now holds the record for the strongest mainland wind gust, measured at 267 kph. It is an ideal base from which to explore the North West Cape region, with its excellent surfing, fishing, snorkelling, diving, boating, windsurfing, bushwalking, birdwatching and photographic opportunities. Most tourist necessities are available locally. Murat Road; (08) 9949 1176 or 1800 287 328; www.exmouth-australia.com

3 CORAL BAY pop. 936   PD
GPS 23° 08.585' S/113° 46.273' E
Coral Bay is breathtakingly beautiful: the coral reef stretches 2 km into the bay to form a magnificent natural lagoon rimmed by white sandy beaches. Boating, snorkelling and swimming are popular and coral-viewing boats operate off the beach. There is a hotel, two caravan parks and a few shops offering basic supplies. Coral Bay Arcade, Robinson Street; (08) 9948 5190.

4 MINILYA ROADHOUSE   PDG
GPS 23° 49.032' S/114° 00.635' E
Minilya Roadhouse offers basic services including food, fuel and local information. It is strategically located near the junction of the Minilya–Exmouth road.

5 CARNARVON pop. 6357   PDG
GPS 24° 50.013' S/113° 39.392' E
Carnarvon, as well as being the commercial capital of the Gascoyne region, supports flourishing fruit and vegetable plantations, irrigated from the Gascoyne River. On Babbage Island, connected to the town by a causeway, the Heritage Maritime Precinct encompasses the original port, One Mile Jetty, a lighthouse and a historic steam train. Most services are available and there is good shopping in town. Markets are held at the Civic Centre on the first Saturday of each month. 11 Robinson Street; (08) 9941 1146; www.outbackcoast.com

CARNARVON TO GERALDTON 491 KM

Authors' choice

✪ Denham Seaside Tourist Village, Denham

Our favourite place to stay in the area, this park is located at the end of the main street and has fabulous panoramic views over the sparkling calm waters of Shark Bay. We recommend this park to anyone keen on fishing: there is easy access to a good boat ramp or you can join a fishing charter just a short stroll away at the town jetty.

For more details see page 363.

✪ Monkey Mia Dolphin Resort, Monkey Mia

If you are keen on wildlife-watching, this large, family park, set on the shores of Shark Bay, is for you. Watch the famous Monkey Mia dolphins play at the water's edge, just metres from the park, or take a catamaran ride on the calm waters in search of dolphins and dugong.

For more details see page 378.

Free camping

Free camping is available at Eagle Bluff, Goulet Bluff, Fowlers Camp Road and Whalebone Road. Campsites cannot be reserved and there are no facilities. You will need to obtain a permit from the Shire of Shark Bay office; 42 Hughes Street, Denham; (08) 9948 1218.

Kalbarri National Park

Travel to Kalbarri National Park, located on the lower reaches of the Murchison River, and explore its many features. Discover its fascinating geological history, coastal cliffs and spectacular gorges carved by the Murchison River over millions of years. See the stunning wildflowers (including grevilleas, banksias, star flowers, featherflowers, smokebushes, kangaroo paws and rare orchids) blooming at their best between July and October – and keep an eye out for emus, kangaroos and thorny devils!

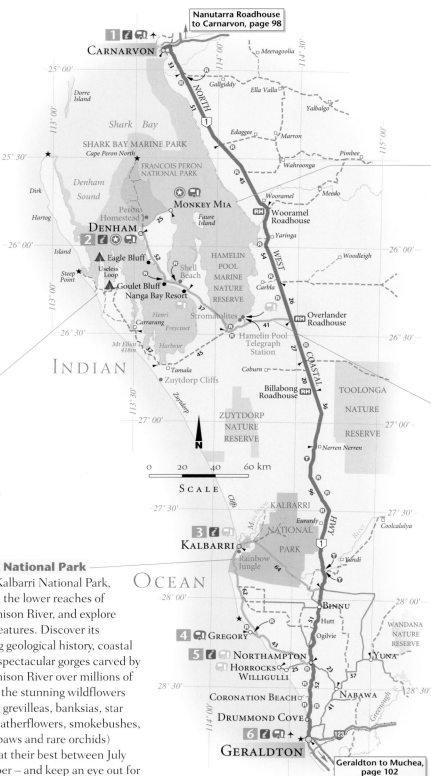

Nanutarra Roadhouse to Carnarvon, page 98

Geraldton to Muchea, page 102

Dolphins at Monkey Mia

Monkey Mia's famous bottlenose dolphins regularly visit the beach and interact with visitors. The dolphins usually appear each day sometime between 8 a.m. and 1 p.m. The Shark Bay World Heritage Area marine life also includes turtles and a large dugong population. Entry fees apply to the Monkey Mia Reserve.

Shark Bay Road

Turn off the highway onto Shark Bay Road, head towards the town of Denham and enjoy the sights along the way. Shell Beach, with tiny white shells stacked metres deep, and the historic Hamelin Pool Telegraph Station are both close to Shark Bay Road and well worth a visit. Near the telegraph station you will find the stromatolites of Hamelin Pool (sedimentary rocks made up of fossilised blue-green algae), the largest group of these amazing fossils in the world.

What's on

JANUARY Geraldton Windsurfing Classic (Australia Day weekend) MARCH Sport Fishing Classic (Kalbarri) APRIL Batavia Coast Fishing Classic (Geraldton) AUGUST Shark Bay Fishing Fiesta (Denham) OCTOBER Airing of the Quilts (Northampton), Sunshine Festival (Geraldton)

Track notes

The North West Coastal Highway is relatively flat along this section of coast and is well serviced with roadhouses. The roads to Monkey Mia and Kalbarri are sealed. In 1999 the road between Kalbarri and Northampton was completed, opening up an excellent alternative route for tourists. It has sealed access to both Gregory and Horrocks.

Town file

1 CARNARVON (see page 99)

2 DENHAM pop. 1140   🅿 PDG
GPS 25° 55.700' S/113° 32.068' E
Denham is a pretty town that is popular with holiday-makers. Monkey Mia Reserve is just 25 km to the north-east. Fishing boats work the waters off Denham and mounds of salt at the Useless Loop saltworks can be seen across the water on clear days. Most services are available. 🛈 Shark Bay Tourist Bureau, 71 Knight Terrace; (08) 9948 1253.

3 KALBARRI pop. 1788   🅿 PDG
GPS 27° 42.654' S/114° 09.838' E
The picturesque holiday town of Kalbarri is almost completely surrounded by Kalbarri National Park. The climate, spectacular cliffs, rugged gorges and windswept beaches all add to the beauty of this town and surrounding area. Kalbarri has most services and a wide selection of accommodation. 🛈 Grey Street; (08) 9937 1104.

4 GREGORY pop. 40   🅿 PD
GPS 28° 11.316' S/114° 15.041' E
With huge white sand dunes, good swimming beaches and interesting convict ruins, Gregory (also known as Port Gregory) is a fishing village worth visiting. Set on a natural, reef-protected harbour, it has operated as a port since 1853.

5 NORTHAMPTON pop. 842   🅿 PDG
GPS 28° 21.051' S/114° 37.864' E
Rich in history, Northampton is one of the oldest settlements outside Perth and is listed by the National Trust as a historic town. Basic services are available in Northampton. North-west of Northampton, and still welcoming tourists, is the Hutt River Province Principality, an 'independent land' since its owner seceded from the Commonwealth of Australia in 1970. 🛈 Hampton Road; (08) 9934 1488.

6 GERALDTON pop. 25 243   🅿 PDG
GPS 28° 46.385' S/14° 36.678' E
Geraldton is a key port and the self-proclaimed lobster capital of the world. The Geraldton Fishermen's Co-operative (Ocean Street) has a live-lobster processing factory and runs free guided tours during the November to June season. Geraldton is one of Australia's top windsurfing destinations, with the best winds occurring between November and April. The Western Australian Museum in Geraldton has an excellent maritime display. 🛈 Chapman Road; (08) 9921 3999.

GERALDTON TO MUCHEA 367 KM

Authors' choice

⊛ **Greenough Rivermouth Caravan Park, Greenough**

Set at the mouth of the Greenough River just 10 km south of Geraldton, this large, well-shaded park is protected from the onshore winds and has very good facilities. Cook in the camp kitchen or buy takeaway food from the park's well-stocked shop. This is an enjoyable place to stay, especially for a family holiday, and we like to stay here and commute to Geraldton. For more details see page 368.

Take the coast road

The proposed sealing of the road between Cervantes and Lancelin will complete the missing link in this great Indian Ocean drive along the coast between Dongara and Perth. The road passes through several small communities and lobster-fishing ports. Travellers are well catered for and we feel sure that this will become a popular tourist route.

The Pinnacles

Visit the famous Pinnacles Desert, a major tourist attraction and definitely worth seeing. When Dutch sailors first saw the Pinnacles from the sea in the 1650s they mistook them for ancient ruins. There are thousands of limestone pillars, some up to 5 m tall. The Pinnacles Desert is part of the Nambung National Park. Entry fee applies.

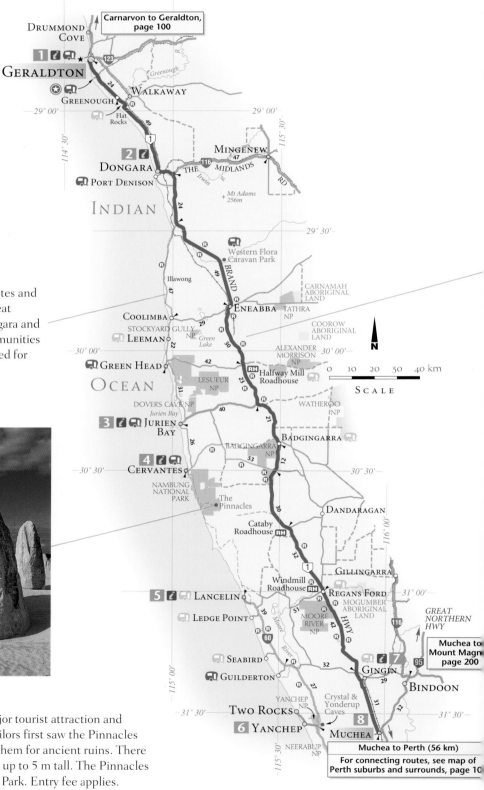

Carnarvon to Geraldton, page 100

Muchea to Mount Magn page 200

Muchea to Perth (56 km)
For connecting routes, see map of Perth suburbs and surrounds, page 10

Travel tip

In springtime consider a visit to the Western Flora Caravan Park. Situated on the highway 22 km north of Eneabba, its 65 hectares contain a diverse range of wildflowers. The owners are passionate about the wildflowers and conduct walks each day at 4 p.m. Their well-stocked shop has a good selection of souvenirs and wildflower books.

Wildflower trail

Stunning wildflowers can be seen along the Brand Highway. Some flowers appear year-round, but in the peak flowering period between July and October thousands of different varieties form an incredibly beautiful picture. Colour, shape and sizes vary and seasonal conditions will cause variations in flowering. Stop off at visitor information centres along the highway for brochures on specific wildflower areas and trails.

What's on

JANUARY Windsurfing Odyssey (Jurien Bay), Ledge to Lancelin Windsurfing Race, Screaming Leeman Windsurfing Tournament EASTER Easter Fair (Jurien Bay), Dune Buggy Championships (Lancelin) JUNE Round of State surfing titles (Flat Rocks)

Track notes

The road has a wide sealed surface and there are a few overtaking lanes. There is regular access to the beach and several coastal towns.

Town file

1 GERALDTON (see page 101)

2 DONGARA–PORT DENISON pop. 1874   ⛽ PDG
GPS 29° 15.083' S/114° 55.857' E (Dongara)
The twin towns of Dongara and Port Denison are popular year-round holiday destinations. The fishing boat harbour houses a large fleet of lobster boats. ℹ 5 Waldeck Street; (08) 9927 1404.

3 JURIEN BAY pop. 636   ⛽ PDG
GPS 30° 18.221' S/115° 02.458' E
Jurien Bay is the largest town along this section of coast. It is located on a sheltered bay with long sandy beaches; swimming, surfing, fishing, diving and windsurfing are all popular. Good catches of fish are common and crabbing is also worthwhile. The town has most basic services. ℹ Shire Office, 110 Bashford Street; (08) 9652 1020.

4 CERVANTES pop. 480   ⛽ PDG
GPS 30° 30.082' S/115° 04.085' E
Close to one of Western Australia's unique tourist attractions – the eerie Pinnacles Desert – Cervantes is a holiday town where fishing and windsurfing are the main pursuits. ℹ Shell Service Station, corner Aragon Street and Seville Street; (08) 9652 7041.

5 LANCELIN pop. 597   ⛽ PDG
GPS 31° 01.200' S/115° 19.923' E
Lancelin is a bustling holiday destination nestled in sand dunes. Windsurfing, surfing and snorkelling are all popular pastimes. The fishing is excellent as is the diving, with 14 shipwrecks between Lancelin and Guilderton. ℹ Lot 102, Gingin Road; (08) 9655 1100.

6 YANCHEP pop. 1790   ⛽ PDG
GPS 31° 32.987' S/115° 37.467' E
Yanchep's beaches are protected by a reef, making them favourites with families and swimmers. Yanchep National Park lies to the east of town.

7 GINGIN pop. 549   ⛽ PDG
GPS 31° 20.890' S/115° 54.307' E
Gingin is a farming centre bypassed by the main highway. It has picturesque parks and is an ideal place for a picnic lunch. The Uniforms of the World Museum (5 Brook Street) houses about 3000 pieces dating as far back as 1799 and the Colamber Bird Park (Mooliabeenie Road) has an extensive array of birds, particularly native parrots. ℹ Shire Offices, 7 Brockman Street; (08) 9575 2211.

8 MUCHEA pop. 336   ⛽ PDG
GPS 31° 34.821' S/115° 58.655' E
Muchea is a centre for many of the small acreage holdings in the area.

PERTH
YOUR GUIDE

With a Mediterranean-type climate and magnificent coastal river setting, Perth is ideal for an outdoor lifestyle. Visitors will find clean surf beaches, tranquil forests and well-kept parklands – all within easy reach of the city centre. Perth is a cosmopolitan city with a population of almost 1.4 million. The Swan River winds through the suburbs, widening to lake size near the city centre, where the serene blue hills of the Darling Range form a distant backdrop.

CITY CENTRE

See map on page 106.

Art Gallery of Western Australia 106 C3
Houses a fine collection of Australian and international works.

Ferry trip 106 C5
From the Barrack Street Jetty, past the exclusive waterside suburbs to Fremantle, South Perth and the Swan Valley wine region.

Kings Park 106 A4
A 404-ha bushland reserve with landscaped gardens, walkways, lakes, a war memorial and good views of the city.

Northbridge 106 C3
Lively arts precinct including the Perth Cultural Centre, the Art Gallery of Western Australia and the Perth Institute of Contemporary Arts; colourful weekend art and craft markets in the Cultural Centre Mall.

Old Mill 106 A6
Picturesque 1838 white-washed windmill; now houses an interesting collection of early colonial artefacts.

Perth Institute of Contemporary Arts (PICA) 106 C3
Sample the latest in visual and performance art.

Perth Mint 106 D4
Houses the world's largest collection of natural gold specimens; lift a gold bar and watch a gold pourer at work.

Perth Zoo 106 B8
Set in a magnificent garden; includes a butterfly house and Australian animal exhibits.

Queens Gardens 106 F5
Site of a 19th-century brickworks; now ornamental lily ponds and garden beds.

WACA Oval 106 F5
Famous venue for national and international cricket and Australian Rules Football matches – Friday and Saturday night games draw huge crowds; tours of the ground and museum run Tuesdays at 10 a.m.

Western Australian Museum 106 C3
Comprehensive collection including two of Perth's oldest buildings: the original Perth Gaol (1856) and an 1860s cottage.

Visitor information

Western Australian Visitors Centre
Corner Forrest Place and Wellington Street
(08) 9483 1111, freecall 1300 361 351
www.westernaustralia.net
www.perthwa.com

Fremantle Tourist Bureau
Fremantle Town Hall
Corner William and Adelaide streets
(08) 9431 7878

Top events

Hopman Cup (January)
Prestigious international tennis event.

Perth International Arts Festival (January–February)
Exciting program with great diversity.

Kings Park Wildflower Festival (September)
Australia's premier native plant and wildflower exhibition.

Rally Australia (November)
Four days of action-packed, world-class motor sport.

SUBURBS AND SURROUNDS

See map on page 107.

Canning Vale Sunday Markets 107 C5
Western Australia's biggest undercover marketplace.

Claremont Museum 107 B4
The former Freshwater Bay School, built in 1862 by convicts; now houses an interesting social history display.

Darling Range 107 D6
Approximately 80 000 ha of escarpment and jarrah forest in the Hills Forest area.

Fremantle Arts Centre and History Museum 107 B4
A striking Gothic building, once a female lunatic asylum; now offers contemporary art exhibitions, Fremantle history displays, a ghost walk and a garden area with cafe.

Fremantle Prison 107 B4
Convict-built from limestone quarried on site in the 1850s; huge, forbidding and full of history.

Lake Monger 107 C4
See Western Australia's famous black swans and other waterbirds.

Ocean beaches 107 B3
Beautiful Indian Ocean beaches for swimming or relaxing; stop off at Sorrento Quay where you will find a marine retail village and a world-class oceanarium, Underwater World.

Subiaco 107 C4
A popular shopping, cafe and market area in one of Perth's oldest suburbs; art and craft stalls in a restored warehouse close to the station run from Thursday to Sunday.

Swan Brewery 107 C5
Tours available of this state-of-the-art brewery renowned for its Swan and Emu beers.

Swan Valley 107 D3
A premier wine-producing district ideal for touring, with historic attractions such as the town of Guildford, and Woodbridge House in West Midland.

University of Western Australia 107 C4
Landscaped gardens and Mediterranean-style buildings; contains the Brendt Museum of Anthropology and the Lawrence Wilson Art Gallery.

Western Australian Maritime Museum 107 B5
Displays include an excellent reconstruction of the 1629 Dutch wreck *Batavia*.

Getting around

The city centre is compact and easy to explore. A free, regular bus service known as the CAT (Central Area Transit) System operates around central Perth. You can also travel free on Transperth buses and trains within the Free Transit Zone in the city centre. Transperth produces a handy tourist guide and map that shows the Free Transit Zone.

A good way to discover the city is on the Perth Tram Co. tours, which operate daily. These replicas of the city's first trams extend east to Burswood International Resort Casino and west to the University of Western Australia. You can break your journey at any point. On weekdays Fremantle Tram Tours operates a 'tram' tour (the vehicle is actually a bus) around the streets of historic Subiaco and out to Lake Monger.

Airport shuttle bus Airport City Shuttle Service (08) 9475 2999; **Motoring organisation** RAC 13 11 11; **Public transport** Transperth 13 62 13; **Tram tours** Perth Tram Company (08) 9322 2006, Fremantle Tram Tours (08) 9339 8719; **Swan River boat cruises** Captain Cook (08) 9325 3341, Boat Torque Cruises (08) 9221 5844; **Taxis** Black and White Taxis 13 10 08, Swan Taxis 13 13 30; **Bicycle hire** Bikewest (08) 9216 8000.

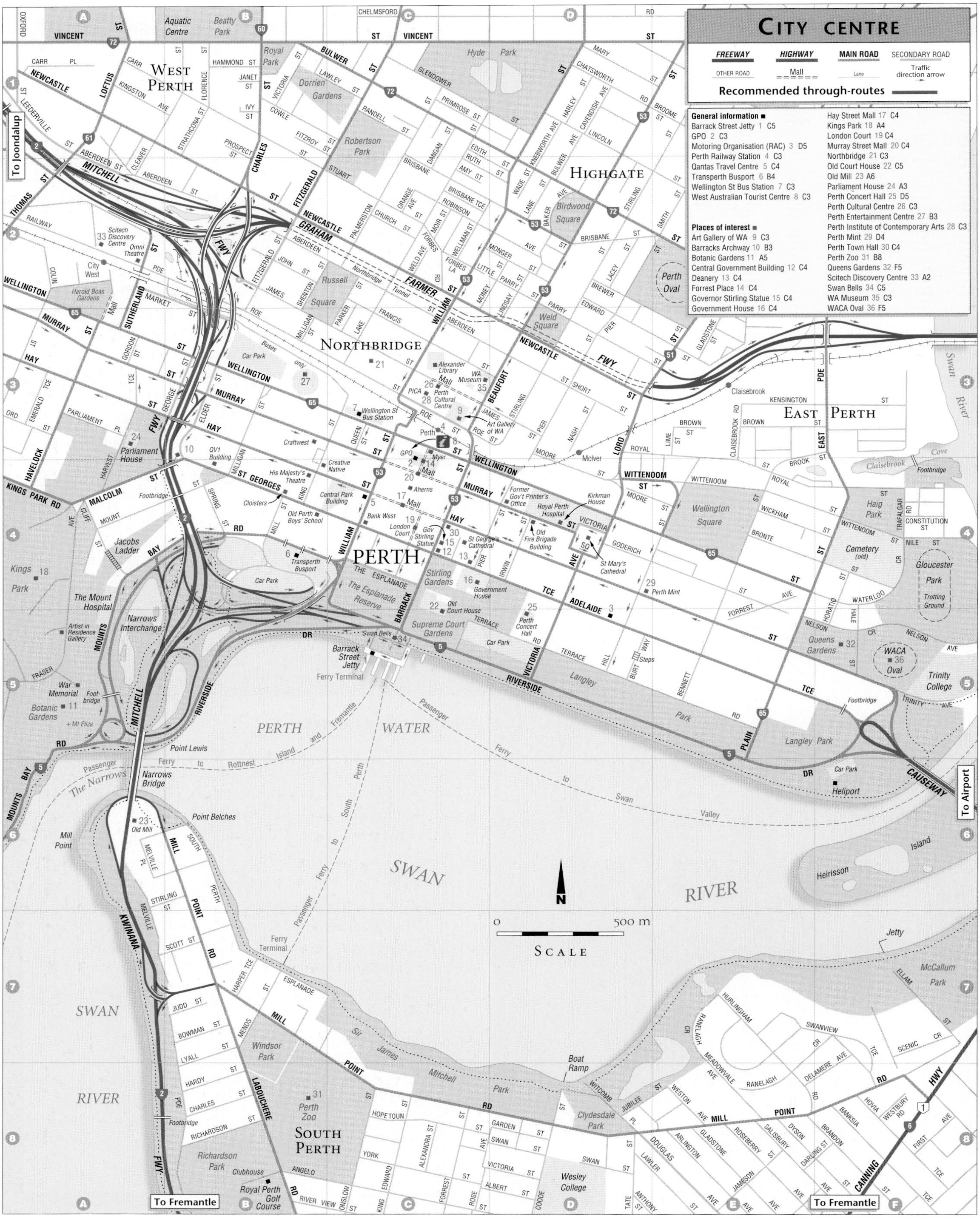

CITY CENTRE

FREEWAY   HIGHWAY   MAIN ROAD   SECONDARY ROAD

OTHER ROAD   ===== Mall   —— Lane   Traffic direction arrow

Recommended through-routes ——

General information ■
Barrack Street Jetty 1 C5
GPO 2 C3
Motoring Organisation (RAC) 3 D5
Perth Railway Station 4 C3
Qantas Travel Centre 5 C4
Transperth Busport 6 B4
Wellington St Bus Station 7 C3
West Australian Tourist Centre 8 C3

Places of interest ■
Art Gallery of WA 9 C3
Barracks Archway 10 B3
Botanic Gardens 11 A5
Central Government Building 12 C4
Deanery 13 C4
Forrest Place 14 C4
Governor Stirling Statue 15 C4
Government House 16 C4

Hay Street Mall 17 C4
Kings Park 18 A4
London Court 19 C4
Murray Street Mall 20 C4
Northbridge 21 C3
Old Court House 22 C5
Old Mill 23 A6
Parliament House 24 A3
Perth Concert Hall 25 D5
Perth Cultural Centre 26 C3
Perth Entertainment Centre 27 B3
Perth Institute of Contemporary Arts 28 C3
Perth Mint 29 D4
Perth Town Hall 30 C4
Perth Zoo 31 B8
Queens Gardens 32 F5
Scitech Discovery Centre 33 A2
Swan Bells 34 C5
WA Museum 35 C3
WACA Oval 36 F5

To Joondalup

To Fremantle

To Fremantle

To Airport

WEST PERTH

HIGHGATE

NORTHBRIDGE

PERTH

EAST PERTH

SOUTH PERTH

KINGS PARK

SWAN RIVER

PERTH WATER

The Narrows

Heirisson Island

McCallum Park

SCALE
0   500 m

N

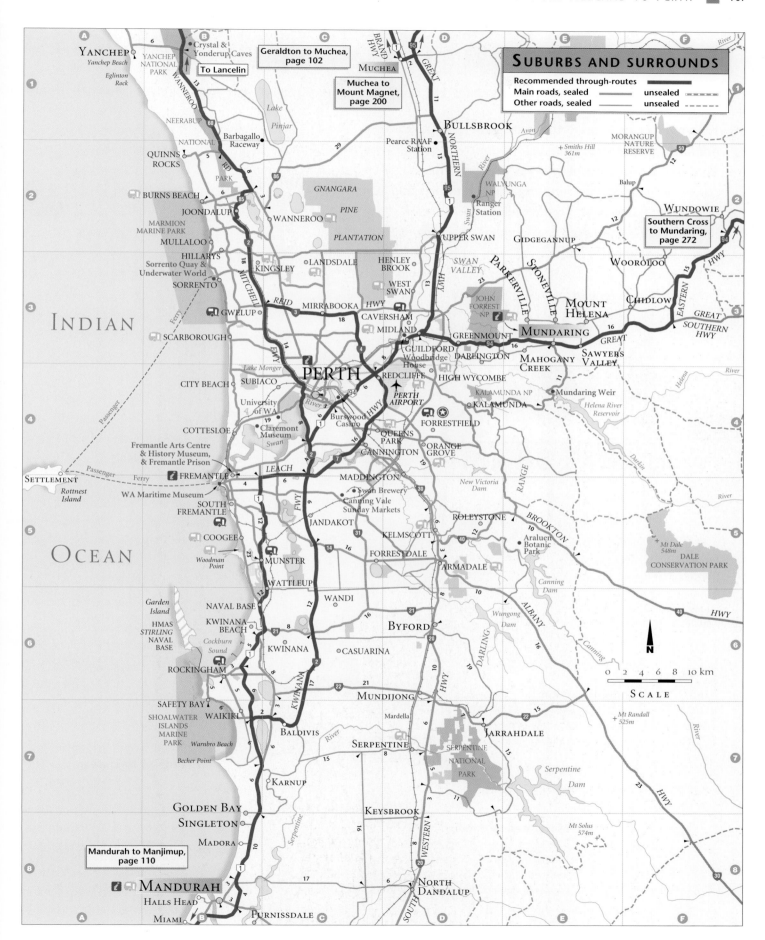

Geraldton to Muchea, page 102

Muchea to Mount Magnet, page 200

SUBURBS AND SURROUNDS

Recommended through-routes	
Main roads, sealed	unsealed
Other roads, sealed	unsealed

Southern Cross to Mundaring, page 272

A

YANCHEP
Yanchep Beach
YANCHEP NATIONAL PARK
Eglinton Rock

Crystal & Yonderup Caves

To Lancelin

WANNEROO

NEERABUP

QUINNS ROCKS

BURNS BEACH

JOONDALUP

MARMION MARINE PARK

MULLALOO

HILLARYS
Sorrento Quay & Underwater World

SORRENTO

INDIAN

Barbagallo Raceway

NATIONAL

PARK

WANNEROO

KINGSLEY

GWELUP

SCARBOROUGH

CITY BEACH

SUBIACO

University of WA

COTTESLOE

Fremantle Arts Centre & History Museum, & Fremantle Prison

SETTLEMENT
Rottnest Island

FREMANTLE
WA Maritime Museum

SOUTH FREMANTLE

COOGEE

OCEAN

MUNSTER
Woodman Point

WATTLEUP

Garden Island
HMAS STIRLING NAVAL BASE

NAVAL BASE

KWINANA BEACH

KWINANA
Cockburn Sound

ROCKINGHAM

SAFETY BAY
WAIKIKI

SHOALWATER ISLANDS MARINE PARK
Warnbro Beach
Becher Point

BALDIVIS

KARNUP

GOLDEN BAY

SINGLETON

MADORA

Mandurah to Manjimup, page 110

MANDURAH

HALLS HEAD

MIAMI

PURNISSDALE

Lake Pinjar

GNANGARA

PINE

PLANTATION

MIRRABOOKA

LANDSDALE

HENLEY BROOK

WEST SWAN

CAVERSHAM

MIDLAND

GUILDFORD
Woodbridge House

REDCLIFFE

PERTH AIRPORT

HIGH WYCOMBE

PERTH

Lake Monger

River

Claremont Museum

Burswood Casino

QUEENS PARK

CANNINGTON

ORANGE GROVE

FORRESTFIELD

MADDINGTON

LEACH

Swan Brewery
Canning Vale Sunday Markets

JANDAKOT

KELMSCOTT

FORRESTDALE

ARMADALE

WANDI

BYFORD

CASUARINA

MUNDIJONG

Mardella

SERPENTINE

KEYSBROOK

NORTH DANDALUP

MUCHEA

BULLSBROOK

Pearce RAAF Station

UPPER SWAN

Swan Valley

JOHN FORREST NP

GREENMOUNT

DARLINGTON

KALAMUNDA NP

KALAMUNDA

ROLEYSTONE

Araluen Botanic Park

New Victoria Dam

WALYUNGA NP
Ranger Station

GIDGEGANNUP

PARKERVILLE

STONEVILLE

MOUNT HELENA

MUNDARING

MAHOGANY CREEK

SAWYERS VALLEY

Mundaring Weir
Helena River Reservoir

RANGE

BROOKTON

Canning Dam

Wungong Dam

Wooroloo

CHIDLOW

WUNDOWIE

Smiths Hill 361m

MORANGUP NATURE RESERVE

Balup

GREAT
SOUTHERN HWY

EASTERN HWY

Helena River

Darkin River

Mt Dale 548m
DALE CONSERVATION PARK

Mt Randall 525m

JARRAHDALE

SERPENTINE NATIONAL PARK

Serpentine Dam

Mt Solus 574m

SCALE
0 2 4 6 8 10 km

N

PERTH TO ADELAIDE

OLD COAST ROAD, SOUTH WESTERN HIGHWAY, SOUTH COAST HIGHWAY, COOLGARDIE ESPERAN

Rich in vineyards and dotted with wineries, quality orchards and towering forests, the south-west of Western Australia is a mecca for tourists. This picturesque area, with numerous beach resorts and large coastal towns, is popular during the warmer holiday periods and holds a special place in our hearts. Crossing the Nullarbor Plain – that wide, flat, featureless geographical barrier separating east from west – is a long drive best broken into sections.

Best time to go

Weather in the south-west can be ideal, although it is often quite windy along the exposed coast. Conditions across the Nullarbor are changeable, but temperatures soar during summer.

John & Jan

ALBANY	J	F	M	A	M	J	J	A	S	O	N	D
Maximum	23	23	22	21	19	17	16	16	17	18	20	22
Minimum	15	15	15	13	11	9	8	8	9	10	12	14
Rainfall (mm)	24	23	39	68	121	132	145	127	101	81	44	30
Raindays	8	8	11	14	19	20	22	21	18	17	12	9

PORT AUGUSTA	J	F	M	A	M	J	J	A	S	O	N	D
Maximum	32	31	30	25	21	18	17	19	23	25	28	31
Minimum	19	19	17	13	10	8	7	8	10	13	15	17
Rainfall (mm)	15	17	17	19	26	27	20	23	22	23	18	16
Raindays	3	2	3	4	6	8	8	8	6	4	3	3

Mandurah to Manjimup

The highway follows the coast south to Bunbury and then drifts through a scenic fruit-growing region where fresh produce is readily available. Manjimup is in the heart of timber country.

Perth

With a Mediterranean-type climate and magnificent coastal river setting, Perth is ideal for an outdoor lifestyle.

South West Capes diversion

This fabulous region, with great surfing and swimming beaches, quality wineries, a host of holiday activities and a range of accommodation, really comes alive during the warmer holiday periods.

Albany to Norseman

The South Coast Highway loops inland through Ravensthorpe, a popular wildflower region, on its way to Esperance and Norseman. Turn off the highway to explore the smaller coastal communities or to visit the extensive Fitzgerald River National Park near Bremer Bay.

Manjimup to Albany

The South Western Highway wends its way through towering forests. Experience the remarkable Tree Top Walk in the Valley of the Giants or spend a day learning about whales and our whaling history at Albany Whaleworld.

...IGHWAY, EYRE HIGHWAY, PRINCES HIGHWAY (3208 KM)

View from Point Ann, Fitzgerald River National Park

Norseman to Border Village

The highway continues across the Nullarbor before dropping onto the coastal plain between Madura and Eucla. Take the diversion to the historic, sand-engulfed Eucla Telegraph Station; it is worth the effort.

Border Village to Ceduna

The spectacular Nullarbor cliffs are a feature of this part of the Eyre Highway, and several rest areas along the clifftops are great observation points, particularly for whale-watching. Further on, Penong is famous for its many windmills.

Ceduna to Port Augusta

The Eyre Highway traverses large expanses of farmland. Consider taking the alternative route along the Eyre Peninsula coast, winding through picturesque fishing villages.

Port Augusta to Two Wells

Travelling south the highway skirts the western foot of the South Flinders Ranges. Take a leisurely drive to the Yorke Peninsula, a favourite holiday destination for Adelaide residents.

Adelaide

The well-planned city of Adelaide is set on the wide curves of the River Torrens. Its immediate location belies the fact that beyond the rolling hills lie great tracts of arid scrubland – Adelaide is the capital of the driest State in Australia.

MANDURAH TO MANJIMUP 232 KM

Tuart Forest National Park

Tuart forests (*Eucalyptus gomphocephala*) once covered much of the coastal strip from Dunsborough to Jurien Bay, growing in a band about 10 km wide, but today little remains. This is the only place in the world in which tuart grows naturally, and the Bunbury old-growth forest at the end of Ocean Drive is one of the best remaining stands and well worth a visit.

What's on
FEBRUARY Mandurah Crab Festival MARCH Bunbury Agricultural Show, World Backpacker Games (Donnybrook) EASTER Apple Festival (Donnybrook) JUNE Manjimup 15 000 Motocross OCTOBER Binningup Fair, Mandurah City Art and Craft Fair

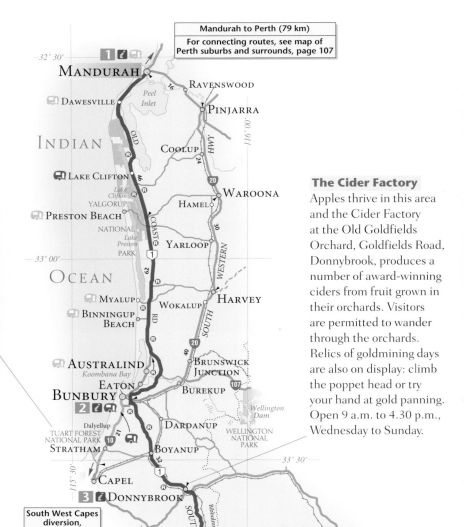

Mandurah to Perth (79 km)
For connecting routes, see map of Perth suburbs and surrounds, page 107

South West Capes diversion, page 112

Manjimup to Albany, page 114

The Cider Factory
Apples thrive in this area and the Cider Factory at the Old Goldfields Orchard, Goldfields Road, Donnybrook, produces a number of award-winning ciders from fruit grown in their orchards. Visitors are permitted to wander through the orchards. Relics of goldmining days are also on display: climb the poppet head or try your hand at gold panning. Open 9 a.m. to 4.30 p.m., Wednesday to Sunday.

Manjimup Regional Timber Park
This delightful park is set on 10 ha with lakes, bridges and woodlands, and incorporates the State Timber Museum. Displays include a historical hamlet, a blacksmith's shop and a sawn karri log that relates world events to the tree's annual growth rings. The Manjimup Tourist Bureau is also located here. Corner Rose and Edward streets; (08) 9771 1831.

Country music

Boyup Brook, 31 km north-east of Bridgetown, is the country music capital of the west, with a country music weekend each September and an awards ceremony in February. Visit Harvey Dickson's Country Music Centre, located in a picturesque farm setting about 5 km out of Boyup Brook. The centre exhibits unique timber sculptures, a wide range of country music and Elvis memorabilia, and various pieces of vintage farming equipment. (08) 9765 1125; Arthur River Road; entry fee applies; booking required for guided tour.

The Diamond Mill

Manjimup is famous for the spectacular karri and jarrah forests nearby, and timber is its major industry. The Diamond Mill, an operating chip mill just to the south of Manjimup, turns forest and mill waste into a valuable export commodity. Fascinating mill tours depart at 9.15 a.m. on Monday, Wednesday and Friday from the Manjimup Tourist Bureau.

Track notes

From Mandurah Highway One runs parallel to the ocean, although it is rarely in sight. Much of it is divided road. Bunbury is bypassed, then the route follows the South Western Highway as it winds through hills, forests and orchards. The road is sealed and well maintained, but in places overtaking is limited. Heavy transports use the South Western Highway.

Town file

1 MANDURAH pop. 35 945 PDG
GPS 32° 32.072' S/115° 43.265' E
Mandurah, 75 km south of Perth, has become a satellite city of the capital. It is a popular beachside destination, as the Peel Inlet is safe for boating and home to numerous small craft. The city has all facilities and a number of caravan parks, but these have only a few tourist sites. 75 Mandurah Terrace; (08) 9550 3999.

2 BUNBURY pop. 24 945 PDG
GPS 33° 19.612' S/115° 38.222' E
Bunbury is the regional capital of the south-west and a working port. It has art and craft studios, numerous restaurants, good shopping and all services. Bunbury's beaches and surf are attractions, as are the dolphins that frolic near the harbour in Koombana Bay; learn about them at the Dolphin Discovery Centre. Old Railway Station, Carmody Place; (08) 9721 7922 or (WA only)1800 2862 879; www.bunburytourism.org.au

3 DONNYBROOK pop. 1635 PDG
GPS 33° 34.343' S/115° 49.430' E
Donnybrook is famous as the home of the Granny Smith apple, grown here since the 1890s. The town lies in a rich agricultural area. Locally quarried sandstone has been used in buildings around the State, while jarrah felled around Donnybrook was used extensively for railway sleepers last century. Most services are available. Railway Station, South Western Highway; (08) 9731 1720.

4 BRIDGETOWN pop. 2123 PDG
GPS 33° 57.458' S/116° 08.234' E
Bridgetown is at the junction of the South Western and Brockman highways. Pine plantations sweep across the undulating country and the Blackwood River, popular for canoeing and trout fishing, flows through town. Basic services are available. Hampton Street; (08) 9761 1740.

5 MANJIMUP pop. 4390 PDG
GPS 34° 14.474' S/116° 08.798' E
Manjimup is a commercial centre surrounded by fertile farming land and majestic forests. There are many timber-related attractions in the area. Grapes from the Warren River Valley, Western Australia's newest wine-producing area, are in high demand. There is a large shopping centre with all services. Corner Rose and Edward streets; (08) 9771 1831.

SOUTH WEST CAPES DIVERSION 342 KM

Authors' choice

✪ Taunton Farm Caravan Park, Cowaramup

We think this is possibly the best base for exploring the wonderful Margaret River region and its many wineries. It is a quality park in a great farm setting and we always enjoy our stays here.
For more details see page 362.

✪ Mandalay Holiday Resort, Busselton

This is an excellent quality caravan park for tourists, one of the best in Australia. It is just across the road from the beach and about 4 km from the town centre. There is a popular resort-style pool, large grassed playing areas and a convenient boat park. Holiday periods are extremely busy, when booking is essential.
For more details see page 359.

What's on

JANUARY Beach Festival (Busselton)
MARCH–APRIL Leeuwin Concert (Margaret River), Margaret River Surfing Masters
NOVEMBER Margaret River Wine Region Festival, Margaret River Agricultural Show

Limestone caves

Travelling from Cape Naturaliste to Cape Leeuwin you will pass over an extensive network of limestone caves. Five of the most accessible caves are regularly open to the public: Ngilgi Caves, Mammoth Cave, Lake Cave, Jewel Cave and Moondyne Cave. Jewel Cave includes the largest straw stalactite in any tourist cave. Phone CaveWorks for opening hours and tour details; (08) 9757 7411; entry fee applies.

Visit world-class wineries

Some of Australia's great wines come from the Margaret River region, which extends from Busselton and Dunsborough in the north to Augusta in the south. Many wineries welcome visitors, most have cellar-door sales and some have restaurants. Regional maps showing vineyard locations are available from visitor information centres.

Discover the local wildlife

Quindalup Fauna Park, 4 km east of Dunsborough, has something different to offer. Apart from the birds and animals on display, there is a fascinating butterfly enclosure and an aquarium stocked with fish from the local Geographe Bay area. 962 Caves Road; (08) 9755 3933; entry fee applies; open daily.

Travel tip

Make sure you allow plenty of time to experience this diverse region. There is so much to see and do: discover majestic forests, explore exciting caves, stroll fabulous beaches with spectacular rolling surf, and savour world-class wineries and gourmet restaurants.

Mandurah to
Manjimup,
page 110

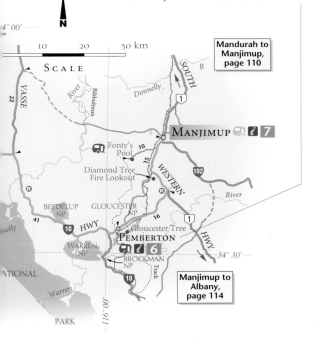

Forest tram trip

Pemberton Tramway operates rides twice daily through the local forests, with longer services on Tuesdays, Thursdays and Saturdays, and steam-train trips on weekends between Easter and November. Pemberton Tramway Company, Pemberton Railway Station, Railway Crescent; (08) 9776 1322.

Mandurah to
Manjimup,
page 110

Manjimup to
Albany,
page 114

Track notes

Most of the main roads in the region are sealed but many wind around the hills and through forests. Holiday traffic can be heavy. The Bussell Highway is wide, mostly divided and well maintained. Caves Road is a popular tourist route allowing good access to vineyards, beaches and the caves.

Town file

1 BUNBURY (see page 111)

2 BUSSELTON pop. 10 642   ⛽ PDG
GPS 33° 39.342' S/115° 19.397' E
Busselton, on the shores of beautiful Geographe Bay, is a key agricultural centre and a popular holiday destination. Over 30 km of white sandy beaches are sheltered from the prevailing winds and the bay is a playground for those who enjoy sailing, fishing, water-skiing, windsurfing and diving. Busselton jetty extends 2 km into the bay, the longest timber jetty in the Southern Hemisphere. There is a large shopping centre and most services. 🛈 Corner Peel Terrace and Causeway Road; (08) 9752 1288; www.downsouth.com.au

3 DUNSBOROUGH pop. 1154   ⛽ PDG
GPS 33° 36.938' S/115° 06.430' E
Dunsborough has a range of shops and a good supermarket. The decommissioned HMAS *Swan* was scuttled off Point Picquet in 1997 and is now an accessible dive wreck. Cape Naturaliste Lighthouse is about 13 km to the north-west of town and includes a maritime museum. 🛈 Seymour Boulevard; (08) 9755 3299; www.downsouth.com.au

4 MARGARET RIVER pop. 2846   ⛽ PDG
GPS 33° 57.056' S/115° 04.433' E
Margaret River, in the midst of the wine-producing region, is a thriving tourist centre. It has a diverse range of shops. 🛈 Corner Tunbridge Road and Bussell Highway; (08) 9757 2911; www.margaretriverwa.com

5 AUGUSTA pop. 1087   ⛽ PDG
GPS 34° 18.915' S/115° 09.566' E
Augusta lies by the mouth of the magnificent Blackwood River. Cape Leeuwin Lighthouse, on the most south-westerly point of the continent, is just 8 km away on a sealed road. You can explore the walking tracks and nearby Jewel Cave. Augusta has basic shopping and services. 🛈 Blackwood Avenue; (08) 9758 0166; www.margaretriverwa.com

6 PEMBERTON pop. 994   ⛽ PDG
GPS 34° 26.685' S/116° 02.101' E
Pemberton is in the midst of towering karri forests. Today the old timber town boasts several galleries, displaying the woodwork of local artisans. The area is developing as a premium wine-producing region. Nearby Gloucester National Park is home to the 60-m-high Gloucester Tree, which has the world's highest treetop fire lookout. 🛈 Brockman Street; (08) 9776 1133 or 1800 671 133; www.pembertontourist.com.au

7 MANJIMUP (see page 111)

MANJIMUP TO ALBANY 235 KM

Authors' choice

⊗ **Middleton Beach Caravan Park, Albany**

A great place for a holiday, this quality park has a fabulous position and fronts onto 500 m of a popular swimming beach. Just 3 km from the Albany post office, it has good amenities and a range of facilities including a new TV room. Albany is a premier holiday destination and bookings are necessary in peak periods. **For more details see page 351.**

A treetop walk

In Walpole–Nornalup National Park, the Valley of the Giants features an awe-inspiring, 600-m-long, 38-m-high Tree Top Walk through a canopy of giant red tingle trees, a species unique to this area. Entry fee applies to walkway only; open daily from 9 a.m.

Climb a 52-m-high tree

The Diamond Tree tower is a fire lookout cabin perched at the top of a massive karri tree (a number of such lookouts were constructed in the area during the 1930s and 1940s). It is located close to the highway just 9 km south of Manjimup and is clearly signposted. Visitors are permitted to climb the tree.

Walking trail

The Bibbulmun Track is an extensive 964-km walking trail from the Perth Hills to Albany. However, campsites along the track are not more than a day's walk apart and it is possible to walk for just a few hours or for a day; alternatively, you can trek for a week or spend eight weeks walking the full length. Contact the Department of Conservation and Land Management on (08) 9334 0265 for more information.

What's on
MARCH Denmark Country Show EASTER Great Southern Wine Festival (Albany) SEPTEMBER Wildflower Week (Walpole)

Map labels:

Mandurah to Manjimup, page 110

MANJIMUP

Fonty's Pool

Diamond Tree Fire Lookout

SIR JAMES MITCHELL

River

102

SOUTH

1

31

Gloucester Tree

PEMBERTON

NATIONAL

PARK

South West Capes diversion, page 112

Warren

34° 30'

50

SHANNON NATIONAL PARK

116° 30'

116° 00'

34° 30'

10

Bibbulmun

Shannon

River

Deep

WESTERN

MOUNT

FRANKLAND

NATIONAL

PARK

Frankland

River

68

117° 00'

Broke Inlet

Track

River

HWY

WALPOLE

2

Tree Top Walk and Valley of the Giants

SOUTH

Bartholomew Meade

WALPOLE–NORNALUP NATIONAL PARK

35° 00'

Rest Point Tourist Centre

Cliffy Head

NORNALUP

Irwin Inlet

Bibbulmun

41

Point Nuyts

PEACEFUL BAY

Point Hillie

116° 30'

117° 00'

SOUTHERN OCEAN

Travel tip

When visiting the picturesque town of Denmark, call in to the Denmark Bakery in Strickland Street – it has an amazingly large range of fresh bread, rolls and cakes. And the bread is not only freshly baked but it keeps particularly well. We always stock up when we pass by.

Sample an ancient beverage

Bartholomews Meadery is one of the few honey meaderies in Australia. Call in and try the mead, the delicious honey ice-cream or just buy a jar of the excellent honey. Located 16 km west of Denmark on the highway; (08) 9840 9349; open 9.30 a.m. to 4.30 p.m. daily.

BARTHOLOMEWS MEADERY

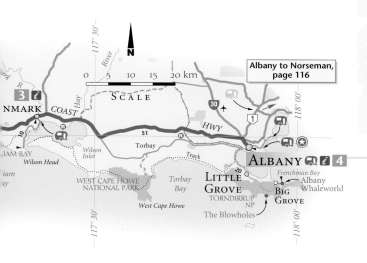

Track notes

The highway between Manjimup and Denmark is quite undulating, winding through forests, across rivers and past farming land. The road is well maintained but overtaking is difficult in some sections. Between Denmark and Albany the country is more open. The Valley of the Giants has parking spaces for cars with caravans and the access road is sealed.

Town file

1 MANJIMUP (see page 111)

2 WALPOLE pop. 337   PDG
GPS 34° 58.559' S/116° 43.934' E
In the 1930s, following the Depression, the Nornalup Land Settlement Scheme gave unemployed city men and their families a new start. They were brought to the area to carve farms out of the virgin bush. Development was slow and today Walpole remains a quiet rural area. The town has basic services. Pioneer Park, South Coast Highway; (08) 9840 1111.

3 DENMARK pop. 1978   PDG
GPS 34° 57.693' S/117° 21.258' E
Denmark, surrounded by picturesque forests, rivers and lakes, is a place that immediately appeals to visitors. The town's history is linked with the timber industry, although since the 1980s the district has benefited from agriculture, tourism and other diverse industries. There is a good shopping strip and most services. A regional art and craft market is held in mid December and early January, and on Easter Saturday. Phone the visitor information centre for specific dates. 60 Strickland Street; (08) 9848 2055.

4 ALBANY pop. 20 493   PDG
GPS 35° 01.4125' S/117° 53.014' E
In 1826, when the brig *Amity* arrived at Princess Royal Harbour with a party of soldiers and convicts, Albany became Western Australia's first settlement. The town has grown into a large rural city surrounded by farmland and forests. It attracts visitors of all ages with its picturesque coast, magnificent harbour and temperate climate. Whaling, once a key industry, has been replaced by whale-watching (August to November). This key centre has all services and good shopping. Old Railway Station, Proudlove Parade; (08) 9841 1088 or 1800 644 088.

Discover our whaling history

Albany Whaleworld is situated at the old Cheynes Beach Whaling Station, closed in 1978 and the last to operate in Australia. The museum, unique because of its creation from a working whaling station, offers a superb insight into one of the less celebrated aspects of our history. Whaling Station Road, Frenchman Bay; (08) 9844 4021; entry fee applies; open 9 a.m. to 5 p.m. daily.

ALBANY TO NORSEMAN 682 KM

⊛ **Esperance Seafront Caravan Park, Esperance**

This large park is just 2 km from the town centre and across the road from the beach – in fact it is possible to walk to town along the beach. The park has good amenities and a lovely grassed playground area that seems to host a serious 'beach' cricket match most summer afternoons. We enjoy spending a few days here.

For more details see page 366.

Take time to visit places off the road: the beaches, national parks and scenery are wonderful between Albany and Norseman. If your visit coincides with school holidays, then be sure to book accommodation or campsites; this region, especially along the coast, can be very busy.

Bush blooms

Wildflowers are abundant between Albany and Esperance. Although you will see many along the roads, if you visit the annual Ravensthorpe Wildflower Show during the first two weeks of September you will be amazed at their profusion: more than 800 local species are displayed.

An ecological wonder

Fitzgerald River National Park, designated as a World Biosphere Reserve, is a wonderful wilderness area and home to many rare and endangered animals, including the ground parrot, heath rat and dibbler. Over 1800 wildflower species grow in the park and these are at their most spectacular in spring. Whales can be seen along the dramatic coast between August and November. There are campsites but services are limited (take your own water). The national park can be reached from either Bremer Bay or the highway.

Manjimup to Albany, page 114

What's on

JANUARY Hopetoun Summer Festival SEPTEMBER Ravensthorpe Wildflower Show (first fortnight) OCTOBER Agricultural Show (Esperance), Festival of the Wind (Esperance, even-numbered years), Show Day (Jerramungup)

Norseman to Southern Cross, page 270

Norseman to Border Village, page 118

Track notes

The South Coast Highway sweeps inland from Albany, through vast tracts of hardwood plantations before reaching wheat and sheep farming areas after Ravensthorpe. The road is well maintained but in places lacks overtaking opportunities; the diversions to Bremer Bay, Hopetoun and Cheyne Beach are sealed. In Fitzgerald River National Park roads are unsealed but mostly suitable for two-wheel drives. From Esperance to Norseman areas of mallee fringe the road and mallee fowl can be seen.

Town file

1 ALBANY (see page 115)

2 BREMER BAY pop. 221   🏕 PD
GPS 34° 23.545' S/119° 22.829' E
Sheltered beaches, great diving, good surfing and excellent fishing make Bremer Bay a popular holiday spot. In spring southern right whales calve in the calm waters. Bremer Bay has several shops, a hotel and a service station. 🛈 Roadhouse; Gnombup Terrace; (08) 9837 4093.

3 RAVENSTHORPE pop. 354   🏕 PDG
GPS 33° 34.904' S/120° 02.853' E
Coppermining was once important around Ravensthorpe and many old mine sites still remain, but sheep and wheat farming are the major industries today. The area is rich in wildflowers and close to Fitzgerald River National Park. Ravensthorpe has basic services. 🛈 Morgan Street; (08) 9838 1277.

4 HOPETOUN pop. 319   🏕 PD
GPS 33° 57.053' S/120° 07.579' E
Named after Australia's first governor-general, Hopetoun began life as a port servicing the Phillips River goldfield near Ravensthorpe. Today it is a relaxing holiday destination, close to Fitzgerald River National Park. The town has limited facilities, including a small general store with fuel.

5 ESPERANCE pop. 8647   🏕 PDG
GPS 33° 51.644' S/121° 53.517' E
Esperance lies on a scenic section of the coast. The bay is a safe harbour and the port handles grain and minerals – it is linked by rail to Kalgoorlie. Esperance is a popular holiday spot with good beaches; Cape Le Grand National Park is nearby. Esperance has all facilities, including a good shopping centre. 🛈 Museum Village, Dempster Street; (08) 9071 2330.

6 NORSEMAN pop. 1516   🏕 PDG
GPS 32° 11.864' S/121° 46.760' E
Norseman lies at the western end of the Nullarbor Plain. One of Australia's richest gold reefs was discovered here in 1892, reputedly by a horse called Hardy Norseman who pawed at the ground and uncovered a large nugget, much to his owner's delight. Mining continues today and agates and opals are found in the area; fossicking permits and information can be obtained from the visitor information centre. Basic services are available. 🛈 68 Robert Street; (08) 9039 1071.

Playful sea lions

The Esperance tanker jetty is a great place to view sea lions. Tankers no longer use it; instead it is maintained for tourists and fishing. The sea lions wait around for handouts from anyone fishing.

NORSEMAN TO BORDER VILLAGE 726 KM

Travel tip

Fuel has always been expensive across the Nullarbor, with prices consistently higher than elsewhere in southern Australia. Mundrabilla Roadhouse, however, usually sells fuel at least 10 per cent cheaper than the average. They get our business!

Limestone caves

This area of the Nullarbor is riddled with sinkholes, caverns and caves such as Haig Cave (pictured) and Cocklebiddy Cave. The latter cave is north-west of Cocklebiddy, along an unmarked track. It is an extensive limestone cave system filled with water and is popular with cave divers, who explore the network of submerged chambers, one of the longest in the world. Even for non-cavers, the still waters of Cocklebiddy Cave and its prolific birdlife are a wonderful attraction.

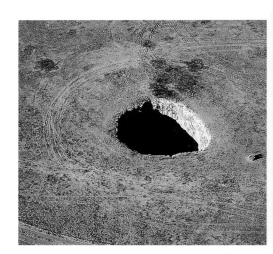

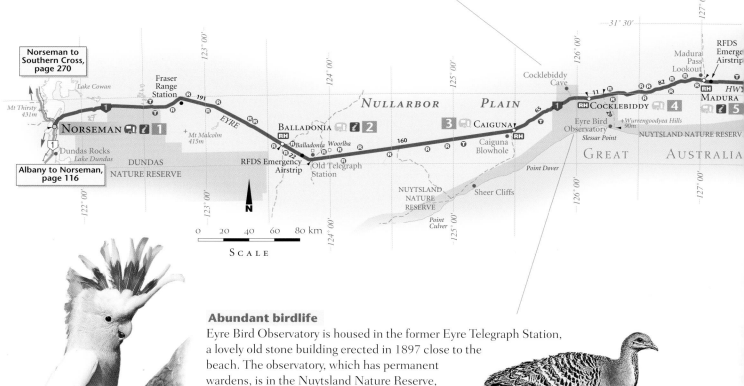

Norseman to Southern Cross, page 270

Albany to Norseman, page 116

Abundant birdlife

Eyre Bird Observatory is housed in the former Eyre Telegraph Station, a lovely old stone building erected in 1897 close to the beach. The observatory, which has permanent wardens, is in the Nuytsland Nature Reserve, 29 km south of the Eyre Highway – the final 12-km section of track is suitable for four-wheel drives only. Over 240 species of birds may be seen in the area. Day visitors are welcome; (08) 9039 3450; entry fee applies.

Travel tip

At Caiguna eastbound travellers should move clocks forward 45 minutes and at Border Village forward another 45 minutes (and vice versa for westbound). South Australia has daylight saving in summer, requiring eastbound travellers to move clocks forward by an additional hour at Border Village, while westbound travellers adjust clocks back by the same amount.

What's on

MAY Golf Classic (Eucla) JUNE–SEPTEMBER Whale-watching (along the coast) OCTOBER Eucla Police Shoot

Border Village to Ceduna, page 120

Old telegraph station

The historic Eucla Telegraph Station, built in 1877 as part of the early telegraph system, is 4 km south of the present town. Today white, shifting sand covers much of the buildings, but they are an evocative and interesting sight. Turn off the highway at Eucla and follow the signs: at the end of the road it is a 50-m walk to the ruins.

Track notes

The Eyre Highway is the main route across Australia and heavy transports are common. Watch out for strong headwinds that can dramatically increase fuel consumption, and incredible turbulence when meeting oncoming transports, especially on a windy day. You will see Royal Flying Doctor Service emergency landing strips painted on the highway. There are spectacular views from a lookout at the top of Madura Pass. Australia's longest section of straight road is a 146.6-km section of the Eyre Highway between Balladonia and Caiguna.

Town file

1 NORSEMAN (see page 117)

2 BALLADONIA pop. 10   🅿 PDG
GPS 32° 21.157' S/123° 37.053' E
Balladonia is a roadhouse and accommodation complex with a small museum. Displays in the museum range from lifesize models of a camel and its Afghan driver to space junk, for in 1979 the NASA Skylab plummeted to earth on Woorlba Station, east of Balladonia.
🛈 (08) 9039 3453; www.users.bigpond.com\balladonia

3 CAIGUNA pop. 10   🅿 PDG
GPS 32° 16.251' S/125° 29.263' E
Caiguna is a roadhouse complex with a caravan park. Caiguna Blowhole, an air-intake point for the limestone cave system beneath, is 5 km to the south-west.

4 COCKLEBIDDY pop. 9   🅿 PDG
GPS 32° 02.262' S/126° 05.824' E
Cocklebiddy is a roadhouse complex with a caravan park.

5 MADURA pop. 8   🅿 PDG
GPS 31° 54.025' S/127° 01.230' E
Lying at the foot of the Madura Pass, Madura is a roadhouse and accommodation complex with a small caravan park. Meals are available.
🛈 Madura Pass Oasis Motel and Roadhouse; (08) 9039 3464.

6 MUNDRABILLA ROADHOUSE   🅿 PD
GPS 31° 49.052' S/128° 13.547' E
Mundrabilla is a roadhouse with accommodation and a small caravan park, lying on the coastal plain beneath the Hampton Tablelands. There is an animal park beside the roadhouse.

7 EUCLA pop. 50   🅿 PDG
GPS 31° 40.594' S/128° 52.942' E
Eucla has a roadhouse with accommodation and a caravan park. The Bureau of Meteorology has an observation station here that welcomes visitors.

8 BORDER VILLAGE pop. 8   🅿 PDG
GPS 31° 38.282' S/129° 00.218' E
Border Village is a roadhouse complex on the Western Australia–South Australia border. There is a fruit and vegetables quarantine checkpoint here for all westbound traffic.

BORDER VILLAGE TO CEDUNA 482 KM

What's on
JUNE–OCTOBER Whale-watching
(along the Great Australian Bight)
SEPTEMBER Ceduna Show OCTOBER
Ceduna Oysterfest (Labour Day weekend)

Cliff lookouts
There are several lookouts close to the Eyre
Highway between Border Village and Nullarbor
offering great views of the fabulous Nullarbor cliffs,
the longest cliff-face in the world. We have also seen
whales from these lookouts during the peak whale-
watching months, June to October. Take care along
the unprotected cliff edge.

Whale-watching
The Head of Bight, adjacent to the Nullarbor National
Park and on Yalata Aboriginal Land, is 11 km along a
sealed road from the Eyre Highway. From a viewing
platform you can watch southern right whales that
venture into this part of the Bight between June and
October; permits are available from local roadhouses
and from White Wells Ranger Station at the Head of
Bight; (08) 8625 6201; entry fee applies.

The Nullarbor

The famous Nullarbor treeless plain extends along the highway ending about 30 km west of Yalata. For as far as the eye can see there are no trees, just a carpet of short plant growth. The Nullarbor National Park also extends along the highway and is entirely desert, with patches of mallee scrub and some ground cover of bluebush and saltbush; it is renowned for its unique desolate beauty.

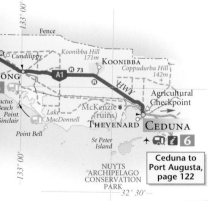

Ceduna to Port Augusta, page 122

Travel tip

Fowlers Bay was one of the first settlements on the coast of western South Australia. Explorers Edward John Eyre and Ernest Giles both used it as a base. Today it is a small village and popular fishing area with a jetty, store and small caravan park. We enjoy calling into Fowlers Bay even though the road is not sealed.

Track notes

The Eyre Highway in this section is a well-maintained sealed road and carries road trains and heavy transports. The highway follows the coast closely in places and strong winds can sometimes make driving uncomfortable, especially towing a caravan. Take care if it is windy. There is an agricultural checkpoint at the Western Australia–South Australia border for all westbound traffic. Fresh fruit and vegetables, plants, flowers, seeds, nuts, honey and used fruit and vegetable containers must all be forfeited. It is best to have discarded them before arrival and plan to buy fresh produce in Western Australia. All eastbound traffic must likewise stop at Ceduna and discard any fruit and vegetables.

Town file

1 BORDER VILLAGE (see page 119)

2 NULLARBOR pop. 13   PDG
GPS 31° 27.020' S/130° 53.814' E
Nullarbor is a roadhouse complex located on the treeless plain after which it is named and includes a caravan park. The Head of Bight, a popular whale-watching area, is to the east and Nullarbor National Park stretches to the west. Basic services for travellers are available.

3 YALATA pop. 273   PD
GPS 31° 29.756' S/131° 48.729' E
Yalata is a small community with a roadhouse owned and operated by the Yalata Aboriginal Community. The Dingo Fence, which runs 6000 km from the cliffs of the Great Australian Bight to Jimbour in Queensland, crosses the Eyre Highway 7 km east of the roadhouse. Whale-watching permits are available from the roadhouse to visit the viewing facility at the Head of Bight.

4 NUNDROO ROADHOUSE   PDG
GPS 31° 47.542' S/132° 13.482' E
Nundroo Roadhouse is an accommodation complex with a caravan park. Basic services are available.

5 PENONG pop. 200   PD
GPS 31° 55.704' S/133° 00.615' E
Penong is a small township known for its windmills: there are working windmills of all shapes and sizes. Cactus Beach, 21 km south along an unsealed road, is a world-renowned surfing beach with both left and right breaking waves. Penong has most basic services and a caravan park.

6 CEDUNA pop. 2599   PDG
GPS 32° 07.558' S/133° 40.535' E
Ceduna is a major commercial centre on the far west of the Eyre Peninsula. The town supports a large agricultural community and a strong oyster industry. There are salt and gypsum works towards Penong, and nearby Thevenard is home to a fishing fleet. The area is a popular spot for fishing, surfing and diving. The town has a good shopping strip and most services.   58 Poynton Street; (08) 8625 2780 or 1800 639 413.

CEDUNA TO PORT AUGUSTA 465 KM

Travel tip

The shortest route to central Australia from the Eyre Highway is the unsealed road from Wirrulla. The 290 km of unsealed road, which joins the Stuart Highway north of Glendambo, is more than 400 km shorter than following the bitumen through Port Augusta. The road is suitable for four-wheel drives and off-road caravans or camper-trailers.

Wadlata Outback Centre

Journey through the Tunnel of Time at the multi-award-winning Wadlata Outback Centre. The centre offers an interpretive and interactive history of the Flinders Ranges and the surrounding outback from 15 million years ago to the present, focusing on the Dreamtime, exploration, early pastoralists, miners and the present day. If you are heading to the Flinders Ranges, a visit here is a must. There is a cafe and gift shop, and the centre offers tourist information for the surrounding area.

41 Flinders Terrace; (08) 8642 4511; entry fee applies; open 9 a.m. to 5.30 p.m. weekdays, 10 a.m. to 4 p.m. weekends.

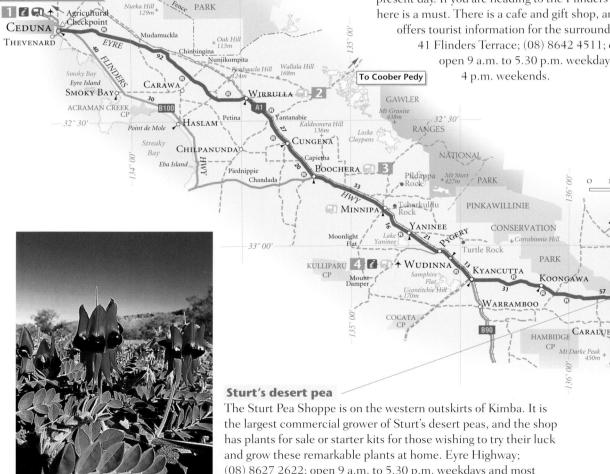

Sturt's desert pea

The Sturt Pea Shoppe is on the western outskirts of Kimba. It is the largest commercial grower of Sturt's desert peas, and the shop has plants for sale or starter kits for those wishing to try their luck and grow these remarkable plants at home. Eyre Highway; (08) 8627 2622; open 9 a.m. to 5.30 p.m. weekdays and most summer weekends.

Desert gardens

The Australian Arid Lands Botanic Garden covers over 250 ha and has 12 km of walking trails. The garden is a wonderful place to spend a couple of hours and provides an insight into arid land ecosystems. Keen birdwatchers will enjoy the wide range of native

birds attracted to the garden. Planting and development is ongoing. There is a visitor centre with interpretive displays, a cafe and a gift shop. Stuart Highway; (08) 8641 1049; fee for guided tours (weekdays only), otherwise entry is free; garden open 7.30 a.m. to sunset; visitor centre open 9 a.m. to 5 p.m. weekdays, 10 a.m. to 4 p.m. weekends.

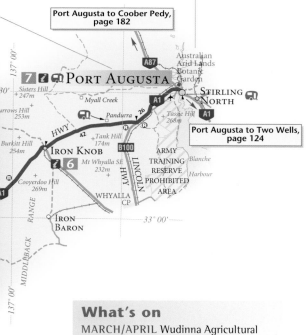

What's on

MARCH/APRIL Wudinna Agricultural Expo (even-numbered years) APRIL Antique and Craft Fair (Port Augusta) AUGUST Camel Cup (Port Augusta) SEPTEMBER Wudinna Show, Kimba Agricultural Show OCTOBER Apex Rodeo (Kimba)

Track notes

The Eyre Highway is well maintained and fully sealed to carry the large volume of heavy transports and road trains travelling the east–west route. During harvest, in early summer, there are also grain trucks and slow-moving farm machinery using the highway.

Town file

1 **CEDUNA** (see page 121)

2 **WIRRULLA** pop. 100   PD
GPS 32° 24.222' S/134° 31.936' E
Wirrulla, similar to many other wheat-belt towns in this area, is close to the railway, the wheat silos and the highway. The town has limited facilities and a tiny caravan park on an unused tennis court. Wirrulla is a good point from which to access the Gawler Ranges.

3 **POOCHERA** pop. 50   PDG
GPS 32° 43.176' S/134° 50.280' E
Poochera is a small wheat-belt town with basic services and a caravan park. The Gawler Ranges are to the north-east and a sealed road stretches to Streaky Bay some 60 km away on the coast.

4 **WUDINNA** pop. 527   PDG
GPS 33° 02.779' S/135° 27.586' E
Wudinna is a service centre for the region. Mount Wudinna, 10 km north of town, is a 261-m-high granite monolith with an easy walking trail and picnic area. The town has a good range of shops, most services and a caravan park. ❷ Council Offices, Burton Terrace; (08) 8680 2002.

5 **KIMBA** pop. 677   PDG
GPS 33° 08.324' S/136° 25.220' E
Kimba is a wheat-producing area with one of the largest inland wheat terminals in South Australia. The town is a good base from which to explore the Gawler Ranges. ❷ The Sturt Pea Shoppe, Eyre Highway; (08) 8627 2622; www.epta.com.au

6 **IRON KNOB** pop. 224   None
GPS 32° 43.845' S/137° 09.012' E
Iron Knob developed to support the BHP mining operations, which began here in 1899. The mine closed in 1998, the hotel burned down and the service station has closed. The town still has a store but very little else in the way of services. ❷ Third Street; (08) 8646 2129.

7 **PORT AUGUSTA** pop. 13 914   PDG
GPS 32° 29.489' S/137° 45.744' E
The regional city of Port Augusta is often referred to as the crossroads of Australia. It is a busy rail centre and is also the junction of two of Australia's most important road transport routes – the Eyre and Stuart highways. A service centre for the north of the State, it has good shopping and all services are available. ❷ Flinders Ranges and Outback Tourist Information, 41 Flinders Terrace; (08) 8641 0793; www.epta.com.au

PORT AUGUSTA TO TWO WELLS 268 KM

Flinders Ranges

One of South Australia's great attractions, the Flinders Ranges extend approximately 420 km from Crystal Brook in the south to Mount Hopeless in the north. Take the time to spend a few days exploring the ranges and you will encounter the Flinders Ranges and Gammon Ranges national parks (including Wilpena Pound), historical Aboriginal sites and spectacular scenery. From the highway take the Stirling North turn-off.

The Yorke Peninsula

Take a tour down the Yorke Peninsula, a popular holiday destination offering some of the best coastal recreation areas in South Australia. Greatly influenced by the Cornish copperminers in the late 1800s, the Yorke Peninsula still retains some of the historic architecture and has museums and festivals that recall the rich local history. There is excellent fishing all along the peninsula's coastline, with jetties at Wallaroo, Moonta Bay, Edithburgh, Stansbury and Port Victoria, and Innes National Park is located at the southern tip of the peninsula.

What's on

JANUARY Annual Festival of the Crab (Port Germein, Australia Day) SEPTEMBER Blessing of the Fleet (Port Pirie) OCTOBER Baroota Rodeo, Country Music Festival (Port Pirie) NOVEMBER Snowtown Street Carnival

Map labels

Port Augusta to Coober Pedy, page 182

Ceduna to Port Augusta, page 122

PORT AUGUSTA
Australian Arid Lands Botanic Garden

To Flinders Ranges

To Peterborough

STIRLING NORTH
Winninowie
Horrocks Pass

ARMY TRAINING RESERVE PROHIBITED AREA
WINNINOWIE CP
Blanche Harbour
Nectar Brook
Hancocks Lookout
MOUNT REMARKABLE NP

Monument Hill 198m
MAMBRAY CREEK
Point Douglas
Backy Point
Barota Reservoir

PORT BONYTHON
Point Lowly
Baroota
TELOWIE GORGE CP

SPENCER
PORT GERMEIN
NELSHABY
NAPPERBY

PORT PIRIE
WARNERTOWN

Jarrold Point
Port Davis
R Broughton
B89
Nurom

SCALE
0 10 20 30 km

Wood Point
WANDEARAH
Wandearah West
MERRITON
CRYSTAL BROOK
NARRIDY

GULF
Fisherman Bay
Clements Gap
REDHILL

PORT BROUGHTON
MUNDOORA
Collinsfield
LAKE VIEW
KOOLUNGA

To Yorke Peninsula

Lincolnfields
WOKURNA
CONDOWIE

BARUNGA GAP
SNOWTOWN
Lake Bumbunga

BUTE
Mona
LOCHIEL
BUMBUNGA

NINNES
NANTAWARRA
Watchman

KULPARA
B85
BEAUFORT
WHITWARTA

To Yorke Peninsula

PORT WAKEFIELD
BOWMANS

INKERMAN
AVON

WILD HORSE PLAINS
LONG PLAINS

WINDSOR
MALLALA

DUBLIN

LOWER LIGHT
TWO WELLS

Two Wells to Adelaide (39 km)
For connecting routes, see map of Adelaide suburbs and surrounds, page 129

Travel tip

Travellers heading to or from the eastern States can take the heavy transport route between Port Augusta and Peterborough via Horrocks Pass, Wilmington and Orroroo. This route joins with the Barrier Highway to Broken Hill. The road is well maintained and sealed, and travels through undulating broadacre farming country.

The Heysen Trail

Running through Mount Remarkable National Park is part of the Heysen Trail, a fabulous 1500-km walking trail from Parachilna Gorge in the Flinders Ranges to Cape Jervis on the south coast of the Fleurieu Peninsula. Most parts of the trail are closed between November and April due to fire risk. Trail information (08) 8463 3059.

Mount Remarkable National Park

Secluded gorges, dramatic scenery and a diverse range of wildlife can all be seen at this national park, located in the South Flinders Ranges. There are some great bushwalks and the Mambray Creek camping area in the park itself is accessible from the Princes Highway approximately 50 km south of Port Augusta. Park information (08) 8634 7068.

Track notes

The Princes Highway linking Port Augusta and Adelaide is the major route north from Adelaide. It is a well-maintained highway and carries a large volume of traffic. There are long sections of divided highway and the balance is a good quality road with several passing lanes. Many of the small towns along the route, including Two Wells, are bypassed, but a number of roadhouses service the needs of passing motorists.

Town file

1 PORT AUGUSTA (see page 123)

2 PORT GERMEIN pop. 235   🅿 PD
GPS 33° 01.371' S/137° 59.956' E
Once a major shipping port with one of the longest jetties in the Southern Hemisphere, Port Germein is today a popular seaside holiday spot and the 1.7-km jetty is now a tourist attraction. The Port Germein Markets are held every second Saturday and basic services are available in town.

3 PORT PIRIE pop. 13 633   🅿 PDG
GPS 33° 10.577' S/138° 00.600' E
Port Pirie is a major commercial and industrial centre and a good base for exploring the South Flinders Ranges. Since 1889 Broken Hill Associated Smelters, the largest silver, lead and zinc smelter in the world, has been smelting ore from the Broken Hill deposits. Port Pirie is also a major port for the export of grain. The town has all services and very good shopping.
🅒 Regional Tourism and Arts Centre, Mary Elie Street; (08) 8633 8700 or 1800 000 424.

4 CRYSTAL BROOK pop. 1323   🅿 PD
GPS 33° 21.192' S/138° 12.372' E
Located at the southern end of the Flinders Ranges, Crystal Brook is worth a visit. The town has a National Trust museum, good shopping, most services and a small caravan park with large shady trees.

5 PORT WAKEFIELD pop. 543   🅿 PDG
GPS 34° 11.105' S/138° 08.891' E
This town is a busy service centre for highway traffic. It has most services and includes a caravan park taken up mostly by annual residents. Northbound traffic travelling to Yorke Peninsula should turn off the Princes Highway just north of town.

6 TWO WELLS pop. 624   🅿 PD
GPS 34° 35.658' S/138° 30.917' E
This is a small residential community on the northern outskirts of greater Adelaide. Many locals commute daily to Adelaide. Much of the surrounding area consists of small crop farms and market gardens along the Gawler River. The town has a small shopping strip and most basic services.

ADELAIDE
YOUR GUIDE

Adelaide is set on the wide curves of the River Torrens between the Mount Lofty Ranges and Gulf St Vincent. It is the only major metropolis in the world where the city's centre is completely encircled by parkland. It has a population of almost 1.1 million, but remains a friendly and open place. The city offers visitors a well-preserved history, the warmth and light of the South Australian outdoors and excellent wining and dining.

CITY CENTRE

See map on page 128.

Adelaide Casino 128 C5
Located in a beautifully restored railway station.

Adelaide Festival Centre 128 C4
One of the best performance venues in the world, with various exhibitions scattered throughout the centre.

Art Gallery of South Australia 128 D5
A superb overview of Australian art from the 18th century on.

Botanic Gardens 128 E4
Join a free tour of these beautiful, formal 16-ha gardens on the edge of the CBD.

Central Market 128 C6
Bustling market with some of the best and cheapest local produce in the country.

Edmund Wright House 128 C5
Historic house that displays travelling exhibitions from the National Museum of Australia; also the home of the State History Centre.

Light's Vision 128 C3
On Montefiore Hill, bronze statue of Colonel Light, the first surveyor-general of the city.

Migration Museum 128 D4
Housed in the former Destitute Asylum; features exhibits charting migrants' lives before, during and after their arrival.

Museum of Classical Archaeology 128 D5
Within the grounds of the University of Adelaide, this museum houses objects that date back to the third millennium BC.

Rundle Mall 128 D5
The major shopping precinct and a vibrant, cosmopolitan cafe strip.

St Peter's Cathedral 128 C3
One of Australia's finest cathedrals, built in 1869 in the Gothic Revival style.

South Australian Museum 128 D5
Features the world's largest collection of anthropological Aboriginal artefacts and a range from the Pacific Islands and Egypt.

Visitor information
South Australian Visitor and Travel Centre
18 King William Street
(08) 8303 2033, freecall 1300 655 276
www.visit.adelaide.on.net

Tandanya – National Aboriginal Cultural Institute 128 E5
Houses displays of Aboriginal culture, art, artefacts and a performance space for dance and theatre.

Treasury Building 128 C6
Dating back to 1839; now a museum charting the fascinating history of exploration and surveying in South Australia.

SUBURBS AND SURROUNDS
See map on page 129.

Adelaide Hills 129 D6
Historic villages, gardens, museums and vineyards sit among bushland and European-style farmland.

Belair National Park 129 C6
The State's oldest national park, established in 1891; includes the impressive gardens of the governor's old summer residence.

Cleland Wildlife Park 129 C6
Excellent park housing native marsupials and aviaries; night-time walks available.

Glenelg 129 B6
Board a tram to this seaside resort with its old-world feel; the amusement centre Magic Mountain is nearby.

McLaren Vale wine region 129 B8
Set among rolling hectares of almond and olive groves, these 53 wineries form one of the country's top wine-producing regions.

South Australian Maritime Museum 129 B4
Re-creations of 19th-century dock life and the immigrant experience, including replicas of parts of old sailing boats.

Victor Harbor (not shown on map)
Popular holiday resort located on the Fleurieu Peninsula; includes a horse-drawn tram, heritage sites, penguins, dolphins and whales.

Getting around
Adelaide's city centre is compact and easily negotiated on foot. The Explorer Tram offers visitors the chance to tour the city's attractions at a leisurely pace and with the benefit of a recorded commentary. A fleet of Popeye motor launches cruise the River Torrens and also provide an ideal means of transport to the Adelaide Zoo. The historic Glenelg tram is the most famous of Adelaide's tourist rides. It departs Victoria Square regularly for a return trip to Adelaide's premier seaside suburb. Car travel is recommended for touring some of the further-flung regions; the roads are excellent and, provided you have a road map, navigation should not be a problem.

Airport shuttle bus Transit Regency Coaches (08) 8381 5311; **Motoring organisation** RAA (08) 8202 4600; **Public transport** Passenger Transport Information Hotline (08) 8210 1000; **Taxis** Suburban Transport Services 13 10 08, United Yellow Cabs 13 22 27; **River Torrens cruises** Popeye Motor Launches (08) 8295 4747; **Port Adelaide cruises** Port Adelaide River Cruises (08) 8341 1194; **Bicycle hire** Contact Bicycle SA for operators (08) 8232 2644.

Top events
Schützenfest (January)
Celebration of South Australia's German heritage.

Adelaide Festival of the Arts and Adelaide Fringe Festival (February–March, even-numbered years)
Highly regarded international festivals.

Glendi Festival (March)
Greek culture, food, song and dance.

500 in Adelaide (April)
V8 supercar race on a modified Grand Prix circuit.

Tasting Australia (October, odd-numbered years)
Sample the latest innovations in food and wine.

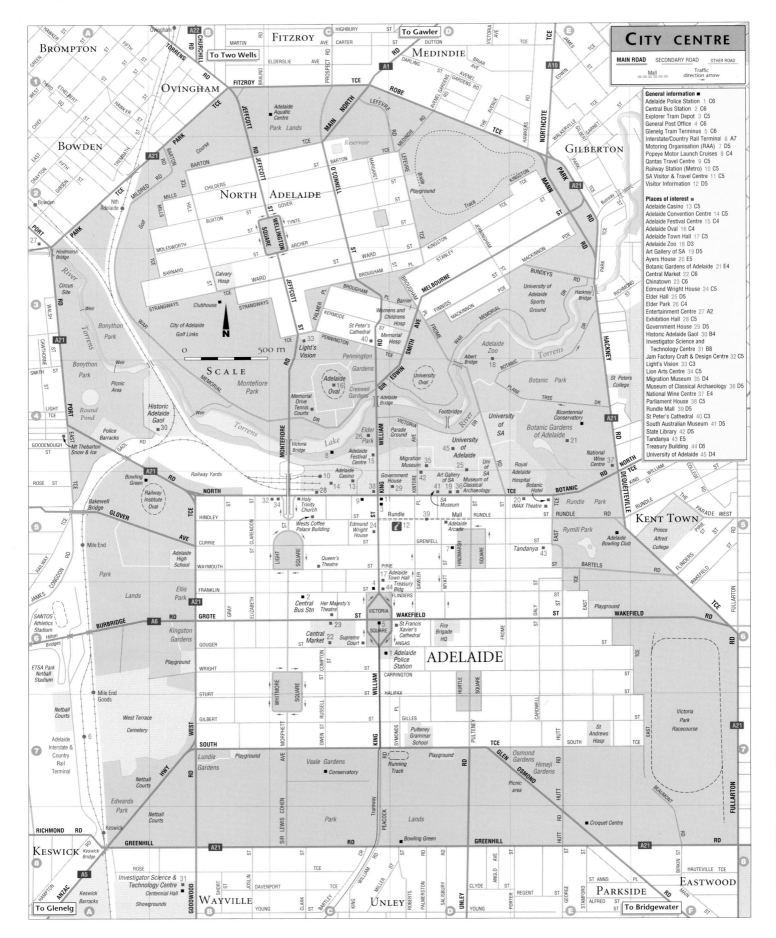

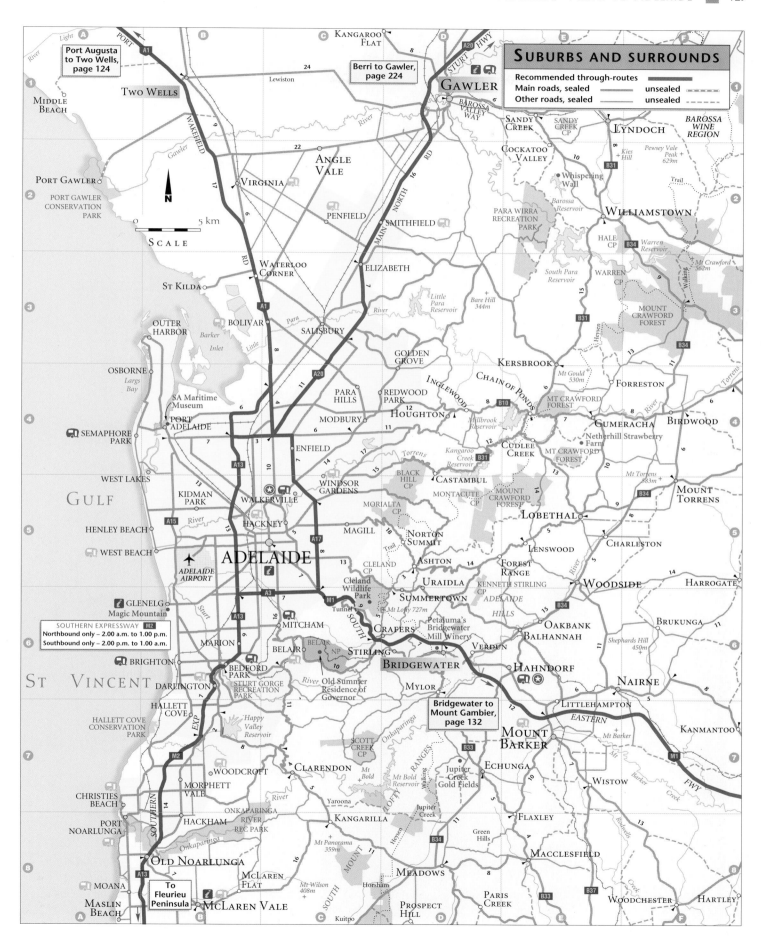

ADELAIDE TO MELBOURNE
SOUTH EASTERN FREEWAY, PRINCES HIGHWAY, PRINCES FREEWAY (921 KM)

The coastal route linking Adelaide with Melbourne is one of Australia's most unforgettable scenic drives. The mystical Blue Lake at Mount Gambier, the seaside town of Portland with some of Victoria's earliest historic buildings, the southern right whales off the coast of Warrnambool, the spectacular Great Ocean Road and the fabulous Otway Ranges ensure that there is something for almost everyone.

Adelaide
The well-planned city of Adelaide is set on the wide curves of the River Torrens. Its immediate location belies the fact that beyond the rolling hills lie great tracts of arid scrubland – Adelaide is the capital of the driest State in Australia.

Blue Lake, Mount Gambier

Bridgewater to Mount Gambier
From the Adelaide Hills the Princes Highway travels through farming country, along the wildlife haven of the Coorong and through forests towards the major regional centre of Mount Gambier.

Mount Gambier to Port Fairy
The highway sweeps inland through neat forests, but the coastal route through Nelson is always a popular alternative. Portland is a busy regional town, while the historic fishing village of Port Fairy is popular for beachside holidays.

Best time to go

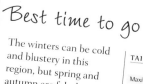

The winters can be cold and blustery in this region, but spring and autumn are fabulous seasons for touring. During the summer holiday periods, tourists flock to many of the popular beaches.

John & Jan

TAILEM BEND

	J	F	M	A	M	J	J	A	S	O	N	D
Maximum	30	29	27	23	19	16	16	17	20	22	25	27
Minimum	14	14	12	10	8	6	6	6	7	9	11	13
Rainfall (mm)	17	21	22	28	40	40	39	40	38	38	28	26
Raindays	3	4	7	11	11	13	13	11	9	6	6	

COLAC

	J	F	M	A	M	J	J	A	S	O	N	D
Maximum	26	26	24	19	16	13	13	14	16	18	21	23
Minimum	11	11	10	8	6	5	4	5	6	7	8	9
Rainfall (mm)	36	35	44	58	72	76	77	89	77	74	57	46
Raindays	8	7	9	13	16	17	19	19	17	16	12	10

Great Ocean Road diversion

One of the country's most spectacular tours, the Great Ocean Road passes exciting surf beaches and popular holiday resorts, and boasts breathtaking scenery. The road winds high above the thundering surf and twists through the dense, green forest of the Otway Ranges.

Colac to Werribee

The highway gets busier as it approaches Melbourne from the west. Geelong is a major Australian regional centre and just a short distance from the popular holiday towns of Ocean Grove and Barwon Heads on the Bellarine Peninsula.

The Twelve Apostles

Port Fairy to Colac

The highway follows the coast from Port Fairy to Warrnambool and then stretches inland through rich dairying country, where dramatic remnants of ancient volcanoes and endless stone fences are prominent features.

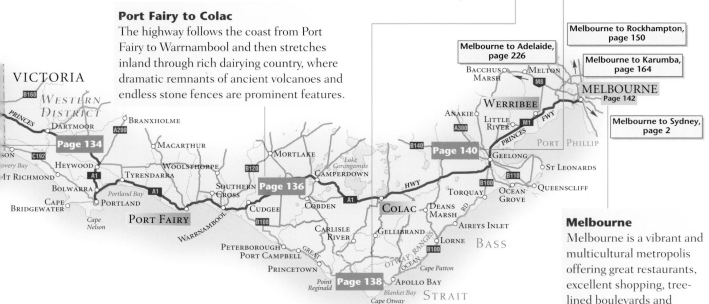

Melbourne to Rockhampton, page 150

Melbourne to Adelaide, page 226

Melbourne to Karumba, page 164

MELBOURNE Page 142

Melbourne to Sydney, page 2

Melbourne

Melbourne is a vibrant and multicultural metropolis offering great restaurants, excellent shopping, tree-lined boulevards and magnificent gardens.

BRIDGEWATER TO MOUNT GAMBIER 426 KM

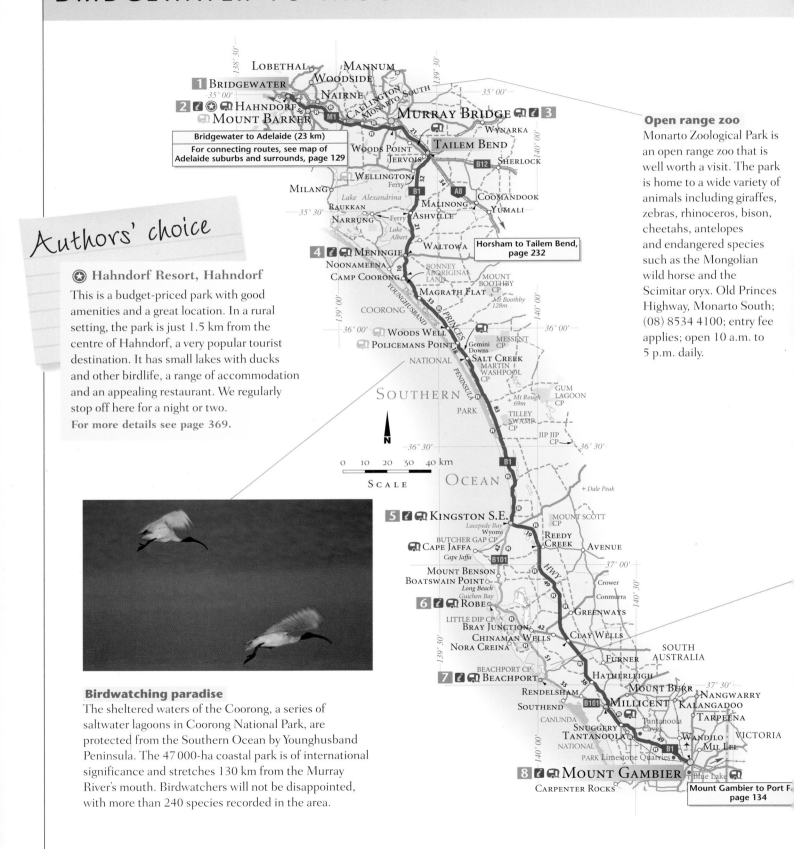

Bridgewater to Adelaide (23 km)
For connecting routes, see map of
Adelaide suburbs and surrounds, page 129

Horsham to Tailem Bend,
page 232

Mount Gambier to Port F.
page 134

Open range zoo

Monarto Zoological Park is an open range zoo that is well worth a visit. The park is home to a wide variety of animals including giraffes, zebras, rhinoceros, bison, cheetahs, antelopes and endangered species such as the Mongolian wild horse and the Scimitar oryx. Old Princes Highway, Monarto South; (08) 8534 4100; entry fee applies; open 10 a.m. to 5 p.m. daily.

Authors' choice

⊛ Hahndorf Resort, Hahndorf

This is a budget-priced park with good amenities and a great location. In a rural setting, the park is just 1.5 km from the centre of Hahndorf, a very popular tourist destination. It has small lakes with ducks and other birdlife, a range of accommodation and an appealing restaurant. We regularly stop off here for a night or two.

For more details see page 369.

Birdwatching paradise

The sheltered waters of the Coorong, a series of saltwater lagoons in Coorong National Park, are protected from the Southern Ocean by Younghusband Peninsula. The 47 000-ha coastal park is of international significance and stretches 130 km from the Murray River's mouth. Birdwatchers will not be disappointed, with more than 240 species recorded in the area.

Travel tip

This section of road follows the coast and the fishing industry is one of the main employers in the region. Many of the small coastal towns along the way have outlets selling lobsters and fish fresh from local waters. We regularly buy fresh fish when travelling in the area.

Historic coastal drive

The alternative coastal route between Kingston S.E. and Millicent is a superb drive through the historic southern port towns of Robe and Beachport. These towns are great tourist destinations, with numerous swimming beaches and good fishing. Lobster fishing is a major industry along this part of the coast.

What's on

JANUARY Cape Jaffa Food and Wine Fair, Lions Regatta Day (Robe), Shutzenfest (German festival, Hahndorf) FEBRUARY Mount Gambier Country Music Festival APRIL Blue Lake Festival (Mount Gambier) NOVEMBER Robe Village Fair, Kingston S.E. Show, Steam and Riverboat Rally (Murray Bridge)

Track notes

This popular tourist route winds out of Adelaide through farming country before sweeping south along the coast, passing through some of the many pine plantations in this area.

Town file

1 BRIDGEWATER pop. 3735   ⛽ PDG
GPS 35° 00.581' S/138° 45.623' E
Bridgewater is a leafy outer suburb on top of the Adelaide Hills with exquisite gardens and a historic mill with wine tastings.

2 HAHNDORF pop. 1726   ⛽ PDG
GPS 35° 01.728' S/138° 48.577' E
Set in the heart of the Adelaide Hills, Hahndorf has a strong German influence. There is a busy main street with gift shops, restaurants and stores selling local produce. ℹ 41 Main Street; (08) 8388 1185.

3 MURRAY BRIDGE pop. 12 831   ⛽ PDG
GPS 35° 07.048' S/139° 16.540' E
Murray Bridge is a centre for water sports and river cruises. The town has all facilities and good shopping. ℹ 3 South Terrace; (08) 8539 1142.

4 MENINGIE pop. 918   ⛽ PDG
GPS 35° 41.419' S/139° 20.208' E
Meningie is set on the shores of the picturesque Lake Albert and has most services and good shopping. ℹ 76 Princes Highway; (08) 8575 1259.

5 KINGSTON S.E. pop. 1431   ⛽ PDG
GPS 36° 49.745' S/139° 51.109' E
Kingston S.E. is set on the shores of Lacepede Bay at the southern end of the Coorong. ℹ The Big Lobster, Princes Highway; (08) 8767 2555.

6 ROBE pop. 816   ⛽ PDG
GPS 37° 09.760' S/139° 45.380' E
Dating back to 1840, the fishing village of Robe has a selection of shops and many fine historic buildings. Long Beach (17 km long) to the north of town is especially popular with visitors. ℹ Robe Institute and Library, Mundy Terrace; (08) 8768 2465.

7 BEACHPORT pop. 441   ⛽ PDG
GPS 37° 28.888' S/140° 00.784' E
Once a whaling station, Beachport has safe swimming beaches and a long jetty. Enjoy the unusual buoyancy properties of the nearby Pool of Siloam, a small lake. Basic services are available. ℹ Millicent Road; (08) 8735 8029.

8 MOUNT GAMBIER pop. 22 037   ⛽ PDG
GPS 37° 49.746' S/140° 46.517' E
Mount Gambier is famous for its spectacular extinct volcano crater lakes, particularly Blue Lake, which changes to a vivid blue from November to March. ℹ The Lady Nelson Visitor and Discovery Centre, Jubilee Highway East; (08) 8724 9750 or 1800 087 187; www.mountgambiertourism.com.au

MOUNT GAMBIER TO PORT FAIRY 184 KM

Authors' choice

⭐ **Narrawong Holiday Park, Narrawong**

This pretty park is in a fabulous, quiet beachside and riverfront position off the main highway. Offering a range of accommodation, it is close to Portland and has good fishing and swimming, and a range of facilities including tennis courts. Campfires are permitted. Just a short walk to the centre of the small community, this park is in a great position and is reasonably priced.

For more details see page 380.

Cave adventures

Princess Margaret Rose Cave, in Lower Glenelg National Park, is 18 km off the highway (or accessible along an unsealed road from Nelson). The old stream cave is adorned with wonderful stalactites, stalagmites and helictites, which can be viewed on a guided tour. (08) 8738 4171; entry fee applies; tours run every hour from 10 a.m. (Victorian time).

Fabulous fishing

Fishing is a great attraction along the coast. Remember, however, that bag limits, size limits and licence requirements apply in both States. You should be aware of the regulations in each State, especially those pertaining to rock lobster and abalone fishing. Information is usually available at caravan parks, visitor information centres and fishing shops.

A treat for divers

Experienced cave divers and snorkellers can enjoy the unique experience of exploring the crystal clear, spring-fed, fresh waters of Ewens Ponds and Piccaninnie Ponds (permit required), both located in conservation parks.

An alternative path

The coastal route between Mount Gambier and Portland via Nelson is a popular alternative to Highway One, with easy access to Lower Glenelg National Park. Nelson is located on the lower reaches of the picturesque Glenelg River.

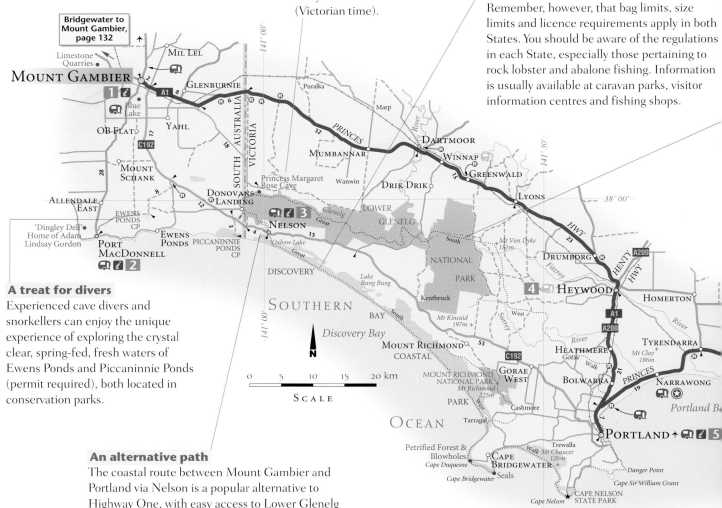

Travel tip

Eastbound travellers should move clocks forward by 30 minutes at the South Australian/Victorian border. During the warmer months (November to March), both States have daylight saving. Westbound travellers should move clocks back by the same amount.

A great walk

The Great South West Walk begins and ends in Portland. The 17 sections that make up the walk cover 250 km between Portland and the Glenelg River. Further information is available from the Portland and Nelson visitor information centres; (03) 5523 2671 or (08) 8738 4051.

What's on

JANUARY Bayside Festival (Port MacDonnell) FEBRUARY Wood, Wine and Roses Festival (Heywood), Go Kart Street Grand Prix (Portland) JUNE Port Fairy Folk Festival NOVEMBER/DECEMBER Admella Surf Boat Marathon (Portland)

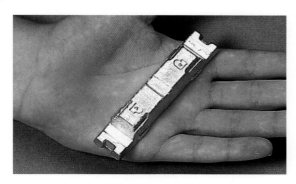

Smelter tours

Portland Aluminium Smelter offers free tours through the smelter and over the adjoining wetlands on Mondays, Wednesdays and Fridays. To book, call (03) 5523 2671.

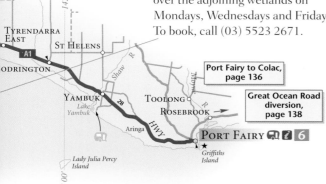

Track notes

The Princes Highway is a well-maintained sealed road that mainly carries local traffic including trucks loaded with timber. A popular alternative is the coastal route through Nelson, which is fully sealed. The roads from Nelson and Mount Gambier to Port MacDonnell are also sealed and in good repair. Many local roads, including the one to Princess Margaret Rose Cave (from Nelson), are unsealed, white limestone roads. Although dusty, they are generally suitable for two-wheel drives.

Town file

1 MOUNT GAMBIER (see page 133)

2 PORT MACDONNELL pop. 662   🅿 PD
GPS 38° 03.278' S/140° 41.982' E
Port MacDonnell was once a busy port, but today it is best known for being the southern rock lobster capital of Australia. It is a busy tourist spot with most basic facilities. 🛈 7 Meylin Street; (08) 8738 2576.

3 NELSON pop. 200   🅿 PD
GPS 38° 02.941' S/141° 00.395' E
The picturesque town of Nelson, on the estuary of the Glenelg River, is named after the *Lady Nelson*, a ship that explored much of the coastline in the area during the early 1800s. The nearby Lower Glenelg National Park, the Discovery Bay Coastal Park and the Princess Margaret Rose Cave all make the town a popular tourist destination. Basic facilities are available. 🛈 Leake Street; (08) 8738 4051.

4 HEYWOOD pop. 1305   🅿 PD
GPS 38° 07.917' S/141° 37.805' E
In its early days, Heywood was one day's travel from Portland and a popular stopover for hopefuls on their way to the goldfields. Today agriculture and timber are the main industries. Located at the junction of the Henty and Princes highways, the town has most basic services.

5 PORTLAND pop. 9664   🅿 PDG
GPS 38° 20.712' S/141° 36.224' E
Portland became the first permanent settlement in Victoria, in 1834. Josephite nun Mary McKillop taught in the town in the 1860s. Today Portland is a busy regional centre with all facilities and a comprehensive shopping centre. 🛈 Portland Maritime Discovery Centre, Lee Breakwater Road; (03) 5523 2671 or 1800 035 567.

6 PORT FAIRY pop. 2625   🅿 PDG
GPS 38° 23.118' S/142° 14.207' E
Port Fairy has a proud seafaring history and commercial abalone, squid and lobster boats still operate out of the picturesque port. The town is a popular holiday destination and has numerous historic buildings. Port Fairy has most services and good shopping. 🛈 Bank Street; (03) 5568 2682; www.greatoceanrd.org.au

PORT FAIRY TO COLAC 141 KM

✪ Ocean Beach Holiday Village, Warrnambool

Across the road from the beach, this well-kept, owner-operated park is ideal for a long holiday or just a few days away. With its excellent facilities including a popular undercover camp kitchen and a new movie room, the park can be busy; it is a good idea to book in holiday periods. (Minimum bookings apply during the Christmas and Easter holidays.) We always enjoy staying here. **For more details see page 393.**

The Stony Rises

Dry stone walls, also known by locals as the Stony Rises, are a special feature of the countryside in the Western District. Most of the walls were built by skilled craftsmen in the 1860s and 1870s, but some date back as far as the 1840s. There are hundreds of kilometres of stone walls still in use in the area today.

What's on

FEBRUARY Wunta Festival (Warrnambool), Tarerer Festival (Warrnambool) MARCH Leura Festival (Camperdown) APRIL Country Music Festival (Colac) APRIL/MAY Irish Festival (Koroit) OCTOBER Warrnambool Agricultural Show

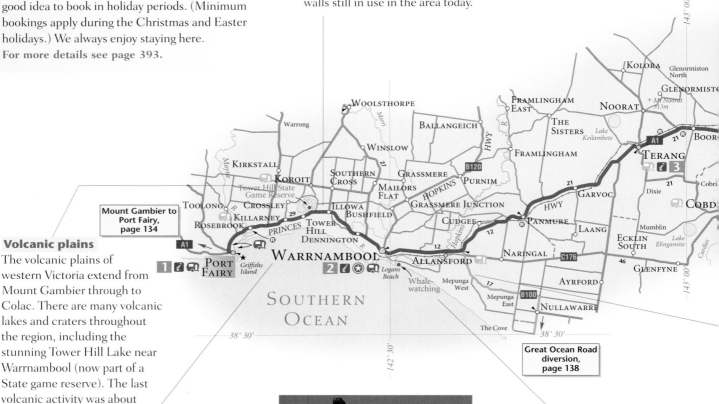

Volcanic plains

The volcanic plains of western Victoria extend from Mount Gambier through to Colac. There are many volcanic lakes and craters throughout the region, including the stunning Tower Hill Lake near Warrnambool (now part of a State game reserve). The last volcanic activity was about 5400 years ago.

Mount Gambier to Port Fairy, page 134

Great Ocean Road diversion, page 138

Re-created maritime village

The unique Flagstaff Hill Maritime Museum complex in Warrnambool is an excellent attraction showcasing the early maritime history of the area and the numerous shipwrecks along the rugged south-west Victorian coastline. There are many replicas of 19th-century buildings, including a town hall, bank and church. 23 Merri Street; (03) 5564 7841; entry fee applies; open 9 a.m. to 5 p.m. daily.

Whale mecca

Logans Beach, just east of Warrnambool, is Victoria's southern right whale nursery. The whales come here to calve between June and September each year. They swim and frolic close to the beach and can be easily viewed from the beach or the specially constructed platform.

Travel tip

The popular holiday centres of Warrnambool and Port Fairy can be extremely busy in the summer and Easter holiday periods. Booking during these periods is essential, so phone ahead to avoid disappointment.

Colac Botanic Gardens

Colac Botanic Gardens, on Gellibrand Street, are situated on the banks of Lake Colac. More than one thousand specimens are included in the gardens, which were listed by the National Trust in 1990.

The unforgettable Great Ocean Road

The Great Ocean Road between Warrnambool and Geelong is a spectacular alternative to the Princes Highway. The coastal scenery, the history of the shipwrecks in the area and the great beaches make this a popular route (see page 138 for more details).

Track notes

The Princes Highway winds through picturesque farming land, often between historic stone walls that give the area a rural Irish feel. The road is well maintained and carries a high level of local traffic. Much of the tourist traffic follows the spectacular Great Ocean Road.

Town file

1 PORT FAIRY (see page 135)

2 WARRNAMBOOL pop. 26 052 PDG
GPS 38° 22.983' S/142° 28.934' E
The city of Warrnambool is a key regional centre and a popular beachside tourist destination. Over one hundred shipwrecks are scattered along the coast to the east and west of town, and the Flagstaff Hill Maritime Museum, which should not be missed, showcases much of this history. Southern right whales visit the coast each winter between June and September, and a whale-watching platform is located to the east of town at Logans Beach. The mysterious *Mahogany Ship*, believed to be a Portuguese caravel last sighted in the 1880s, lies buried in the sands between Warrnambool and Port Fairy, and is often the subject of enthusiastic searches. The Hillside Markets are held at the Showgrounds on the second Sunday of each month. The city has all services and very good shopping. 600 Raglan Parade (Princes Highway); (03) 5564 7837 or 1800 637 725; www.warrnamboolinfo.com.au

3 TERANG pop. 1867 PDG
GPS 38° 14.482' S/142° 55.139' E
The small town of Terang services the local agricultural industry. The National Trust has classified some of the town's beautiful avenues of deciduous trees. Terang has most basic services. Clarke Saddlery, 105 High Street; (03) 5592 1164.

4 CAMPERDOWN pop. 3153 PDG
GPS 38° 13.934' S/143° 08.768' E
Camperdown is located on the side of Mount Leura, a volcanic cone. Nearby, lakes Gnotuk and Bullen Merri are two spectacular crater lakes where fishing for trout and Chinook salmon is popular. Camperdown has most services and good shopping with a craft market held on the first Sunday of each month. Old Courthouse, Manifold Street; (03) 5593 3390.

5 COLAC pop. 9793 PDG
GPS 38° 20.388' S/143° 35.130' E
Colac is a service centre for the surrounding, closely populated agricultural areas and the local timber industry. The town lies on the eastern edge of a volcanic plain that covers most of western Victoria. Lake Colac to the north of town is a large freshwater lake popular for boating and fishing. The town has most services and good shopping. Corner Murray and Queen streets (Princes Highway); (03) 5231 3730.

GREAT OCEAN ROAD DIVERSION 273 KM

Authors' choice

⊛ **Zeally Bay Caravan Park, Torquay**
Great for a family holiday and just across the
road from the beach, this quality caravan
park caters especially for tourists and families.
Facilities include a tennis court and a cafe,
and the park is only 1.2 km north of the
town centre.
For more details see page 391.

The tragic story of the *Loch Ard*

Loch Ard Gorge is named after the three-masted
clipper *Loch Ard*, which was wrecked in 1878 on
Mutton Bird Island, just off the coast near Port
Campbell. There were just two survivors from
the shipwreck, and their amazing story of survival
is told on a signposted walk above the gorge.

What's on

JANUARY Pier to Pub
Swim (Lorne), Agricultural
Show (Apollo Bay) **MARCH**
Music Festival (Apollo Bay)
EASTER Bells Beach
Surfing Classic
DECEMBER High Tide
Festival (Torquay)

The spectacular Twelve Apostles

Among Australia's most photographed
geographic features, the Twelve Apostles
are stunning limestone formations
standing erect in the pounding Southern
Ocean. A visitor information centre offers
tourists an insight into this remarkable
stretch of coast.

Shipwreck coast

The rugged, isolated Cape Otway is the northern landfall on the
treacherous entrance to Bass Strait. During the 19th century many
ships entering the strait foundered along this dangerous coast,
resulting in the loss of more than 160 vessels and countless lives.
Cape Otway Lighthouse began operation in 1848 and is now open
to the public. Entry fee applies; open daily from 9 a.m.

Map labels

Mount Gambier to Port Fairy, page 134

Port Fairy to Colac, page 136

WARRNAMBOOL (see page 136)
PANMURE
Logans Beach
ALLANSFORD
NARINGAL
Mepunga West
AYRFORD
NULLAWARRE
The Cove
NIRRANDA
TIMBOON
Buttress Point
Nirranda South
CURDIE VALE
Paaratte
SOUTHERN
Bay of Islands
Newfield
KENNEDYS CREEK
The Arch
PETERBOROUGH
PORT CAMPBELL
Chapple Vale
BEECH FOREST
Mt Sabine 583m
Grotto
London Bridge
Mutton Bird Island
Gibson Steps
Mt Chapple 550m
Weeaproinah
Tanybryn
OTWAY
Loch Ard Gorge, Blowhole & Thunder Cave
The Twelve Apostles
PRINCETOWN
MELBA GULLY STATE PARK
LAVERS HILL
SKENES CREEK
Paradise
APOLLO BAY
PORT CAMPBELL NATIONAL PARK
Moonlight Head
Point Reginald
Yuulong
Johanna Beach
JOHANNA
Castle Cove
Glenaire
OTWAY NP
MARENGO
OCEAN
OTWAY NATIONAL PARK
Blanket Bay
BA
Cape Otway Lighthouse
Cape Otway

SCALE
0 5 10 15 20 km

N

Travel tip

This is one of Australia's greatest scenic routes. The views are breathtaking, the geographic coastal features awesome, the towns friendly and there is a wide selection of caravan parks. The winter months bring a totally different beauty to the area, but remember to bring your winter woollies! Visit www.greatoceanrd.com.au for more information.

Track notes

The busy Great Ocean Road hugs the coastline, crosses rugged headlands and drifts through farmland and towering forests.

Town file

1 WARRNAMBOOL (see page 137)

2 PORT CAMPBELL pop. 281 🅿 PDG
GPS 38° 37.198' S/142° 59.682' E
Port Campbell is central to a fabulous stretch of coast that includes the Twelve Apostles, Loch Ard Gorge, London Bridge and sheer limestone cliffs. With several shipwrecks nearby, diving is popular. The town has basic facilities. 🅘 26 Morris Street; (03) 5598 6053 or 1300 137 255.

3 APOLLO BAY pop. 979 🅿 PDG
GPS 38° 45.300' S/143° 40.141' E
Tucked between the Otway Ranges and rugged coastline, this picturesque village boasts a number of galleries, gift shops and cafes. Fishing and exploring the Otway forests are two popular pastimes. Fresh seafood is available from the Fisherman's Cooperative on the jetty. 🅘 Great Ocean Road Visitor Information Centre, 100 Great Ocean Road; (03) 5237 6529.

4 LORNE pop. 1082 🅿 PDG
GPS 38° 32.501' S/143° 58.521' E
Lorne has beautiful beaches, an exquisite gallery and boutiques, and a variety of entertainment. It is a great base from which to explore the Otways and the hinterland. 🅘 144 Mountjoy Parade; (03) 5289 1152.

5 AIREYS INLET pop. 761 🅿 PDG
GPS 38° 27.536' S/144° 06.410' E
Aireys Inlet is ideal for a relaxing holiday. The main landmark, Split Point Lighthouse, was built in 1891 and still operates. There is a 3.5-km cliff-top walk between the lighthouse and Sunnymeade Beach with fabulous views. The nearby coastal heathland has abundant wildflowers in spring.

6 ANGLESEA pop. 1995 🅿 PDG
GPS 38° 24.303' S/ 144° 11.344' E
Anglesea has a wide, sandy beach great for swimming and surfing, while the more protected waters at Point Roadknight are popular with families. The local golf course, set in native bushland, is dotted with kangaroos that happily graze on the wide green fairways.

7 TORQUAY pop. 5984 🅿 PDG
GPS 38° 19.915' S/144° 19.404' E
Torquay is close to the great surfing beaches, Jan Juc and Bells. Its Surf City Plaza has numerous stores selling surf apparel and equipment. The centre also houses the Surfworld Museum – a fabulous interactive experience. 🅘 Surf City Plaza, Beach Road; (03) 5261 4219.

8 GEELONG (see page 141)

Carvings that tell a tale
Worth a look are the large woodcarvings that adorn the foreshore park alongside the visitor information centre in Apollo Bay. Carved from local wood, each piece depicts an aspect of the region's relationship with the sea.

COLAC TO WERRIBEE 113 KM

Authors' choice

✪ Beacon Resort, Queenscliff

This is one of Victoria's few five-star caravan parks. The award-winning establishment has all the trimmings you would expect from a five-star park, including very good recreational facilities – an indoor heated swimming pool and tennis courts. In addition to all this, it is just a short walk to the beach.

For more details see page 385.

Travel tip

Market gardens in Werribee South grow a wide range of vegetables. Take a drive through the area and buy fresh in-season produce at the farm gate. Also worth a visit are the wineries on the Bellarine Peninsula. There are now some 20 wineries there, with a number offering sales to the public.

Historic mansion

Located in Werribee Park is a historic 60-room mansion, built in the 1870s and opulently furnished in the style and time of the original occupants. It is now a fascinating museum and worth a visit. Also at Werribee Park is the Victoria State Rose Garden. K Road; (03) 9741 2444; entry fee applies; open 10 a.m. to 5 p.m. daily, 10 a.m. to 4 p.m. in winter.

Coastal diversion

For a scenic alternative route, drive the coastal loop around the Bellarine Peninsula, travelling through the seaside towns of Barwon Heads (where the popular TV series *SeaChange* was filmed), Ocean Grove, Queenscliff and Portarlington. To take this scenic diversion, turn off onto the B100 route shortly before Geelong and head towards Torquay. Soon after turn left onto the Barwon Heads road.

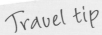

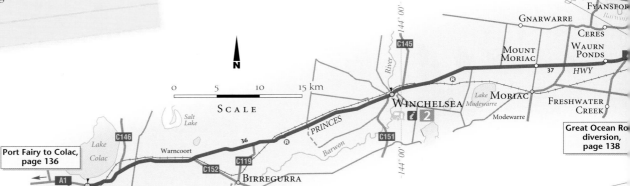

Fort tours

Fort Queenscliff, protecting the entrance to Port Phillip, was built in 1882 as a strategic part of Victoria's defence from a feared foreign invasion. Tours of the well-preserved fort are held on weekends, public holidays and school holidays. King Street; (03) 5258 1488; entry fee applies.

Open range zoo

Werribee Zoo showcases a range of animals, including rhinoceros, giraffes, zebras, antelopes, monkeys and cheetahs, on 200 ha of parkland. Join a guided tour to view these marvellous animals up close. K Road; (03) 9731 9600; entry fee applies; open 9 a.m. to 5 p.m. daily.

Ferry trip

The Queenscliff to Sorrento Ferry is a great way of bypassing Melbourne. The drive-on, drive-off ferry operates six or more times daily. The crossing takes around 50 minutes. Larkin Parade, Queenscliff; (03) 5258 3244; fee applies.

What's on

FEBRUARY Australian International Airshow (Avalon Airport, Geelong, odd-numbered years) MARCH/APRIL The Otway Harvest Festival (Colac) APRIL Country Carnival (Winchelsea) JUNE National Wool Week (Geelong) OCTOBER Bellarine Food and Wine Fair (Drysdale) NOVEMBER Queenscliff Music Festival

Track notes

Between Colac and Geelong the route is well maintained and sealed, winding through farming country. Overtaking lanes are common and the highway carries local traffic and large transports travelling to and from the south-west of the State. The highway between Geelong and Werribee is a divided multi-lane road, bypassing the two cities.

Town file

1 COLAC (see page 137)

2 WINCHELSEA pop. 1027   🅿 PDG
GPS 38° 14.600' S/143° 59.400' E
Winchelsea is a small community on the Princes Highway mainly servicing the surrounding farming area. It has a couple of lovely galleries and the historic Barwon Bridge, opened in 1867, with its graceful stone arches. The town has basic services and a small selection of shops. 🛈 Old Shire Hall Tearooms, Princes Highway; (03) 5267 2769.

3 GEELONG pop. 125 382   🅿 PDG
GPS 38° 08.916' S/144° 21.439' E
Located on the western shore of Corio Bay, Geelong is Victoria's largest provincial city. It is an industrial city with a large shipping and export grain terminal, and is home to the Ford Motor Company's engine plant. The city is less than an hour's drive from Melbourne. All services are available and there are a number of shopping centres. 🛈 Stead Park, Corio (on Princes Highway); (03) 5275 5797 or 1800 620 888.

4 QUEENSCLIFF pop. 3832   🅿 PDG
GPS 38° 16.046' S/144° 39.668' E
The beachside holiday resort of Queenscliff lies on the western side of the entrance to Port Phillip. Both the Maritime Museum and Queenscliff Fort are popular attractions. The town has good restaurants and shops, and offers basic facilities. 🛈 55 Hesse Street; (03) 5258 4843.

5 PORTARLINGTON pop. 2407   🅿 PDG
GPS 38° 06.896' S/144° 39.108' E
On the Bellarine Peninsula, Portarlington is a popular tourist destination during the summer and Easter holidays. The bayside beach is a safe family beach and popular fishing area. The local caravan park is one of the largest we have found. Portarlington is only 29 km from the city of Geelong.

6 WERRIBEE pop. 23 461   🅿 PDG
GPS 37° 54.191' S/144° 39.484' E
Werribee is a satellite city, bypassed by the freeway, midway between Geelong and Melbourne. The town has a large shopping centre and all community services. Extensive market gardens to the south of the town grow a range of fresh vegetables. The historic mansion at Werribee Park and the Werribee Zoo adjoin the State Equestrian Centre in Werribee South. Werribee South is situated in a picturesque location on the shores of Port Phillip and is a popular picnic area.

MELBOURNE
YOUR GUIDE

Described as the world's most livable city, Melbourne is a vibrant and multi-cultural metropolis offering great restaurants, excellent shopping and world-class sporting venues. It also boasts stunning new buildings, tree-lined boulevards and magnificent public gardens. Situated at the head of Port Phillip and centred on the north bank of the Yarra River, the city has a population of about 3.4 million. Visitors will find there is always something happening in Melbourne, whether it be a lively festival or a major sporting event.

CITY CENTRE

See map on page 145.

The Block Arcade 145 C5
The oldest arcade in Australia, with a mosaic floor, glass and iron-lace roof and stylish shops, including tearooms.

Chinatown 145 D4
Packed with fascinating restaurants, shops and a fine museum.

Crown Entertainment Complex 145 B6
Shop, wine and dine or have a flutter at the casino.

Federation Square 145 D5
Shops, restaurants, the National Gallery of Victoria and the Australian Centre for the Moving Image.

Fitzroy Gardens 145 F4
Beautiful gardens with Captain Cook's Cottage, the Fairy Tree and Model Tudor Village.

Ian Potter Centre: National Gallery of Victoria 145 D5
A fine collection of Australian and international masterpieces at the new Federation Square site.

Koorie Heritage Centre 145 D3
An insight into Victorian Aboriginal cultural life.

Melbourne Aquarium 145 B6
The magic of marine life – over 270 species from the Southern Ocean and inland waterways.

Melbourne Central 145 C4
Huge retail complex featuring a 20-storey glass cone that encloses a historic shot tower.

Melbourne Cricket Ground (MCG) 145 F5
The hallowed venue for Australian-rules football and national and international cricket; also contains the Australian Gallery of Sport, an Olympic Museum and a Melbourne Cricket Club Museum.

Melbourne Museum 145 D2
A superb introduction to Melbourne and Australia.

Old Melbourne Gaol 145 C3
Contains chillingly macabre exhibits, including the gallows where Ned Kelly swung.

Queen Victoria Market 145 B3
A large range of fresh fish, meat, fruit, vegetables and delicatessen lines along with clothing and general merchandise are on offer at this Melbourne landmark; open Tuesdays and Thursdays to Sundays.

Rialto Towers Observation Deck 145 B5
Stunning 360-degree views of the city from Australia's tallest building.

Royal Botanic Gardens 145 F8
Melbourne's showpiece and considered to be among the best in the world.

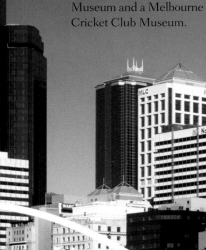

Visitor information

Melbourne Visitor Information Centre
Melbourne Town Hall
Corner Swanston and Little Collins streets
(03) 9658 9658

Information kiosks
Flinders Street Station and Bourke Street Mall

Victorian Tourism Information Service
13 28 42
www.melbourne.vic.gov.au
www.visitvictoria.com

St Patrick's Cathedral 145 E3
Massive 19th-century bluestone building, and one of the world's best examples of Gothic Revival architecture.

Southgate 145 C6
Riverside promenade with restaurants, shops, wine bars and outdoor eating areas, along with fabulous sculptures.

State Library of Victoria 145 C3
Begun in 1854 and completed in 1913, the library holds more than one million books.

Victoria Police Museum 145 A6
Houses memorabilia from some of Victoria's most famous criminal cases, including Ned Kelly's armour.

Victorian Arts Centre 145 D6
Contains three theatres, the Performing Arts Museum and the George Adams Gallery.

SUBURBS AND SURROUNDS
See map on pages 146–7.

Dandenong Ranges 147 I4
Scenic hills and native rainforests only 50 km from city; extensive gardens, galleries, and craft shops for leisurely browsing.

Gulf Station 147 J2
Oldest working farm in the Yarra Valley, first occupied in the 1850s, with old slab-timber farmhouse, stables, barns, animals and early farm implements and machinery.

Healesville Sanctuary 147 K2
The 32-ha wildlife sanctuary is world-renowned, with over 200 animal and bird species.

Melbourne Cemetery 146 F4
Dating back to the 1850s; explore Melbourne's history on a guided tour.

Melbourne Zoo 146 F4
An essential stop for animal lovers; see the magnificent butterfly house and walk the 'people cage' through the lions' enclosure.

Montsalvat 147 G3
An artists' colony established in the 1930s, featuring medieval-style buildings and with residents' artworks and crafts for sale; a popular jazz festival is held each January.

Museum of Modern Art at Heide 147 G3
Set in the tranquil parklands of Bulleen, one of Australia's most renowned art spaces, housing a collection of the great Australian modernists and new artists.

Top events

The Australian Open (January)
Grand Slam tennis excitement.

The Australian Formula One Grand Prix (March)
The fastest fun around.

Moomba Festival (March)
The idea of Moomba is just to enjoy yourself.

Melbourne Food and Wine Festival (March)
Taste the best of the world's food and wine.

Melbourne International Comedy Festival (April)
International and local laughs.

AFL Grand Final (September)
Heroes of the footy field battle it out.

Royal Melbourne Show (September)
The country comes to the city.

Melbourne Festival (October)
Celebrating the city's heart and soul, with art, dance, opera and theatre.

Spring Racing Carnival (October–November)
Includes the Melbourne Cup.

MELBOURNE (CONTINUED)

YOUR GUIDE

Organ Pipes National Park
146 D2
An 85-ha park named after its unusual 20-m wall of basalt columns; they were formed over one million years ago from lava flow from local volcanoes.

Puffing Billy Railway 147 I5
Old-fashioned steam train with open carriages and restaurant car that travels 25 km through forest from Belgrave to Gembrook and back again.

Rippon Lea 146 F5
National Trust Romanesque mansion with 5 ha of beautiful English-style landscaped gardens and resident peacocks.

St Kilda 146 F5
Lively beachside suburb that hosts an art and craft market on the Esplanade every Sunday; Acland Street is famous for its continental cake shops.

Scienceworks 146 E4
Exciting interactive science and technology museum, with new Planetarium, and Australia's first plane and car on display.

Studley Park Boathouse
146 F4
Hire a boat or just sit by the Yarra and enjoy the Devonshire teas and bush atmosphere.

William Ricketts Sanctuary
147 I4
William Ricketts lived and worked at this mountain-side sanctuary until his death at age 94; his sculptures, scattered through the forest, were inspired by Aboriginal people and their affinity with nature.

Williamstown 146 E5
Take a ferry from St Kilda to Melbourne's oldest suburb, a former maritime village with quaint pubs, churches and cottages.

Yarra Valley 147 J2
Good scenery, excellent wineries, fine food outlets, historic gardens and forest.

Getting around

The city centre is easy to explore, with its wide streets laid out in a grid system. Parking in the centre consists of mainly short-term parking meters and undercover carparks, which at peak times can be difficult to find or expensive. Outside the centre there is usually no problem finding a parking spot.

Public transport is excellent, particularly the tram system. There are free City Circle trams around the perimeter of the central grid, in both directions. Normal tram services criss-cross the city on their way to the suburbs. The main terminus for the suburban train lines is Flinders Street Station. Trains from here go round an underground loop that can be used instead of the City Circle tram to explore Melbourne. Buses cover major routes that are not reached by trams or trains.

A good way to explore the city is on the City Wanderer (summer only) or the City Explorer, the former extending as far as the Westgate Bridge and Williamstown. Both buses operate daily.

The Yarra River has a variety of tour boats, including water taxis and ferries. Many are moored at Southgate or Princes Bridge, and destinations include Williamstown, St Kilda and the bay.

Airport shuttle bus Skybus (03) 9335 3066; **CityLink** A toll road linking the Tullamarine, West Gate and Monash freeways. There are no toll booths. Travellers can buy an e-TAG or a Day Pass, or pay by credit card afterwards, within 24 hours of making a journey. Prices vary and motorhomes and commercial vehicles, including utilities, cost more. There is no additional fee for towing a caravan. Call 13 26 29; **Motoring organisation** RACV 13 19 55; **Public transport** Trams, including free City Circle trams, suburban trains and buses 13 16 38; **Tourist Bus** City Explorer, City Wanderer (03) 9563 9788; **Taxis** Bay City Cabs Combined 13 22 27, Embassy 13 17 55, Northern Suburban 13 11 19, Silver Top 13 10 08, West Suburban (03) 9689 1144; **Yarra River boat trips** Melbourne River Cruises (03) 9629 7233, Southbank Cruises (03) 9645 9944, Williamstown Bay and River Cruises (03) 9682 9555, Penguin Waters Cruises (03) 9386 2986.

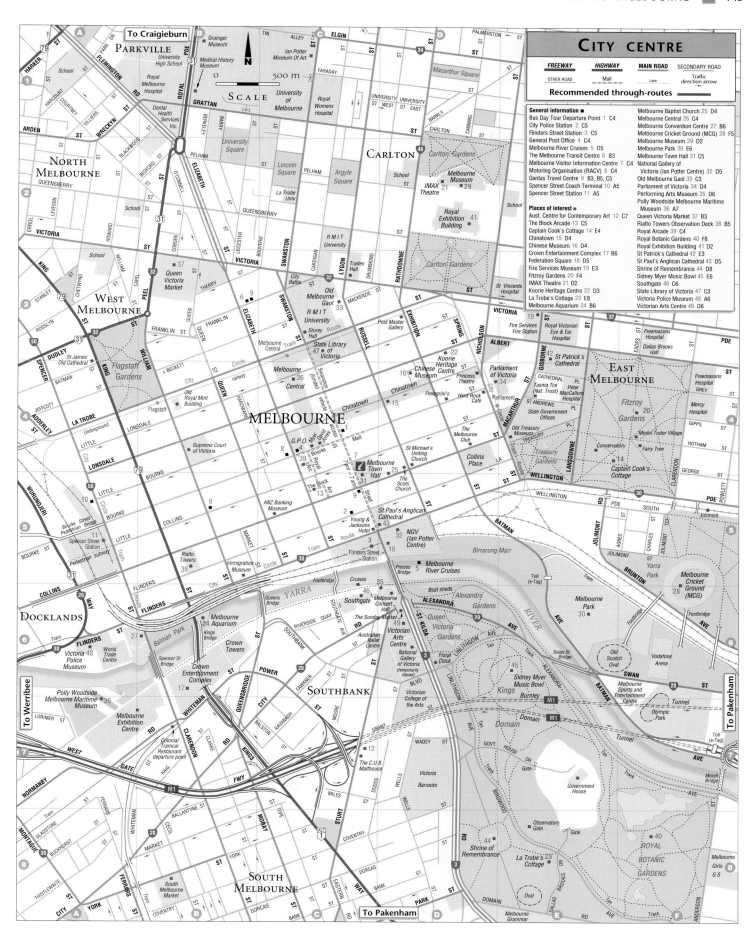

SUBURBS AND SURROUNDS

Recommended through-routes
Main roads, sealed   unsealed
Other roads, sealed   unsealed

Melton to Ballarat,
page 228

Craigieburn
to Shepparton,
page 152

Colac to Werribee,
page 140

SCALE
0   2   4   6   8   10 km

N

Pakenham to Sale,
page 4

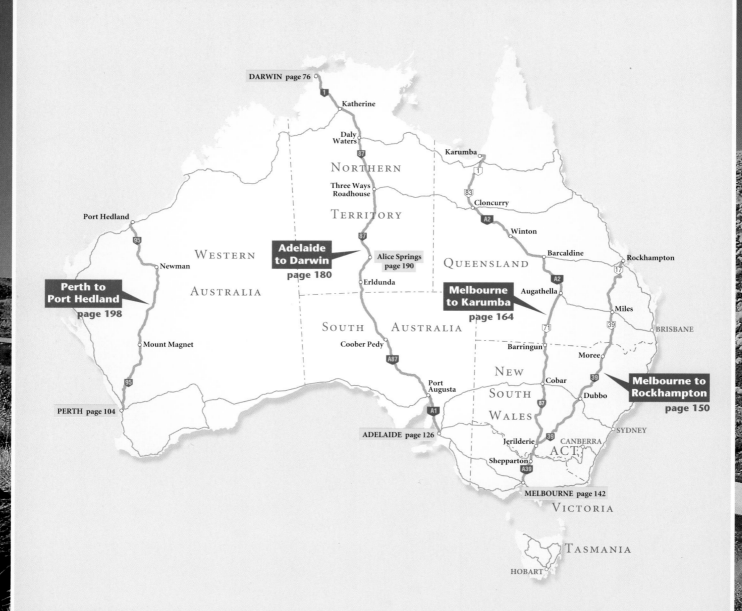

Chapter 2

Great inland highways: south–north

GETTING AS FAR north or south as possible is at the top of many people's holiday agendas, and there are some great highways that can get you to these distant spots.

In the east, Route 39 links Melbourne with Rockhampton. It winds through Victorian dairy country and onwards to the rice-producing area of southern New South Wales. From there it passes the magnificent Warrumbungles before entering Queensland. Cotton crops and mining towns fill the view before the road leads to the wonderful tropical coast. If Rockhampton is not as far north as you would like, then there is another route through Queensland's outback to Karumba, a major fishing port nestled in the Gulf of Carpentaria.

You cannot miss the Adelaide to Darwin route, the road that cuts up through the middle of the continent. The deep-ochre outback and the royal-blue skies are a visual feast, but just wait until you get to Uluru, that giant red monolith rising out of the flat Central Australian landscape.

In the west of the country, the Great Northern Highway links Perth with Port Hedland on an inland route. Journey through grain-growing territory and, if you have timed your trip accordingly, through endless wildflowers. Before you hit Port Hedland, the gorges and the rust-red hills of the Pilbara will take your breath away.

MELBOURNE TO ROCKHAMPTON

HUME FREEWAY, GOULBURN VALLEY HIGHWAY, NEWELL HIGHWAY, LEICHHARDT HIGHWAY, BURN

If you are heading north from Melbourne, one of your choices is to travel on Route 39, a major inland highway network linking Melbourne and the central Queensland coast. The route spans three States, crosses some of Australia's important rivers and links many of our great agricultural regions. Along the way you will pass dairy farms and fruit orchards in the Goulburn Valley, extensive rice fields in the Riverina, manicured cotton fields in northern New South Wales and Queensland, and some of Australia's most productive cattle country.

Dubbo to Moree
The Warrumbungle Range stands starkly on the horizon as the highway approaches Coonabarabran. The Warrumbungle National Park and the two nearby observatories are popular tourist attractions. North of Coonabarabran the highway sweeps through the enormous Pilliga Nature Reserve.

Jerilderie to Dubbo
The Newell Highway links Narrandera, West Wyalong, Forbes, Parkes and Dubbo, all of which are important regional centres servicing the surrounding grazing and cropping region. The Western Plains Zoo at Dubbo is a great tourist destination.

Shepparton to Jerilderie
Crossing the Murray River at Tocumwal, the highway leaves the northern Victorian dairy country and enters a large rice-producing area. Jerilderie's visitor information centre has a detailed history of the Kelly Gang, who robbed the bank here in 1879.

Melbourne
Melbourne is a vibrant and multicultural metropolis offering great restaurants, excellent shopping, tree-lined boulevards and magnificent gardens.

Craigieburn to Shepparton
The busy Hume Freeway heads north from Melbourne, bypassing towns. The road gradually climbs through the ranges and passes some of the State's notable vineyards before reaching Shepparton.

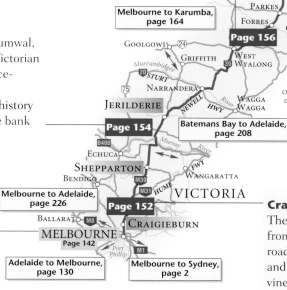

Rockhampton to Three Ways Roadhouse, page 256

Brisbane to Cair page 42

Brisbane to Augathella, page 248

Melbourne to Karumba, page 164

Sydney to Adelaide, page 234

Batemans Bay to Adelaide, page 208

Melbourne to Adelaide, page 226

Adelaide to Melbourne, page 130

Melbourne to Sydney, page 2

GHWAY (1964 KM)

Miles to Rockhampton

The Leichhardt Highway winds north from Miles, skirts the central Queensland coalfields, and links the historic mining town of Mount Morgan with Rockhampton on the coastal plain. Rockhampton is a major Queensland coastal city and at the centre of Australia's beef cattle industry.

Moree to Miles

Moree is surrounded by fertile, black-soil plains supporting thriving cotton fields where the crops reach the highway's edge. Further north across the Queensland border, the route drifts through broadacre farms and large cattle properties.

Best time to go

While this is a busy route year-round, traffic increases between April and November as travellers drift north to escape the southern winter. The temperatures climb during the summer months.

John & Jan

NARRANDERA

	J	F	M	A	M	J	J	A	S	O	N	D
Maximum	32	32	28	23	19	15	14	16	19	23	27	30
Minimum	17	17	14	10	7	4	3	4	6	9	12	15
Rainfall (mm)	41	35	32	45	48	39	40	46	45	51	37	37
Raindays	5	4	4	6	8	9	9	10	9	8	6	5

MILES

	J	F	M	A	M	J	J	A	S	O	N	D
Maximum	33	32	31	27	23	20	19	21	25	29	31	33
Minimum	20	19	.17	12	8	5	4	5	9	13	16	18
Rainfall (mm)	97	74	59	37	41	39	39	29	32	55	66	89
Raindays	8	7	6	4	4	5	5	4	4	6	7	8

The Breadknife, Warrumbungle National Park

CRAIGIEBURN TO SHEPPARTON 151 KM

Authors' choice

⊛ Victoria Lake Holiday Park, Shepparton

Set on the shores of Lake Victoria, this picturesque park is centrally located on the main highway 1 km south of the city centre (although there are long-term plans to construct a bypass around Shepparton). With good facilities and great waterfront sites, it is the park we like to stay at when in Shepparton.

For more details see page 387.

Award-winning wines

The Goulburn Valley is home to Mitchelton Wines, with an art gallery at its cellar door, and the historic Tahbilk Winery and Vineyard (pictured), dating from 1860, plus other boutique wineries. Some wineries serve food, giving visitors a complete gourmet experience. Mitchelton Wines, Mitchellstown Road; (03) 5794 2710; cellar door open 10 a.m. to 5 p.m. daily. Tahbilk Winery and Vineyard, off Goulburn Valley Highway; (03) 5794 2555; cellar door open 9 a.m. to 5 p.m. Monday to Saturday, 11 a.m. to 5 p.m. Sunday and public holidays.

Scenic lake

Lake Nagambie was formed by the construction of the Goulburn Weir in 1891 and the town is laid out picturesquely along the lake's shore. It is a popular recreation and water-sports destination, where regular rowing regattas and water-ski events are held.

Shepparton to Jerilderie, page 154

What's on

FEBRUARY Bush Market Day (Shepparton) MARCH Seymour Rafting Festival, Toolamba Pumpkin Festival (Shepparton), Shepparton Arts Festival JUNE Celtic Festival (Kilmore)

Craigieburn to Melbourne (24 km)
For connecting routes, see map of Melbourne suburbs and surrounds, pages 146–7

Travel tip

Whether heading off on holiday, on an around-Australia trip or just north to beat the southern winter, you should stop in Shepparton and Mooroopna for bargains at the Ardmona and SPC factory outlets respectively. On our last around-Australia odyssey we loaded several cases of fruit into our Winnebago. We love those Goulburn Valley peaches!

Fine Australian ceramics

The Shepparton Art Gallery is world renowned for its ceramics collection. Here you will see works by the Boyd family, the Bendigo Pottery and many Aboriginal ceramic artists. Its prestigious biennial Sidney Myer Fund International Ceramics Award attracts entries from many countries. Civic Centre, Welsford Street; (03) 5832 9861; open 10 a.m. to 4 p.m. daily, 1 p.m. to 4 p.m. public holidays.

Discount fruit

Local food processors Ardmona and SPC have factory sales outlets where you can buy their products at considerable discounts. It is a good idea to stop if passing through the area and stock up with their fruit. Ardmona, McLennan Street (Midland Highway), Mooroopna; (03) 5825 2444; open 9 a.m. to 5 p.m. daily. SPC, Andrew Fairley Avenue, Shepparton; (03) 5833 3777; open 9 a.m. to 5 p.m. daily.

Track notes

The Hume Freeway and Goulburn Valley Highway are major interstate routes carrying heavy traffic. The Goulburn Valley Highway is well surfaced but still mainly two lanes. Heavier traffic sometimes makes overtaking a little difficult, although the traffic usually flows well.

Town file

1 CRAIGIEBURN pop. 12 919   🅿 PDG
GPS 37° 35.526' S/144° 56.491' E
Craigieburn, once an outlying community, is now linked with the northern suburbs of Melbourne and is a densely populated residential suburb.

2 KILMORE pop. 2710   🅿 PDG
GPS 37° 17.518' S/144° 57.060' E
Settled in 1841, Kilmore is Victoria's oldest inland town, with numerous historic buildings. The area is well known for horse breeding and training. Small rural residential lots have developed here, with many residents commuting to work in Melbourne. On the Northern Highway, Kilmore has most services and good country-town shopping. 🛈 Kilmore Library, 12 Sydney Street; (03) 5781 1319.

3 SEYMOUR pop. 6294   🅿 PDG
GPS 37° 01.493' S/145° 08.147' E
Seymour is a regional centre with most services and good shopping, bypassed by the freeway. A few kilometres from town is the Puckapunyal Military Base, an important training centre for World War II soldiers and national servicemen until the 1970s. It is still a major military base and home to the Army Tank Museum. 🛈 Old Court House, Emily Street; (03) 5799 0233.

4 NAGAMBIE pop. 1335   🅿 PDG
GPS 36° 47.114' S/145° 09.237' E
Nagambie is a service centre for a diverse range of agriculture including dairying, vineyards, orchards, sheep and cattle grazing and grain growing. Some buildings in the town have been classified by the National Trust. Nagambie has most services and a good country-town selection of shops. 🛈 145 High Street; (03) 5794 2647.

5 SHEPPARTON pop. 31 945   🅿 PDG
GPS 36° 22.813' S/145° 23.973' E
Shepparton is a large, multicultural regional centre. The irrigated surrounds have a reputation for quality fruit and dairy produce; some of Australia's largest food processors are located in the area. Shepparton has all services, excellent shopping and a good range of accommodation and restaurants. Victoria Park Lake, close to the centre of the city, is popular for picnics. There is a craft market in Queens Gardens on the third Sunday of each month. 🛈 534 Wyndham Street; (03) 5831 4400 or 1800 808 839.

SHEPPARTON TO JERILDERIE 143 KM

Authors' choice

⊛ **Boomerang Way Tourist Park, Tocumwal**

This well-cared-for, owner-operated park is 500 m from the centre of Tocumwal and away from the highway's noise. The park has a large swimming pool as well as a covered barbecue area and is ideal both for an overnight stay or an entire holiday. Minimum bookings apply during the Christmas, January and Easter holiday periods. **For more details see page 390.**

Rice paddies

You will see fields of rice if you drive through here in spring and summer, for the irrigated region from the Murray River north to Griffith is a major rice-growing area. Seeds are usually planted by aircraft beginning in October; the crops reach maturity and harvesting starts in late February. Harvested rice is transported by road to local mills.

Camp beside the Murray

Parks and reserves along the Victorian bank of the Murray River, including the Tocumwal Regional Park, are managed by Parks Victoria. Most areas are available for camping, subject to guidelines. For more information ring Parks Victoria on 13 19 63.

What's on

JANUARY Country Music Festival (Finley), Rodeo (Finley) FEBRUARY Jerilderie Show JUNE Country Craft Fiesta (Tocumwal) DECEMBER Murray River Marathon (passes through Tocumwal)

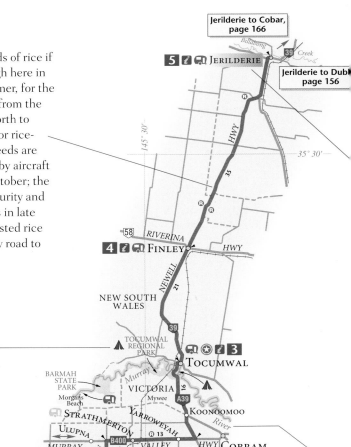

Jerilderie to Cobar, page 166

Jerilderie to Dubb, page 156

5 🚐 ℹ 🚗 JERILDERIE

4 ℹ 🚗 FINLEY 58 RIVERINA HWY

NEW SOUTH WALES

TOCUMWAL REGIONAL PARK

🚗 ⊛ ℹ **3** TOCUMWAL

BARMAH STATE PARK

Morgans Beach

VICTORIA

Mywee

STRATHMERTON YARROWEYAH KOONOOMOO

ULUPNA VALLEY COBRAM

MURRAY

Albury to Echuca, page 218

Baulkamaugh

KATUNGA

WAAIA

NUMURKAH 🚐 ℹ **2**

Broken Creek

WUNGHNU

Mundoona

MARUNGI

BUNBARTHA TALLYGAROOPNA SCALE

0 5 10 15 km

ZEERUST

CONGUPNA

Lemnos

Craigieburn to Shepparton, page 152

MOOROOPNA Ardmona River SHEPPARTON 🚐 ⊛ ℹ **1**
(see page 152)

Travel tip

Where to dine out is often a difficult decision in an unknown town. Licensed clubs often have bistros and some even have fine-dining restaurants. Clubs welcome genuine travellers to their facilities. We enjoy a meal at the Tocumwal Golf Club when in the area.

Kelly country

The Kelly Gang held up Jerilderie's Bank of New South Wales in 1879. Here Ned dictated the famous document known as the 'Jerilderie Letter', in which he outlined how the authorities had mistreated the Kelly family, admitted crimes he had committed and denied some he had been blamed for. See Kelly memorabilia at the Willows museum and historic home. 11 Powell Street; (03) 5886 1666; open 10 a.m. to 2 p.m. Wednesdays and weekends, and the first Monday of each month.

The 'big one'

Most people fishing in the Murray River system are usually out to catch the 'big one', a Murray cod. These fish are a sought-after catch but a meal of golden perch (yellow-belly) or redfin is delicious also. You will need a New South Wales fishing licence to fish the Murray River. Other fishing regulations may apply, such as bag and size limits; check with the local fisheries office or visitor information centre for up-to-date information.

Track notes

This route is the interstate link between Melbourne and Brisbane; both the Goulburn Valley and Newell highways thus carry a large volume of traffic including heavy transports. Road trains are permitted between Tocumwal and Morundah (north of Jerilderie). The road passes through the northern Goulburn Valley where dairy farming and orchards predominate, then crosses the Murray River at Tocumwal where rice fields soon become evident.

Town file

1 SHEPPARTON (see page 153)

2 NUMURKAH pop. 3128   PDG
GPS 36° 05.434' S/145° 26.540' E
Numurkah is the centre of local government for an irrigated dairying area that was developed by the Murray River Valley Settlers scheme. The town has most services and a good shopping centre. The Goulburn Valley Highway skirts the edge of town. ❓ 25 Quinn Street; (03) 5862 3458.

3 TOCUMWAL pop. 1453   PDG
GPS 35° 48.731' S/145° 34.033' E
Once a river port, this township has most services and a small shopping strip. Tocumwal is a popular holiday centre with miles of Murray River bends where holiday-makers camp. It has a 36-hole golf course and is the perfect place for a relaxing holiday. The largest World War II aerodrome in the Southern Hemisphere was in Tocumwal, and was used for training Liberator bomber crews: today it is an important gliding centre. ❓ Foreshore Park; (03) 5874 2131 or 1800 677 271.

4 FINLEY pop. 2137   PDG
GPS 35° 38.397' S/145° 34.729' E
Finley, at the crossroads of the Newell and Riverina highways, is at the centre of a diverse agricultural region with a mixture of irrigated and dry-land farming. The town has most basic services and a good selection of shops. ❓ Finley and District Historical Museum and Log Cabin, Newell Highway; (03) 5883 2195.

5 JERILDERIE pop. 871   PDG
GPS 35° 21.364' S/145° 43.663' E
Jerilderie lies on the banks of the Billabong Creek in a rich farming region: wool, rice, wheat, canola, beans, onions, tomatoes and grapes are all grown locally. The Kelly Gang visited Jerilderie in 1879. The telegraph station, where the gang cut communications, still stands. The town has most services and a selection of shops. ❓ The Willows, 11 Powell Street; (03) 5886 1666.

JERILDERIE TO DUBBO 504 KM

Authors' choice

✪ Forbes River Meadows Caravan Park, Forbes

Located about 1.5 km south of Forbes, alongside the highway, this owner-operated park is a convenient and ideal overnight stop. It has shady trees, large expanses of lawn, spotless amenities and a pool. We like staying here.
For more details see page 366.

✪ Dubbo City Caravan Park, Dubbo

Enjoy the sights of Dubbo from this quality park. Conveniently located on the Newell Highway about 2 km from the city centre and just a short drive from the Western Plains Zoo, this park has a selection of accommodation, plush lawns and good facilities, including a car-washing bay.
For more details see page 364.

What's on

MARCH Lachlan River Carp-a-thon (Forbes) MAY Agricultural Show (Dubbo) AUGUST Jazz Festival (Dubbo) SEPTEMBER Agricultural Show (Forbes), Rodeo (West Wyalong) OCTOBER Country Music Spectacular (Parkes)

A bushranger's resting place

Visit the Forbes Cemetery to see the grave of famous bushranger Ben Hall. He was leader of one of the most feared gangs of the mid-19th century, holding up mail coaches, plundering hotels and shops, even holding a police magistrate for ransom. Hall died, aged only 28, in a shoot-out with police at Billabong Creek near Forbes in 1865. Bogan Gate Road.

Dubbo to Moree, page 158
Dubbo to Cobar, page 242
Orange to Du[bbo] page 240
(see page 242)
Jerilderie to Cobar, page 166
Jerilderie to Cobar, page 166
Shepparton to Jerilderie, page 154

The dish

The Parkes Observatory, with its famous radio telescope, is 25 km north of Parkes. The dish (64 m in diameter) has been probing outer space for radio emissions since 1961, and played a vital part in tracking the Apollo moon landings. Stop in at the adjacent Australia Telescope Visitors Centre for videos and a 3-D show, explaining radio astronomy. (02) 6861 1776; admission free but entry fee applies to theatre presentations; open 8.30 a.m. to 4.30 p.m. daily.

Stone cells and convicts' chains

The Old Dubbo Gaol offers a fascinating self-guided tour through an 1870s gaol that operated until 1966. See the original gallows, stop a moment in the solitary confinement cell, and listen while animatronic models tell the convicts' stories. Macquarie Street (next to the Colonial Bank); (02) 6882 8122; entry fee applies; open 9 a.m. to 5 p.m. daily.

A great zoo

Home to over a thousand animals from across the world in more than 300 ha of bushland, the Western Plains Zoo is justifiably one of the State's most popular inland attractions. It is well worth a visit and definitely our favourite attraction in the area. Obley Road (off Newell Highway); (02) 6882 5888; entry fee applies; open 9 a.m. to 5 p.m. daily.

Travel tip

Dubbo is about midway between Melbourne and Brisbane. Between April and October, large demands are placed on facilities; it is sometimes difficult to find accommodation or sites. We recommend calling ahead to reserve a spot. It is not necessary to organise days in advance but do ring to book the next evening's accommodation.

Track notes

The Newell Highway carries tourists, locals and heavy transports, although road trains are not permitted between Morundah and Dubbo. This enjoyable drive passes through scenic country.

Town file

1 JERILDERIE (see page 155)

2 NARRANDERA pop. 4678 🅿 PDG
GPS 34° 44.823' S/146° 33.183' E
On the Murrumbidgee River, Narrandera, with most services and good shops, supplies an irrigated agricultural area. Look out for the meticulously restored Tiger Moth. 🅸 Cadell Street (Newell Highway); (02) 6959 1766 or 1800 672 392.

3 WEST WYALONG pop. 3419 🅿 PDG
GPS 33° 55.416' S/147° 12.306' E
This former goldmining town has most services, and shops line the famous crooked Main Street, formed from bullock tracks that wound through the diggings. 🅸 89–91 Main Street; (02) 6972 3645.

4 FORBES pop. 7467 🅿 PDG
GPS 33° 23.118' S/148° 00.468' E
The 1861 discovery of gold brought prospectors flooding to Forbes. The town's historic features include the Albion Hotel, formerly a Cobb & Co. office, plus a network of tunnels used to move gold from local banks to coaches. Forbes has all services and good shopping. 🅸 Old Railway Station, Union Street; (02) 6852 4155; www.forbes.nsw.gov.au

5 PARKES pop. 10 094 🅿 PDG
GPS 33° 08.327' S/148° 10.441' E
Parkes is at the centre of a rich farming region. Again, its beginnings were linked with gold: the Northparkes Mine still produces gold and copper. Parkes has all services and good shopping. 🅸 Kelly Reserve, Newell Highway; (02) 6862 4365.

6 PEAK HILL pop. 1061 🅿 PDG
GPS 32° 43.429' S/148° 11.443' E
The town services the local farming community and an open-cut mine. It has accommodation (including two caravan parks) and is a popular stopover, with basic services and a small shopping strip.

7 DUBBO pop. 30 102 🅿 PDG
GPS 32° 14.709' S/148° 36.201' E
Dubbo, the hub of central New South Wales, is a popular destination: attractions include the Western Plains Zoo and the Dubbo Military Museum. Dubbo has all services and very good regional shopping. 🅸 Corner Newell Highway and Macquarie Street; (02) 6884 1422; www.dubbo.com.au

DUBBO TO MOREE 373 KM

Therapeutic waters

Moree Hot Mineral Baths attract people from all around Australia. The invigorating natural artesian waters, which rise from the ground at a delightful 41 degrees Celsius, are reputed to have therapeutic value. Anne Street; (02) 6752 7480; entry fee applies; open 6 a.m. to 8.30 p.m. weekdays, 7 a.m. to 7 p.m. weekends and public holidays.

Starry, starry nights

The night sky in this area is remarkably clear and there are a couple of great observation spots. Skywatch Night and Day Observatory has interactive displays, a planetarium, night sky viewing and Astro Mini Golf. Warrumbungle National Park Road; (02) 6842 3303; entry fee applies; open daily 2 p.m. to 5 p.m. and from 6.30 p.m. with guided sessions at 7 p.m. and 8 p.m. Siding Springs houses the largest optical telescope in Australia, capable of seeing stunning astronomical sights such as the horsehead nebula (pictured); there are also interactive displays, a gift shop and a cafe. Warrumbungle National Park Road; (02) 6842 6291; entry fee applies; open 9.30 a.m. to 4 p.m. daily.

The beautiful Warrumbungles

Approximately 30 km of marked walking trails are a feature of the Warrumbungle National Park. Walks range from the 14.5-km Grand High Tops to shorter 1-km walks on paved paths suitable for wheelchairs. The Breadknife is a volcanic plug that has eroded into a 90-m-high thin blade of rock; Belougery Spire is also worth viewing. There are camping grounds in the national park, with varying facilities. (02) 6825 4364; entry fee applies; visitor information centre open 9 a.m. to 4 p.m. daily.

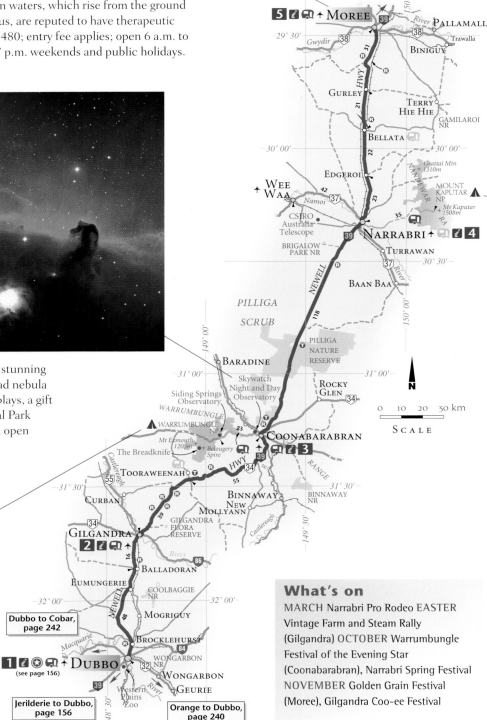

Moree to Miles, page 160

Dubbo to Cobar, page 242

Jerilderie to Dubbo, page 156

Orange to Dubbo, page 240

What's on

MARCH Narrabri Pro Rodeo EASTER Vintage Farm and Steam Rally (Gilgandra) OCTOBER Warrumbungle Festival of the Evening Star (Coonabarabran), Narrabri Spring Festival NOVEMBER Golden Grain Festival (Moree), Gilgandra Coo-ee Festival

See New South Wales

Mount Kaputar National Park is the dramatic remnants of a once mighty volcano. From the top of Mount Kaputar you can see a tenth of New South Wales in a panoramic 360-degree view. You can drive right to the summit or, more energetically, walk 3.5 km from the main carpark through beautiful forest. However, the twisty road to the park has unsealed sections and is unsuitable for caravans; it is fine for two-wheel drives. Camping is permitted and there are good facilities. Off Old Gunnedah Road, Narrabri; (02) 6792 7300.

Travel tip

Moree has its well-known commercial thermal spas, but the Gwydir Carapark in Moree also has its very own artesian-fed hot mineral baths for use by patrons. After a long day on the road book in and have a relaxing dip in their pools.

Track notes

This is a major route carrying road trains and heavy transports. The road passes through the roughly half-million hectares of Pilliga scrub between Coonabarabran and Narrabri. This huge expanse of mallee-type growth protects a large number of native species including kangaroos and emus. Traffic normally flows well on the highway and there are ample overtaking opportunities.

Town file

1 DUBBO (see page 157)

2 GILGANDRA pop. 2822   🅿 PDG
GPS 31° 42.663' S/148° 40.141' E
Gilgandra lies at the junction of the Newell, Oxley and Castlereagh highways, on the banks of the Castlereagh River and at the southern end of the Warrumbungle Range. The town is at the centre of a rich farming area producing grain, oilseed, wool and cattle. Visit Gilgandra Observatory, a private observatory where you can look at the stars through a telescope. Willie Street; (02) 6847 2646; entry fee applies; open from dusk to 10 p.m. Monday to Saturday. Gilgandra has most services and good country-town shopping. 🄘 Coo-ee Heritage Centre, Coo-ee March Memorial Park, Newell Highway; (02) 6847 2045.

3 COONABARABRAN pop. 3012   🅿 PDG
GPS 31° 16.424' S/149° 16.632' E
Coonabarabran claims the title of the astronomy capital of Australia: there are four observatories in the area with about 15 telescopes between them. The Warrumbungle National Park is a very obvious natural attraction in the region. Coonabarabran is a regional centre with good facilities and good shopping. 🄘 Newell Highway; (02) 6842 1441 or 1800 242 881.

4 NARRABRI pop. 6419   🅿 PDG
GPS 30° 19.613' S/149° 47.027' E
Narrabri is at the centre of an intensive agricultural area: grain and cotton are the main crops. Mount Kaputar (1508 m) lies to the east of town and there are varying grades of walking tracks in the spectacular surrounding national park. The most powerful radio telescope complex in the Southern Hemisphere (CSIRO Australia Telescope) is west of town; its visitor information centre is open on weekdays. Narrabri has most services and good shopping. 🄘 Newell Highway; (02) 6799 6760.

5 MOREE pop. 9270   🅿 PDG
GPS 29° 27.800' S/149° 50.569' E
Moree is a major regional centre surrounded by diverse agriculture including cotton farms, olive plantations and the Trawalla pecan nut farm. The town has a number of historic buildings but is best known for the hot mineral baths. Moree has all services and good regional shopping. Markets are held at Jellicoe Park on the first Sunday of each month. 🄘 Corner Newell and Gwydir highways; (02) 6757 3350.

MOREE TO MILES 343 KM

Authors' choice

⊛ Possum Park Caravan and Camping Park, Miles

We always enjoy staying at this unique caravan park – once a World War II munitions dump, the underground bunkers have been converted to cabins! Owner-operated, it is a great park set in a quiet location alongside the Leichhardt Highway, 20 km north of Miles. It has clean amenities and good facilities.

For more details see page 378.

The Goondiwindi Grey

The legendary racehorse Gunsynd, often called the 'Goondiwindi Grey', won 29 races from his 54 starts, finished second on seven occasions, third on eight occasions and was also third in the 1972 Melbourne Cup. A statue of this famous horse can be found in Apex Park.

Travel tip

Whether travelling north or south from Moree it is worth remembering that the price of fuel can differ between New South Wales and Queensland. Fuel is usually several cents cheaper in Queensland, where it has a lower level of tax. Goondiwindi and Boggabilla prices are usually similar.

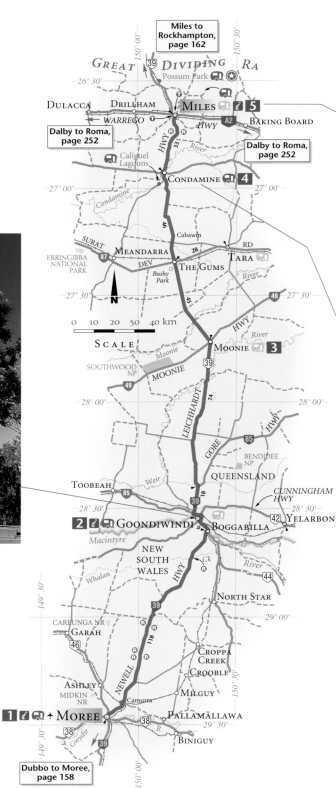

Miles to Rockhampton, page 162

Dalby to Roma, page 252

Dalby to Roma, page 252

Dubbo to Moree, page 158

Travel tip

Queensland and New South Wales both operate on Eastern Standard Time (EST). However, New South Wales introduces daylight saving throughout the warmer months. From November to March, at the border northbound travellers should adjust clocks and watches back by one hour and southbound travellers forward by one hour.

A fascinating historical village

Visit Miles Historical Village and Museum to see 21 authentic buildings from the pioneering days, including a dairy, church, school and police cells. There is also a world-class shell collection and the only community-supported war museum outside Canberra. Murilla Street (Warrego Highway); (07) 4627 1492; entry fee applies; open 8 a.m. to 5 p.m. daily.

Cowbells

The famous 'Condamine Bell' was a strong cowbell, once hung around the neck of working bullocks. It made it easier for teamsters to locate the working team after a night's grazing. You can see a large replica of this bell in the park, or buy one: traditional bells are available in Condamine.

What's on

APRIL Goondiwindi Show MAY Miles Show OCTOBER Condamine Rodeo, Goondiwindi Spring Festival, Back to the Bush Weekend (Miles)

Track notes

The Newell Highway from Moree to Goondiwindi carries road trains and heavy transports but a lot of this traffic heads to Brisbane and south-east Queensland. The Leichhardt Highway is also a main route but carries less traffic. Its road surface is good but not the same quality as south of the border.

Town file

1 MOREE (see page 159)

2 GOONDIWINDI pop. 4374   🅿 PDG
GPS 28° 32.789' S/150° 18.480' E
Goondiwindi is on the northern bank of the Macintyre River, which forms this part of the Queensland–New South Wales border. The town is a large regional centre servicing a strong pastoral industry and an intensive cotton industry. Goondiwindi has all services and a good shopping centre. Traffic travelling between Goondiwindi and Brisbane can choose between the Cunningham Highway or the Gore Highway through Toowoomba, the latter being just a few kilometres shorter.
🛈 Corner McLean and Bowen streets; (07) 4671 2653; www.qldsoutherndowns.org.au

3 MOONIE pop. 60   🅿 PD
GPS 27° 43.041' S/150° 22.232' E
Moonie was the site of Australia's first commercial oilfield following the discovery of oil in 1961. The field still operates today but only accounts for a small proportion of the national production. The small township is little more than a crossroads, with roadhouses being the main providers of services.

4 CONDAMINE pop. 120   🅿 PD
GPS 26° 55.602' S/150° 08.120' E
Condamine was once an important local administrative centre and a changing post on Cobb & Co.'s Dalby-to-Roma route. The town's importance decreased when the railway and the Warrego Highway bypassed the town to the north. The surrounding farms are predominantly cattle-grazing and broadacre grain properties. Condamine has limited facilities.

5 MILES pop. 1187   🅿 PDG
GPS 26° 39.556' S/150° 11.172' E
Miles is situated at the crossroads of the Leichhardt and Warrego highways. First settled in 1844, the township was originally called Dogwood Crossing. It was subsequently re-named in 1878 after the then member for Maranoa and minister for railways, Mr William Miles, the owner of Dulacca Station. 🛈 Historical Village, Murilla Street (Warrego Highway); (07) 4627 1492.

MILES TO ROCKHAMPTON 426 KM

Authors' choice

⭐ Glebe Weir, via Taroom

Fishing is the main attraction at this popular, out-of-the-way camping area, 52 km north-east of Taroom. The weir is a renowned spot for yellow-belly and saratoga. The camping ground is reached along a narrow bitumen road from the highway. Amenities are basic and the showers are cold water only, but there are a number of powered sites. This is a great park for the budget conscious and is suitable for larger motorhomes. **For more details see page 367.**

Steam along

The Mount Morgan Railway operates a 1904 Hunslett 'Saddle Tank' steam engine from the historic (Victorian) Mount Morgan railway station. The track includes a tunnel and a bridge over the Dee River. Railway Parade; (07) 4938 2312; ring for operating times.

A sandstone maze

Isla Gorge National Park is a maze of sandstone gorges and cliffs. The park has no walking tracks and only well-equipped and experienced walkers should attempt to explore the gorge system. Use the Queensland Department of Natural Resources and Mines 1:50 000 Isla Gorge map. However, there is a lookout close to the highway from which you can gaze down into the extraordinary gorge; a caravan and camping area is close by. Queensland Parks and Wildlife Service ranger (07) 4627 3358.

What's on

MAY Golden Mount Festival (Mount Morgan), Mount Morgan Rodeo, Australian Bush Festival (Rockhampton) JULY Bauhinia Arts Festival (Rockhampton) AUGUST Leichhardt Festival (Taroom) SEPTEMBER Capricorn Country Music Festival (Rockhampton)

Rockhampton to Mackay page 50

Gin Gin to Rockhampton, page 48

Rockhampton to Barcaldine, page 258

Moree to Miles, page 160

(see page 160)

0 10 20 30 40 km

SCALE

Beef it up

Rockhampton, the beef capital of the nation, has larger-than-life statues of various breeds of bulls on the approaches to, and main roads throughout, the city. These statues attract more than their share of attention, with a history of senseless vandals stealing their vital parts.

Superb gardens

The Rockhampton Botanic Gardens consist of 38 ha of spectacular tropical and subtropical gardens. They contain many species of palms, ferns and cycads, and there is a delightful Japanese garden that brings peace to the visitor. Stop for refreshment at the tearooms, under a giant banyan fig, or use the barbecues there. These fabulous gardens are alongside the main highway through town. Spencer Street; (07) 4922 1654.

Travel tip

Looking for a few quiet days, or a rest? We love the peace and quiet of Glebe Weir. It is a 27-km drive from the Leichhardt Highway along a narrow sealed road. The weir offers great water-skiing. There is limited power, and cold showers only, but then camping here is only $5 per night.

Track notes

The Leichhardt Highway is generally well maintained and signposted. At Dululu most heavy traffic for Rockhampton diverts to the Capricorn Highway, as the road through Mount Morgan is a winding, steep descent (it is suitable for caravans but it requires caution).

Town file

1 MILES (see page 161)

2 WANDOAN pop. 432   ⛽ PD
GPS 26° 07.527' S/149° 47.676' E
The small community of Wandoan developed around a hotel built in the 1890s. *i* Juandah Heritage Centre, Royds Street; (07) 4627 5227.

3 TAROOM pop. 662   ⛽ PD
GPS 25° 38.461' S/149° 47.779' E
Taroom is set on the banks of the Dawson River. Ludwig Leichhardt passed through here on his great trip to Port Essington: a tree in the main street is blazed 'LL 1844'. Taroom services a local pastoral industry, and has basic services and a small selection of shops. *i* The Old Pub, 43 Yaldwyn Street; (07) 4628 6113.

4 THEODORE pop. 508   ⛽ PD
GPS 24° 57.324' S/150° 04.459' E
In the 1920s a dam and major irrigation scheme was proposed near Theodore, but never proceeded, although coal mining is a future possibility. The town was named after Edward Theodore, Queensland premier from 1919 to 1925, and was designed by Walter Burley Griffin. Theodore has basic services and shopping. *i* The Boulevard; (07) 4993 1900.

5 BANANA pop. 50   ⛽ PDG
GPS 24° 28.339' S/150° 07.688' E
Banana, at the junction of the Leichhardt and Dawson highways, has basic services.

6 MOUNT MORGAN pop. 2487   ⛽ PD
GPS 23° 38.746' S/150° 23.238' E
Mount Morgan is one of Australia's great historic mining towns, with over 240 tonnes of gold and 360000 tonnes of copper produced during 109 years until the mine closed in 1991. In the mine's heyday, around 1910, the town had 14000 people. The town has many historic buildings and relics from that era. Mount Morgan has most services and shops. *i* Heritage Railway Station, 1 Railway Parade; (07) 4938 2312.

7 ROCKHAMPTON (see page 49)

MELBOURNE TO KARUMBA

KIDMAN WAY, MITCHELL (MATILDA) HIGHWAY, LANDSBOROUGH (MATILDA) HIGHWAY, CAPRICO

Sweeping northwards from Melbourne, this network of highways has become popular due to the strong marketing of the Kidman Way and Matilda Highway tourist route. The fully sealed route crosses three States and many tourists travel north to escape the cold southern winters for the balmy tropics. The wineries of the Murrumbidgee Irrigation Area, Tambo's famous teddy bears and the Australian Stockman's Hall of Fame at Longreach are all must-see attractions for travellers visiting this area.

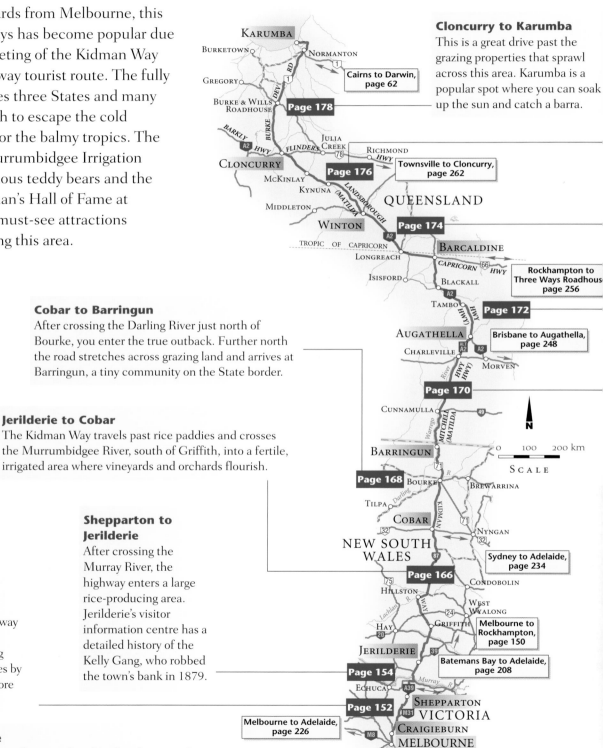

Cloncurry to Karumba
This is a great drive past the grazing properties that sprawl across this area. Karumba is a popular spot where you can soak up the sun and catch a barra.

Cobar to Barringun
After crossing the Darling River just north of Bourke, you enter the true outback. Further north the road stretches across grazing land and arrives at Barringun, a tiny community on the State border.

Jerilderie to Cobar
The Kidman Way travels past rice paddies and crosses the Murrumbidgee River, south of Griffith, into a fertile, irrigated area where vineyards and orchards flourish.

Shepparton to Jerilderie
After crossing the Murray River, the highway enters a large rice-producing area. Jerilderie's visitor information centre has a detailed history of the Kelly Gang, who robbed the town's bank in 1879.

Craigieburn to Shepparton
The busy Hume Freeway streams north from Melbourne, bypassing towns. The road passes by notable vineyards before reaching Shepparton.

Melbourne
Melbourne is a vibrant and multicultural metropolis offering great restaurants, excellent shopping, tree-lined boulevards and magnificent gardens.

IGHWAY, BURKE DEVELOPMENTAL ROAD (MATILDA HIGHWAY) (2909 KM)

Winton to Cloncurry

This stretch of highway is probably best known for the famous Blue Heeler Hotel in Kynuna and the Walkabout Creek Hotel in McKinlay, which featured in the movie *Crocodile Dundee*.

Barcaldine to Winton

Longreach's famous Australian Stockman's Hall of Fame, and historic Qantas hangar and Winton's spectacular Waltzing Matilda Centre will take some time but are all on the 'must see' list.

Augathella to Barcaldine

See the delightful handcrafted Tambo Teddies, the historic Blackall Wool Scour and Barcaldine's Tree of Knowledge – all worth a visit.

Barringun to Augathella

The Mitchell Highway stretches north across the plains to Augathella. Take the time in Charleville to learn more about the Royal Flying Doctor Service at their excellent visitors centre.

Australian Stockman's Hall of Fame and Outback Heritage Centre, Longreach

Best time to go

Western Queensland and the Gulf country are best experienced in the balmy winter months, while the Murray River area is a popular summer playground.

GRIFFITH

	J	F	M	A	M	J	J	A	S	O	N	D
Maximum	32	31	28	23	18	15	14	16	20	23	27	30
Minimum	16	16	14	9	6	4	3	4	6	9	12	15
Rainfall (mm)	30	28	34	33	38	37	33	40	33	41	29	31
Raindays	4	4	4	6	8	10	11	10	8	7	5	5

CLONCURRY

	J	F	M	A	M	J	J	A	S	O	N	D
Maximum	37	36	35	32	28	25	25	28	31	35	37	38
Minimum	25	24	23	19	15	12	10	12	16	20	23	24
Rainfall (mm)	117	113	64	18	15	12	8	4	7	16	30	67
Raindays	8	7	5	2	2	1	1	1	1	2	3	6

John & Jan

JERILDERIE TO COBAR 501 KM

Authors' choice

⊛ Griffith Tourist Caravan Park, Griffith

This owner-operated park stands out because of its excellent facilities and the fact that it is a great base from which to explore the interesting Griffith area. It has a large number of ensuite sites, a pool, a spa and a tennis court. We always enjoy staying at Griffith.

For more details see page 369.

A rich copper lode

Cobar is rich in mining history. Copper was discovered in 1869, and Cobar became a magnet for Cornish miners: many local surnames are Cornish in origin. Large deposits of gold, silver, zinc and lead were later found, and mining continues today. Visit the Great Cobar Heritage Centre, a terrific museum, for a glimpse of Cobar's history; there is a walkway to the original open-cut mine. Barrier Highway; (02) 6836 2448; entry fee applies; open 8.30 a.m. to 5 p.m. weekdays, 9 a.m. to 5 p.m. weekends and public holidays.

Travel tip

Some caravan parks throughout this area may, from time to time, be home to seasonal workers. Cotton chippers, fruit pickers and processing plant workers follow the work across Australia. To be sure of a site it may be wise to phone ahead and book, or at least check site availability. Most caravan parks do, however, retain some sites for tourists even during the busiest times.

Cobar to Barringun, page 168

Cobar to Broken Hill, page 244

Dubbo to Cobar, page 242

Shepparton to Jerilderie, page 154

Jerilderie to Dubbo, page 156

What's on

FEBRUARY Jerilderie Show EASTER Festival of Griffith APRIL Hillston Picnic Races AUGUST Festival of the Miner's Ghost (Cobar) SEPTEMBER Hillston Show OCTOBER Festival of Gardens (Griffith)

Beyond the Black Stump

The small community of Merriwagga has an area officially referred to as the 'Black Stump' district. The name arose from the unfortunate death of Barbara Blaine, a bullocky's wife, who burnt to death in a campfire in 1886. Her remains, according to her husband when he found them, resembled a black stump.

McWilliam's Wines

There are several significant wineries in the Griffith area, including the McWilliam's winery at Hanwood, which was established in 1913. This winery is close to Kidman Way and has a unique, barrel-shaped wine-tasting centre, as well as a museum of winery memorabilia in a building shaped like a bottle. Jack McWilliam's Road; (02) 6963 0001; open 9 a.m. to 5 p.m. Monday to Saturday, guided winery tours by appointment.

Mighty merinos

The Riverina is famous for its merinos, in particular the historic Peppin stock, which produce fine wool. Jerilderie is home to many merino studs, and there is a prestigious annual merino show here.

Track notes

The Kidman Way between Jerilderie and Hillston carries local traffic, occasional slow-moving tractors and, during the rice harvest, numerous trucks. The road is well maintained and sealed; however, the surface's quality and width varies.

Town file

To get from Melbourne to Jerilderie, see Craigieburn to Shepparton, page 152, and Shepparton to Jerilderie, page 154.

1 JERILDERIE (see page 155)

2 COLEAMBALLY pop. 647 ⛽ PD
GPS 34° 48.321' S/145° 52.883' E
Coleambally was established in 1968 as a centre for this major rice-growing area; north of town is a large rice mill. The town has basic facilities and a picturesque rest area among large pines.

3 DARLINGTON POINT pop. 881 ⛽ PD
GPS 34° 34.076' S/146° 00.014' E
This old town on the Murrumbidgee was established as a river crossing point. The first bridge, built in 1905 and replaced in 1979, now forms the entrance to the caravan park. Basic facilities are available.

4 GRIFFITH pop. 14 209 ⛽ PDG
GPS 34° 17.280' S/146° 02.785' E
Griffith is at the centre of a great wine and food area, due to the Murrumbidgee Irrigation Scheme. The city (designed by Walter Burley Griffin) has craft shops, galleries and great restaurants. Griffith has all services and comprehensive shopping. 🛈 Corner Banna and Jondaryan avenues; (02) 6962 4145 or 1800 681 141.

5 GOOLGOWI pop. 375 ⛽ PD
GPS 33° 58.839' S/145° 42.719' E
Located at the intersection of the Kidman Way and the Mid Western Highway, Goolgowi has a hotel, roadhouse, small shopping centre and a basic caravan park.

6 HILLSTON pop. 1099 ⛽ PDG
GPS 33° 29.136' S/145° 31.879' E
Hillston is an agricultural centre with most services and basic shopping. 🛈 High Street; (02) 6967 2555.

7 COBAR pop. 4524 ⛽ PDG
GPS 31° 29.978' S/145° 50.302' E
Cobar, with a long mining history, has numerous fine buildings, some listed by the National Trust; many date from the 1860s and 1870s. Cobar is at the junction of the Kidman Way and the Barrier Highway, a crossroads at the virtual centre of New South Wales. Most services are available and Cobar has a good shopping strip. There is no fuel available between Cobar and Bourke, to the north. 🛈 The Great Cobar Heritage Centre, Barrier Highway; (02) 6836 2448.

COBAR TO BARRINGUN 294 KM

Fred Hollows – an inspiring example

The famous Professor Fred Hollows, who worked so hard to improve the health of Aboriginal people, is buried at the Bourke cemetery. This revered eye specialist was known internationally for his marvellous work preventing blindness among the world's poorer nations, especially in Nepal, Eritrea and South-East Asia. His message – and work – lives on in the Fred Hollows Foundation: 'Leave the world a better place'.

Travel tip

Throughout this region wildlife regularly graze beside the road, often wandering across it. Kangaroos, emus and wild pigs are the most common and can cause extensive damage to a vehicle. Kangaroos are more obvious around sunrise and sunset. Animals can usually be seen from some distance, but anticipating their direction of travel can be difficult: be cautious.

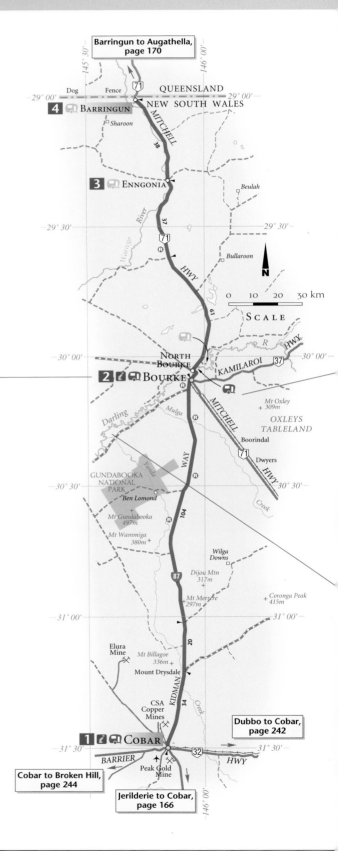

Barringun to Augathella, page 170

Cobar to Broken Hill, page 244

Jerilderie to Cobar, page 166

Dubbo to Cobar, page 242

Travel tip

Queensland and New South Wales both operate on Eastern Standard Time (EST). However, New South Wales introduces daylight saving throughout the warmer months. From November to March at the border, northbound travellers should adjust clocks and watches back by one hour and southbound travellers forward by one hour.

Cotton growing

Cotton was introduced to the Bourke area in 1966 and is now a major and valuable crop: 94 per cent of Australian cotton is exported. The cotton plants reach maturity in the late summer and harvesting usually takes place during March.

The Darling paddle-steamers

The Darling River forms part of the Murray–Darling river system, the largest such system in Australia. Paddle-steamers once plied the river as far north as Bourke, carrying bales of wool downstream, the last one being the *JG Arnold* with its barge, the *Ukee*, in 1932. There is a replica of the historic Bourke Jetty in Sturt Street.

Track notes

The Kidman Way is growing in popularity with tourists since the final section was sealed. The road carries local traffic and interstate heavy transports and road trains. Between Bourke and Barringun the Mitchell Highway is sealed, but in places the surface is narrow and can be a little rough. There are also a number of grids along this section and we recommend slowing down for these as some are rough.

Town file

1 COBAR (see page 167)

2 BOURKE pop. 2775   ⛽ PDG
GPS 30° 05.398' S/145° 56.195' E
Bourke holds a unique place in Australian folklore. Remote places are often referred to as being at 'the back o' Bourke'. The town was the port at the head of the Darling River and until the 1930s paddle-steamers carried the local wool clip from Bourke to market. The town has several well-maintained buildings from those early days. Bourke has a long agricultural history and cotton, introduced in 1966, is now an important local crop. Citrus fruit, grapes and a range of horticultural crops also contribute greatly to the local economy. Bourke provides major regional services to the local agricultural industries. The town has good shopping and most services. For northbound travellers, Bourke is the last chance to fill up with petrol and diesel before Barringun, while gas is not available until Queensland. There is no fuel between Bourke and Cobar, to the south. ℹ Old Railway Station, Anson Street; (02) 6872 2280; www.backobourke.com.au

3 ENNGONIA pop. 30   ⛽ None
GPS 29° 19.197' S/145° 50.801' E
Enngonia is a small residential community 98 km north of Bourke, and the hotel is the only tourist service. The Mitchell Highway passes through town. The surrounding area is sheep-grazing country and many of the local stations are quite large.

4 BARRINGUN pop. 15   ⛽ PD
GPS 29° 00.603' S/145° 42.747' E
Barringun is a tiny settlement just south of the New South Wales–Queensland border. A roadhouse and a hotel are the extent of the services for travellers. It can be tempting to drive straight through the town, but the roadhouse often has a selection of freshly baked cakes that are worth stopping for.

What's on

EASTER Fishing Competition (Bourke)
SEPTEMBER Mateship Festival (Bourke), Enngonia
Race Meeting OCTOBER Back o' Bourke Stampede

BARRINGUN TO AUGATHELLA 401 KM

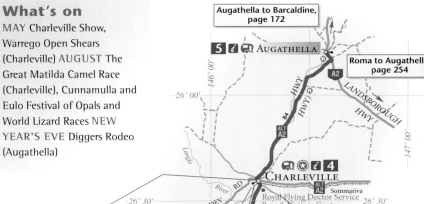
Augathella to Barcaldine,
page 172

Roma to Augathell
page 254

Authors' choice

⊛ Bailey Bar Caravan Park, Charleville

We regularly stay at this very good owner-operated park. Set in a quiet, off-highway location 1.5 km from the town centre, the park has great lawns, clean amenities and good facilities. It offers a range of accommodation and runs bush poetry events during the middle months of the year.

For more details see page 360.

What's on

MAY Charleville Show, Warrego Open Shears (Charleville) AUGUST The Great Matilda Camel Race (Charleville), Cunnamulla and Eulo Festival of Opals and World Lizard Races NEW YEAR'S EVE Diggers Rodeo (Augathella)

Grand hotel

The luxurious Corones Hotel in Charleville was an illustrious social meeting place in the 1930s and 1940s. Take a guided tour of this grand establishment and hear the interesting tales of its famous guests and of days gone by. Tours begin at 2 p.m. most days. The tour fee includes afternoon tea. Corner Galatea and Wills streets; (07) 4654 1022.

Travel tip

Queensland and New South Wales both operate on Eastern Standard Time (EST). However, New South Wales introduces daylight saving throughout the warmer months. From November to March at the border, northbound travellers should adjust clocks and watches back by one hour and southbound travellers forward by one hour.

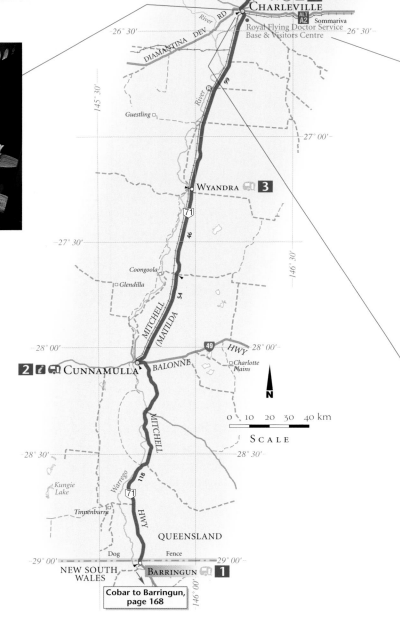

Cobar to Barringun,
page 168

Travel tip

Visitor information centres, found in most towns around Australia, are the single greatest source of up-to-date information for travellers. Most operate between 9 a.m. and 5 p.m. daily with a mix of permanent and volunteer staff; however, in the off-season (usually October to April) the visitor information centres in Cunnamulla and Charleville only open on weekdays.

See the Flying Doctors at work

The Royal Flying Doctor Service Visitors Centre at Charleville has a small cinema that shows a film depicting everyday life in this important service. It also has a display of past and present equipment and a shop stocked with a range of RFDS merchandise. Old Cunnamulla Road; (07) 4654 1233; entry fee applies; open 8.30 a.m. to 5 p.m. Monday to Friday, 9 a.m. to 5 p.m. weekends.

Look to the heavens

The Charleville Cosmos Centre is a fascinating astronomy centre; gaze at the night skies with the help of an expert guide. Indigenous cosmology is also explained in the newly expanded centre. Airport Road; (07) 4654 3057; entry fee applies; open daily, but phone first.

Track notes

The Mitchell Highway between Cunnamulla and Augathella is a well-maintained sealed road. Between Barringun and Cunnamulla, however, the sealed surface is generally much narrower and in parts the edges are broken, rough, soft and prone to becoming boggy in wet conditions. Care is needed along this stretch where it is often necessary to move off the sealed section to pass oncoming heavy transports. This is a major route carrying road trains and interstate transports.

Town file

1 BARRINGUN (see page 169)

2 CUNNAMULLA pop. 1450   PDG
GPS 28° 041.151' S/145° 40.945' E
Located on the banks of the Warrego River, Cunnamulla is a service centre for the local pastoral industry and a crossroads for traffic heading west to Innamincka or the south-west Queensland oil and gas fields. The town has a large number of historic buildings, a caravan park and a range of other accommodation. Basic shopping and services are available. *i* Jane Street, Centenary Park; (07) 4655 2481.

3 WYANDRA pop. 60   PD
GPS 27° 14.791' S/145° 58.854' E
Wyandra is a small township midway between Cunnamulla and Charleville. The town has several residents but also a large number of unoccupied buildings. There is a hotel but little else in the way of services, other than a small camping area where powered sites are free to overnight campers. The camping area has toilets and cold showers.

4 CHARLEVILLE pop. 3400   PDG
GPS 26° 24.071' S/146° 14.381' E
Charleville is a major regional centre and a key base for the Royal Flying Doctor Service. The town has numerous historic buildings, including the grand Corones Hotel. Cobb & Co. operated a coach-building factory here for 34 years before closing in 1920 when motorised vehicles replaced their coach services. In the past two decades, the town has been twice ravaged by the flooded Warrego River. Charleville is an important service centre for a large sheep and cattle industry, and also an important railway terminal on the Brisbane to Quilpie line. Markets are held at Historical House on the first Sunday of each month. *i* Sturt Street; (07) 4654 3057.

5 AUGATHELLA pop. 450   PDG
GPS 25° 47.713' S/146° 35.127' E
Other than the roadhouse, motel and caravan park, the township of Augathella is not immediately visible from the highway, but it is worth the detour. There are basic services and one of the attractions for travellers may be the large, well-stocked craft shop at the far end of the main street. It has an extensive range of local handicrafts and doubles as the visitor information centre. *i* Boadicea Arts and Craft, Main Street; (07) 4654 5116.

AUGATHELLA TO BARCALDINE 324 KM

The historic Tree of Knowledge

The Tree of Knowledge is a stately ghost gum outside the Barcaldine Railway Station in Oak Street. Beneath this tree the shearers' strike meetings of 1891 were held, leading to the formation of the Australian Labor Party.

Legendary shearer

On Alice Downs Station in 1892, Jackie Howe, gun shearer, managed to shear 321 sheep in 7 hours and 40 minutes with blade shears. Jackie lived and died in Blackall and is buried in the town cemetery. His incredible record stood until electric shears were introduced in the 1950s. A memorial to Jackie's achievement stands outside the visitor information centre in Short Street.

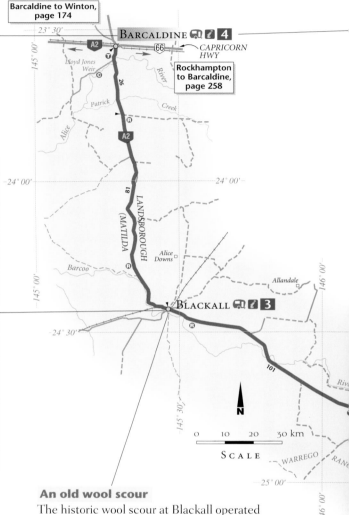

Barcaldine to Winton, page 174

Rockhampton to Barcaldine, page 258

An old wool scour

The historic wool scour at Blackall operated until 1978 and is the last remaining example of a steam-powered plant in Australia. The scour is located next to a natural artesian bore and there is also a 20-stand shearing shed attached to the plant. Tours are available every hour until 3 p.m. Evora Road (5 km north of Blackall); (07) 4657 4637; entry fee applies; open 8 a.m. to 4 p.m. daily from April to November.

Travel tip

When it comes to satisfying the appetite, there are many great places to dine out along the Landsborough (Matilda) Highway. One of our favourites is the Blackall Caravan Park, which offers sumptuous meals cooked in a camp-oven on most nights during the winter tourist season.

Tambo Teddies

See how they toiled

The Australian Workers Heritage Centre at Barcaldine showcases the experiences of workers and the difficult conditions in which they often laboured in days gone by. This popular tribute is in the centre of town on 2 ha of landscaped gardens. 94 Ash Street; (07) 4651 2422; entry fee applies; open 9 a.m. to 5 p.m. Monday to Saturday, 10 a.m. to 5 p.m. Sunday.

Teddy central

Tambo Teddies, in the main street of Tambo, has an amazing range of teddy bears made from sheepskin. A number of local women handcraft the bears, which have become prized possessions. We definitely recommend a visit to this fabulous shop. 17 Arthur Street; (07) 4654 6223; open 9 a.m. to 5 p.m. weekdays and Saturday mornings.

Track notes

The Landsborough (Matilda) Highway is a major route carrying tourist traffic, stock trucks, road trains and heavy transports. The road is fully sealed, in good condition and well maintained. Visibility is good and there are always opportunities to overtake. The road passes through open grazing country.

Town file

1 **AUGATHELLA** (see page 171)

2 **TAMBO** pop. 378   PDG
GPS 24° 52.941' S/146° 15.401' E
Tambo is a rural service town located to the west of the rugged limestone country of the Carnarvon Ranges. The town is the oldest in central-western Queensland, dating back to 1863. There are basic services for travellers and a visit to the unique Tambo Teddies shop in Arthur Street should not be missed. *i* Tambo Shire Council, Arthur Street; (07) 4654 6133.

3 **BLACKALL** pop. 2066   PDG
GPS 24° 25.460' S/145° 27.899' E
Located on the Barcoo River, Blackall is the centre of a merino sheep farming area with many large stations nearby. Jackie Howe, the famous gun shearer, lived in Blackall and set both blade and mechanical shearing records on local stations. Surveyors used an astro-station reference point, dubbed the 'Black Stump', in Blackall in the 1880s in the surveying of western Queensland. A replica marking the 1887 astro-station location can be seen in Thistle Street. Like many western Queensland towns, the town water supply is from an artesian bore. Blackall has all basic services and shopping. *i* Short Street; (07) 4657 4637.

4 **BARCALDINE** pop. 1592   PDG
GPS 23° 33.232' S/145° 17.315' E
Barcaldine lies at the junction of the Capricorn and Landsborough (Matilda) highways. The town was founded in 1886 when the railway pushed west from Rockhampton. Soon after, Barcaldine became famous as the centre of the shearers' strike of 1891, and the Australian Labor Party was founded as a result of the strike meetings. The Australian Workers Heritage Centre is a major attraction in town. Barcaldine has good basic shopping and most services. *i* Oak Street; (07) 4651 1724.

What's on

MARCH Claypan Boogie Country Music Festival (Blackall) MAY Blackall Agricultural Show, Barcaldine Show JUNE Artesian Festival (Barcaldine, even-numbered years) JULY Black Stump Camel Race Festival (Blackall)

Barringun to Augathella, page 170

Roma to Augathella, page 254

BARCALDINE TO WINTON 282 KM

Winton to Cloncurry, page 176

4 Winton

To Lark Quarry Conservation Park

BLADENSBURG NATIONAL PARK

LANDSBOROUGH (MATILDA)

Oondooroo

Creek

Lorraine Station

109 A2 Chorregon

Clyde

Maneroo

Creek

Evesham

Darr River Downs

Morella

HWY (HWY 65)

Darr

Longway

Thomson River

Onkley

Qantas Founders Outback Museum

TROPIC

LONGREACH **3**

ILFRACOMBE **2**

Dart

N

| 0 | 10 | 20 | 30 km |

SCALE

Travel tip

When on your travels, it can often be a difficult decision choosing which tourist attractions to visit and which to pass by. This area in particular has some unique major attractions. If possible, try to budget a little more time (and money) at this point so that you do not miss the interesting experiences along this route.

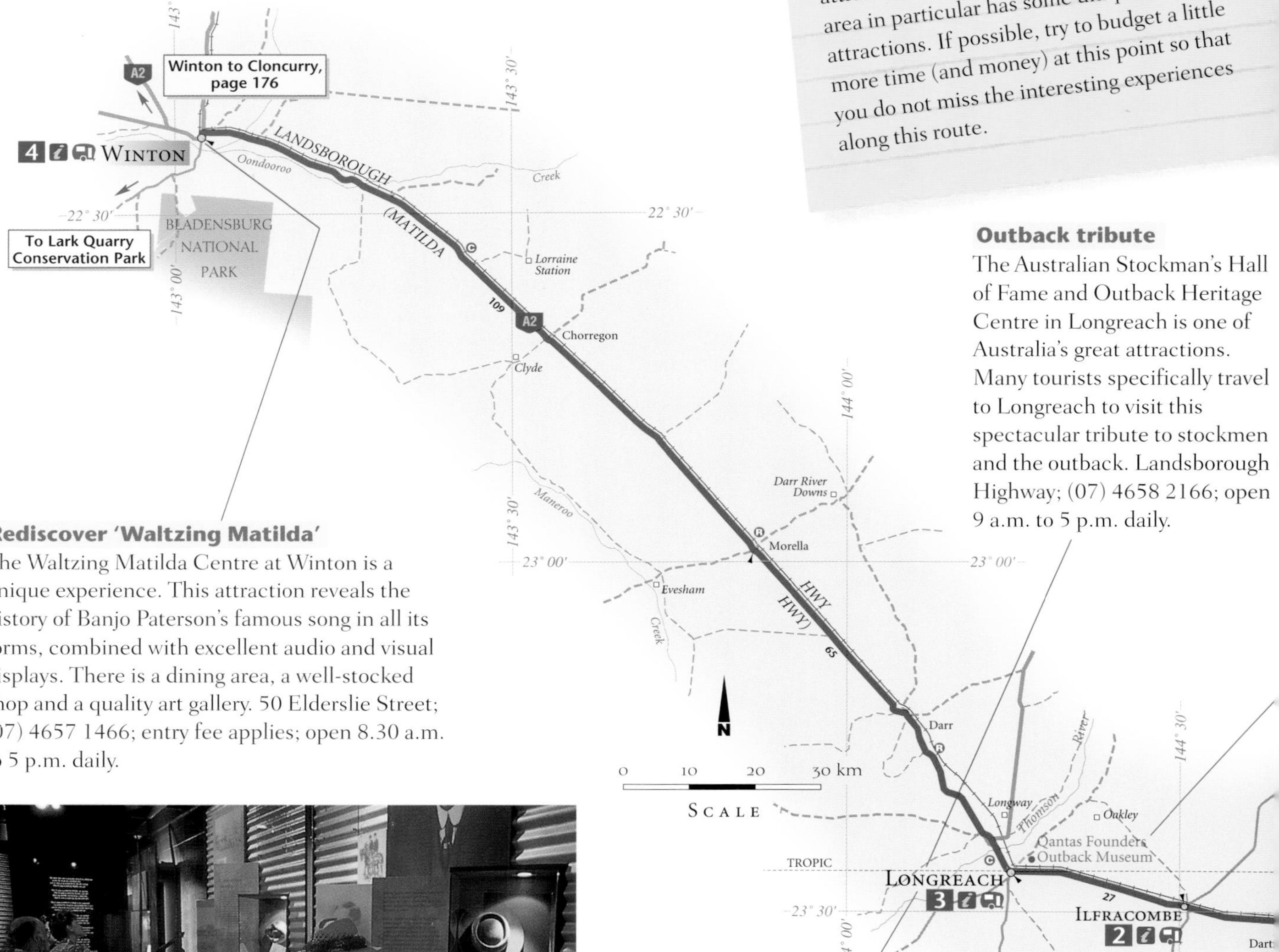

Outback tribute

The Australian Stockman's Hall of Fame and Outback Heritage Centre in Longreach is one of Australia's great attractions. Many tourists specifically travel to Longreach to visit this spectacular tribute to stockmen and the outback. Landsborough Highway; (07) 4658 2166; open 9 a.m. to 5 p.m. daily.

Rediscover 'Waltzing Matilda'

The Waltzing Matilda Centre at Winton is a unique experience. This attraction reveals the history of Banjo Paterson's famous song in all its forms, combined with excellent audio and visual displays. There is a dining area, a well-stocked shop and a quality art gallery. 50 Elderslie Street; (07) 4657 1466; entry fee applies; open 8.30 a.m. to 5 p.m. daily.

Outback education

Longreach School of Distance Education (LSODE) was established in 1987 to educate pupils previously enrolled through the School of the Air. The centre caters for some 300 students in western Queensland. Tours of the centre are available at 9 a.m. and 10 a.m. weekdays. Sir James Walker Drive; (07) 4658 4222.

What's on

EASTER Easter in the Outback (Longreach, Winton and Ilfracombe) APRIL Waltzing Matilda Art and Bush Poetry Competitions (Winton) JUNE Winton Show JULY Diamond Shears Competition (Longreach)

The first home of Qantas

The Qantas Founders Outback Museum is located in the company's original hangar at Longreach. Discover some of the early history of one of the world's great airlines. There is a full-size replica of an AVRO 504K, the first type of aircraft operated by Qantas. Longreach Airport; (07) 4658 3737; entry fee applies; open 9 a.m. to 5 p.m. daily.

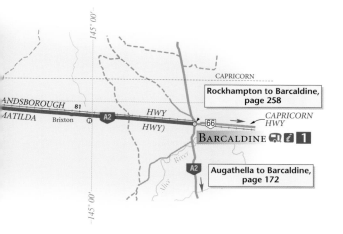

Track notes

The Capricorn and Landsborough (Matilda) highways are major routes carrying road trains and heavy transports. The quality of the road has greatly improved in recent years with a newly completed section west of Longreach crossing the Thomson River flood plain. The road runs alongside the railway line for most of the way and trainloads of cattle heading to market are a common sight.

Town file

1 BARCALDINE (see page 173)

2 ILFRACOMBE pop. 200   🏕 PD
GPS 23° 29.358' S/144° 30.417' E
Once the transport centre for Wellshot Station, this small township now provides basic services for travellers. There is an interesting machinery display that stretches the length of town along the roadside. The first motorised mail service in Queensland operated from Ilfracombe in 1910. The 'Back to the Bush Show' is a popular attraction at the Wellshot Hotel. 🛈 Shire Offices, Devon Street; (07) 4658 2233; www.ilfracombe.qld.gov.au

3 LONGREACH pop. 3766   🏕 PDG
GPS 23° 26.470' S/144° 15.002' E
Longreach is the important regional centre for a big sheep- and cattle-farming area. It is home to a large agricultural college and a number of excellent tourist attractions including the Australian Stockman's Hall of Fame and Outback Heritage Centre. Qantas relocated its operations to Longreach Airport early in its history and the company's original hangar is now the Qantas Founders Outback Museum. Longreach is a popular tourist destination during the cooler winter months and has a comprehensive shopping centre along with all services. 🛈 Qantas Park, Eagle Street; (07) 4658 3555.

4 WINTON pop. 1142   🏕 PDG
GPS 22° 23.421' S/143° 02.359' E
Winton abounds with outback history. The first public performance of Banjo Paterson's 'Waltzing Matilda' was in 1895 at the North Gregory Hotel, and the Waltzing Matilda Centre in the main street now pays tribute to this famous song. Winton was also the home of Qantas's first registered office, opened in 1920. The remarkable Lark Quarry Conservation Park dinosaur 'stampede' prints are located about 110 km south-west of town. Winton has most services and basic shopping. 🛈 Waltzing Matilda Centre, 50 Elderslie Street; (07) 4657 1466; www.matildacentre.com.au

WINTON TO CLONCURRY 343 KM

Cloncurry to Karumba,
page 178

Cloncurry to
Three Ways Roadhouse,
page 260

CLONCURRY

Hughenden to Cloncurry,
page 266

Beenfields

McKINLAY

To BHP
Cannington Mine

KYNUNA

Combo
Waterhole

COMBO
CONSERVATION
PARK 1 & 2

Kerrs Table Mtn
305m

Remembering the Flying Doctors

At John Flynn Place the founders of the Royal Flying Doctor Service are remembered. Exhibits include one of the first pedal wirelesses and a scale model of the *Victory*, the first plane that took off with a doctor on board, in 1928. Daintree Street, Cloncurry; (07) 4742 1251; entry fee applies; open 8 a.m. to 4.30 p.m. weekdays throughout the year, 9 a.m. to 3 p.m. weekends April to October.

Authors' choice

⊛ Gilbert Park Tourist Village, Cloncurry

We regularly stay at this quality family-operated park, located on the main highway 2 km east of the town centre. Relax in the pool and spa or enjoy a meal at the covered barbecue area. With clean amenities and a range of facilities, the park also adjoins a small rocky hill known as Sunset Hill, the perfect place to sit and enjoy the sunset.
For more details see page 361.

What's on

APRIL Kynuna Campdraft and Rodeo JUNE McKinlay Annual Race Meeting, Cloncurry Annual Show JULY Stockman's Challenge (Cloncurry) AUGUST/SEPTEMBER Kynuna Surf Carnival

Paterson's inspiration

Events at Combo Waterhole on the Diamantina River in 1894 that involved a striking shearer are believed to have provided the inspiration for Banjo Paterson's 'Waltzing Matilda'. The turn-off to the waterhole is signposted 16 km east of Kynuna, after which there is an 8 km unsealed track and a short walk.

Travel tip

Sunset Hill is a short walk from the Gilbert Park Tourist Village in Cloncurry. The hill offers superb 360-degree views of town and is an ideal spot to relax at the day's end and watch or photograph the vivid winter sunsets.

The legend of 'Waltzing Matilda'
Matilda Expo at Kynuna is the base of Richard Magoffin, a local authority on Banjo Paterson's 'Waltzing Matilda'. There are live performances every day and night during the tourist season.
Matilda Highway; (07) 4746 8401.

Track notes

The Landsborough (Matilda) Highway forms part of the main road-train thoroughfare from Brisbane to Darwin. It is also a popular tourist route, with some great tourist attractions along the way. The road surface is fully sealed and well maintained. The distances between centres along this stretch of the highway are long, so take adequate breaks.

Town file

1 WINTON (see page 175)

2 KYNUNA pop. 18   🅿 PDG
GPS 21° 34.734' S/141° 55.217' E
Originally an important staging post for Cobb & Co., Kynuna still caters for travellers with the famous Blue Heeler Hotel, a roadhouse and Richard Magoffin's Matilda Expo. Banjo Paterson composed 'Waltzing Matilda' at nearby Dagworth Station, and the original manuscript and other associated material are on display at the expo. Two caravan parks in town offer basic facilities.

3 McKINLAY pop. 30   🅿 PDG
GPS 21° 16.322' S/141° 17.398' E
McKinlay is best known for the Walkabout Creek Hotel, which, along with other buildings in the town, featured in the movie *Crocodile Dundee*. In recent years the hotel has been relocated to front the highway. The BHP Cannington Mine, opened in 1997, is located 85 km south-west of town, and is the world's largest single mine producer of silver and lead.

4 CLONCURRY pop. 2459   🅿 PDG
GPS 20° 42.339' S/140° 30.328' E
Located at the junction of the Flinders and Landsborough (Matilda) highways, Cloncurry has always been a frontier town. Coppermining played a major role in the town's early history but mining waned after World War I. In 1922 Qantas operated its first regular air service between Cloncurry and Charleville, and the Royal Flying Doctor Service was launched in 1928. Today there has been a resurgence in mining and large cattle properties sprawl across the area. *ℹ* Mary Kathleen Park, McIlwraith Street; (07) 4742 1361.

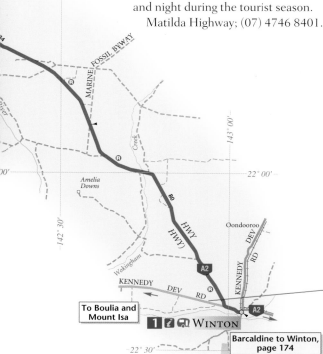

Alternative route

The route from Winton to Mount Isa via Boulia is an alternative, fully sealed route taking in the remote outback towns of Middleton, Boulia and Dajarra.

CLONCURRY TO KARUMBA 446 KM

Authors' choice

⭐ Karumba Point Tourist Park, Karumba Point

We like this popular, quality park, located 7.5 km from Karumba. It has a unique attraction: a free fish barbecue for guests each Wednesday and Saturday night during the winter tourist season. The park is always busy during the tourist season so booking is necessary.

For more details see page 372.

Bag a barra

The Gulf Barramundi Restocking Association at Karumba is a community project. There are guided tours daily and souvenirs for sale to help support this exciting initiative. Yappar Street; (07) 4745 9359; open 1 p.m. to 5 p.m. daily.

Outback train adventures

The *Gulflander* is one of the world's unique train trips. The railway has operated continually since 1891 and the diesel railmotor departs year-round from Normanton each Wednesday at 8.30 a.m. for the 152-km journey to Croydon, returning Thursday. Normanton Railway Station; (07) 4745 1391; fare applies.

What's on

EASTER Barra Classic Fishing Tournament (Normanton) MAY Kajabbi Yabbi Races, Gregory River Marathon Canoe Race (Gregory Downs, Queensland Labour Day weekend) JUNE Normanton Show, Rodeo and Gymkhana

Karumba to Weipa Barge Service

Normanton to Hells Gate Roadhouse, page 68

Mount Garnet to Normanton page 66

To Gregory Downs

Burke & Wills Roadhouse

Hughenden to Cloncurry, page 266

Cloncurry to Three Ways Roadhouse, page 260

Winton to Cloncurry, page 176

(see page 176)

SCALE
0 10 20 30 km

Fabulous fishing

The quality of the sports fishing in this region's river estuaries and in the Gulf of Carpentaria is one of the great attractions of this area. Barramundi are the prize catch. There are boats for hire in Karumba and Normanton along with several charter fishing boats. If you are not so keen on catching it yourself, fresh seafood is readily available in both Karumba and Normanton.

A monster croc

At almost 9 m long, 'Krys the Savannah King' is reputedly the largest estuarine crocodile ever caught. A lifesize replica of this monster sits in the park next door to the council offices in Haig Street, Normanton.

Travel tip

Our Authors' choice, Karumba Point Tourist Park, provides a free fish barbecue for guests twice a week during the winter tourist season. The fish is delicious and it is a great chance to catch up with other travellers, particularly to discuss the best fishing spots, the condition of the road and interesting attractions in the area.

Track notes

The Burke Developmental Road (Matilda Highway) between Cloncurry and Normanton is fully sealed, but has long, narrow stretches where it is not possible to overtake or pass without one or both vehicles leaving the bitumen. The road shoulders are stony in places and it is important to reduce speed to avoid stone damage when passing. Road trains use the road, and it may be necessary to pull off the sealed section to allow them to pass.

Town file

1 CLONCURRY (see page 177)

2 KAJABBI pop. 50   ⛽ PD
GPS 20° 00.546' S/140° 02.042' E
Years have passed since the last train came through town but this historic mining area was also once the railhead for cattle being sent to the eastern markets. The Kalkadoon Hotel at Kajabbi is one of those unique outback pubs; it was moved here from the nearby mining fields. Prospectors and fossickers still scour the nearby hills. The town has no facilities other than the hotel.

3 BURKE AND WILLS ROADHOUSE   ⛽ PDG
GPS 19° 13.610' S/140° 20.834' E
In the midst of Gulf Savannah cattle country, the Burke and Wills Roadhouse is a strategically located service complex. Sited at the crossroads of the Burke Developmental Road (Matilda Highway) and the roads to Julia Creek and Gregory Downs, it provides fuel, accommodation and meals. The Gregory Downs Road now carries heavy traffic for the giant Century Zinc mine. This is the last stop for autogas northbound before Atherton, Queensland, or Daly Waters, Northern Territory.

4 NORMANTON (see page 67)

5 KARUMBA pop. 1043   ⛽ PD
GPS 17° 29.207' S/140° 50.257' E
Karumba is a major prawn-fishing port and a great tourist destination. Good access to the Gulf of Carpentaria, excellent fishing, a warm winter climate and its location at the northernmost end of the fully sealed Matilda Highway all contribute to Karumba's popularity. There are three large caravan parks in Karumba (including Karumba Point), and all are extremely busy during the winter tourist season. For several years, we have heard rumours that Karumba caravan parks will only take bookings for long periods; however, we do not believe this is the case and the two parks we recommend have assured us that they will accept reservations for any period. Most supplies are available in town.

ADELAIDE TO DARWIN

STUART HIGHWAY (3032 KM)

Bisecting Australia's dry red centre, the Stuart Highway sweeps across vast plains, weaves through the rugged MacDonnell Ranges and passes by lonely roadhouses. The route is the country's major south–north inland route, offering easy access to awesome scenery, remote deserts and the fabulous gorges close to Alice Springs. Alice Springs, Uluru and Kings Canyon are major tourist attractions.

Darwin
Darwin has interesting museums, great restaurants and a good range of tourist and leisure activities.

Best time to go

The most popular time to travel through the red centre is during the cooler months, between April and October. The days are usually warm and sunny and rain is less likely during this period.

John & Jan

Kata Tjuṯa (the Olgas)

WOOMERA

	J	F	M	A	M	J	J	A	S	O	N	D
Maximum	34	34	30	25	20	17	17	19	22	26	30	32
Minimum	19	19	17	13	9	7	6	7	9	12	15	18
Rainfall (mm)	15	20	15	12	21	16	16	15	16	16	17	14
Raindays	3	3	3	3	5	5	6	6	5	5	4	3

DALY WATERS

	J	F	M	A	M	J	J	A	S	O	N	D
Maximum	37	36	35	34	31	29	29	32	35	38	39	38
Minimum	24	23	22	19	16	13	12	13	17	21	24	24
Rainfall (mm)	161	163	118	23	5	6	2	2	5	23	59	108
Raindays	12	12	8	3	1	1	0	0	1	3	6	10

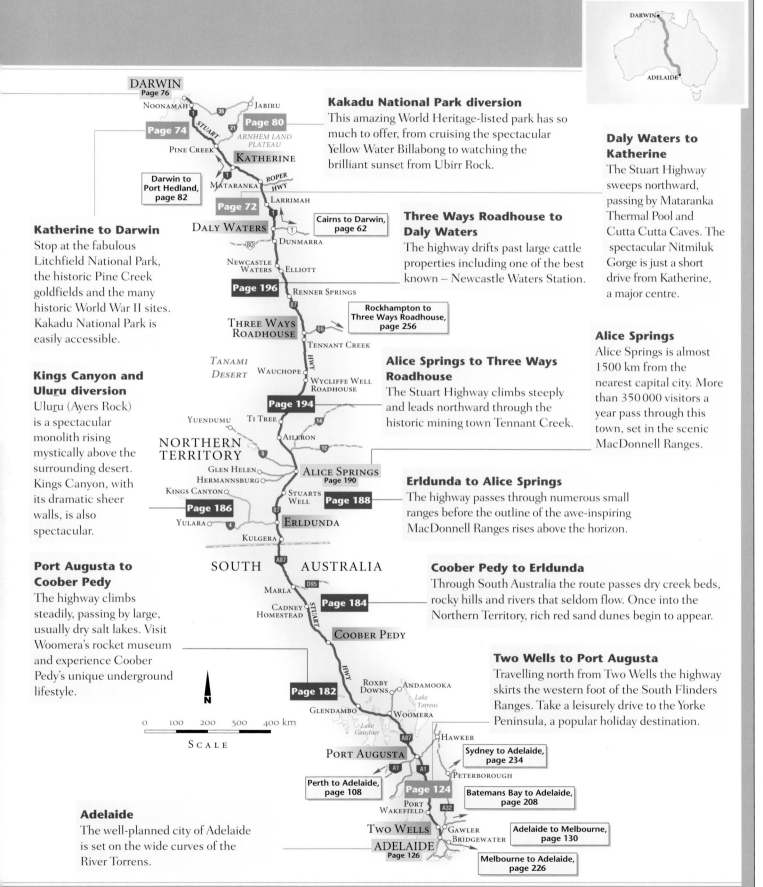

DARWIN
Page 76
NOONAMAH○ ○JABIRU
Page 74
STUART
36
21
Page 80
ARNHEM LAND
PLATEAU
PINE CREEK
KATHERINE

Darwin to Port Hedland, page 82
MATARANKA ROPER HWY
LARRIMAH
Page 72
DALY WATERS
DUNMARRA
Cairns to Darwin, page 62
80
NEWCASTLE WATERS○ ○ELLIOTT
Page 196
RENNER SPRINGS
87
THREE WAYS ROADHOUSE
86
Rockhampton to Three Ways Roadhouse, page 256
TENNANT CREEK
TANAMI DESERT
HWY
WAUCHOPE
WYCLIFFE WELL ROADHOUSE
Page 194
YUENDUMU○ TI TREE
14
AILERON
NORTHERN TERRITORY
12
5
GLEN HELEN
HERMANNSBURG○
KINGS CANYON○
YULARA○
4
ALICE SPRINGS
Page 190
STUARTS WELL
Page 188
ERLDUNDA
KULGERA
SOUTH
A87
AUSTRALIA
MARLA
D95
Page 184
CADNEY HOMESTEAD
STUART HWY
COOBER PEDY
Page 182
ROXBY DOWNS○ ○ANDAMOOKA
Lake Torrens
GLENDAMBO○ ○WOOMERA
Lake Gairdner
○HAWKER
Sydney to Adelaide, page 234
PORT AUGUSTA
A87 A1
○PETERBOROUGH
A1
Perth to Adelaide, page 108
Page 124
Batemans Bay to Adelaide, page 208
PORT WAKEFIELD
A32
TWO WELLS ○GAWLER
Adelaide to Melbourne, page 130
○BRIDGEWATER
ADELAIDE
Page 126
Melbourne to Adelaide, page 226

N

0   100   200   300   400 km
SCALE

Kakadu National Park diversion
This amazing World Heritage-listed park has so much to offer, from cruising the spectacular Yellow Water Billabong to watching the brilliant sunset from Ubirr Rock.

Daly Waters to Katherine
The Stuart Highway sweeps northward, passing by Mataranka Thermal Pool and Cutta Cutta Caves. The spectacular Nitmiluk Gorge is just a short drive from Katherine, a major centre.

Katherine to Darwin
Stop at the fabulous Litchfield National Park, the historic Pine Creek goldfields and the many historic World War II sites. Kakadu National Park is easily accessible.

Three Ways Roadhouse to Daly Waters
The highway drifts past large cattle properties including one of the best known – Newcastle Waters Station.

Alice Springs
Alice Springs is almost 1500 km from the nearest capital city. More than 350 000 visitors a year pass through this town, set in the scenic MacDonnell Ranges.

Kings Canyon and Uluru diversion
Uluru (Ayers Rock) is a spectacular monolith rising mystically above the surrounding desert. Kings Canyon, with its dramatic sheer walls, is also spectacular.

Alice Springs to Three Ways Roadhouse
The Stuart Highway climbs steeply and leads northward through the historic mining town Tennant Creek.

Erldunda to Alice Springs
The highway passes through numerous small ranges before the outline of the awe-inspiring MacDonnell Ranges rises above the horizon.

Port Augusta to Coober Pedy
The highway climbs steadily, passing by large, usually dry salt lakes. Visit Woomera's rocket museum and experience Coober Pedy's unique underground lifestyle.

Coober Pedy to Erldunda
Through South Australia the route passes dry creek beds, rocky hills and rivers that seldom flow. Once into the Northern Territory, rich red sand dunes begin to appear.

Two Wells to Port Augusta
Travelling north from Two Wells the highway skirts the western foot of the South Flinders Ranges. Take a leisurely drive to the Yorke Peninsula, a popular holiday destination.

Adelaide
The well-planned city of Adelaide is set on the wide curves of the River Torrens.

PORT AUGUSTA TO COOBER PEDY 540 KM

Authors' choice

⊛ Stuart Range Caravan Park, Coober Pedy

Located close to the Stuart Highway, this park has good facilities including an extensive range of accommodation, a pool and barbecues. Stop for dinner at the park's very popular pizza shop. There are no water hook-ups in the Coober Pedy parks due to the shortage of water; most parks have coin-in-the-slot water points for filling tanks.

For more details see page 361.

A prohibited area

Much of this section of the trip passes through the Woomera Prohibited Area, which covers 12.7 million ha. Although you can drive along the Stuart Highway, access to the rest of the area is by permit only. Camping is not allowed in the prohibited area.

A short cut

If you are travelling from Central Australia to the west, consider taking the unsealed road to Wirrulla from the Stuart Highway, 53 km north of Glendambo. This is the shortest route between Central Australia and the Eyre Highway. At 290 km, it is more than 400 km shorter than following the bitumen through Port Augusta. The road is suitable for four-wheel drives and off-road caravans or camper-trailers.

Coober Pedy to Erldunda, page 184

What's on

EASTER Opal Festival (Coober Pedy)
JUNE Glendi Festival (Coober Pedy)
OCTOBER Coober Pedy Races

Rocket museum

Woomera Heritage Centre and Missile Park is located in the centre of town. The outdoor display of rockets and missiles is complemented by a substantial indoor museum in the Oasis Centre. Corner Dewrang and Banool streets; (08) 8673 7042; entry fee applies; open 9 a.m. to 5 p.m. daily.

The beauty of opal

Mysterious and alluring stones, opals are much sought after. Australia produces the majority of the world's opal and most of it is mined close to Coober Pedy, a town famous for its underground buildings. Opals and opal jewellery are available from outlets in and around Coober Pedy.

Track notes

The Stuart Highway is a major route carrying tourist traffic, road trains and heavy transports. The road passes close to a number of large salt lakes and traverses undulating country between Port Augusta and Pimba. Woomera and Roxby Downs are reached along sealed roads from the turn-off at Pimba.

Town file

To get from Adelaide to Port Augusta see page 124.

1 **PORT AUGUSTA** (see page 123)

2 **WOOMERA** pop. 1349   🅿 PDG
GPS 31° 11.999' S/136° 49.482' E

Woomera was established in 1947 as a rocket launching site. There is a joint defence satellite communications facility nearby. In recent years asylum seekers have been detained near Woomera while their refugee claims are processed. Woomera is run by the Department of Defence and the town has basic facilities. 🛈 Oasis Centre, corner Dewrang and Banool streets; (08) 8673 7042.

3 **GLENDAMBO** pop. 30   🅿 PDG
GPS 30° 58.196' S/135° 45.026' E

Glendambo is a small settlement offering roadhouses, an accommodation complex, a caravan park and a tavern. The township has developed since the highway was re-routed and sealed in 1982. If travelling north, this is the last spot for fuel until Coober Pedy (254 km).

4 **COOBER PEDY** pop. 2762   🅿 PDG
GPS 29° 00.771' S/134° 45.271' E

In the arid centre of South Australia, Coober Pedy is a busy, cosmopolitan opal-mining town. Opal was discovered here in 1915 and Coober Pedy now yields about 85 per cent of Australia's opal output. Many residents live underground in 'dugouts' to escape the searing heat, and the town has several underground buildings including a hotel, a motel, galleries and churches. Coober Pedy has a good selection of shops and all services. If travelling south, it is the last spot for fuel until Glendambo (254 km). 🛈 Council Offices, Hutchison Street; (08) 8672 5298 or 1800 637 076; www.opalcapitaloftheworld.com.au

Travel tip

Coober Pedy's water comes from artesian bores and is treated at a reverse-osmosis plant, so it is quite expensive. Water to fill jerry cans or tanks is available from coin-in-the-slot dispensers located at the water authority in Hutchison Street and some caravan parks. This water is good quality and we fill our tanks here when we get the opportunity, despite the cost.

Port Augusta to Two Wells, page 124

Ceduna to Port Augusta, page 122

COOBER PEDY TO ERLDUNDA 489 KM

An opal town

The small opal-mining community of Mintabie, 33 km to the west of Marla, is reached along an unsealed road. The town's population fluctuates but basic services are available. Most of the opal here is open-cut mined with bulldozers. The town and rich opal field lie on Aboriginal land so a permit is required to visit Mintabie; you can obtain one from the police station at Marla for a small fee.

A great train ride

The passenger train service from Adelaide to Alice Springs, the *Ghan*, completed its first journey in 1929. In 1980 a new, more westerly line that parallels the Stuart Highway was opened. Construction of the railway from Alice Springs to Darwin is now under way.

Breakaways Reserve

This reserve is an area of low, coloured hills 34 km north of Coober Pedy. It has two lookouts and the area is best visited in the early morning or late afternoon as the colours of the hills change with the light. Turn east off the Stuart Highway 23 km north of town and obtain a self-issued national park entry pass on site.

Erldunda to Alice Springs, page 188

LASSETER HWY

RH ERLDUNDA 🚐 5

Kings Canyon and Uluru diversion, page 186

Lyndavale

4 🚐 KULGERA
RH

Victory Downs

Mount Cavenagh

NORTHERN TERRITORY

SOUTH AUSTRALIA

Alberga

STUART

CENTRAL AUSTRALIA

+ *Mt Howe 519m*

PITJANTJATJARA

Marble Hill + 523m

IWANTJA (INDULKANA)

Mt Chandler + 551m *Chandler*

River

ABORIGINAL

To Oodnadatta

MARLA 🚐 3

OODNADATTA   D95

Welbourn Hill

TRACK

MINTABIE

LAND

33

N

+ *Ammaroodinna Hill 359m*

Wintinna

The Painted Desert

0   20   40   60 km

SCALE

AUSTRALIA

Cadney Homestead
RH

2 🚐

32 *Copper Hills*

Mount Willoughby

Mt Arckaringa 243m ●

73

Arckaringa

Evelyn Downs

TALLARINGA CONSERVATION PARK

RAILWAY

HWY

Creek

Pootnoura

WOOMERA PROHIBITED AREA

Pootnoura

129

A87

Dog   *Fence*

BREAKAWAYS RESERVE

Ck *Mabel Creek*

Manguri

117

23

Port Augusta Coober Pedy page 182

COOBER PEDY

1 🛈 ✪ 🚐 ✈

(see page 182)

Travel tip

Northern Territory and South Australia both operate on Central Standard Time (CST). However, South Australia introduces daylight saving throughout summer (and one month either side). During daylight saving, northbound travellers should adjust clocks back by one hour and southbound travellers should move clocks forward by one hour at the border.

A legendary track

The legendary Oodnadatta Track closely follows the original *Ghan* railway line. This unsealed but maintained track is a popular route for travellers in four-wheel drives.

The colours of nature

The Painted Desert (Arckaringa Hills) is located between Cadney Homestead and Oodnadatta, to the east of the highway. These strikingly colourful hills, which change colour during the day as the light varies, are popular with photographers and painters. The Painted Desert is also known for its flora and fauna. All roads in the area are unsealed and really only suitable for four-wheel drives. Copper Hills Homestead is a good base from which to explore the area.

Track notes

This section of the Stuart Highway is a major route carrying tourist traffic, road trains and heavy transports. The road sweeps across wide plains through cattle-grazing country. The unsealed Oodnadatta Track meets the highway at Marla, as does the unsealed road to the opal-mining town of Mintabie.

Town file

1 COOBER PEDY (see page 183)

2 CADNEY HOMESTEAD 🅿 PDG
GPS 27° 54.317' S/134° 03.424' E
Cadney Homestead is a roadhouse with accommodation and a caravan park. Basic services are available.

3 MARLA pop. 80 🅿 PDG
GPS 27° 18.265' S/133° 37.371' E
Marla is located at the junction of the Oodnadatta Track and the Stuart Highway. The small township is a key highway service centre with all basic services.

4 KULGERA pop. 18 🅿 PDG
GPS 25° 50.391' S/133° 18.023' E
Kulgera is a roadhouse with accommodation. Basic services are available. The unsealed road to Finke that starts here is also the access route to the Lambert Centre (Australia's centre of gravity), 138 km east of Kulgera.

5 ERLDUNDA pop. 21 🅿 PDG
GPS 25° 11.886' S/133° 12.052' E
Erldunda is strategically located at the junction of the Stuart and Lasseter highways. The roadhouse accommodation complex has fuel, various styles of accommodation, a caravan park and a restaurant. Basic requirements are available.

Travel tip

The highway traverses the arid outback. In winter the days can be clear and sunny, but during summer temperatures can soar to 50 degrees Celsius. High temperatures place additional stresses on both motor vehicles and people. Carry adequate drinking water and drive to suit the conditions. Most of the highway is fenced but be aware that there still may be wandering stock.

KINGS CANYON AND ULURU DIVERSION 862 KM (RETURN)

Authors' choice

⊛ Kings Creek Station, Kings Canyon

This large camping area on a cattle station is our choice of places to stay when we visit the Kings Canyon area. It caters solely for tourists and has numerous sites in bush settings. The facilities include a pool, barbecues, a restaurant and a shop. The station also offers several fabulous activities including camel rides, helicopter flights and quad (four-wheel motorbike) rides. Kings Canyon is 39 km away along a sealed road.
For more details see page 373.

Travel tip

Two popular activities in the region are climbing Uluru (Ayers Rock) and taking the rim walk at Kings Canyon. Both are strenuous (especially Uluru) but worth the effort. Carry plenty of drinking water and avoid walking in the hotter part of the day. Bear in mind, however, that Uluru lies in the territory of the Anangu people and they prefer tourists not to climb Uluru. There are four guided walks offered as alternatives.

Dramatic domes

The first European discovery of Kata Tjuta (the Olgas) was by one of Australia's great explorers, Ernest Giles. These rounded granite domes stand sentinel-like on the red sandy plain and their vivid colours change from red to grey to purple. A visit here will live in the memory forever. Entry fee applies at Uluru–Kata Tjuta National Park.

The magnificence of Uluru

Uluru (Ayers Rock) is an Australian icon. The colours of this magnificent monolith, as it rises above the surrounding desert, are astounding. Visitors can climb to the summit, flock to the viewing points at sunrise and sunset, take flights over the Rock and travel around it on any number of tours. Entry fee applies at Uluru–Kata Tjuta National Park.

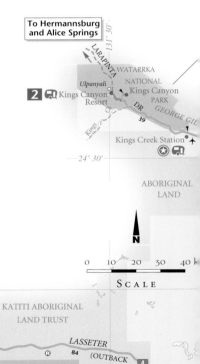

The wonders of Kings Canyon

Kings Canyon, in the Watarrka National Park, has been carved by Kings Creek slicing through the rugged George Gill Range. The canyon has two walks: one along the canyon floor or a more arduous but more spectacular rim-edge walk. The rich, stunning colours of the canyon walls, the weathered domes and the lush Garden of Eden along the creek make this a particularly beautiful destination.

Track notes

The Lasseter Highway between the Stuart Highway and Yulara is sealed. The road west from Yulara is sealed as far as Kata Tjuta (the Olgas). Luritja Road to Kings Canyon is also sealed. The Ernest Giles Road between the Stuart Highway and Luritja Road is unsealed and best tackled in a four-wheel drive as it can be quite rough.

Town file

1 ERLDUNDA (see page 185)

2 KINGS CANYON RESORT pop. 50   PDG
GPS 24° 15.058' S/131° 30.679' E
Kings Canyon Resort is located 7 km from Kings Canyon. Services include a roadhouse, tavern, fine-dining restaurant, cafe and small supermarket. Larapinta Drive (Mereenie Loop Road) between Kings Canyon Resort and Hermannsburg is a popular unsealed route to Alice Springs.

3 YULARA pop. 2754   PDG
GPS 25° 14.506' S/130° 58.984' E
Yulara is the major service point for the Uluru–Kata Tjuta National Park. There is a range of accommodation, a good caravan park and camping ground, a shopping centre with all basic requirements and a busy industrial estate. This is the only base for exploring the national park as no camping is permitted within the park and bush camping outside the park is prohibited.   (08) 8957 7377.

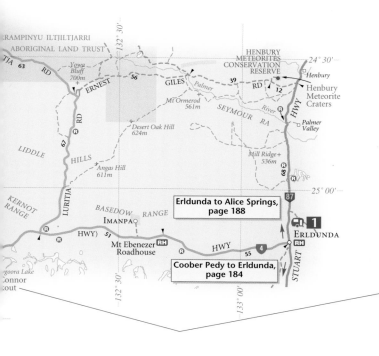

What's on

SEPTEMBER The Great Pram Battle (Yulara)

Outback lookout

Mount Connor is a striking, flat-topped mountain south of the Lasseter Highway and can be seen from this lookout. Tourists often mistake Mount Connor as a distant sighting of Uluru (Ayers Rock). Climb the sand dune opposite the lookout for a view across a salt lake.

ERLDUNDA TO ALICE SPRINGS 201 KM

⊛ MacDonnell Range Holiday Park, Alice Springs

Enjoy a delicious, free pancake breakfast every Sunday morning at this large, quality park – one of the Alice Springs parks we choose to stay at. It has numerous activities during the tourist season (April to October), including nightly talks on the stars, bush tucker and other subjects, and has a great range of tourist park facilities. Located 4.5 km south of the city centre, it is a great base for exploring the region. Bookings are essential in the tourist season.

For more details see page 352.

Sacred rock carvings

At Ewaninga Rock Carvings Conservation Reserve, 34 km south-east of Alice Springs via the unsealed Old South Road (accessible by two-wheel drive), sandstone outcrops beside a small claypan form natural galleries, where the Arrernte Aboriginal people have carved a great variety of sacred petroglyphs – shallow rock engravings. They are best viewed in the early morning and late afternoon, when shadows make the carvings more obvious. Follow the walk with explanatory signs.

Preserving the railway

Once operating between Marree and Alice Springs, the original narrow-gauge *Ghan* line has mostly been dismantled. However, the Ghan Preservation Society still operates both steam and diesel locomotives along a 22-km section of track between the MacDonnell Sidings (just outside Alice Springs) and Ewaninga Rock Carvings Conservation Reserve. There is also a museum preserving the history of the *Ghan*. Norris Bell Avenue, off Stuart Highway; entry fee applies; open daily. Trains operate April to September on Wednesday, Friday and Sunday; fee applies; (08) 8955 5047.

Meteorite craters

The Henbury craters were created when a meteor slammed into Earth about 4700 years ago. There are 12 craters; the largest is 180 m across and around 15 m deep. An easy self-guided walk from the carpark takes about 45 minutes. Ranger (08) 8952 1013.

Kings Canyon and Uluru diversion, page 186

Coober Pedy to Erldunda, page 184

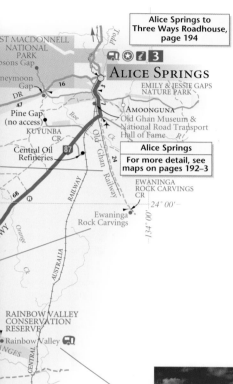

Alice Springs to
Three Ways Roadhouse,
page 194

ALICE SPRINGS

EMILY & JESSIE GAPS
NATURE PARK

Alice Springs
For more detail, see
maps on pages 192–3

Track notes

This section of the Stuart Highway is a major route, carrying road trains and heavy transports. The highway passes through some scenic country and crosses the Finke and Palmer rivers. The roads to Rainbow Valley and Henbury Meteorite Craters are unsealed but maintained and usually accessible by two-wheel drives with care. Visitors to Kings Canyon can travel on the all-sealed route or can take the unsealed Ernest Giles Road, which is best negotiated in a four-wheel drive – it can be rough at times.

Town file

1 **ERLDUNDA** (see page 185)

2 **STUARTS WELL** pop.10   ⛽ PD
GPS 24° 20.409' S/133° 27.550' E
Stuarts Well is a roadhouse complex with a caravan park and a licensed inn. Visit Noel Fullerton's famous camel farm; the camel rides on offer vary from a couple of minutes to 14-day safaris. Basic requirements are available in Stuarts Well.

3 **ALICE SPRINGS** (see page 190)

A rainbow in stone

Rainbow Valley lies in the James Ranges. This stunning, much photographed formation is a sandstone cliff face with bands of rock that resemble a rainbow. The brilliant range of colours is most spectacular in the late afternoon. Sometimes, after good rains, the cliff face is beautifully reflected in the water-filled claypan in front of it. There are several camping sites here (fee applies) and free gas barbecues. Ranger (08) 8952 1013.

An ancient river

The Finke River is the oldest river in the world that still follows its original course. Cutting through the MacDonnell Ranges west of Alice Springs, the Finke flows into the desert towards Lake Eyre in South Australia. While short sections regularly flow, it has only flowed over its full length once since European occupation of Central Australia. It is, however, exhilarating to walk along the dry riverbed.

What's on

JUNE Finke Desert Race (Alice Springs) JULY Camel Cup (Alice Springs) AUGUST Springs Rodeo (Alice Springs), Lockwood/Henley-on-Todd Regatta (Alice Springs)

ALICE SPRINGS

YOUR GUIDE

Alice Springs, at the heart of the Red Centre and almost 1500 km from the nearest capital city, is en route to many attractions including Uluru (Ayers Rock). More than 350000 visitors a year pass through this well-maintained town in the scenic MacDonnell Ranges. Between May and September days are warm and nights are cold. For the rest of the year daytime temperatures rise to the high 30s but nights are milder. Rains, usually brief, can come at any time of the year.

CITY CENTRE

See map on page 192.

Aboriginal Art and Culture Centre 192 D4
Displays of Arrernte culture and music. Didgeridoo and spear-throwing lessons available; billy tea, damper and bush tucker are all served.

Alice Springs Reptile Centre 192 C4
Close-up encounters at the largest reptile display in the Territory.

Araluen Centre for Arts and Entertainment 192 A3
Contains three major art galleries that feature work by Albert Namatjira, as well as other Aboriginal and contemporary art.

Central Australian Aviation Museum 192 A4
Houses two early flying doctor planes, interesting accounts of aviation history and memorabilia.

Museum of Central Australia 192 A3
Replicas of local ancient megafauna including the world's largest bird, and an impressive meteorite display.

Panorama Guth 192 D3
Includes a remarkable 360-degree panorama painted by resident artist Henk Guth, along with many other original paintings and prints.

Royal Flying Doctor Service Base 192 C4
Audiovisual presentations and an interactive museum at a working base of this important service.

ALICE SPRINGS AND SURROUNDS

See map on page 193.

Alice Springs Desert Park 193 H3
Desert animals and plants, and information about their traditional use by Aboriginal people; film and interactive displays.

Alice Springs Telegraph Station Historical Reserve 193 J1
Original stone buildings and equipment, guided tours, bushwalking and wildlife.

Visitor information

Central Australian Tourism Industry Association
60 Gregory Terrace, Alice Springs
(08) 8952 5800
www.centralaustraliantourism.com

ALICE SPRINGS REGION

See map on pages 192–3.

Arltunga Historical Reserve 193 K5

Site of Central Australia's first gold discovery in 1887; now a ghost town; wander through the old camps, buildings and mines.

Glen Helen Gorge 192 B6

Walk along the Finke River bed, between towering cliffs; the permanent waterhole is a haven for birdlife.

Hermannsburg Historic Precinct 192 B7

Former Lutheran Mission and once the home of Albert Namatjira; the 1870s German-style buildings have been restored and include a museum, an art gallery of Aboriginal works, and tearooms.

National Road Transport Hall of Fame 193 G7

Houses a large collection of trucks, cars and related memorabilia; much of the history of remote transport and early road trains can be found here.

Old Ghan Museum 193 G7

Houses engines, carriages and memorabilia from the old *Ghan*; tells the story of the laying of the railway.

Ormiston Gorge and Pound 192 B6

Arresting scenery and incredibly high cliffs; walk to the Pound: a bowl in the mountains formed by erosion.

Ross River Homestead 193 J6

Experience outback culture; accommodation, horseriding, whip-cracking and other pursuits are all on offer.

Ruby Gap Nature Park 193 L5

Boasts an 850-million-year-old landscape including the garnet-strewn gorge at Glen Annie and also at Hale River; strictly four-wheel drive access only.

Simpsons Gap 192 F6

Here red cliffs tower several hundred metres above a waterhole; spot black-footed rock wallabies in the early morning or late afternoon.

Standley Chasm 192 E6

Reached by a 20-minute walk down a lush gully beside a creek and through cycads and ferns; at about midday the chasm becomes spectacularly coloured by the sun, the red rocks glowing unforgettably.

Tnorala (Gosse Bluff) Conservation Reserve 192 A7

A huge crater formed over 130 million years ago when a meteor fell to earth; there is a four-wheel drive track to the inside of the crater.

Trephina Gorge Nature Park 193 I5

Excellent walking trails and picturesque scenery; swim in the refreshingly cold waters of the John Hayes Rockhole.

Getting around

The roads leading to Alice Springs are long but sealed. The city is small, and easy to negotiate. All the main attractions are within walking distance. There are six marked tourist trails around the city, each with a different theme. Pick up the theme brochures and maps from the visitor information centre on Gregory Terrace.

Airport shuttle bus Alice Springs Airport Shuttle (08) 8953 0310; **Motoring organisations** AANT (08) 8952 1087, Northern Territory Road Report 1800 246 199; **Taxis** Alice Springs Taxis (08) 8952 1877, Fisher Taxis (08) 8955 5552.

Top events

Country Music Festival (April)
Plenty of toe-tapping fun.

Finke Desert Race (June)
Car and motorbike racing.

Camel Cup (July)
A huge event, with camel races and a carnival atmosphere.

Lockwood/Henley-on-Todd Regatta (August)
Crews carry or wheel bottomless boats along the dry riverbed.

Masters Games (October)
Mature-age athletic carnival, even-numbered years.

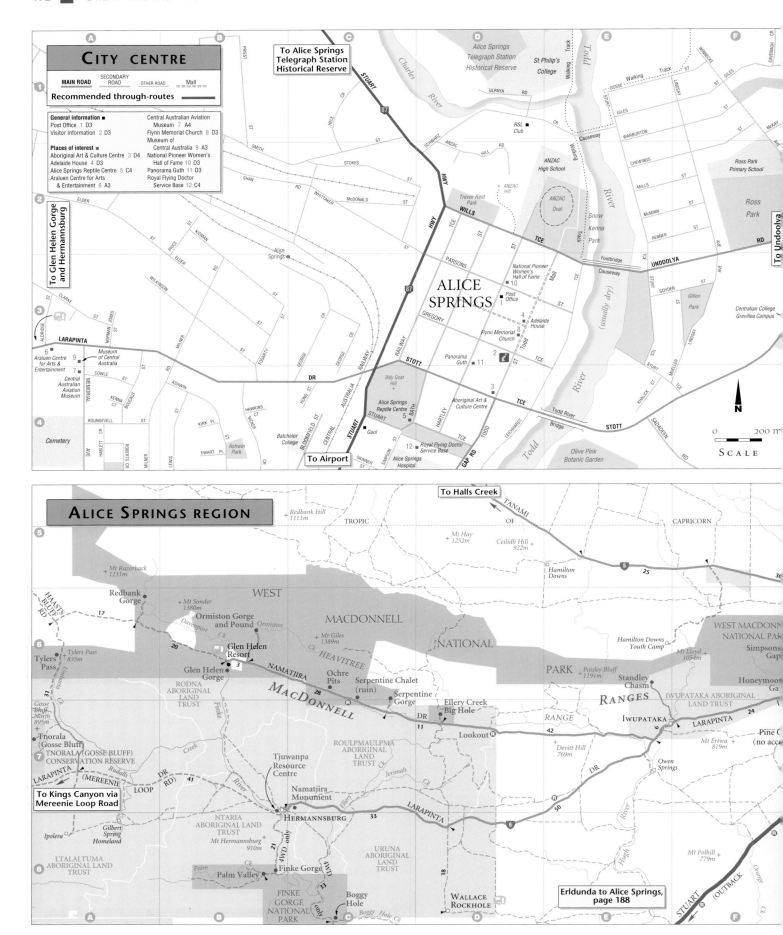

CITY CENTRE

MAIN ROAD SECONDARY ROAD OTHER ROAD Mall

Recommended through-routes

General information ■
Post Office 1 D3
Visitor Information 2 D3

Places of interest ■
Aboriginal Art & Culture Centre 3 D4
Adelaide House 4 D3
Alice Springs Reptile Centre 5 C4
Araluen Centre for Arts
& Entertainment 6 A3

Central Australian Aviation
Museum 7 A4
Flynn Memorial Church 8 D3
Museum of
Central Australia 9 A3
National Pioneer Women's
Hall of Fame 10 D3
Panorama Guth 11 D3
Royal Flying Doctor
Service Base 12 C4

To Alice Springs
Telegraph Station
Historical Reserve

To Glen Helen Gorge
and Hermannsburg

ALICE SPRINGS

To Undoolya

To Airport

ALICE SPRINGS REGION

To Halls Creek

To Kings Canyon via
Mereenie Loop Road

Erldunda to Alice Springs,
page 188

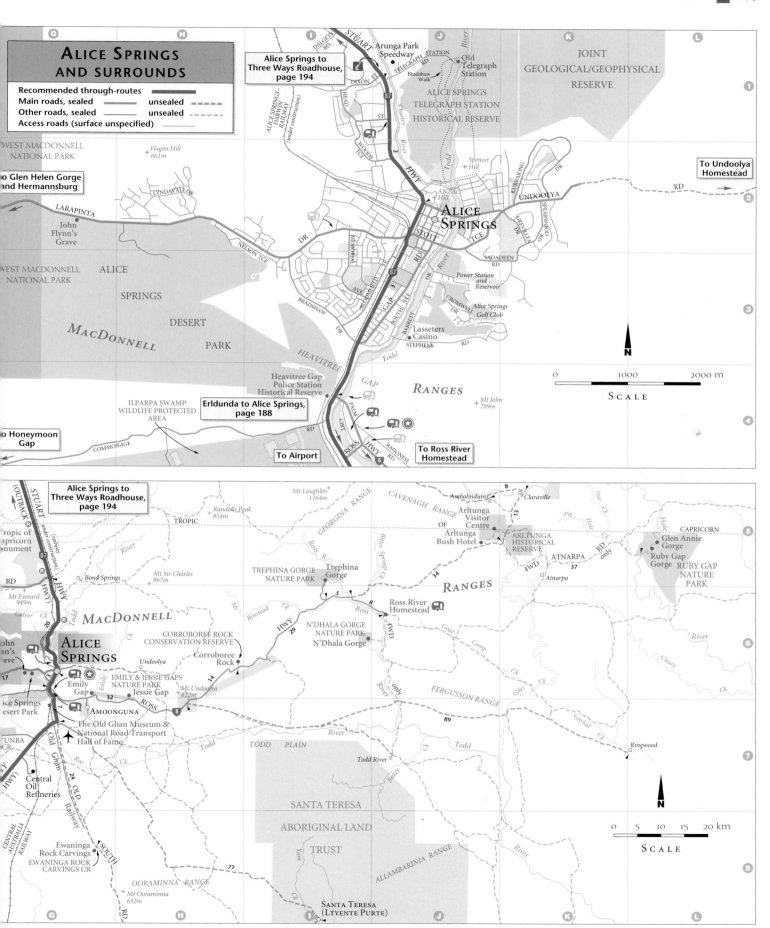

ALICE SPRINGS AND SURROUNDS

Recommended through-routes ▬▬▬
Main roads, sealed ▬▬▬ **unsealed** ▬ ▬ ▬
Other roads, sealed ▬▬ **unsealed** ─ ─ ─
Access roads (surface unspecified) ───

Alice Springs to Three Ways Roadhouse, page 194

Erldunda to Alice Springs, page 188

To Undoolya Homestead

To Glen Helen Gorge and Hermannsburg

To Honeymoon Gap

To Airport

To Ross River Homestead

WEST MACDONNELL NATIONAL PARK

ALICE SPRINGS DESERT PARK

MacDONNELL RANGES

ILPARPA SWAMP WILDLIFE PROTECTED AREA

JOINT GEOLOGICAL/GEOPHYSICAL RESERVE

ALICE SPRINGS TELEGRAPH STATION HISTORICAL RESERVE

Arunga Park Speedway

Old Telegraph Station

Bradshaw Walk

ALICE SPRINGS

Lasseters Casino

Power Station and Reservoir

Alice Springs Golf Club

Heavitree Gap Police Station Historical Reserve

Mt John 789m

Flagon Hill 661m

John Flynn's Grave

SCALE 0 1000 2000 m

N

Alice Springs to Three Ways Roadhouse, page 194

MacDONNELL RANGES

ALICE SPRINGS

Alice Springs Desert Park

John Flynn's Grave

Central Oil Refineries

The Old Ghan Museum & National Road Transport Hall of Fame

Ewaninga Rock Carvings
EWANINGA ROCK CARVINGS CR

Emily Gap
EMILY & JESSIE GAPS NATURE PARK
Jessie Gap
Mt Undoolya 822m

Amoonguna
Undoolya

CORROBOREE ROCK CONSERVATION RESERVE
Corroboree Rock

TREPHINA GORGE NATURE PARK
Trephina Gorge

N'DHALA GORGE NATURE PARK
N'Dhala Gorge

Ross River Homestead

ARLTUNGA HISTORICAL RESERVE
Arltunga Visitor Centre
Arltunga Bush Hotel

Glen Annie Gorge
Ruby Gap
RUBY GAP NATURE PARK

Mt Laughlen 1164m
Randalls Peak 854m
Mt Sir Charles 867m
Bond Springs
Mt Everard 949m

GEORGINA RANGE
CAVENAGH RANGE
Ambalindum
Claraville
FERGUSSON RANGE

SANTA TERESA ABORIGINAL LAND TRUST

Ringwood

TODD PLAIN
Todd River

OORAMINNA RANGE
Mt Ooraminna 652m

ALLAMBARINJA RANGE

Santa Teresa (Ltyente Purte)

TROPIC OF CAPRICORN

SCALE 0 5 10 15 20 km

N

ALICE SPRINGS TO THREE WAYS ROADHOUSE 531 K

Authors' choice

⊛ Outback Caravan Park, Tennant Creek

This large, well-appointed park is just 1 km from the town centre and off the highway. We find it an ideal base for a few days exploring this interesting area. Facilities include a pool, spa and new entertainment area, for bush cooking and poetry recitals.

For more details see page 390.

Battery Hill Mining Centre

This impressive complex, 1.5 km east of Tennant Creek, showcases the rich mining history of the area. It boasts a working underground mine, one of only three 10-stamp batteries still operational in Australia, and a host of historic mining equipment. The Battery Hill Mineral Museum is part of the centre and houses some unique and fascinating mineral specimens. The complex adjoins the visitor information centre in Peko Road; (08) 8962 1281; entry fee applies; open 9 a.m. to 5 p.m. daily with underground mine and battery tours every morning and afternoon.

Historical reserve

In 1860 the explorer John McDouall Stuart calculated that Mount Stuart marked the centre of Australia, as it was equidistant from the south and north coasts, and equidistant from the east and west coasts. Today there is a small reserve with a monument at the base of the mountain marking the centre. A visitor information board is also located at the foot of the mountain.

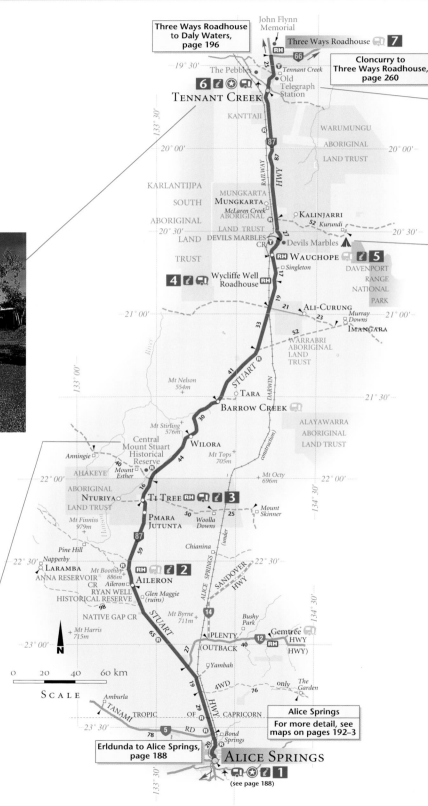

Three Ways Roadhouse to Daly Waters, page 196

Cloncurry to Three Ways Roadhouse, page 260

Erldunda to Alice Springs, page 188

Alice Springs
For more detail, see maps on pages 192–3

The Overland Telegraph

Completed in 1872, the Overland Telegraph was a major technological feat for its time. The 1800-km-long single overhead wire, along with an undersea cable that ran to Java, linked Australia to the rest of the world for the first time. Long since surpassed by new technology, many remnants of the Telegraph remain, including the repeater stations at Alice Springs, Barrow Creek and Tennant Creek.

The Devils Marbles

According to Aboriginal Dreamtime mythology, the Devils Marbles, 106 km south of Tennant Creek, are the fossilised eggs of the Rainbow Serpent. These hundreds of huge, rounded granite boulders are a favourite subject for photographers. There is bush camping available (fee applies).

What's on

MAY Tennant Creek Cup Race Day JULY Tennant Creek Show AUGUST Barrow Creek Races SEPTEMBER Desert Harmony Festival of Arts and Culture (Tennant Creek)

Travel tip

Gemtree, 135 km north-east of Alice Springs, is the centre of a world-class gemfield where zircon, garnet, beryl and tourmaline can all be found. Fossicking equipment can be hired and experienced guides will show you the best places to try your luck. The fields are a 70-km-drive along a sealed section of the Plenty Highway. There is a caravan park at Gemtree and it sells supplies, fuel and gemstones.

Track notes

The Stuart Highway in this section is wide, well maintained and sealed. While there are no slow-vehicle lanes, it is possible to overtake on longer straight sections. However, take care when overtaking road trains as some are up to a staggering 53.5 m in length.

Town file

1 **ALICE SPRINGS** (see page 190)

2 **AILERON** pop. 10   ⛽ PDG
GPS 22° 22.621' S/132° 22.126' E
A popular rest stop on the Stuart Highway, Aileron is 133 km north of Alice Springs. The Aileron Roadhouse complex has a range of accommodation. Gemstones can be cut and set at the historic Aileron homestead. Basic services are available. 🛈 Aileron Roadhouse, Stuart Highway; (08) 8956 9703.

3 **TI TREE** pop. 50   ⛽ PDG
GPS 22° 07.853' S/133° 24.987' E
In this small township the roadhouse is the main service centre for travellers. Fruit and vegetables can be bought from local farms; follow the signs. There is a gallery of local Aboriginal art on the west side of the highway. 🛈 Ti Tree Roadhouse, Stuart Highway; (08) 8956 9741.

4 **WYCLIFFE WELL ROADHOUSE**   ⛽ PDG
GPS 20° 47.727' S/134° 14.225' E
This area claims the title of UFO capital of Australia. Press clippings that record many unusual sightings are on display in the roadhouse. The roadhouse complex has a shop, caravan park and large dam stocked with barramundi. If you have a four-wheel drive, this is an ideal base from which to explore the Davenport Ranges, roughly 160 km east. 🛈 Stuart Highway; (08) 8964 1966; www.wycliffe.com.au

5 **WAUCHOPE** pop. 7   ⛽ PDG
GPS 20° 38.428' S/134° 13.350' E
Wauchope, settled in the 1930s, has a hotel, roadhouse and caravan park complex located just a few kilometres south of the Devils Marbles. 🛈 The Wauchope Hotel, Stuart Highway; (08) 8964 1963.

6 **TENNANT CREEK** pop. 3856   ⛽ PDG
GPS 19° 38.635' S/134° 11.489' E
Gold was discovered here in the 1930s, starting Australia's last gold rush. Today gold is still mined on the rich Tennant Creek fields and fossickers also come to try their luck. 🛈 Battery Hill Visitor Information Centre, Peko Road; (08) 8962 3388; www.tennantcreektourism.com.au

7 **THREE WAYS ROADHOUSE**   ⛽ PDG
GPS 19° 26.235' S/134° 12.489' E
One of Australia's best known intersections, 'Three Ways' is the junction of the Barkly and Stuart highways. The roadhouse provides fuel, meals and accommodation for travellers.

THREE WAYS ROADHOUSE TO DALY WATERS 379 KM

The Overland Telegraph Monument

Less than 30 km south of Dunmarra, a monument marks the place where the last historic join occurred in the single-wire Overland Telegraph, on 22 August 1872. A few remaining telegraph poles are also visible immediately alongside the Stuart Highway.

What's on

SEPTEMBER Daly Waters Rodeo and Campdraft, Spellbore Campdraft (Newcastle Waters Station)

Newcastle Waters

Also known as Marlinja, this historic droving town was at the junction of the busy north–south Murranji and Barkly stock routes. The Jones Store (listed by the National Trust), the old hotel and a larger-than-life bronze tribute to drovers make this town an interesting deviation. There are no services available.

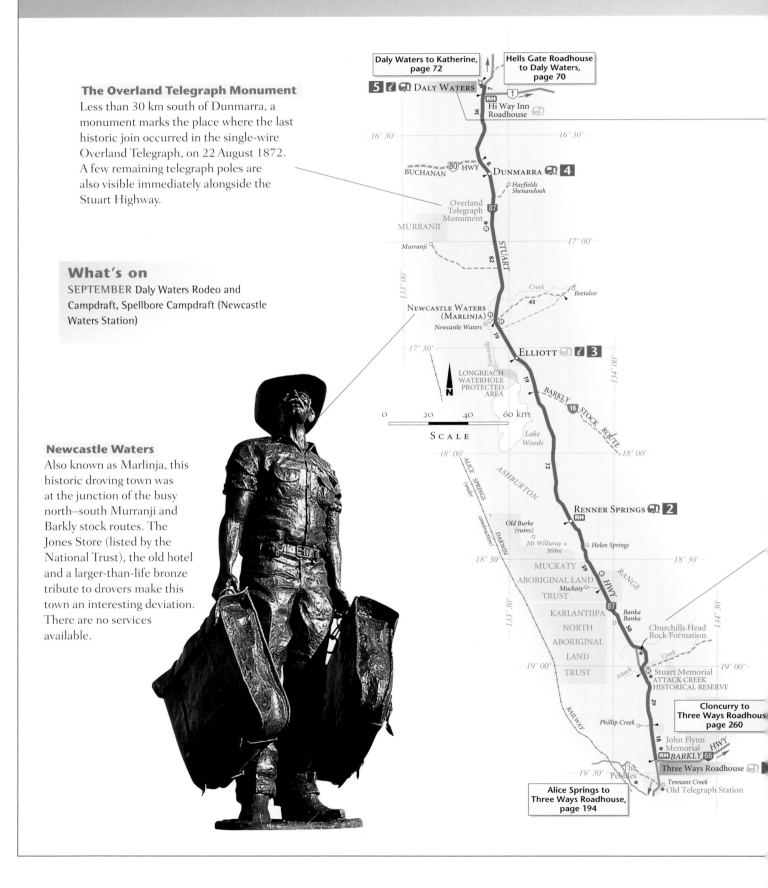

Daly Waters to Katherine, page 72

Hells Gate Roadhouse to Daly Waters, page 70

Cloncurry to Three Ways Roadhouse page 260

Alice Springs to Three Ways Roadhouse, page 194

Daly Waters

Hi Way Inn Roadhouse

BUCHANAN HWY 80

DUNMARRA 4

Hayfields Shenandoah

Overland Telegraph Monument

MURRANJI

Murranji

STUART

Creek Beetaloo

NEWCASTLE WATERS (MARLINJA)

Newcastle Waters

LONGREACH WATERHOLE PROTECTED AREA

ELLIOTT 3

N

BARKLY STOCK ROUTE

Lake Woods

0 20 40 60 km

SCALE

ALICE SPRINGS (under construction)

ASHBURTON

DARWIN

RENNER SPRINGS 2

Old Burke (ruins)

Mt Willieray + 369m

Helen Springs

MUCKATY ABORIGINAL LAND TRUST

Muckaty

HWY

RANGE

KARLANTIJPA NORTH ABORIGINAL LAND TRUST

Banka Banka

Churchills Head Rock Formation

Creek

Attack

Stuart Memorial ATTACK CREEK HISTORICAL RESERVE

Phillip Creek

RAILWAY

John Flynn Memorial BARKLY 66 HWY

Three Ways Roadhouse

The Pebbles

Tennant Creek Old Telegraph Station

A legendary pub

The historic Daly Waters Pub, on Stuart Street, was built in the 1930s to service the crew and passengers of international aircraft. Today it still caters for travellers, with most now arriving by road to enjoy the famous nightly Beef and Barra Barbecue during the tourist season (April to October).

Churchills Head

This unusual rock formation (said to resemble Winston Churchill) is at the crest of a cutting on the old highway alignment. The scenic detour is easily located about 60 km north of Three Ways Roadhouse, with clearly signposted turn-offs at the northern and southern entrances.

Travel tip

During the winter tourist season, the Daly Waters Pub Caravan Park is extremely popular. No bookings are taken and space is available on a 'first in, first served' basis, so get in early. The informal, open-plan park has no site allocations and power is available from a small number of power boxes. The relaxed nature of the park is similar to what can be experienced next door at the historic pub.

Track notes

The Stuart Highway from Three Ways Roadhouse to Daly Waters is a wide sealed road with a number of rest areas. Some of these on the Stuart and Barkly highways are clearly signposted for trucks only, while there are other adequate rest areas for caravans, motorhomes and other vehicles.

Town file

1 THREE WAYS ROADHOUSE (see page 195)

2 RENNER SPRINGS pop. 11   ⛽ PDG
GPS 18° 19.120' S/133° 47.731' E
Life revolves around the roadhouse complex in this tiny highway town, named after Frederick Renner who was the doctor to workers on the Overland Telegraph. Dr Renner discovered springs in the area when he observed flocks of birds gathering there. The service station, motel and caravan park form a convenient service point for travellers on the busy Stuart Highway. Meals, fuel, phones and accommodation are available. We think the sandwiches here are quite special – the roadhouse still bakes its own bread each day.

3 ELLIOTT pop. 432   ⛽ PDG
GPS 17° 33.344' S/133° 32.892' E
A large shaded rest area is a welcome sight for tourists entering the highway town of Elliott. Named after Captain Elliott, the officer in charge of a camp for troops during World War II, it has basic services for travellers including two caravan parks, and fuel, meals, accommodation and limited supplies are available. On the southern outskirts of town, there is the site of a World War II camp. ⓘ Elliott Hotel, Stuart Highway; (08) 8969 2069.

4 DUNMARRA pop. 10   ⛽ PDG
GPS 16° 40.790' S/133° 24.756' E
The service station, accommodation and caravan park complex forms the centre of this small town. The final section of the Overland Telegraph line was completed just a few kilometres from here in 1872, joining the northern and southern sections of the vast project. Food, fuel, phones and accommodation are available.

5 DALY WATERS (see page 71)

To continue on to Darwin, see Daly Waters to Katherine, page 72, and Katherine to Darwin, page 74.

PERTH TO PORT HEDLAND
GREAT NORTHERN HIGHWAY (1649 KM)

The Great Northern Highway is an important, direct inland route linking Perth with the far north of Western Australia. It crosses the rich grain-growing areas of the south, the sheep properties in the centre of the State and the larger cattle properties in the north. Many of the frontier towns along this route are steeped in mining history, and mining still continues at several large sites alongside the highway, including the BHP iron-ore operations at Newman. The spectacular, rugged red Pilbara gorges are easily reached from this route before the highway rolls into busy Port Hedland.

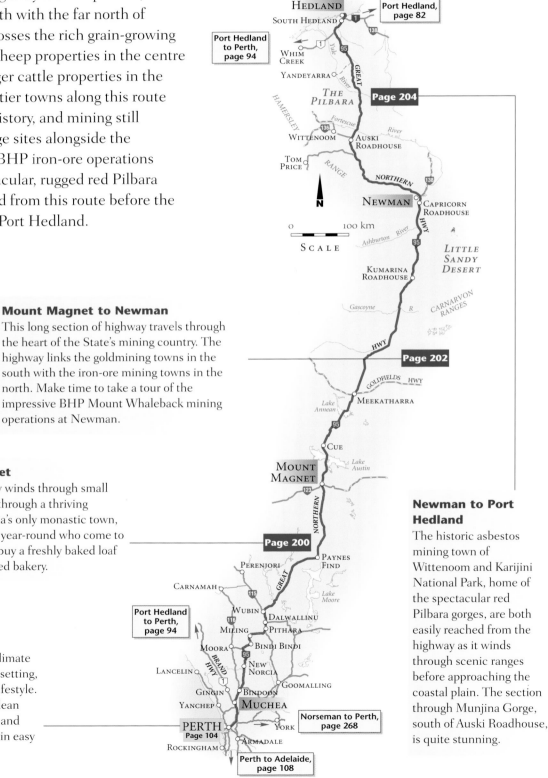

Mount Magnet to Newman
This long section of highway travels through the heart of the State's mining country. The highway links the goldmining towns in the south with the iron-ore mining towns in the north. Make time to take a tour of the impressive BHP Mount Whaleback mining operations at Newman.

Muchea to Mount Magnet
The Great Northern Highway winds through small rural towns as it heads north through a thriving grain-growing region. Australia's only monastic town, New Norcia, attracts tourists year-round who come to enjoy a guided tour or just to buy a freshly baked loaf from the monastery's renowned bakery.

Perth
With a Mediterranean-type climate and magnificent coastal river setting, Perth is ideal for an outdoor lifestyle. Visitors to this city will find clean surf beaches, tranquil forests and well-kept parklands – all within easy reach of the city centre.

Newman to Port Hedland
The historic asbestos mining town of Wittenoom and Karijini National Park, home of the spectacular red Pilbara gorges, are both easily reached from the highway as it winds through scenic ranges before approaching the coastal plain. The section through Munjina Gorge, south of Auski Roadhouse, is quite stunning.

Walga Rock, near Cue

Best time to go

The best time to travel far north is in the cooler, drier months from April to October, while in the south, year-round travel is possible.

John & Jan

PAYNES FIND	J	F	M	A	M	J	J	A	S	O	N	D
Maximum	37	36	33	28	23	19	18	20	24	27	31	35
Minimum	21	21	18	14	9	7	5	6	8	11	15	18
Rainfall (mm)	18	22	27	25	42	46	35	28	14	10	10	12
Raindays	2	2	3	4	6	8	8	6	4	3	2	2

NEWMAN	J	F	M	A	M	J	J	A	S	O	N	D
Maximum	39	37	36	32	26	22	22	25	29	34	37	39
Minimum	25	24	23	19	13	10	8	10	14	18	22	24
Rainfall (mm)	51	80	39	25	23	25	12	11	4	4	10	28
Raindays	7	7	5	4	4	4	2	1	1	1	3	5

MUCHEA TO MOUNT MAGNET 513 KM

Stay at a station

Several station properties along the Great Northern Highway offer camping to visitors during the winter months and also when the wildflowers are blooming. These include Wogarno, Kirkalocka and Ninghan. The turn-offs to the stations are well signposted with caravan park symbols. Some are close to the highway, while others are many kilometres off.

Australia's only monastic town

A visit to New Norcia is an unforgettable experience. This monastic town was founded on the Victoria Plains in 1846 in an attempt to 'help' the local Aboriginal people. Today it is still owned and operated by the Benedictine monastic community. Two-hour walking tours of the town depart daily from the museum gift shop at 11 a.m. and 1.30 p.m.

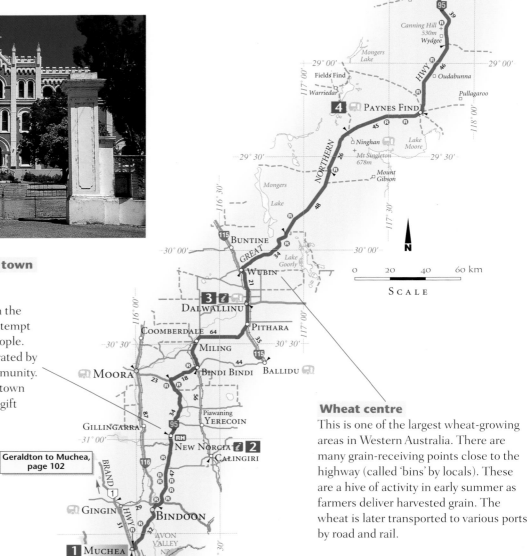

Mount Magnet to Newman, page 202

Geraldton to Muchea, page 102

Muchea to Perth (56 km)
For connecting routes, see map of Perth suburbs and surrounds, page 107

Wheat centre

This is one of the largest wheat-growing areas in Western Australia. There are many grain-receiving points close to the highway (called 'bins' by locals). These are a hive of activity in early summer as farmers deliver harvested grain. The wheat is later transported to various ports by road and rail.

Wildflowers

Between July and November this area of Western Australia can be ablaze with wildflowers, including the unusual wreath flower. Wattles are the dominant plant in the region, with more than 80 varieties found. Depending on the rains, you may also see stunning displays of white, yellow and pink everlasting daisies.

What's on

SEPTEMBER Wattle Week Festival (Dalwallinu)

Travel tip

The Benedictine monks of New Norcia produce a range of wonderful products, including olive oil, table wine and their famous long-life nut cake. A variety of fresh bread is also baked each day in the monastery's 100-year-old wood-fired bakery. The produce is available from the museum gift shop or the roadhouse.

Track notes

This is a major route carrying road trains and heavy transports, many of which travel to Port Hedland, Broome and towns further north. Progress can be a little slow through some hilly sections, but generally the road is a good, wide sealed highway. The route passes through broadacre grain-farming areas and sheep country, where many local grain trucks use the road during the wheat harvest in early summer.

Town file

1 MUCHEA (see page 103)

2 NEW NORCIA pop. 75   ⛽ PD
GPS 30° 58.371' S/116° 12.808' E
Founded in 1846, New Norcia is Australia's only monastic town. Twenty-seven of its buildings are classified by the National Trust and the whole town is registered on the National Estate. It is home to a community of Benedictine monks who own and operate the town. In recent years the monastery has opened its doors to visitors, and tours depart twice daily from the museum gift shop. The fascinating New Norcia Museum and Art Gallery houses a fine collection of heritage material. A roadhouse and general store cater for travellers. 🛈 Museum and Art Gallery, Great Northern Highway; (08) 9654 8056; www.newnorcia.wa.edu.au

3 DALWALLINU pop. 697   ⛽ PDG
GPS 30° 06.464' S/116° 37.965' E
This town is a regional centre for wheat and sheep farming and the shire is the largest wheat-producing area in Western Australia. From July to November the area is rich in wildflowers. Dalwallinu has all facilities, a caravan park and good shopping. 🛈 Johnston Street; (08) 9661 1001.

4 PAYNES FIND pop. 9   ⛽ PDG
GPS 29° 15.781' S/117° 41.164' E
Paynes Find is another of Western Australia's historic goldmining towns. The Paynes Find goldmine battery is certainly worth a visit, but not much else remains apart from the hotel, which caters for travellers' needs. Meals, fuel, accommodation and cold beer along with a range of shop items are available. There is a small caravan park behind the hotel.

5 MOUNT MAGNET pop. 747   ⛽ PDG
GPS 28° 03.821' S/117° 50.934' E
Mount Magnet is the oldest operating gold settlement in Western Australia; gold was discovered here in 1891. It is still mined close to the town, and a tourist trail map is available that guides you around the local mining sites, both past and present. The town has a museum displaying pioneering and mining artefacts and there are many buildings of historic significance. Beautiful wildflowers appear in spring. Just north of town you will find the Granites, with Aboriginal rock art and a picnic spot nearby, and the ghost town of Lennonville. Take care as there are dangerous old mine shafts in the area. Most facilities are available in town. 🛈 Hepburn Street; (08) 9963 4172.

MOUNT MAGNET TO NEWMAN 619 KM

Mount Whaleback Mine

Tours of the BHP Mount Whaleback mining operations depart Monday to Saturday from the Newman Visitor Information Centre. The tour takes about 90 minutes and includes a video presentation and a bus tour to the mine site. Bookings are required; (08) 9175 2888; a small tour fee applies.

Travel tip

Along this section, the Great Northern Highway traverses some of the drier and hotter parts of the State. While the winter months can be very pleasant for travelling, during the height of summer daytime temperatures can soar into the forties, placing stress on vehicles and people.

Newman to Port Hedland, page 204

What's on
AUGUST Fortescue Festival (Newman)
SEPTEMBER Newman Campdraft and Rodeo

Muchea to Mount Magnet, page 200

Opthalmia Dam

Stop for lunch at Opthalmia Dam, an integral part of Newman's water supply and a popular recreational area for the locals. It is approximately 15 km from Newman and a good spot for a swim or a picnic (there are barbecues). Camping is permitted but the only facilities are toilets.

Meekatharra Meteorological Office

Take a tour of this interesting operation, or attend the launching of weather balloons (every morning and evening). Campbell Road near the airport; (08) 9981 1191, phone before arrival; tours conducted daily.

Historic Cue

This town boasts a number of historic buildings, some dating back to the late 19th century, with many classified by the National Trust. The old hospital ruins, the Great Fingal Mine Office and the Masonic Lodge in Dowley Street (built largely of corrugated iron) are just some to look out for. Details of the Cue Heritage Trail can be obtained from the Cue Visitor Information Centre.

Track notes

The Great Northern Highway is a wide sealed road used by lengthy road trains and other heavy traffic. The distance from Meekatharra to Newman is in excess of 400 km and Kumarina Roadhouse is all that lies between. Beware of wildlife on the road in this section.

Town file

1 MOUNT MAGNET (see page 201)

2 CUE pop. 374   PDG
GPS 27° 25.370' S/117° 53.939' E
The many magnificent old buildings are a feature of this historic goldmining town, where gold was discovered in 1892. Wildflowers are spectacular between July and October, carpeting the area. Cue has most basic services for travellers. ℹ Lot 35, Robinson Street; (08) 9963 1216.

3 MEEKATHARRA pop. 1270   PDG
GPS 26° 35.486' S/118° 29.772' E
First settled by prospectors in 1896, this town has a rich goldmining history, and mining is still a major industry today. Meekatharra is an important base for the Royal Flying Doctor Service, and its operation is open to the public in the mornings from Monday to Friday. The town also has a Meteorological Office at the airport and a School of the Air base in High Street. A park in Main Street has mining relics on display, including the old State battery. The town has most facilities, including a very good supermarket. ℹ Meekatharra Shire Council Office, Main Street; (08) 9981 1002; www.meekashire.wa.gov.au

4 KUMARINA ROADHOUSE   PDG
GPS 24° 42.467' S/119° 36.283' E
This roadhouse complex is situated on the Great Northern Highway between Meekatharra and Newman. Fuel, meals and accommodation are available and there is a caravan camping area.

5 NEWMAN pop. 4790   PDG
GPS 23° 21.462' S/119° 43.778' E
The mining town of Newman was built to house the workers at BHP's Mount Whaleback Mine, the largest open-cut iron-ore mine in the world. There are several other ore deposits now being mined near Newman. Ore from these mines is transported by train to Port Hedland on BHP's own rail network. The town has good facilities, including a shopping centre with supermarket and specialty shops. There are two caravan parks, and bush camping at Opthalmia Dam is only a short drive from town.
ℹ Corner Fortescue Avenue and Newman Drive; (08) 9175 2888.

NEWMAN TO PORT HEDLAND 461 KM

Iron-ore tour

Take a 1.5-hour tour of BHP's Nelson Point facilities in Port Hedland for a closer look at the company's local operations, state-of-the-art technology and massive machinery. Tours operate each weekday departing at 9.30 a.m. from the Port Hedland Tourist Bureau in Wedge Street; tour fee applies.

Great fishing

Fishing is popular along the north-west coast of the State and people flock to the several caravan parks and resorts between Broome and Port Hedland in the cooler dry months. This coast is subject to large tidal movements so check tide charts (available from visitor information centres) before venturing onto tidal flats. Also note that poisonous stone fish inhabit the coastal waters, so wear strong footwear if walking on rocky reef areas. Fishing charter operators are based in Port Hedland.

Karijini National Park

Karijini is one of the great national parks of Australia, renowned for extraordinary gorges, multicoloured walls, and hidden pools and waterfalls. Brilliant wildflowers carpet the rust-red hills in spring. The spectacular gorges can be seen from several easily accessible viewing points, and walks into the gorges are rated on a scale of difficulty. There are camping areas in the park, the best of which is possibly Dales Gorge. It is also the easiest to reach from the Great Northern Highway. Entry fee applies.

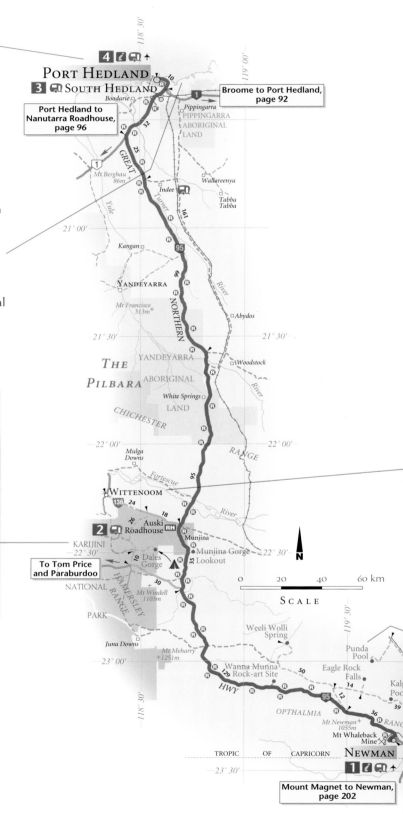

Port Hedland to Nanutarra Roadhouse, page 96

Broome to Port Hedland, page 92

To Tom Price and Paraburdoo

Mount Magnet to Newman, page 202

Track notes

This is a major route carrying road trains and heavy transports. The road passes through some scenic range country and the section through Munjina Gorge, south of Auski Roadhouse, is quite spectacular. Take the time to stop at the Munjina Gorge Lookout; the view makes the stop worthwhile. The only refuelling point along this section is at Auski Roadhouse, Munjina. The road to Tom Price and Paraburdoo is fully sealed and joins the North West Coastal Highway at Nanutarra Roadhouse.

Town file

1 **NEWMAN** (see page 203)

2 **AUSKI ROADHOUSE** ⛽ PDG
GPS 22° 22.654' S/118° 41.456' E
The Auski Roadhouse, at the intersection of the Great Northern Highway and Wittenoom Road in the locality of Munjina, is nestled at the base of the Hamersley Range. It provides fuel, meals, accommodation and a camping ground. During the cooler tourist season a helicopter is based at the roadhouse, offering scenic flights over the remarkable Karijini gorges.

3 **SOUTH HEDLAND** (see page 93)

4 **PORT HEDLAND** (see page 93)

Wittenoom

This was a thriving town for almost 20 years, but its decline was rapid after the closure of the asbestos mines in 1966. Just a small number of residents remain, against the advice of government and health officials that there are dangerous properties of blue asbestos. Wittenoom Gem Shop has an amazing collection of minerals and gemstones on display and for sale.

"I've been to WITTENOOM and Lived"

The Newman waterholes

Kalgan Pool, Eagle Rock Falls, Punda Pool and Weeli Wolli Spring are waterhole areas north-west of Newman. Some have gorges, others feature waterfalls and river-gum scenery. All these areas can be reached from Newman within 90 minutes, but most are accessible by four-wheel drive only.

Travel tip

A worthwhile detour is to follow the Hamersley Iron railway from Tom Price to Dampier. Suitable for most vehicles, this is the quickest link between Tom Price, Millstream–Chichester National Park, Dampier and Karratha. A permit is required (obtained during office hours from the Tom Price mine gatehouse office or the Hamersley Iron office at Parker Point, Dampier).

What's on

JUNE Black Rock Stakes (Whim Creek to Port Hedland)
AUGUST Port Hedland Cup SEPTEMBER Pilbara Music Festival (Port Hedland) SEPTEMBER/OCTOBER Ninji Ninji Festival (Port Hedland)

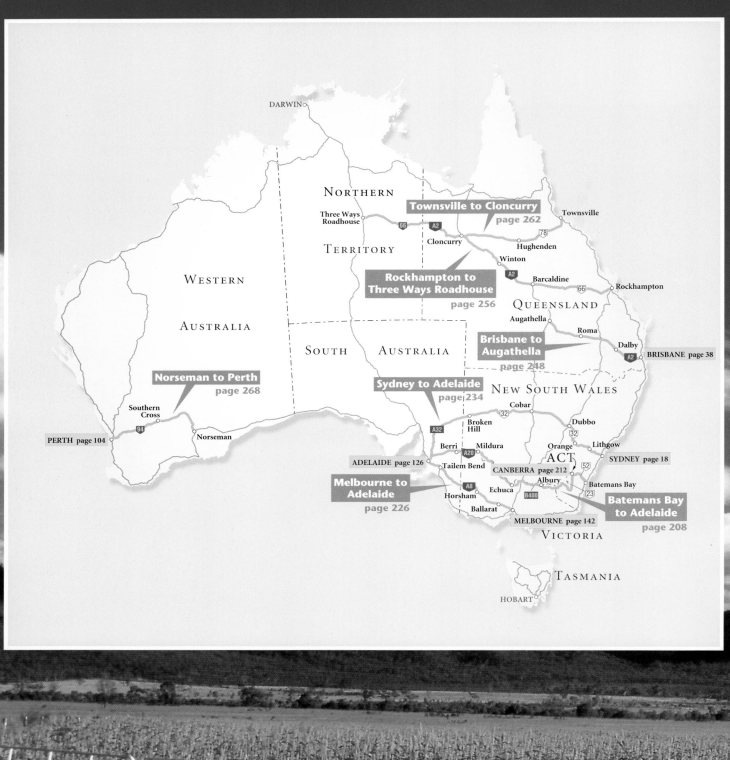

DARWIN

NORTHERN

TERRITORY

WESTERN

AUSTRALIA

Three Ways
Roadhouse

Townsville to Cloncurry
page 262

Townsville

66   A2

78

Cloncurry

Hughenden

Winton

A2

Barcaldine

66

Rockhampton

**Rockhampton to
Three Ways Roadhouse**
page 256

QUEENSLAND

SOUTH   AUSTRALIA

Augathella

Roma

**Brisbane to
Augathella**
page 248

Dalby

A2

BRISBANE page 38

Norseman to Perth
page 268

Sydney to Adelaide
page 234

NEW SOUTH WALES

Southern
Cross

A32

Cobar

32

Dubbo

PERTH page 104

94

Norseman

Broken
Hill

32

Orange

Lithgow

ACT

SYDNEY page 18

Berri

Mildura

ADELAIDE page 126

A20

52

Tailem Bend

CANBERRA page 212

Albury

Batemans Bay

**Melbourne to
Adelaide**
page 226

A8

Echuca

B400

23

**Batemans Bay
to Adelaide**
page 208

Horsham

Ballarat

MELBOURNE page 142

VICTORIA

TASMANIA

HOBART

Chapter 3

Great inland highways: east–west

A WEB-LIKE NETWORK of highways criss-crosses the Australian continent – many of these great highways travel east to west.

If you begin on the east coast, you can take the Warrego Highway, which winds west from Brisbane and climbs through the rich Darling Downs. Townsville and Rockhampton are linked to the major inland industrial centres of Mount Isa and Tennant Creek by the Capricorn, Barkly and Flinders highways. The Great Western, Mitchell and Barrier highways connect Sydney and Adelaide, passing the picturesque Blue Mountains and historic Broken Hill. Melbourne and Adelaide are linked by the Western and Dukes highways, which wind through the site of the Eureka Stockade.

A spectacular route joins Batemans Bay with Adelaide. The Kings Highway takes you first to the national capital then joins a summer-only route through the Snowy Mountains, past Australia's highest town. On the next leg of the route the Murray Valley Highway tracks one of the country's great rivers, passing rich irrigated dairying country, orchards and vineyards. After Mildura this route takes you down through another great wine-producing region, the Barossa Valley.

From Perth the Great Eastern and Coolgardie Esperance highways form the most direct route east, traversing through wheat fields, salt lakes and old goldmining centres. Take any of these routes to get a glimpse of Australia's rich inland.

BATEMANS BAY TO ADELAIDE

KINGS HIGHWAY, MONARO HIGHWAY, SNOWY MOUNTAINS HIGHWAY, TOOMA ROAD, MURRA

The interconnecting highways in this section climb from the New South Wales south coast, pass by the national capital and cross the Snowy Mountains to the headwaters of the Murray River. The route then follows the lush Murray Valley through dairy farms, extensive vineyards, rich fruit-growing land and on to the famous wine-producing region of the Barossa Valley. There are snowfields in the alpine areas, spectacular mountain scenes, superb golf courses, miles of shady river bends and wineries galore.

Best time to go

The warm, sunny summer and the balmy spring and autumn are features of the Murray Valley and Riverland regions. Expect cooler summers and cold, snowy winters in the alpine areas.

John & Jan

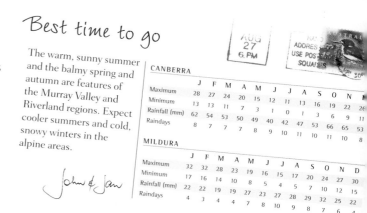

CANBERRA	J	F	M	A	M	J	J	A	S	O	N	D
Maximum	28	27	24	20	15	12	11	13	16	19	22	26
Minimum	13	13	11	7	3	1	0	1	3	6	9	11
Rainfall (mm)	62	54	53	50	49	40	42	47	53	66	65	53
Raindays	8	7	7	8	9	10	11	10	11	11	10	8

MILDURA	J	F	M	A	M	J	J	A	S	O	N	D
Maximum	32	32	28	23	19	16	15	17	20	24	27	30
Minimum	17	16	14	10	8	5	4	5	7	10	12	15
Rainfall (mm)	22	22	19	19	27	23	27	28	29	32	25	22
Raindays	4	3	4	4	7	8	10	9	8	7	6	4

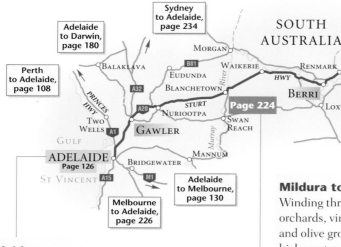

Adelaide

Adelaide is set on the wide curves of the River Torrens, belying the fact that beyond the rolling hills lie great tracts of scrubland – Adelaide is the capital of the driest State in Australia.

Snow gums in Kosciuszko National Park

Mildura to Berri

Winding through orchards, vineyards and olive groves, the highway traverses this irrigated Riverland region. Hire a houseboat to cruise the Murray River.

Berri to Gawler

Once through the Riverland the highway climbs before dropping into the Barossa Valley, one of Australia's best known wine regions. Visitors flock to the Barossa to enjoy the magnificent wineries, dine in excellent restaurants and soak up the fascinating Germanic history of this region.

Echuca to Mildura

The highway follows the Murray Valley through thriving dairy country, picturesque orchards and neat vineyards. The warm climate, numerous wineries, manicured golf courses and a rich history attract tourists year-round.

Albury to Echuca

This sun-drenched region of the Murray Valley is a popular holiday playground. There are excellent golf courses, large lakes, river beaches and the fabulous Rutherglen wine region.

VALLEY HIGHWAY, STURT HIGHWAY (1595 KM)

Murray River, South Australia

Canberra to Albury

Climbing high through the Snowy Mountains on seasonally closed roads, the alpine scenery is breathtaking. Admire the engineering feats of the Snowy Mountains Scheme or stop for a few days and fish for trout.

Canberra

Canberra, capital of Australia, is a model metropolis set graciously on the shores of Lake Burley Griffin. This small city claims some of the nation's most significant institutions, including a magnificent art gallery and one of the best war museums in the world.

Batemans Bay to Canberra

The Kings Highway climbs from the Clyde Valley through abundant forests to the higher farming country and then Canberra. Soak up some of the local history in Braidwood or stroll around the superb craft shops in Bungendore.

BATEMANS BAY TO CANBERRA 148 KM

Authors' choice

✪ Nelligen Park, Nelligen

What makes this park so appealing is its lovely setting on a grassy bend of the Clyde River. The township of Nelligen, just 10 km from Batemans Bay, is a great place to stay for a few days or even just overnight. The park is only a short walk from the town centre and the local hotel, which is well known for its meals. This park has good facilities and great expanses of green grass, spacious enough for a game of cricket.
For more details see page 380.

✪ White Ibis Holiday Village, Sutton

Take the time to sit by the lake, relax and feed the ducks at White Ibis, one of our favourite parks. Located in a spacious rural setting around a lake, it is just 14 km north of Canberra and easily accessible from the Federal Highway. This is a good base for exploring Canberra and the park's facilities include a range of accommodation, a well-stocked shop and a tennis court. We enjoy staying here.
For more details see page 388.

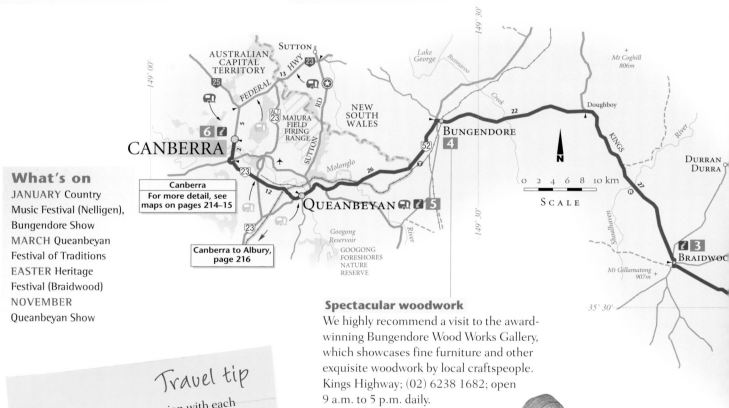

What's on

JANUARY Country Music Festival (Nelligen), Bungendore Show
MARCH Queanbeyan Festival of Traditions
EASTER Heritage Festival (Braidwood)
NOVEMBER Queanbeyan Show

Spectacular woodwork

We highly recommend a visit to the award-winning Bungendore Wood Works Gallery, which showcases fine furniture and other exquisite woodwork by local craftspeople. Kings Highway; (02) 6238 1682; open 9 a.m. to 5 p.m. daily.

Travel tip

This is a popular tourist region with each town offering something unique, but Bungendore holds a special place in our hearts. The Wood Works Gallery, the leather shop, the fabulous photography gallery and the quality restaurants make this destination popular with many travellers. We recommend that you take the time to stop and look around this remarkable town.

Historic Braidwood

Braidwood has numerous historic buildings and a self-guided walking tour is an ideal way to view them. Collect a tour brochure from the visitor information centre in Wallace Street. Well worth a visit is the Braidwood Museum, housed in the historic Royal Hotel and considered one of the State's finest country museums. Wallace Street; (02) 4842 2310; entry fee applies; open 10 a.m. to 4 p.m. Friday to Monday.

Kings Highway

The Kings Highway winds over Clyde Mountain between Nelligen and Braidwood through beautiful forest, offering spectacular views of the ocean through the trees. The climb from the coast is slow and steep but there are ample overtaking lanes. If you are towing a caravan, exercise caution when climbing and descending the range.

Track notes

The Kings Highway links Batemans Bay with the national capital. The road skirts Budawang National Park, passing through wide grassy valleys and dense forests on the coastal plain before winding through the Great Dividing Range. Along the highway, the towns of Nelligen, Braidwood and Bungendore are all popular weekend tourist destinations. This is a pretty drive year-round with ample passing lanes through the steeper ranges.

Town file

1 BATEMANS BAY (see page 13)

2 NELLIGEN pop. 120   🛢 PD
GPS 35° 38.779' S/150° 08.117' E
The pretty village of Nelligen, on the banks of the Clyde River, was proclaimed a town in 1854. Nelligen's wharf became an important port for the town of Braidwood and the surrounding goldfields. The township has several historic buildings, a picturesque camping area and the popular Steam Packet Hotel, but other facilities are limited. The town is just 10 km north-west of Batemans Bay.

3 BRAIDWOOD pop. 940   🛢 PDG
GPS 35° 26.537' S/149° 47.996' E
The entire town of Braidwood has the special distinction of being classified by the National Trust. The area was settled in the 1820s and grew steadily until gold was discovered in 1851, when thousands more poured onto the goldfields seeking their fortune. Today Braidwood services local agriculture and is home to several talented artists and craftspeople. The town has most services and basic shopping.
🛈 Wallace Street; (02) 4842 1144.

4 BUNGENDORE pop. 1348   🛢 PDG
GPS 35° 15.277' S/149° 26.650' E
Bungendore grew out of early settlement in the area during the 1830s. The small town has an abundance of craft and pottery galleries, antique shops and the remarkable Wood Works Gallery. Tourists flock to the area on weekends and there is a selection of B&B-style accommodation in town. Limited facilities and basic shopping are available.

5 QUEANBEYAN pop. 25 689   🛢 PDG
GPS 35° 21.062' S/149° 14.040' E
Queanbeyan, situated just 14 km from Canberra, is a major regional centre servicing a widespread and diverse agricultural industry. Tourism and leisure pursuits also contribute greatly to the city's economy. The town, on the banks of the Molonglo River, has all facilities and a good shopping precinct. 🛈 Farrer Place; (02) 6298 0241 or 1800 026 192; www.queanbeyan.nsw.gov.au

6 CANBERRA (see page 212)

CANBERRA
YOUR GUIDE

Canberra, capital of Australia, is a model metropolis set graciously on the shores of Lake Burley Griffin. The cultural as well as the political life of the country is on show here. This small city, with a population of only 310 000, claims some of the nation's most significant institutions, including a magnificent art gallery and one of the best war museums in the world. Grand public buildings and monuments complement the order and beauty of the city's original design.

CITY CENTRE
See map on page 214.

Australian War Memorial 214 E2
Probably the world's largest war museum with an estimated four million items; also on site is the Bradbury Aircraft Hall and Anzac Hall, housing large relics.

Blundell's Cottage 214 D4
Built in 1858, this cottage re-creates the struggle of the labouring classes in those early farming years.

National Capital Exhibition 214 C4
See exhibits on the history and development of the city and take in the views of the parliamentary precinct.

National Gallery of Australia 214 D5
A brilliant overview of Australian art, including an extensive Aboriginal collection.

National Library of Australia 214 C5
This grand neo-classical structure contains over six million books, including the diaries of Captain Cook's *Endeavour* voyages.

National Museum of Australia 214 B4
Housing an extraordinary collection of Aboriginal artefacts and bark paintings, the museum also features displays and gardens that document our history from European settlement.

Old Parliament House 214 C6
Wander through for a fascinating recollection of the events and intrigues of Australian political life; the National Portrait Gallery is also housed here.

Parliament House 214 B7
Take a free tour of Canberra's centrepiece, with more than 4500 rooms and 3000 artworks, and watch the politicians at work.

Questacon – The National Science and Technology Centre 214 C5
Fascinating hands-on displays and experiments within five galleries.

ScreenSound Australia 214 B2
Dedicated to the preservation of Australia's film and sound archive, the museum has regularly updated displays and a 1930s cinema.

SUBURBS AND SURROUNDS
See map on page 215.

Australian Institute of Sport 215 C3
Tour the complex where the top athletes train.

Visitor information
Canberra Visitors Centre
330 Northbourne Avenue, Dickson
(02) 6205 0044, 1300 554 114
www.canberratourism.com.au

Top events
Summernats Car Festival (January)
A major meeting of street-machine enthusiasts.

Royal Canberra Show (February)
Rural displays, fireworks and a grand parade.

National Multicultural Festival Canberra (February)
Capital arts and culture.

Australian Science Festival (August)
Science and technology at their interactive best.

Floriade (September–October)
One of the country's best botanic events.

Australian National Botanic Gardens 215 C3
The largest collection of native plant species in the country; also includes a rainforest gully and an Aboriginal plant-use walk.

Calthorpes' House 215 C4
A 1927 house in Spanish Mission style containing original furnishings and providing a glimpse of middle-class domestic life in the fledgling capital.

Canberra Deep Space Communications Complex 215 B6
Assisting NASA with its deep-space tracking, this impressive complex has an excellent museum and display area with astronaut suits and space food.

Cockington Green 215 C2
A miniature re-creation of an English rural village.

Cuppacumbalong Craft Centre 215 C7
Near the town of Tharwa on the Murrumbidgee River, this old homestead and its beautiful 19th-century gardens have become the showroom for quality works by Canberra's craftspeople.

Federation Square and Ginninderra Village 215 C2
The Square boasts excellent speciality shops and a walk-in aviary; opposite, Ginninderra Village has craft studios and art galleries housed in historic buildings.

Fyshwick Markets 215 D4
The city's fresh produce markets with fruit and vegetables sold at very reasonable prices.

Lanyon Homestead 215 C7
One of Australia's most beautiful 19th-century homesteads; one section of this restored 1850s farmhouse now houses the Sidney Nolan Gallery.

Mount Ainslie Lookout 215 D3
Drive to the lookout for great views of the city and surrounding mountain ranges.

Mount Stromlo Observatory 215 B4
Houses a huge telescope that charts the night skies; visitors can tour the facility and learn about the wonders of the galaxy.

Namadgi National Park 215 A7
A stretch of alpine wilderness with fabulous bushwalks; it has a visitor information centre near Tharwa.

National Aquarium and Wildlife Park 215 C4
Featuring an amazing collection of freshwater fish and a wildlife sanctuary where all the Australian favourites are on display.

Royal Australian Mint 215 C4
Producing around two million coins each day, visitors can view the production process here and learn about the history of money minting.

Telstra Tower Lookout 215 C3
Also known as Black Mountain Tower, it gives superb views of Canberra and surrounds.

Tidbinbilla Nature Reserve 215 A6
This 5500-ha area of bushland is a refuge for many species of native wildlife; there are walking tracks, picnic spots and a cafe.

Getting around

Canberra is a city with a very high rate of car usage and it is easy to see why: wide roads cater for bus-only public transport that can be variable at off-peak times. For a convenient way to get around the main attractions, catch a double-decker City Sightseeing bus departing from the Melbourne Building. The road infrastructure is probably the best in Australia and visitors will find that they can cover long distances in a short time. Clean air, wide streets and plenty of parkland make Canberra a great place to explore on foot or by bicycle. A boat cruise of Lake Burley Griffin is an essential visitor experience; tours depart from the Southern Cross Yacht Club at Lotus Bay.

Motoring organisation NRMA 13 21 32; Public transport ACTION Buses 13 17 10; Taxis Canberra Cabs 13 22 27; Lake cruises Canberra Steam Boat Cruises 0419 418 846, Lakeside Boat Hiring and Charters 0418 828 357, Southern Cross Cruises (02) 6273 1784.

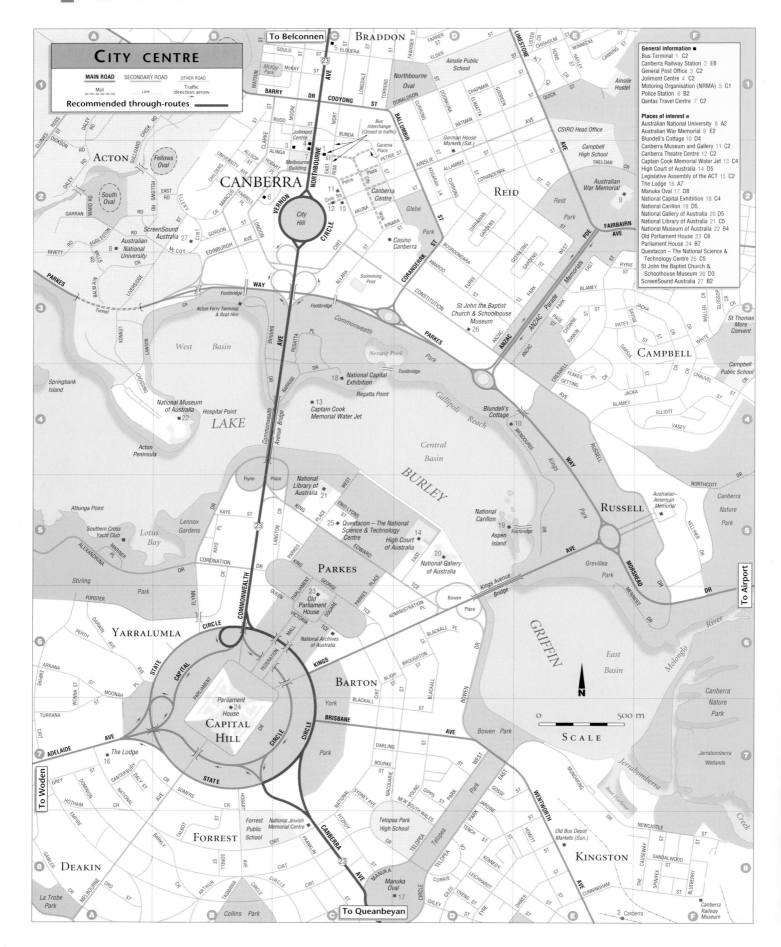

To Belconnen

CITY CENTRE

MAIN ROAD   SECONDARY ROAD   OTHER ROAD

Mall   Lane   Traffic direction arrow

Recommended through-routes

General information ■
Bus Terminal 1 C2
Canberra Railway Station 2 E8
General Post Office 3 C2
Jolimont Centre 4 C2
Motoring Organisation (NRMA) 5 C1
Police Station 6 B2
Qantas Travel Centre 7 C2

Places of interest ■
Australian National University 8 A2
Australian War Memorial 9 E2
Blundell's Cottage 10 D4
Canberra Museum and Gallery 11 C2
Canberra Theatre Centre 12 C2
Captain Cook Memorial Water Jet 13 C4
High Court of Australia 14 D5
Legislative Assembly of the ACT 15 C2
The Lodge 16 A7
Manuka Oval 17 D8
National Capital Exhibition 18 C4
National Carillon 19 D5
National Gallery of Australia 20 D5
National Library of Australia 21 C5
National Museum of Australia 22 B4
Old Parliament House 23 C6
Parliament House 24 B7
Questacon – The National Science &
  Technology Centre 25 C5
St John the Baptist Church &
  Schoolhouse Museum 26 D3
ScreenSound Australia 27 B2

To Woden

To Adelaide

To Queanbeyan

To Airport

N

0   500 m

SCALE

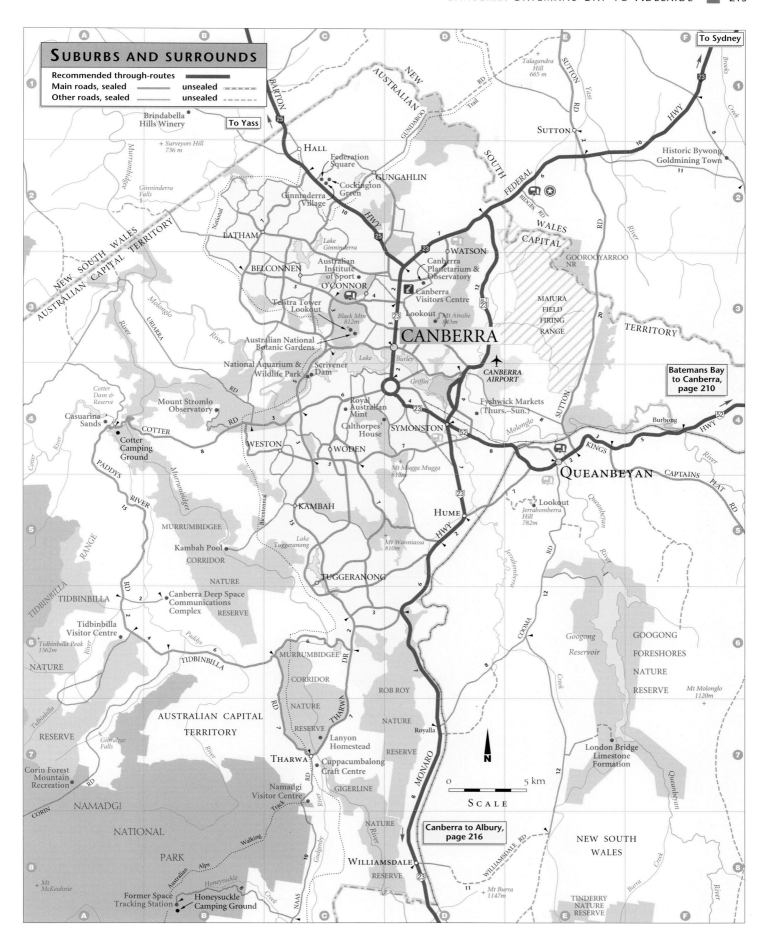

CANBERRA TO ALBURY 435 KM

⭐ Boathaven Holiday Park, Ebden

Located about 12 km east of Wodonga, this park is one of Australia's few five-star rated caravan parks. Set on 4 ha of landscaped grounds on the shores of Lake Hume, Boathaven offers a range of recreational facilities including a pool, spa, tennis court, volleyball court and canoe and bicycle hire. There is a large kiosk and a number of pleasant, shaded sites.

For more details see page 364.

The Man from Snowy River

Corryong is the final resting place of Jack Riley, the man said to be the inspiration for A. B. Paterson's *The Man from Snowy River*. He was buried in the Corryong Cemetery in 1914. The Man from Snowy River Folk Museum features Riley's hut and classic clothing and ski collections. Hanson Street; (02) 6076 1114; open 10 a.m. to noon, 2 p.m. to 4 p.m. daily except in winter (open by appointment only).

Tumut 2 Power Station is just a few kilometres from Cabramurra and visitors can tour this unique underground power station. The visit is well worthwhile; however, the sealed road to the station includes a very steep descent, so if you are towing a caravan you may choose to leave it at Cabramurra to make the trip down and back. Phone 1800 623 776 for tour information.

Military memories

The Army Museum at Bandiana houses an extensive collection of military memorabilia, equipment and vehicles from several branches of the service. Murray Valley Highway; (02) 6055 2525; entry fee applies; open 9.30 a.m. to 4 p.m. Sunday to Friday.

Catch a trout

Trout fishing is one of the great recreational pursuits in this high country region, and the many lakes, rivers and streams are home to both brown and rainbow trout. State fishing licences are required in both New South Wales and Victoria, and are usually readily available from a retail shop in each town. (A New South Wales licence is required for the Murray River.)

Canberra
For more detail, see
maps on pages 214–15

A technological achievement

The Snowy Mountains Scheme is one of
the world's great engineering feats. Stop off
at the Snowy Mountains Authority Visitor
Information Centre in Cooma for an
overview of this remarkable hydro-electric
scheme. Yulin Street, off Monaro Highway;
(02) 6452 1777 or 1800 623 776; open daily.

What's on

MARCH Tallangatta Show, Cooma Show
APRIL Man from Snowy River Bush Festival
(Corryong) EASTER Adaminaby Easter Fair
OCTOBER Coomafest (Cooma) NOVEMBER
Monaro Merino Week (Adaminaby)

Track notes

The Snowy Mountains Highway between Adaminaby and Kiandra climbs
across the ranges and is a relatively easy drive apart from a couple of
steeper climbs and descents. From Kiandra to Khancoban turn-off the
road is sealed but travel will be slower. Again there are some steep
climbs and descents but the views are spectacular. The road between
Cabramurra and Khancoban is closed at times of heavy snow.

Town file

1 CANBERRA (see page 212)

2 COOMA pop. 7150   ⛽ PDG
GPS 36° 14.055' S/149° 07.425' E
Cooma is both a busy tourist town and a key service centre for the area's
large pastoral industry. The Snowy Mountains Authority headquarters are
here. Cooma has most services and a wide range of shops. 🛈 119 Sharp
Street; (02) 6450 1742 or 1800 636 525.

3 ADAMINABY pop. 366   ⛽ PDG
GPS 35° 59.852' S/148° 46.485' E
Adaminaby is a popular fishing spot and in the town centre you will find the
world's largest trout, a structure reaching several metres high. It is also the
closest accommodation to the Mount Selwyn ski fields. 🛈 The Bakerhouse,
Denison Street; (02) 6454 2453; www.snowymountains.com.au

4 CABRAMURRA pop. 203   ⛽ PD
GPS 35° 56.198' S/148° 22.831' E
At 1488 m, Cabramurra is Australia's highest town. The local store
displays a range of interesting books on, and memorabilia from, the
Snowy Mountains Scheme including a collection of photographs
depicting the difficult conditions endured by the construction workers.

5 CORRYONG pop. 1215   ⛽ PD
GPS 36° 11.753' S/147° 54.253' E
Located in the Murray River Valley, Corryong offers a wide range of
leisure pursuits including hang-gliding, whitewater rafting, trail-riding,
walking, four-wheel driving and fishing. The town has most services and
a good range of shops. 🛈 Hanson Street; (02) 6076 2277.

6 WODONGA pop. 25 825   ⛽ PDG
GPS 36° 07.373' S/146° 53.287' E
Along with its sister city, Albury, Wodonga is a key service centre on the
busy Murray Valley and Hume highways. The nearby Lake Hume is a
popular tourist destination. 🛈 Gateway Visitor Information Centre,
Lincoln Causeway; 1300 796 222; www.albury.wodonga.com

7 ALBURY pop. 41 491   ⛽ PDG
GPS 36° 04.862' S/146° 55.074' E
Albury is located across the Murray River from Wodonga. The Rotary
Markets are worth a visit, held on Sunday mornings in the Tax Office
carpark, on Townsend Street.

ALBURY TO ECHUCA 241 KM

Cruise on a paddle-steamer

Echuca is still a busy paddle-steamer port. Cruises on beautifully restored riverboats are available daily, departing the historic wharf at the restored port precinct.

Something special for golfers

The towns of Corowa, Yarrawonga–Mulwala, Cobram–Barooga and Echuca–Moama all boast world-class championship golf courses. Not surprisingly, this area along the Murray River attracts large numbers of keen golfers, many on golfing holidays.

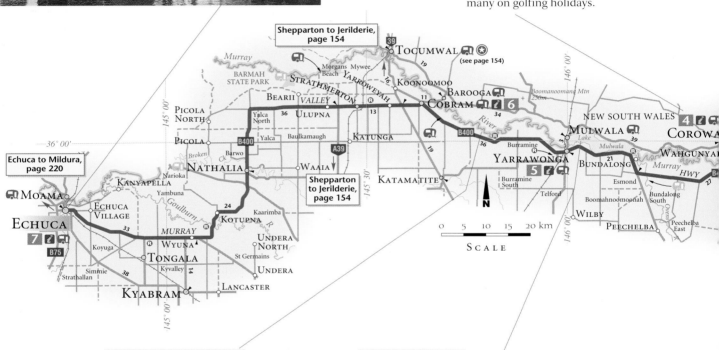

The Great Murray Cod

There is plenty of good fishing in this area and the Murray River is home to the popular yet elusive Murray Cod, a large freshwater fish that can grow to enormous proportions. Specimens have been known to exceed 100 kg. (A New South Wales fishing licence is required to fish the Murray River.)

Aquatic paradise

Lake Mulwala at Yarrawonga is the lowest major water storage on the Murray River. This aquatic paradise is a popular location for water-skiing, sailing, fishing and powerboat racing. Its diversion weir supplies irrigation water to both New South Wales and Victorian farmers.

Travel tip

The region along the Murray Valley is a rich fruit and vegetable growing area. In season produce can be bought direct from the growers at farm-gate stalls throughout the area. Juicy oranges and delicious stone fruit such as peaches and apricots are our favourites.

Wine-tasting

Rutherglen is a historic wine-producing region that is renowned for its top quality wines, especially the rich dessert wines. Numerous vineyards conduct cellar-door sales. Most are open daily.

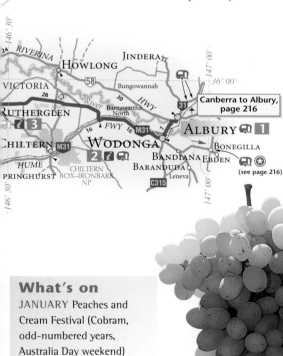

What's on

JANUARY Peaches and Cream Festival (Cobram, odd-numbered years, Australia Day weekend) FEBRUARY Echuca– Moama Jazz, Food and Wine Festival JUNE Winery Walkabout (Rutherglen, Queen's Birthday weekend) DECEMBER Murray River Red Cross Marathon (canoe event, starts at Yarrawonga)

Track notes

The Murray Valley Highway is a well-maintained, fully sealed road that carries large volumes of local and regional traffic. Milk tankers, slow-moving farm machinery and local traffic all use the highway. There are few overtaking lanes; however, long, straight sections and flat country make overtaking relatively easy.

Town file

1 ALBURY (see page 217)

2 WODONGA (see page 217)

3 RUTHERGLEN pop. 1904   ⛽ PDG
GPS 36° 03.278' S/146° 27.655' E
This historic town is at the centre of a legendary wine-producing region and its wine industry attracts a large number of tourists to the area. There is a small shopping centre along with restaurants, cafes and basic services. ℹ 57 Main Street; (02) 6032 9166 or 1800 622 871.

4 COROWA pop. 5161   ⛽ PDG
GPS 35° 59.870' S/146° 23.472' E
The Federation movement first met in Corowa in 1893, and the story of nationhood is told at the town's Federation Museum. The quality golf course, the bowling greens and the Murray River attract tourists year-round. Good shopping and most services are available. ℹ 88 Sanger Street; (02) 6033 3221 or 1800 814 054.

5 YARRAWONGA pop. 3435   ⛽ PDG
GPS 36° 00.596' S/146° 00.271' E
On the shores of the artificial Lake Mulwala, Yarrawonga and its twin town Mulwala have been a popular tourist destination for decades. The town has most services, good shopping, three large clubs and an excellent golf course. The Rotary Markets are held on the third Sunday of each month. ℹ Irvine Parade; (03) 5744 1989 or 1800 062 260.

6 COBRAM pop. 3865   ⛽ PDG
GPS 35° 55.195' S/145° 38.948' E
This Murray River town services a major fruit-growing and dairy area. The river draws many tourists, offering sandy river bends and shady river gums. Water sports, fishing, golf, bowls and tennis are all popular. Cobram has most services and good shopping. The Lions Markets are held on the first Saturday of each month. ℹ 2 Station Street; (03) 5872 2132 or 1800 607 607.

7 ECHUCA pop. 10 014   ⛽ PDG
GPS 36° 07.699' S/144° 45.006' E
The city of Echuca was once Australia's largest inland port and its historic riverside precinct is a bustling tourist attraction. The town has all services, good shopping and numerous restaurants and cafes. ℹ 2 Heygarth Street; (03) 5480 7555 or 1800 804 446; www.echucamoama.com

ECHUCA TO MILDURA 375 KM

Horticultural centre

In addition to its numerous vineyards and produce farms, Mildura is the regional home of Australia's dried fruit industry. Many small vineyards grow and then sun-dry fruit on racks.

Authors' choice

⭐ River Beach Camping Ground, Mildura

The beautiful setting of this park – shady trees, green lawns and the river winding by – makes it a favourite of ours. Large and spacious, the park is located 4 km west of Mildura opposite a popular swimming beach. Sit back and enjoy the scenery with a fresh lunch from the park's takeaway shop. **For more details see page 378.**

Take another path

An alternate route for touring through this area is to turn off the highway at Robinvale and, once you reach Bannerton, follow the Robinvale–Hattah Road and the Calder Highway to Mildura. On this route you can visit Hattah–Kulkyne National Park (pictured) and Murray–Sunset National Park, both noted for their untamed beauty, wide variety of wildlife, large tracts of wilderness and fabulous bushwalks.

What's on

JANUARY Summer Fruits Harvest Festival (Swan Hill)
EASTER Quambatook Tractor Pull, Lake Boga Yacht Club
Regatta SEPTEMBER Country Music Festival (Mildura),
Festival of Vintage Tractors (Red Cliffs, even-numbered years)
NOVEMBER Sunraysia Jazz, Food and Wine Festival (Mildura)

Travel tip

The award-winning Hudaks Bakery was established in Mildura in 1947. There are now three family-owned shops including the cafe bakery in Fifteenth Street (Calder Highway). The cafe has good parking and is a convenient place to grab lunch or just stock up on fresh bakery items.

Step back in time

The Swan Hill Pioneer Settlement Museum is a re-created port town of the historic paddle-steamer days. The 3-ha site has a 19th-century main street and numerous artefacts and restored vehicles. There is also an interesting display on local Aboriginal culture. Make sure you take a trip on a horse-drawn carriage, or a cruise on the PS *Pyap*. Horseshoe Bend; (03) 5036 2410; entry fee applies; open 9 a.m. to 5 p.m. daily.

A wildlife haven

Gunbower Island, Australia's largest inland island, is covered in red gum and box forest, and is home to abundant birdlife, kangaroos and emus. The island is part of the Gunnawarra Wetlands, which include forests, marshes and waterways. There are picnic and barbecue facilities on the island, along with walking tracks. River cruises are a great way to view the wetlands; the island can be reached by bridge from Cohuna.

Track notes

The highways throughout this section are wide, sealed main routes carrying a variety of traffic. The vineyards and orchards are generally on smaller holdings and this results in more local and slow-moving traffic. Some of the bridges crossing the Murray, including the one at Robinvale, are old and narrow by modern standards. Along the route there are several roadside, or farm-gate, fruit and vegetable stalls.

Town file

1 ECHUCA (see page 219)

2 COHUNA pop. 1979 ⛽ PDG
GPS 35° 48.560' S/144° 13.183' E
Cohuna is located on Gunbower Creek, an anabranch of the Murray River, which forms Gunbower Island. Cohuna has basic services.

3 KERANG pop. 3883 ⛽ PDG
GPS 34° 44.032' S/143° 55.217' E
The Kerang area is scattered with a vast network of lakes, marshes and streams forming large and significant wetlands. The area is a breeding ground for many waterbirds and Australia's largest ibis rookery is found on Reedy Lake. Kerang has most services and good shopping. Murrabit, 27 km north, is home to Australia's largest country market, on the first Saturday of each month.

4 SWAN HILL pop. 9385 ⛽ PDG
GPS 35° 20.325' S/143° 33.577' E
The mild weather, the Murray River and the surrounding lakes make Swan Hill a popular holiday spot. It is well known for its good fishing, boating and water sports as well as the fascinating heritage museum, the Pioneer Settlement. The town has all services and great shopping.
🅘 306 Campbell Street; (03) 5032 3033 or 1800 625 373.

5 ROBINVALE pop. 1758 ⛽ PDG
GPS 34° 35.050' S/142° 46.460' E
On the banks of the Murray, Robinvale is a popular tourist destination, particularly during the Christmas and Easter holidays when many people camp along the river. The town is central to the local fruit industry, and the area abounds with vineyards and orchards. Fishing and water-skiing are popular. There is general shopping and most services are available.
🅘 Kyndalyn Park Information Centre, Bromley Road; (03) 5026 1388.

6 MILDURA pop. 24 142 ⛽ PDG
GPS 34° 11.199' S/142° 09.906' E
Enjoying a warm, almost Mediterranean climate, Mildura is located amid an oasis of irrigated vineyards and orchards. The city is a favourite holiday destination offering a diverse selection of accommodation including houseboats for hire. The magnificent Murray River winds by, providing a fabulous venue for many water activities. The city has good shopping facilities. 🅘 180–190 Deakin Avenue; (03) 5018 8380 or 1300 550 858; www.milduratourism.com

MILDURA TO BERRI 163 KM

Authors' choice

⊛ Renmark Riverfront Caravan Park, Renmark

This park makes a perfect holiday destination and we have stayed here many times. It is an ideal base from which to explore the area. Set on the Murray River about 2 km from the town centre, it has shady grassed areas – great for relaxing picnics – and good facilities.
For more details see page 385.

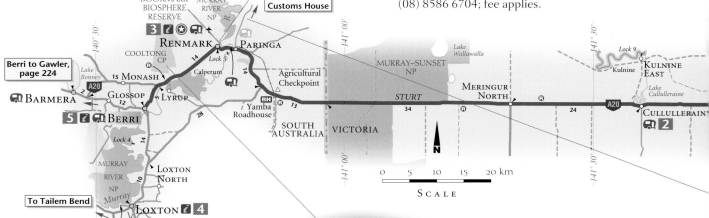

Grand paddle-steamers

Many paddle-steamers used to travel the Murray, including the PS *Industry*, built in 1911. This grand paddle-steamer still cruises the Murray River on the first Sunday of each month and on long weekends. It operates from the visitor information centre at Renmark. 84 Murray Avenue; (08) 8586 6704; fee applies.

A globally important area

The Bookmark Biosphere Reserve provides an area for ecological and environmental research with the intention of conserving the habitat of the region's plants and animals. It is part of a worldwide UNESCO program. The 900000-ha reserve consists of a number of national parks and conservation parks and reserves, including Murray River National Park, Cooltong Conservation Park and the Calperum Wetlands, an important breeding area for waterbirds. Eagles, like the wedge-tailed eagle pictured, show up in the area from time to time.

Travel tip

At the Victoria–South Australia border westbound travellers should move clocks back 30 minutes while eastbound travellers should adjust clocks forward by the same amount. During the summer months both States have daylight saving.

River trade

The old Customs House (1884) at Border Cliffs now operates as a store servicing the Murray River and tourist trade. This historic customs port, which highlights how important the Murray once was as a trading route, is 27 km north of Paringa, in the Chowilla Regional Reserve. It can be reached along a fully sealed road.

What's on

JANUARY Riverland Rodeo (Berri) FEBRUARY Loxton Mardi Gras, Loxton Gift SEPTEMBER Riverland Field Days (Loxton) OCTOBER Rose Festival (Renmark)

Track notes

The Sturt Highway is a major road carrying local and long-distance traffic. It passes between irrigated vineyards and orchards, and through thick mallee scrub and open farming land. The highway is well signposted; however, older maps show the road passing through Berri but it now runs through Monash to the north. You can still travel via Berri and Glossop and we usually take this route, as there is negligible difference in distance. The fully sealed roads from Berri via Loxton to Pinnaroo or Tailem Bend link with the Mallee, Dukes and Princes highways. At Yamba Roadhouse, near the Victoria–South Australia border, there is a fruit fly quarantine checkpoint. All westbound traffic must stop. No fresh fruit or vegetables are permitted beyond this point.

Town file

1 **MILDURA** (see page 221)

2 **CULLULLERAINE** pop. 30 ⛽ PD
GPS 34° 16.691' S/141° 35.794' E
The tiny settlement of Cullulleraine is a service point on the Sturt Highway with a roadhouse and two caravan parks. Its great asset is Lake Cullulleraine, a lake filled from the Murray River, which attracts both travellers seeking a peaceful camping area and those enjoying water sports or fishing.

3 **RENMARK** pop. 4366 ⛽ PDG
GPS 34° 10.259' S/140° 44.979' E
The riverfront town of Renmark is renowned for its local produce, especially quality fruit, nuts and wine. Irrigated orchards and vineyards surround the town. Renmark has sunshine year-round and is a popular tourist destination with a large fleet of houseboats for hire. The town has all services and very good shopping. 🛈 84 Murray Avenue; (08) 8586 6704.

4 **LOXTON** pop. 3310 ⛽ PDG
GPS 34° 27.071' S/140° 34.187' E
Turn left off the highway after Yamba Roadhouse to get to Loxton, a quiet country town servicing the local Riverland area. The region is home to numerous vineyards and large orchards. Loxton is popular during the summer months, when holiday-makers visit the area to enjoy water sports or to find a quiet place to fish. The town has most services and good shopping. 🛈 Bookpurnong Terrace; (08) 8584 7919.

5 **BERRI** pop. 3912 ⛽ PDG
GPS 34° 17.121' S/140° 36.104' E
Berri is the main business centre of the Riverland region, with all services and very good shopping. The riverfront parkland is a town feature that appeals to tourists, and the Berri area in general is dotted with peaceful picnic and fishing areas. The Berri Fruit Juice factory is a major employer and visitors are welcome. The huge Berri Estates winery and distillery are in the nearby town of Glossop. 🛈 Riverview Drive; (08) 8582 5511.

BERRI TO GAWLER 189 KM

Authors' choice

⊛ **Tanunda Caravan and Tourist Park, Tanunda**

Enjoy the Barossa Valley experience from this popular park. Situated right in the heart of the Barossa Valley, it is a great base for exploring this fabulous wine-producing region. Located 1.5 km from the town centre, with easy access, it offers patrons a good range of accommodation and facilities, including bicycle hire.

For more details see page 389.

Travel tip

We always stop off at the popular Waikerie Bakery, on the Sturt Highway at Waikerie. The cafe-style bakery has a wide range of delicious products, is easy to find, has parking and even has a drive-through service for those in a hurry!

What's on

MARCH Celtic Festival (Kapunda)
EASTER Barossa Valley Vintage Festival (odd-numbered years) JUNE Riverland Country Music Festival and Awards (Barmera) SEPTEMBER/ OCTOBER International Barossa Music Festival (Barossa Valley) OCTOBER Barmera Sheepdog Trials NOVEMBER Lavender Festival (Lyndoch)

A rich copper town

Kapunda became the first town in Australia to mine significant amounts of metal after copper was discovered here in 1842. By 1850 the mine produced 100 tonnes of ore monthly but it closed in 1878. Today a large statue of a Cornish miner celebrates Kapunda's mining history. Kapunda was once South Australia's most important commercial centre north of Adelaide.

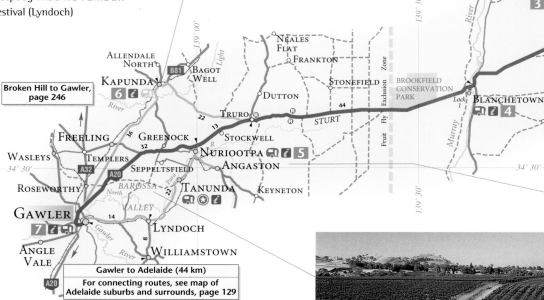

Tour the wineries

The Barossa Valley is perhaps Australia's best known premium wine-producing region. This celebrated tourist destination has more than 60 wineries, most with cellar-door sales. There is a great selection of galleries, historic buildings and restaurants throughout the valley. The Barossa Wine and Visitor Centre, 66–68 Murray Street, Tanunda, (08) 8563 0600, is a good starting point for a tour of the local wineries.

Broken Hill to Gawler, page 246

Gawler to Adelaide (44 km)
For connecting routes, see map of Adelaide suburbs and surrounds, page 129

An environmental winery

Banrock Station Winery and Wetland Centre offers not only wine-tasting and light meals but also several boardwalks through the magnificent wetlands. A new 7-km boardwalk has been constructed; bookings are essential for this walk. Vines grow on only 250 ha of the 1700-ha property; the rest has been returned to its natural state. There is 12 km of river frontage and over 400 ha of wetland. Native wildlife abounds and revegetation is continuing. Holmes Road, Kingston-on-Murray; (08) 8583 0299; entry fee applies for boardwalks; open 10 a.m. to 5 p.m. daily.

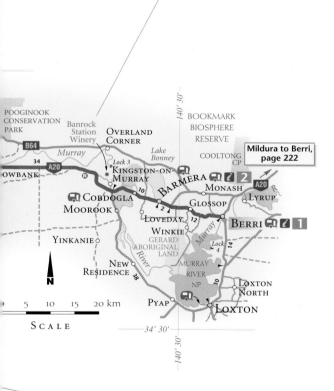

Fruit delight

The Riverland region is a major fruit-producing centre. As well as vineyards, citrus and stone-fruit orchards flourish, and a range of other produce grows well in this irrigated area. Locally grown fruit is regularly available at farm gates and in Angaston you will find the shopfront for Australia's biggest processor of dried fruit – Angus Park Fruit Company.

Track notes

The Sturt Highway carries a large volume of interstate transport and crosses the Murray River several times. South Australia's pioneer heritage is noticeable: look out for the distinctive German architecture.

Town file

1 BERRI (see page 223)

2 BARMERA pop. 1837   ⛽ PDG
GPS 34° 15.130' S/140° 27.908' E
Beside Lake Bonney, Barmera is surrounded by vineyards and orchards and is a popular holiday destination, particularly for water sports enthusiasts. It has most services as well as a nudist caravan park. The highway bypasses Barmera. 🛈 Barwell Avenue; (08) 8588 2289.

3 WAIKERIE pop. 1798   ⛽ PDG
GPS 34° 10.756' S/139° 59.178' E
Waikerie services farmers and is also a popular gliding centre. Most services are available and there is good country shopping; again, the town is bypassed. 🛈 The Orange Tree, Sturt Highway; (08) 8541 2332.

4 BLANCHETOWN pop. 256   ⛽ PDG
GPS 34° 21.117' S/139° 36.741' E
A holiday town at the Murray River's Lock 1, Blanchetown has basic services and shopping. 🛈 Russ and Di's Deli, Takeaway and Hardware, Merrivale Street; (08) 8540 5305.

5 NURIOOTPA pop. 3486   ⛽ PDG
GPS 34° 28.381' S/138° 59.749' E
With the Para River running through town, marked by fine parks and picnic spots, Nuriootpa is the commercial centre of the Barossa Valley. In addition to Nuriootpa, Tanunda, Greenock and Angaston lie in the Barossa Valley. All have most services and good shopping, plus extensive accommodation. In Nuriootpa, Maggie Beer's Farm Shop sells the delicious gourmet products that have made her name famous. The visitor information centre is located in Tanunda. 🛈 Barossa Wine and Visitor Centre, 66–68 Murray Street, Tanunda; (08) 8563 0600 or 1800 812 662; www.barossa-region.org

6 KAPUNDA pop. 2195   ⛽ PDG
GPS 34° 20.467' S/138° 54.906' E
The historic mining town of Kapunda has basic services and a good choice of shops. 🛈 7 Hill Street; (08) 8566 2902.

7 GAWLER pop. 15 484   ⛽ PDG
GPS 34° 35.893' S/138° 44.951' E
Gawler has a rich industrial history. Most of the heavier industry has now gone, but being close to Adelaide while offering the advantage of country living, Gawler has survived. Gawler is a historic town with all services and very good shopping. It is bypassed, but the detour is worthwhile. 🛈 2 Lyndoch Road; (08) 8522 6814; www.gawler.sa.gov.au

MELBOURNE TO ADELAIDE
WESTERN FREEWAY, WESTERN HIGHWAY, DUKES HIGHWAY, SOUTH EAST FREEWAY (737 KM)

Explore the grand old mining city of Ballarat or go bushwalking in the magnificent Grampians as you head west on Route 8, a busy interstate highway linking the two capital cities of Melbourne and Adelaide. It skirts the northern fringe of the Grampians National Park near Dadswells Bridge, passes by some of the oldest properties in the wine industry and descends through the picturesque Adelaide Hills to the festival city of Adelaide.

Adelaide
The well-planned city of Adelaide is set on the wide curves of the River Torrens. Its immediate location belies the fact that beyond the rolling hills lie great tracts of arid scrubland – Adelaide is the capital of the driest State in Australia.

Best time to go

This is a popular route year-round, but most beautiful through spring and autumn. Visit Ballarat in March to catch the city's fabulous annual Begonia Festival.

John & Jan

BALLARAT	J	F	M	A	M	J	J	A	S	O	N	D
Maximum	25	25	22	18	14	11	10	11	14	17	19	23
Minimum	11	11	10	8	6	4	3	4	5	6	8	9
Rainfall (mm)	39	44	44	53	68	64	68	76	74	69	56	52
Raindays	8	7	10	13	16	18	20	20	17	16	13	11

TAILEM BEND	J	F	M	A	M	J	J	A	S	O	N	D
Maximum	30	29	27	23	19	16	16	17	20	22	25	27
Minimum	14	14	12	10	8	6	6	6	7	9	11	13
Rainfall (mm)	17	21	22	28	40	40	39	40	38	38	28	26
Raindays	3	4	4	7	11	11	13	13	11	9	6	6

Tailem Bend to Bridgewater
From Tailem Bend you join part of the Bridgewater to Mount Gambier route from Chapter one. This will take you to Bridgewater, set in the leafy Adelaide Hills 26 km from Adelaide.

Horsham to Tailem Bend
The Wimmera, a major grain-growing region, slips slowly by as the highway crosses into South Australia. Stop off at the Little Desert National Park near Dimboola to see its beautiful show of spring wildflowers. Mixed farming country interrupted by patches of mallee eucalypts fringes the highway to Tailem Bend.

Grampians National Park

Melton to Ballarat
Leaving Melbourne, the highway sweeps towards Ballarat. Ballarat was a rich goldmining centre in the 1850s and the site of the Eureka uprising. Sovereign Hill, one of the city's major attractions, re-creates the excitement and events of that era and should not be missed.

Melbourne
Melbourne is a vibrant and multicultural metropolis offering great restaurants, excellent shopping, tree-lined boulevards and magnificent gardens.

Ballarat to Horsham
Beyond Ballarat the highway passes through fertile grazing country and by flourishing vineyards at Ararat and Great Western. A highlight is the rugged Grampians National Park, rising abruptly in the west, with walking trails, captivating views and native wildlife.

Melbourne to Karumba, page 164

Melbourne to Rockhampton, page 150

Adelaide to Melbourne, page 130

Melbourne to Sydney, page 2

MELTON TO BALLARAT 73 KM

Authors' choice

⊛ Ballarat Goldfields Holiday Park, Ballarat

Centrally located (only 2 km from the city centre) and easily accessible, this quality tourist park has a wide range of accommodation and very good facilities, including a heated pool and spa, free barbecues, bathrooms for children and families, and recreation rooms. We especially like it because it is just a short distance from Sovereign Hill, one of Ballarat's major tourist attractions and our favourite place to visit in the area.

For more details see page 353.

Blooming begonias

Ballarat has many beautiful parks, and the Ballarat Botanical Gardens on the western shores of Lake Wendouree have an outstanding display of magnificent trees and gardens. During March the tremendous show of begonias in the Conservatory forms the main attraction of the city's annual Begonia Festival, while in the gardens you can ride a vintage tram and visit poet Adam Lindsay Gordon's cottage.

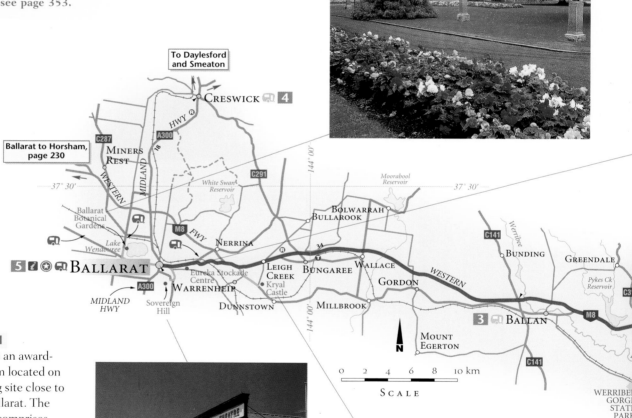

Sovereign Hill

Sovereign Hill is an award-winning museum located on a historic mining site close to the centre of Ballarat. The re-created park comprises 25 ha and tells the city's story from 1851 to 1861. There is a gold-rush settlement, a fascinating Gold Museum and activities that include panning for gold and a tour of a goldmine. Main Street; (03) 5331 1944; entry fee applies; open 10 a.m. to 5 p.m. daily.

Knights and ladies

Kryal Castle, 9 km east of Ballarat, is a re-created medieval castle with exhibits of heraldry and other displays. This is a spot for family entertainment. Forbes Road, Warrenheip; (03) 5334 7388; entry fee applies; open 10 a.m. to 5 p.m. weekends, public holidays and school holidays.

Travel tip

The Western Freeway from Melbourne is a busy road bypassing all towns, including Ballarat. Most important for travellers, there is no roadside stop with toilet facilities on the eastbound lanes between Ballarat and the Melbourne suburbs. There is just one westbound, close to Ballarat, and a westbound-only service centre at Ballan. All other facilities are off the freeway.

Eureka Stockade

To experience part of the history of Australia, visit the Eureka Stockade Centre at Ballarat. It is built on the site of the 1854 uprising. The centre interprets Australia's only armed insurrection, the Eureka Rebellion, when miners angry at licence fees being imposed on them raised the flag of the Southern Cross and fought against government troops. Eureka Street; (03) 5333 1854; entry fee applies; open 9 a.m. to 4.30 p.m. daily.

What's on

JANUARY Shindig Festival (Bacchus Marsh), Organs of the Ballarat Goldfields FEBRUARY Super Southern Swap Meet (Ballarat) MARCH Begonia Festival (Ballarat) APRIL Food, Wine and All That Jazz Festival (Smeaton)

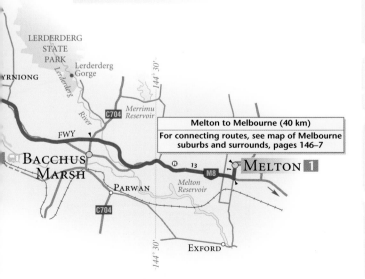

Melton to Melbourne (40 km)
For connecting routes, see map of Melbourne suburbs and surrounds, pages 146–7

Track notes

The Western Freeway and the Western Highway form the busy route between Melbourne and Adelaide. This section of the road is excellent and well signposted. There is a long climb up the Pentland Range from Bacchus Marsh. This major route carries heavy transports, local traffic and many commuters to Melbourne from as far afield as Ballarat. For those heading to Geelong and the Great Ocean Road, the Midland Highway linking Ballarat and Geelong is a popular, well-maintained and well-signposted route.

Town file

1 **MELTON** pop. 30 304   ⛽ PDG
GPS 37° 40.995' S/144° 34.931' E
Melton has developed as a residential satellite city of Melbourne. The area is known for horse studs and small, modern 'rural living' properties. Melton offers most services and has very good shopping.

2 **BACCHUS MARSH** pop. 11 279   ⛽ PDG
GPS 37° 40.559' S/144° 26.307' E
Once a small town in the rich valleys of the Lerderderg and Werribee rivers, Bacchus Marsh has expanded into a busy community close to the west of Melbourne and bisected by the freeway. Irrigated market gardens and apple orchards flourish. The town has all services and very good shopping.

3 **BALLAN** pop. 1414   ⛽ PDG
GPS 37° 36.009' S/144° 13.586' E
The area, notable for wool, was first settled in 1838, but Ballan developed as people headed to the goldfields in the 1850s. Ballan is off the freeway on the upper reaches of the Werribee River. The town has few services and basic shopping.

4 **CRESWICK** pop. 2327   ⛽ PD
GPS 37° 25.515' S/143° 53.643' E
Creswick nestles picturesquely amid pine forests 18 km north of Ballarat. Once a prosperous goldmining town on one of the world's richest alluvial goldfields, Creswick is now small, with many residents commuting to Ballarat to work. Basic services and limited shopping are available. The town of Daylesford is 28 km north-east and is an attractive weekend destination with galleries, antique shops and heritage buildings.

5 **BALLARAT** pop. 64 831   ⛽ PDG
GPS 37° 33.715' S/143° 51.514' E
Ballarat, Victoria's largest inland city, is grand, with many historic buildings. Gold was discovered in 1851 and mining continues today. Ballarat is a major centre with one of Australia's best regional art galleries (the original Eureka Flag is displayed) and great attractions including Sovereign Hill. It has very good services and excellent shops. A trash and trivia market is held at the showgrounds every Sunday. ℹ 39 Sturt Street; (03) 5332 2694 or 1800 648 450; www.ballarat.com

BALLARAT TO HORSHAM 191 KM

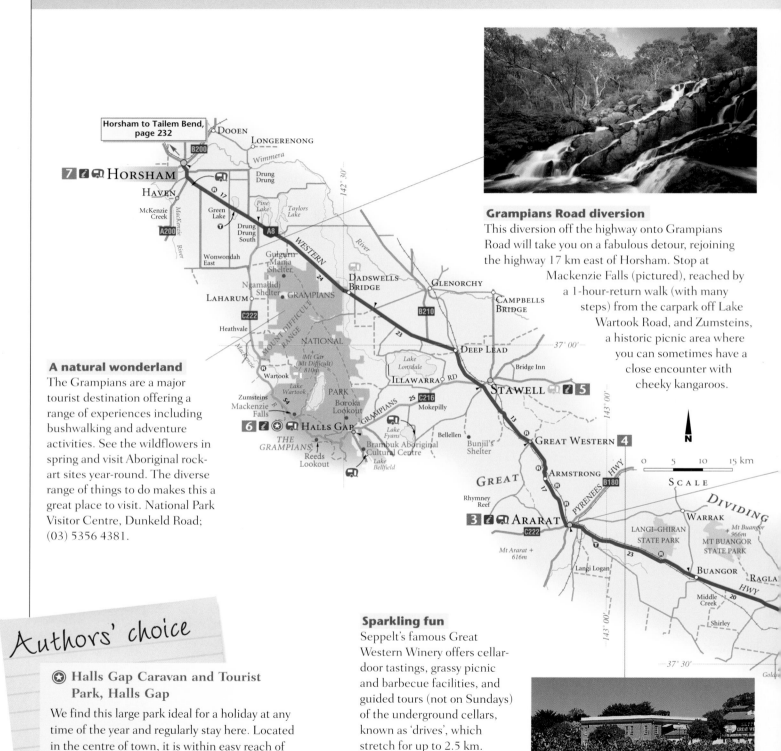

Grampians Road diversion

This diversion off the highway onto Grampians Road will take you on a fabulous detour, rejoining the highway 17 km east of Horsham. Stop at Mackenzie Falls (pictured), reached by a 1-hour-return walk (with many steps) from the carpark off Lake Wartook Road, and Zumsteins, a historic picnic area where you can sometimes have a close encounter with cheeky kangaroos.

A natural wonderland

The Grampians are a major tourist destination offering a range of experiences including bushwalking and adventure activities. See the wildflowers in spring and visit Aboriginal rock-art sites year-round. The diverse range of things to do makes this a great place to visit. National Park Visitor Centre, Dunkeld Road; (03) 5356 4381.

Authors' choice

⍟ Halls Gap Caravan and Tourist Park, Halls Gap

We find this large park ideal for a holiday at any time of the year and regularly stay here. Located in the centre of town, it is within easy reach of most of the area's attractions and makes a good base for exploring the Grampians. Minimum bookings apply during all holidays.

For more details see page 369.

Sparkling fun

Seppelt's famous Great Western Winery offers cellar-door tastings, grassy picnic and barbecue facilities, and guided tours (not on Sundays) of the underground cellars, known as 'drives', which stretch for up to 2.5 km. Western Highway, Great Western; (03) 5361 2239; entry fee applies for tours; open 10 a.m. to 5 p.m. daily.

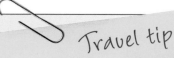

Travel tip

The Grampians are one of the prettiest spots in Australia, with rugged ranges, lakes, waterfalls and stunning scenery. It can, however, turn bitterly cold without notice. If you are planning a visit to this wonderful area then ensure that you pack some warm clothing. For walking, a small day pack and a water bottle are important.

What's on

MARCH Ararat Jailhouse Rock Festival EASTER Stawell Gift JUNE Stawell Hot Air Balloon Festival SEPTEMBER/OCTOBER Australian Cymbidium Orchid Festival (Ararat) OCTOBER Horsham Spring Garden Festival, Golden Gate Festival (Ararat) DECEMBER Kanamaroo Rock'n'Roll Festival (Horsham)

A lunatic asylum

J Ward, formerly an institution for the criminally insane, at Ararat, has been restored. It started life as a prison in 1859, but began holding the insane in the 1880s; it was not closed until 1991. Tours offer an informative look at the bluestone buildings and their grim history. Girdlestone Street; (03) 5352 3357; entry fee applies; open 11 a.m. to 3 p.m. Sundays and school holidays (tours hourly), 11 a.m. and 2 p.m. Monday to Saturday (tours only).

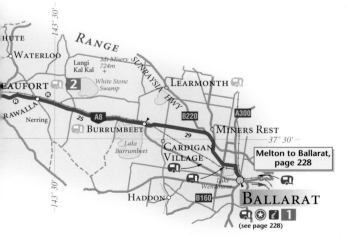

Track notes

The Western Highway is an important route with much traffic but there are many overtaking areas. A diversion through the Grampians is a great drive but the road does narrow and climb; although it is still of a very good standard, vehicles usually travel much slower here.

Town file

1 BALLARAT (see page 229)

2 BEAUFORT pop. 1039   🅿 PDG
GPS 37° 25.781' S/143° 22.962' E
This small town services the local grazing industry. From Melbourne it is the first community encountered, the freeway bypassing all others. Beaufort has basic services and shopping.

3 ARARAT pop. 6890   🅿 PDG
GPS 37° 17.044' S/142° 55.698' E
This area was first explored by Sir Thomas Mitchell in 1836. His glowing report brought early pastoralists and then gold was discovered in the 1850s. Today Ararat, with lovely gardens and historic bluestone buildings, services a grazing industry and vineyards. ℹ 91 High Street; (03) 5352 2096 or 1800 657 158; www.ararat.asn.au

4 GREAT WESTERN pop. 192   🅿 PD
GPS 37° 09.086' S/142° 51.223' E
This small town has been home to a thriving wine industry since 1865. Several wineries, including Seppelt's Great Western, are close. The town has basic facilities.

5 STAWELL pop. 6272   🅿 PDG
GPS 37° 03.392' S/142° 46.803' E
Gold was discovered at Stawell in 1853; today the mine is Victoria's largest gold producer. Stawell is a strong industrial and pastoral centre, close to the Grampians and home of the Stawell Easter Gift, Australia's best known professional foot race. The town has good shopping. ℹ 50–52 Western Highway; (03) 5358 2314 or 1800 330 080.

6 HALLS GAP pop. 256   🅿 PDG
GPS 37° 08.366' S/142° 31.146' E
Halls Gap, an extremely popular holiday destination, is a great base from which to explore the Grampians. It has a cluster of shops and a wide range of accommodation. ℹ Grampians Road; (03) 5356 4616 or 1800 065 599.

7 HORSHAM pop. 12 591   🅿 PDG
GPS 36° 42.800' S/142° 11.787' E
Horsham is an important commercial and administrative centre for the Wimmera region. It has all services and very good shopping. ℹ 20 O'Callaghan Parade; (03) 5382 1832 or 1800 633 218.

HORSHAM TO TAILEM BEND 333 KM

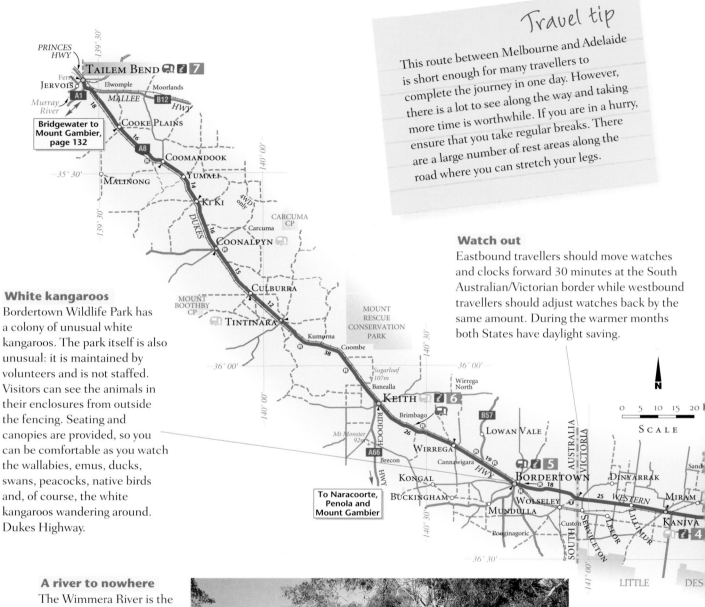

PRINCES HWY
TAILEM BEND 🚐 ℹ 7
Ferry
JERVOIS
Elwomple   Moorlands
Murray River
MALLEE HWY
A1
18
B12
Bridgewater to Mount Gambier, page 132
COOKE PLAINS
16
A8
COOMANDOOK
MALINONG
14
YUMALI
KI KI
DUKES
16
CARCUMA CP
4WD only
Carcuma
COONALPYN 🚐
15
CULBURRA
MOUNT BOOTHBY CP
12
TINTINARA 🚐
Kumorna
MOUNT RESCUE CONSERVATION PARK
38
Coombe
Sugarloaf 107m
Banealla
Wirrega North
KEITH ℹ 6
Brimbago
LOWAN VALE
B57
RIDDOCH
Mt Monster 92m
26
WIRREGA
A66
Brecon   Cannawigara
19
BORDERTOWN 🚐 ℹ 5
KONGAL
18
DINYARRAK
BUCKINGHAM
AUSTRALIA
VICTORIA
MIRAM
HWY
WOLSELEY
25
WESTERN
LILLIMUR
KANIVA 🚐 ℹ 4
MUNDULLA
Custon
SENISCETON
LEEOR
SOUTH
Pooginagoric
LITTLE DES

To Naracoorte, Penola and Mount Gambier

N

0 5 10 15 20
SCALE

Travel tip

This route between Melbourne and Adelaide is short enough for many travellers to complete the journey in one day. However, there is a lot to see along the way and taking more time is worthwhile. If you are in a hurry, ensure that you take regular breaks. There are a large number of rest areas along the road where you can stretch your legs.

Watch out

Eastbound travellers should move watches and clocks forward 30 minutes at the South Australian/Victorian border while westbound travellers should adjust watches back by the same amount. During the warmer months both States have daylight saving.

White kangaroos

Bordertown Wildlife Park has a colony of unusual white kangaroos. The park itself is also unusual: it is maintained by volunteers and is not staffed. Visitors can see the animals in their enclosures from outside the fencing. Seating and canopies are provided, so you can be comfortable as you watch the wallabies, emus, ducks, swans, peacocks, native birds and, of course, the white kangaroos wandering around. Dukes Highway.

A river to nowhere

The Wimmera River is the only major watercourse in this dry area. Rising in the hills to the north of Stawell the river flows north-west through Horsham and Dimboola, draining into Lake Hindmarsh (north of Dimboola) and then further north via Outlet Creek to Lake Albacutya. This is a land-locked river system.

Flowers in the desert

The Little Desert National Park bursts into a colourful carpet of flowers during spring. There are many nature walks, and you may be lucky enough to see a mallee fowl nest site – look for a large sandy mound. Conventional vehicle access to day visitor areas (which also have camping) on the fringes of the park is from Dimboola or Kiata. The network of national park tracks is mainly suitable for four-wheel drives only.

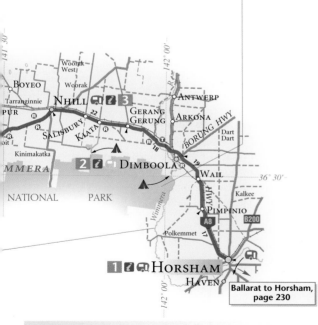

What's on

MARCH Nhill Country Music Festival APRIL Wimmera German Fest (Dimboola) SEPTEMBER Little Desert Festival (Nhill) OCTOBER Bordertown Show NOVEMBER Nhill Agricultural Show

Track notes

This is a well-maintained highway with few overtaking lanes but ample opportunities to overtake. The maximum speed limit in South Australia is 110 kph unless otherwise posted; in Victoria it is 100 kph unless otherwise posted. Speed limits are vigorously enforced around the border.

Town file

1 HORSHAM (see page 231)

2 DIMBOOLA pop. 1557   ⛽ PDG
GPS 36° 27.321' S/142° 01.649' E
Dimboola services a farming community and has access to the Little Desert National Park. Camping is permitted in the national park along the Wimmera River, a few kilometres from town. Dimboola has most basic services. 🛈 Dim E-Shop, 109–111 Lloyd Street; (03) 5389 1588.

3 NHILL pop. 1890   ⛽ PDG
GPS 36° 19.974' S/141° 39.000' E
Nhill is a wheat-belt town that services a rural community and claims to have the largest single-bin silo in the Southern Hemisphere (in Davis Avenue). Nhill has most services and good country-town shops, plus access to the Little Desert National Park. 🛈 Victoria Street; (03) 5391 3086.

4 KANIVA pop. 765   ⛽ PDG
GPS 36° 22.715' S/141° 13.312' E
In the west Wimmera town of Kaniva there are historical walks and a museum with a large local history collection. On the western outskirts, Rotary Fauna Park has nature walks and a bird hide. Kaniva has basic services. 🛈 Apricot House, 41 Commercial Street; (03) 5392 2418.

5 BORDERTOWN pop. 2337   ⛽ PDG
GPS 36° 18.665' S/140° 46.417' E
Bordertown is at the centre of a diverse agricultural region: a vast underground water supply is used for irrigation. Bordertown was the childhood home of past prime minister Bob Hawke. The town has most services and good shopping. 🛈 81 North Terrace; (08) 8752 0700.

6 KEITH pop. 1089   ⛽ PDG
GPS 36° 05.898' S/140° 21.225' E
Keith is called 'the gateway to the South East' as the Riddoch Highway leads from here to Naracoorte, Penola and Mount Gambier. The former Congregational Church in Heritage Street has leadlight windows of the town's history. 🛈 Penny Farthing, Heritage Street; (08) 8755 1061.

7 TAILEM BEND pop. 1488   ⛽ PDG
GPS 35° 15.259' S/139° 27.282' E
Tailem Bend, on the banks of the Murray River, is close to the junction of the Princes, Dukes and Mallee highways. It is an important highway service centre. 🛈 51 Railway Terrace; (08) 8572 4277.

To continue on to Adelaide, see Bridgewater to Mount Gambier, page 132.

SYDNEY TO ADELAIDE

GREAT WESTERN HIGHWAY, MITCHELL HIGHWAY, BARRIER HIGHWAY (1685 KM)

The Great Western Highway climbs west through the spectacular Blue Mountains, a formidable barrier shielding inland New South Wales from the coast. The busy tourist centres of Leura and Katoomba soon give way to numerous large towns and small villages. Broken Hill is a destination with character – the historic mining town is now home to a strong artistic community. Silverton, a ghost town to the west, has also attracted some excellent artists. The highway drifts westward into South Australia across boundless plains before swinging south to Burra, a historic coppermining centre. Gawler is the northern gateway to Adelaide, and just a short drive from the famous Barossa Valley.

Bathurst Gaol

Cobar to Broken Hill

The towns are few and far between in the hot, far west of New South Wales, but Broken Hill is a unique destination, well known for both its community of talented artists and its mining past.

Adelaide

The well-planned city of Adelaide is set on the wide curves of the River Torrens. Its immediate location belies the fact that beyond the rolling hills lie great tracts of arid scrubland – Adelaide is the capital of the driest State in Australia.

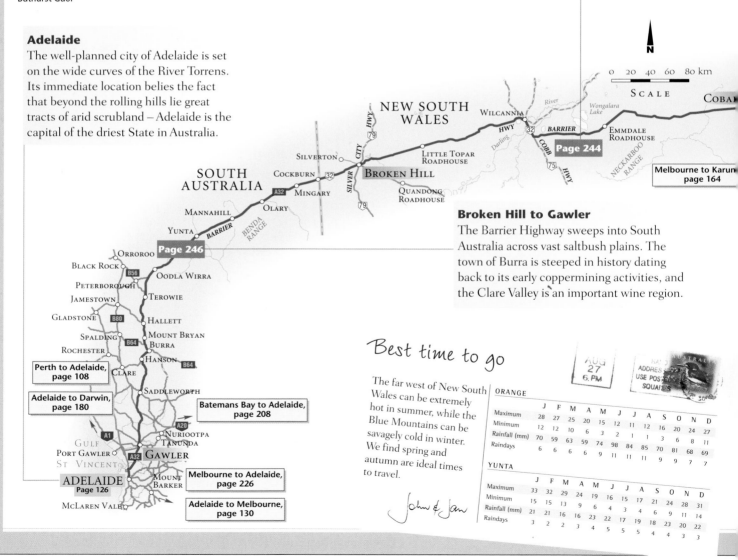

Broken Hill to Gawler

The Barrier Highway sweeps into South Australia across vast saltbush plains. The town of Burra is steeped in history dating back to its early coppermining activities, and the Clare Valley is an important wine region.

Melbourne to Karun
page 164

Perth to Adelaide,
page 108

Adelaide to Darwin,
page 180

Batemans Bay to Adelaide,
page 208

Melbourne to Adelaide,
page 226

Adelaide to Melbourne,
page 130

Best time to go

The far west of New South Wales can be extremely hot in summer, while the Blue Mountains can be savagely cold in winter. We find spring and autumn are ideal times to travel.

John & Jan

ORANGE	J	F	M	A	M	J	J	A	S	O	N	D
Maximum	28	27	25	20	15	12	11	12	16	20	24	27
Minimum	12	12	10	6	3	1	1	1	4	6	8	11
Rainfall (mm)	70	59	63	59	74	98	84	85	70	81	68	69
Raindays	6	6	6	6	9	11	11	11	9	9	7	7

YUNTA	J	F	M	A	M	J	J	A	S	O	N	D
Maximum	33	32	29	24	19	16	15	17	21	24	28	31
Minimum	15	15	13	9	6	4	3	4	6	9	11	14
Rainfall (mm)	21	21	16	16	22	23	22	17	19	18	23	20
Raindays	3	2	3	3	4	5	5	4	4	4	3	3

Silverton, near Broken Hill

Lithgow to Orange

The route passes through Bathurst, where it is possible to drive around the public roads that make up Mount Panorama, the famous motor-racing circuit. Watch the speed limit though!

Glenbrook to Lithgow

The highway winds steeply into the Blue Mountains, passing by Leura, where lush manicured gardens thrive, and on to Katoomba, near one of Australia's most photographed geographic features, the Three Sisters.

Dubbo to Cobar

The highway passes through the large town of Narromine, a popular gliding centre, beyond the cotton fields near Nevertire and on to the historic mining town of Cobar.

Orange to Dubbo

The limestone caves at Wellington are worth a stop along this section, while in Dubbo the superb Old Gaol and the fascinating Western Plains Zoo are great tourist attractions.

Sydney

Sydney is one of the world's most beautiful cities, with its sweeping surf beaches, soaring cliffs and the glittering waters of Sydney Harbour. Combined with great restaurants, superb architecture and interesting historic sites, this city is an irresistible destination.

GLENBROOK TO LITHGOW 84 KM

Maxvision

The Edge Maxvision Cinema offers the unique opportunity of watching a movie on a six-storey-high 'maxvision' screen. You will feel as though you are actually experiencing the thrills portrayed on the screen. The cinema shows several films, but the most popular is *The Edge*, featuring extreme exploration of the local area. 225–237 Great Western Highway, Katoomba; (02) 4782 8900; entry fee applies.

Guns from around the world

The Lithgow Small Arms Museum showcases a comprehensive collection of small firearms from around the world, including many manufactured at the Lithgow Small Arms Factory since 1912. Methven Street; (02) 6351 4452; entry fee applies; open 10 a.m. to 4 p.m. weekends and public holidays.

Travel tip

It is easy to visit many Blue Mountains attractions without having to deviate too far from the highway or walk long distances. Some can be viewed from lookouts or reached along walking tracks. It is possible to park close to many attractions. We find it easy to spend a few days here, but beware – it can be cool and the weather can be ordinary.

Soar over the Jamison Valley

Katoomba's Scenic Skyway is the only gondola ride in Australia, while the new Sceniscender is Australia's steepest cable-car ride and the Scenic Railway is the world's steepest incline railway. All are popular tourist attractions operated by Blue Mountains Scenic World. The Skyway and Sceniscender take you over the Jamison Valley, with views of the Three Sisters. Corner Cliff Drive and Violet Street; (02) 4782 2699; fare applies; open 9 a.m. to 5 p.m. daily.

The Three Sisters

Katoomba's most famous natural attraction, the Three Sisters, sits majestically above the Jamison Valley. The Queen Elizabeth Lookout at Echo Point offers an excellent view of this eroded sandstone rock formation (floodlit at night). The name comes from an Aboriginal legend that three sisters were turned to stone by a witchdoctor to protect them, but the witchdoctor was killed before he could restore their bodies.

Lithgow to Orange, page 238

To Jenolan Caves

Zig Zag Railway

The fabulous Zig Zag Railway, completed in the 1860s, is a great engineering feat. Ride the railway in a steam train on Wednesdays, weekends, public holidays and most school holidays or take a vintage railmotor on other days. Bells Line of Road, Clarence; (02) 6351 4826 for recorded timetable or (02) 6353 1795; fare applies; departs 11 a.m., 1 p.m. and 3 p.m. daily.

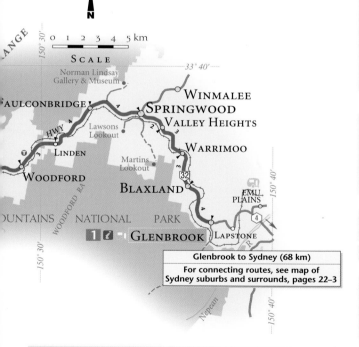

Glenbrook to Sydney (68 km)
For connecting routes, see map of
Sydney suburbs and surrounds, pages 22–3

What's on

MARCH Lithgow Show, Blue Mountains Festival of Folk, Roots and Blues (Katoomba) JUNE Winter Magic Festival (Katoomba) OCTOBER Leura Village Fair NOVEMBER Spring Festival (Glenbrook), Rhododendron Festival (Blackheath)

Track notes

Blaxland, Wentworth and Lawson crossed the Blue Mountains in May 1813; by December 1814 the first road through the range had been completed. Today the road is an easy multi-lane climb. The steepest section is from the west up Victoria Pass; modern vehicles handle it with relative ease. This major highway carries plenty of local traffic and heavy transports to western New South Wales and beyond.

Town file

1 GLENBROOK pop. 5059   PDG
GPS 33° 46.015' S/150° 37.318' E
Glenbrook is the first community west of the M4. There are a number of shops and lovely parklands perfect for picnics. Glenbrook provides access to the southern section of the Blue Mountains National Park.
i Blue Mountains Tourism, Great Western Highway; 1300 653 408.

2 LEURA pop. 3777   PDG
GPS 33° 42.790' S/150° 19.864' E
Some of Australia's most beautiful and famous private gardens thrive in Leura. A mall shopping strip with coffee shops, boutiques and restaurants completes the scene. Leura's Village Fair in October attracts people from all around the country. *i* Leura Mall; (02) 4784 2222.

3 KATOOMBA pop. 11 795   PDG
GPS 33° 42.980' S/150° 18.668' E
Katoomba, at the heart of the Blue Mountains, has many natural features and superb scenery. The area, an extremely popular tourist destination, offers activities like bushwalking, abseiling and canyoning. Katoomba has a wide range of accommodation, several art galleries, great restaurants and good shops. *i* Blue Mountains Tourism, Echo Point; 1300 653 408; www.bluemountainstourism.org.au

4 BLACKHEATH pop. 4119   PD
GPS 33° 38.155' S/150° 17.153' E
Blackheath is the highest town in the Blue Mountains. Local attractions include Govetts Leap Lookout, Evans Lookout and Walls Cave. Blackheath is renowned for its fabulous Rhododendron Gardens. The cemetery contains some of the area's earliest graves, of both convicts and free settlers. Blackheath has basic services and limited shopping. *i* Heritage Centre, Govetts Leap Road; (02) 4787 8877.

5 LITHGOW pop. 11 441   PD
GPS 33° 28.854' S/150° 09.436' E
Rich in heritage, Lithgow has a history in coal and steel. The Small Arms Factory is unique in Australia: both military and sporting weapons have been manufactured here. Lithgow is a railway centre and the historic Zig Zag Railway is nearby. Lithgow has most services and a comprehensive shopping centre. The turn-off to the spectacular Jenolan Caves is 12 km south of Lithgow (the caves are 46 km south-west from the turn-off).
i 1 Cooerwull Road; (02) 6353 1859.

LITHGOW TO ORANGE 117 KM

Authors' choice

⊙ East's Bathurst Holiday Park, Kelso

This park is owned by one of the East brothers, well known in the caravan park industry. It is a quality park on the Great Western Highway, 5 km east of the centre of Bathurst, and offers a range of accommodation and great facilities. Minimum bookings apply during the Easter holidays, the October long weekend and Mount Panorama race weekends.

For more details see page 372.

Miss Traill's House

This Colonial Georgian house, in an old-world garden of daisies and roses, was built in 1845. Miss Traill, who lived here from 1931 to 1976, was a descendant of Bathurst pioneers. Family furnishings and memorabilia fill the house. 321 Russell Street; (02) 6332 4232; entry fee applies; open 10 a.m to 3 p.m Friday, Saturday and Sunday (tours hourly).

The Man from . . . Orange

Orange is the birthplace of the great Australian poet A. B. (Banjo) Paterson, author of *The Man from Snowy River*, who spent his early years in Yeoval (80 km north-west). His birthday is celebrated in Orange with the Banjo Paterson Festival each February/March.

What's on

FEBRUARY/MARCH Banjo Paterson Festival (Orange) APRIL Royal Bathurst Show, Food of Orange District (Orange) OCTOBER Orange Region Winefest, V8 Supercar 1000 (Bathurst)

National Motor Racing Museum

This fascinating museum houses a selection of racing cars and bikes, including several cars that won the Bathurst 1000 and the fabulous Matchless G50 ridden by the late Ron Toombs in the early 1970s. Murrays Corner, Mount Panorama; (02) 6332 1872; entry fee applies; open 9 a.m. to 4.30 p.m. daily.

The Mount Panorama race circuit is a public road and it is possible to complete a lap or two in your private vehicle. We have even taken our Winnebago around the course! There is a speed limit that is vigorously enforced at all times other than under race conditions. Take care, as the road carries two-way traffic.

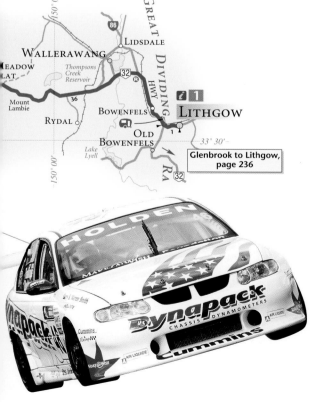

Track notes

The Great Western and Mitchell highways wind through undulating farming country. The road has a good wide surface and a number of overtaking lanes. Extreme winter weather, with snow and ice, can occasionally create hazardous driving conditions. Fog is quite common: it is permissible to drive with hazard lights flashing in foggy conditions.

Town file

1 LITHGOW (see page 237)

2 BATHURST pop. 26 029   ⛽ PDG
GPS 33° 24.998' S/149° 34.844' E
Bathurst, proclaimed in 1815, is Australia's oldest inland settlement. Gold was first discovered in the area in 1823, but it was not until the discoveries at Ophir and Sofala in the 1850s that the town boomed: in 1862 Bathurst supported 50 hotels. Past prime minister Ben Chifley was born and lived in Bathurst and the City Council maintains the Chifley Home at 10 Busby Street just as it was when the Chifleys lived there. The Mount Panorama motor-racing circuit hosts one of Australia's premier motor-racing events, the Bathurst 1000. The city has all services and good shopping. *i* 28 William Street; (02) 6332 1444.

3 LUCKNOW pop. 200   ⛽ PD
GPS 33° 20.754' S/149° 09.687' E
Lucknow is the site of the Wentworth Goldfields. The goldfields were unique in two respects: not only was the quality of the gold good but the gold, discovered in 1851, was on private land where public prospecting was not permitted. Gold was mined in Lucknow until 1938 and several mining relics are still obvious. The town has limited services.

4 ORANGE pop. 30 705   ⛽ PDG
GPS 33° 17.022' S/149° 06.015' E
Known as Australia's Colour City, Orange experiences very distinct seasons and the city's trees change through the spectrum of greens to reds and oranges. In 1851 gold was discovered at Ophir, 30 km north of Orange. Since 1983 grapevines have been planted in the area and now more than 50 vineyards are dotted through the area. The Orange region has developed a reputation for producing quality food and wine. Orange has all services, excellent shopping and some very good restaurants.
i Corner Byng and Peisley streets; (02) 6393 8226 or 1800 069 466.

Glenbrook to Lithgow, page 236

Mount Panorama

The world-class Mount Panorama motor-racing circuit is a few kilometres south of the centre of Bathurst. The racetrack – which in fact is a public road that closes for race meetings – is home to the exciting Bathurst 1000 and other major events.

ORANGE TO DUBBO 149 KM

Authors' choice

⊛ Caves Caravan Park, Wellington

Relax and let a few days slip by at this spacious park, located 6 km south of the town centre alongside the Wellington Caves, a popular tourist attraction. It is a quality park and makes an ideal stopover.

For more details see page 393.

Stone cells and convicts' chains

The Old Dubbo Gaol is more than just another museum: it is a fascinating self-guided tour through an 1870s gaol that operated until 1966. See the original gallows, stop a moment in the solitary confinement cell, and listen while animatronic models tell the convicts' stories. Macquarie Street; (02) 6882 8122; entry fee applies; open 9 a.m. to 5 p.m. daily.

The world's largest stalagmite

The Wellington Caves and Phosphate Mine are spectacular and many fossils have been found here. Guided tours visit Cathedral Cave (pictured), which boasts the world's largest stalagmite, the Gaden Cave, renowned for cave 'coral', and the Phosphate Mine. The mine is a chance to see how miners worked during World War I. Caves Road (off Mitchell Highway); (02) 6845 1418 or 1800 621 614 for full listing of tour times; entry fee applies; tours depart between 9 a.m. and 4 p.m. daily with extra tours on weekends and holidays.

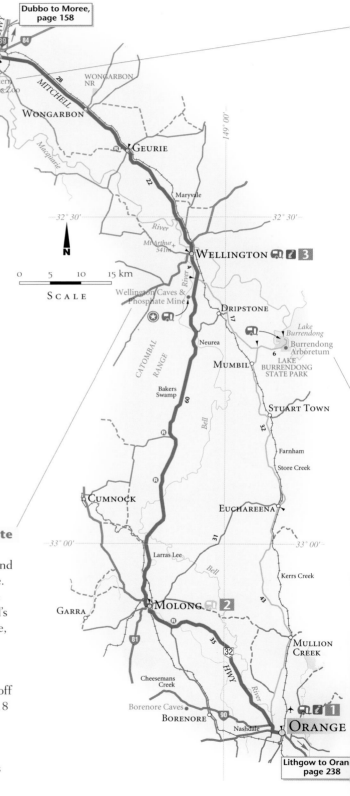

Dubbo to Cobar, page 242

Dubbo to Moree, page 158

Jerilderie to Dubbo, page 156

DUBBO (see page 156)

Lithgow to Oran page 238

A great zoo

Home to over a thousand animals from across the world in more than 300 ha of bushland, the Western Plains Zoo is justifiably one of the State's most popular inland attractions. It is well worth a visit and definitely our favourite attraction in the area. Obley Road (off Newell Highway); (02) 6882 5888; entry fee applies; open 9 a.m. to 5 p.m. daily.

What's on

MARCH Boot Race Festival (Wellington, horseraces), Sheepdog Trials (Molong) MAY Dubbo Show AUGUST Dubbo Annual Jazz Festival OCTOBER Festivale (Wellington) DECEMBER Molong Rodeo

Lake Burrendong and the arboretum

Take the sealed diversion between Orange and Wellington to reach Lake Burrendong, a large water-storage area where water sports, fishing and relaxing are popular. Lake Burrendong State Park has a picturesque camping area by the lake, while Burrendong Arboretum also overlooks the water. This is a major botanical garden (167 ha), with over 50 000 plants from more than 2000 native species. The gardens will delight naturalists and gardeners, especially from late winter to early summer when many plants are in bloom. 1 Tara Road, Mumbil; (02) 6846 7454; entry fee applies; open 7.30 a.m. to sundown daily.

Track notes

The highway meanders across open farming country, passing through several smaller towns and the larger community of Wellington. The highway is well maintained and clearly signposted. This is a major route for heavy transport.

Town file

1 ORANGE (see page 239)

2 MOLONG pop. 1604 ⛽ PDG
GPS 33° 05.525' S/148° 52.175' E
Molong is a charming rural town on the Mitchell Highway. Cobb & Co. coaches once ran through Molong, and in later years transhipped passengers onto the railway. Sadly, the train no longer stops in Molong. About 2 km east of town is the grave of Yuranigh, the Aboriginal guide of explorer Sir Thomas Mitchell. The town has basic facilities and limited shopping, but there are some good craft and gift shops.

3 WELLINGTON pop. 4920 ⛽ PDG
GPS 32° 33.348' S/148° 56.627' E
Wellington, set at the junction of the Macquarie and Bell rivers, is the second oldest town west of the Blue Mountains but is perhaps best known for its spectacular caves. The limestone caves house one of the world's largest stalagmites, located in the spectacular Cathedral Cave. In town there is a historical museum in the old bank, built in 1883 (corner Percy and Warner streets), and the Orana Aboriginal Corporation (Swift Street) sells Aboriginal ceramics, paintings, clothing and artefacts. The nearby Lake Burrendong is a large constructed lake that attracts water-sports enthusiasts from around the region. The Burrendong Arboretum is a botanic garden showcasing more than 2000 different types of Australian plants. ℹ Cameron Park, Nanima Crescent; (02) 6845 1733 or 1800 621 614.

4 DUBBO (see page 157)

Travel tip

If you are planning to visit the Western Plains Zoo, our experience has been that many animals are more active in the cooler morning, and tend to lie in the shade during the middle of the day. If possible, plan your visit early and make sure you allow adequate time. We feel a minimum of about four hours is required. There are some welcoming picnic areas in the zoo so pack your picnic basket.

DUBBO TO COBAR 297 KM

Authors' choice

⊛ Rose Gardens Tourist Park, Narromine

Within the grounds of this quality owner-operated park you will find a historic church, built in 1872. Along with this unusual feature the park offers a range of accommodation, including an ensuite railway carriage, and bicycles for hire. It is set alongside the Mitchell Highway on the eastern approach to Narromine and, in our opinion, is a great park at a very competitive price. **For more details see page 380.**

⊛ Riverside Caravan Park, Nyngan

We really like it when a lot of effort has gone into a park and this is the case with Riverside. The park is set in a quiet riverfront location on the western side of Nyngan and strategically located near the junction of the Mitchell and Barrier highways. It has most of the normal park facilities and, while it has highway frontage, it is set well back in large spacious grounds. **For more details see page 381.**

What's on

MAY Narromine Annual Chrysanthemum Show
AUGUST Festival of the Miner's Ghost (Cobar)
SEPTEMBER Cobar Rodeo, Narromine Agricultural Show, Spring into Nyngan

Riches from the rocks

Cobar is rich in mining history. Copper was discovered in 1869, and Cobar became a magnet for Cornish miners: many local surnames are Cornish in origin. Large deposits of gold, silver, zinc and lead were later found, and mining continues today. Visit the Great Cobar Heritage Centre, a terrific museum, for a glimpse of Cobar's history; there is a walkway to the original open-cut mine. Barrier Highway; (02) 6836 2448; entry fee applies; open 9 a.m. to 5 p.m. daily.

Raising goats

For decades farmers in the central west of New South Wales tried hard to eradicate wild goats from their properties. However, today the tables have turned as goat meat is low in fat and cholesterol and is in demand. Goats are being allowed to breed on properties, and are then mustered and shipped to abattoirs.

Travel tip

Travelling west on the Barrier Highway late in the day can be difficult as the sun drops low into the sky. The setting sun can be blinding, so take extra care or try to avoid driving this part of the road late in the day.

Local crops

Both cotton and soy (pictured) are major crops in the Macquarie River valley around the Trangie and Warren area. Cotton crops reach maturity in late summer and harvesting usually begins in March. The harvested cotton is moved in modules on special trucks to local cotton gins for processing. Soy beans are usually planted in November and December and harvested during April and May.

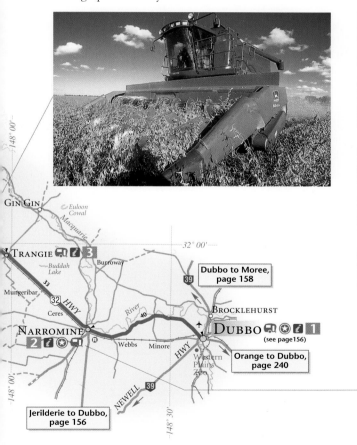

Track notes

The Mitchell and Barrier highways carry a large number of heavy vehicles. Both are good roads with ample overtaking opportunities. The distance between towns becomes greater in this section and it is important to ensure you have adequate fuel to reach the next town; there are not always refuelling points between major centres.

Town file

1 DUBBO (see page 157)

2 NARROMINE pop. 3486 ⛽ PDG
GPS 32° 13.806' S/148° 36.058' E
Narromine is on the banks of the Macquarie River. The town services the local farming area, where grazing and grain growing have been a way of life for more than a century. Narromine is a popular gliding and ultra-light centre; there is an aviation museum at the airport. For gardeners, Swane's Rose Nursery is 5 km from town. Narromine has most services and good country-town shopping. ℹ Dubbo Road; (02) 6889 4596; www.narromine.nsw.gov.au

3 TRANGIE pop. 951 ⛽ PDG
GPS 32° 01.814' S/147° 58.880' E
Trangie is at the centre of a rich irrigation area where cotton is the predominant crop. The weir at nearby Gin Gin on the Macquarie River is popular for boating, fishing and swimming. Trangie has most basic services and a selection of shops. ℹ Mitchell Highway; (02) 6888 7712.

4 NYNGAN pop. 2240 ⛽ PDG
GPS 31° 33.762' S/147° 11.793' E
Situated on the banks of the Bogan River, at the junction of the Mitchell and Barrier highways, Nyngan is an important centre for a large mixed-farming district. The town's recent history includes major floods and the amazing water depths are marked on some of the shops in the main street. Nyngan has most services and a selection of shops. ℹ Nyngan Video Parlour, 105 Pangee Street; (02) 6832 1155.

5 COBAR (see page 167)

Soar away

Narromine is known worldwide as an excellent centre for gliding. Its advantages are many: there are few airspace restrictions; the terrain is flat; the hot, dry climate is excellent for soaring; and there are plenty of safe places to land in the surrounding area. Narromine is also a popular ultra-light centre. For those not ready to take to the skies, there is an aviation museum at the Narromine airport 1.8 km north-west of town. It tells the history of the airport – once one of Australia's most significant regional air centres. (02) 6889 7131; entry fee applies; open 10 a.m to 4 p.m. daily.

COBAR TO BROKEN HILL 456 KM

Authors' choice

⊛ Broken Hill Caravan Park, Broken Hill

With its heated pool, covered barbecues and well-stocked kiosk, this large park is our pick of the Broken Hill parks and we regularly stay here. It is easily accessible from the Barrier Highway and is a good base in Broken Hill.

For more details see page 357.

Desert sculptures

The Living Desert Sculptures are located north of Broken Hill, on a hill overlooking the city. These majestic sculptures, hand-carved from sandstone by a group of sculptors from all over the world, can be reached by a 20-minute walk or by vehicle. People driving must first obtain a key to the gate (for a small fee) from the visitor information centre (details on opposite page). Access is wheelchair friendly.

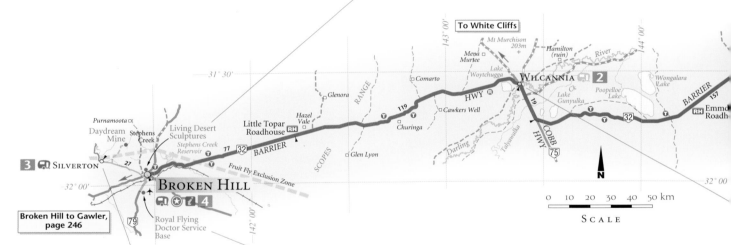

The ghost remains

The historic mining town of Silverton has been a virtual ghost town for more than a century; however, several historic buildings, a popular hotel and a small number of gifted local artists attract large numbers of tourists. The town has also proven popular with film-makers, *Mad Max 2* being one film shot in the area. While here, drive a little further and take a tour of the Daydream Mine, no longer in operation, north-east of town; (08) 8088 5682; tours hourly from 10 a.m. to 3.30 p.m. daily.

Flying doctors

Australia's world-famous Royal Flying Doctor Service has a base and visitor centre at the Broken Hill airport, to the south of the city. You can take a tour through the base and see the organisation at work. The centre has a theatrette, museum and gift shop. (08) 8080 1714; entry fee applies; open 9 a.m. to 5 p.m. weekdays, 11 a.m. to 4 p.m. weekends.

What's on

MAY Broken Hill Agfair (even-numbered years)
JULY Quickshear (Wilcannia) SEPTEMBER Silver City Show (Broken Hill) OCTOBER Broken Hill Country Music Festival

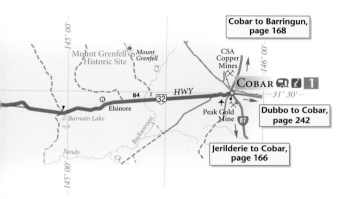

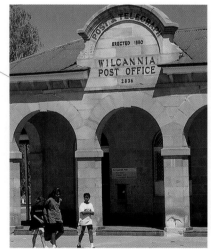

Historic Wilcannia

Wilcannia lies on the Darling River and was once Australia's third largest port, carrying wool from north-western New South Wales downstream by paddle-steamer. It is now much smaller, but a self-guided heritage trail gives a hint of the town's former glory. Following it you will see Wilcannia's magnificent sandstone buildings and many other points of interest.

Travel tip

Broken Hill, although in New South Wales, operates on Central Standard Time, the same as South Australia 50 km to the west. The reason is that the city's business dealings are generally with South Australia and this is purely a matter of convenience. Broken Hill's ore is shipped to Port Pirie for refining and most general supplies are sourced from South Australia.

Track notes

The Barrier Highway between Cobar and Broken Hill is a long, flat road broken only by Wilcannia. The surface is good and there are ample opportunities in this countryside for overtaking. The highway is mostly flanked by grazing land and scrub where wildlife, especially kangaroos and emus, roam freely. Take care as the animals, startled by approaching vehicles, often dash across the road.

Town file

1 COBAR (see page 167)

2 WILCANNIA pop. 688   ⛽ PDG
GPS 31° 33.483' S/143° 22.651' E
Once a key Darling River paddle-steamer port, Wilcannia grew into a strong regional administrative centre for a sparse grazing industry. Today many of the classic sandstone buildings remain but most of the businesses have moved on. The town services travellers on the Barrier Highway. The main access road to the opal-mining town of White Cliffs is from Wilcannia (about 35 km of this road remains unsealed).

3 SILVERTON pop. 65   ⛽ None
GPS 31° 53.126' S/141° 13.380' E
Silverton was a significant commercial centre for silver-mining operations at the end of the 19th century. The town's fortunes soon withered, however, and the municipal council closed in 1899. Today several historic buildings remain in what has become a ghost town. The hotel still operates and a number of prominent artists reside within the historic precinct. Tourists flock to the area although, apart from the hotel, the town has no services.

4 BROKEN HILL pop. 20 963   ⛽ PDG
GPS 31° 57.493' S/141° 27.965' E
In 1883 the rich Broken Hill silver, lead and zinc deposits were discovered and by 1885 the Broken Hill Proprietary Company had been formed to mine the ore. Over more than a century the infrastructure, highways, roads and water supply have improved to transform this once-remote frontier mining town into a modern city, well connected with the larger coastal cities. As mining has declined over recent decades, tourism has grown and Broken Hill is now a busy tourist centre noted for its red sandy surrounds and its extremely talented and prolific art community. The city has many galleries including those of Pro Hart, Jack Absalom, Roxanne Minchin and other acclaimed artists. The city has all services and very good shopping. 🛈 Corner Blende and Bromide streets; (08) 8087 6077; www.murrayoutback.org.au

BROKEN HILL TO GAWLER 470 KM

Authors' choice

⊛ Burra Caravan and Camping Park, Burra

This picturesque park is situated along a creek just two minutes walk from the centre of Burra – a historic mining town. The park has good basic facilities and plenty of large shady trees. It is an excellent base from which to explore the town. Minimum bookings are required at Easter and on long weekends.

For more details see page 358.

Shortcut to Port Augusta

The route from Peterborough to Port Augusta via Orroroo and Wilmington is a popular shortcut for travellers heading to Port Augusta. The road is fully sealed, in good condition and well signposted. The route passes through the picturesque Horrocks Pass.

All aboard

Peterborough was once an important railway centre. Steamtown is an operating museum maintaining a working link with Peterborough's narrow-gauge railway heritage. The attractions include Australia's only remaining triple-gauge turntable. Main Street; (08) 8651 2730; tours 11 a.m., 1.30 p.m. and 3.30 p.m. daily.

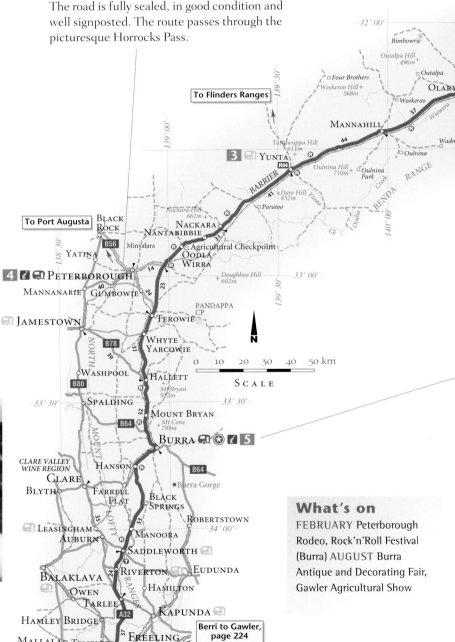

What's on

FEBRUARY Peterborough Rodeo, Rock'n'Roll Festival (Burra) AUGUST Burra Antique and Decorating Fair, Gawler Agricultural Show

Berri to Gawler, page 224

Gawler to Adelaide (44 km)
For connecting routes, see map of Adelaide suburbs and surrounds, page 129

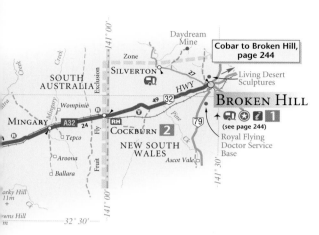

A key to Burra's past

The unique 'Burra Heritage Passport', which can be bought at the Burra Visitor Centre, comes with a key that allows you entry to eight locked historic sites. The heritage trail is 11 km in length: ride a bike, walk or drive round the trail, which includes the Burra Mine Site, the 1847 lockup, the 1856 gaol, brewery cellars and miners' dugouts. This is our pick of things to do in this area. Burra Visitor Centre, 2 Market Square; (08) 8892 2154.

Travel tip

The Barrier Highway is a popular route between Sydney and Adelaide. It passes through relatively dry, saltbush, sheep-grazing country. Large kangaroos are often a problem in this area. They are most common around dawn and dusk and are difficult to see at night. A collision with a kangaroo can cause extensive damage to vehicles so it is very important to take care when driving this route.

Track notes

This is an important route used by road trains carrying freight between Sydney and Perth. Westbound road trains leave the highway at the Peterborough turn-off for Port Augusta. The road surface is mostly very good and improves south of Burra. In summer local grain trucks carrying harvested wheat use the highway. At Oodla Wirra there is an agricultural checkpoint for fruit fly for westbound travellers: no fresh fruit or vegetables are permitted beyond this point. Eastbound traffic is not affected. Broken Hill operates on Central Standard Time (South Australian time). This is an anomaly in the normal time zone system. Road signs north, south and east of Broken Hill advise where the time zone changes between Central Standard Time and Eastern Standard Time. During the warmer months both States have daylight saving.

Town file

1 **BROKEN HILL** (see page 245)

2 **COCKBURN** pop. 40 ⛽ PD
GPS 32° 04.695' S/141° 00.060' E
Cockburn, near the State border, services passing traffic. It was once an important rail terminal (freight was transferred from trains to camels carrying supplies north to outback settlements). Cockburn's services are a police station and roadhouse.

3 **YUNTA** pop. 90 ⛽ PD
GPS 32° 34.889' S/139° 33.754' E
Yunta is a small town servicing the local pastoral community and highway traffic. Roadhouses are the main feature here. The unsealed road north from Yunta is a popular route to the Flinders Ranges. Yunta's roadhouses have minimal services.

4 **PETERBOROUGH** pop. 1855 ⛽ PDG
GPS 32° 58.386' S/138° 50.372' E
Peterborough is an old railway town and a regional centre for the grazing and agricultural industries. Visit Steamtown in Main Street and Rann's Museum in Moscow Street, with exhibits from the 19th century, including farm implements. Peterborough has a range of services and shops. The town is not on the highway, but it is a popular overnight stop and the deviation is worthwhile. *i* Main Street; (08) 8651 2708.

5 **BURRA** pop. 1008 ⛽ PDG
GPS 33° 40.947' S/138° 56.295' E
This former coppermining centre, located 158 km north of Adelaide, is one of the country's best-preserved mining towns. Copper was discovered here in 1845 and Cornish miners soon followed; Burra became a pastoral centre when mining ceased in 1877. The town has numerous historic buildings and a mining infrastructure. *i* 2 Market Square; (08) 8892 2154.

6 **GAWLER** (see page 225)

BRISBANE TO AUGATHELLA
WARREGO HIGHWAY, LANDSBOROUGH HIGHWAY (737 KM)

Enjoy the friendly country hospitality on offer as you travel along the Warrego Highway, the major westerly route from Brisbane. It crosses the fertile Lockyer Valley and travels through market gardens before abruptly climbing the Great Dividing Range to the picturesque city of Toowoomba. Tourists flock to Toowoomba for its impressive parks and gardens and wonderful show of flowers during spring time. Further west the highway narrows as it traverses the Darling Downs, an intensive farming region where crops of wheat, corn and sorghum grow along the road's edge. The towns of Dalby, Miles, Roma and Mitchell all service busy farming regions.

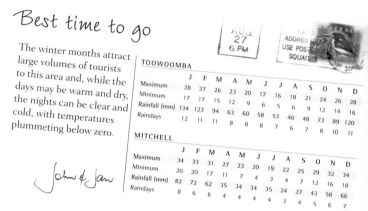

Best time to go

The winter months attract large volumes of tourists to this area and, while the days may be warm and dry, the nights can be clear and cold, with temperatures plummeting below zero.

John & Jan

TOOWOOMBA	J	F	M	A	M	J	J	A	S	O	N	D
Maximum	28	27	26	23	20	17	16	18	21	24	26	28
Minimum	17	17	15	12	9	6	5	6	9	12	14	16
Rainfall (mm)	134	123	94	63	60	58	53	40	48	73	89	120
Raindays	12	11	11	8	8	8	7	6	7	8	10	11

MITCHELL	J	F	M	A	M	J	J	A	S	O	N	D
Maximum	34	33	31	27	23	20	19	22	25	29	32	34
Minimum	20	20	17	11	7	4	3	4	7	12	16	18
Rainfall (mm)	82	72	62	35	34	34	35	24	27	43	58	66
Raindays	8	6	6	4	4	4	4	3	4	5	6	7

Dalby to Roma

Cotton crops are harvested around Dalby during late autumn and the cotton is transported to a local gin for processing. The highway travels through dry grazing country as it passes through Chinchilla and Miles en route to Roma, a town at the heart of Queensland's early oil industry.

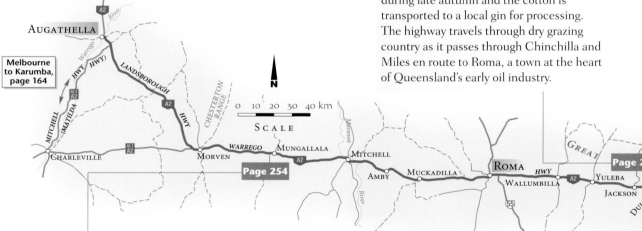

Roma to Augathella

Take a break in Mitchell and have a dip in the artesian pools in the main street or stop and learn about the region's legendary bushrangers, the Kenniff brothers. The highway passes through cropping and grazing country before sweeping northward to meet the Mitchell (Matilda) Highway south of Augathella.

Brisbane

The city of Brisbane straddles the lazy curves of the Brisbane River, which winds its way through the suburbs to Moreton Bay. The long fingers of Moreton and Stradbroke islands create a barrier to the Pacific Ocean, providing the city with a vast body of calm water at its foreshore. Inland, a hilly subtropical terrain provides breathing space and a beautiful backdrop for the city with a population of more than 1.6 million.

Ipswich to Dalby

Sweeping westward, the Warrego Highway passes market gardens and roadside fruit stalls where we regularly stop to buy fresh produce. The road climbs steeply up the range to the main regional centre of Toowoomba, and then through rich farming land further west.

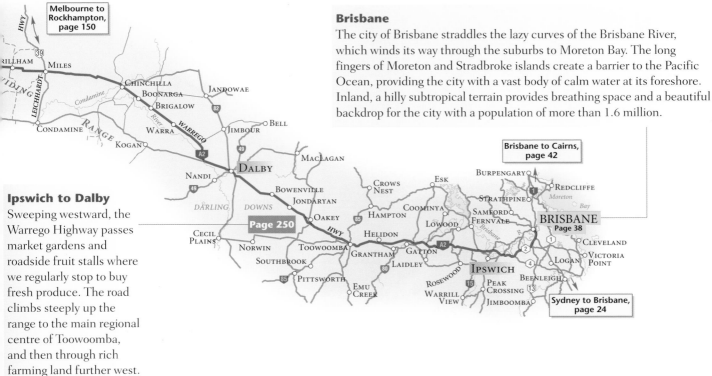

Melbourne to Rockhampton, page 150

Brisbane to Cairns, page 42

Sydney to Brisbane, page 24

IPSWICH TO DALBY 174 KM

Authors' choice

⭐ Myall Creek Caravan Park, Dalby

Enjoy dinner at one of the local bistros, pop into the RSL club for a drink or walk to the centre of town – all possible from this conveniently located park. Owner-operated, it is a good quality park with clean, modern amenities and easy access to the highway.
For more details see page 363.

The great Bernborough

Bernborough was one of Australia's greatest racehorses. He won 26 of his 38 races, including an amazing 15 races in a row in Sydney, Melbourne and Brisbane. He was bought by movie mogul Louis B. Mayer and retired to stud after breaking down in 1946, becoming a very successful sire in Kentucky. A lifesize bronze statue of this local Queensland champion stands proudly outside the council offices in Oakey.

Dalby to Roma, page 252

Pioneer farming

Visit the Pioneer Park Museum in Dalby to see their extensive collection of early model tractors and other agricultural machinery from the area's pioneering days. A working tractor field day is held on the second Sunday of May each year. There are also historic buildings, such as a blacksmith's shed and watch-house. Black Street, Dalby; (07) 4662 4760; entry fee applies; open 8 a.m. to 5 p.m. daily.

Click go the shears

Built in 1859, Jondaryan Woolshed is the oldest woolshed in Queensland. Today it is a popular attraction with fascinating tours and demonstrations of shearing, blacksmithing, working horses and damper making. There are many historic buildings, re-creating a sheep station village. Evanslea Road, Jondaryan; (07) 4692 2229; entry fee applies; open 9 a.m. to 4 p.m. daily; demonstrations Wednesday to Sunday.

What's on
MARCH Cotton Week (Dalby) MAY Heavy Horse
Field Days (Gatton) JUNE Winternational Drag
Racing Championships (Ipswich) SEPTEMBER
Carnival of Flowers (Toowoomba) OCTOBER Potato
Carnival (Gatton), Jacaranda Festival (Ipswich)

Winged history
The Flypast Museum of Australian Army Flying is
located at the Oakey Army Airfield, just on the
outskirts of the small town. There are numerous
military aircraft displayed, dating back to a 1914
Bristol Boxkite. Army Aviation Centre, Oakey;
(07) 4691 7666; entry fee applies; open 10 a.m. to
4 p.m. Wednesday to Sunday and public holidays.

Stagecoach days
Freeman Cobb established his coaching business
in 1853, and the name Cobb & Co. became
synonymous with transport in rural Australia and the
outback. The Cobb & Co. Museum, part of the
Queensland Museum, is a glimpse into our
pioneering history, showcasing Australia's finest
collection of horse-drawn vehicles. 27 Lindsay
Street, Toowoomba; (07) 4639 1971; entry fee
applies; open 10 a.m. to 4 p.m. daily.

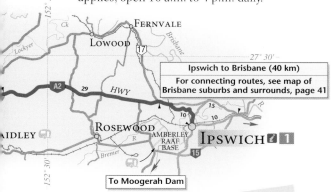

Ipswich to Brisbane (40 km)
For connecting routes, see map of
Brisbane suburbs and surrounds, page 41

To Moogerah Dam

Travel tip
There are always bargains to be found
when buying fresh fruit and vegetables
from roadside stalls between Ipswich and
Toowoomba. Fresh local produce can be
bought at very competitive, sometimes
exceptional, prices. We often stop along this
road to stock our shelves. One of the fruit
stalls even incorporates a bakery and
takeaway food shop.

Track notes
The busy Warrego Highway between Brisbane and Toowoomba is
mostly dual lane and divided, although the Gatton bypass is still two
lanes. West of Toowoomba the highway is two lanes and overtaking
opportunities are limited. Care is needed around dawn or dusk as glare
reduces visibility.

Town file

1 IPSWICH pop. 66 048   ⛽ PDG
GPS 27° 36.542' S/152° 46.038' E
Ipswich is a large city with all services. It dates back to convict days but
more recently coal mining, railways, foundries and the Amberley RAAF
base have been major employers. The scenic Moogerah Dam is 60 km
south. ℹ Corner Brisbane Street and D'Arcy Doyle Place; (07) 3281 0555.

2 GATTON pop. 5328   ⛽ PDG
GPS 27° 33.460' S/152° 16.595' E
Gatton is at the centre of the rich Lockyer Valley, an intensively irrigated
area. Potatoes, cabbages, carrots, onions and much more thrive and there
are numerous fresh produce stands along the highway. Gatton has good
country town shopping and a wide range of services. ℹ Lake Apex Drive;
(07) 5462 3430.

3 TOOWOOMBA pop. 83 350   ⛽ PDG
GPS 27° 34.142' S/151° 57.115' E
Toowoomba, an important regional centre with good shopping
and all services, perches high above the Lockyer Valley. Known as the
'garden city', it has fine colonial buildings and magnificent parks and
gardens. ℹ Corner James and Kitchener streets; (07) 4639 3797 or
1800 331 155; www.toowoomba.qld.gov.au

4 OAKEY pop. 3396   ⛽ PD
GPS 27° 26.064' S/151° 43.267' E
Oakey, a small town at the heart of the Darling Downs, is home to
the Australian Army Aviation wing. Oakey has limited shopping and
basic services.

5 JONDARYAN pop. 120   ⛽ PD
GPS 27° 22.130' S/151° 35.573' E
Jondaryan has a roadhouse, a hotel and not much else. It is best known
for the popular attraction Jondaryan Woolshed.

6 DALBY pop. 9517   ⛽ PDG
GPS 27° 11.030' S/151° 15.811' E
Dalby is at the centre of one of Australia's richest grain-growing and
cotton-growing regions, one of few places in the world where both
summer and winter crops are grown in the same soil. The neat town has
a good selection of shops and all services. ℹ Thomas Jack Park, corner
Drayton and Condamine streets; (07) 4662 1066.

DALBY TO ROMA 267 KM

For more details see page 386.

Authors' choice

⊛ Villa Holiday Park, Roma

This is our choice of places to stay in Roma. A winery and shop adjoin the park, and there are large grassed areas, modern facilities and a large selection of cabins. The park is well maintained and located about 2 km from the town centre. The quality of this park means it gets very busy during the tourist season and space is often scarce. We recommend you book.
For more details see page 386.

Visit a historical village

Take a stroll through the past at the Miles Historical Village and Museum. The buildings are authentic (not replicas) and there is an interesting display of local Aboriginal culture and history. Murilla Street, Miles; (07) 4627 1492; entry fee applies; open 8 a.m. to 5 p.m. daily.

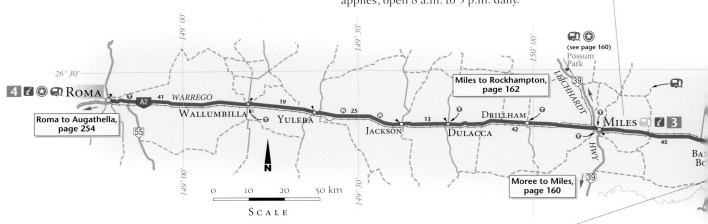

(see page 160)
Roma to Augathella, page 254
Miles to Rockhampton, page 162
Moree to Miles, page 160

Travel tip

An unusual memento of your trip can be found in Chinchilla: petrified wood. A very large deposit of wood that grew more than 100 million years ago was found here in 1871. Today pieces of the petrified wood are cut and polished by local craftspeople into attractive ornaments, and you will find a wide selection on sale at local shops.

Chinchilla Historical Society Museum

Spend some time at this museum for an insight into the area's rural history. You can see a fully operational vintage steam sawmill, the original town gaol, a pioneer slab hut, a collection of restored steam traction engines and one of the first two tickets issued by Qantas. Villiers Street, Chinchilla; (07) 4662 7014; entry fee applies; open 9 a.m. to 4 p.m. Tuesday to Sunday.

What's on

FEBRUARY Melon Festival (Chinchilla, odd-numbered years) JULY Polocrosse Carnival (Chinchilla) SEPTEMBER Back to the Bush (Miles, includes Wildflower Festival)

The Chinchilla Melon Festival

While this area is well known for its rockmelons, strawberries and grapes, the Chinchilla Melon Festival celebrates the booming local industry in watermelons. Occurring every two years in February, the festival includes a large parade down the main street and a competition for the heaviest melon, as well as numerous other activities, such as the Melon Triathlon.

Boonarga Cactoblastis Memorial Hall

Prickly pear, imported from the USA as food for the cochineal beetle, became a noxious weed. By 1926, over 24 million ha of Queensland were covered with it, preventing agriculture or grazing. Settlers despaired, many quitting the land. This hall, listed on the Queensland Heritage Register, was erected in 1936 to commemorate the control of prickly pear by the Cactoblastis moth. Warrego Highway, Boonarga.

Track notes

The highway between Dalby and Roma is a wide, two-lane, fully sealed road that is well maintained and generally in very good condition. Be careful of slow-moving agricultural machinery along this section of road. There is usually ample opportunity to overtake slower vehicles although overtaking lanes are few and far between. There are a number of rest areas dotted along this part of the highway, although some of the better ones seem to be in the smaller settlements such as Warra, Dulacca and Wallumbilla.

Town file

1 DALBY (see page 251)

2 CHINCHILLA pop. 3247 🅿 PD
GPS 23° 44.333' S/150° 37.725' E
The explorer Ludwig Leichhardt named the area in 1844 after the local Aboriginal name for cypress pines, *jinchilla*. Today Chinchilla is a prosperous town, with grain-growing the traditional industry, as well as cattle, sheep, pigs, timber and, more recently, grapes, cotton and watermelons. There is good general shopping here, including banks and supermarkets. 🄸 Warrego Highway; (07) 4668 9564.

3 MILES (see page 161)

4 ROMA pop. 5744 🅿 PDG
GPS 26° 34.462' S/148° 48.015' E
Admire the Roma bottle trees in Heroes' Avenue, which were planted to commemorate local soldiers who died in World War I. The adjacent park has picnic facilities. Visitors can also visit Romaville, which is the oldest and one of the largest vineyards in Queensland. Roma has a range of services and good shopping. 🄸 Corner Warrego Highway and Riggers Road; (07) 4622 4355.

Ipswich to Dalby, page 250

Jimbour House

Acclaimed as one of the best stately homes in Australia, this 40-room mansion was built in 1874 from local sandstone and timber. It has french doors, delicate colonnades and verandahs. Visitors are welcome to view the extensive and magnificent gardens, in which there is a tiny timber chapel. Jandowae Road, Jimbour; (07) 4663 6108; open 10 a.m. to 4 p.m. daily.

ROMA TO AUGATHELLA 266 KM

Authors' choice

⭐ Major Mitchell Caravan Park, Mitchell

Soak away your aches at the artesian spa pools or wander into the centre of town for a bit of sightseeing, both just a short walk from this popular, modern park. Its greatest attraction, however, is the unique offer of the first two nights free. This park gets very busy during the tourist season and space is often scarce. **For more details see page 378.**

Ooline trees

The Tregole National Park (day visitor facilities only) is 10 km south of Morven along a sealed road. This 7500-ha park preserves a large stand of ooline trees, a species that originated in the rainforest when Australia was a much wetter continent. Ooline trees are noted for their delicate flowers. A 2.1-km walking track that starts and ends at the day-access area weaves through the ooline forest.

Augathella to Barcaldine, page 172

5 ℹ 🚐 AUGATHELLA

Barringun to Augathella, page 170

CHESTERTON RANGE NP

MORVEN CP

WARREGO

MORVEN 4

TREGOLE NATIONAL PARK

Alice Downs

Womalilla

MUNGALLALA 3

Neil Turner Weir

MITCHELL

AMBY

SCALE
0   10   20   30 km

What's on

EASTER MONDAY Easter Race Meeting (Augathella) **NEW YEAR'S EVE** Diggers Rodeo (Augathella)

A cattle-duffing past

The town of Mitchell was the centre of activity for the Kenniff brothers, habitual horse and cattle rustlers, who were convicted of murdering a policeman and station manager sent to arrest them, and sentenced to death. Patrick Kenniff was the last man hanged in Queensland, in 1903, while his brother James's sentence was changed to 16 years. Kenniff Courthouse has a collection of historic, related information. Cambridge Street; (07) 4623 1133; open daily.

Relaxing spas

The Great Artesian Spa forms part of the
Mitchell swimming pool complex. Visitors can
enjoy relaxing in the artesian pools – one hot,
one cooler – that are landscaped with Australian
flora. Cambridge Street; (07) 4623 1073; entry
fee applies; open 8 a.m. to 7 p.m. daily.

Rural memories

West of Roma on the Warrego Highway is
the Meadowbank Museum, where visitors
can see horse-drawn vehicles, antique
farm machinery, a doll collection and
much more. Open by appointment;
(07) 4622 3836.

Track notes

The Warrego Highway between Roma and Morven is fully sealed and
well maintained, as is the Landsborough Highway from Morven to
Augathella. In places the edges tend to break up and summer rainfall
can cause surface damage. The highways carry road trains and heavy
transports. It is a rural route, passing through a mix of wooded areas,
open cultivated farmland and grazing country.

Town file

1 ROMA (see page 253)

2 MITCHELL pop. 967   🅿 PD
GPS 26° 29.339' S/147° 58.700' E
Mitchell has become very tourist friendly in recent years and there is
much to see in and around town. A soak in the Great Artesian Spa, a visit
to the historic Kenniff Courthouse and a cruise on the Maranoa River are
a few such experiences. The town has well-cared-for gardens and much-
photographed bottle trees in the main street. Mitchell has most services
and a good shopping strip. *i* Great Artesian Spa Complex, Cambridge
Street; (07) 4623 1073; www.maranoa.org.au

3 MUNGALLALA pop. 130   🅿 PD
GPS 26° 26.776' S/147° 32.589' E
Mungallala is a community midway between Morven and Mitchell. The
only businesses in town are the Club Hotel and the Mungallala Cafe, a
one-stop post office, store and eatery. The Cobb & Co. rest area at the
western edge of town, once a changing station for horses, has barbecues,
a shelter shed and toilets.

4 MORVEN pop. 200   🅿 PD
GPS 26° 24.923' S/147° 06.777' E
Morven is somewhat smaller today than it was in the late 1800s, when
it was a regular stop for bullock teams travelling between Mitchell and
Charleville, and an overnight stop on the Cobb & Co. coach route. The
town has basic facilities, with a large roadhouse 2 km to the east.

5 AUGATHELLA (see page 171)

Dalby to Roma,
page 252

ROMA
(see page 252)

Travel tip

Boadicea Arts and Crafts in Augathella
caught Jan's eye. This large shop has a great
selection of handicrafts, with locally made
and imported items as well as Aboriginal
art. You can also sample their homemade
goodies with a cup of tea. Main Street;
(07) 4654 5116; open 9 a.m. to 4 p.m.
weekdays April to November and 9 a.m. to
2.30 p.m. weekdays for the rest of the year.

ROCKHAMPTON TO THREE WAYS

CAPRICORN HIGHWAY, LANDSBOROUGH (MATILDA) HIGHWAY, BARKLY HIGHWAY (1955 KM)

Explore Central Queensland on the highways that link Rockhampton on the east coast to the Stuart Highway in the heart of the Northern Territory. This popular tourist route passes through the heart of Australia's cattle country, the Central Queensland coalfields and the cosmopolitan mining centre of Mount Isa. Further west the highway crosses the stark Mitchell grass plains of the Barkly Tableland before joining the Stuart Highway at Three Ways Roadhouse, north of the historic goldmining centre of Tennant Creek. Major tourist attractions in this area include Longreach's Stockman's Hall of Fame and the Waltzing Matilda Centre in Winton.

Cloncurry to Three Ways Roadhouse

The Barkly Highway winds slowly through the picturesque ranges as it approaches Mount Isa, a busy mining centre and residential city. Take some time and enjoy a tour of the mine or visit the Riversleigh Fossils Centre. Further west the highway stretches across the black soil plains of the Barkly Tableland, a major cattle-grazing region.

Winton to Cloncurry

This interesting stretch of highway, with some photogenic mesa-shaped hills, is probably best known for the famous Blue Heeler Hotel in Kynuna and the Walkabout Creek Hotel in McKinlay, which featured in the movie *Crocodile Dundee*.

ROADHOUSE

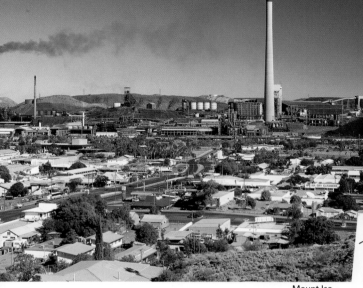

Mount Isa

Page 174

Barcaldine to Winton

Longreach's famous Stockman's Hall of Fame, and historic QANTAS hangar, and Winton's spectacular Waltzing Matilda Centre will take some time but are all on the 'must see' list.

Best time to go

During the winter months the weather is pleasant; however, temperatures and humidity rise during the build-up to the wet season towards the end of the year. The best time to travel is between April and November.

John & Jan

EMERALD	J	F	M	A	M	J	J	A	S	O	N	D
Maximum	34	33	32	30	26	23	23	25	28	32	34	35
Minimum	21	21	20	16	12	9	7	8	12	16	19	21
Rainfall (mm)	103	100	69	36	35	34	29	21	24	40	59	91
Raindays	8	8	6	4	4	3	3	3	3	5	6	7

CAMOOWEAL	J	F	M	A	M	J	J	A	S	O	N	D
Maximum	37	36	35	33	29	26	26	28	32	36	37	38
Minimum	24	24	22	18	14	10	9	11	15	20	22	24
Rainfall (mm)	95	90	57	13	12	10	6	3	6	14	28	58
Raindays	8	8	5	1	1	1	1	1	1	3	4	6

Rockhampton to Barcaldine

The Capricorn Highway reaches westward through this cattle region. Enormous coal trains thunder along the major rail link between the Central Queensland coalfields and the export ports. The highway runs alongside this railway for much of its length. Barcaldine is home to the Tree of Knowledge, the birthplace of the Australian Labor Party.

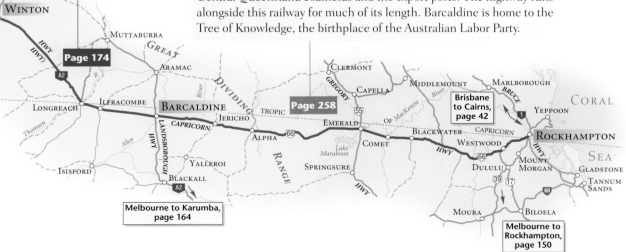

Page 258

Brisbane to Cairns, page 42

Melbourne to Karumba, page 164

Melbourne to Rockhampton, page 150

ROCKHAMPTON TO BARCALDINE 574 KM

Authors' choice

⊛ Blue Gem Caravan and Tourist Park, Sapphire

For those interested in trying their luck in the gemfields, this award-winning park is a good base. It forms part of a shop and service station complex and is centrally located in Sapphire on the banks of Retreat Creek, where sapphires were first discovered in 1875. Facilities at this park are excellent for the price.

For more details see page 387.

Sparkling sapphires

The towns of Rubyvale, Sapphire, Willows Gemfields and Anakie are at the heart of the Central Queensland gemfields. The fields produce a wide range of attractive coloured sapphires, most notably yellow and parti-coloured crystals. Try your luck fossicking or buy stones and finished jewellery from various shops in the area.

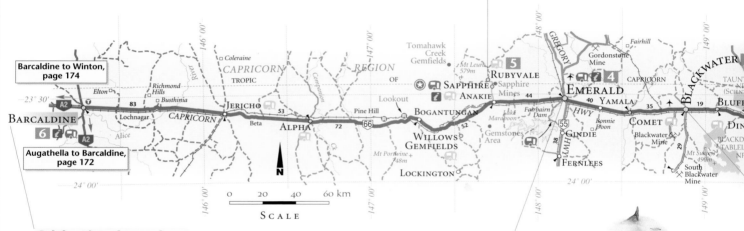

Celebrating the workers

Barcaldine was the site of one of the first Australian industrial disputes, in the great shearers' strike of 1891. Today the Australian Workers Heritage Centre showcases the experiences of working conditions in bygone days. This popular attraction is in the centre of town on 2 ha of landscaped gardens. Ash Street; (07) 4651 1579; entry fee applies; open 9 a.m. to 5 p.m. Monday to Saturday, 10 a.m. to 5 p.m. Sunday.

A sea of white cotton

Cotton is a major crop in the Emerald agricultural area, which produces 25 per cent of Queensland's cotton. The crops reach maturity in late summer, when the fields will be covered with white, fluffy bolls, and harvesting usually begins in March. The crop is processed at local cotton gins.

Travel tip

While large commercial operations or boutique bakeries have taken over in the cities, many small country towns still have traditional bakeries. Snow's Bakery in the small railway township of Alpha produces a wide range of pies, breads and cakes. The quality is good and we stock up each time we pass through.

Track notes

The Capricorn Highway is fully sealed and well maintained. It passes through coalfields, rich agricultural land around Emerald, then gemfields and cattle country. West of Anakie the road carries less traffic and is narrower, but sections are being widened.

Town file

1 ROCKHAMPTON (see page 49)

2 DUARINGA pop. 276   PDG
GPS 23° 42.881' S/149° 40.331' E
Duaringa is the local government base for the area. It has basic facilities and a convenient rest area alongside the highway, with showers and toilets, where overnight stops are permitted.

3 BLACKWATER pop. 5931   PDG
GPS 23° 34.996' S/148° 52.823' E
There are several large mines around Blackwater. Some offer tours; check with the information stand (located in the historic railway siding). Blackwater has most services, two caravan parks and a shopping centre.

4 EMERALD pop. 9345   PDG
GPS 23° 31.544' S/148° 09.680' E
Emerald is the major centre in this area. Gemfields lie to the west, while around town there is agricultural land growing cotton, oilseed, sorghum and citrus. Nearby Fairbairn Dam is a popular recreational area. Emerald has good shopping and services. *i* Apex Park, Clermont Street; (07) 4982 4142.

5 RUBYVALE pop. 602   PD
GPS 23° 25.176' S/147° 41.894' E
Rubyvale is one of four communities on the Central Queensland gemfields. These have developed around the gemfield workings. The hotel is built from local 'billy boulders', a popular construction method on the gemfields. Basic services and supplies are available. Visitor information is located in Anakie. *i* 1 Anakie Road, Anakie; (07) 4985 4525.

6 BARCALDINE (see page 173)

To continue on to Winton and Cloncurry, see Barcaldine to Winton, page 174, and Winton to Cloncurry, page 176.

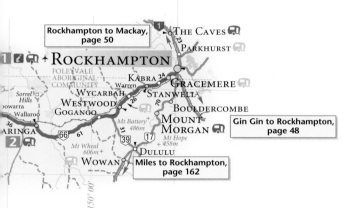

Rockhampton to Mackay, page 50

Gin Gin to Rockhampton, page 48

Miles to Rockhampton, page 162

A coal town

Blackwater lies in the Bowen Basin and is a mining town – the 'Coal Capital of Queensland'. Approximately 15 million tonnes of coal are transported annually from local mines to the coastal terminal at Gladstone.

What's on

EASTER Sunflower Festival (Emerald) **MAY** Barcaldine Show **JUNE** Artesian Festival (Barcaldine, even-numbered years) **JULY** World Dingo Trap Throwing Championships (Dingo) **AUGUST** Gemfest (Emerald) **SEPTEMBER** Country Music Spectacular (Emerald)

CLONCURRY TO THREE WAYS ROADHOUSE 756 KM

Authors' choice

⊛ Sunset Caravan Park, Mount Isa

Relax by the pool or enjoy a meal in the pleasant barbecue area at this popular owner-operated park, situated 1.6 km from the centre of town and away from highway traffic. We feel that this is the best caravan park in Mount Isa and it may be necessary to book during the peak winter months.

For more details see page 379.

Travel tip

The family-owned butcher shop in Camooweal, on the Barkly Highway, caters for locals, properties and travellers. They sell good-quality locally grown and butchered beef along with most other things you would expect to find in a butcher shop, including cooked meats. We have bought meat here for some years. They cut your meat to order and vacuum-pack it while you wait.

Great grazing

The Barkly Tableland covers a large area of the midlands of the Northern Territory and rich Mitchell grass plains stretch to the horizon both north and south of the Barkly Highway. This is some of Australia's great cattle country.

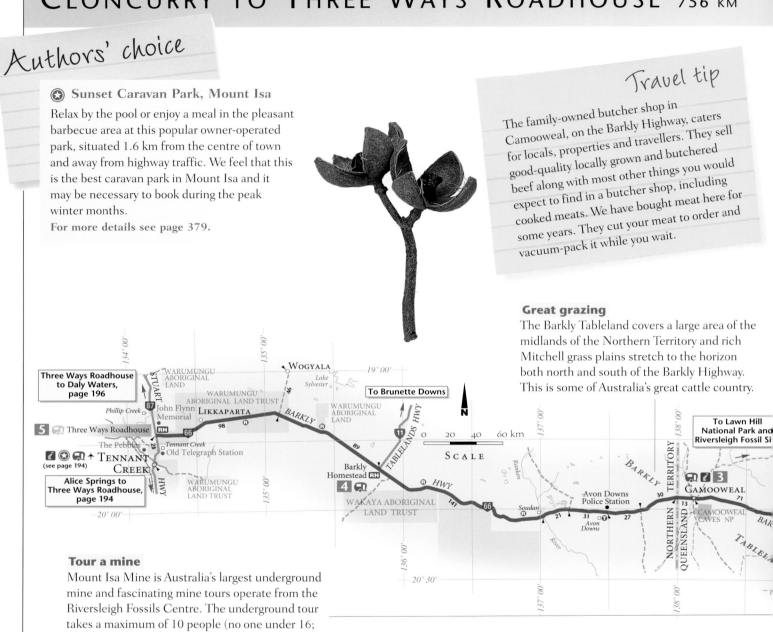

Tour a mine

Mount Isa Mine is Australia's largest underground mine and fascinating mine tours operate from the Riversleigh Fossils Centre. The underground tour takes a maximum of 10 people (no one under 16; age and medical restrictions apply; book well in advance). Depart from 19 Marian Street; (07) 4749 1555; fee applies; tours available.

Welcome to Barkly Homestead
Powered Site's

Please place this form under your windscreen wiper

Name TAIT

Rego 867STS   Date 17-11-0

Site No. 3   Key No. 6

We hope you enjoy your stay

The Riversleigh fossils

The unique Riversleigh Fossils Centre in Mount Isa gives a great insight into the World Heritage-listed fossils excavated during 1976 on Riversleigh Station. Here is a rare glimpse of exotic animals that lived in the area 25 million years ago. There are many displays, a theatrette and fossil material. The actual fossil site is approximately 190 km north of Camooweal. 19 Marian Street; (07) 4749 1555; entry fee applies; open 9 a.m. to 4.30 p.m. weekdays, 9 a.m. to 2 p.m. weekends.

Remote oasis

Discover the stunning Lawn Hill National Park, 245 km north of Camooweal. Lawn Hill Gorge has colourful cliffs rising 60 m to the surrounding plateau. On the gorge walls are Aboriginal rock paintings, and middens also remain. Visitors can see these from the boardwalk and viewing platforms. The creek has permanent water and offers a habitat for tropical vegetation. The water attracts various bird species and reptiles including freshwater crocodiles, tortoises and water monitors. There are several walking tracks in the park. The road into the park is very rough in some places, so four-wheel drives are recommended.

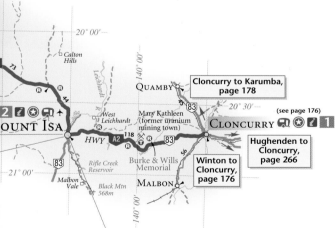

Flying doctors

The Royal Flying Doctor Service operates its regional base from Mount Isa. The service offers care to those injured or seriously ill in the outback, as well as regular clinic care to remote regions. Visit the RFDS Visitor Centre for an insight into its vital work. 11 Barkly Highway; (07) 4742 4125; entry fee applies; open 9 a.m. to 5 p.m. weekdays.

Track notes

The Barkly Highway between Cloncurry and Mount Isa is narrow, rough bitumen with poor road shoulders. Take great care with oncoming traffic, especially road trains; it is often necessary to pull off the sealed surface to allow oncoming vehicles to pass. Camooweal to Three Ways Roadhouse is a wide bitumen road in very good condition.

Town file

1 CLONCURRY (see page 177)

2 MOUNT ISA pop. 21 751   ⛽ PDG
GPS 20° 43.523' S/139° 29.675' E

Mount Isa is the largest industrial and commercial centre in north-west Queensland. It owes its spectacular history to silver, lead and zinc. The city has very good shopping and services and much accommodation including several caravan parks. Like many mining towns, the caravan parks cater predominantly for permanent dwellers. We have found good-value meals at some of the city's clubs. 🛈 Riversleigh Fossils Centre, 19 Marian Street; (07) 4749 1555 or 1300 659 660.

3 CAMOOWEAL pop. 258   ⛽ PDG
GPS 19° 55.288' S/138° 07.138' E

Proclaimed a town in 1887, Camooweal was an important pre-Federation customs outpost on the Queensland border. Today it is a popular tourist stop, especially during the cooler winter months. Many stop to look through Freckleton's Historic Store or visit the Camooweal Caves National Park, 24 km south of Camooweal along the unsealed Urandangi Road. Only properly equipped and experienced cavers should enter this complex dolomite labyrinth, and it is recommended that caving is restricted to the dry season. Most basic services are available. This is the last fuel stop before Barkly Homestead for westbound travellers (263 km). 🛈 Barkly Highway; (07) 4748 2022.

4 BARKLY HOMESTEAD   ⛽ PDG
GPS 19° 42.653' S/135° 49.661' E

The roadhouse, a key service centre on the Barkly Highway, is situated at its junction with the Tablelands Highway. It sells fuel, and there is a bar, restaurant, motel, extensive camping area and caravan park with predominantly drive-through powered sites – a convenient overnight stop. For eastbound travellers, this is the last fuel stop before Camooweal (263 km). Keep your eye out for mahogany seed pods (pictured on facing page) around the roadhouse.

5 THREE WAYS ROADHOUSE (see page 195)

What's on

APRIL Camooweal Races JUNE Brunette Downs Races, Camooweal Campdraft, Mount Isa Show AUGUST Mount Isa Rotary Rodeo

TOWNSVILLE TO CLONCURRY

FLINDERS HIGHWAY (774 KM)

Travel deep into the Queensland outback down the
Flinders Highway, a strategic route linking the major
coastal city of Townsville with inland industrial centres.
Although the highway deteriorates west of Torrens
Creek, the attractions along this route are great: the
historic mining centre of Charters Towers is an exciting
town to explore and the fascinating dinosaur trail
through Hughenden and Richmond certainly make
the journey worthwhile.

Former Australian Bank of Commerce, Charters Towers

Hughenden to Cloncurry

After crossing large pastoral leaseholds, the highway passes through
the small towns of Richmond and Julia Creek. Once part of an ancient
inland sea, Richmond is home to the fascinating Richmond Marine
Fossil Display where some of Australia's best examples of vertebrate
fossils are exhibited. The route intersects with the Landsborough
(Matilda) Highway at Cloncurry, an important mining and cattle centre.

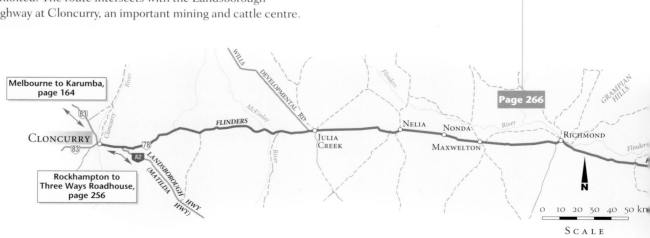

Melbourne to Karumba,
page 164

Page 266

Rockhampton to
Three Ways Roadhouse,
page 256

CLONCURRY
FLINDERS
JULIA CREEK
NELIA
NONDA
MAXWELTON
RICHMOND
GRAMPIAN HILLS

0 10 20 30 40 50 km
SCALE

Best time to go

The summers in this region can be hot and humid, so the warm days and cool nights of the temperate months between May and October are the best time to travel.

John & Jan

CHARTERS TOWERS

	J	F	M	A	M	J	J	A	S	O	N	D
Maximum	34	33	32	30	27	25	25	27	30	32	34	35
Minimum	22	22	21	18	15	12	11	12	15	18	20	21
Rainfall (mm)	137	130	104	43	24	27	17	13	15	22	41	87
Raindays	10	10	8	5	4	4	3	2	2	3	4	7

JULIA CREEK

	J	F	M	A	M	J	J	A	S	O	N	D
Maximum	38	37	36	33	30	27	26	29	33	36	38	38
Minimum	24	24	22	18	15	10	9	11	15	19	21	23
Rainfall (mm)	121	114	58	18	16	11	8	3	6	17	31	68
Raindays	8	8	4	2	1	1	1	1	1	2	3	6

Brisbane to Cairns, page 42

Page 264

Townsville to Hughenden

The Flinders Highway leads inland to busy Charters Towers, a historic mining town with many magnificent buildings from the 1880s and 1890s. Further west the highway passes through several small communities before arriving in the town of Hughenden, an important regional centre where a lifesize *Muttaburrasaurus langdoni* replica is the first indication of the town's strong prehistoric history.

TOWNSVILLE TO HUGHENDEN 378 KM

Authors' choice

⊛ **Exchange Hotel Van and Camping Park, Torrens Creek**

This park has an unusual appeal and we like it. It is small, well maintained and conveniently located next to the Exchange Hotel. It is good value, being budget priced but with plenty of grass, although there are only a small number of powered sites.

For more details see page 391.

Travel tip

Bushwalkers in the White Mountains National Park must register with the ranger and bookings are required for camping. Register and obtain information at the National Parks offices in Hughenden, (07) 4741 1113, or Charters Towers, (07) 4787 3388.

Dinosaur country

Hughenden Dinosaur Display houses a lifesize replica of the 7-m-long, bird-footed dinosaur *Muttaburrasaurus langdoni*, and several other fascinating fossils collected from the region. Gray Street; (07) 4741 1021; entry fee applies; open 9 a.m. to 5 p.m. daily.

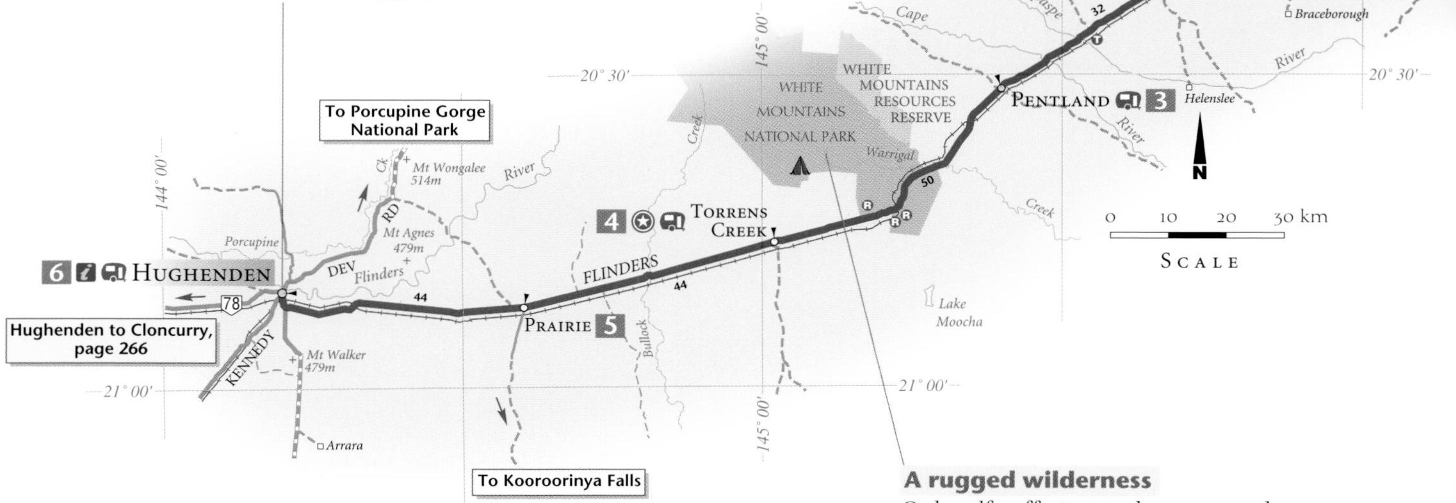

A rugged wilderness

Only self-sufficient and experienced bushwalkers should enter the White Mountains National Park. For those well prepared, however, this wilderness park rewards with spectacular scenery and many varieties of wildflowers that flower in late winter and spring.

What's on

MAY Mingela Rodeo, Pentland Campdraft, Country Music Festival (Charters Towers) JULY/AUGUST Dinosaur Festival (Hughenden, even-numbered years), Race Meeting (Prairie)

To Porcupine Gorge National Park

To Koorooyinya Falls

Hughenden to Cloncurry, page 266

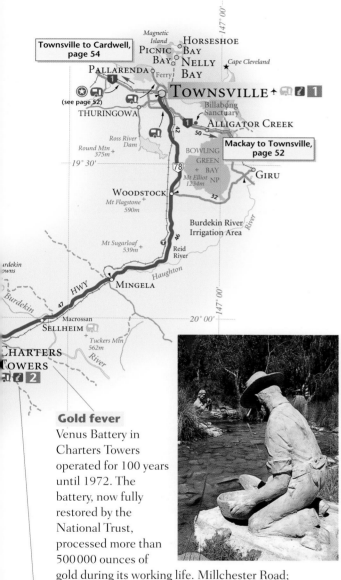

Track notes

The Flinders Highway is a major route carrying heavy traffic, including road trains. Between Townsville and Charters Towers it is wide, sealed and well maintained. From Charters Towers to Torrens Creek the road is in a reasonably good state of repair; however, west of Torrens Creek it deteriorates with sharp edges, an uneven surface and broken asphalt. Drivers, especially those towing campers and caravans, must exercise extreme caution between Torrens Creek and Hughenden.

Town file

1 TOWNSVILLE (see page 53)

2 CHARTERS TOWERS pop. 8893   ⛽ PDG
GPS 20° 04.574' S/146° 15.474' E
Gold was discovered here in 1871 and by the 1890s Charters Towers was a prosperous city, the second largest in Queensland. It is now the heart of a busy cattle-raising industry and an important education centre for western Queensland, with both private boarding schools and State schools. The city has all services. 🛈 Mosman Street; (07) 4752 0314.

3 PENTLAND pop. 200   ⛽ PD
GPS 20° 31.402' S/145° 23.948' E
Pentland grew out of the Cape River goldfields with the arrival of the railway in 1884 and was once a cattle centre. Today Pentland is a small settlement providing basic services.

4 TORRENS CREEK pop. 12   ⛽ PD
GPS 20° 46.211' S/145° 01.165' E
Torrens Creek, now a very small community, was once an important staging post for Cobb & Co. and an ammunition dump in World War II. It is close to White Mountains National Park. The railway passes through the township, which has a hotel and small caravan park.

5 PRAIRIE pop. 60   ⛽ PD
GPS 20° 52.270' S/144° 36.028' E
Prairie is a small service centre with basic services and a hotel built in the 1860s. The Kooroorinya Falls, approximately 60 km south of Prairie, are a popular nearby attraction, offering birdwatching, fishing and swimming. The road to the falls is fairly rough (especially in the wet season) so four-wheel drives are recommended.

6 HUGHENDEN pop. 1444   ⛽ PDG
GPS 20° 50.565' S/144° 12.032' E
Hughenden is a major pastoral centre on the Flinders River in an area once home to dinosaurs and marine species, while the surrounds are still rich in gemstones. A lifesize replica of a *Muttaburrasaurus langdoni* stands on the median strip in the town centre. Porcupine Gorge National Park lies approximately 50 km to the north. The town has most services and basic shopping. 🛈 Gray Street; (07) 4741 1021.

Gold fever

Venus Battery in Charters Towers operated for 100 years until 1972. The battery, now fully restored by the National Trust, processed more than 500 000 ounces of gold during its working life. Millchester Road; (07) 4787 2222; entry fee applies; open 9 a.m. to 3 p.m. daily. In another tribute to the town's goldmining history, monuments (pictured) can be seen in gardens off the highway.

Historic architecture and lacework verandahs

The central business area of Charters Towers is a historic area retaining many wonderfully preserved buildings from the 1880s and 1890s. The old-world architecture is prominent and the Stock Exchange, City Hall and the Australian Bank of Commerce buildings are great examples of this.

HUGHENDEN TO CLONCURRY 396 KM

Australian uranium

The Mary Kathleen Uranium Mine was opened by the prime minister, Robert Menzies, in 1958. The mine, between Cloncurry and Mount Isa, was abandoned and is no longer accessible, but has been immortalised in Cloncurry's Mary Kathleen Park and Museum. Four buildings re-erected in the park house much of the mine's history, including an 18 000-piece mineral display. McIlwraith Street (Flinders Highway); (07) 4742 1361; entry fee applies; open 8 a.m. to 4.30 p.m. weekdays throughout the year and 9 a.m. to 3 p.m. weekends April to October.

Remembering the flying doctors

At John Flynn Place the founders of the Royal Flying Doctor Service are remembered. Exhibits include one of the first pedal wirelesses and a scale model of the *Victory*, the first plane that took off with a doctor on board, in 1928. Daintree Street, Cloncurry; (07) 4742 4125; entry fee applies; open 8.30 a.m. to 4.30 p.m. weekdays throughout the year and 9 a.m. to 3 p.m. weekends April to October.

Dramatic sunsets

Sunset Hill is a short walk from the Gilbert Park Tourist Village in Cloncurry. The hill offers superb 360-degree views of the town and is an ideal spot to relax at the day's end and watch or photograph the vivid winter sunsets.

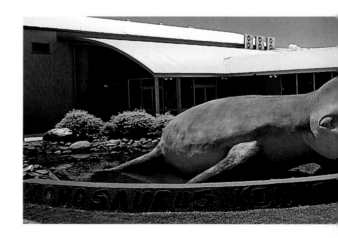

What's on

MAY Julia Creek Dirt and Dust Festival, Julia Creek Campdraft, Fossil Festival (Richmond, odd-numbered years) JUNE Maxwelton Races JULY/AUGUST Merry Muster Rodeo (Cloncurry)

Exotic perfume

The sandalwood factory and mill in Richmond is the only operational sandalwood plant in Queensland. The oil that is extracted from the wood is exported to Asian markets. Simpson Street.

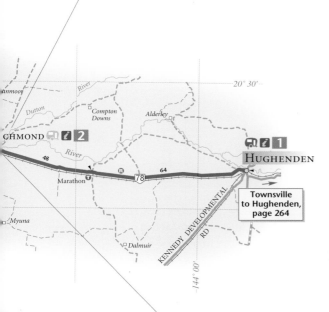

Kronosaurus Korner

Kronosaurus Korner in Richmond houses the amazing Richmond Marine Fossil Display. A 5-m-long pliosaur and the armoured Minmi, both on display, are two of the most complete and well-preserved fossils of their type in the world. 91–93 Goldring Street; (07) 4741 3429; entry fee applies; open 8.30 a.m. to 4.45 p.m. daily.

Track notes

The Flinders Highway between Hughenden and Cloncurry is a fully sealed road badly in need of major repair. The surface is uneven, the edges poor and there are patches of broken asphalt. In a small number of places the road surface has been reconstructed but elsewhere extreme care is required. The road carries heavy traffic including road trains.

Town file

1 **HUGHENDEN** (see page 265)

2 **RICHMOND** pop. 733   🅿 PDG
GPS 20° 43.757' S/143° 08.496' E
Despite now being 500 km from the ocean, the area Richmond lies in was once an inland sea and the major marine fossil finds in the area are some of the most notable examples in the world. Kronosaurus Korner houses an amazing display of local fossils. Located on the banks of the Flinders River (Queensland's longest), the town is a service centre for many large cattle properties. The rich Mitchell and Flinders grass plains and a reliable artesian water supply ensure this is some of the north's best cattle country. Richmond has most basic services and supplies.
🛈 Kronosaurus Korner, 91–93 Goldring Street; (07) 4741 3429.

3 **JULIA CREEK** pop. 519   🅿 PDG
GPS 20° 39.428' S/141° 44.726' E
Julia Creek is a regional service centre, near the junction of the Flinders Highway and Wills Developmental Road. The first pastoralists moved into the area in 1862, just a year after Burke and Wills had passed through the area and the town still has strong ties with the pastoral industry. Julia Creek has most basic services. 🛈 Shire offices, Burke Street; (07) 4746 7166.

4 **CLONCURRY** (see page 177)

Travel tip

Being overtaken on a bad surface can be frightening, especially if you are towing a caravan. Consider pulling onto the shoulder to allow oncoming or overtaking traffic as much road as possible. This is even more important if the vehicle is a road train as while the driver will attempt to keep to the correct half of the road, the following trailers can wander.

NORSEMAN TO PERTH
COOLGARDIE ESPERANCE HIGHWAY, GREAT EASTERN HIGHWAY (720 KM)

Travel to Perth through historic goldmining towns and golden
wheat fields on Route 94, the most direct road linking the
eastern States with the cosmopolitan coastal city. The
Coolgardie Esperance Highway intersects with Highway One
at the historic mining town of Norseman on the western end
of the Nullarbor Plain crossing. Visit the intriguing Kalgoorlie
and Coolgardie goldfields or watch the sun slip behind the
horizon over expanses of wheat in the Merredin region.

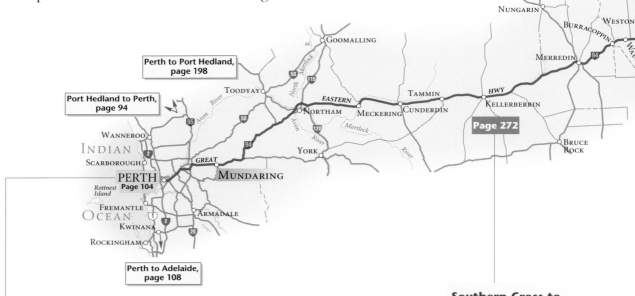

Perth to Port Hedland,
page 198

Port Hedland to Perth,
page 94

Page 272

Perth to Adelaide,
page 108

Perth
With a Mediterranean-type
climate and magnificent coastal
river setting, Perth is ideal for an
outdoor lifestyle. Visitors to this
city will find clean surf beaches,
tranquil forests and well-kept
parklands – all within easy reach
of the city centre.

Southern Cross to Mundaring
The Great Eastern Highway
travels along the goldfields'
water pipeline for much of
the route, passing through
Merredin, the heart of the
State's wheat industry, and
Meckering, the site of a
devastating earthquake in
1968. The small, historic
towns of Northam and York are
worth a stop-off before the
highway begins the climb
through the hills towards
Perth.

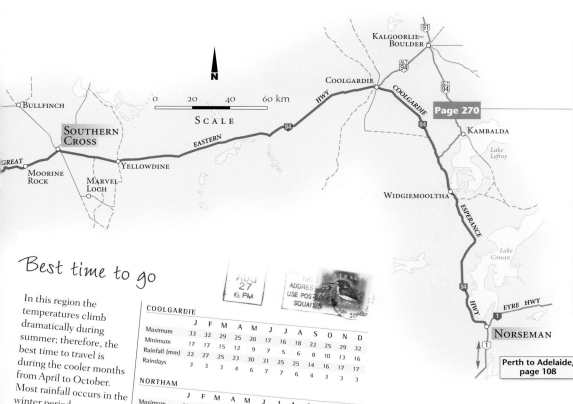

Norseman to Southern Cross

The Coolgardie Esperance Highway swings north from Norseman across kilometres of mallee country and salt lakes before ending in the once-thriving historic goldmining city of Coolgardie. Kalgoorlie–Boulder, now the prosperous key city in the goldfields, is a short and worthwhile deviation from the main route.

Page 270

Perth to Adelaide, page 108

Best time to go

In this region the temperatures climb dramatically during summer; therefore, the best time to travel is during the cooler months from April to October. Most rainfall occurs in the winter period.

John & Jan

COOLGARDIE

	J	F	M	A	M	J	J	A	S	O	N	D
Maximum	33	32	29	25	20	17	16	18	22	25	29	32
Minimum	17	17	15	12	9	7	5	6	8	10	13	16
Rainfall (mm)	22	27	25	23	30	31	25	25	14	16	17	17
Raindays	3	3	3	4	6	7	7	6	4	3	3	3

NORTHAM

	J	F	M	A	M	J	J	A	S	O	N	D
Maximum	34	34	31	26	21	18	17	18	21	24	28	32
Minimum	17	17	15	12	9	7	6	6	7	9	12	15
Rainfall (mm)	10	13	19	23	57	83	84	62	37	25	12	9
Raindays	2	2	2	5	11	15	16	14	11	7	4	2

Wheat fields near Merredin

NORSEMAN TO SOUTHERN CROSS 352 KM

Authors' choice

⊛ Kalgoorlie Accommodation Village, Kalgoorlie–Boulder

Excellent quality and convenience make this a stand-out park in our opinion, and it is a great base from which to explore the goldmining history of Kalgoorlie. Located off the main road, close to the airport and about 2 km from the centre of Boulder, it has a wide range of facilities to suit both overnight travellers or those staying longer. There is a pool, a camp kitchen and a range of accommodation. We always stay here when we pass through Kalgoorlie.

For more details see page 371.

Pan for gold

Hannans North Historic Mining Reserve produced gold for 60 years. The Australian Prospectors and Miners Hall of Fame now at the site displays a substantial collection of mining equipment, offers demonstrations of gold panning and pouring, and has underground tours. Closed footwear (no open-toed sandals) is essential. Broadarrow Road; (08) 9091 4074; entry fee applies; open 9 a.m. to 4.30 p.m. daily.

Unusual bottles

The Goldfields Exhibition Museum is housed in the historic Coolgardie Warden's Court. Here you will find fascinating displays, including the largest bottle collection in Western Australia, and Aboriginal artefacts upstairs. 62 Bayley Street; (08) 9026 6090; entry fee applies; open 9 a.m. to 5 p.m. daily.

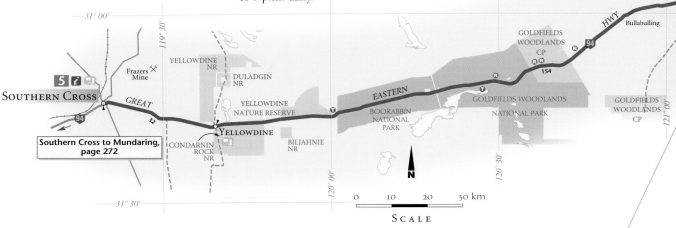

Southern Cross to Mundaring, page 272

Travel tip

When travelling in this area, Kalgoorlie–Boulder is a 'must see'. Make a round trip from the highway through Kambalda to Kalgoorlie–Boulder and rejoin the highway at Coolgardie, or vice versa. The best selection of caravan parks, accommodation and shopping is at Kalgoorlie–Boulder. The town continues to improve and we enjoy visiting it.

Lavish architecture

The early architecture on the goldfields can be best studied in some of the grand old buildings in Coolgardie. Make sure you see the historic railway station, the courthouse, the gaol and the National Trust-restored Warden Finnerty's residence, among others.

What's on

MARCH St Patrick's Day Parade (Kalgoorlie–Boulder) APRIL
Norseman Gold Cup Race Meeting JUNE Menzies to Kalgoorlie
Cycle Race SEPTEMBER Balzano Barrow Race (Kanowna to
Kalgoorlie–Boulder), Fishing in the Desert (Kambalda)

Track notes

The Great Eastern and Coolgardie Esperance highways are wide roads
that wind through undulating country and across plains. There are
almost no overtaking lanes and sometimes few opportunities to
overtake. Be patient. This route is the main thoroughfare to and from
the eastern States and carries much heavy traffic.

Town file

1 NORSEMAN (see page 117)

2 KAMBALDA pop. 3598   🅿 PD
GPS 31° 12.239' S/121° 40.070' E
Kambalda was a battling goldmining town until the 1960s, when nickel
was discovered and the town boomed. Extensive mining continues in the
area. Kambalda has a range of facilities and land sailing is a popular and
exhilarating sport on nearby Lake Lefroy, a huge salt lake. Kambalda
actually has two town centres, Kambalda East and Kambalda West.
ℹ Emu Rocks Road; (08) 9027 0192.

3 COOLGARDIE pop. 1258   🅿 PDG
GPS 30° 57.278' S/121° 09.858' E
Once the third largest settlement in Western Australia, Coolgardie was
a thriving goldmining city. Today it is one of Australia's great frontier
towns and is best known for its historic buildings. The famous explorer
Ernest Giles is buried in the cemetery. Basic services are available.
ℹ 62 Bayley Street; (08) 9026 6090.

4 KALGOORLIE–BOULDER pop. 28 087   🅿 PDG
GPS 30° 44.819' S/121° 28.379' E (Kalgoorlie)
At the heart of the goldfields, Kalgoorlie–Boulder has all services.
Shopping is very good and there are several caravan parks. The
famous Golden Mile is recognised as the richest square mile of gold-
bearing ore in the world, while the Super Pit is the largest goldmine in
Australia. There is a lot to see: the famous two-up school still operates
6 km north of town on the Menzies Road and a newer attraction,
Langtrees Bordello, offers tours of its extravagant premises in
historic Hay Street. ℹ 250 Hannan Street; (08) 9021 1966;
www.kalgoorlieandwagoldfields.com.au

5 SOUTHERN CROSS pop. 1147   🅿 PDG
GPS 31° 13.904' S/119° 19.692' E
The town was named after the constellation that early prospectors used
to find their way here after gold was first discovered in 1887. Southern
Cross has had its ups and downs but many goldmines still operate today.
At the eastern entrance to town a pioneer cemetery contains early
headstones. The town has most facilities including a caravan park.
ℹ Yilgarn Shire Office, Antares Street; (08) 9049 1001.

SOUTHERN CROSS TO MUNDARING 334 KM

Authors' choice

✪ Merredin Caravan Park and Av-a-Rest Village, Merredin

This park is of a quality that is rarely found in an inland town the size of Merredin and we highly recommend it. From here it is a comfortable 260 km to Perth or 335 km to Kalgoorlie; Merredin is an excellent choice for an overnight stop. The park facilities include a pool and camp kitchen, and the adjoining roadhouse serves meals.

For more details see page 377.

Swanning around

Black swans are the emblem of Western Australia; however, the Avon River at Northam is home to a happy family of European white swans. The swans were introduced in 1896 and have bred successfully since then. Northam's swan warden feeds the swans each day but you can also buy some feed at the visitor information centre and feed the birds yourself.

Whitewater adventure

The Northam Avon Descent is a classic 133-km whitewater event held annually on the first weekend in August, and is a fabulous event to watch. There are numerous classes of competition for various crafts and vessels, including surf skis and powerboats, as well as the more traditional canoes and kayaks.

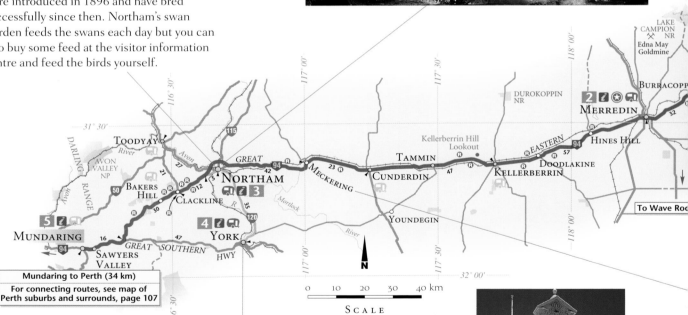

Convicts and cars

York is a historic town and one of Western Australia's finest tourist destinations. The historic buildings, dating back as far as the 1840s, are the major drawcard. The Residency Museum and the Old Gaol and Courthouse should not be missed, while the mechanically minded might enjoy a visit to the York Motor Museum.

Travel tip

Merredin lies roughly midway between Perth and the goldfields and is perfect for an overnight stop. The excellent caravan park, the good supermarket and shopping, plus a choice of places to eat, all combined with cheerful service, help to make Merredin a pleasant stop. We usually enjoy a relaxed bistro-style meal at the roadhouse just 30 m from the caravan park.

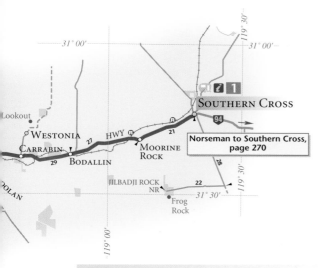

What's on

MARCH Vintage on Avon Motorsport (Northam)
EASTER York Antique and Collectors Fair AUGUST Avon Descent (Northam), Avon River Festival (Northam) SEPTEMBER York Jazz Weekend NOVEMBER Mundaring Arts Festival

Rare earthquake

At 10.59 a.m. on Monday, 14 October 1968, an earthquake struck Meckering and many of the buildings in and around town tumbled down. The quake measured 6.9 on the Richter scale, making it the second largest earthquake ever in Australia. Information about the earthquake is displayed on a board in the town's park.

Track notes

The Great Eastern Highway is the major and most direct route between Perth and the eastern States, so it carries a large amount of heavy traffic. The surface is good, although at times the road does wander through hilly country, making travel a little slower. The water pipeline from Mundaring Weir to the goldfields mostly follows the highway.

Town file

1 SOUTHERN CROSS (see page 271)

2 MERREDIN pop. 2911   🅿 PDG
GPS 31° 28.926' S/118° 16.697' E
This large regional town serves an intensive agricultural area where much of the State's wheat is grown. Merredin is home to two popular museums: the Military Museum in Barrack Street and the Old Railway Station Museum on the Great Eastern Highway. There are most facilities including good shopping and a very good caravan park. Wave Rock, a 2.7-billion-year-old piece of granite, 15 m high and 100 m long, is 193 km south along Maj Road. *i* Barrack Street; (08) 9041 1666.

3 NORTHAM pop. 6300   🅿 PDG
GPS 31° 39.116' S/116° 39.593' E
Situated on the Avon River, Northam is Western Australia's second largest inland town and a large agricultural centre. An excellent visitor information centre on the banks of the Avon should be the first port of call for tourists and from here it is possible to see, and photograph, the town's famous white swans. There is excellent shopping and all services in Northam. *i* 2 Grey Street; (08) 9622 2100; www.avon.net.au/~northam

4 YORK pop. 1923   🅿 PDG
GPS 31° 53.313' S/116° 46.106' E
York is a historic town on the Avon River first settled in 1831, two years after the Swan River Colony was founded. This is a rich agricultural area with an even richer history. While not on the Great Eastern Highway the deviation to York is very worthwhile. Whether you prefer exploring the historic buildings or enjoying an al fresco lunch at one of the many cafes, York is memorable. *i* 81 Avon Terrace; (08) 9641 1301.

5 MUNDARING pop. 1912   🅿 PDG
GPS 31° 54.113' S/116° 10.005' E
Situated 34 km inland from Perth, Mundaring sits in the hills of the Darling Range. Mundaring Weir supplies water to goldfields as far away as Norseman; the pipeline was completed in 1903 and there are several pumping stations along the route to Kalgoorlie–Boulder and Norseman, with the pipeline's route following the Great Eastern Highway for much of its 563-km length. Mundaring has most basic facilities. *i* 7225 Great Eastern Highway; (08) 9295 0202.

TASMANIA

Smithton

A2

Somerset

1

Devonport

A10

1

Launceston

A3

A3

Rosebery

**Devonport to Hobart
(via Midlands)**
page 276

Bicheno

Derwent
Bridge

1

A10

**Devonport to Hobart
(via west coast)**
page 286

A3

**Hobart to
Launceston**
page 296

A10

1

1

A3

HOBART page 282

Chapter 4

Touring Tasmania

TASMANIA IS A PLACE where you really can see everything. It is easy to bypass many worthwhile places on the mainland simply because of the sheer immensity of the continent, but in Tasmania you can take your time, so why not make the most of it?

Devonport, where the ferry docks midway along the north coast, is a natural starting point. From Devonport there are three routes to follow. You could take one south, one to return north, and the third in part or full if you have some extra time.

The route that cuts through the centre of Tasmania takes you first to Launceston then down through the Midlands, a farming region dotted with historic places. A trip along the west coast to Hobart takes you through a vast network of rivers – some of the State's best trout-fishing areas – to the Cradle Mountain–Lake St Clair National Park. This park is a vast and unspoilt wilderness famous the world over. On the third route, along the east coast, you can visit some of Tasmania's gorgeous coastline. The diversion to Port Arthur gives you a glimpse of Tasmania's penal history, and another diversion to Freycinet National Park will take you to beaches straight out of a postcard. Whichever route you choose, Tasmania is a terrific place to start or end a trip around Australia.

DEVONPORT TO HOBART (VIA MIDLANDS)

BASS HIGHWAY, MIDLAND HIGHWAY (303 KM)

Head deep into the fertile, undulating plains of Tasmania's Midlands on the Bass and Midland highways, the main route linking the north coast and Devonport with Hobart. The road passes through some major agricultural regions where, in addition to wheat, oats and barley, farmers grow unique crops such as poppies for medicinal use and pyrethrum for use in insecticides. Tourists flock to many of the delightful historic towns in this part of the State, including Longford, Evandale, Ross and Oatlands. The distances in Tasmania are not great, and driving from Devonport to Hobart takes just a pleasant few hours.

Cataract Gorge Reserve, near Launceston

Best time to go

The winters in Tasmania are cold, so spring and autumn are the most popular times to travel. Though warmer, the summers are still very comfortable for touring.

John & Jan

DELORAINE

	J	F	M	A	M	J	J	A	S	O	N	D
Maximum	21	23	20	17	13	11	10	11	13	16	18	20
Minimum	8	9	6	5	3	1	1	1	3	4	5	7
Rainfall (mm)	51	47	51	73	88	104	122	115	93	85	65	64
Raindays	8	7	8	11	13	14	16	16	14	13	11	9

OATLANDS

	J	F	M	A	M	J	J	A	S	O	N	D
Maximum	22	22	19	16	12	10	9	11	13	15	17	20
Minimum	9	9	8	6	3	2	1	2	3	5	6	8
Rainfall (mm)	44	39	40	48	43	47	44	45	42	54	50	56
Raindays	10	8	10	13	15	16	18	18	15	15	13	12

Devonport to Launceston

This section of the route rolls through beautiful coastal hills where flower farms bloom in the spring. The road then sweeps inland through regional farming communities to Launceston, the 'Garden City' of the north. Before you head south, take a diversion from Devonport to Port Sorell, a popular coastal holiday resort.

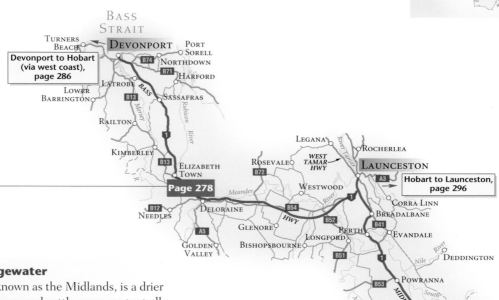

Launceston to Bridgewater

This area of the State, known as the Midlands, is a drier farming region where sheep and cattle graze contentedly and wheat crops stand tall. Many towns and properties have excellent historic buildings, several of which are regularly open to the public. Do not miss Woolmers Estate near Longford, which dates back to 1817 and is considered Australia's most significant colonial property.

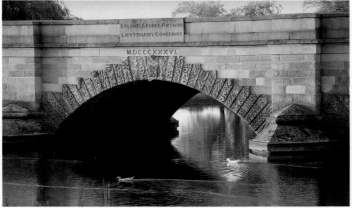

Ross Bridge

Hobart

Hobart, Australia's second oldest and most southerly city, is situated on the broad estuary of the River Derwent under the spell of majestic Mount Wellington. A strong maritime flavour and sense of the past give Hobart an almost European air. This feeling is heightened in winter, when daytime temperatures drop to a crisp average 12 degrees Celsius.

DEVONPORT TO LAUNCESTON 102 KM

Authors' choice

⊛ Port Sorell Lions Caravan Park, Port Sorell

This popular beachfront park is owned and operated by the Lions Club. It is close to the centre of town, adjacent to the boat ramp and ideal for family holidays. It is an easy drive to the Devonport ferry terminal from here. Bookings are required in holiday periods.
For more details see page 384.

Holiday town

Take the short deviation to Port Sorell, the oldest township on the north-west coast, for fabulous river and sea fishing, swimming, boating and bushwalking. Across the estuary is Narawntapu National Park with numerous isolated beaches, sand dunes and grasslands covered in wildflowers.

Travel tip

Caravan parks near the Bass Strait ferry terminal in Devonport are often filled by people who have just arrived or are about to leave on the ferry. Devonport is an easy drive from several towns and numerous caravan parks along the north coast, including those at Port Sorell and Kelso, and those further west at Stanley and Wynyard.

What's on

JANUARY Henley-on-the-Mersey (Latrobe), Summer Festival (Port Sorell) FEBRUARY Festivale (Launceston), Launceston Cup OCTOBER Royal Show (Launceston) NOVEMBER Tasmanian Craft Fair (Deloraine)

Platypuses

Platypuses are shy and rarely seen by people. However, the Latrobe Landcare group operates guided tours daily at dawn and dusk in the Warrawee Forest Reserve along the Mersey River – a chance to see these entrancing creatures in their natural habitat. Bookings are essential. Book at Carnation Connection, 153 Gilbert Street, Latrobe; (03) 6426 2877; fee applies.

Gorgeous gorge

The towering granite walls of the Cataract Gorge channel the waters of the South Esk River to its junction with the River Tamar. Scenic cruises operate through the gorge and there are walking tracks through the surrounding parkland, while a chairlift carries the more adventurous across the gorge.

Tractors and traction engines

Pearn's Steam World claims to house the best collection of agricultural steam engines in the Southern Hemisphere. Some machines date back more than a century. Steam spectaculars are held on each long weekend during the warmer months of the year. Old Bass Highway, Westbury; (03) 6393 1414; entry fee applies; open 9 a.m. to 4 p.m. daily.

Track notes

The Bass Highway from Devonport is wide, with overtaking lanes at slower points. Near Launceston the highway becomes dual carriageway. Many towns, including Latrobe and Deloraine, are bypassed but are worth visiting.

Town file

1 DEVONPORT pop. 22 299   PDG
GPS 41° 10.823' S/146° 21.762' E
Tasmania's north-west is rich farming land. Devonport is a busy port exporting local produce, the dock for the *Spirit of Tasmania* ferries and a regional centre with good shopping and most services. It is an ideal base from which to see northern Tasmania. *i* Tasmanian Travel and Information, 92 Formby Road; (03) 6424 8176; www.dcc.tas.gov.au

2 PORT SORELL pop. 1818   PD
GPS 41° 11.963' S/146° 23.915' E
Port Sorell, once a shipbuilding town, is now a fast-growing residential area. It is 15 minutes' drive from Devonport and popular for holidays, with good beaches, fishing spots and walks.

3 LATROBE pop. 2765   PD
GPS 41° 14.102' S/146° 24.449' E
Latrobe is rich in history: more than 80 properties are classified by the National Trust. Bells Parade Reserve on the Mersey River is soon to become home to the Australian Axemen's Hall of Fame. Latrobe has basic shopping and good services, including a modern hospital. *i* 70 Gilbert Street; (03) 6426 2693.

4 DELORAINE pop. 2168   PD
GPS 41° 31.454' S/146° 39.477' E
Deloraine, established at a crossing over the Meander River, has many colonial buildings. It is a service centre for the surrounding agricultural community, and is well known for its quality art and craft. *i* Great Western Tiers Visitor Centre, 98–100 Emu Bay Road; (03) 6362 3471.

5 WESTBURY pop. 1280   PDG
GPS 41° 31.590' S/146° 49.951' E
A rural village, Westbury has many old buildings, limited country-town shopping and basic services.

6 LAUNCESTON pop. 67 701   PDG
GPS 41° 26.201' S/147° 08.264' E
Tasmania's second largest city, Launceston lies at the head of the River Tamar valley, renowned for its vineyards and fine foods. The city has gracious old buildings, very good shopping and all services, and makes a good base from which to explore the region. *i* Gateway Tasmania Travel Centre, corner St John and Paterson streets; (03) 6336 3133.

Bicheno to Launceston, page 302

Launceston to Bridgewater, page 280

LAUNCESTON TO BRIDGEWATER 178 KM

Woolmers Estate

Be sure to visit Australia's oldest family-owned property, Woolmers Estate outside Longford. The house was built in about 1817 and six generations of the Archer family lived here, until 1994. The property has a unique collection of historic farm buildings, including an 1819 woolshed and a convicts' chapel, antiques, vintage cars and equipment. Woolmers Lane, near Longford; (03) 6391 2230; entry fee applies; open 10 a.m. to 4.30 p.m. daily.

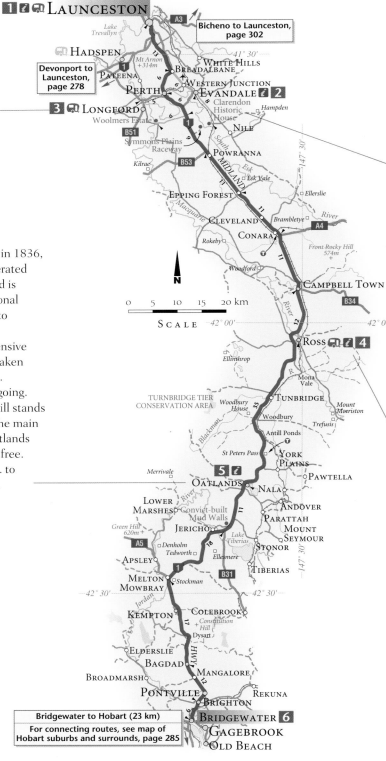

Wind power

Callington Mill, built in 1836, is the oldest wind-operated mill in the country and is classified by the National Trust. The mill fell into disrepair early in the 20th century, but extensive restoration work has taken place since the 1970s.

Restoration is ongoing. Callington Mill stands proudly in the main street of Oatlands and entry is free. Open 9 a.m. to 5 p.m. daily.

What's on

JANUARY Woodstock Music Festival (Longford) FEBRUARY National Penny Farthing Championships (Evandale), Village Fair (Evandale), Rodeo (Oatlands) MARCH Tasmanian Highland Games (Campbell Town) OCTOBER Longford Agricultural Show

Bicheno to Launceston, page 302

Devonport to Launceston, page 278

Bridgewater to Hobart (23 km)
For connecting routes, see map of Hobart suburbs and surrounds, page 285

Travel tip

Several of the small towns along this route have historic attractions, and some historic properties are also open to the public. We especially enjoy the areas surrounding Longford and Evandale. The Longford Bakery is a great choice for a relaxing lunch, while the Teddy Bear Shop in Oatlands sells some of the best biscuits we have tried.

Historic houses

Evandale is a marvellously historic town, founded in 1829. The town remains unspoilt and many buildings here are of architectural significance, especially in High Street. Clarendon Historic House, an extraordinarily grand Georgian mansion set in formal gardens and parkland, lies 8 km south of Evandale, near Nile. It has been restored by the National Trust. Off Nile Road; (03) 6398 6220; entry fee applies; open 10 a.m. to 5 p.m. daily in summer and 10 a.m. to 4 p.m. daily in winter.

Stone arches

At Ross the Macquarie River is spanned by one of Australia's oldest and most beautiful bridges (circa 1836). The convict-built bridge displays many fine carvings and earned pardons for two of the stonemasons responsible for the workmanship.

Track notes

The Midland Highway winds through Tasmania's Midland region, an area well known for broadacre grain and sheep farming. This highway is the direct route between Launceston and Hobart, and carries both local and tourist traffic and some heavy transports. The road is clearly signed and well maintained.

Town file

1 LAUNCESTON (see page 279)

2 EVANDALE pop. 1033 ⛽ PD
GPS 41° 34.284' S/147° 14.843' E
Evandale retains fine old buildings, some dating back to 1809, and is noted for numerous antique and craft shops. Markets are held each Sunday at Falls Park. Evandale has quaint resort-style shopping and few services. 🛈 Tourism and History Centre, 18 High Street; (03) 6391 8128.

3 LONGFORD pop. 2829 ⛽ PD
GPS 41° 35.730' S/147° 07.318' E
On the banks of the Macquarie River, Longford was first settled in 1813 and has a unique village green. Longford has good country-town shopping and most services.

4 ROSS pop. 275 ⛽ PD
GPS 42° 14.575' S/147° 24.336' E
Classified by the National Trust, Ross is a historic township with many colonial sandstone buildings. It is bypassed by the highway but is a fascinating place to visit. The town is at the centre of a farming region respected for its fine merino wool and is home to the Tasmanian Wool Centre museum. Do not miss the Female Factory Historic Site (off Bond Street), the most archaeologically intact female convict site in Australia. Ross has basic shopping. 🛈 Tasmanian Wool Centre, Church Street; (03) 6381 5466.

5 OATLANDS pop. 539 ⛽ PD
GPS 42° 17.963' S/147° 22.351' E
Classified by the National Trust, the town of Oatlands claims the most pre-1837 buildings in Australia. Several significant buildings are prominent in the town, which has a small country-town shopping strip and limited services. 🛈 Central Tasmanian Tourism Centre, 85 High Street; (03) 6254 1212.

6 BRIDGEWATER pop. 4250 ⛽ PDG
GPS 42° 43.949' S/147° 14.248' E
Bridgewater was established in 1812 around a bridge crossing the Derwent River, as a military post to protect travellers who changed coaches here. The crossing was built by convicts in the 1830s; during construction over 2 million tonnes of clay and rock were moved by wheelbarrow. Bridgewater has a shopping centre and most services.

HOBART

YOUR GUIDE

Hobart, Australia's second oldest and most southerly city, is situated on the broad estuary of the River Derwent under the spell of majestic Mount Wellington. A strong maritime flavour and sense of the past give Hobart an almost European air. This feeling is heightened in winter, when daytime temperatures drop to a crisp average 12 degrees Celsius. However, it is also very much an Australian city, surrounded as it is by bushland and boasting prime examples of distinctive colonial architecture.

CITY CENTRE

See map on page 284.

Anglesea Barracks 284 D6
The oldest military establishment in Australia, dating back to 1846, with beautiful Georgian buildings; guided tours on Tuesday mornings.

Antarctic Adventure 284 E5
Explore the world's most isolated continent; exhibits range from a blizzard simulator ride to evocative accounts of explorers and researchers.

Battery Point 284 E6
Former mariners' village; tearooms, restaurants and an antique shop around every corner.

Constitution Dock 284 E4
Historic hub of Hobart's busy waterfront; buy fresh seafood on the dock.

Maritime Museum of Tasmania 284 E4
Treasure chest of seafaring relics from when Hobart was a famous sea-port.

Parliament House 284 D5
Originally a customs house designed by John Lee Archer and constructed by convicts in the late 1830s; visitors may inspect the restored Legislative Council Chamber.

Penitentiary Chapel Historic Site 284 D3
View the tunnels, courtrooms and solitary confinement cells; ghost tours operate most evenings.

Royal Tasmanian Botanical Gardens 284 E1
The State's horticultural jewel, contained within convict-built walls; includes the Botanical Discovery Centre, which houses an Interpretation Gallery, a Plant House and a restaurant.

Visitor information

Tasmanian Travel and Information Centre
Corner Elizabeth and Davey streets, Hobart
(03) 6230 8233
www.discovertasmania.com.au

Top events

Australian Wooden Boat Festival (February)
Hobart's waterfront at its colourful best.

10 Days on the Island (March–April)
Local and international arts, music, dance, film and theatre.

Tulip Festival of Tasmania (September)
Hobart welcomes spring.

Sydney and Melbourne to Hobart yacht races (December)
Party time at Constitution Dock.

Taste of Tasmania (December)
The very best of Tasmanian food and wine.

St Davids Park 284 D5
A good place to rest; Hobart's first colonial burial ground was here with gravestones dating back to 1804.

Salamanca Place 284 E5
Setting for the bustling Saturday market; historic 1830s warehouses now house quality arts and crafts, cafes and restaurants.

Tasmanian Museum and Art Gallery 284 E4
Notable for its magnificent colonial landscape paintings, Aboriginal history and the convict experience.

Theatre Royal 284 D4
Australia's oldest theatre still in operation.

Van Diemen's Land Memorial Folk Museum (Narryna) 284 D6
Colonial collection in historic townhouse.

SUBURBS AND SURROUNDS
See map on page 285.

Cadbury Schweppes Chocolate Factory 285 D2
A chocolate-lover's dream come true; tours on weekdays and free samples.

Cascade Brewery 285 D3
Set in the foothills of Mount Wellington and over 150 years old; offers tours on weekdays.

D'Entrecasteaux Channel 285 B8
A leisurely drive from Hobart along the coastline of this deep-blue channel takes you through tiny towns and boutique produce farms; stunning views.

Derwent Valley 285 B2
Neat agricultural landscapes, rolling hills and historic buildings.

Mount Wellington 285 D3
Superb views of the D'Entrecasteaux Channel and the Derwent Valley, 1270 m above the city.

Richmond 285 E2
Probably Australia's best preserved Georgian Colonial village; boasts the country's oldest bridge, built by convicts in the 1820s; the local gaol pre-dates Port Arthur.

Runnymede 285 D3
National Trust Georgian-style house with lovely gardens.

Tudor Court Model Village 285 D4
Fascinating model of a Tudor Village: traditional thatched cottages, shingled shops, manor house, windmill and other period houses along with minute gardens and inhabitants dressed in historic costume.

Getting around
Traffic flows freely throughout Hobart; however, be warned that many of the streets are one way. Metered street parking is readily available and the Council operates several carparks at modest rates. Metro Tasmania operates a bus service that runs frequently during business hours, with a limited evening/weekend timetable. Walking is the best way to appreciate the rich history of the city centre, waterfront and Battery Point. Ferries and cruise boats leave regularly from Franklin Wharf and Brooke Street Pier at Sullivans Cove. During summer, sailing vessels run charter tours as far afield as Port Arthur and Bruny Island. There are also a number of coach tours, including a daily tour of the city and suburbs.

Airport shuttle bus Tasmania's Own Redline Coach Services 1300 360 000; Motoring organisation RACT 13 11 11; Public transport Metro Tasmania 13 22 01; Taxis City Cabs 13 10 08, Taxi Combined 13 22 27; River Derwent cruises The Cruise Company (03) 6234 9294, Captain Fells Ferries (03) 6223 5893.

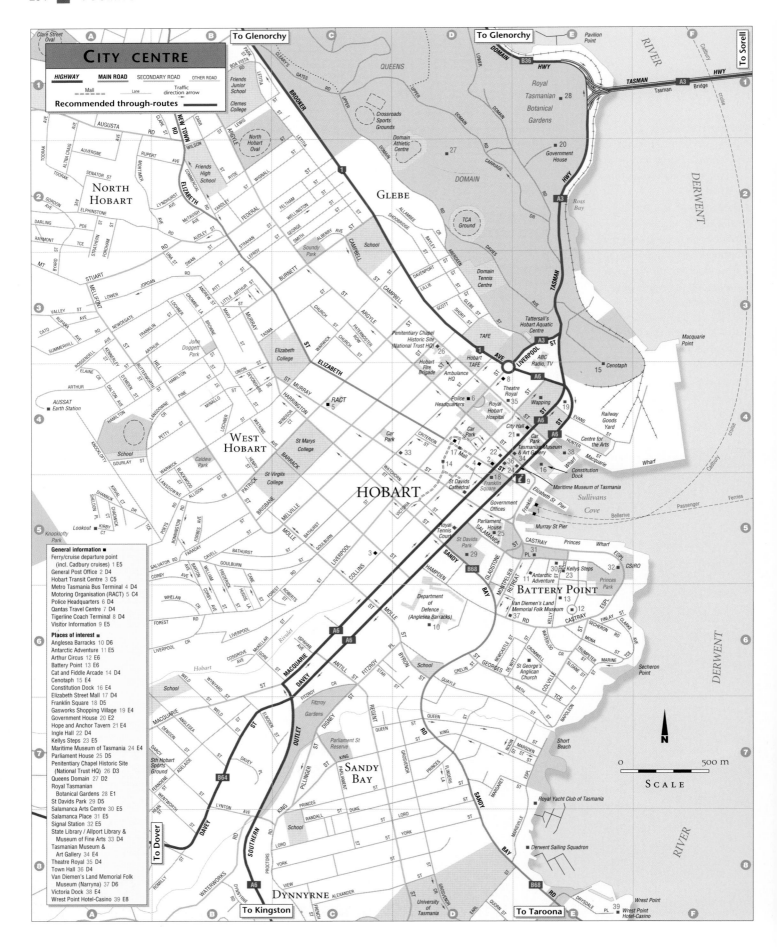

CITY CENTRE

HIGHWAY   MAIN ROAD   SECONDARY ROAD   OTHER ROAD

===== Mall   ——— Lane   → Traffic direction arrow

Recommended through-routes ———

To Glenorchy

To Glenorchy

To Sorell

RIVER

Tasman HWY

B35

A3

TASMAN HWY

Tasman Bridge

Royal Tasmanian Botanical Gardens

QUEENS

Crossroads Sports Grounds

Domain Athletic Centre

■ 27

Government House

■ 20

DOMAIN

NORTH HOBART

Friends Junior School

Clemes College

Friends High School

North Hobart Oval

GLEBE

Soundy Park

TCA Ground

Domain Tennis Centre

Ross Bay

DERWENT

Macquarie Point

Pavilion Point

TAFE

Penitentiary Chapel Historic Site National Trust HQ ■ 26

Hobart Fire Brigade

Ambulance HQ

Police Headquarters ■ 6

Royal Hobart Hospital

Tattersall's Hobart Aquatic Centre

Cenotaph ■ 15

ABC Radio, TV

Theatre Royal ■ 35

Wapping

City Hall

Car Park

Tasmanian Museum & Art Gallery

Centre for the Arts

Railway Goods Yard

Cenotaph

Hope and Anchor Tavern

WEST HOBART

John Doggett Park

Elizabeth College

St Marys College

St Virgils College

Caldew Park

AUSSAT Earth Station

School

Lookout

Knocklofty Park

HOBART

Criterion St

Car Park

■ 33

■ 17 Mall

■ 14

■ 22

■ 5

■ 4

■ 36

■ 18

■ 24

■ 34

■ 16

■ 9

Macquarie Wharf

Constitution Dock

Maritime Museum of Tasmania

Sullivans Cove

Wharf

St Davids Cathedral

Franklin Square

Government Offices

Parliament House ■ 25

Elizabeth St Pier

Murray St Pier

Princes Wharf

Passenger Ferries

Bellerive

Royal Tennis Court

St Davids Park ■ 29

SALAMANCA

■ 31

■ 30 ■ 23 ■ 32

Kellys Steps

Princes Park

CSIRO

Antarctic Adventure ■ 11

BATTERY POINT

■ 13

■ 12

■ 37

Van Diemen's Land Memorial Folk Museum

Department of Defence (Anglesea Barracks)

■ 10

HAMPDEN

B68

SANDY BAY

St George's Anglican Church

School

Secheron Point

Short Beach

Fitzroy Gardens

Parliament St Reserve

Sth Hobart Sports Ground

DYNNYRNE

SANDY BAY

University of Tasmania

School

Royal Yacht Club of Tasmania

Derwent Sailing Squadron

Wrest Point

■ 39 Wrest Point Hotel-Casino

RIVER

DERWENT

To Dover

To Kingston

To Taroona

N

0   500 m

SCALE

General information ■

Ferry/cruise departure point (incl. Cadbury cruises) 1 E5
General Post Office 2 D4
Hobart Transit Centre 3 C5
Metro Tasmania Bus Terminal 4 D4
Motoring Organisation (RACT) 5 C4
Police Headquarters 6 D4
Qantas Travel Centre 7 D4
Tigerline Coach Terminal 8 D4
Visitor Information 9 E5

Places of interest ■

Anglesea Barracks 10 D6
Antarctic Adventure 11 E5
Arthur Circus 12 E6
Battery Point 13 E6
Cat and Fiddle Arcade 14 D4
Cenotaph 15 E4
Constitution Dock 16 E4
Elizabeth Street Mall 17 D4
Franklin Square 18 D5
Gasworks Shopping Village 19 E4
Government House 20 E2
Hope and Anchor Tavern 21 E4
Ingle Hall 22 D4
Kellys Steps 23 E5
Maritime Museum of Tasmania 24 E4
Parliament House 25 D5
Penitentiary Chapel Historic Site (National Trust HQ) 26 D3
Queens Domain 27 D2
Royal Tasmanian Botanical Gardens 28 E1
St Davids Park 29 D5
Salamanca Arts Centre 30 E5
Salamanca Place 31 E5
Signal Station 32 E5
State Library / Allport Library & Museum of Fine Arts 33 D4
Tasmanian Museum & Art Gallery 34 E4
Theatre Royal 35 D4
Town Hall 36 D4
Van Diemen's Land Memorial Folk Museum (Narryna) 37 D6
Victoria Dock 38 E4
Wrest Point Hotel-Casino 39 E8

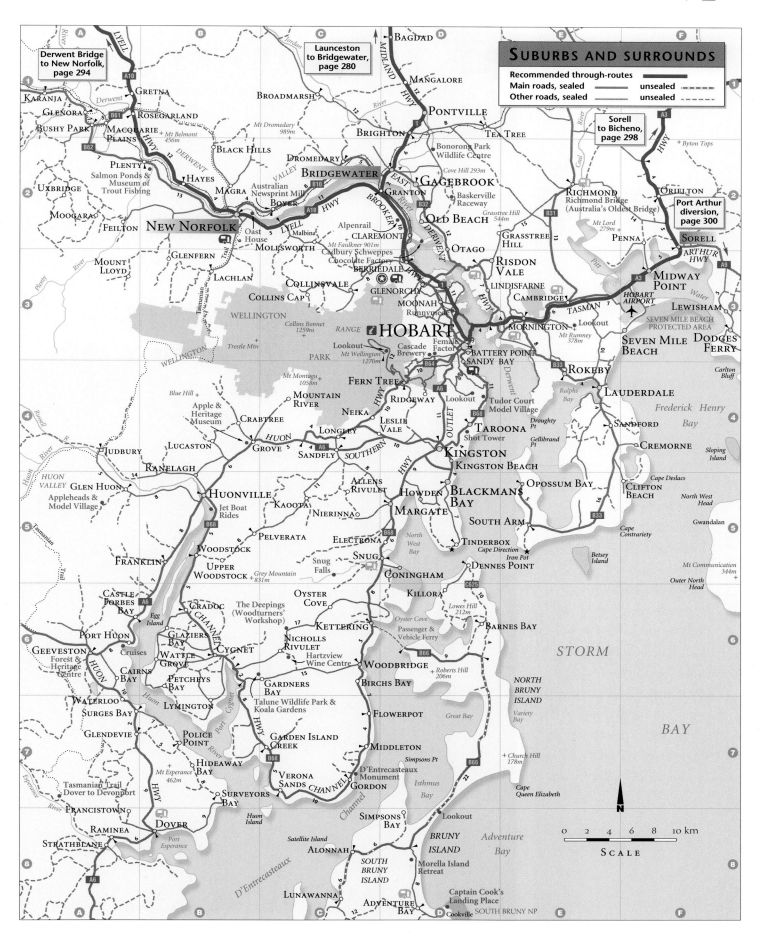

Derwent Bridge to New Norfolk, page 294

Launceston to Bridgewater, page 280

SUBURBS AND SURROUNDS

Recommended through-routes
Main roads, sealed — unsealed
Other roads, sealed — unsealed

Sorell to Bicheno, page 298

Port Arthur diversion, page 300

BAGDAD

MANGALORE

BROADMARSH

PONTVILLE

TEA TREE

BRIGHTON

Bonorong Park Wildlife Centre

Cove Hill 293m

RICHMOND
Richmond Bridge (Australia's Oldest Bridge)

ORIELTON

KARANJA

GRETNA

GLENORA

ROSEGARLAND

Mt Dromedary 989m

DROMEDARY

BRIDGEWATER

GAGEBROOK

Baskerville Raceway

Grasstree Hill 544m

PENNA

+ Byton Tops

BUSHY PARK

MACQUARIE PLAINS

+ Mt Belmont 456m

BLACK HILLS

GRANTON

OLD BEACH

GRASSTREE HILL

SORELL

PLENTY

HAYES

MAGRA

BOYER

Australian Newsprint Mill

Alpenrail

CLAREMONT

Otago

RISDON VALE

MIDWAY POINT

ARTHUR HWY

UXBRIDGE

Salmon Ponds & Museum of Trout Fishing

Malbina

Mt Faulkner 901m

Cadbury Schweppes Chocolate Factory

Mt Lord 279m

LEWISHAM

MOOGARA

FEILTON

NEW NORFOLK

Oast House

MOLESWORTH

BERRIEDALE

LINDISFARNE

CAMBRIDGE

TASMAN

HOBART AIRPORT

SEVEN MILE BEACH PROTECTED AREA

GLENFERN

COLLINSVALE

GLENORCHY

MOONAH

Runnymede

SEVEN MILE BEACH

DODGES FERRY

MOUNT LLOYD

LACHLAN

Collins Cap

Collins Bonnet 1259m

WELLINGTON

MORNINGTON

Mt Rumney 378m

Carlton Bluff

HOBART

ROKEBY

LAUDERDALE

Frederick Henry Bay

Trestle Mtn

RANGE

Lookout

Cascade Brewery

Female Factory

Battery Point
Sandy Bay

Ralphs Bay

Mt Montagu 1058m

Mt Wellington 1270m

PARK

WELLINGTON

Blue Hill +

FERN TREE

RIDGEWAY

Lookout

Tudor Court Model Village

Droughty Pt

Sandford

CREMORNE

Sloping Island

Cape Deslacs

MOUNTAIN RIVER

NEIKA

LESLIE VALE

Shot Tower

Gellibrand Pt

CLIFTON BEACH

North West Head

Apple & Heritage Museum

CRABTREE

LONGLEY

TAROONA

Apple & Heritage Museum

LUCASTON

GROVE

SANDFLY

SOUTHERN

KINGSTON

Kingston Beach

OPOSSUM BAY

JUDBURY

HUON VALLEY

RANELAGH

GLEN HUON

Appleheads & Model Village

HUONVILLE

Jet Boat Rides

KAOOTA

NIERINNA

ALLENS RIVULET

HOWDEN

MARGATE

BLACKMANS BAY

SOUTH ARM

Cape Contrariety

Mt Communication 344m

Outer North Head

FRANKLIN

PELVERATA

WOODSTOCK

UPPER WOODSTOCK

Grey Mountain + 831m

ELECTRONA

SNUG

North West Bay

Snug Falls

TINDERBOX

Cape Direction

Iron Pot

DENNES POINT

Betsey Island

STORM

CASTLE FORBES BAY

CRADOC

Egg Island

The Deepings (Woodturners' Workshop)

OYSTER COVE

KILLORA

CONINGHAM

Oyster Cove Passenger & Vehicle Ferry

Lowes Hill 212m

PORT HUON

GEEVESTON

Forest & Heritage Centre

Cruises

GLAZIERS BAY

WATTLE GROVE

CYGNET

NICHOLLS RIVULET

Hartzview Wine Centre

KETTERING

BARNES BAY

BIRCHS BAY

WOODBRIDGE

Roberts Hill 206m

NORTH BRUNY ISLAND

CAIRNS BAY

PETCHEYS BAY

GARDNERS BAY

Talune Wildlife Park & Koala Gardens

WATERLOO

SURGES BAY

LYMINGTON

FLOWERPOT

Great Bay

Variety Bay

BAY

GLENDEVIE

POLICE POINT

GARDEN ISLAND CREEK

MIDDLETON

Church Hill 178m

Mt Esperance 462m

HIDEAWAY BAY

Tasmanian Trail Dover to Devonport

SURVEYORS BAY

VERONA SANDS

GORDON

D'Entrecasteaux Monument

Simpsons Pt

Isthmus Bay

Cape Queen Elizabeth

FRANCISTOWN

Huon Island

SIMPSONS BAY

Lookout

RAMINEA

DOVER

Port Esperance

BRUNY ISLAND

Adventure Bay

STRATHBLANE

Satellite Island

ALONNAH

SOUTH BRUNY ISLAND

Morella Island Retreat

Captain Cook's Landing Place

N

0 2 4 6 8 10 km

SCALE

LUNAWANNA

ADVENTURE BAY

Cookville

SOUTH BRUNY NP

DEVONPORT TO HOBART (VIA WEST COAST,

BASS HIGHWAY, MURCHISON HIGHWAY, ZEEHAN HIGHWAY, LYELL HIGHWAY (639 KM)

Best time to go

The north-west coast has a mild climate (by Tasmanian standards), while the higher country further south has cold and snowy winters. Late spring and early autumn are the best times to travel.

John & Jan

BURNIE

	J	F	M	A	M	J	J	A	S	O	N	D
Maximum	21	21	20	18	15	13	13	13	14	16	18	19
Minimum	13	13	12	10	8	7	6	6	7	8	10	11
Rainfall (mm)	44	49	52	78	98	105	130	110	87	89	71	65
Raindays	10	8	10	11	15	15	18	18	16	15	13	11

TARRALEAH

	J	F	M	A	M	J	J	A	S	O	N	D
Maximum	19	20	17	14	11	9	8	9	11	14	16	18
Minimum	7	7	6	4	2	0	0	1	2	3	5	6
Rainfall (mm)	70	62	71	98	105	99	117	123	116	111	102	93
Raindays	13	11	14	17	19	17	21	21	19	19	17	16

Most tourists who drive around Tasmania will choose to travel on this popular route, especially as there is good, sealed access to both ends of the spectacular Cradle Mountain–Lake St Clair National Park. The highway climbs over the famous stark hills surrounding Queenstown and crosses a great trout-fishing region in the centre of the State. The breathtaking west-coast town of Strahan is a very popular tourist destination where the cruise boats ply the tannin-stained waters of the mighty Gordon River.

Cradle Mountain

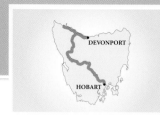

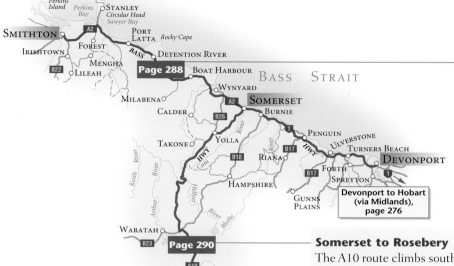

Devonport to Smithton

The moderate climate along the north-west coast makes this a popular tourist region. The highway closely follows the sea and the coastal towns along the way all have interesting attractions. The Nut, an unusual rocky formation overlooking the historic township and fishing port of Stanley, has a chairlift from which to take in the wonderful views.

Devonport to Hobart (via Midlands), page 276

Somerset to Rosebery

The A10 route climbs south from the coast into lush forests, and distant mountain peaks soon become visible. The small, historic mining town of Waratah is a worthwhile diversion to the west. Cradle Mountain–Lake St Clair National Park, with its abundant wildlife and rewarding bushwalks, can be reached from this route.

Rosebery to Derwent Bridge

Located on the shores of Macquarie Harbour, Strahan is an incredibly popular tourist resort, while the historic mining towns of Zeehan and Queenstown also attract visitors. The highway climbs steeply around the bare hills above Queenstown en route to Derwent Bridge, a small community at the southern end of tranquil Lake St Clair.

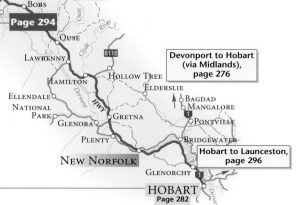

Devonport to Hobart (via Midlands), page 276

Hobart to Launceston, page 296

Derwent Bridge to New Norfolk

Winding down through the ranges, the highway runs along rivers, travels through small rural towns and passes some of the State's best trout-fishing areas. New Norfolk is an important regional town with many well-preserved historic buildings.

Hobart

Hobart, Australia's second oldest city, is situated on the broad estuary of the River Derwent under the spell of majestic Mount Wellington. A strong maritime flavour and sense of the past give Hobart an almost European air.

DEVONPORT TO SMITHTON 137 KM

Authors' choice

⊛ Stanley Cabin and Tourist Park, Stanley

This park, on the water's edge, is a 200-m stroll from the centre of town – a perfect base for exploring historic Stanely. It has very good amenities and nicely grassed sites, and booking is necessary in holiday periods.

For more details see page 388.

Stanley's Nut

In Stanley, the Nut, a 152-m-high basalt monolith rising from the sea, is the most obvious natural feature; the town shelters at its base. Take the chairlift to the summit (there is also a walking track for the more energetic) for a terrific view. From the top it is possible to view a shearwater (muttonbird) rookery between November and April.

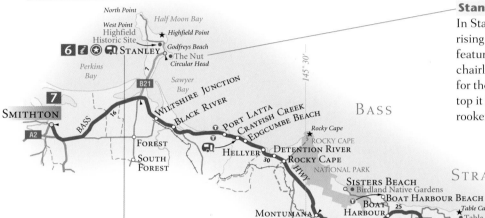

Van Diemen's Land Company

Stanley was the headquarters of the Van Diemen's Land Company, and the historic property Highfield, north of Stanley, was home to the company's chief agent from 1834 to 1856. Highfield Historic Site is open to the public. Greenhills Road; (03) 6458 1100; entry fee applies; open 10 a.m. to 4 p.m. daily October to April.

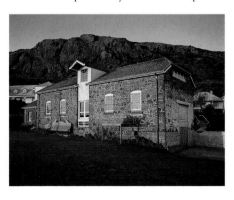

A wealth of attractions

Wings Farm at Gunns Plains has trout fishing, bushwalking, kayaking, golf, a wildlife menagerie and a very good reptile display. There is also a caravan park (and camping areas). 137 Winduss Road; (03) 6429 1335; entry fee applies; open 10 a.m. to 4 p.m. daily.

What's on
MARCH Wynyard Agricultural Show **MAY** Mount Roland Folk Festival (Sheffield) **OCTOBER** Daffodil Show (Sheffield), Tulip Festival (Wynyard) **NOVEMBER** Sheffield Agricultural Show, North West Food Festival (Burnie), Penguin Festival (Penguin) **DECEMBER** Circular Head Agricultural Show (Stanley), Mardi Gras (Ulverstone)

Travel tip

Stanley's historic buildings, spectacular Nut, fairy penguins on Godfreys Beach and excellent caravan park make it one of our favourite Tasmanian destinations. Stanley's buildings date from the early 1800s, with some connected to the historic Van Diemen's Land Company.

Steam back in time

The Don River Railway has the largest collection of steam locomotives in Tasmania, dating back to 1879. Steam-train rides operate on Sundays and public holidays, along a section of the State's oldest line, between Don and Coles Beach north of Devonport, while diesel engines operate Monday to Saturday. (03) 6424 6335; fare applies; departs from Don on the hour from 10 a.m. to 4 p.m., departs Coles Beach 20 minutes past the hour from 10.20 a.m. to 4.20 p.m.

A town of murals

Sheffield was experiencing an economic downturn in the late 1980s and it was decided to revitalise the town with a mural project. Now almost every possible wall has been painted: the many spectacular murals depict local scenes and snippets of the area's local history. Today many people visit Sheffield to see these murals. It is a detour from the route, but an enjoyable experience.

Track notes

The Bass Highway is a sealed, well-maintained road with some overtaking lanes. It winds along the coast and the sea is rarely out of sight. Roadside rest areas are uncommon. Trucks and milk tankers use the highway.

Town file

1 DEVONPORT (see page 279)

2 ULVERSTONE pop. 9792   ⛽ PD
GPS 41° 09.247' S/146° 10.924' E
Ulverstone's warm summers and sandy beaches attract holiday-makers. Beach and estuary fishing are popular. The town meets local needs with a country-town shopping centre and basic facilities. *i* Car Park Lane (rear of post office); (03) 6425 2839.

3 PENGUIN pop. 3030   ⛽ PD
GPS 41° 05.327' S/146° 00.639' E
Penguin is next to the beach and fairy penguins can be viewed at dawn and dusk. The town has a small shopping centre and limited facilities. *i* Main Street; (03) 6437 1421.

4 BURNIE pop. 16 007   ⛽ PDG
GPS 41° 03.203' S/145° 54.316' E
Burnie, on the shores of Emu Bay, is a major industrial and regional centre, with government services and offices. Its port is a terminal for mining produce, farm produce and paper. Burnie has very good regional shopping and all services. *i* Tasmanian Travel and Information Centre, Little Alexander Street; (03) 6434 6111.

5 WYNYARD pop. 4509   ⛽ PD
GPS 40° 59.291' S/145° 43.815' E
The centre of a rich farming area and a fishing port, Wynyard is a popular base for trout fishing, especially in the Inglis and Flowerdale rivers. The lookout on Table Cape offers exceptional views. Wynyard has basic shopping and limited facilities. *i* Corner Hogg and Goldie streets; (03) 6442 4143.

6 STANLEY pop. 543   ⛽ PD
GPS 40° 45.846' S/145° 17.746' E
The Van Diemen's Land Company, which developed and settled much of Tasmania's north-west, established its headquarters here in 1826. The Nut towers behind the town. Stanley has limited shopping and services. *i* 45 Main Road; (03) 6458 1330.

7 SMITHTON pop. 3313   ⛽ PDG
GPS 40° 50.450' S/145° 07.415' E
Smithton is a regional centre, with an economy based mainly on fishing, timber, dairying and vegetable production. It offers country-town shopping.

Map showing Devonport area including Ulverstone, Turners Beach, Coles Beach, Spirit of Tasmania Ferries, Forth, Don, Don River Railway & Museum, Botsham, Alford, Quoiba, Spreyton, Kindred, Melrose, Paloona, Latrobe, Lower Barrington, Railton, Nook, Barrington, Lake Paloona, Sheffield, Stoodley.

Devonport to Launceston, page 278

To Cradle Mountain

SOMERSET TO ROSEBERY   119 KM

Authors' choice

★ **Cradle Mountain Tourist Park, Cradle Mountain**

Set in bushland just outside the World Heritage-listed wilderness area, this quality park has good facilities including a large recreational building with open fireplaces. It is a popular camping site for walkers from around the world who come to walk the renowned Overland Track in the Cradle Mountain–Lake St Clair National Park.

For more details see page 362.

Tasmania's highest waterfall

The spectacular Montezuma Falls are Tasmania's highest waterfall, tumbling 113 m. They are 8 km south-west of Rosebery by road, plus a 3-km walk from the parking area along a disused railway track, gently graded, through lush temperate rainforest.

A former mining town

Waratah is a historic tin-mining town and the site of what was once the world's richest tin mine, at Mount Bischoff. Take a walk around the old mining area to soak up its history, or a self-drive tour of the town – brochures are available.

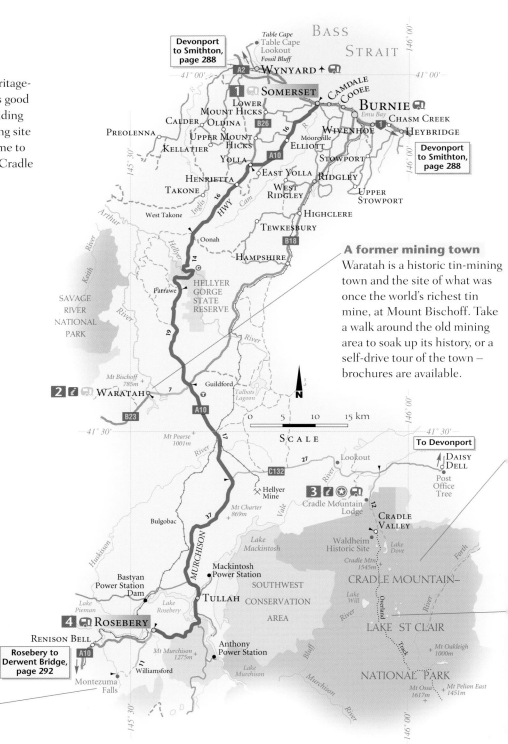

Devonport to Smithton, page 288

Devonport to Smithton, page 288

Rosebery to Derwent Bridge, page 292

Cradle Mountain–Lake St Clair National Park

The Cradle Mountain–Lake St Clair National Park is famous worldwide for its unspoilt beauty and the richness of its plant and animal life. The park has two main focal points, each with its own visitor information centre: Cradle Mountain in the north and Lake St Clair in the south. This deep and tranquil lake – the deepest in Australia – lies in a basin gouged out by ancient glaciers.

Walking tracks for everyone

There are many walking tracks in the Cradle Mountain–Lake St Clair National Park, graded to suit all levels of fitness, taking in temperate rainforest, waterfalls and moorland. Pick up information leaflets from the park's visitor information centres. Perhaps the most famous walk is the 85-km Overland Track, which links the striking Cradle Mountain with the serene Lake St Clair. Another enjoyable walk is the Lake Dove Boardwalk (pictured).

Track notes

The Murchison Highway winds rapidly from the coastal plain to the mountains, passing great scenery and remote mining sites. This wide sealed highway carries an assortment of traffic and provides good access to Cradle Mountain via Route C132. The Hellyer River crossing is a popular rest spot.

Town file

1 SOMERSET pop. 1000 ⛽ PD
GPS 41° 52.735' S/145° 23.191' E

Somerset is a small community west of Burnie at the junction of the Bass and Murchison highways. Shopping and services are available in Burnie, just a few kilometres east.

2 WARATAH pop. 230 ⛽ PD
GPS 41° 26.456' S/145° 31.444' E

Once the site of the world's richest tin mine, now closed, Waratah is a tiny town amid heathland. The dams that used to service the mines now provide good trout fishing. Waratah Park, in the centre of town, is a popular place for a picnic or barbecue. The town has basic shopping.
ℹ Council Offices, Smith Street; (03) 6439 7100.

3 CRADLE MOUNTAIN LODGE ⛽ P
GPS 41° 35.717' S/145° 55.699' E

The Cradle Mountain Lodge resort is at the entrance to the World Heritage-listed Cradle Mountain–Lake St Clair National Park. The park is an extremely popular destination for tourists, who can find information on the walking tracks, amazing landscape and natural features at the Cradle Mountain Visitor Information Centre just inside the park entrance. A local shop is the extent of the services. Park entry fee applies.
ℹ Cradle Mountain; (03) 6492 1110; www.parks.tas.gov.au

4 ROSEBERY pop. 1439 ⛽ PD
GPS 41° 46.749' S/145° 32.405' E

In 1893 gold was discovered in Rosebery Creek and shortly afterwards lead and zinc were found in the region. The township developed with the mining activity that followed and mining has continued for more than 100 years. Rosebery is located on the highway and offers travellers a range of shops and services.

What's on

MARCH Miners, Axemen, Bush and Blarney Festival (Rosebery), Wynyard Agricultural Show OCTOBER Jazz West Festival (Tullah), Tulip Festival (Wynyard) NOVEMBER North West Food Festival (Burnie)

ROSEBERY TO DERWENT BRIDGE 135 KM

Authors' choice

⊛ **Strahan Caravan and Tourist Park, Strahan**

Explore the fabulous western coastal region from this popular resort-style park, only 1.5 km west of the centre of Strahan. It has basic but good amenities. We stay here when we visit Strahan. **For more details see page 388.**

An alien landscape

The unique, almost bare mountain landscape surrounding Queenstown is the town's most notable feature. The hills were stripped of timber to fuel the copper smelters and subsequent erosion left the rock exposed. The naked mountains are quite spectacular, but look so strange that many visitors feel they are unearthly. The landscape certainly has made an impression on us.

Sarah Island

The extremely harsh conditions of the Sarah Island penal settlement are well documented in Marcus Clarke's novel *For the Term of His Natural Life*; the convict settlement was established on Sarah Island in 1822 and operated until 1833. A visit to Sarah Island and its convict ruins – a historic site – is evocative; the island is reached by boat cruise from Strahan.

What's on
JANUARY Mount Lyell Picnic (Strahan) MARCH Piners Festival (Strahan) OCTOBER Robert Sticht Festival (Queenstown)

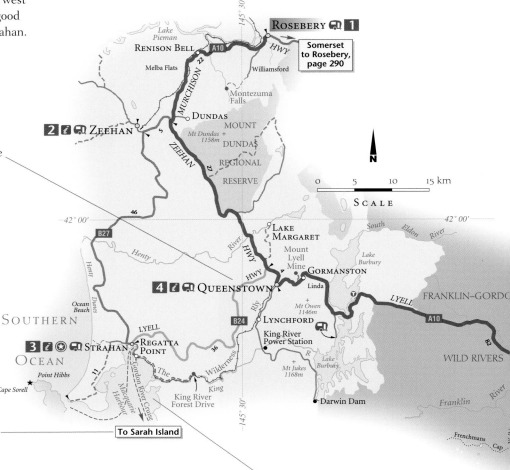

Somerset to Rosebery, page 290

To Sarah Island

River cruises

A very popular trip is the cruise from Strahan across Macquarie Harbour and up the dark tannin-stained waters of the Gordon River. Temperate rainforest hugs the riverbanks, where the remaining Huon pines still stand majestically above the forest.

Franklin–Gordon Wild Rivers National Park
This 446 000-ha national park forms the central portion of Tasmania's World Heritage Area. The Lyell Highway runs through the park and excellent short walks lead off the highway to rainforests, waterfalls and lookouts.

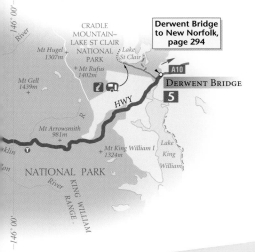

Derwent Bridge to New Norfolk, page 294

Travel tip

The Lake St Clair Visitor Centre is on the shores of Lake St Clair and within the park, so park-use fees have to be paid to reach it. The centre has a shop retailing books, clothing and souvenirs, a busy cafe and a range of park information. The adjoining caravan park has a good range of facilities.

Track notes

The route follows the A10 through the centre of the State. It is very windy around Queenstown, where it also climbs abruptly. The route passes through eucalypt forests in the Franklin–Gordon Wild Rivers National Park and crosses the headwaters of the River Derwent at Derwent Bridge. The road is well maintained and has a good surface. There are some overtaking opportunities.

Town file

1 ROSEBERY (see page 291)

2 ZEEHAN pop. 1116   ⛽ PD
GPS 41° 53.091' S/145° 20.261' E
Zeehan became a thriving town after the discovery of silver and lead in 1882. Classified by the National Trust, the historic town is named after Abel Tasman's ship on his discovery voyage in 1642. A railway once linked Zeehan with Strahan in 1862, but a road to the remote town was not opened until 1962. Zeehan's history is preserved in the West Coast Pioneers Memorial Museum. The town has a basic shopping centre and basic services. 🛈 West Coast Pioneers Memorial Museum, Main Street; (03) 6471 6225.

3 STRAHAN pop. 701   ⛽ PDG
GPS 42° 09.182' S/145° 19.709' E
On Macquarie Harbour, the only safe anchorage on Tasmania's west coast, Strahan was established in 1883 to service the area's mining settlement. Huon pine was milled here for many years. The picturesque waterfront village has a wide selection of tourist accommodation and a resort-style shopping centre with craft shops, galleries and eateries. 🛈 The Esplanade; (03) 6471 7622.

4 QUEENSTOWN pop. 2631   ⛽ PD
GPS 42° 04.880' S/145° 33.411' E
This historic town nestles at the bottom of a valley surrounded by stark mountains almost totally devoid of vegetation. Copper, silver and gold have been mined here since the 1880s (more than 20 000 kg of gold have been extracted); tours of the mine are available. Queenstown, the largest township in western Tasmania, has adequate shopping and most services. 🛈 Queenstown Gallery Museum, Corner of Sticht and Driffield streets; (03) 6471 1483.

5 DERWENT BRIDGE pop. 117   ⛽ PDG
GPS 42° 07.898' S/146° 13.969' E
Derwent Bridge is a small community 5 km from Cradle Mountain–Lake St Clair National Park Visitor Centre. The area, surrounded by forests and buttongrass plains, is popular with bushwalkers and great for trout fishing. There is a roadhouse and hotel but other services are limited. 🛈 Lake St Clair; (03) 6289 1172.

DERWENT BRIDGE TO NEW NORFOLK 131 KM

Travel tip

A visit to the Mount Field National Park or the Great Lake area can be full of surprises. This central region of Tasmania is steeped in history, having been settled soon after the Hobart area. There are many historic towns and lots to see; however, the past does not always immediately present itself and it may be necessary to look a little harder.

(Map showing route from Derwent Bridge to New Norfolk, including Cradle Mountain–Lake St Clair NP, Lake St Clair, Central Plateau Conservation Area, Bronte Park, Lake Big Jim, Lake Samuel, To Miena and Great Lake, Laughing Jack Lagoon, Nive River, Bronte Lagoon, Bradys Trail, Lake Binney, Tarraleah Power Station, Tarraleah, Franklin–Gordon Wild Rivers NP, Liapootah Power Station, Wayatinah, Wayatinah Lagoon, Black Bobs, Wayatinah Power Station, Lake Catagunya, Repulse Power Station, Cluny Power Station, Lawrenny, Glen, Ellendale, Mount Field NP, Russell Falls, National Park)

Rosebery to Derwent Bridge, page 292

Power from water

Tasmania's first hydro-electric power station was constructed in 1910. There are currently 30 hydro-electric power stations operating in the State and many are close to this route; all have large water storages and many have huge pipes conducting water to the turbines.

Mount Field National Park

This national park is one of Tasmania's popular ski fields. The scenery is also spectacular, with several waterfalls including the well-known Russell Falls, a delightful three-tier fall. Mount Field was the first national park to be declared in Tasmania, back in 1916, and it has much to offer visitors: vegetation ranges from a forest of huge tree ferns and swamp gums to alpine species, while the eastern barred bandicoot, nationally listed as vulnerable, is often seen here.

Plenty of salmon

Take an alternative route to Plenty to see the Salmon Ponds, a delightful fish hatchery in a garden setting, where rustic bridges cross the pools that lie like goldfish ponds amid well-tended lawns – a lovely place for a picnic. The hatchery, now run by the Inland Fisheries Commission, began operation in 1864, when trout and salmon ova were imported from England. There is also a fascinating Museum of Trout Fishing here. (03) 6261 1076; entry fee applies; open 9 a.m. to 5 p.m. daily.

What's on

MARCH Hop Harvest Festival (New Norfolk) AUGUST Winter Challenge (New Norfolk) OCTOBER Spring in the Valley (New Norfolk) NOVEMBER Tasmanian Trout Fishing Championships (Miena)

Cast your line

Trout fishing – generally for wild brown trout, although there are populations of rainbows – is the major recreational activity in central Tasmania. There are numerous dams and lakes throughout the region, and trout are found in almost every permanent stream and river. Fly-fishing is extremely popular and the fishing season reaches a peak in January and February. Have a go: there is nothing more delicious than a freshly caught brown trout.

A historic church

St Peter's Anglican Church in Hamilton is one of Australia's oldest churches. It was built in 1834, at a time when Van Diemen's Land was in the Diocese of Calcutta, India. The stone church has only one door: the popular explanation for this is that it was to prevent the convict congregation escaping!

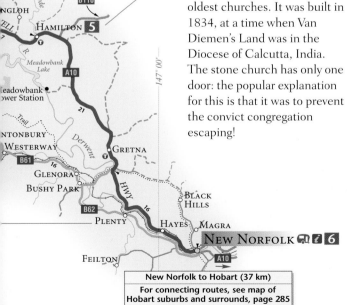

New Norfolk to Hobart (37 km)
For connecting routes, see map of Hobart suburbs and surrounds, page 285

Track notes

Linking Strahan with Hobart, the Lyell Highway winds by lakes and rivers, passes power stations and visits historic towns. It is well signposted and well maintained, and carries a diverse mix of traffic. There are several small townships but few roadside stops.

Town file

1 DERWENT BRIDGE (see page 293)

2 TARRALEAH pop. 398   ⛽ None
GPS 42° 18.285' S/146° 26.746' E
Tarraleah, a hydro-electricity township, houses electricity commission workers and has a small commercial centre. Pipes slope down nearby hills to the power station, where an information board helps visitors understand the magnitude of the scheme.

3 WAYATINAH pop. 122   ⛽ PD
GPS 42° 23.137' S/146° 30.325' E
Wayatinah is another hydro-electric town; the small community's needs are serviced by a shop, tavern and caravan park. Trout fishing is popular, wildlife abounds and platypuses are common.

4 OUSE pop. 158   ⛽ PD
GPS 42° 29.100' S/146° 42.640' E
Ouse, on the banks of the River Derwent, has several historic buildings, including the St John the Baptist Anglican church (consecrated in 1867) with impressive stained-glass windows. Cawood is a two-storey Georgian stone house (1820s) and the Millbrook water mill (circa 1843) is in Victoria Valley Road. Ouse has a hotel but little else in the way of services.

5 HAMILTON pop. 150   ⛽ PD
GPS 42° 33.344' S/146° 50.050' E
Hamilton is a small colonial township on the banks of the Clyde River. Its many historic buildings include St Peter's Anglican Church and Glen Clyde House (circa 1840), now a large craft shop and gallery. The region's farming history dates back to the early 1800s. Hamilton has limited shopping.

6 NEW NORFOLK pop. 5286   ⛽ PD
GPS 42° 46.632' S/147° 04.138' E
This fascinating town is the location of some of Australia's oldest homes, after being first settled in 1808. This area is the major producer of the hops used by Australian breweries, with paper mills at nearby Boyer (4 km east) the other regional industry. The town has good shopping and most services. Markets are held each Saturday. ℹ The Oast House, Lyell Highway; (03) 6261 1322.

HOBART TO LAUNCESTON

TASMAN HIGHWAY (432 KM)

Experience the popular east coast of Tasmania by travelling north-east from Hobart on the Tasman Highway. From Sorell take the diversion to the spectacular Tasman Peninsula, one of the most treasured historic areas in the State and the location of the Port Arthur Historic Site. The main route largely follows the coast until St Helens, then turns west to climb through forested ranges before heading towards Launceston, Tasmania's major northern city. The highway also links the picturesque Freycinet Peninsula and several holiday resorts dotted along the coast.

Wineglass Bay, Freycinet Peninsula

Best time to go

The temperate east coast has beautiful weather during spring and autumn, but is cold in the depths of winter and warm at the height of summer.

AUG 27 6. PM

ORFORD

	J	F	M	A	M	J	J	A	S	O	N	D
Maximum	22	22	21	19	16	13	13	14	16	17	19	20
Minimum	12	12	11	8	6	4	3	4	6	7	9	10
Rainfall (mm)	49	46	48	60	62	52	62	60	50	61	65	67
Raindays	10	8	10	11	12	12	13	13	12	13	14	12

SCOTTSDALE

	J	F	M	A	M	J	J	A	S	O	N	D
Maximum	23	23	21	18	15	13	12	13	14	17	19	21
Minimum	11	11	10	8	6	4	3	4	5	6	8	9
Rainfall (mm)	60	41	55	86	110	103	127	119	101	88	74	71
Raindays	10	8	9	12	14	14	16	17	16	15	12	12

John & Jan

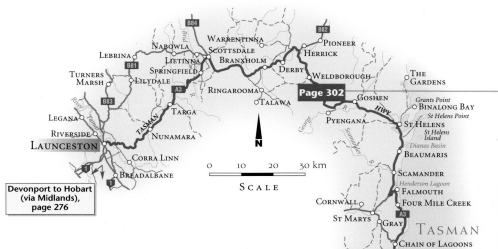

Page 302

Devonport to Hobart
(via Midlands),
page 276

Bicheno to Launceston

This pretty drive winds along the coastline and through towering forests. St Helens is a seaside holiday resort with good swimming beaches, and the cascading St Columba Falls are just a short drive from the highway near Pyengana. Further west is the busy centre of Scottsdale, with a strong farming community.

Hobart

Hobart, Australia's second oldest and most southerly city, is situated on the broad estuary of the River Derwent under the spell of majestic Mount Wellington. A strong maritime flavour and sense of the past give Hobart an almost European air. This feeling is heightened in winter, when daytime temperatures drop to a crisp average 12 degrees Celsius.

Sorell to Bicheno

The Tasman Highway sweeps along the coast towards the small crayfishing town of Bicheno. The Freycinet Peninsula is a short, worthwhile diversion from the main route and is especially popular with bushwalkers, who enjoy exploring its beaches and taking in the stunning views.

Page 298

Devonport to Hobart
(via Midlands),
page 276

Devonport to Hobart
(via west coast),
page 286

HOBART
Page 282

Page 300

Port Arthur diversion

Visiting the Tasman Peninsula and the Port Arthur Historic Site is a must. The highway twists across the narrow Eaglehawk Neck isthmus towards the eerie penal settlement. The Tasman Arch and the extraordinary Tessellated Pavement are also worth a look.

SORELL TO BICHENO 156 KM

Leather tanning

Swansea Bark Mill (circa 1880s), just north of Swansea, processed wattle bark until 1930 for use in the leather tanning process. The restored mill still houses the original operational machinery as well as showcasing local wine and wool products. 96 Tasman Highway; (03) 6257 8382; entry fee applies; open 9 a.m. to 5 p.m. daily.

Richmond: much to enjoy

The small village of Richmond is Tasmania's most important historic town. The historic buildings from the 1820s and 1830s, the quality art and craft, the quaint shopping and the selection of restaurants and eateries attract large numbers of visitors. We recommend picking up a brochure for a self-guided walk. Be sure to see the picturesque stone bridge (1823), the gaol (entry fee applies) and Bridge Street, which has numerous historic buildings.

Bicheno to Launceston, page 302

Sorell to Hobart (26 km)
For connecting routes, see map of Hobart suburbs and surrounds, page 285

Port Arthur diversion, page 300

What's on

MARCH Rotary Carnival (Orford) SEPTEMBER Swansea Agricultural Show NOVEMBER Bushranger Festival (Sorell), Fun Fish (Swansea)

Travel tip

The church of St John the Baptist (circa 1846) in Buckland has a stained-glass window depicting the life of this saint. The window dates back to the 14th century and is believed to have come from Britain's Battle Abbey. The church is alongside the Tasman Highway.

A beautiful beach

Wineglass Bay in the Freycinet National Park is a picture-postcard beach – a new moon of white sand in a secluded bay, protected from the ocean by its curved sides. It is also one of Tasmania's great walking destinations. A 1-hour-return walk to the spectacular lookout overlooking the bay or a 2.5-hour-return walk to Wineglass Bay beach are among the more popular. Camping is available at the entrance to the park. Park entry fee applies.

Convicts and fossils

Maria Island was the site of the Darlington Penal Settlement. Smaller but older than Port Arthur, it dates from the 1840s. The gaol is the most popular attraction but the island, now a national park, also has excellent bushwalking, camping, birdwatching and fishing, and there are fossil deposits at Painted Cliffs. No food is available on Maria Island: self sufficiency is a must. Ferries depart from Eastcoaster Resort, Louisville, north of Orford, three–four times daily. (03) 6257 1589; fare applies.

Track notes

The Tasman Highway winds through hills and along the coast. Its surface is generally good. There are a few overtaking lanes in the hills but several long sections without overtaking opportunities.

Town file

1 SORELL pop. 3199   PD
GPS 42° 46.903' S/147° 33.774' E
Sorell has a modern shopping centre and most services. It is 26 km from Hobart, at the junction of the Tasman and Arthur highways, the latter leading to the Tasman Peninsula and Port Arthur. ℹ 16 Gordon Street (Main Road); (03) 6265 6438.

2 ORFORD pop. 461   PD
GPS 42° 36.452' S/147° 42.993' E
Orford is a holiday town on the estuary of the Prosser River. Scuba-diving and fishing are popular and charter fishing boats operate.

3 TRIABUNNA pop. 766   PD
GPS 42° 30.574' S/147° 54.922' E
Triabunna was a historic garrison town and whaling port. Today abalone and scallop fishing boats operate from here and there is a large woodchip mill: tours of the mill are available. Local beaches are good for swimming and fishing. Triabunna has basic shopping. ℹ Corner Charles Street and Esplanade West; (03) 6257 4090.

4 SWANSEA pop. 495   PD
GPS 42° 07.374' S/148° 04.450' E
This township is one of Tasmania's oldest, with numerous colonial buildings. Fairy penguins come ashore at dusk along Coswell Beach. ℹ Swansea Bark Mill, 96 Tasman Highway; (03) 6257 8382.

5 COLES BAY pop. 120   PD
GPS 42° 07.229' S/148° 17.057' E
Coles Bay, gateway to the Freycinet National Park, focuses upon the park's attractions: Wineglass Bay and the protected coves and beaches. Swimming, sailing, windsurfing and kayaking are popular. ℹ Freycinet National Park; (03) 6256 7000.

6 BICHENO pop. 700   PD
GPS 41° 52.516' S/148° 18.264' E
Bicheno, a whaling and sealing base as early as 1803, is now a crayfishing port. It is also a holiday destination, with sandy beaches and great fishing. Fresh crayfish can be purchased locally in season. A 3-km foreshore footpath follows the bay to the north. Bicheno has good resort-style shopping.

PORT ARTHUR DIVERSION 164 KM (RETURN)

Sorell to Bicheno, page 298

Sorell to Hobart (26 km)
For connecting routes, see map of Hobart suburbs and surrounds, page 285

Authors' choice

⊛ Port Arthur Caravan and Cabin Park, Port Arthur

Explore the historic Port Arthur area from this popular, quality caravan park, only 1 km from the Port Arthur Historic Site. It offers a good range of facilities and lots of shady trees. Bookings are recommended during busy holiday periods.

For more details see page 383.

Devils!

The Tasmanian Devil Park at Taranna has a good collection of native animals and houses recuperating Tasmanian devils. Devils are nocturnal marsupials, voracious feeders on small mammals and carrion, and known for ferocity and aggression. The devils are fed at 11 a.m. at the park: this is a real experience for those with strong stomachs. (03) 6250 3230 or 1800 641 641; entry fee applies; open 9 a.m. to 5 p.m. daily.

Travel tip

The Tasman Peninsula has numerous tourist attractions and the Port Arthur Historic Site tops the list, but we also enjoy staying at the Port Arthur Caravan and Cabin Park, and visiting the Tasmanian Devil Park. Watching devils being fed is an amazing half-hour experience. The little devils rarely stop for long enough to be photographed.

Final resting place

The Isle of the Dead is the resting place of 1769 convicts and 180 free people who died at Port Arthur. A visit here is a moving experience. The tiny island (0.8 ha) is offshore from the main Port Arthur site, and boat cruises take tourists daily except in June and July. Book through Port Arthur Historic Site Visitor Centre, (03) 6251 2310.

An unusual pavement

The Tessellated Pavement near Eaglehawk Neck is an unusual geological formation, which appears like a large tiled area of flat stone at the water's edge. It is clearly explained on a nearby information board and is just a short walk from the carpark.

Port Arthur: not to be missed

Port Arthur Historic Site is Tasmania's most visited attraction and one of our favourites. The penal colony operated from 1830 to 1877 and today showcases the incredible hardships, cruelty and suffering undergone by an estimated 12 500 prisoners. Take a day to see it all. The buildings include both ruins and restored period houses: visit the penitentiary, asylum, commandant's house and church, all set in magnificent gardens. (03) 6251 2310; entry fee applies; grounds open 8.30 a.m. to dusk, restored buildings open 9 a.m. to 5 p.m. daily.

Track notes

The highway to the Forestier and Tasman peninsulas is fully sealed and well signposted, but has few overtaking possibilities.

Town file

1 SORELL (see page 299)

2 DUNALLEY pop. 286   🛢 PD
GPS 42° 53.204' S/147° 48.179' E
Dunalley is on a narrow isthmus. A canal connects this busy fishing village to Frederick Henry Bay; a swing bridge allows vessels through to the east coast. Cafes, galleries and craft shops cater for tourist needs.

3 EAGLEHAWK NECK pop. 209   🛢 PD
GPS 43° 01.192' S/147° 55.192' E
Eaglehawk Neck is a 100-m-wide isthmus linking the Forestier and Tasman peninsulas. To prevent prisoners escaping from Port Arthur a 'dog line' of fierce dogs once guarded it; bushranger Martin Cash escaped by swimming around them. A garrison was based here and the officers' quarters (1832) is the oldest timber building in Australia (now a museum).

4 DOO TOWN pop. 40   🛢 None
GPS 43° 02.168' S/147° 56.348' E
Doo Town is a unique, much-photographed village. Many house names play on the word 'Doo'. The practice was allegedly started by a holiday home named Doo Little; names now include Love Me Doo, Gunadoo, This Will Doo and more. The village is near remarkable coastal features including the Tasman Arch, Tasman Blowhole and Devils Kitchen. There are no shops or services.

5 PORT ARTHUR pop. 190   🛢 PD
GPS 43° 06.691' S/147° 44.176' E
The legendary penal settlement at Port Arthur is now Tasmania's most popular tourist attraction. It has a fascinating information centre and various cafes. The small township of Port Arthur has limited shopping and few services. 🛈 Port Arthur Historic Site Visitor Centre; (03) 6251 2310 or 1800 659 101; www.portarthur.org.au

6 NUBEENA pop. 264   🛢 PD
GPS 43° 05.864' S/147° 44.590' E
Nubeena is the largest town on the Tasman Peninsula, on the shores of Wedge Bay. Known for its great surf, at White and Roaring beaches, the town is popular for fishing and surfing. Today Nubeena lies at the centre of a farming area; coal, however, was once mined nearby. The Coal Mines Historic Site, north of Saltwater River, preserves the ruins of sandstone buildings from the convict mine.

BICHENO TO LAUNCESTON 250 KM

Authors' choice

✪ Scamander Forest Campground, Scamander

Enjoy the peace and quiet at this Forestry Tasmania camping area, set in a forested area on the banks of the upper Scamander River. Access is along 10 km of unsealed roads; just follow the signs. It is ideal for motorhomes and camper-trailers and camping is free. **For more details see page 387.**

Gunpowder mills

Penny Royal World is a collection of restored buildings (a millwright, wheelwright, watermill and more) that re-create the past. The Penny Royal Gunpowder Mills, set in the old quarry site at Cataract Gorge Reserve, are unique – they are the only remaining set of working gunpowder mills in the world. 147 Paterson Street, Launceston; (03) 6331 6699; entry fee applies; open January to April.

Classic cars

The National Automobile Museum of Tasmania showcases a selection of superbly restored cars and classic motorcycles. See a 1923 Alfa Romeo, a Ferrari F40, a Bentley S3, a Rolls Royce Silver Wraith and many more. This is a fascinating visit for the car and bike enthusiast. 86 Cimitiere Street, Launceston; (03) 6334 8888; entry fee applies; open daily 9 a.m. to 5 p.m. in summer and 10 a.m. to 4 p.m. in winter.

What's on

FEBRUARY Launceston Cup APRIL Surf Fishing Carnival (St Helens) JUNE Suncoast Jazz Festival (St Helens) OCTOBER Royal Show (Launceston) NOVEMBER Agricultural Show (Scottsdale)

Devonport to Launceston, page 278

Launceston to Bridgewater, page 280

A sea of purple

Bridestowe Estate Lavender Farm at Nabowla is the largest lavender farm in the Southern Hemisphere, boasting 48 ha of the exquisite purple flowers. December is the best month to walk among the vivid, perfumed display, just prior to harvest season in January. Visitors can also observe the processing plant and purchase a wide range of lavender products in the farm shop. 296 Gillespies Road, (03) 6352 8182; entry fee applies; open daily October to April, open weekdays May and September, and closed during winter.

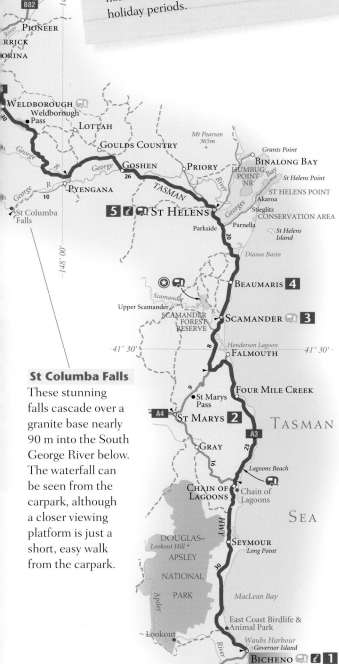

Travel tip

The Lagoons Beach camping area, 32 km north of Bicheno, is an ideal place to rest for a few days at virtually no expense for the fully self-sufficient traveller. Beside the beach and away from town, this is a quiet bushland area; nonetheless, it is usually busy during peak holiday periods.

St Columba Falls

These stunning falls cascade over a granite base nearly 90 m into the South George River below. The waterfall can be seen from the carpark, although a closer viewing platform is just a short, easy walk from the carpark.

Sorell to Bicheno, page 298

Track notes

From Bicheno the highway follows the coast before sweeping inland north of St Helens, then climbing abruptly over the Weldborough Pass, offering great views. Numerous communities dot the route, which passes through farming land and forests and is used by logging trucks.

Town file

1 BICHENO (see page 299)

2 ST MARYS pop. 588   ⛽ PD
GPS 41° 34.516' S/148° 11.024' E
St Marys developed when convicts cleared land and built roads during the 1830s. Dairy farming and coal mining became the main industries. Just before the turn-off to St Marys is the Chain of Lagoons, a series of tidal pools. The road north-east from St Marys crosses the precipitous, convict-built St Marys Pass. The town has basic country-town shopping and most services.

3 SCAMANDER pop. 435   ⛽ PD
GPS 41° 27.707' S/148° 15.799' E
Scamander is popular for fishing. Farms grow poppies, which flower in summer, for medicinal use. The town has basic shopping and services.

4 BEAUMARIS pop. 60   ⛽ None
GPS 41° 24.919' S/148° 16.656' E
Beaumaris is a popular coastal resort: holiday homes are tiered up the hill from the beach. Its mild climate, long beaches and great fishing attract holiday-makers. Beaumaris has limited facilities.

5 ST HELENS pop. 1280   ⛽ PDG
GPS 41° 19.511' S/148° 14.987' E
St Helens draws holiday-makers, especially for its fishing. Once a whaling and sealing port (dating from around 1830), it lies on Georges Bay, and is now busy with crayfish and abalone boats. St Helens has good shopping and all services. 🛈 61 Cecilia Street; (03) 6376 1744.

6 SCOTTSDALE pop. 1922   ⛽ PD
GPS 41° 09.709' S/147° 30.930' E
At the centre of a busy forestry region and a rich farming area, Scottsdale is a major regional town. Its crops include vegetables that are grown and processed locally, softwood timber, poppies and hops. Scottsdale has good regional shopping and most services.

7 LAUNCESTON (see page 279)

Chapter 5

Making the most of your trip

THINKING ABOUT a holiday raises questions:
Where do we start? How much time do we have?
How much is it going to cost? When will we go?
How long should we go for? If you are planning an
extended trip in a caravan, you need to add to this
list: What kind of van do we need? Is the car up to
the job? Have we got the right towing equipment?
What do we need to pack to be self-sufficient?
How do we choose a caravan park that is right for
us? What are the issues in terms of safe driving
while towing? This chapter is full of practical
information to help you find the right answers to
these questions and, in doing so, ensure that you
have the best caravan holiday possible.

PREPARING YOUR RIG

The 'rig' refers to the combination of the camping vehicle, towing vehicle and related towing equipment. It is essential that you find the combination that is right for you. Equipping your van and towing vehicle properly is equally important and will take time, research and legwork. Getting these things right at the outset is the best guarantee of a stress-free holiday.

■ CHOOSING THE RIGHT UNIT

We have travelled with off-road camper-trailers, tray-top campers, an off-road caravan, campervans and motorhomes. In every instance we have thoroughly enjoyed our travels. There are many options when it comes to choosing a caravan or motorhome. Ultimately it is a matter of finding the unit that suits you, your travel plans, your budget and the kind of lifestyle you wish to enjoy while travelling.

Types of units

Full-height caravans

Caravans come in all shapes and sizes. Most people touring Australia travel in vans less than 7 m in length. Caravans provide a good level of comfort and many are well appointed with appliances not unlike those enjoyed at home. Beds can remain made, fridges can be stocked, everyday utensils are readily available and clothing can be stored in robes and drawers. Many units are airconditioned and most are fitted with annexes or awnings to provide outdoor living shelter. There are numerous options in terms of axles (single, double and even triple), door position and sleeping capacity. There is also a choice between on- and off-road models. Prices range from $15 000 to $70 000.

Folding caravans and campers

These units are constructed of lightweight materials. The internal appointments are similar to those of a regular caravan. The roof section is usually raised mechanically to expose canvas walls, and usually the ends slide out to accommodate the beds. Some manufacturers also call these camper-trailers.

On- and off-road models are available; prices start at around $10 000 and peak at $30 000.

Pop-tops

Pop-top caravans are just like regular vans, except the top section of a pop-top folds down. This makes them easier to tow: the lower profile means far less drag. They lack overhead cupboard space and require slightly more maintenance. On- and off-road models are available; prices range from $15 000 to around $45 000.

Camper-trailers

These units come in a variety of models. Accommodation ranges from couple-only units through to big family set-ups. When collapsed, each model fits into a small, easily towed unit. Two- and four-wheel drive configurations are available.

Most units include a built-in bed and many include a functional camping kitchen. Prices range from $5000 to $30 000.

Campervans

These vehicles are designed specifically as delivery vans before undergoing extensive fit-outs that convert them to camping units. Sizes range from small models suitable for couples through to larger units with good facilities including, in some cases, a shower and toilet. They are easy to drive and can often double as the family car.

Motorhomes

These all-in-one vehicles are nearly always constructed on a truck base. They range in size from 5 m to 12 m. The smaller units, which have many of the attributes of a caravan, can be driven on a normal car licence. The larger units, some of which are spectacularly appointed with luxury fittings, require a truck licence. People buy motorhomes for the convenience of not having to tow, and for the high degree of self-sufficiency they allow. On the downside, they are difficult to park (particularly the larger vehicles), and they restrict mobility: every time you want to use your vehicle, you have to dismantle your campsite.

Many owners of larger motorhomes overcome this latter problem by towing a trailer loaded with a small vehicle; others carry bicycles. Motorhomes range in price from $50 000 to $650 000.

Slide-on or tray-top campers

These units are great for people who own a utility: they can be simply attached to the vehicle as needed. They are popular with off-road enthusiasts, and with travellers who want to be able to tow a boat or other kind of trailer. Costs range from $10 000 to $25 000.

Layout and fixtures

The interior layout of your caravan or motorhome is important. There are a number of things to consider. One is the size of the bed. Double beds in caravans are often smaller than the real thing. Sometimes beds are shaped with rounded corners, which means it is impossible to use a fitted sheet. Similar problems can occur with beds in motorhomes. In campervans, beds can be bigger than king-size so, again, sheets may be a problem. The choice of single beds versus double beds is personal

Caravan kitchens can be surprisingly well equipped

and is entirely dependent on what sleeping arrangements you prefer. Think also about whether you want a fold-up bed, so you can enjoy extra space during the day, and where you want the bed positioned: some travellers prefer an island bed, others are happy for it to be flush against the caravan side.

Make sure the unit you choose has good usable storage space both inside and outside. The wardrobe should have hanging capacity. The question of rear-door versus side-door entry in caravans is a perennial one; we have had both and have experienced no problems with either. The dust sealing on rear-door models is important and a scupper vent in the roof to pressurise the van is good for minimising dust.

Many vans these days come equipped with showers, toilets and hot-water services. But if you are planning on spending most of your nights in caravan parks, you will end up with duplicate facilities. Showers and toilets require regular cleaning – of course – and take up valuable space. They usually come as a unit, with the toilet built into the shower cubicle. Larger motorhomes may have separate toilets. We have had motorhomes with both but have found that, while we use the toilet, we prefer to use external shower facilities when they are available.

We strongly recommend a microwave oven as an essential feature (most modern vans are equipped with one). Airconditioning is more a matter of personal choice. It is readily available these days, but whether you use it or not will depend on where you intend to travel. Both microwaves and airconditioning units are generally 240-v appliances.

Many new caravans are built to order, which means you have the option of customising some features to suit your own taste. These features are usually limited, possibly including minimal floor-plan changes and some choice in terms of trim fabrics, fridge and stove models, and maybe window furnishings.

Authors' tip

Take a tape measure when you go to inspect caravans and motorhomes. Many units have good headroom, but some do not. The latter can result in quite a few accidents, even for those of average height.

Shopping for your caravan, campervan or motorhome

Draw up a list of 'must haves' and take it with you as you shop. Have a look at a number of different kinds of units (caravan, motorhome, camper) in both the new and second-hand markets in order to establish what you can get for your money. The leisure market is large these days and we have learnt that there is no need to rush in.

Caravan and leisure shows are a good way to get an overview of various products at one convenient location. You can make comparisons without getting 'trapped' by pushy salespeople. If you have already researched your potential purchase and decided that a new unit is what you want, think about buying the unit on the spot: show-only discounts often represent good value.

New caravans, campervans, camper-trailers and motorhomes are all available through dealers or, in some cases, direct from the manufacturer. Used units are available through dealers or privately through the classified ads in newspapers, trader publications and leisure magazines.

■ UNDERSTANDING AND EQUIPPING YOUR CARAVAN, CAMPERVAN OR MOTORHOME

Caravans and camper-trailers have to be registered separately to your vehicle, and serviced regularly. Before you set off on your trip, it is worthwhile spending some time getting familiar with the workings of your unit and all its components. Although many features are now standard, particularly in new vans, there will still be some 'furnishing' to do.

Servicing

Wheel bearings and brakes need regular attention on caravans. We have our wheel bearings checked every 20 000 km or annually. The garage that services our cars generally carries out this level of service on our vans. We carry a spare set of wheel bearings with us, and we know how to replace them if necessary. Brakes are a little more complex. We do have them checked for wear by our garage, but occasionally we find it necessary to visit a brake specialist. Most other service items on caravans are related to checking function and operation, such as checking battery and light functions and making minor operational adjustments. These can be done by service centres or by owners who know what they are looking for.

Power supply

Caravans are usually wired to operate on 12 v and 240 v. The 240-v supply must be a plug-in supply such as that obtained from a powered campsite or a home power point. They require 15-amp plugs, which are not normally fitted in homes. Most caravans have a 12-v house battery (their own) to operate the electrics in the caravan and this must be charged regularly by

Buying a van

Our last caravan was a 14-foot (4.25 m) Supreme Getaway. We bought it second-hand: it had already toured the continent. We were looking for an off-road van with good suspension and a pop-top, to reduce the drag. We also wanted an island double bed. We looked at several vans and finally selected a unit that was in good condition and well maintained. It did not have airconditioning, however, so we did some research and found that we could have airconditioning installed at a later date. We bargained a little and eventually purchased the van for a very good price.

charger or via the car when it is running. Some caravans and motorhomes are fitted with switch-mode chargers, which charge house batteries on demand while the vehicle is plugged into 240-v power. We highly recommend this accessory.

Many modern motorhomes, especially the larger models, are built with on-board generators. There are also portable 240-v and 12-v generators available, which seem to be used by a fair number of travellers. If you are planning on staying mostly in caravan parks, a generator will be a surplus item. Other points detracting from their favour include their heavy weight, large size and noisy operation. We have never yet travelled with a generator.

Any unit that utilises the towing vehicle's alternator to charge house batteries should be fitted with an isolation device to ensure that the batteries can be separated when the vehicle is not running. These isolators range from a simple key-operated switch through to very expensive and sophisticated management systems. We prefer the simple managed solenoid system, which costs around $200.

Refrigeration

Refrigeration is a big issue for owners of caravans and motorhomes. For many years the three-way fridge, which can operate on 12 v, 240 v or gas, has been standard. While these are not bad in terms of their operation, they are not the most efficient refrigeration system. They generally operate reasonably well on 240 v, a little bit better on gas, but only just hold on 12 v despite using an enormous amount of power. Some of the newer models perform better. Performance can be slightly improved by installing a ventilator fan behind the fridge to improve airflow. These are available at caravan accessory shops.

Gas supply

Most caravans, campervans and motorhomes have gas-operated stoves, ovens and hot-water services. Gas is efficient, clean and quite safe. We use a system with two gas bottles so that we can use one until it is totally empty and then switch to the other. This saves us from having to refill bottles that may not yet be empty. Even when camping in a tent we take two small 2-kg bottles for the same reason. Always stand gas bottles in a vertical position. Make sure a regulator is fitted; this will turn off the gas if a major leak occurs.

Lifestyle extras

Televisions and video recorders, even DVDs, are increasingly popular items to travel with. Most Australian towns have some kind of television reception but for those who want reliable reception, there is the option of installing a satellite dish on your motorhome, offering access to a selection of free-to-air and cable channels. Televisions and videos come in 12 v and 240 v.

A full annexe, complete with floor, can add thousands of dollars to the cost of a new van. It may seem like a desirable item but, if you are moving around a lot, you may find as we have that it gets used rarely. Awnings tend to be more useful as they are much easier to set up.

Authors' tip

Check that your gas bottles are not out of date. The date is stamped on the collar of the bottle, and it should indicate that the bottle has been checked within the last 10 years. It is against the law for a reseller to fill out-of-date gas bottles.

An outdoor table setting is an important addition to your camping equipment. Also desirable are a couple of comfortable chairs to relax in. With these kinds of purchases, you tend to get what you pay for in terms of quality.

Another fairly indispensable item is an outdoor stove or barbecue. Cooking outdoors while caravanning is sociable and pleasurable, and it means not having to live and sleep with the smell of cooked meat or fish. Most parks have barbecue areas, but these can be in high demand.

Portable chemical toilets are used by those travelling in smaller campervans or with caravans that do not have a built-in facility. They require regular emptying and the chemicals have to be replenished. They are popular with older travellers who do not relish the idea of navigating a course to the amenity block during the small hours.

Blocks and chocks

Not every caravan site is going to be perfectly flat, so you will need to carry levelling blocks to rectify the situation where necessary. These come in the form of shaped wedges (or you can use a thick, flat board). They are placed on the site and the caravan is driven onto them. Some motorhomes have built-in self-levelling supports.

A pair of shaped wheel-chocks is very handy for stabilising your van. Chocks can be bought commercially or easily made at home. They should be placed on the downhill side of the caravan's wheels to prevent the unit rolling.

■ THE TOWING VEHICLE

Ensuring that your towing vehicle is compatible with the caravan, safe, well maintained and well equipped is an essential part of planning a caravan holiday.

Size and towing capacity

The majority of travellers do not have the luxury of choosing a special towing vehicle to suit their new van; in most cases it is a matter of finding a van that will suit an existing vehicle.

Car manufacturers stipulate a safe towing weight for each vehicle and Australia's national regulations are built around these specifications (see Towing limits, page 311). As a general rule of thumb, the most suitable vehicle is one that is heavier than the unit it is going to tow. This will then allow for the fully loaded weight of the unit that is to be towed. Small cars are usually limited to towing camper-trailers, folding caravans, and small caravans or pop-tops. Bigger cars can manage caravans and pop-tops at the larger end of the market. In addition to weight, it is important to take into account the overall measurements of the unit you intend to tow: very high, wide units will need extra power to overcome wind resistance.

Off-road vehicles

Four-wheel drives have become very popular tow vehicles and are extremely capable. They are able to tow larger vans, and manage the dinghy and a few other items as well. Many travellers use off-road vehicles without ever venturing off the bitumen. Others travel extensively in the outback, unhitching the van when the terrain gets too rough.

Transmission

The choice between manual and automatic transmission is one of personal preference. In the past we have tended to choose manual transmission for our touring vehicles. That said, modern improvements in automatic transmissions have prompted us to consider a change. Automatic four-wheel drives seem to perform well off-road.

Tools and spares

When setting out on an extended touring holiday it is important to carry a tool kit in order to undertake minor repairs to your vehicle and to carry out those household repair jobs around the caravan. A tool kit should include the following items:
- Phillips head screwdrivers
- blade screwdrivers
- set of spanners to suit your car and van

You can feel at ease travelling in remote areas if you know your vehicle is in order

- hammer
- pliers
- small adjustable shifter
- larger shifter for gas bottles
- scissors
- wheel spanner
- set of spike-resistant jumper leads
- tyre-pressure gauge
- tow rope or tow strap.

Make sure that the jack and handle are fitted in the vehicle and that the jack is in good working order. Make sure that the same jack will fit both your vehicle and caravan.

Carry a jacking board, about 250 sq. mm, to place beneath the jack when the ground is soft, uneven or wet. A piece of checker-plate aluminium is our choice.

The wheel brace that suits your car may not necessarily fit the wheel studs on your caravan. Check before leaving home.

Carry a good spare tyre for your vehicle and one for your caravan. If you plan to travel off the beaten track, you will need two spares for each unit. On some camper-trailers, the wheels are interchangeable with those of the towing vehicle. If this is the case, a total of two spares will be adequate in most circumstances. (See Tyre pressure, page 328.)

■ TOWING EQUIPMENT AND MODIFICATIONS

Fitting towing equipment and modifying towing vehicles are specialist activities and should only be done by professionals. Dealers will often fit tow bars to new vehicles if requested. You will have to specify that you need one to match the vehicle's *maximum* towing capacity so that you do not end up with something only suitable for towing a small household trailer. If you already have a vehicle, contact a specialist tow-bar retailer and mechanic; check the *Yellow Pages* under 'Towing'.

Towing equipment

All commercially manufactured tow bars in Australia are built to a standard and should perform well. Different makes and models will have different features and different prices.

Most lightweight bars are suitable for towing trailers and vans with a gross mass of 1000 kg or even less. Heavy-duty bars, such as those fitted to large four-wheel drives, have the capacity to tow a mass of up to 3500 kg. Each tow bar has a specified maximum trailer mass and a maximum static ball weight. The latter, which is the difference in weight between the caravan on and off the vehicle, should be around 10 per cent of the total trailer weight. So, if the loaded trailer weight is 1000 kg, the ball weight should be around 100 kg. All tow bars are restricted to the maximum recommended capacity of the vehicle. To make absolutely sure you are not towing more than

Towing limits

In 1999 the National Road Transport Commission (NRTC) introduced a set of recommended towing limits, which were adopted by all States and Territories. Until that point up to five different towing limits applied across Australia, which meant a lot of confusion for caravanners crossing State and Territory borders.

The national regulations, as laid out by the NRTC, state that the weight of the loaded caravan must not exceed the recommended limit as prescribed by the manufacturer of the towing vehicle, or the stated capacity of the towing apparatus fitted to the vehicle. If the manufacturer has not specified limits, which, surprisingly, is not that unusual, the weight of the loaded caravan should be no more than one and a half times the unloaded weight of the towing vehicle, provided the caravan is fitted with brakes. If the caravan is not fitted with brakes, then the loaded caravan should equal the weight of the unloaded car. If you have any difficulty establishing the parameters of these requirements, seek the advice of your dealer or an independent tow-bar manufacturer. For further information on the regulations contact the NRTC; (03) 9321 8444; www.nrtc.gov.au

you should be, get your caravan weighed fully loaded. Exceeding towing limits can result in accidents, fines and non-payment of insurance claims.

Tow bars are fitted with a choice of towing hitches. Most standard caravans and trailers get by with a 50 mm ball, while off-road models may require a more complex off-road hitch.

Caravans and trailers must be fitted with safety chains; these must be securely attached to the towing vehicle.

Weight distribution

We have all seen the car and caravan combination with the hitch almost dragging on the road. Weight-distribution bars, widely available at caravan accessory shops, can be used to maintain a more level profile of the car and van. These tend to be standard equipment for larger vans, but should really be considered for all but the lightest of vans. The issue can also be addressed by correct loading. If the movable load within the caravan is all packed forward of the axle, this will greatly increase the ball weight (see Towing equipment, this page). If the load is more evenly distributed throughout the van, then the ball weight is less likely to be adversely affected. Never load a caravan or trailer with more weight behind the axle than forward of the axle. (It is wise to secure items to prevent movement.)

Other modifications

Brakes

If your caravan is fitted with electric brakes, you will need to have a brake controller fitted to the towing vehicle. This enables the driver to increase or decrease the caravan's braking efficiency from the driver seat. Most controllers are fitted with a tell-tale light that helpfully indicates the level of braking selected.

Cooling system

Towing vehicles are regularly placed under duress. All systems should be maintained in excellent condition, particularly radiators and cooling systems. Owners of automatic towing vehicles often opt to have transmission coolers fitted. Most are fitted as original equipment, but some after-market models are available.

Suspension

Rear suspension is often adversely affected by towing. The rig can be levelled using weight distribution bars (see Weight distribution, above). In some vehicles, particularly four-wheel drives, up-rated rear springs can be fitted, or air bags can be placed inside the spring to provide a range of adjustments.

Mirrors

Most caravans are wider than the towing vehicle, which means that extension mirrors should be regarded as standard safety equipment. Most caravan accessory shops have a wide range of mirrors. Many do not require professional fitting – most just clip to the existing rear-view mirror.

PLANNING YOUR TRIP

This section details the many travel decisions you have to make and the practical tasks you need to carry out before leaving home, from organising mail and banking to arranging permits, booking sites, choosing a route and packing food. Plan carefully to make sure your holiday is as stress-free as possible, but do not get bogged down in the details: some decisions, such as where to go next and how long to stay in one place, are sometimes best left for the road.

■ WHEN TO TRAVEL

Whether you are taking a week's leave or embarking on an extended tour of the continent, your first decision is *when* to travel. The weather, the timing of school and public holidays and the calendar of events in the areas you intend to visit will all influence your decision. Some travellers also think about how they can fit special occasions or visits to family and friends into their schedule.

Weather

The vast Australian continent crosses several climatic zones, giving it incredible extremes of weather. Travelling through western New South Wales one balmy spring we discovered that – although we were enjoying mild temperatures – the north-east coastal area of the State was sweltering in 40 degrees Celsius heat and the alpine regions in the south were blanketed in snow.

Such extremes are not uncommon, but travellers can plan their holidays according to reasonably predictable weather patterns, making some allowances for occasional variations and anomalies.

The southern States have four clearly identifiable seasons. Summers are warm to hot, winters cool to cold. Most rain falls in the winter months but other seasons can be prone to the occasional shower or downfall. Snow falls on the Australian Alps and the Tasmanian Highlands in winter, early spring and sometimes in late autumn.

Northern Australia has a dry and a wet season. The dry season runs from April to November, give or take a few weeks. Little or no rain falls and the countryside turns from lush green to a dusty brown. The wet season, with high temperatures and oppressive humidity, lasts from December until March. Tropical storms regularly dump large volumes of rain, and cyclones are not uncommon.

The centre of Australia is arid or semi-arid. Rain can fall throughout the year or not at all. From May to September daytime temperatures are mild but can drop dramatically at night. Summer temperatures can be extremely high.

The best time to travel through Australia's northern and central regions is between April and November. Year-round travel is possible in the south, with spring and autumn offering mild

Autumn can be a beautiful time to travel

Bureau of Meteorology information services

www.bom.gov.au

Recorded phone information services (calls charged at 77 cents per minute including GST, higher for mobile phones):

• Directory of all services	1900 926 113
• Australia-wide forecasts	1900 955 369
• Australia-wide marine forecasts	1900 955 370
• Australian capital cities	1900 926 161
• Australian three-month seasonal outlook	1900 926 162
• Australian Capital Territory	1900 955 362
• New South Wales	1900 955 361
• Northern Territory	1900 955 367
• Queensland	1900 955 360
• South Australia	1900 955 965
• Tasmania	1900 955 364
• Victoria	1900 955 363
• Western Australia	1900 955 366

and pleasant conditions. Southerners begin drifting northward in early May and return south around September.

Detailed weather information can be found by contacting services offered by the Bureau of Meteorology. (See the table of telephone numbers above.)

School and public holidays

For those without children, travelling during school holidays is best avoided, particularly during Easter, Christmas and New Year periods. At these times accommodation is in heavy demand and many establishments also put their prices up.

Australia's mainland States each have a four-term year. While the holiday periods from State to State do not necessarily align exactly, they do tend to overlap. The holiday periods generally are:

• two weeks in April usually coinciding with Easter
• two weeks in late June or early July
• two weeks in late September or early October
• six weeks from mid December until the end of January including Christmas and New Year.

Tasmania has a three-term year with holidays in June, September and from December through to the middle of February.

Long weekends are a popular time to get away. Check when public holidays fall in the different States to avoid crowds in holiday regions, particularly areas close to the capital cities.

Local events

There is an ever-growing list of cultural and sporting events in regional Australia. Some are minor affairs that may be fun to stumble across. Others, such as the Laura–Cape York Aboriginal Dance Festival in Queensland and the Port Fairy Folk Festival in Victoria are large, well organised and very enjoyable. Phone visitor information centres for event guides, and check out the What's on information in the earlier chapters of this book.

■ FINDING YOUR WAY

Once you have chosen your basic route, linking together all the places you want to visit, you will need some practical tools to help you find your way. At a basic level this means getting maps and guides, and those who delight in technology may look at installing a Global Positioning System, or GPS, good for travelling off main roads.

Global Positioning System (GPS)

GPS, a navigation system developed by the American military, is now widely used by professionals and recreational travellers.

A GPS receiver determines the user's position, accurate to within 10 m, by collecting distance and time measurements from satellites. GPS can also be used to determine speed of travel, altitude, and distance (in a straight line) to a proposed destination and estimated time of arrival. Most GPS receivers have the capacity to remember at least several routes, thus

Taking a GPS reading is not difficult

enabling return trips to be plotted. The preloaded data may include information on road networks and major geographical features. GPS receivers and antennae range in price from several hundred dollars to a couple of thousand.

A laptop computer, loaded with interactive mapping software downloaded from a CD-ROM and connected to a GPS receiver, offers a hi-tech visual navigational aid. We employed this to collect the mapping data used in this book.

Hand-held GPS receivers usually operate on replaceable batteries; as the battery life is very short, however, it is necessary to carry a supply of replacement batteries. An alternative is to purchase a power pack, which will allow the receiver to be plugged into your vehicle's power supply.

Maps and guides

If you are going off-road in remote areas, you will need more detailed maps – a selection of these will be available at better map shops.

Travellers who stick to highways and main roads will get by with a good road atlas (try *The Touring Atlas of Australia* or *The Australian Road Atlas*). These publications provide broad coverage region by region, and detailed coverage of cities and towns. They are best if replaced every three years or so.

Visitor information centres are a good source of local maps, generally reproduced in free brochures or leaflets. These maps tend to be quite detailed and useful in exploring the local area.

Specialised books and guides covering localities and holiday activities fill the shelves of bookshops including map shops, national park shops and specialist environmental stores. Good all-round publications include *Explore Australia* and, for the outback adventurer, *Explore Australia by Four-wheel Drive*.

Visitor information centres

Many Australian towns have a visitor information centre. Addresses and phone numbers of local centres are listed in the touring section of this book. The staff offer information on

Main State and Territory visitor information centres

Australian Capital Territory

Canberra Visitors Centre
330 Northbourne Avenue
Dickson 2602
(02) 6205 0044
1300 554 114
www.canberratourism.com.au

New South Wales

Sydney Visitor Centre The Rocks
106 George Street
The Rocks 2000
(02) 9255 1788
www.sydney.com.au
New South Wales Visitor Information Line
13 20 77
www.visitnsw.com.au

Northern Territory

Tourism Top End
Corner Mitchell and Knuckey streets
Darwin 0800
(08) 8936 2499
www.nttc.com.au

Central Australian Tourism Industry
Association (CATIA)
60 Gregory Terrace
Alice Springs 0870
(08) 8952 5800
www.centralaustraliantourism.com

Queensland

Brisbane Visitor Information Centre
Queen Street Mall
Brisbane 4000
(07) 3006 6290
www.brisbanetourism.com.au

Tourism Tropical North Queensland
51 The Esplanade
Cairns 4870
(07) 4051 3588
www.tropicalaustralia.com.au

Tourism Queensland Information Line
13 88 33
www.tq.com.au

South Australia

South Australian Visitor and Travel Centre
1 King William Street
Adelaide 5000
(08) 8303 2033
1300 655 276
www.visit.adelaide.on.net
www.southaustralia.com

Tasmania

Tasmanian Travel and Information Centre
Corner Elizabeth and Davey streets
Hobart 7000
(03) 6230 8233
www.discovertasmania.com.au

Victoria

Melbourne Visitor Information Centre
Melbourne Town Hall
Corner Swanston and Little Collins streets
Melbourne 3000
(03) 9658 9658
www.melbourne.vic.gov.au

Victorian Tourism Information Line
13 28 42
www.visitvictoria.com

Western Australia

Western Australian Visitors Centre
Corner Forrest Place and Wellington Street
Perth 6000
(08) 9483 1111
1300 361 351
www.perthwa.com
www.westernaustralia.net

local accommodation, caravan parks, businesses and tourist attractions by phone or face-to-face. For a general overview of a State or region, contact the main State or Territory visitor information centre. Details are listed on the previous page.

■ PERMITS, PARKS AND PRIVATE LAND

There are many areas of Australia where access is prohibited, restricted or subject to particular requirements.

Aboriginal land

Aboriginal communities own large tracts of land in areas such as Central Australia, the Kimberley and Cape York. Travellers wishing to visit areas of Aboriginal-owned land must first apply to the relevant authority for a permit (see Aboriginal land authorities, below). Always ring first, as some areas of Aboriginal land may be completely out of bounds for tourists and permits therefore are not an option. The permit-processing period can be quite long and travellers should get things moving well ahead of leaving home.

Visitor information centres in the area that you are heading off to will offer advice on which lands are covered by what authorities. In some areas – particularly areas with high tourist traffic – permits can be purchased or obtained on the spot, although this tends to be the exception rather than the rule.

Permits are not usually required for travel along the *public* roads in Australia that traverse Aboriginal land, though notable exceptions include the Great Central Road that links Yulara in

Aboriginal land authorities

Northern Territory

Central Lands Council
31–33 Stuart Highway
Alice Springs 0871
(08) 8951 6211
www.clc.org.au

Northern Lands Council
9 Rowlings Street
Casuarina 0810
(08) 8920 5100
www.nlc.org.au

Tiwi Land Council
(Melville and Bathurst islands)
Unit 5, 3 Bishop Street
Stuart Park 0820
(08) 8981 4898

Ngaanyatjarra Council
(including Great Central Road)
Shop 6, 58 Head Street
Alice Springs 0871
(08) 8950 1711

Queensland

Queensland Aboriginal
Coordinating Council
17 Aclin Street (PO Box 6512)
Cairns 4870
(07) 4031 2623

South Australia

Anangu Pitjantjatjara Yankunytjatjara
Land Council
PMB 227 Umuwa
via Alice Springs NT 0872
(08) 8954 8111

Maralinga Tjarutja Lands
43 McKenzie Street (PO Box 435)
Ceduna 5690
(08) 8625 2946

Western Australia

Aboriginal Lands Trust
Level 1, 197 St Georges Terrace
(PO Box 7770 Cloister Square)
Perth 6850
(08) 9235 8000
www.dia.wa.gov.au

Tnorala (Gosse Bluff) is on Aboriginal land west of Alice Springs

the Northern Territory with Warburton in Western Australia. Respect should be of utmost importance when travelling through Aboriginal lands, whether a permit is required or not.

National parks

Australia's 500 or so national parks protect the continent's unique flora, fauna, famous landscapes and natural icons.

Each State and Territory administers its own parks. The federal body, Parks Australia, oversees the management of a small number of parks, including Kakadu and Uluru–Kata Tjuta, and Booderee at Jervis Bay.

In some States, permits are required to visit national parks. These can be purchased in advance by contacting the central authority (see National park offices, below), or on the day within the park. No forward planning is required unless you intend to camp. If this is the case, you should contact the relevant authority to make sure camping is permitted and, if necessary, book a site. In some parks, sites are heavily booked well in advance, particularly during peak periods.

Unlike commercial caravan parks where you can expect a range of standard facilities, national park camping areas vary a great deal. To make sure you know what you are getting, phone ahead and ask the following questions:
- Are the camping grounds likely to be open?
- Are the sites suitable for vans?
- What are the facilities like?
- Are there fire restrictions?
- Is there a ranger station in the area?
- Is it necessary to pre-book a site?

For further information see Camping in national parks, page 331.

Private land

There are tracts of private land, particularly in the remote northern half of Australia, where owners allow travellers to camp and sometimes fish. Most of these places are rural stations located off the beaten track and are generally known about by word-of-mouth. Always get permission to camp on private land. The nearest visitor information centre (see Main State and Territory visitor information centres, page 314) can, in some instances, provide you with details of the land-holder, or try local directories or businesses. Failing that, it may be a matter of stopping in at the homestead once you are on the road.

■ INSURANCE AND ROADSIDE ASSISTANCE

Covering yourself in the event of an accident or breakdown is crucial when you are a long way from home on a holiday and completely dependent upon your car and van or motorhome for transport and accommodation.

National park offices

Most park organisations have a location in the relevant capital city where travellers can purchase passes and collect brochures, maps and other information. Addresses are provided where relevant. Many of the larger and more popular parks have information centres on site.

Parks Australia

Northern Australia
(08) 8946 4300

Southern Australia
(02) 6274 2320
www.ea.gov.au/parks

New South Wales

New South Wales Parks and Wildlife Service
102 George Street
The Rocks 2000
1300 361 967 (within NSW)
(02) 9253 4600
www.npws.nsw.gov.au

Northern Territory

Parks and Wildlife Commission of the Northern Territory
(08) 8999 5511
www.nt.gov.au/ipe/paw

Queensland

Naturally Queensland Information Centre (Department of Environment)
160 Ann Street
Brisbane 4000
(07) 3227 8186
www.env.qld.gov.au/environment/park

South Australia

The Environment Shop (Department of Environment and Heritage)
77 Grenfell Street
Adelaide 5000
(08) 8204 1910
www.environment.sa.gov.au

Tasmania

Tasmanian Parks and Wildlife Service
134 Macquarie Street
Hobart 7000
(03) 6233 6191
www.dpiwe.tas.gov.au

Victoria

Parks Victoria
13 19 63
www.parkweb.vic.gov.au

Western Australia

Department of Conservation and Land Management
17 Dick Perry Avenue
Kensington 6151
(08) 9334 0333
www.calm.wa.gov.au

Travelling with pets

Around 14 per cent of the population take their dogs on regular holidays. This makes sense for caravanners who go away for longish periods. You will not have to worry about costly kennels or the wellbeing of your animal while you are gone and, depending on the dog, you might even get an extra source of security. Against this, you will be restricted to staying in parks with pet-friendly policies, which, as we have discovered, are decreasing in number. Caravan park proprietors have had enough of irresponsible dog owners who do not pick up droppings or use a leash and do not prevent their animals from barking all night. If you travel with a dog, you will need to find out the rules for each caravan park and stick to them. Do not, for example, wash your dog in the shower as we have heard often happens!

This remote Western Australian caravan park makes its pet policy clear

Travelling with a dog means planning a route that takes you through towns with pet-friendly caravan parks. You will also need to consider where the animal will sleep, how often it will have to be walked, what it will eat, and how it will cope with long periods in the car. You must ask yourself if you are going to be comfortable giving up activities like visits to national parks and boat cruises, just because you cannot take your dog with you. Dogs should never be left alone in caravans or cars.

In our travels we have taken note of the parks we recommend that permit dogs. A few of these parks even have special dog facilities, like washing bays. These are listed in the Caravan park directory (page 350). A more extended list of places can be found in the Life Be In It publication titled *Holidaying with Dogs*, widely available in the travel section of most bookshops.

Insurance

The benefits of comprehensive insurance on your vehicle and caravan are obvious: the loss of some personal items within a vehicle is covered, as is damage to the vehicle through theft, vandalism or accident.

Understanding what your insurance covers is important. Make sure it covers the activities you have planned within the areas you intend to visit. This is particularly the case if off-road travel is involved. Many companies offer extra cover for extra money, including such items as free car hire in the event of an accident and rating-one protection. Take the time to shop around for the best package. Prices can vary according to the criteria applied by different insurance companies at any given time. Carry copies of your policies with you.

Roadside assistance

Many new motor vehicles are sold with a manufacturer's warranty that includes roadside assistance in the event of a breakdown. The warranty varies from one to three years depending on the make and model of the vehicle. Details of your roadside assistance package, including contact numbers, are usually contained in the glove-box folder. Check your policy carefully before you go. Make sure it covers the kind of travel you intend and the places you want to go.

Motorists without a new vehicle warranty, or who do not believe that their warranty is adequate, should become a member of their State-based motoring organisation (see Motoring organisations, page 318). For a small annual fee these organisations provide breakdown assistance around Australia. All organisations offer reciprocal membership to members from other States. Different levels of membership are offered. Drivers who plan on putting their vehicles to the test should go for top-level cover, which, in most areas, offers unlimited service calls and free towing. Motoring organisations also have one or more shopfront branches in their State that offer travel advice and sell maps, guides and car accessories. Once you have used the services of a motoring organisation, you may decide that the membership fee was the best money you ever spent.

Motoring organisations

Australian Capital Territory

National Roads and Motorists Association (NRMA)
92 Northbourne Avenue
Canberra 2601
13 21 32
www.nrma.com.au

New South Wales

National Roads and Motorists Association (NRMA)
74–76 King Street
Sydney 2000
13 21 32
www.nrma.com.au

Northern Territory

Automobile Association of NT (AANT)
81 Smith Street
Darwin 0800
(08) 8981 3837
www.aant.com.au

Queensland

Royal Automobile Club of Queensland (RACQ)
GPO Building
261 Queen Street
Brisbane 4000
13 19 50
www.racq.com.au

South Australia

Royal Automobile Association of SA (RAA)
41 Hindmarsh Square
Adelaide 5000
13 11 11
www.raa.net

Tasmania

Royal Automobile Club of Tasmania (RACT)
Corner Murray and Patrick streets
Hobart 7000
13 11 11
www.ract.com.au

Victoria

Royal Automobile Club of Victoria (RACV)
360 Bourke Street
Melbourne 3000
13 19 55
www.racv.com.au

Western Australia

Royal Automobile Club of WA (RAC)
228 Adelaide Terrace
Perth 6000
13 11 11
www.rac.com.au

■ MONEY MATTERS

Put your finances into order before going on holiday, particularly if you are planning a long trip. Work out a budget, plan your cash flow and arrange for the payment of bills.

Budgets

Working out a budget will give you an idea of how much your planned trip might cost. Important items to include are:
- fuel costs, allowing for increases in remote areas and increased consumption if towing a van
- vehicle servicing costs
- campsite costs
- food, including both groceries and dining out
- entry fees and other costs associated with tours and activities
- gifts and souvenirs.

If you are planning a long trip of several months, budget in smaller blocks. One month at a time is very manageable. If after the first month your budget does not reflect actual spending, use the trends to modify the budget.

Be prepared for the range of small emergencies that can occur on the road. Most are vehicle-related expenses: tyres, windscreens and mechanical repairs. Consider also the possibility of expenses arising through injury or illness. To ensure that you can continue in comfort and without anxiety, set aside a small reserve of easily accessed money.

Set out on the facing page is the budget we devised for a recent two-week holiday.

Banking and bills

Before you go, think about what services your bank may be able to provide while you travel. We have chosen the facilities offered by one of the major banks because they have many more branches across a wider range of locations. Australia Post, through its Giropost service, offers a range of banking services for a range of small banks and credit unions, as well as a couple of the big players. These services include cheque deposits, cash withdrawals and transfers. Ring Australia Post (13 13 18) or your own bank for details.

Phone and internet banking can be of great benefit, taking away the hassle of having to find bank branches or post offices. Both services allow travellers to gain access to account information, transfer funds, make credit card and mortgage payments and pay bills. With most banks you have to register to use these services, so make your enquiries before you travel.

Sample budget

Fuel	Distance: 2700 km
	Consumption: 12 litres per 100 km
	Fuel cost (average): 83c per litre
	Calculation: 2700 x (12÷100) x 0.83
	Total fuel: $269
Service for car	No service required
	Total service: $0
Camping fees	10 days @ $22.00
	4 days free
	Total camping: $220
Food	Groceries: $275
	Dining out 3 nights at $35 for 2 per night: $105
	Total food: $380
Entertainment	One day fishing on charter boat for 2 @ $175 each: $350
	Movies 2 nights for 2 @ $12.50 per admission: $50
	Total entertainment: $400
Gifts	Gifts for grandchildren: $50
	Total gifts: $50
Miscellaneous	Total miscellaneous: $200
	Total budget: $1519

An extended holiday will require you to arrange payment of bills. Most major companies, ranging from insurers to phone and electricity companies, now have direct-debit facilities. You can have the amount of your monthly, quarterly or yearly payment deducted from your account.

If you want to keep an eye on finances, arrange to have your bills posted to you along with other mail (see Post, page 322). Payments can be made in the following ways:

- Use a mobile phone or payphone and a credit card or a bill-pay service. The latter, which draws on your savings or cheque account for the amount of the bill, can be reached through your bank or Australia Post.
- Use the internet by logging on to your bank site, the site of the creditor or a specialised bill-paying site. Many caravan parks around Australia now provide an internet service.
- Pay in person at an Australia Post outlet. A wide range of bills, from tax to car registration, can be paid in this way.

Cheques are still a useful way of paying bills. You will, however, rarely come across a retail outlet prepared to accept a personal cheque. If you have a strong preference for paying by cheque, contact the business first.

Using credit and EFTPOS

When travelling we mostly use a credit card linked to our bank accounts. This allows us to use an ATM, bank or EFTPOS transaction to replenish cash, pay for purchases using credit or EFTPOS, obtain a summary of transactions each month and pay bills using a mobile phone.

Many outlets impose a minimum amount on card transactions of between $10 and $25. Major outlets will accept most kinds of credit cards but many smaller businesses only accept MasterCard, Visa and Bankcard.

Cash

Cash still has its uses. Many small businesses – markets, takeaway food outlets and cafes among others – do not have card facilities and many more will not accept cards for small amounts. Paying cash for incidental items, such as refreshments, magazines and entertainment admissions, is easier than having to worry about checking off a large number of small amounts against credit-card statements. If your bank charges ATM withdrawal fees, you may want to get out an amount sufficient to last you a week or so. Do a cash budget by working out how you plan to pay for the items you will need on your holiday (see Sample budget, this page). Avoid carrying large amounts of cash. Cash is rarely insurable and certainly not replaceable, and large amounts will only cause you worry.

■ WHAT TO PACK

Packing for a holiday is a fine art, more so when you are contemplating several months on the road. Spend some time thinking about what you can live without, and what you cannot. Make lists and consult friends who have undertaken similar trips. The old adage 'less is more' is generally useful advice for travellers. Even so, you should not deprive yourself of the kind of creature comforts that may help make a trip more enjoyable. This section covers your day-to-day domestic and leisure requirements. For some advice on larger, more permanent items and specialist camping equipment see the section on Understanding and equipping your caravan, campervan or motorhome, page 308.

Authors' tip

Credit cards can be lost or stolen so we always carry a second credit card, issued by another bank. We keep this second credit card in a safe place – not with our other cards – and use it only in emergencies.

Seniors discounts

Many businesses across Australia offer discounts to senior citizens and old-age pensioners. Make a point of asking, as these discounts may not be advertised. Each State and Territory government issues a permanent lifetime card to eligible seniors entitling them to discounts on a range of products and services, including some government services. Cardholders receive a booklet listing all the participating providers. Seniors cards are not means tested and most are accepted Australia wide. The national website is www.seniors.com.au and contact numbers are:

Australian Capital Territory
(02) 6282 3777

New South Wales
1300 364 758

Northern Territory
1800 777 704

Queensland
1800 175 500 or (07) 3224 2788

South Australia
(08) 8226 6852

Tasmania
1800 678 174 or (03) 6222 7651

Victoria
(03) 9616 8241

Western Australia
(08) 9220 1123

Food

New travellers often have difficulty working out what food to take. Our advice is aim for a balanced diet such as you would enjoy at home. A permanent supply of the following non-perishable items will ensure that you always have the makings of a meal or a snack on hand:

- coffee
- tea
- dried herbs
- cereals
- condiments
- rice
- pasta
- legumes
- oil and vinegar
- salt and pepper
- a small range of canned goods.

Do not attempt to carry enough food to last the whole trip: shop as you go. Supermarkets across Australia carry the same basic grocery lines, although certain gourmet items now standard in big-city stores may be hard to get in rural areas.

Prices are reasonably stable across the country except for fresh fruit and vegetables. Restrictions on availability, particularly in remote areas, can force the prices of fresh produce to fluctuate wildly. One way around this is to look out for the regional in-season produce offered at roadside stalls. In many coastal towns fresh fish can be bought off the wharf or from a beachside kiosk. Gourmet produce is offered in some regions so keep your eye out for producers selling olives, oil, honey, cheeses, game and prepared meats and, of course, local wines.

Remember there are restrictions on the movement of fruit, vegetables and some foodstuffs, such as honey, across some State borders.

We regularly buy meat, but only purchase larger quantities if we can have it individually cryovac (vacuum) packaged in meal-size portions to minimise wastage. The packaging helps to keep the meat fresh for quite a while, with beef lasting up to three or four weeks in the refrigerator.

Cooking equipment

Most caravans and motorhomes are equipped with a microwave oven so a limited selection of plastic microwave cooking bowls is a good investment. They usually pack inside each other, do not rattle or break and are not expensive. A few pots and pans are essential for stove cooking. A kettle and a toaster are also important, as is a frying pan. We have a favourite cast-iron frying pan that has travelled with us for years – just as good on the gas stove in the motorhome as it is on an open fire.

Kitchen utensils should include tongs, an egg slice, a breadboard, bottle and can openers, one or two good quality knives, a wooden spoon and an ovenproof holder. An all-purpose barbecue tool is essential for outside cooking.

Try to avoid travelling with fragile, easily breakable pieces. We use unbreakable crockery and drinking vessels. Inexpensive plastic storage containers with secure lids will come in handy for storing biscuits and loose food.

We have learned over many years that, with cooking equipment, least is best – if you are in doubt about needing a particular item, leave it at home.

Clothing

Travellers heading north will need lightweight clothing and something warm for those cold nights. Travellers heading south will need a range of warm- and cool-weather items. Thermal underwear is very effective in very cold areas. If you are planning

Authors' tip

Whether you are packing most food items or shopping as you travel, avoid items with flimsy packaging. Lightweight plastic bottles for cooking oil are notorious for splitting and leaking. Choose glass or metal containers, and store in a plastic tub for extra protection.

Pack the right gear if you plan on doing any bushwalking

Other necessary and useful items

Pack good supplies of sheets, towels and tea towels. While you will not need the entire contents of your linen cupboard, you do not want to have to plan your holiday around your next laundry date. For beach use, pack separate towels that can be used many times without washing.

Think about what you use around the house on a day-to-day basis and pack accordingly. You will need some cleaning

to do any bushwalking, check out the extremely light but very warm clothes made from high-tech synthetic fabrics available at specialist camping stores. Regardless of where you are going, always pack something lightweight with long sleeves to wear around dusk when the mosquitoes arrive. Carry items like swimwear, towels, spare socks and jumpers in a bag that can be kept within easy reach. Sunhats and sunglasses are essential.

Footwear is important. You should include a pair of light-weight casual shoes or sandals for general daily wear; a sturdier pair of shoes for walking, for when it rains or for cold weather; and a pair of rubber thongs or plastic sandals for wearing to public shower blocks.

Health and safety items

A good first-aid kit is a high priority and can be bought from camping stores or St John Ambulance. Some kits are designed for administering first aid in major trauma situations. While these items are necessary, even if never used, you should also carry the bits and pieces that will see you through minor injuries and upsets (see First-aid kit, this page). Make sure you check your first-aid kit regularly in order to get rid of out-of-date items and replenish stock.

If you take prescription medicine, ask your doctor to provide sufficient prescriptions to last the trip, particularly if you are spending time in remote regions. Repeats cannot normally be filled all at once so it may be necessary to stop at a pharmacy every few weeks to get more stock.

If you need specialist non-prescription medicines and other health products, particularly of a non-traditional nature, you should carry enough stock to last the trip, or at least the length of time between major centres. Do not forget sunscreen and insect repellent. Pack brands that you have used before as these products can cause skin irritations and allergic reactions.

First-aid kit

You first-aid kit should contain:

- first-aid handbook to help identify and treat various conditions
- tweezers to remove splinters and prickles
- scissors to cut dressings, tape and so on
- gauze bandages to hold dressings in place and protect wounds
- cotton wool and buds to clean and dress wounds
- elastic bandages to support joint injuries and treat spider or snake bites
- pins or clips to hold elastic bandages in place
- triangular bandages to use as a sling, to secure a splint, and to cover head wounds
- bandaids (various shapes and sizes) to dress all types of small wounds, cuts and abrasions
- non-adhesive dressings to cover wounds and abrasions
- anti-itch cream to treat bites, stings and some rashes
- antiseptic to treat open cuts and wounds
- alcohol swabs to clean around wounds
- cold pack to treat sprains, swellings and some bites
- latex gloves to prevent the spread of infection
- diarrhoea tablets
- anti-nausea tablets
- motion-sickness tablets
- aspirin or paracetamol
- throat lozenges
- eye soother
- lip balm
- antihistamines to treat allergic reactions.

products and utensils: dishwashing detergent, an all-round cleaner, sponges, garbage bags and a dustpan and brush. You will need all the usual toiletries: toothpaste, toilet paper and shaving gear. Unless you have a yen for particularly hard-to-get products, there is no need to pre-buy sufficient supplies to last your entire trip. Matches and a torch are also essential items.

A portable clock-radio makes a good companion on a long trip. So does a carefully selected supply of books and other reading matter. A camera is highly desirable if not essential. A video or digital recorder will further help preserve memories of your holiday.

Pack appropriate equipment for the leisure activities you regularly enjoy, or you may want to hire equipment rather than bring your own gear.

■ COMMUNICATIONS

Whether you are on a short holiday or an extended trip, being able to contact people and also be contacted by them may be important, even crucial, particularly if you are travelling through remote areas.

Email

Email is fast becoming a major mail carrier. Internet cafes around the country enable you, for a fee, to send and receive messages. If you already use email at home, contact your service provider and find out how to send and receive mail from remote destinations, using your own address. Otherwise, you can set up a portable Hotmail or Yahoo! address at any internet outlet (just ask staff), which you can use as you travel. Some mobile phones can receive and send email messages. If you are really serious, do what we do and carry a laptop and mobile phone, which have been set up for internet and email access.

Post

You will need to make arrangements for the delivery of your mail before you go away. Your local post office will hold your mail for you for a pre-arranged period of time. Be sure to make enquiries well in advance of travelling. Ask a friend or neighbour to check that the service is operating as intended. We once returned from holiday to find our mail blowing down the street. The post office had continued delivering our mail despite our arrangement to have it held at the post office.

An alternative to the post office service is to have a reliable friend collect your mail and forward it on using a pre-paid envelope. Alternatively, you can have your mail sent to a post office in the area you are next visiting. Ask the sender to mark the envelope 'post restante' and take identification when you go to pick up your mail.

If you do not want to impose on friends or neighbours, or you have sold up and are without an address, contact Landbase Australia (see Communications contacts, page 323). The service was set up to provide an address for yachties sailing the world and is now available to all travellers. For a fee, the service will receive your mail and then forward it on to a location of your choice.

Mobile phones

Mobile phones are used widely throughout Australia and there are now a good number of carriers in the marketplace. As well as calls, most mobile phones can receive voice and text messages. Some can be linked to a computer to gain access to internet and email services.

A disadvantage of travelling with a mobile phone in Australia is that in many areas of the country your phone will be out of range. We have found the Telstra digital network is best suited, in most instances, to our travelling lifestyle.

It is important to remember that it is illegal to use a mobile phone when driving, unless it has a hands-free attachment.

Public phones

Public phones can be an inexpensive alternative to mobile phones, although if you are on a good mobile plan you may find the reverse is true. There are around 30 000 payphones dotted around Australia and, contrary to popular perceptions, most of them work most of the time.

Whether you intend to use public phones exclusively, or only as backup when your mobile is out of range, a phone card is a must. The coin slots in payphones often malfunction as a result of coin jams and vandalism, whereas problems rarely seem to occur with the card slots. The Telstra Phonecard, prepaid in amounts of $5, $10, $20 and $50, can be purchased at newsagents and general stores almost everywhere. Alternatively, you can use a Telstra Telecard, which allows you to make calls from public or private phones using a card number and pin number. The cost is then charged back to your home or office account. Ring Telstra (see Communications contacts, page 323) at least a couple of weeks before you intend to travel to arrange for a card.

Satellite phones

Satellite phones, in operation in Australia since 1994, are now used by anyone needing access to a mobile phone outside Australia's geographically limited mobile network. The satellite network covers every inch of the continent, no matter how remote. Units are available to buy or to hire but in both instances the costs are steep. Call costs are also high. See 'Satellite equipment and services' in the *Yellow Pages* for details of suppliers and service providers. A word of warning: while the satellite network is generally very reliable, a clear reception cannot be guaranteed 100 per cent of the time. Calling from

Authors' tip

To enhance the performance and extend the range of your mobile phone, install an 'in-car kit', which includes a cradle, a power supply and, most importantly, an external antenna. That way, you will be contactable in most places.

within a thickly wooded area or a deep valley, or beneath a very cloudy sky, may reduce a phone's effectiveness and disappoint you if you have paid a lot of money for it.

CB radio

Citizen Band (CB) radio is a useful device for people travelling in convoys of two or more vehicles. Sets start at around $100. CB radios should not be relied upon for life-saving communication as interference regularly causes problems with transmission.

Ultra High Frequency (UHF) CB radios are more expensive than the simple CB sets but have clearer transmission. A network of repeater stations across the country ensures that UHF units usually have a good range as well.

HF radio

High Frequency (HF) radio is a reliable form of outback communication. HF radios have traditionally been known as 'Flying Doctor' radios. These sets have been around for many years and were favoured by remote operators and pastoralists in the outback who often had no other method of communication. The radios are mostly used for long-distance communication. They have the ability to be interconnected with the phone system to make phone calls via technology known as radphone: you make a radio call and an operator connects you to the phone number you require. Despite the advent of satellite technology, HF radio is still used by many organisations and individuals, including the Royal Flying Doctor Service (RFDS).

There is little privacy on HF radio transmissions and sets are reasonably expensive, although good quality second-hand units can be purchased for between $1000 and $1500. Hiring is also an option. The RFDS once provided a range of HF services but these have recently been scaled back. Contacting other travellers through RFDS frequencies is still possible provided, first, that it does not interfere with a control station's operations and, second, you have purchased an outpost licence from the Australian Communications Authority. RFDS remains an important contact for travellers who find themselves in emergency situations. HF radio users should contact the RFDS for a list of their control stations and relevant frequencies.

Many travellers using HF subscribe to VKS-737, the Australian National 4WD Radio Network. The service, operated by volunteer enthusiasts, offers five dedicated frequencies; weather and road updates; a point of contact for emergencies and links to relevant emergency services; and limited radphone facilities. Travellers wishing to use radphone regularly should hook up with a specialist service provider; VKS-737 recommends the Newcastle-based Radtech.

See Communications contacts, below, for details of organisations who can provide further information on HF radios.

Emergency Position Indicator Radio Beacon

Emergency Position Indicator Radio Beacons (EPIRBs) are used to locate vessels, planes, vehicles and individuals in distress. The user can activate an emergency call signal that sends a series of radio beeps to the headquarters of Australian Search and Rescue (AusSAR). This organisation then contacts the relevant State-based or maritime rescue bodies. Beacons are used only to track location – not for voice communication. The availability of inexpensive, personal beacons (406 MHz units) has made the technology available to recreational users including bushwalkers, outback travellers and anglers. The units cost a couple of hundred dollars and can be purchased in electronics stores. A beacon should *only* be activated in extreme life-threatening situations. Wrongful use may attract large fines. If the unit is inadvertently activated, the user should attempt to contact AusSAR as soon as possible.

Communications contacts

Email

Hotmail
www.hotmail.com

Yahoo!
www.yahoo.com.au

Post

Australia Post
13 13 18
www.austpost.com.au

Landbase Australia
(mail forwarding and messaging service)
Locked Bag 25
Gosford NSW 2250
0408 686 461
www.ozemail.com.au/~lbase/

Public phone

Telstra Telecard
1800 038 000

HF Radio

Australian Communications Authority
Canberra office: (02) 6219 5555
(or see the *White Pages* for the office in your State)
www.aca.gov.au

VKS-737 Australian National 4WD Radio Network Inc.
(08) 8287 6222
www.vks737.on.net

Radtech Communications
(02) 4982 6570

Royal Flying Doctor Service

National office: (02) 9241 2411
www.rfds.org.au

EPIRB

AusSAR Coordination Centre
1800 641 792
1800 815 257

ON THE ROAD

Once you set out, much of the hard work of getting ready for your trip is behind you. That said, there are still plenty of things to attend to as you travel. You will have to make sure your rig is well maintained and that you are well versed in the driving techniques needed for a safe trip. There are daily checks to be made, fuel use to be calculated, caravan parks to be selected and settled into, and daily health and safety issues to be considered. The information contained in this section will help you take care of these tasks as efficiently as possible to allow plenty of time in the day for relaxation and leisure activities.

It is easy to enjoy the open road once all the pre-trip preparations are behind you

■ SAFE TOWING

Towing a caravan or camper is not just a matter of hooking up and heading off. Specialist driving skills are needed and regulations must be observed.

Towing regulations

Australia has a set of national regulations for weight limits for towing vehicles (see Towing limits, page 311). Speed limits may also apply. In most States, motorists are required only to observe normal speed limits as signed. On some of the Northern Territory's outback roads where there are no limits, caravanners are asked to drive at what they would consider a safe towing speed. In Tasmania a 90 km/h limit applies. In Western Australia a 90 km/h limit applies where the caravan weighs over 750 kg and 100 km/h for caravans under 750 kg. For further information contact the National Road Transport Commission; (03) 9321 8444; www.nrtc.gov.au

Towing skills

If you have not towed a caravan before, you should get some practice before leaving home. Waiting until you are on the road to perfect your techniques will mean you may annoy other drivers, attract bemused spectators and have to contend with poorly maintained roads and bad weather conditions.

Learn to reverse

Reversing is one of the most important towing skills. You will regularly need to reverse your caravan 90 degrees into a space, and often across a kerb. Take your van to a large paved parking area on a quiet day and practise until you feel confident. After that, all parking and reversing should not be a problem.

Overtaking

Allow adequate distance for the reduced acceleration of your rig. Also make allowances when veering left back into the driving lane. If you are being overtaken, slow down and move to the left but not far enough to force the wheels on your van off the sealed surface.

Avoid trailer sway

Crosswinds can be a problem when towing because the caravan's slab sides act like sails. The combination of high speed and crosswinds can cause trailer sway, which dangerously destabilises both towing vehicle and caravan. You will feel it happen first and a glance in the rear-view mirror will confirm the problem. Rectify the situation by easing back on your speed. Brake, if necessary, very gently to avoid compounding the problem. Resume speed gradually.

Be courteous to other drivers

Caravans and motorhomes should travel as safely as they can with the flow of traffic. We have all seen cars towing caravans cruising along a main highway at about 50 km/h, with an endless stream of traffic following. If you desire to travel at a slower speed and the traffic does build behind you, you should regularly pull off the road to let the traffic flow by. On a recent motorhome trip in New Zealand we noted that – almost without exception – slower moving vehicles were in the habit of easing off the road at every opportunity to allow faster moving traffic to pass by.

Allow for extra weight

Towing a van will make the acceleration and braking on your vehicle much slower. A couple of driving techniques can help. On long, steep uphill sections, select a gear that the towing vehicle is comfortable with. Keep the revs to the higher end of the operating range to help prevent overheating. Avoid letting the engine lug at low revs in a higher gear. On long, steep downhill sections, keep your speed under control and keep the brakes as cool as possible. Select a lower gear and let the engine do as much braking as possible. Increasing the efficiency of the electric trailer brakes on the controller will allow the van to help slow the towing vehicle. Many motorhomes are fitted with engine brakes, which work very efficiently on long downhill sections.

Take special care when crossing rivers, especially while towing a caravan

■ ROAD RULES AND SAFE DRIVING

Safe driving is paramount when towing a van. Take some time before you travel to re-acquaint yourself with road safety rules.

Australian road rules

Uniform national road rules apply in Australia but some rules vary to suit local conditions. A number of outback roads in the Northern Territory have no speed limit. In Melbourne, to ensure the smooth and safe running of trams, vehicles must pull to the left and not queue across tram tracks when turning right at marked intersections; not overtake a tram on the right; and stop behind a tram when it is stationary. For more information on road rules, and the differences between States and Territories, contact the National Road Transport Commission; (03) 9321 8444; www.nrtc.gov.au

Concentration

Observing the following tips can help to keep your focus on the road, avoiding the biggest single cause of all road accidents:
- Wear lightweight, non-restrictive clothing and good quality anti-glare sunglasses.
- Drive with both hands all the time.
- Sit at a comfortable distance from the wheel.
- Make all seat, belt and rear-view mirror adjustments before you take off.
- Do not allow conversations to distract you – resolve issues likely to prove contentious before you take off, or pull over if something comes up that cannot wait.
- Do not use a mobile phone while driving.

Fatigue

Fatigue is a killer. Driving while tired is a major contributor in up to 25 per cent of serious road accidents. Studies have shown that chronically tired drivers are as ineffective as drunk drivers. To avoid driving fatigue, observe the following tips:

- Do not drive when you would normally sleep, such as very early in the morning or late at night.
- Have nutritious snacks every couple of hours, rather than big meals at longer intervals.
- Take a 10- to 15-minute break every two hours and a longer break every four hours.
- Get plenty of sleep before you travel.
- Limit driving to a maximum of 10 hours per day.
- Share the driving if possible. With another driver the distance you must drive is halved.
- Watch out for fatigue symptoms such as daydreaming, drowsiness, sore eyes, boredom, restlessness and aches and pains. Self-awareness is crucial to staying safe.

Fuel consumption			100	150	200	250	300	350	400	450
Litres per 100 km	Km per litre	Miles per gallon								
8.0	12.5	35.6	8.0	12.0	16.0	20.0	24.0	28.0	32.0	36.0
8.5	11.8	33.5	8.5	12.8	17.0	21.3	25.5	29.8	34.0	38.3
9.0	11.1	31.6	9.0	13.5	18.0	22.5	27.0	31.5	36.0	40.5
9.5	10.5	29.9	9.5	14.3	19.0	23.8	28.5	33.3	38.0	42.8
10.0	10.0	28.4	10.0	15.0	20.0	25.0	30.0	35.0	40.0	45.0
10.5	9.5	27.1	10.5	15.8	21.0	26.3	31.5	36.8	42.0	47.3
11.0	9.1	25.9	11.0	16.5	22.0	27.5	33.0	38.5	44.0	49.5
11.5	8.7	24.7	11.5	17.3	23.0	28.8	34.5	40.3	46.0	51.8
12.0	8.3	23.7	12.0	18.0	24.0	30.0	36.0	42.0	48.0	54.0
12.5	8.0	22.8	12.5	18.8	25.0	31.3	37.5	43.8	50.0	56.3
13.0	7.7	21.9	13.0	19.5	26.0	32.5	39.0	45.5	52.0	58.5
13.5	7.4	21.1	13.5	20.3	27.0	33.8	40.5	47.3	54.0	60.8
14.0	7.1	20.3	14.0	21.0	28.0	35.0	42.0	49.0	56.0	63.0
14.5	6.9	19.6	14.5	21.8	29.0	36.3	43.5	50.8	58.0	65.3
15.0	6.7	19.0	15.0	22.5	30.0	37.5	45.0	52.5	60.0	67.5
15.5	6.5	18.4	15.5	23.3	31.0	38.8	46.5	54.3	62.0	69.8
16.0	6.3	17.8	16.0	24.0	32.0	40.0	48.0	56.0	64.0	72.0
16.5	6.1	17.2	16.5	24.8	33.0	41.3	49.5	57.8	66.0	74.3
17.0	5.9	16.7	17.0	25.5	34.0	42.5	51.0	59.5	68.0	76.5
17.5	5.7	16.3	17.5	26.3	35.0	43.8	52.5	61.3	70.0	78.8
18.0	5.6	15.8	18.0	27.0	36.0	45.0	54.0	63.0	72.0	81.0
18.5	5.4	15.4	18.5	27.8	37.0	46.3	55.5	64.8	74.0	83.3
19.0	5.3	15.0	19.0	28.5	38.0	47.5	57.0	66.5	76.0	85.5
19.5	5.1	14.6	19.5	29.3	39.0	48.8	58.5	68.3	78.0	87.8
20.0	5.0	14.2	20.0	30.0	40.0	50.0	60.0	70.0	80.0	90.0
20.5	4.9	13.9	20.5	30.8	41.0	51.3	61.5	71.8	82.0	92.3
21.0	4.8	13.5	21.0	31.5	42.0	52.5	63.0	73.5	84.0	94.5
21.5	4.7	13.2	21.5	32.3	43.0	53.8	64.5	75.3	86.0	96.8
22.0	4.5	12.9	22.0	33.0	44.0	55.0	66.0	77.0	88.0	99.0
22.5	4.4	12.6	22.5	33.8	45.0	56.3	67.5	78.8	90.0	101.3
23.0	4.3	12.4	23.0	34.5	46.0	57.5	69.0	80.5	92.0	103.5
23.5	4.3	12.1	23.5	35.3	47.0	58.8	70.5	82.3	94.0	105.8
24.0	4.2	11.9	24.0	36.0	48.0	60.0	72.0	84.0	96.0	108.0
24.5	4.1	11.6	24.5	36.8	49.0	61.3	73.5	85.8	98.0	110.3
25.0	4.0	11.4	25.0	37.5	50.0	62.5	75.0	87.5	100.0	112.5

Travel times

Always set yourself realistic daily distances. This means different things to different people. Many caravanners like to travel around 300 km in one day whereas others easily accomplish 500 km or more. It can depend on what is on offer in the region you are visiting. Unless you are in a rush to get somewhere, holidays are vastly improved by stopping along the way. Advance planning should help overcome the impatience that can compromise safety and ruin the fun of the holiday.

■ FUEL

Fuel is readily available across Australia, particularly around areas with high populations. The price of fuel varies greatly between States, and between city and country areas. Most towns have a petrol station or two. In remote regions you will have to consider the distances between the lonely highway roadhouses. Many Aboriginal communities in Australia's north have outlets selling fuel to travellers but in the remoter areas they may not carry a supply of leaded petrol.

Distance in kilometres										
500	550	600	650	700	750	800	850	900	950	1000
Litres										
40.0	44.0	48.0	52.0	56.0	60.0	64.0	68.0	72.0	76.0	80.0
42.5	46.8	51.0	55.3	59.5	63.8	68.0	72.3	76.5	80.8	85.0
45.0	49.5	54.0	58.5	63.0	67.5	72.0	76.5	81.0	85.5	90.0
47.5	52.3	57.0	61.8	66.5	71.3	76.0	80.8	85.5	90.3	95.0
50.0	55.0	60.0	65.0	70.0	75.0	80.0	85.0	90.0	95.0	100.0
52.5	57.8	63.0	68.3	73.5	78.8	84.0	89.3	94.5	99.8	105.0
55.0	60.5	66.0	71.5	77.0	82.5	88.0	93.5	99.0	104.5	110.0
57.5	63.3	69.0	74.8	80.5	86.3	92.0	97.8	103.5	109.3	115.0
60.0	66.0	72.0	78.0	84.0	90.0	96.0	102.0	108.0	114.0	120.0
62.5	68.8	75.0	81.3	87.5	93.8	100.0	106.3	112.5	118.8	125.0
65.0	71.5	78.0	84.5	91.0	97.5	104.0	110.5	117.0	123.5	130.0
67.5	74.3	81.0	87.8	94.5	101.3	108.0	114.8	121.5	128.3	135.0
70.0	77.0	84.0	91.0	98.0	105.0	112.0	119.0	126.0	133.0	140.0
72.5	79.8	87.0	94.3	101.5	108.8	116.0	123.3	130.5	137.8	145.0
75.0	82.5	90.0	97.5	105.0	112.5	120.0	127.5	135.0	142.5	150.0
77.5	85.3	93.0	100.8	108.5	116.3	124.0	131.8	139.5	147.3	155.0
80.0	88.0	96.0	104.0	112.0	120.0	128.0	136.0	144.0	152.0	160.0
82.5	90.8	99.0	107.3	115.5	123.8	132.0	140.3	148.5	156.8	165.0
85.0	93.5	102.0	110.5	119.0	127.5	136.0	144.5	153.0	161.5	170.0
87.5	96.3	105.0	113.8	122.5	131.3	140.0	148.8	157.5	166.3	175.0
90.0	99.0	108.0	117.0	126.0	135.0	144.0	153.0	162.0	171.0	180.0
92.5	101.8	111.0	120.3	129.5	138.8	148.0	157.3	166.5	175.8	185.0
95.0	104.5	114.0	123.5	133.0	142.5	152.0	161.5	171.0	180.5	190.0
97.5	107.3	117.0	126.8	136.5	146.3	156.0	165.8	175.5	185.3	195.0
00.0	110.0	120.0	130.0	140.0	150.0	160.0	170.0	180.0	190.0	200.0
02.5	112.8	123.0	133.3	143.5	153.8	164.0	174.3	184.5	194.8	205.0
05.0	115.5	126.0	136.5	147.0	157.8	168.0	178.5	189.0	199.5	210.0
07.5	118.3	129.0	139.8	150.5	161.3	172.0	182.8	193.5	204.3	215.0
10.0	121.0	132.0	143.0	154.0	165.0	176.0	187.0	198.0	209.0	220.0
12.5	123.8	135.0	146.3	157.5	168.8	180.0	191.3	202.5	213.8	225.0
15.0	126.5	138.0	149.5	161.0	172.5	184.0	195.5	207.0	218.5	230.0
17.5	129.3	141.0	152.8	164.5	176.3	188.0	199.8	211.5	223.3	235.0
20.0	132.0	144.0	156.0	168.0	180.0	192.0	204.0	216.0	228.0	240.0
22.5	134.8	147.0	159.3	171.5	183.8	196.0	208.3	220.5	232.8	245.0
25.0	137.5	150.0	162.5	175.0	187.5	200.0	212.5	225.0	237.5	250.0

Additional fuel may have to be carried on some outback highways. Fuel should only be stored in approved containers, such as metal or approved plastic jerry cans. You will also need a funnel, pourer or siphon hose to transfer the fuel from the container to the tank. Fuel containers should be stored in racks on vans or trailers, or on the roof-rack of a four-wheel drive. Fuel containers must never be stored inside the passenger compartment of your vehicle.

Your vehicle will use a lot more fuel when towing. Before setting out on your trip, do a trial run in built-up areas and on the open road to gauge your fuel efficiency. Fuel outlets can be scarce in remote areas. Use the fuel calculator table (page 326) to work out your fuel requirements over particular distances and avoid the major hassle of running out of fuel.

■ DAILY CHECKS AND CHORES

Daily checks, regular maintenance, careful packing and ensuring you are informed on the conditions ahead can prevent unwelcome incidents that can delay or, in the worst circumstances, cut short a holiday.

Packing

Limit the items carried in the passenger compartment to necessities. If you are travelling in a sedan, secure the heavier items in the boot. In a station wagon, have a safety barrier or net fitted to protect passengers from flying luggage in the event of an accident. Dispose of litter as soon as possible, particularly glass bottles and cans. For information on packing your van safely see Weight distribution, page 311.

Checklist

Organise a checklist of what to do when packing up and taking off. These are the things that must be done every time you head off, regardless of whether you have been stationary for a week or a day. Get into a routine and share the tasks. Place the list behind a visor where it is easily scanned. The list should include the following:
- Stow television antenna.
- Secure jockey wheels on caravans.
- Secure corner stabilisers.
- Stow step away.
- Clip fridge door.
- Secure cupboard doors.
- Close vents.
- Collect chocks or levelling wedges.
- Secure pop-tops.
- Roll up power lead.
- Stow waste-water hoses.

Authors' tip

We find it useful to always carry a tyre gauge. When a tyre is correctly inflated it should sit with just a small bulging at the bottom. If the tyre walls are straight, then the pressure is likely to be too great.

Tyre pressure

When it comes to basic vehicle maintenance the issue of tyre pressures is one that causes particular confusion. It is our experience that many tyre fitters do not fully understand correct inflation. On your vehicle you will find a tyre placard, which indicates the correct tyre pressure. This is fine for normal loading. For abnormal loading, however, the amount of pressure should be calculated according to the amount of weight being borne by that tyre. The manufacturer of your tyres should be able to provide you with a chart that shows your tyre size, the weight it will bear and the correct pressure for those specifications. The general rule of thumb is: the greater the load on a tyre, the greater the tyre pressure required.

Inflating your caravan's tyres is not simply a matter of using the same pressure as used for the tyres on your vehicle. Recommended tyre pressures are stamped on your caravan's Vehicle Identification Number (VIN) plate. You will have to take into account the laden weight of your van and calculate accordingly.

- Check all lights and indicators.
- Adjust rear-vision mirrors.
- Check electric brakes.
- Release caravan handbrake.
- Secure safety chain.
- Secure awning.
- Fasten caravan door/s.

Roadside maintenance

If you take your vehicle and caravan to a mechanic for a full service on a regular basis, you will probably be able to carry out basic maintenance on your rig yourself. (For a list of useful equipment see Tools and spares, page 310.) Commonsense and an ability to read the danger signs of your vehicle should suffice in most instances.

Carry out these basic tasks to keep things in order:
- Check that the oil level is close to the full mark and above the low mark.
- Ensure the lights are working after the van is hitched.
- Ensure the safety chains are secure.
- Examine the tow hitch after the first 200 m.
- Fill the washer bottle.
- Check the coolant level.
- Clean the windscreen.
- In diesel vehicles, look for sediment or water in glass-bowl-type filters.

Once a week you will need to check:
- the electrolyte level of your battery (add distilled water if it is low)
- for damp spots, leaks or loose fittings beneath the vehicle
- tyre pressures when cold (see Tyre pressure, facing page)
- brakes and brake operation on both your van and your vehicle
- brake and clutch fluids to make sure both sit between the high and low lines.

Every 1000 km or so you should also check the tread on your tyres for uneven or unusual wear and the tyre walls for damage.

■ CARAVAN PARKS AND OTHER SPOTS

Deciding where to stay will take time and energy. Most people choose to stay in caravan parks but there are, however, a core group of independently minded travellers who prefer, wherever possible, to stay in the bush or by the side of the road. Think about what you expect from a camping area, be it park or bush, and what is expected of you in terms of being a good neighbour in a confined living environment.

Choosing a caravan park

The caravan park for you is the one that suits your individual needs. Children need a park with a playground or a swimming pool. Pets require a park with a pet-friendly policy. A large van or motorhome demands a suitably large site, perhaps even a drive-through site. Travellers concerned about privacy may require a park with ensuite facilities.

Location is important. Proximity to shops, the beach and other facilities will reduce car use. This is important to those with motorhomes and campervans because using the car means dismantling the campsite.

Word-of-mouth can be the best way of choosing a park after you have exhausted the information contained in the Caravan park directory (page 350). Make a point of talking to people who have just returned from the places you intend to visit next. These exchanges, which, more often than not, take place in the laundries of caravan parks, are a great source of up-to-date information on where to go and where to avoid. But remember that travellers have very different ideas of what makes a good caravan park, so filter any suggestions carefully.

Australia's auto clubs publish guides to caravan parks based on star ratings. A problem with this system is that for a park to earn more stars it must offer an increasing range of services and facilities. Average campers, who would happily settle for a shady site, friendly service and spotless amenities, find themselves paying for a range of facilities they do not necessarily need or want, such as putt-putt golf and trampolines.

We have generally found that owner-operated parks provide that little bit more in the way of service. We also look out for well-tended grounds as an indication of what lies in store.

Sites with water frontage are always popular

Choosing a site

Every caravan park has a different layout and sites of varying size. Your choice of site will be limited during holiday periods and in popular parks that are busy year-round. If you book well in advance, you may be able to specify a site, or a general area of the park, where you wish to be located. Sites with beach or river frontage are always popular, and tend to attract higher site fees.

When checking into a park, ask if there is a choice of site. You may want to be near the amenities, away from a busy road, or close to friends. Most proprietors will do their best to meet your preferences.

Most parks have sites with and without power. Sites without power, generally reserved for people with tents and small camper-trailers, can, in some parks, be of poor quality. We sometimes find it better to take a powered site even if we do not intend to use the power. In other parks, sites without power can be of a very good quality indeed, with grassy expanses and close proximity to the amenities block. A good example is the camping section of the Ayers Rock Resort.

Authors' tip

Tune in to the FM tourist radio network, which operates in many towns around Australia, giving information on the local area. The service is advertised on blue and white road signs, usually located just outside the town. The frequency is generally FM 88.

There are some beautiful bush camping areas in Australia

Prices and bookings

Caravan park prices vary dramatically across Australia. Some parks offer seasonally structured pricing. Others have heavy loadings on site fees during holiday periods and attractive discounts in non-peak periods. In our experience, site fees range from around $10 per night for a basic park in a non-tourist area to $40 per night during the summer holidays in a good quality park near a popular beach. Parks often have a policy of minimum bookings over holiday periods: around four days over Easter and up to a week in the summer holidays. Look out for discounts, such as seven nights for the price of five, but make sure the normal nightly rate is competitive with other parks in the area.

Three major caravan-park chains operate in Australia (see Australia's caravan chains, this page). If you are planning an extended tour around the country, we recommend you join at least one and possibly all. The parks associated with these three chains are generally of better than average quality. The cost of the membership is quickly recouped through the membership discounts. The usual discount is 10 per cent of the scheduled fee with a maximum discount of between $15 and $25 per stay.

Authors' tip

If you are allocated a site beneath trees, always have a good look for dead or unstable limbs, particularly in riverside parks with lots of red gums. The shade is wonderful but branches can, and do, come crashing down, causing injuries and even fatalities.

Australia's caravan chains

Big4
1800 632 444
www.big4.com.au

Family Parks of Australia
1800 682 492
www.familyparks.com.au

Top Tourist
(08) 8363 1905
www.toptouristparks.com.au

Bush camping

Camping in the bush or along the roadside has been common in Australia for as long as we can remember. In recent years, rising concerns about security have seen a drop-off in the numbers of roadside campers but many still enjoy the pleasures of self-sufficiency, particularly owners of motorhomes and campervans. The best places to stay are the many recognised bush and roadside camping areas where a small gathering of overnight campers can usually be found. Avoid camping alone if you can.

Camping in national parks

Camping in national parks is very popular. Most sites are designed for tents. Vans are allowed but in some parks they are poorly accommodated. A common problem is the positioning of the post and rail fences that are used to delineate camping areas. Vans cannot pass through, forcing them to park on the roadside. That said, a handful of national parks cater very well for vans, offering generous sites. Few offer powered sites.

Most sites in national parks require a degree of self-sufficiency but camping fees tend to be much cheaper than in commercial caravan parks. Contact the park before you travel to find out about caravan access. In some parks the handful of caravan sites available are booked up for weeks or months in advance. For further information and contact details see National parks, page 316.

Camping etiquette

Life becomes a little less private on a camping holiday. At caravan parks, roadside stops and in the bush you will find yourself living in very close proximity to all sorts of fellow travellers. You can generally avoid most of the difficulties that can arise by observing the following basic points of camping courtesy:

- If it is not yours, do not touch it.
- If you do not know how to operate it, do not use it.
- Walk around, not through, other people's campsites.
- Do not take anything that does not belong to you; this includes what you may think of as inconsequential items such as toilet paper, plugs and hoses.
- Empty night toilet buckets in the toilets and do not rinse them in the bathroom sinks or camp kitchens.
- Do not empty hot water on lawns or gardens.
- Wash your vehicle only in the area prescribed.
- Do not refuel cars on lawns.
- Do not camp on the road adjoining a caravan park.
- If you bring it with you, take it with you.
- Be careful with rubbish and plastic bags.
- Do not burn or bury rubbish.
- If bins are full or overflowing in a roadside stop area, take your rubbish with you.
- Respect others and keep noise to a minimum at night. This especially applies to using stereos.
- Park your car on your caravan-park site.
- Brief your children on how to behave in camping areas.
- Keep your pets on leads at all times (see Travelling with pets, page 317).

Camping is permitted in designated areas in the Flinders Ranges National Park

Caring for the environment

Tourism has a demonstrable environmental impact. The following guidelines will help you preserve Australia's magnificent landscapes for the generations of travellers who will follow in your footsteps:

- Drive only along defined roads and tracks. Do not drive along closed roads.
- Take all your rubbish with you. Do not throw rubbish from your vehicle. Do not deposit bags of rubbish alongside overflowing bins at roadside stops and do not burn or bury rubbish.
- Do not cut down standing timber for firewood. Collect a minimum amount of ground wood if you must have a fire.
- Do not use detergent, soap or shampoo in rivers, streams or lakes.
- Respect private land, including Aboriginal land.
- Protect native flora and fauna. Some States impose substantial penalties for picking wildflowers. All native fauna is generally protected.

■ AVOIDING DANGER

While Australia is very much a safe and friendly country, there are things – of both a criminal and environmental nature – that can threaten your safety if you are not aware and do not employ some basic precautions.

Personal safety

Stay in touch with a trusted friend or relative. Keep them informed of your travel plans, particularly if you are travelling in remote or outback regions. The contact person should have the responsibility of notifying authorities if you fail to get in touch. Discuss this thoroughly with them before leaving home. Make sure you agree on a margin of time to allow for poor weather, mechanical breakdown and other problems.

Keep your vehicle and caravan locked when you are not there, even if you plan to be absent for only a few minutes at a service station, public toilet, shop or lookout: petty criminals are attracted to such places. Do not leave expensive items on display. If you have valuables, such as cash, cheques, papers and jewellery, you may consider buying one of the small, fibre-style car safes now on the market. Take care when withdrawing money at ATMs and only withdraw small amounts of cash.

Be cautious on the road. Do not pick up hitchhikers, a practice that is illegal in some States. If someone flags you down, keep your doors locked and talk to them through a partially opened window until you can work out what is going on. Report any suspicious behaviour to the local police.

Creature hazards

Although Australia's unique wildlife is universally appealing, some species are extremely dangerous and direct contact with them should be avoided. There are some fairly simple precautions that you can take.

Box jellyfish
Found in Australia's northern tropical waters from October to May, these creatures have a sting that is fatal to humans. Prompt medical attention can and does save lives. Authorities prohibit swimming on beaches north of Rockhampton during the stinger season. Outside of the season, check with locals first before entering the water.

Stonefish
These fish are another resident of northern waters with a very poisonous sting. Wear sandshoes in the water and do not over-turn rocks and coral.

Blue-ringed octopus
Common in rock pools all around Australia, these creatures have a sting that can cause paralysis followed by death. Wear shoes to explore rocky areas and avoid handling the marine life you come across.

Sharks
The best way to avoid sharks is to swim at patrolled beaches. Otherwise, avoid areas of low visibility, do not swim at night and check with locals about whether or not they consider an area safe.

Crocodiles
Two varieties are found in northern Australia. Saltwater crocs are extremely dangerous and are found on the coast and in rivers up to 300 km inland. Freshwater crocodiles tend to avoid humans, but not always. Both varieties lurk beneath the surface of the water. They are hard to see and, if you are not an expert, hard to tell apart. Heed local warning signs. Do not swim or paddle in crocodile areas. Do not feed or clean fish by the water's edge.

Spiders and snakes
Leave them alone and they will generally not bother you. Avoid contact by wearing sturdy boots when walking, and checking bedding, shoes and other likely spots for stowaways.

Water safety

Most of Australia's coastline is unpatrolled and dangerous, not just because of harmful creatures but also because of powerful rips and currents. The only safe way to swim in coastal waters is between the flags at patrolled beaches. Know your swimming ability and watch out for warning signs and beach closures.

You should always swim between the flags and heed any box jellyfish warnings, even at a beach like Airlie Beach

Survival in the bush and outback

The Australian bush is a harsh environment, subject to many droughts, floods, bushfires and cyclones. Most Australians have a basic awareness of the dangers and how to avoid them. If you are planning to travel into a threatened area, get an idea of what awaits you: listen to local radio, read the local press and make contact with a relevant authority who can possibly give you information about conditions such as police, emergency services, park rangers and even the local visitor information centre.

If your travels take you into isolated or remote areas, your most serious threat is that of becoming stranded. Always let someone know where you are travelling and when you expect to return. Check in when you arrive at your destination. In particularly remote places, you should inform police or other authorities, such as national park rangers, of your travel plans.

Becoming stranded is common: cars get bogged; dinghies break down; bushwalkers wander off the track. The best insurance against a simple mishap turning into a life-threatening situation is to carry a suitable communication device (see Communications, page 322). In addition, observe these basic survival tips:

- Do not try to walk out of a remote area for assistance.
- Stay with, or close to, your vehicle or boat.
- If the weather is hot or wet, set up shelter from the elements.
- Wear sensible clothing including a hat and footwear.
- Conserve your food and water supplies in anticipation of a long wait.
- Conserve your energy.
- Try to signal for help using fire, or scratch the word 'help' into the ground or sand.

The most important thing is not to panic. We regularly travel alone in the most remote deserts, and along tracks that never seem to be used, but rarely do we fail to run into a fellow traveller: it may not happen immediately, but sooner or later (within days, not weeks) a vehicle will appear on the horizon.

Drinking adequate fluids is even more important than eating food. Without a supply of water, you have little chance of surviving in places of extreme heat. If you intend to travel in the desert or remote outback areas, prepare for the worst and carry 4 to 5 litres of water per person for every day you expect to be on the road. Then carry extra water for three or four days to cover you in the event of a breakdown.

AUSTRALIAN ROAD ATLAS

MAP SYMBOLS

ROUTES by CHAPTER

Chapter 1: Around Australia on Highway One

sealed   unsealed

Chapter 2: Great inland highways: south–north

Chapter 3: Great inland highways: east–west

Chapter 4: Touring Tasmania

ROADS

FREEWAY / HIGHWAY	HIGHWAY
sealed	unsealed
MAIN ROAD	MAIN ROAD
sealed	unsealed
MINOR ROAD	MINOR ROAD
sealed	unsealed

VEHICULAR TRACK

RAILWAY

◄——— 152 ———►
distance in kilometres

ROUTE MARKERS

1 **A2**   National highway route markers

1 **A8**   National route markers

16 **B500**   State route markers

TOWN and POINT SYMBOLS

State capital city	◉ **ADELAIDE**
Town, over 50 000 inhabitants	◉ **Wollongong**
Town, 10 000–50 000 inhabitants	◉ **Cessnock**
Town, 5000–10 000 inhabitants	◉ Broome
Town, 1000–5000 inhabitants	◦ Coober Pedy
Town, 200–1000 inhabitants	◦ Northampton
Town, under 200 inhabitants	◦ Lake King
Aboriginal community	◦ Doomadgee
Roadhouse	**RH** Hells Gate Roadhouse
Place of interest	● Bungle Bungles
Landmark feature	● Poeppel Corner
Mine site	⚒ Tanami Mine

AREA FEATURES

ABORIGINAL LAND	PROHIBITED AREA	NATIONAL PARK
OTHER RESERVE	LAKE RESERVE	

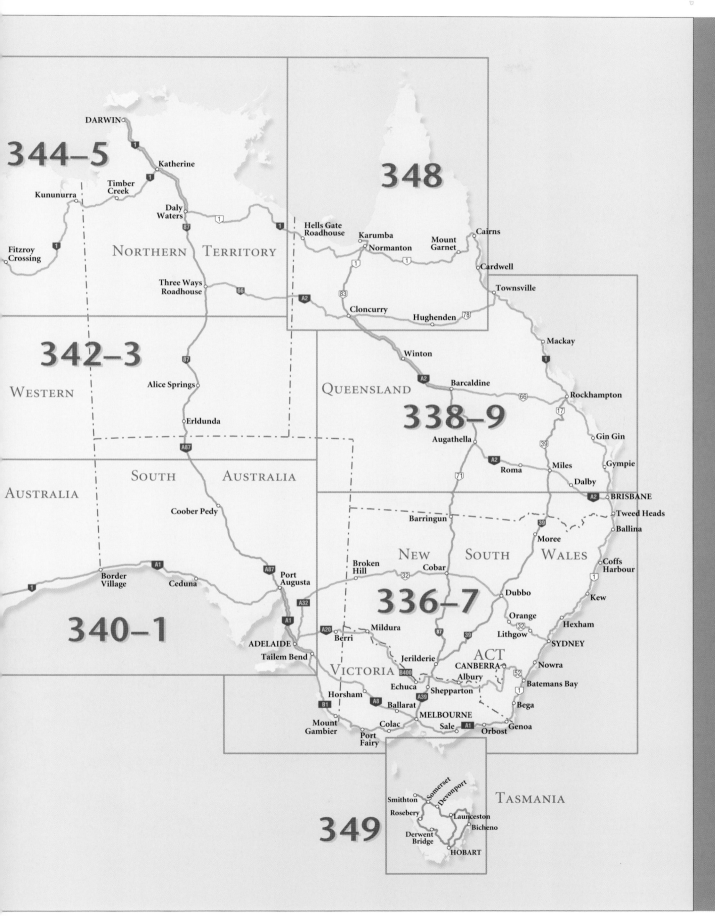

344–5

DARWIN

Katherine

Timber
Creek

Kununurra

Daly
Waters

Fitzroy
Crossing

NORTHERN   TERRITORY

Hells Gate
Roadhouse

Karumba

Normanton

Mount
Garnet

Cairns

348

Cardwell

Three Ways
Roadhouse

Cloncurry

Hughenden

Townsville

342–3

Mackay

Winton

WESTERN

Alice Springs

Barcaldine

QUEENSLAND

Rockhampton

Erldunda

338–9

Gin Gin

AUSTRALIA

Augathella

Gympie

SOUTH   AUSTRALIA

Roma

Miles

Dalby

Coober Pedy

BRISBANE

Tweed Heads

Barringun

Ballina

NEW   SOUTH   WALES

Moree

Coffs
Harbour

Broken
Hill

Cobar

Border
Village

Ceduna

Port
Augusta

336–7

Dubbo

Kew

340–1

Mildura

Orange

Hexham

Berri

Lithgow

SYDNEY

ADELAIDE

Jerilderie

ACT

Nowra

Tailem Bend

CANBERRA

Albury

Batemans Bay

Victoria

Echuca

Shepparton

Horsham

Ballarat

Bega

Mount
Gambier

Colac

MELBOURNE

Sale

Genoa

Port
Fairy

Orbost

Somerset

Devonport

TASMANIA

Smithton

Rosebery

Launceston

349

Bicheno

Derwent
Bridge

HOBART

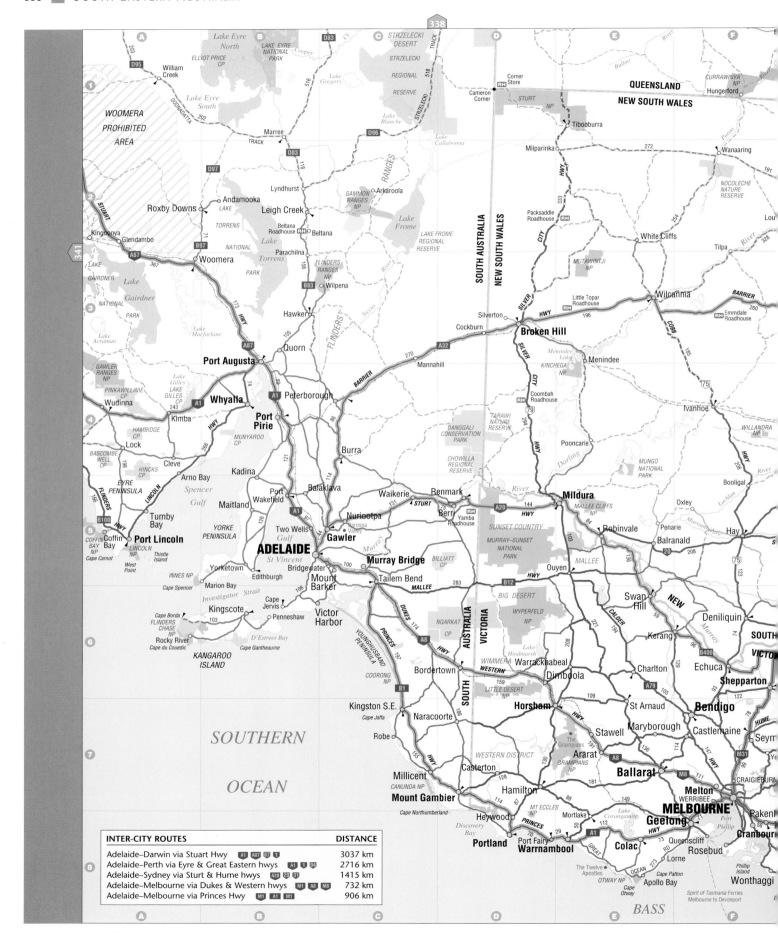

INTER-CITY ROUTES	DISTANCE
Adelaide–Darwin via Stuart Hwy A1 A87 87 1	3037 km
Adelaide–Perth via Eyre & Great Eastern hwys A1 1 94	2716 km
Adelaide–Sydney via Sturt & Hume hwys A20 20 31	1415 km
Adelaide–Melbourne via Dukes & Western hwys M1 A8 M8	732 km
Adelaide–Melbourne via Princes Hwy M1 A1 M1	906 km

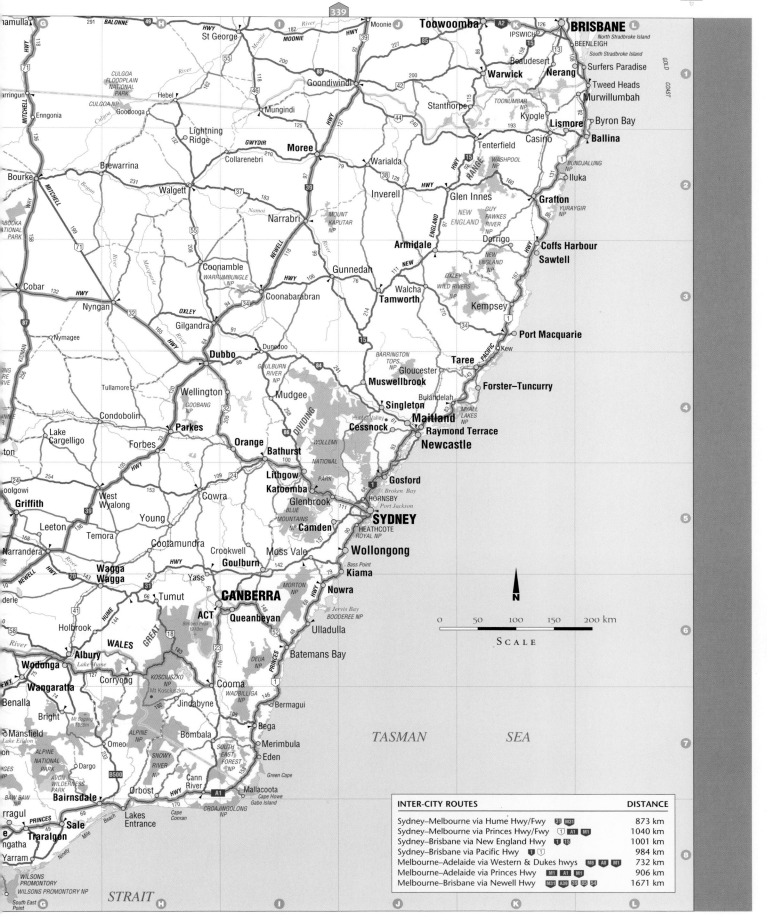

INTER-CITY ROUTES DISTANCE

Route		Distance
Sydney–Melbourne via Hume Hwy/Fwy	31 M31	873 km
Sydney–Melbourne via Princes Hwy/Fwy	1 A1 M1	1040 km
Sydney–Brisbane via New England Hwy	1 15	1001 km
Sydney–Brisbane via Pacific Hwy	1 1	984 km
Melbourne–Adelaide via Western & Dukes hwys	M8 A8 M1	732 km
Melbourne–Adelaide via Princes Hwy	M1 A1 M1	906 km
Melbourne–Brisbane via Newell Hwy	M31 A39 85 54	1671 km

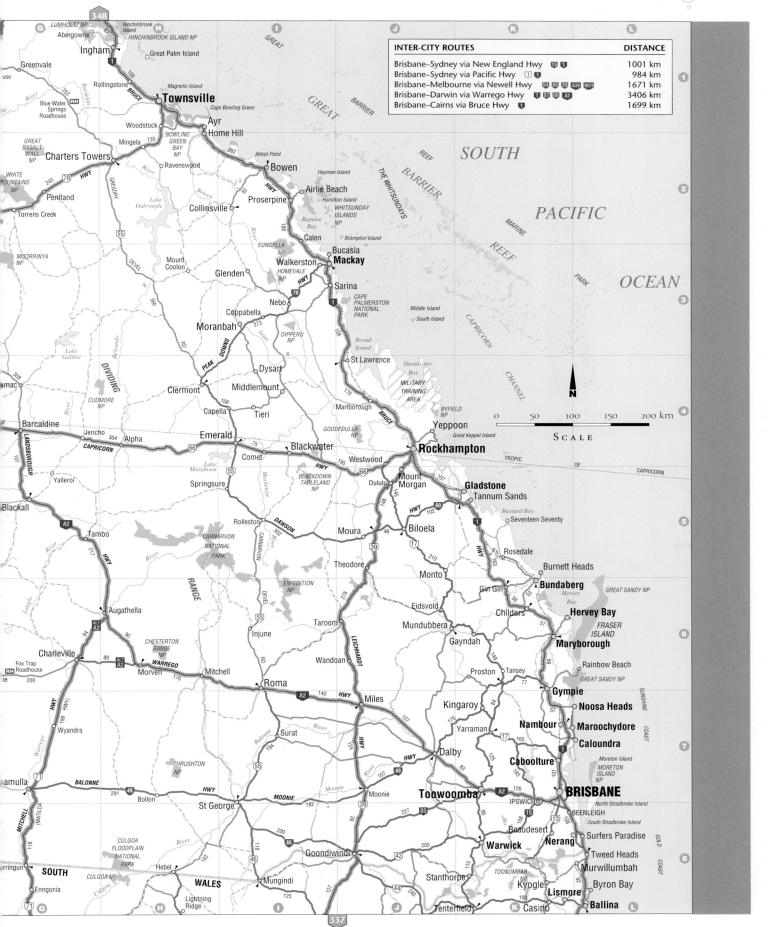

INTER-CITY ROUTES		DISTANCE
Brisbane–Sydney via New England Hwy **15** **1**		1001 km
Brisbane–Sydney via Pacific Hwy **1** **1**		984 km
Brisbane–Melbourne via Newell Hwy **54** **39** **A39** **M31**		1671 km
Brisbane–Darwin via Warrego Hwy **1** **87** **66** **A2**		3406 km
Brisbane–Cairns via Bruce Hwy **1**		1699 km

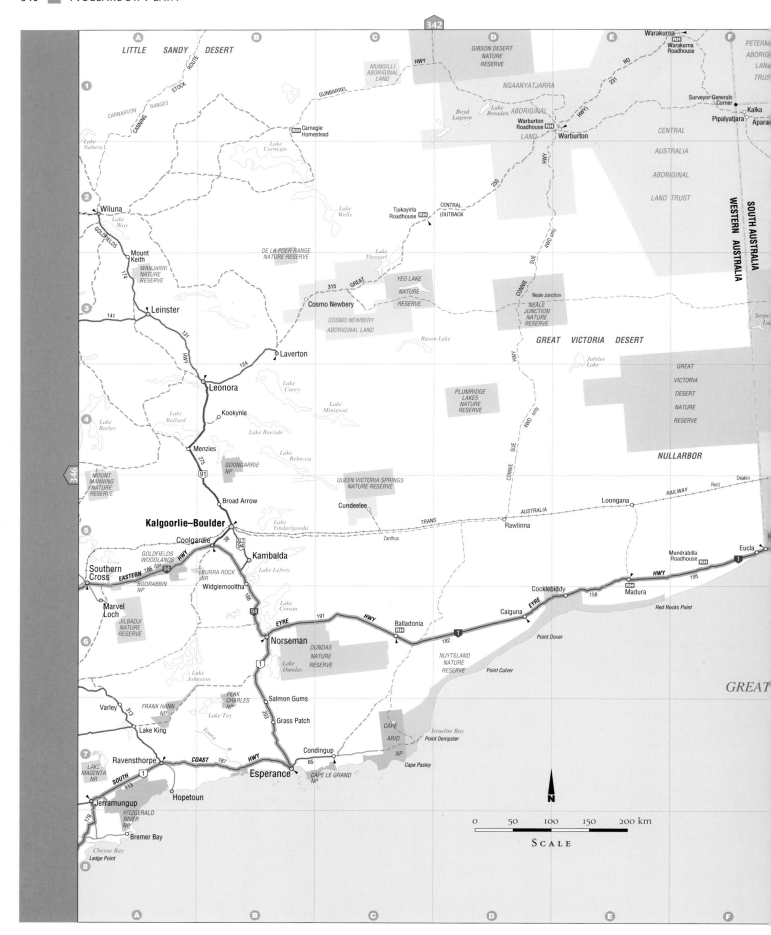

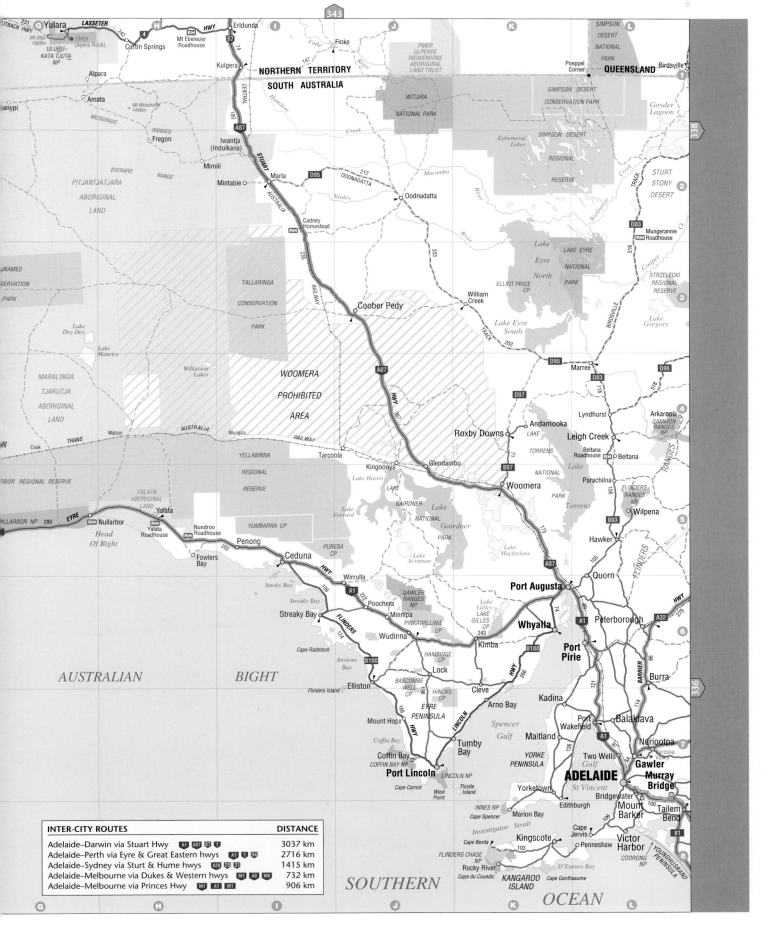

343

231 Yulara
LASSETER HWY
Erldunda
UTBACK HWY
Mt Olga 1069m
Uluru (Ayers Rock)
ULURU–KATA TJUTA NP
Curtin Springs
Mt Ebenezer Roadhouse
242
4
RH
87
74
I
Finke
Finke River
SIMPSON DESERT NATIONAL PARK
L
Poeppel Corner
Birdsville
QUEENSLAND

Kulgera
NORTHERN TERRITORY
SOUTH AUSTRALIA
147
PMER ULPERRE INGWEMIRNE ABORIGINAL LAND TRUST
1

Alpara
Amata
MUSGRAVE
Mt Woodroffe 1440m
RANGES
180
CENTRAL
Hamilton
Creek
WITJIRA NATIONAL PARK
Goyder Lagoon

anypi
Fregon
A87
Iwantja (Indulkana)
STUART
WOOMERA
Simpson Desert Conservation Park
SIMPSON DESERT REGIONAL RESERVE
STURT STONY DESERT
2

PITJANTJATJARA ABORIGINAL LAND
EVERARD RANGE
Mimili
Mintabie
Marla
D95
212 OODNADATTA
Ephemeral Lakes
Neales
Macumba
River
D83
Mungerannie Roadhouse RH
516

AUSTRALIA
Cadney Homestead
235
RH
Oodnadatta
River
Lake Eyre North NATIONAL PARK
Strzelecki Regional Reserve
3

UNAMED SERVATION PARK
Lake Dey Dey
Lake Maurice
MARALINGA TJARUTJA ABORIGINAL LAND
Wilkinson Lakes
TALLARINGA CONSERVATION PARK
RAILWAY
A87
HWY
203
William Creek
ELLIOT PRICE CP
Lake Eyre South
BIRDSVILLE TRACK
Lake Gregory
4

Coober Pedy
202
Marree
D95
D83
118
Arkaroola
GAMMON RANGES NP

ARBOR REGIONAL RESERVE
Watson
AUSTRALIA
Mungala
WOOMERA PROHIBITED AREA
307
D97
D96
518
Lyndhurst
Andamooka
Roxby Downs
LAKE TORRENS
Leigh Creek
Beltana Roadhouse RH
Beltana
FLINDERS RANGES

Cook
TRANS
AUSTRALIA RAILWAY
YELLABINNA REGIONAL RESERVE
Tarcoola
B97
Woomera
NATIONAL
95
Parachilna
Wilpena
RANGES
5

EYRE
Nullarbor RH
280
Yalata RH
Yalata Roadhouse RH
Nundroo Roadhouse RH
YUMBARRA CP
Kingoonya
Glendambo
71
LAKE TORRENS NATIONAL PARK
Lake Torrens
173
B83
Hawker
Sliccr R.

W
LLARBOR NP
Head Of Bight
Yalata
Penong
202
Ceduna
Fowlers Bay
PUREBA CP
Lake Everard
LAKE GAIRDNER NATIONAL PARK
Lake Gairdner
Lake Macfarlane
A87
105
Quorn
FLINDERS

HWY
Wirrulla
108
A1
222
Poochera
Minnipa
GAWLER RANGES NP
Lake Acraman
Port Augusta
74
A1
Peterborough
A32
270

Smoky Bay
Streaky Bay
Streaky Bay
124
Wudinna
PINKAWILLINIE CP
LAKE GILLES CP
243
Whyalla
86
Burra

Cape Radstock
FLINDERS
166
HAMBIDGE CP
Kimba
HWY
266
B100
Port Pirie
121
Balaklava

Anxious Bay
B100
Elliston
BASCOMBE WELL CP
196
HINCKS CP
Lock
Cleve
Kadina
114
Nuriootpa
Barossa Valley

Flinders Island
Mount Hope
166
EYRE PENINSULA
Arno Bay
Port Wakefield
Maitland
A1
128
Two Wells
Gawler
44

Coffin Bay
Tumby Bay
LINCOLN HWY
Spencer Gulf
YORKE PENINSULA
ADELAIDE
Murray Bridge

COFFIN BAY NP
Port Lincoln
LINCOLN NP
Cape Carnot
West Point
Thistle Island
Yorketown
Edithburgh
St Vincent
Bridgewater
Mount Barker
106
100
Tailem Bend
B1

FLINDERS CHASE NP
Rocky River
Cape du Coedic
Marion Bay
Cape Spencer
INNES NP
KANGAROO ISLAND
Kingscote
103
Penneshaw
D'Estrees Bay
Cape Gantheaume
Cape Jervis
COORONG NP
Victor Harbor
YOUNGHUSBAND PENINSULA

AUSTRALIAN
BIGHT
SOUTHERN
OCEAN

Investigator Strait
Cape Borda

INTER-CITY ROUTES	DISTANCE
Adelaide–Darwin via Stuart Hwy A1 A87 87 1	3037 km
Adelaide–Perth via Eyre & Great Eastern hwys A1 1 94	2716 km
Adelaide–Sydney via Sturt & Hume hwys A20 20 31	1415 km
Adelaide–Melbourne via Dukes & Western hwys M1 A8 M8	732 km
Adelaide–Melbourne via Princes Hwy M1 A1 M1	906 km

G   H   I   J   K   L

338

336

Ⓐ Ⓑ Ⓒ 344 Ⓔ Ⓕ

Kununurra
KEEP RIVER NP
46 36
191
VICTORIA
34
Amanbidji
WAGURU ABOBIG LAND Tr
PRINCE REGENT NATURE RESERVE
KUNMUNYA ABORIGINAL RESERVE
Hall Point
GARDNER PLATEAU
Drysdale R
284
DOON DOON ABORIGINAL LAND
Lake Argyle
151
Ⓐ1 Koolan
Collier Bay
Churnley River
Gibb River
151
Mistake Creek
MALNGIN ABORIGINAL LAND TRUST

THE KIMBERLEY
Mount Barnett Roadhouse RH
Turkey Creek Roadhouse RH
Turkey Creek (Warmun)
161
HWY
PURNULULU NP
Bungle Bungles

Cape Leveque
One Arm Point
Lombadina
Isdell River
Kupingarri
Chamberlain River
Durack River

Pender Bay
Beagle Bay
365
KING LEOPOLD RANGES CP
KING LEOPOLD RANGES
Ord River

Cape Baskerville
Coulomb Point
BEAGLE BAY ABORIGINAL RESERVE
Meda River
DEVONIAN REEF
Fitzroy River
RANGES
80
404

Ⓐ2 POINT COULOMB NR
Derby
43
NATIONAL PARKS
Halls Creek
1

Willare Bridge Roadhouse RH
219
GREAT
Fitzroy Crossing
DENISON PLAINS
DUNCAN

Cape Boileau
Roebuck Roadhouse RH
145
Looma
NOOGOORA BURR QUARANTINE AREA

Broome 34
NORTHERN
288
Sturt

Ⓐ3 Roebuck Bay
Cape Villaret
Gourdon Bay
HWY
Fitzroy River

False Cape Bossut
Bidyadanga
286
Cape Jaubert

WARNINGS: In outback Australia, long distances separate some towns. Travellers should familiarise themselves with prevailing conditions before departure and take care to ensure their vehicle is roadworthy. Adequate supplies of petrol, water and food should be carried at all times.

In northern Australia, rainfall during the wet season (October to March) can make some roads impassable. Full information on road conditions should be obtained from local authorities before departure.

If visitors intend diverting off public roads within Aboriginal Land areas, a permit is required from the relevant Aboriginal authority.

Beware of crocodiles in rivers, estuaries and coastal areas.

Biliiluna (Mindibungu)
404
TANAMI
RD
5
Tanam (no a

Balgo Hills

Beach
1
NORTHERN
ROUTE
Lake Gregory
KEARNEY ABORIGINAL LAND

Eighty
Mile
RH
Sandfire Roadhouse
Ⓐ4 GREAT

GREAT SANDY DESERT

De Grey River
Tobin Lake
Lake Wills

Ⓐ5 Lake Waukarlycarly
Percival Lakes
Lake Mackay

N
0 50 100 150 200 km
SCALE

347
Oakover River
Lake Dora
Lake Auld
Lake George
RUDALL RIVER NATIONAL PARK
STOCK

Ⓐ6 River
Kiwirrkurra
Lake Macdonald
Kintor

CAPRICORN
TROPIC OF CAPRICORN
Lake Earnham
GIBSON DESERT
CENTRAL
Lake Hopkins

WALAGUNYA ABORIGINAL LAND
Jigalong
Lake Disappointment
GIBSON DESERT NATURE RESERVE
AUSTRALIA
Kaltukatjara (Docker River)
105

JIGALONG ABORIGINAL LAND
Warakurna RH
Warakurna Roadhouse

Ⓐ7 LITTLE SANDY DESERT
231 HWY
NGAANYATJARRA
Surveyor Generals Corner
Pipalyatjara

CANNING
CARNARVON RANGES
GUNBARREL
MUNGILLI ABORIGINAL LAND
HWY
Lake Breaden
Boyd Lagoon
ABORIGINAL LAND
Warburton Roadhouse RH
Warburton
ABORIGINAL LAND TRUST

Ⓐ8 Lake Naberu
Carnegie Homestead RH
Lake Carnegie
GREAT 250 (OUTBACK
CENTRAL

Ⓐ Ⓑ Ⓒ 340 Ⓓ Ⓔ Ⓕ

NORTHERN TERRITORY
WESTERN AUSTRALIA

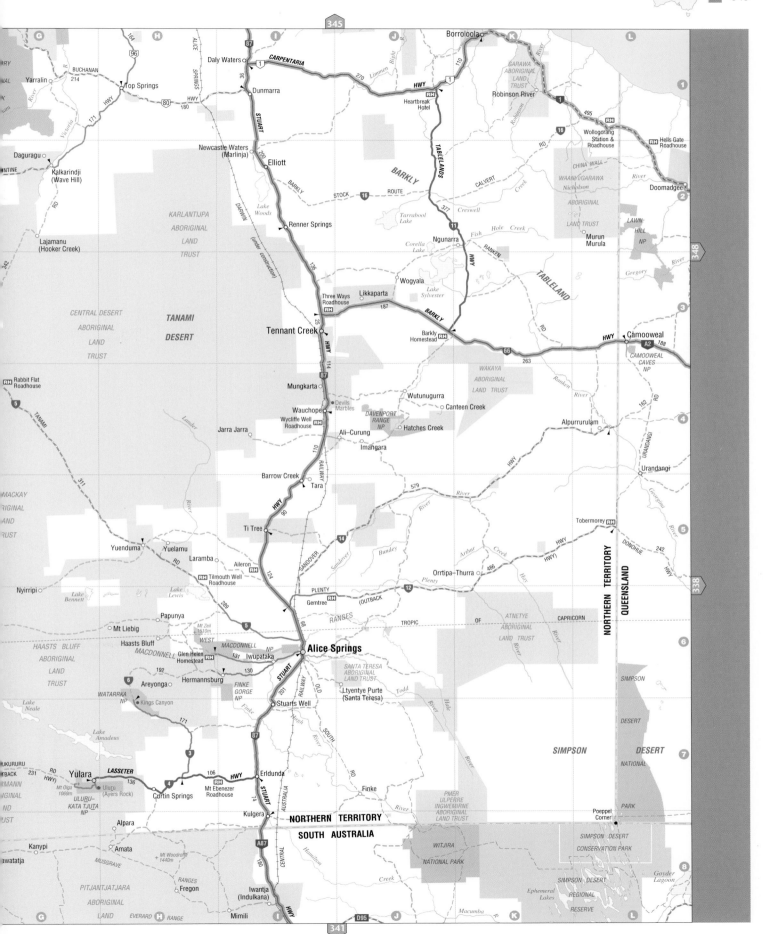

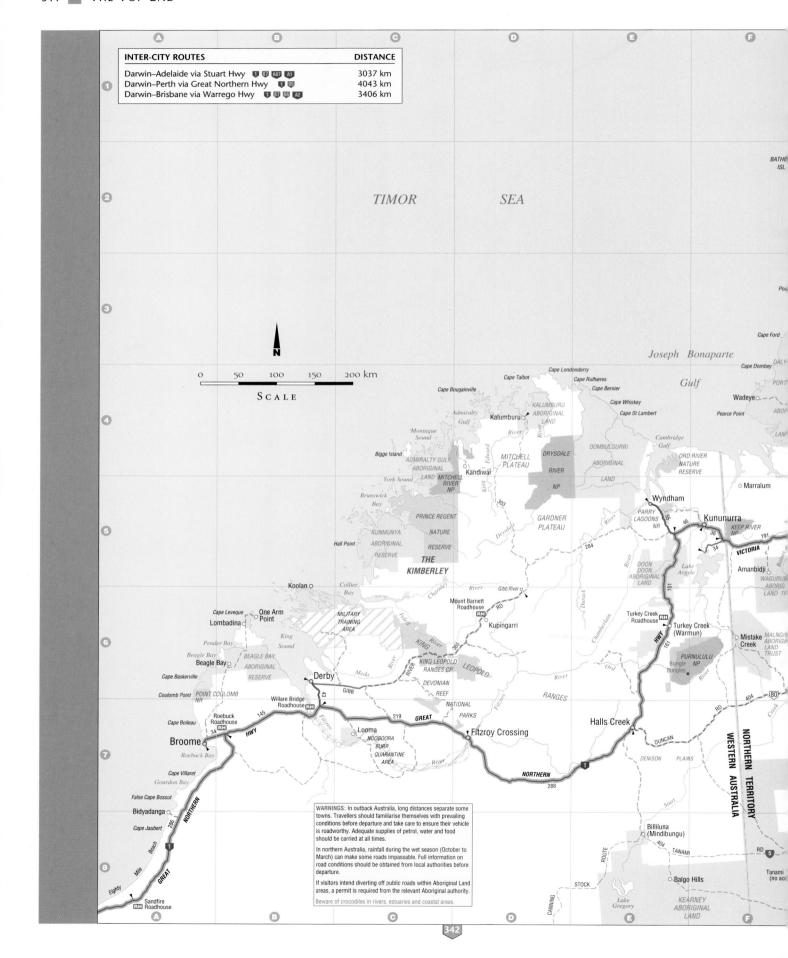

INTER-CITY ROUTES	DISTANCE
Darwin–Adelaide via Stuart Hwy	3037 km
Darwin–Perth via Great Northern Hwy	4043 km
Darwin–Brisbane via Warrego Hwy	3406 km

TIMOR SEA

N

SCALE
0   50   100   150   200 km

Joseph Bonaparte Gulf

WARNINGS: In outback Australia, long distances separate some towns. Travellers should familiarise themselves with prevailing conditions before departure and take care to ensure their vehicle is roadworthy. Adequate supplies of petrol, water and food should be carried at all times.

In northern Australia, rainfall during the wet season (October to March) can make some roads impassable. Full information on road conditions should be obtained from local authorities before departure.

If visitors intend diverting off public roads within Aboriginal Land areas, a permit is required from the relevant Aboriginal authority.

Beware of crocodiles in rivers, estuaries and coastal areas.

ARAFURA SEA

GULF
OF
CARPENTARIA

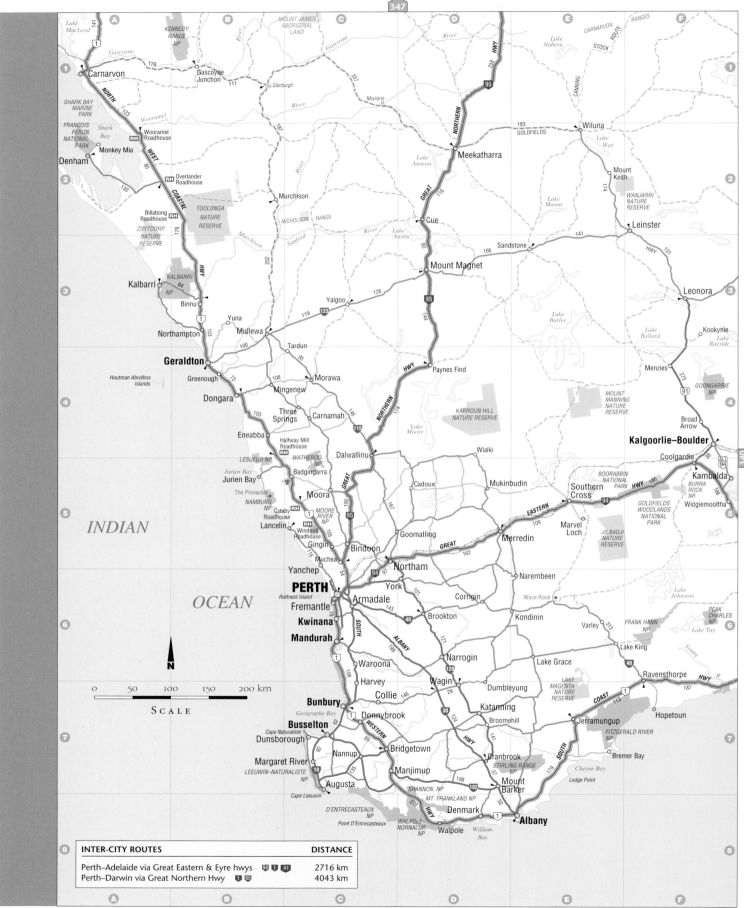

INDIAN

OCEAN

N

| 0 | 50 | 100 | 150 | 200 km |

SCALE

PERTH

INTER-CITY ROUTES		DISTANCE
Perth–Adelaide via Great Eastern & Eyre hwys		2716 km
Perth–Darwin via Great Northern Hwy		4043 km

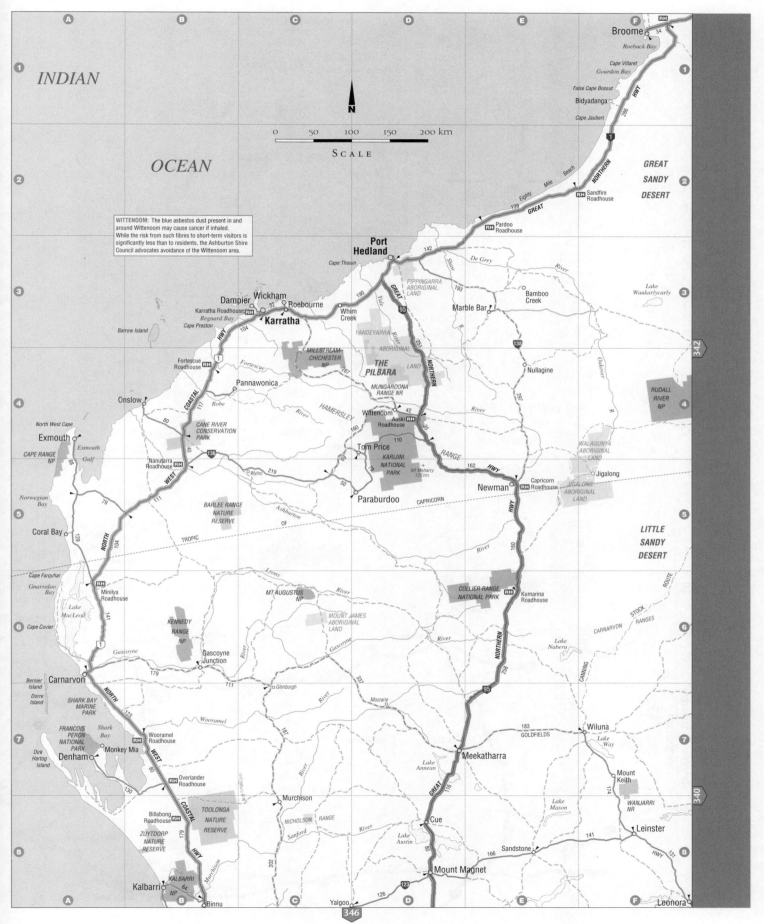

INDIAN

OCEAN

WITTENOOM: The blue asbestos dust present in and around Wittenoom may cause cancer if inhaled. While the risk from such fibres to short-term visitors is significantly less than to residents, the Ashburton Shire Council advocates avoidance of the Wittenoom area.

GREAT SANDY DESERT

Broome
Roebuck Bay
Cape Villaret
Gourdon Bay
False Cape Bossut
Bidyadanga
Cape Jaubert
Eighty Mile Beach
Sandfire Roadhouse
Pardoo Roadhouse

Lake Waukarlycarly

Port Hedland
Cape Thouin
De Grey River
Shaw River
PIPPINGARRA ABORIGINAL LAND
Marble Bar
Bamboo Creek
Nullagine
Oakover River

RUDALL RIVER NP

Dampier
Wickham
Roebourne
Karratha Roadhouse
Regnard Bay
Cape Preston
Karratha
Barrow Island
Whim Creek
YANDEYARRA ABORIGINAL LAND
MILLSTREAM-CHICHESTER NP
THE PILBARA
Fortescue Roadhouse
Fortescue River
Pannawonica
MUNGAROONA RANGE NR
HAMERSLEY
Wittenoom
Auski Roadhouse
WALAGUNYA ABORIGINAL LAND
Robe River
Onslow
Cane River Conservation Park
Tom Price
KARIJINI NATIONAL PARK
Mt Meharry 1251m
RANGE
Jigalong
JIGALONG ABORIGINAL LAND
North West Cape
Exmouth
CAPE RANGE NP
Exmouth Gulf
Nanutarra Roadhouse
Wyloo
Paraburdoo
Newman
Capricorn Roadhouse
HWY
Norwegian Bay
BARLEE RANGE NATURE RESERVE
Ashburton River
OF
Coral Bay
TROPIC
CAPRICORN
LITTLE SANDY DESERT
Cape Farquhar
Gnarraloo Bay
Minilya Roadhouse
MT AUGUSTUS NP
Lyons River
COLLIER RANGE NATIONAL PARK
Kumarina Roadhouse
STOCK ROUTE
Lake MacLeod
Cape Cuvier
KENNEDY RANGE NP
MOUNT JAMES ABORIGINAL LAND
Lake Naberu
CARNARVON RANGES
Gascoyne River
Gascoyne Junction
Bernier Island
Carnarvon
Dorre Island
Glenburgh
Moorarie
CANNING
SHARK BAY MARINE PARK
Wooramel River
Lake Annean
FRANCOIS PERON NATIONAL PARK
Shark Bay
Wooramel Roadhouse
Wiluna
Lake Way
Dirk Hartog Island
Monkey Mia
Denham
GOLDFIELDS
Mount Keith
Overlander Roadhouse
Meekatharra
WANJARRI NR
Billabong Roadhouse
TOOLONGA NATURE RESERVE
Murchison
Lake Mason
ZUYTDORP NATURE RESERVE
NICHOLSON RANGE
Sanford River
Cue
Lake Austin
Sandstone
Leinster
KALBARRI NP
Kalbarri
Binnu
Mount Magnet
Yalgoo
Leonora

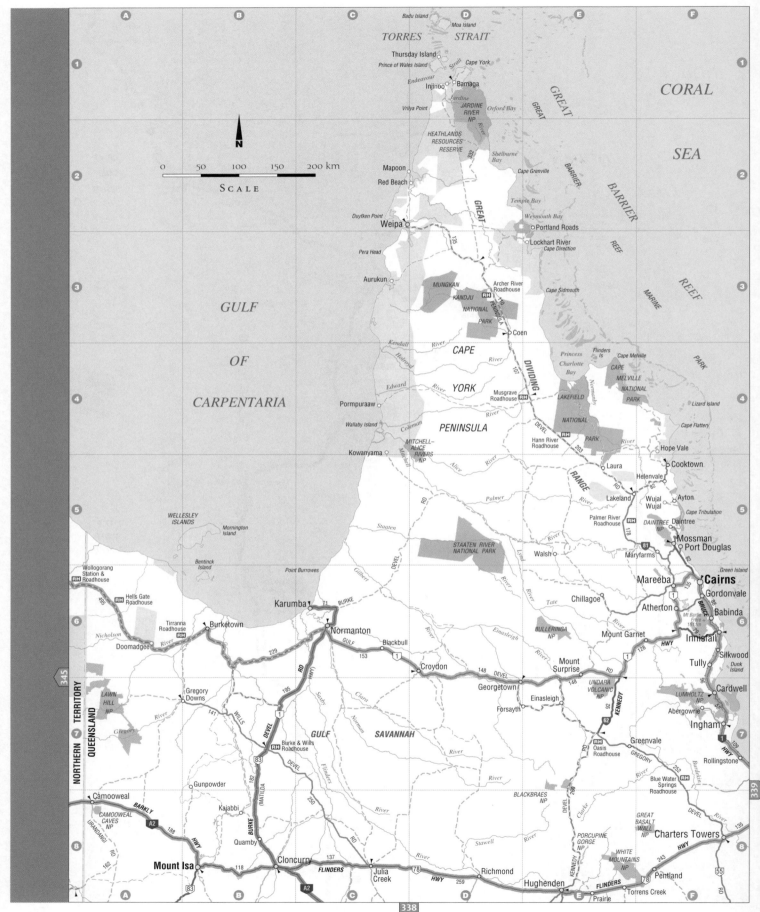

SCALE

0   50   100   150   200 km

N

TORRES STRAIT

Badu Island
Moa Island
Thursday Island
Prince of Wales Island
Cape York
Endeavour Strait
Injinoo Bamaga
Jardine River NP
Vrilya Point
Orford Bay

GREAT

CORAL

Mapoon
Red Beach

Duyfken Point
Weipa

Pera Head

Heathlands Resources Reserve
Shelburne Bay
Cape Grenville
Temple Bay
Weymouth Bay
Portland Roads
Lockhart River
Cape Direction

Aurukun

MUNGKAN KANDJU NATIONAL PARK
Archer River Roadhouse
Cape Sidmouth

Coen

SEA

BARRIER

REEF

MARINE

Pormpuraaw
Wallaby Island

Kowanyama

GULF

OF

CARPENTARIA

CAPE YORK PENINSULA

Kendall River
Holroyd River
Edward River
Coleman River
Mitchell River
MITCHELL-ALICE RIVERS NP
Alice River

GREAT DIVIDING RANGE

Princess Charlotte Bay
Flinders Is
Cape Melville
CAPE MELVILLE NATIONAL PARK
LAKEFIELD NATIONAL PARK
Musgrave Roadhouse
Hann River Roadhouse
Normanby River
Lizard Island
Cape Flattery

PARK

Hope Vale
Cooktown
Helenvale
Laura
Lakeland
Wujal Wujal
Ayton
Cape Tribulation
Palmer River Roadhouse
DAINTREE NP
Daintree
Mossman
Port Douglas

WELLESLEY ISLANDS
Mornington Island
Bentinck Island
Point Burrowes

Staaten River
STAATEN RIVER NATIONAL PARK

Palmer River
Walsh River
Walsh
Maryfarms

Green Island

Mareeba
Cairns
Gordonvale

Wollogorang Station & Roadhouse
Hells Gate Roadhouse
Tirranna Roadhouse
Burketown
Doomadgee
Nicholson River

Karumba
BURKE
Normanton
GULF
Blackbull
Croydon

Gilbert River

Einasleigh River

Chillagoe
BULLERINGA NP
Mount Garnet

Atherton
Mt Bartle Frere
Babinda
Innisfail
Silkwood
Dunk Island
Tully

LAWN HILL NP

NORTHERN TERRITORY
QUEENSLAND

Gregory Downs

Gregory River

GULF

SAVANNAH

Tate River

Mount Surprise
Georgetown
Einasleigh
Forsayth

UNDARA VOLCANIC NP

KENNEDY

Greenvale
Oasis Roadhouse
GREGORY

LUMHOLTZ NP
Abergowrie
Ingham
Rollingstone

Gunpowder
Kajabbi
Burke & Wills Roadhouse

Flinders River
Norman River
Clara River
Saxby River

Cloncurry

Camooweal
CAMOOWEAL CAVES NP
BARKLY HWY
URANDANGI RD

Quamby
Mount Isa
Julia Creek

FLINDERS HWY
Richmond
Hughenden
Prairie
Torrens Creek

BLACKBRAES NP

Clarke River
Stawell River

PORCUPINE GORGE NP
GREAT BASALT WALL NP
WHITE MOUNTAINS NP

Blue Water Springs Roadhouse
Burdekin River

Charters Towers
Pentland

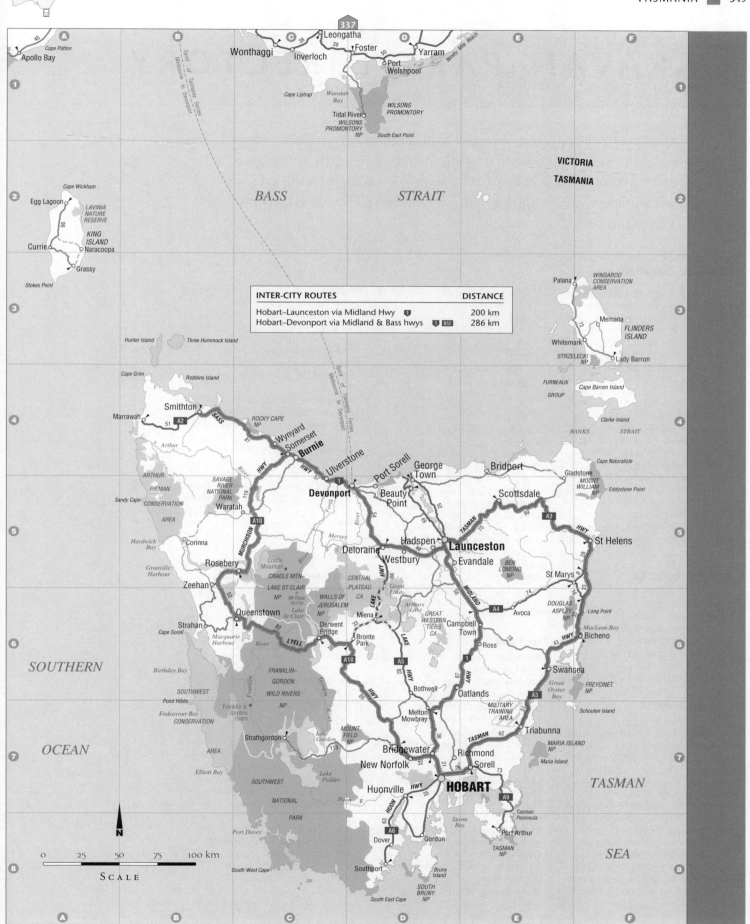

337

A · B · C · D · E · F

Cape Patton
Apollo Bay

1

Wonthaggi   Leongatha
Inverloch   Foster
              Port
              Welshpool   Yarram
Ninety Mile Beach

Cape Liptrap
Waratah Bay
WILSONS PROMONTORY
Tidal River
WILSONS PROMONTORY NP
South East Point

BASS   STRAIT

VICTORIA
TASMANIA

2

Cape Wickham
Egg Lagoon
LAVINIA NATURE RESERVE
KING ISLAND
Currie   Naracoopa
Grassy
Stokes Point

Palana
WINGAROO CONSERVATION AREA

3

Hunter Island   Three Hummock Island

Memana
FLINDERS ISLAND
Whitemark
STRZELECKI NP   Lady Barron

INTER-CITY ROUTES · **DISTANCE**
Hobart–Launceston via Midland Hwy · 1 · 200 km
Hobart–Devonport via Midland & Bass hwys · 1 B52 · 286 km

FURNEAUX GROUP
Cape Barren Island

4

Cape Grim   Robbins Island
Smithton
Marrawah
ROCKY CAPE NP
Wynyard
Somerset
Burnie
A2   BASS   Ulverstone
BASS HWY
Arthur River

ARTHUR PIEMAN CONSERVATION AREA
SAVAGE RIVER NATIONAL PARK
Sandy Cape

Port Sorell   George Town   Bridport
Beauty Point   Gladstone
Scottsdale   MOUNT WILLIAM NP   Eddystone Point
Cape Naturaliste

Clarke Island
BANKS   STRAIT

5

Hardwick Bay   Corinna
Waratah   A10   MURCHISON HWY
Rosebery
Zeehan   Granville Harbour

Cradle Mountain
CRADLE MTN–LAKE ST CLAIR NP
Mt Ossa 1617m
Lake St Clair
WALLS OF JERUSALEM NP
Miena

Deloraine   Hadspen   Launceston
Westbury   Evandale
CENTRAL PLATEAU CA
Great Lake
GREAT WESTERN TIERS CA
Arthurs Lake

TASMAN HWY
BEN LOMOND NP
A3 HWY   St Helens
St Marys
DOUGLAS APSLEY NP   Long Point
MacLean Bay
Bicheno

6

Queenstown   LYELL HWY
Strahan
Cape Sorell   Macquarie Harbour
FRANKLIN–GORDON WILD RIVERS NP
Birthday Bay
Point Hibbs
Franklin & Gordon rivers
Endeavour Bay CONSERVATION AREA

Derwent Bridge   A10
Bronte Park
A5   LAKE HWY
Campbell Town
Ross
A4   Avoca
MIDLAND HWY

Bothwell
Oatlands   MILITARY TRAINING AREA
Swansea
Great Oyster Bay
FREYCINET NP
Schouten Island

7

SOUTHERN   OCEAN
SOUTHWEST CONSERVATION AREA
Strathgordon
Lake Gordon
MOUNT FIELD NP
Elliott Bay
Lake Pedder
SOUTHWEST NATIONAL PARK
Port Davey

Melton Mowbray
Bridgewater   Richmond   Triabunna
New Norfolk   Sorell
MARIA ISLAND NP
Maria Island

Huonville   HUON HWY
HOBART   A9
TASMAN   SEA

8

SCALE
0 · 25 · 50 · 75 · 100 km
South West Cape

Dover   A6
Gordon
Southport   Bruny Island   SOUTH BRUNY NP
South East Cape

Tasman Peninsula
Port Arthur
TASMAN NP
Storm Bay

TASMAN

A · B · C · D · E · F

CARAVAN PARK DIRECTORY

This directory is our independent assessment of the best caravan parks on or near the tour routes. We have provided details on all the parks we recommend (those indicated by a purple caravan symbol on the tour maps). Our recommendation is based on factors such as facilities, cleanliness, service and location – no park has paid to be in this directory or any other part of this book.

How to use this directory

It was often difficult to work out what place-name a park entry should come under, especially for those not near a town or city centre. Our policy has been to be as specific as possible. For a park attached to an outback roadhouse on the map, look under the name of that roadhouse. For a park attached to a landmark or place of interest and not within 5–10 km of a town, look under the name of that landmark or place of interest. However, for those parks that are attached to a landmark or place of interest close to a town, look under the name of the town. For parks in cities and urban areas such as the Gold Coast, look under the name of the city not the suburb. And parks within national parks come under the name of the national park, except if they are located in a town inside the national park. If you are unsure of what place-name to look under, our extensive cross-referencing should help you.

Authors' choice

All the parks in this directory are recommended by us, but there are some that are our stand-out favourites. We have called these parks the Authors' choice parks – ones that we especially recommend – and marked them with a star. These parks are also included in a special feature at the front of the book called Our favourite parks (see page xii).

Prices/seasons

Symbols represent the starting price for a powered site for two people per night. (Prices were correct at the time of going to press.) Prices in peak seasons and school holidays will often differ, and peak seasons differ around the country. In southern Australia the tourist season runs from October to April, peaking around December and January. In northern Australia the tourist season is roughly the reverse. For the far north of Australia, such as Darwin, Cairns and Kununurra, the period from April to October is their dry season. The rest of the year is the wet season, with extremely high humidity that most visitors find unbearable.

Parks will often have peak and off-peak rates based on their seasons.

$⑤$ = free
$\$$ = under \$13
$\$\$$ = \$13–\$18
$\$\$\$$ = \$18–\$24
$\$\$\$\$$ = \$24 and over

Sites

Tent sites: area for tents, usually unpowered.
Powered sites: powered sites for caravans.
Drive-thru sites: sites that a caravan and towing vehicle (or a motorhome) can drive in and out of without reversing or unhitching.
Ensuite sites: powered sites with individual amenities.
Fits big motorhomes: has sites that accommodate motorhomes over 9 m in length; phone before arrival as these sites may be limited.
Cabins: on-site accommodation for rent (separate to on-site vans) such as cabins, chalets, villas, dongas, motel rooms.
On-site vans: on-site caravans for rent.

Facilities

Toilets: toilets, which in the case of national parks may be pit or dry-mulch.
Showers: showers, which in the case of national parks may be cold only.
Disabled access: wheelchair access to shower and toilet blocks, often a designated disabled bathroom.
Laundry: washing tubs, a washing machine and a clothesline nearby; may have a clothes dryer.
Sewer dump-point: location where the contents of chemical toilets and motorhome blackwater tanks can be emptied.
Telephone: public telephone available; may be up to 100 m outside the park.
Kiosk/shop: shop that sells some grocery lines; may be up to 100 m outside the park.
LP gas refills: LP gas available; may be at a business up to 100 m outside the park.

Ice: ice available; may be at a business up to 100 m outside the park.
Camp kitchen: camp kitchen with a minimum of a stove, a refrigerator and a sink with hot and cold water; may also have a barbecue and microwave.
Pool: swimming pool; may be a public swimming pool up to 100 m outside the park.
Playground: playground for children; may be up to 100 m outside the park.
Boat ramp: boat ramp within the park's boundary or up to 500 m outside the park.
TV cables: a TV plug in the power boxes of some powered sites, enabling free-to-air television reception.
Internet terminal: a computer set up with the internet and available for use, usually for a fee.
Pets: pets permitted; park policies differ so pet owners should check policy prior to arrival.

Bookings/payment details

Bookings required: most parks will require bookings for powered sites in their peak and holiday periods; listed here only if applicable year-round.
Credit cards: major credit cards accepted, usually Visa, Bankcard and MasterCard; minimum transactions in some cases.
Holiday loading: rates for sites are higher in a park's peak period/s.
Pensioners: discounts for aged pensioners; may be offered only in the off-peak season.
Seniors: discounts for seniors-card holders; may be offered only in the off-peak season.
2nd night: discount on nightly rate offered for the 2nd night of stay; other variations include 3rd, 4th and 5th night discounts.
Weekly: discounts for a booking of one week, for example 7 nights for the price of 6; may be offered only in the off-peak season.
Big4, Top Tourist, Family Parks of Australia (FPA): three national chains that we have recognised; each offer their members a discount along with other services.

ADAMINABY (NSW)

See Anglers Reach and Old Adaminaby.

ADELAIDE (SA) p. 129

Adelaide Beachfront Tourist Park

349 Military Road, Semaphore Park 5019
Ph (08) 8449 7726 or 1800 810 140,
fax (08) 8449 5877
Email info@adelaidebeachfront.com.au
Website www.adelaidebeachfront.com.au

With very good amenities and a wide range of facilities, this quality park is close to the Port Adelaide region, Football Park and the West Lakes shopping complex, as well as only 10 km from the city centre. It is one of Adelaide's most popular beachfront parks. Facilities include two pools and a free shuttle bus that runs four times a day to the train station and beyond. $$$

❑ Tent sites, powered sites, ensuite sites, fits big motorhomes, cabins.

❑ Toilets and showers, laundry, sewer dump-point, telephone, kiosk/shop, LP gas refills, ice, pool, playground, no pets.

❑ Credit cards, holiday loading. Discounts: weekly, Top Tourist.

Brighton Caravan Park and Holiday Village

Burnham Road, Kingston Park 5049
Ph (08) 8377 0833, fax (08) 8377 0628
Email brighton@senet.com.au
Website www.brightoncaravanpark.com.au

Just 17 km from Adelaide city, this tourist park enjoys absolute beach frontage and has a nice, relaxed feel. It is a popular family park and bookings are essential during the busy holiday periods. $$$

❑ Tent sites, powered sites, drive-thru sites, fits big motorhomes, cabins.

❑ Toilets and showers (disabled access), laundry, sewer dump-point, telephone, kiosk/shop, LP gas refills, ice, camp kitchen, playground, boat ramp, no pets.

❑ Credit cards, holiday loading. Discounts: weekly, FPA.

Brownhill Creek Caravan Park

Brownhill Creek Road, Mitcham 5062
Ph (08) 8271 4824 or 1800 626 493,
fax (08) 8373 2293
Email info@brownhillcreekcaravanpark.com.au
Website www.brownhillcreekcaravanpark.com.au

This picturesque owner-operated park is set in the Adelaide foothills, 7 km south-east of the city. Its 120-acre bushland setting offers lots of shade and the facilities include a TV room, a pool and a tennis court. A minimum booking applies during holiday periods. $$$

❑ Tent sites, powered sites, drive-thru sites, ensuite sites, fits big motorhomes, cabins, on-site vans.

❑ Toilets and showers, laundry, telephone, kiosk/shop, LP gas refills, ice, pool, playground, TV cables, no pets.

❑ Credit cards, holiday loading. Discounts: seniors, weekly, Top Tourist.

◎ Levi Park Caravan Park

69 Lansdowne Terrace, Walkerville 5081
Ph (08) 8344 2209 or 1800 442 209,
fax (08) 8342 5733
Email contact@levipark.com.au
Website www.levipark.com.au

Levi Park is just 6 km from the city and a very good base for exploring central Adelaide. It has shady caravan sites and pleasant grassed tent sites, all located in a magnificent historic garden. The River Torrens flows by the park. $$$

❑ Tent sites, powered sites, fits big motorhomes, cabins.

❑ Toilets and showers (disabled access), laundry, sewer dump-point, telephone, kiosk/shop, LP gas refills, ice, camp kitchen, playground, no pets.

❑ Bookings required, credit cards, holiday loading. Discounts: weekly, Big4.

Marion Holiday Park

323 Sturt Road, Bedford Park 5042
Ph (08) 8276 6695 or 1800 063 193,
fax (08) 8357 4330
Email bookings@marionholidaypark.com.au
Website www.marionholidaypark.com.au

This tourist park in the southern suburbs is close to the enormous Marion shopping centre. It has very good amenities, shaded areas and good facilities including a recreation room and a tennis court. It makes a good base from which to explore Adelaide or a convenient park for a short stay. A minimum booking is required at Christmas, Easter and long weekends. $$$

❑ Tent sites, powered sites, ensuite sites, fits big motorhomes, cabins.

❑ Toilets and showers (disabled access), laundry, sewer dump-point, telephone, kiosk/shop, LP gas refills, ice, camp kitchen, pool, playground, no pets.

❑ Credit cards, holiday loading. Discounts: weekly, Big4.

ADELAIDE RIVER (NT) p. 74

Mount Bundy Station Homestead

Haynes Road, Adelaide River 0846
Ph (08) 8976 7009, fax (08) 8976 7113
Email mt.bundy@octa4.net.au

This is a unique riverfront farmstay camping area, 3 km from Adelaide River, with basic but good amenities. The station raises water buffaloes for export and horseriding is on offer during the tourist season. The camping area is nicely grassed and close to the homestead. $$$

❑ Tent sites, powered sites, drive-thru sites, fits big motorhomes, cabins.

❑ Toilets and showers (disabled access), laundry, telephone, ice, camp kitchen, pool, no pets.

❑ Bookings required, credit cards. Discounts: weekly.

AIREYS INLET (VIC) p. 139

Aireys Inlet Holiday Park

19 Great Ocean Road, Aireys Inlet 3231
Ph (03) 5289 6230 or 1800 668 866,
fax (03) 5289 7399
Email info@aicp.com.au
Website www.aicp.com.au

Located on the Great Ocean Road just 100 m from the town centre, this quality park has a wide range of facilities. Minimum bookings apply during the Christmas, January and Easter holiday periods. We have always enjoyed our stays here. $$$

❑ Tent sites, powered sites, drive-thru sites, ensuite sites, fits big motorhomes, cabins.

❑ Toilets and showers, laundry, sewer dump-point, telephone, LP gas refills, ice, camp kitchen, pool, playground, internet terminal, no pets.

❑ Credit cards, holiday loading. Discounts: weekly, Top Tourist.

AIRLIE BEACH (QLD) p. 53

See also Shute Harbour.

Adventure Whitsunday Resort Caravan Park

25–29 Shute Harbour Road, Airlie Beach 4802
Ph (07) 4946 1166 or 1800 640 587,
fax (07) 4946 1595
Email resort@whitsunday.net.au
Website www.adventurewhitsunday.com.au

This is a very good quality park in an exceptionally popular holiday destination. The park has many features including a pool, a kids club, a boat park and mini-golf. $$$

❑ Tent sites, powered sites, drive-thru sites, fits big motorhomes, cabins, on-site vans.

❑ Toilets and showers (disabled access), laundry, sewer dump-point, telephone, kiosk/shop, LP gas refills, ice, camp kitchen, pool, playground, TV cables, internet terminal, no pets.

❑ Credit cards, holiday loading. Discounts: weekly, Big4.

ALBANY (WA) p. 115

See also Cheyne Beach.

Emu Beach Holiday Park

8 Medcalf Parade, Albany 6330
Ph (08) 9844 1147 or 1800 984 411,
fax (08) 9844 8662
Email ebhp@iinet.net.au
Website www.emubeach.com

This quality, popular beachside park is 7 km from the centre of Albany. It has a wide range of facilities including a shop, a games room and mini-golf. Bookings are necessary in peak holiday periods. $$$

❑ Tent sites, powered sites, fits big motorhomes, cabins.

❑ Toilets and showers (disabled access), laundry, sewer dump-point, telephone, kiosk/shop, LP gas refills, ice, camp kitchen, playground, no pets.

❑ Bookings required, credit cards, holiday loading. Discounts: weekly, Top Tourist.

Kalgan River Chalets and Caravan Park

Nanarup Road, Albany 6330
Ph (08) 9844 7937 or 1800 447 937,
fax (08) 9844 8202

Situated 11 km east of Albany on the Kalgan River, this park suits travellers looking for plenty of space. There are large sites and big rigs can be accommodated. Its features include a cafe, canoes for hire, a nine-hole golf course and a tennis court. $$

❑ Tent sites, powered sites, drive-thru sites, fits big motorhomes, cabins, on-site vans.

❑ Toilets and showers (disabled access), laundry, telephone, kiosk/shop, LP gas refills, ice, camp kitchen, playground, boat ramp, TV cables, no pets.

❑ Credit cards, holiday loading. Discounts: weekly, FPA.

◎ Middleton Beach Caravan Park

28 Flinders Parade, Albany 6330
Ph (08) 9841 3593 or 1800 644 674,
fax (08) 9842 2088
Email big4@iinet.com.au
Website www.holidayalbany.com

A great place for a holiday, this quality park has a fabulous position and fronts onto 500 m of a popular swimming beach. Just 3 km from the Albany post office, it has good amenities and a range of facilities including a new TV room. Albany is a premier holiday destination and bookings are necessary in peak periods. $$$

❑ Tent sites, powered sites, fits big motorhomes, cabins.

❑ Toilets and showers (disabled access), laundry, sewer dump-point, telephone, kiosk/shop, LP gas refills, ice, camp kitchen, playground, internet terminal, no pets.

❑ Credit cards, holiday loading. Discounts: weekly, Big4.

Mount Melville Caravan Park

22 Wellington Street (off Albany Highway), Albany 6330
Ph (08) 9841 4616 or 1800 888 617,
fax (08) 9841 4806
Email annetah@iinet.com.au

The closest park to the centre of Albany, this is a good-quality place with a well-stocked shop, a tennis court and a native animal enclosure. The park is in a quiet, off-the-main-road position, well protected from the prevailing winds. $$$

❏ Tent sites, powered sites, drive-thru sites, ensuite sites, fits big motorhomes, cabins, on-site vans.

❏ Toilets and showers (disabled access), laundry, sewer dump-point, telephone, kiosk/shop, LP gas refills, ice, camp kitchen, playground, internet terminal, no pets.

❏ Credit cards, holiday loading. Discounts: weekly, Big4.

ALBURY (NSW) p. 216

See also Wodonga.

Albury Caravanna Caravan Park

443 Wagga Road, Lavington 2641
Ph (02) 6025 1489, fax (02) 6040 0838
Email lovescaravanna@hotkey.net.au

This small park is conveniently located on the Hume Highway (Wagga Road) close to the clubs and shopping centre of Lavington, on the northern outskirts of greater Albury. $$

❏ Tent sites, powered sites, drive-thru sites, ensuite sites, fits big motorhomes, cabins, on-site vans.

❏ Toilets and showers, laundry, sewer dump-point, telephone, kiosk/shop, LP gas refills, ice, pool, pets.

❏ Bookings required, credit cards, holiday loading. Discounts: seniors, weekly.

Albury Central Tourist Park

286 North Street, Albury 2640
Ph (02) 6021 8420, fax (02) 6021 8420

This centrally located park is about 2 km from the city centre in a quiet, off-highway location. It has good facilities including a pool and a tennis court. There are sufficient basic amenities and it is a good base for exploring the Albury area. $$

❏ Tent sites, powered sites, drive-thru sites, fits big motorhomes, cabins.

❏ Toilets and showers, laundry, sewer dump-point, telephone, kiosk/shop, LP gas refills, ice, pool, playground, pets.

❏ Credit cards, holiday loading. Discounts: weekly.

Lake Hume Tourist Park

Riverina Highway, Lake Hume Village 2640
Ph (02) 6026 4677, fax (02) 6026 4081
Email lakehume@albury.net.au
Website www.lakehume.albury.net.au

On the shores of Lake Hume and 14 km from Albury, this park makes an ideal holiday base. It features a licensed bistro, tennis courts, pool and general store, with a good takeaway-food selection. Minimum bookings apply on long weekends and at Easter. $$$

❏ Tent sites, powered sites, fits big motorhomes, cabins.

❏ Toilets and showers (disabled access), laundry, telephone, kiosk/shop, LP gas refills, ice, pool, playground, boat ramp, no pets.

❏ Credit cards, holiday loading. Discounts: weekly, FPA.

Trek 31 Tourist Park

Corner Wagga Road and Catherine Crescent, Lavington 2641
Ph (02) 6025 4355, fax (02) 6025 5051
Email trek31@austarnet.com.au

Located on the northern outskirts of greater Albury, this is a convenient park with good facilities, great for an overnight stay or longer. $$$

❏ Tent sites, powered sites, drive-thru sites, ensuite sites, fits big motorhomes, cabins.

❏ Toilets and showers, laundry, sewer dump-point, telephone, kiosk/shop, LP gas refills, ice, camp kitchen, pool, playground, pets.

❏ Bookings required, credit cards, holiday loading. Discounts: 5th night, Top Tourist.

ALEXANDRA BRIDGE (WA) p. 112

Alexandra Bridge Camping Ground

Alexandra Bridge Road (off Brockman Highway), via Karridale 6288

This large open camping area alongside the Blackwood River is 11 km east of Karridale. It is a quiet area that will suit self-sufficient campers for a convenient overnight stop or a couple of days rest. The turn-off to the camping ground is well signposted on the east side of the river. $

❏ Tent sites, fits big motorhomes.

❏ Toilets, boat ramp, pets.

❏ No credit cards.

ALICE SPRINGS (NT) pp. 189, 193

See also Ross River.

G'day Mate Tourist Park

Palm Circuit, Alice Springs 0870
Ph (08) 8952 9589, fax (08) 8952 2612

With its barbecues, pool and clean amenities, this is one of the parks we stay at when we visit Alice each year. The park does not cater for tourist buses or school groups, which normally means it is fairly quiet. The park can be busy, however, and bookings are required in the popular winter months. $$$

❏ Tent sites, powered sites, ensuite sites, fits big motorhomes, cabins, on-site vans.

❏ Toilets and showers, laundry, sewer dump-point, telephone, kiosk/shop, LP gas refills, ice, camp kitchen, pool, internet terminal, no pets.

❏ Credit cards, holiday loading. Discounts: pensioners, seniors, weekly.

◉ MacDonnell Range Holiday Park

Palm Place, Alice Springs 0870
Ph (08) 8952 6111 or 1800 808 373, fax (08) 8952 5236
Email macrange@macrange.com.au
Website www.macrange.com.au

Enjoy a delicious, free pancake breakfast every Sunday morning at this large, quality park – one of the Alice Springs parks we choose to stay at. It has numerous activities during the tourist season (April to October), including nightly talks on the stars, bush tucker and other subjects, and has a great range of tourist park facilities. Located 4.5 km south of the city centre, it is a great base for exploring the region. Bookings are essential in the tourist season. $$$

❏ Tent sites, powered sites, drive-thru sites, ensuite sites, fits big motorhomes, cabins.

❏ Toilets and showers (disabled access), laundry, sewer dump-point, telephone, kiosk/shop, LP gas refills, ice, camp kitchen, pool, playground, internet terminal, no pets.

❏ Credit cards, holiday loading. Discounts: weekly, Big4.

Wintersun Gardens Caravan Park

Stuart Highway, Alice Springs 0870
Ph (08) 8952 4080, fax (08) 8952 4588

Located on the Stuart Highway on the north side of Alice Springs, this tourist park's facilities include a pool and barbecue area, and there are pleasant, shady grassed sites. This is a quality park and also a good base for exploring this central Australian region. Good access to the highway is a feature of the park. $$$

❏ Tent sites, powered sites, drive-thru sites, fits big motorhomes, cabins.

❏ Toilets and showers, laundry, sewer dump-point, telephone, LP gas refills, camp kitchen, pool, no pets.

❏ Credit cards. Discounts: pensioners, weekly.

ANGLERS REACH (NSW) p. 216

Providence Holiday Park

Snowy Mountains Highway, Adaminaby 2630
Ph (02) 6454 2357, fax (02) 6454 2420
Email svensan@snowy.net.au

This park, on the banks of Lake Eucumbene and 17 km from Adaminaby, is popular for trout fishing. It has a large number of unpowered sites and only a few powered sites available to tourists. The park is also popular during winter months with cross-country skiers visiting the nearby Mount Selwyn ski fields. There is fishing boat hire on site and a shop with a good range of fishing tackle. $$$

❏ Tent sites, powered sites, cabins, on-site vans.

❏ Toilets and showers, laundry, telephone, kiosk/shop, LP gas refills, ice, boat ramp, pets.

❏ Credit cards, holiday loading.

ANGLESEA (VIC) p. 139

Anglesea Family Caravan Park

Cameron Road, Anglesea 3230
Ph (03) 5263 1583 or 1800 040 455, fax (03) 5263 3055
Email info@angleseafcp.com.au
Website www.angleseafcp.com.au

This large beachfront and riverfront park is centrally located and just 500 m from the town centre. It has large expanses of lawn, shady sites and a range of good facilities. Minimum bookings apply during the Christmas and Easter holiday periods. $$$

❏ Tent sites, powered sites, drive-thru sites, fits big motorhomes, cabins.

❏ Toilets and showers (disabled access), laundry, sewer dump-point, telephone, LP gas refills, ice, camp kitchen, playground, no pets.

❏ Credit cards, holiday loading. Discounts: Top Tourist.

ANNA BAY (NSW) p. 28

◉ One Mile Beach Holiday Park

260 Gan Gan Road, Anna Bay 2316
Ph (02) 4982 1112 or 1800 650 035, fax (02) 4982 2832
Email ombhp@bmr.net.au
Website www.onemilebeach.com

This quality, award-winning caravan park is located in the popular Port Stephens region, just a few kilometres south of Nelson Bay. Set alongside a popular patrolled surf beach, it has excellent amenities and great recreational facilities including mini-golf, a tennis court and a resort-style swimming pool. A real favourite with us – we always enjoy staying here. $$$

❏ Tent sites, powered sites, drive-thru sites, ensuite sites, fits big motorhomes, cabins.

❏ Toilets and showers (disabled access), laundry, sewer dump-point, telephone, kiosk/shop, LP gas refills, ice, camp kitchen, pool, playground, TV cables, no pets.

❏ Credit cards, holiday loading. Discounts: seniors, weekly, Top Tourist.

ANNABURROO (NT) p. 80

Bark Hut Caravan Park

Arnhem Highway, Annaburroo 0822
Ph (08) 8978 8988, fax (08) 8978 8932
Email barkhutinn@bigpond.com

This popular, convenient roadhouse and caravan park complex is roughly midway between Jabiru and Darwin's suburbs. $$$

❏ Tent sites, powered sites, drive-thru sites, fits big motorhomes.

❏ Toilets and showers (disabled access), laundry, sewer dump-point, telephone, kiosk/shop, LP gas refills, ice, pool, no pets.

❏ Credit cards. Discounts: weekly, seniors.

APOLLO BAY (VIC) p. 138

Pisces Caravan Resort

311 Great Ocean Road, Apollo Bay 3233
Ph (03) 5237 6749, fax (03) 5237 6326
Website www.greatoceanroad.org/pisces

This is a quality park with a range of accommodation and a great outlook. Situated on a rise overlooking the sea, it is 1.5 km to the town centre and only a short stroll to the beach. The park has minimum booking periods during Christmas and Easter holidays. $$$

❏ Tent sites, powered sites, fits big motorhomes, cabins.

❏ Toilets and showers (disabled access), laundry, telephone, ice, camp kitchen, playground, TV cables, no pets.

❏ Credit cards, holiday loading. Discounts: weekly.

ARARAT (VIC) p. 230

Acacia Caravan Park

6 Acacia Avenue, Ararat 3377
Ph (03) 5352 2994, fax (03) 5352 1733
Email acacia@netconnect.com.au

This is a good, basic, budget-priced park near the highway and close to the town centre. The park has a solar-heated pool, covered barbecues and a range of accommodation. We think this is a good park at a good price. **$$**

❏ Tent sites, powered sites, drive-thru sites, fits big motorhomes, cabins, on-site vans.

❏ Toilets and showers, laundry, kiosk/shop, LP gas refills, ice, camp kitchen, pool, playground, pets.

❏ Credit cards. Discounts: weekly, FPA.

ARRAWARRA (NSW) p. 32

Arrawarra Beach Holiday Park
46 Arrawarra Beach Road, Arrawarra 2456
Ph (02) 6649 2753, fax (02) 6649 1270
Email thebiga@midcoast.com.au

A popular budget-priced, beachfront park with good facilities, it is the closest recommended park to the centre of Arrawarra. **$$$**

❏ Tent sites, powered sites, fits big motorhomes, cabins, on-site vans.

❏ Toilets and showers, laundry, telephone, kiosk/shop, LP gas refills, ice, camp kitchen, boat ramp, no pets.

❏ Credit cards, holiday loading. Discounts: weekly.

Darlington Beach Resort
104–134 Eggins Drive, Arrawarra 2456
Ph (02) 6649 2977 or 1800 888 999,
fax (02) 6649 2480
Email darlo@bigpond.com

This popular park, a few kilometres north of Arrawarra, has very good quality facilities. It has absolute beach frontage, a restaurant and its own nine-hole golf course, tennis courts, outdoor bowling area and archery range. **$$$$**

❏ Tent sites, powered sites, drive-thru sites, ensuite sites, fits big motorhomes, cabins, on-site vans.

❏ Toilets and showers (disabled access), laundry, sewer dump-point, telephone, kiosk/shop, LP gas refills, ice, camp kitchen, pool, playground, internet terminal, no pets.

❏ Bookings required, credit cards, holiday loading. Discounts: weekly, Big4.

The Lorikeet Tourist Park
Old Pacific Highway, Arrawarra 2456
Ph (02) 6649 2717 or 1800 555 858,
fax (02) 6649 2811
Email lorikeet@midcoast.com.au
Website www.lorikeet.contact.com.au

This wonderful park has excellent facilities, including a games room and tennis, basketball and volleyball courts. It is easily accessible from the highway, with good access to long stretches of beach. This park is very close to the Darlington Beach Resort. **$$$**

❏ Tent sites, powered sites, drive-thru sites, ensuite sites, fits big motorhomes, cabins.

❏ Toilets and showers (disabled access), laundry, sewer dump-point, telephone, kiosk/shop, LP gas refills, ice, camp kitchen, pool, playground, no pets.

❏ Bookings required, credit cards, holiday loading. Discounts: weekly, Top Tourist.

ATHERTON (QLD) p. 64

Atherton Woodlands Tourist Park
141 Herberton Road, Atherton 4883
Ph (07) 4091 1407, fax (07) 4091 3449

On the outskirts of Atherton, about 2 km from the town centre, this tidy park has large shady trees and makes a good base for a few days of exploring the area. **$$$**

❏ Tent sites, powered sites, drive-thru sites, fits big motorhomes, cabins.

❏ Toilets and showers (disabled access), laundry, sewer dump-point, telephone, LP gas refills, camp kitchen, pool, no pets.

❏ Credit cards. Discounts: weekly.

AUGATHELLA (QLD) pp. 170, 254

Augathella Motel and Caravan Park
Landsborough (Matilda) Highway,
Augathella 4477
Ph (07) 4654 5177, fax (07) 4654 5353

This is a good owner-operated park with basic facilities, ideal for an overnight stop. It is conveniently located next to the BP roadhouse on the highway, where meals are available around the clock. **$$**

❏ Tent sites, powered sites, drive-thru sites, fits big motorhomes.

❏ Toilets and showers, laundry, sewer dump-point, telephone, LP gas refills, ice, pets.

❏ Credit cards.

AUGUSTA (WA) p. 112

Doonbanks Caravan Park
Blackwood Avenue, Augusta 6290
Ph (08) 9758 1517, fax (08) 9758 1517
Email doonbank@netserv.net.au
Website www.netserv.net.au/doonbank

On the waterfront and close to the town centre, this park has easy access to the beach, great for surfing, windsurfing and fishing. The park has good basic facilities. **$$**

❏ Tent sites, powered sites, fits big motorhomes, cabins, on-site vans.

❏ Toilets and showers, laundry, telephone, camp kitchen, playground, boat ramp, pets.

❏ Credit cards, holiday loading. Discounts: weekly.

Turner Caravan Park
1 Blackwood Avenue, Augusta 6290
Ph (08) 9758 1593, fax (08) 9758 1593
Email turnercp@amrsc.wa.gov.au

This is a large waterfront park in the heart of town, with wide sprawling lawns and all the usual holiday park features. **$$**

❏ Tent sites, powered sites, drive-thru sites, fits big motorhomes.

❏ Toilets and showers (disabled access), laundry, sewer dump-point, telephone, boat ramp, no pets.

❏ Credit cards, holiday loading. Discounts: pensioners, seniors.

AUSKI ROADHOUSE (WA) p. 204

Auski Tourist Village
Corner Great Northern Highway and
Wittenoom Road, Munjina
Ph (08) 9176 6988, fax (08) 9176 6973

The park is part of the Auski Roadhouse complex and a convenient base from which to explore Wittenoom and the surrounding Pilbara gorges. This good basic caravan park can be reached along bitumen roads whereas some of the nearby national park camping areas require travel on often badly corrugated roads. Helicopter flights over Karijini National Park operate from here during the tourist season. **$$$**

❏ Tent sites, powered sites, drive-thru sites, fits big motorhomes.

❏ Toilets and showers (disabled access), laundry, telephone, kiosk/shop, LP gas refills, ice, camp kitchen, pets.

❏ Credit cards.

AYERS ROCK (NT)

See Yulara.

AYR (QLD) p. 52

Silver Link Caravan Village
34 Norham Road, Ayr 4807
Ph (07) 4783 3933 or 1800 335 261,
fax (07) 4783 5015
Email silverlink@tpg.com.au

This park is in a quiet, off-highway position and has recently upgraded its amenities. **$$$**

❏ Tent sites, powered sites, drive-thru sites, fits big motorhomes, cabins, on-site vans.

❏ Toilets and showers (disabled access), laundry, telephone, kiosk/shop, LP gas refills, ice, camp kitchen, pool, playground, no pets.

❏ Credit cards. Discounts: weekly, Big4.

BAIRNSDALE (VIC) p. 6

Mitchell Gardens Holiday Park
2 Main Street, Bairnsdale 3875
Ph (03) 5152 4654, fax (03) 5152 3294
Email mitchell.gardens@net-tech.com.au

This park is located at the river end of the main street (Princes Highway), just 500 m from the centre of town. With beautifully maintained surrounds, the park is located on the banks of the Mitchell River. It has good amenities and the facilities include a heated pool. **$$**

❏ Tent sites, powered sites, drive-thru sites, fits big motorhomes, cabins.

❏ Toilets and showers (disabled access), laundry, telephone, LP gas refills, ice, pool, playground, no pets.

❏ Credit cards, holiday loading. Discounts: weekly.

BALGAL (QLD) p. 54

Balgal Beach Camping Area
Balgal 4816

This small area offers free camping for a maximum of 48 hours. 🄢

❏ Tent sites, drive-thru sites, fits big motorhomes.

❏ Toilets (disabled access), telephone, kiosk/shop, LP gas refills, ice, boat ramp, pets.

BALLARAT (VIC) p. 228

A Ballarat Windmill Holiday Park
Remembrance Drive (Avenue of Honour),
Alfredton 3350
Ph (03) 5334 1686 or 1800 256 633,
fax (03) 5334 1559
Email windmill@qonline.com.au
Website www.ballaratwindmill.com.au

This well-established, quality park is in a quiet rural area 6 km west of the city on the old Western Highway. It has a great range of facilities including a spa, sauna, tennis court and recreation room. Minimum bookings apply on long weekends and during Easter holidays. **$$$**

❏ Tent sites, powered sites, drive-thru sites, ensuite sites, fits big motorhomes, cabins, on-site vans.

❏ Toilets and showers, laundry, telephone, kiosk/shop, camp kitchen, pool, playground, no pets.

❏ Credit cards, holiday loading. Discounts: Big4.

A Welcome Stranger Holiday Park
Corner Water Street and Scott Parade,
Ballarat 3350
Ph (03) 5332 7722 or 1800 622 777,
fax (03) 5331 2062
Email welcome@welcomestranger.com.au
Website www.welcomestranger.com.au

Located 2.5 km east of Ballarat, this is a good quality park in a quiet, easily accessible area on the east of the city. The park has a large number of sites, a heated pool, a spa, mini-golf, an adventure playground and a tennis court. We sometimes stay here as it is a good base from which to explore the area. Minimum bookings apply during special events, long weekends and Easter holidays. **$$$**

❏ Tent sites, powered sites, drive-thru sites, ensuite sites, fits big motorhomes, cabins.

❏ Toilets and showers, laundry, sewer dump-point, telephone, kiosk/shop, LP gas refills, ice, camp kitchen, pool, playground, internet terminal, no pets.

❏ Credit cards, holiday loading. Discounts: weekly, Big4.

⊙ Ballarat Goldfields Holiday Park
108 Clayton Street, Ballarat 3350
Ph (03) 5332 7888 or 1800 632 237,
fax (03) 5332 4244
Email stay@ballaratgoldfields.com.au
Website www.ballaratgoldfields.com.au

Centrally located (only 2 km from the city centre) and easily accessible, this quality tourist park has a wide range of accommodation and very good facilities, including a heated pool and spa, free barbecues, bathrooms for children and families, and recreation rooms. We especially like it because it is just a short distance from Sovereign Hill, one of Ballarat's major tourist attractions and our favourite place to visit in the area. **$$$**

❏ Tent sites, powered sites, drive-thru sites, ensuite sites, fits big motorhomes, cabins.

❑ Toilets and showers, laundry, sewer dump-point, telephone, LP gas refills, camp kitchen, pool, playground, internet terminal, no pets.

❑ Bookings required, credit cards, holiday loading. Discounts: Big4.

Lake Wendouree Tourist Park
195 Gillies Street, Ballarat 3350
Ph (03) 5338 1381 or 1800 333 994,
fax (03) 5339 4327
Email lakewendouree@giant.net.au
Website www.ballarat.com/lwtp.htm

This central park is a short distance from the spectacular Ballarat Botanical Gardens, Lake Wendouree and the Wendouree shopping centre. It is a very good quality park offering a good range of facilities including a solar-heated swimming pool, a tennis court and covered barbecues. A popular walking track circumnavigates the nearby lake. **$$$**

❑ Tent sites, powered sites, drive-thru sites, ensuite sites, fits big motorhomes, cabins.

❑ Toilets and showers, laundry, sewer dump-point, telephone, kiosk/shop, LP gas refills, ice, camp kitchen, pool, playground, internet terminal, no pets.

❑ Credit cards. Discounts: Top Tourist.

BALLINA (NSW) p. 32

Ballina Central Caravan Park
1 River Street, Ballina 2478
Ph (02) 6686 2220, fax (02) 6681 6340
Email central@lis.net.au

This park is across the road from the water, at the end of the main street and just walking distance from the shops. The park has good amenities and good basic facilities. **$$$**

❑ Tent sites, powered sites, fits big motorhomes, cabins.

❑ Toilets and showers (disabled access), laundry, telephone, LP gas refills, ice, boat ramp, no pets.

❑ Bookings required, credit cards, holiday loading. Discounts: weekly.

Ballina Headlands Leisure Park
Skennars Head Road, Ballina 2478
Ph (02) 6687 7450 or 1800 181 208,
fax (02) 6687 7165
Email bhlp@bigpond.net.au
Website www.ballina-headlands. contact. com.au

On a popular holiday coast, this park is about 500 m from the water and 9 km north-east of Ballina off the Beach Road. It is a good base when visiting the area and has a heated pool for winter months. **$$$**

❑ Tent sites, powered sites, drive-thru sites, ensuite sites, fits big motorhomes, cabins.

❑ Toilets and showers, laundry, sewer dump-point, telephone, kiosk/shop, LP gas refills, ice, camp kitchen, pool, playground, TV cables, no pets.

❑ Bookings required, credit cards, holiday loading. Discounts: weekly, Top Tourist.

Ballina Lakeside Holiday Park
Fenwick Drive, Ballina East 2478
Ph (02) 6686 3953 or 1800 888 268,
fax (02) 6686 8755
Email info@ballinalakeside.com.au
Website www.ballinalakeside.com.au

This is a very good quality park on the lakeside, about 3 km from the centre of town.

The park has many features including a mini-golf course and a mini-mart. This is an ideal park for a holiday or a short break. **$$$**

❑ Tent sites, powered sites, drive-thru sites, ensuite sites, fits big motorhomes, cabins.

❑ Toilets and showers (disabled access), laundry, sewer dump-point, telephone, kiosk/shop, LP gas refills, ice, camp kitchen, pool, playground, internet terminal, no pets.

❑ Credit cards, holiday loading. Discounts: weekly, Big4.

BAMBAROO (QLD)

See Jourama Falls.

BARALABA (QLD) p. 162

Baralaba Picnic Area and Camping Site
Baralaba 4702

This basic camping area is on the shores of a picturesque expanse of the Dawson River, about 500 m from the centre of the small town. The park has very basic facilities and cold showers, and a two-day limit on stays. This is a good out-of-the-way place for self-sufficient travellers to spend a few quiet days. ⓢ

❑ Tent sites, drive-thru sites, fits big motorhomes.

❑ Toilets and showers, pets.

BARCALDINE (QLD) pp. 172, 258

Homestead Caravan Park
Blackall Road (Landsborough Highway), Barcaldine 4725
Ph (07) 4651 1308, fax (07) 4651 1308

This park is on the Landsborough Highway just a few blocks from the town centre. It has good facilities and each night during the winter tourist season, billy tea and damper are served. Discount fuel is also available to park guests. **$$**

❑ Tent sites, powered sites, drive-thru sites, fits big motorhomes, cabins.

❑ Toilets and showers, laundry, sewer dump-point, telephone, kiosk/shop, LP gas refills, ice, pets.

❑ Credit cards. Discounts: weekly.

BARGARA (QLD) p. 46

Bargara Beach Caravan Park
Nielsen Park, Bargara 4670
Ph (07) 4159 2228, fax (07) 4159 2228
Email bargarabeach@optusnet.com.au

This quality beachside tourist park is in a popular holiday destination. The park is large and snorkelling, diving and fishing are popular in the surrounding waters. Bargara is a small coastal community not far from Bundaberg. The Mon Repos turtle rookery is nearby. **$$$**

❑ Tent sites, powered sites, drive-thru sites, fits big motorhomes, cabins, on-site vans.

❑ Toilets and showers (disabled access), laundry, sewer dump-point, telephone, kiosk/shop, LP gas refills, ice, camp kitchen, playground, no pets.

❑ Credit cards. Discounts: weekly.

Turtle Sands Tourist Park
Mon Repos Road, Mon Repos 4670
Ph (07) 4159 2340, fax (07) 4159 2737
Email turtlesands@bigpond.com
Website www.turtlesands.com.au

This park, on 5 ha of wonderful beachfront, adjoins the turtle rookery. The park has good facilities and will suit those looking for a beachside park in a quieter area. **$$**

❑ Tent sites, powered sites, drive-thru sites, cabins, on-site vans.

❑ Toilets and showers, laundry, telephone, kiosk/shop, LP gas refills, ice, no pets.

❑ Credit cards. Discounts: weekly.

BARKLY HOMESTEAD (NT) p. 260

Barkly Homestead Caravan Park
Corner Barkly and Tablelands Highways, Tablelands 0860
Ph (08) 8964 4549, fax (08) 8964 4543

Forming part of the Barkly Homestead Roadhouse complex, this park is a popular overnight stop 210 km east of Tennant Creek. The complex has a range of accommodation options and the adjoining roadhouse is licensed and offers a good selection of meals. The park becomes very busy during the winter tourist season as it is a key stopping point between Mount Isa and Tennant Creek. The complex runs on generator power. **$$$**

❑ Tent sites, powered sites, drive-thru sites, fits big motorhomes.

❑ Toilets and showers, laundry, telephone, kiosk/shop, LP gas refills, ice, pets.

❑ Credit cards.

BARMERA (SA) p. 225

Lake Bonney Holiday Park
Lakeside Drive, Barmera 5345
Ph (08) 8588 2234, fax (08) 8588 1974
Email lbhp@sa.ozland.net.au
Website www.murrayriver.com.au/ accommodation/bonnie

On the shores of Lake Bonney, this popular park is a great holiday base or ideal for an overnight stop. The park is about 1.5 km from the town centre, has a range of accommodation, good amenities and facilities, and shade. **$$$**

❑ Tent sites, powered sites, drive-thru sites, ensuite sites, fits big motorhomes, cabins.

❑ Toilets and showers, laundry, telephone, kiosk/shop, LP gas refills, ice, playground, boat ramp, no pets.

❑ Bookings required, credit cards. Discounts: weekly, FPA.

BAROOGA (NSW) p. 218

See also Cobram.

Cobram Barooga Golf Resort Caravan Park
Golf Course Road, Barooga 3644
Ph (03) 5873 4523 or 1800 181 880,
fax (03) 5873 4132
Email golfresort@cnl.com.au
Website www.golfresort.com.au

Adjacent to one of the Murray Valley's renowned golf courses, this park is very good quality and just 1.5 km from the town centre.

The park's facilities include a pool and a tennis court. This would be a great base for visitors to the area, especially those coming to play golf. **$$$**

❑ Tent sites, powered sites, drive-thru sites, fits big motorhomes, cabins.

❑ Toilets and showers (disabled access), laundry, telephone, kiosk/shop, ice, camp kitchen, pool, playground, no pets.

❑ Credit cards, holiday loading. Discounts: Big4.

BAROSSA VALLEY (SA)

See Nuriootpa and Tanunda.

BARWON HEADS (VIC) p. 141

Barwon Heads Caravan Park
Ewing Blyth Drive, Barwon Heads 3227
Ph (03) 5354 1115, fax (03) 5254 2762

This is a large park fronting the wide picturesque estuary of the Barwon River close to the river mouth. It is a popular summer beachside park and just a short walk from the town centre. Minimum bookings apply during the Christmas, January and Easter holiday periods. **$$$**

❑ Tent sites, powered sites, drive-thru sites, cabins.

❑ Toilets and showers (disabled access), laundry, telephone, playground, boat ramp, no pets.

❑ Credit cards, holiday loading. Discounts: weekly.

BATCHELOR (NT) p. 74

See also Litchfield National Park.

Batchelor Caravillage
Rum Jungle Road, Batchelor 0845
Ph (08) 8976 0166 or 1800 260 166,
fax (08) 8976 0230
Email big4.batchelor.nt@bigpond.com

The park is 500 m from the Batchelor town centre and a good base to explore nearby Litchfield National Park. The park has good facilities including a pool, mini-golf and bicycles for hire. **$$$$**

❑ Tent sites, powered sites, drive-thru sites, fits big motorhomes, cabins.

❑ Toilets and showers, laundry, sewer dump-point, telephone, kiosk/shop, ice, pool, playground, no pets.

❑ Credit cards. Discounts: weekly, Big4.

BATEAU BAY (NSW) p. 26

ⓢ **Blue Lagoon Beach Resort**
Bateau Bay Road, Bateau Bay 2261
Ph (02) 4332 1447 or 1800 680 036,
fax (02) 4334 6888
Email info@bluelagoonbeachresort.com.au
Website www.bluelagoonbeachresort.com.au

Tucked away at the water's edge, this beachfront park has a pool, spa and even its own restaurant. It is an ideal place for a quiet break, although it is busy at the height of the Christmas and Easter holidays, when we recommend that you book. **$$$$**

❑ Tent sites, powered sites, drive-thru sites, cabins.

❑ Toilets and showers (disabled access), laundry, sewer dump-point, telephone, kiosk/shop, LP gas refills, ice, pool, playground, no pets.

❑ Credit cards, holiday loading. Discounts: weekly.

Sun Valley Tourist Park
2 Bateau Bay Road, Bateau Bay 2261
Ph (02) 4332 1107, fax (02) 4334 7822

This large, council-operated beachside park has good, basic facilities. There are a large number of permanent holiday vans and the park will be very busy during the peak holiday periods when a booking is essential. Prices go up at weekends. $$$

❑ Tent sites, powered sites, drive-thru sites, cabins, on-site vans.

❑ Toilets and showers (disabled access), laundry, telephone, kiosk/shop, LP gas refills, ice, playground, no pets.

❑ Bookings required, credit cards, holiday loading. Discounts: weekly.

BATEHAVEN (NSW) pp. 12, 211

Glenhaven Van Village
51 Beach Road, Batehaven 2536
Ph (02) 4472 4541, fax (02) 4472 4520
Email glenhaven@batemansbay.com
Website www.southcoast.com.au/glenhaven

This owner-operated beachfront park is about 3 km from the centre of Batemans Bay. It has good amenities and is home to a large number of permanent holiday vans. It gets busy during holiday periods. $$$

❑ Tent sites, powered sites, drive-thru sites, fits big motorhomes, cabins, on-site vans.

❑ Toilets and showers (disabled access), laundry, sewer dump-point, telephone, ice, playground, no pets.

❑ Credit cards, holiday loading. Discounts: weekly.

Pleasurelea Caravan Park
438 Beach Road, Batehaven 2536
Ph (02) 4472 4258 or 1800 639 396,
fax (02) 4472 5079
Email info@pleasurelea.com.au
Website www.pleasurelea.com.au

This good quality, owner-operated holiday park is just a short walk from the beach. There is a range of accommodation on site and facilities include a tennis court. Small dogs are permitted outside holiday times. $$$

❑ Tent sites, powered sites, drive-thru sites, cabins, on-site vans.

❑ Toilets and showers (disabled access), laundry, telephone, kiosk/shop, LP gas refills, ice, camp kitchen, pool, playground, pets.

❑ Credit cards, holiday loading. Discounts: seniors, weekly, Top Tourist.

BATEMANS BAY (NSW) pp. 12, 211

Coachhouse Marina Resort
49 Beach Road, Batemans Bay 2536
Ph (02) 4472 4392 or 1800 670 715,
fax (02) 4472 4852
Email bookings@coachhouse.com.au
Website www.coachhouse.com.au

Located on the water's edge just 1.5 km from the centre of town, this resort-style

establishment is a popular holiday destination with very good amenities. Facilities include a licensed restaurant, kids club and tennis courts. Minimum booking periods apply at Christmas and Easter. $$$$

❑ Tent sites, powered sites, fits big motorhomes, cabins, on-site vans.

❑ Toilets and showers (disabled access), laundry, telephone, kiosk/shop, pool, playground, boat ramp, internet terminal, no pets.

❑ Credit cards, holiday loading.

East's Riverside Holiday Park
Wharf Road, Batemans Bay 2536
Ph (02) 4472 4048 or 1800 447 404,
fax (02) 4472 4058
Email holiday@easts.com.au
Website www.easts.com.au

The East family name is well known in the caravan park industry and this park is owned by one of the three East brothers. Superbly located on the north bank of the Clyde River, this park has good amenities and lovely views across the water to town. $$$

❑ Tent sites, powered sites, ensuite sites, cabins.

❑ Toilets and showers, laundry, sewer dump-point, telephone, LP gas refills, ice, camp kitchen, TV cables, no pets.

❑ Bookings required, credit cards, holiday loading. Discounts: weekly, Big4.

BATHURST (NSW)

See Kelso.

BAWLEY POINT (NSW) p. 14

⊗ **Racecourse Beach Tourist Park**
381 Murramarang Road, Bawley Point 2539
Ph (02) 4457 1078 or 1800 659 545,
fax (02) 4457 1489
Email racecourse@racecoursebeach.com
Website www.racecoursebeach.com

It is hard to resist staying at a wonderful, award-winning beachside park such as this. Just 9 km from the Princes Highway, it has good facilities including mini-golf, a heated pool, a sauna and a tennis court. Minimum bookings apply in peak holiday periods. $$$

❑ Tent sites, powered sites, fits big motorhomes, cabins.

❑ Toilets and showers (disabled access), laundry, sewer dump-point, telephone, kiosk/shop, LP gas refills, ice, camp kitchen, pool, playground, internet terminal, no pets.

❑ Bookings required, credit cards, holiday loading. Discounts: Big4.

BEACHPORT (SA) p. 132

Southern Ocean Tourist Park
Somerville Street, Beachport 5280
Ph (08) 8735 8153, fax (08) 8735 8218
Email sotp@seol.net.au

This is a large, spacious park in a popular south-east resort town. The park has very good amenities and sites are reasonably priced. It is situated in an area where fishing and recreational water activities are the main attractions. The area will be busy during the Christmas and Easter holiday periods. $$$

❑ Tent sites, powered sites, drive-thru sites, fits big motorhomes, cabins.

❑ Toilets and showers (disabled access), laundry, telephone, LP gas refills, ice, camp kitchen, playground, no pets.

❑ Bookings required, credit cards. Discounts: pensioners, seniors, weekly.

BEAUMARIS (TAS)

See Scamander.

BELMONT (NSW) p. 26

Belmont Pines Tourist Park
24 Paley Crescent, Belmont 2280
Ph (02) 4945 4750, fax (02) 4645 8197
Email belmont.pines@hunterlink.net.au
Website www.huntertourism.com/belmontpines

This park is in a superb lakeside position, not far south of Newcastle's town centre. It is a good family park and an ideal base for water-sports enthusiasts. $$

❑ Tent sites, powered sites, cabins, on-site vans.

❑ Toilets and showers (disabled access), laundry, telephone, pool, playground, boat ramp, no pets.

❑ Bookings required, credit cards, holiday loading. Discounts: pensioners, weekly.

BENARABY (QLD) p. 48

See also Lake Awoonga.

Greenacres Motel and Caravan Park
Bruce Highway, Benaraby 4680
Ph (07) 4975 0136, fax (07) 4975 0136

This is an older, basic park easily accessed from the Bruce Highway and very convenient for an overnight stay. The owner operators have a limited number of tourist sites and a range of accommodation at a budget price. Tannum Sands Sportsmens Club runs a courtesy bus to the park on Thursdays–Sundays. $$

❑ Tent sites, powered sites, drive-thru sites, fits big motorhomes, on-site vans.

❑ Toilets and showers, laundry, telephone, ice, camp kitchen, pool, TV cables, internet terminal, pets.

❑ Credit cards. Discounts: weekly.

Willowgrove On The River
Bruce Highway, Benaraby 4680
Ph (07) 4975 0163 or 1800 002 234,
fax (07) 4975 0470
Email willowgrove@bigpond.com
Website www.willowgroveontheriver.com.au

This is a very good park with river and highway frontage. The park has very good amenities and nice grassed areas all the way to the river. It is a very convenient overnight stop for those travelling the Bruce Highway or a good base close to Gladstone. $$$

❑ Tent sites, powered sites, drive-thru sites, fits big motorhomes, cabins.

❑ Toilets and showers, laundry, telephone, kiosk/shop, LP gas refills, ice, camp kitchen, pool, boat ramp, TV cables, internet terminal, no pets.

❑ Credit cards. Discounts: Big4.

BENDALONG (NSW) p. 14

Bendalong Point Tourist Park
Bendalong Road, Bendalong 2539
Ph (02) 4456 1167 or 1300 733 025,
fax (02) 4456 1167
Email holidayhaven@shoalhaven.com.au
Website www.holidayhaven.com.au

Located on the beach at Red Point, this well managed council park is close to surfing and swimming beaches. There are good amenities and the facilities include a playground, camp kitchen and gas and wood barbecues. Minimum bookings apply over Christmas, Easter and long weekends. $$$$

❑ Tent sites, powered sites, drive-thru sites, fits big motorhomes, cabins.

❑ Toilets and showers (disabled access), laundry, LP gas refills, ice, camp kitchen, playground, boat ramp, no pets.

❑ Credit cards, holiday loading. Discounts: pensioners, seniors, weekly.

BERMAGUI (NSW) p. 12

Zane Grey Caravan Park
Lamont Street, Bermagui 2546
Ph (02) 6493 4382, fax (02) 6493 3222
Email zanegrey@asitis.net.au

Close to the centre of town, this good quality park is popular with holidaymakers. The park was so named because the American writer Zane Grey once had a fishing shack on this piece of land. The undercover barbecues and playground area are among this park's good facilities. Pets are allowed outside busy seasons. $$

❑ Tent sites, powered sites, drive-thru sites, fits big motorhomes, cabins.

❑ Toilets and showers, laundry, sewer dump-point, telephone, ice, playground, pets.

❑ Credit cards, holiday loading. Discounts: weekly.

BEROWRA (NSW)

See Sydney.

BERRI (SA) p. 222

Berri Riverside Caravan Park
Riverview Drive, Berri 5343
Ph (08) 8582 3723 or 1800 332 255,
fax (08) 8582 2578
Email berririv@riverland.net.au
Website www.riverland.net.au/berricp

This is a large, quiet park about 1 km from town and just across the road from the Murray River. The park has very good amenities and extensive facilities including a pool and a tennis court. This is a good park and we stay here when passing through Berri. $$$$

❑ Tent sites, powered sites, drive-thru sites, ensuite sites, fits big motorhomes, cabins, on-site vans.

❑ Toilets and showers (disabled access), laundry, sewer dump-point, telephone, LP gas refills, ice, camp kitchen, pool, playground, boat ramp, pets.

❑ Credit cards, holiday loading. Discounts: Top Tourist.

BERRY SPRINGS (NT) p. 74

The Lakes Resort Caravan Park
Doris Road (off Cox Peninsula Road),
Berry Springs 0837
Ph (08) 8988 6277, fax (08) 8988 6118

The park is 2.5 km from Berry Springs. Its lakeside position and close proximity to the Territory Wildlife Park make it a popular stopping place. The park has good amenities and is a convenient base in the area. $$$

❏ Tent sites, powered sites, drive-thru sites, fits big motorhomes, cabins.

❏ Toilets and showers, laundry, sewer dump-point, telephone, kiosk/shop, LP gas refills, ice, camp kitchen, pool, playground, boat ramp, pets.

❏ Credit cards. Discount: weekly, Top Tourist.

BIGGERA WATERS (QLD)

See Gold Coast.

BLACKALL (QLD) p. 172

Blackall Caravan Park
53 Garden Street, Blackall 4472
Ph (07) 4657 4816, fax (07) 4657 4327

Easily accessible from the Landsborough (Matilda) Highway, the park is just a short walk from the town centre. It is popular during the winter tourist season, offering camp-oven meals each evening. $$

❏ Tent sites, powered sites, drive-thru sites, fits big motorhomes, cabins.

❏ Toilets and showers, laundry, kiosk/shop, LP gas refills, ice, pets.

❏ Credit cards.

BLACKBULL (QLD) p. 66

Blackbull Siding
Great Top Road, Blackbull 4871
Ph (07) 4745 3510, fax (07) 4745 3510

Blackbull Siding is 61 km west of Croydon. The siding has basic unpowered camping sites at a budget price and the *Gulflander* railmotor, running on an 1890 track, stops here every Wednesday and Thursday for morning tea. $

❏ Tent sites, drive-thru sites, fits big motorhomes.

❏ Toilets and showers, ice, pets.

❏ No credit cards.

BLACKHEATH (NSW) p. 236

Blackheath Caravan Park
Prince Edward Street, Blackheath 2785
Ph (02) 4787 8101, fax (02) 4787 8101

In the heart of the Blue Mountains, this park is situated in a pretty parkland setting opposite the remarkable Rhododendron Gardens. The park is within walking distance of the town centre and Govetts Leap Lookout. There are good basic facilites and just over the road is a playground and free seasonal swimming pool. $$$$

❏ Tent sites, powered sites, fits big motorhomes, cabins.

❏ Toilets and showers (disabled access), laundry, sewer dump-point, telephone, kiosk/shop, playground, no pets.

❏ Credit cards, holiday loading.

BLANCHETOWN (SA) p. 224

Riverside Caravan Park
Sanders Street, Blanchetown 5357
Ph (08) 8540 5070 or 1800 425 070,
fax (08) 8540 5278
Email riverside@noelscaravans.com.au

This well-maintained park is in a picturesque spot on the banks of the Murray River, just below the Blanchetown lock. It is a smaller, good quality park with a range of accommodation, about 500 m from the town centre. $$$

❏ Tent sites, powered sites, fits big motorhomes, cabins, on-site vans.

❏ Toilets and showers, laundry, camp kitchen, playground, TV cables, no pets.

❏ Credit cards. Discounts: pensioners, seniors, Big4.

BLI BLI (QLD)

See Maroochydore.

BLUE LAKE (SA)

See Mount Gambier.

BLUEWATER (QLD) p. 55

Bluewater Creek Rest Area
Bluewater 4818

This is a popular rest area with a 24-hour maximum stay. At the time of publication it was free. The area is well grassed and has a few shady trees. It is adjacent to the highway and is also a great lunch stop. Ⓢ

❏ Tent sites, drive-thru sites, fits big motorhomes.

❏ Toilets, pets.

BOAT HARBOUR (NSW)

See Anna Bay.

BOMBAH POINT (NSW) p. 28

Myall Shores Eco-Tourist Resort
Myall Lakes National Park, Bombah Point 2423
Ph (02) 4997 4495, fax (02) 4997 4600
Email resort@myallshores.com.au
Website www.myallshores.com.au

Situated on the shores of Myall Lakes, this park is reached from Bulahdelah along a 16 km unsealed road. Located in a picture-postcard position close to the vehicle ferry crossing, it has good facilities and a cafe. Bushwalking, canoeing, fishing, sailing, swimming and water-skiing are all popular activities. It is very easy to spend a few days here lazing on the banks of the lakes. $

❏ Tent sites, powered sites, fits big motorhomes, cabins.

❏ Toilets and showers (disabled access), laundry, sewer dump-point, telephone,

kiosk/shop, LP gas refills, ice, boat ramp, no pets.

❏ Bookings required, credit cards, holiday loading.

BONEGILLA (VIC)

See Albury, Ebden and Wodonga.

BONGAREE (QLD) p. 44

Bongaree Caravan Park
Welsby Pde, Bongaree, Bribie Island 4507
Ph (07) 3408 1054, fax (07) 3408 1054

Bribie Island is a popular holiday destination and this park overlooks the southern end of the Pumicestone Passage, a safe protected fishing destination. $$$

❏ Tent sites, powered sites, cabins.

❏ Toilets and showers (disabled access), laundry, telephone, kiosk/shop, LP gas refills, ice, boat ramp, no pets.

❏ No credit cards, holiday loading. Discounts: weekly.

BONNY HILLS (NSW) p. 30

Bonny Hills Caravan Park
Ocean Drive, Bonny Hills 2445
Phone (02) 6585 5276, fax (02) 6585 5276
Email bonnyhillscaravanp@fasternet.com.au

This park is excellent value when considering the great views out to sea. $$

❏ Tent sites, powered sites, fits big motorhomes, cabins.

❏ Toilets and showers, laundry, telephone, LP gas refills, ice, pets.

❏ Credit cards, holiday loading. Discounts: pensioners, weekly.

BORDERTOWN (SA) p. 232

Bordertown Caravan Park
Penny Terrace, Bordertown 5268
Ph (08) 8752 1752

This is a tidy park with good facilities, right in the heart of town. It is just a short 200 m walk to the shopping centre and the park is easily accessible from the highway. $$$

❏ Tent sites, powered sites, drive-thru sites, fits big motorhomes, cabins.

❏ Toilets and showers (disabled access), laundry, telephone, LP gas refills, ice, pets.

❏ Credit cards. Discounts: pensioners, seniors, weekly.

BORROLOOLA (NT) p. 70

McArthur River Caravan Park
Lot 781 Robinson Road, Borroloola 0854
Ph (08) 8975 8734, fax (08) 8975 8712

This park is located in the main street of Borroloola. The park has basic facilities and although there is little shade, it is a popular stopover to explore the local area or spend some time fishing the McArthur River. $$$

❏ Tent sites, powered sites, drive-thru sites, fits big motorhomes, cabins.

❏ Toilets and showers, laundry, kiosk/shop, pets.

❏ Credit cards. Discounts: weekly.

BOURKE (NSW) p. 168

Kidman's Camp Van and Cabin Park
Mitchell Highway (Kidman Way), Bourke 2840
Ph (02) 6872 1612, fax (02) 6872 3107

Located 8 km north of town, this riverfront park has good facilities, plenty of lawn and open space. The park is in a quiet, out-of-town location backing onto the Darling River. $$$

❏ Tent sites, powered sites, drive-thru sites, fits big motorhomes, cabins.

❏ Toilets and showers (disabled access), laundry, camp kitchen, playground, pool, no pets.

❏ No credit cards.

Mitchell Caravan Park
Mitchell Street, Bourke 2840
Ph (02) 6872 2791, fax (02) 6872 3107
Email simmonds@lisp.com.au

This caravan park is located in a quiet, off-highway position about 1 km from the town centre. The park has modern, clean amenities and good basic facilities. It is a good base for those exploring Bourke. $$

❏ Tent sites, powered sites, drive-thru sites, ensuite sites, fits big motorhomes, cabins.

❏ Toilets and showers, laundry, playground, pets.

❏ No credit cards. Discounts: weekly.

BOWEN (QLD) p. 52

Coral Coast Caravan Park
Soldiers Road, Bowen 4805
Ph (07) 4785 1262, fax (07) 4785 1428
Email cccpbowen@boweninternet.com.au

Bowen is a popular coastal town and this park has absolute beach frontage, with excellent facilities and spotless amenities. Swimming, snorkelling and walking the beaches are all popular activities here. $$

❏ Tent sites, powered sites, drive-thru sites, fits big motorhomes, cabins, on-site vans.

❏ Toilets and showers (disabled access), laundry, telephone, LP gas refills, ice, pool, playground, boat ramp, no pets.

❏ Credit cards. Discounts: weekly.

BOWENFELS (NSW)

See Lithgow.

BOYNE ISLAND (QLD) p. 48

Boyne Tannum Caravan Park
1 Jacaranada Drive, Boyne Island 4680
Ph (07) 4973 8888, fax (07) 4973 7359

This is a large, good quality park close to the beach. The park has a good range of accommodation and facilities, including a boat park and covered barbecues. This is a popular park and bookings are necessary in peak holiday periods. $$

❏ Tent sites, powered sites, fits big motorhomes, cabins, on-site vans.

❏ Toilets and showers, laundry, telephone,

kiosk/shop, LP gas refills, ice, pool, playground, boat ramp, TV cables, no pets.

❑ Credit cards. Discounts: weekly, Top Tourist.

BREMER BAY (WA) p. 116

Bremer Bay Caravan Park
Borden Bremer Bay Road, Bremer Bay 6338
Ph (08) 9837 4018, fax (08) 9837 4021
Email bremercarapark@wn.com.au

This is a large park in a popular holiday destination across the road from the water. The kiosk only operates during holiday periods. $$$

❑ Tent sites, powered sites, drive-thru sites, fits big motorhomes, cabins, on-site vans.

❑ Toilets and showers, laundry, telephone, kiosk/shop, LP gas refills, ice, playground, no pets.

❑ Bookings required, credit cards, holiday loading. Discounts: weekly.

Fishery Beach Tourist Park
Wellstead Road, Bremer Bay 6338
Ph (08) 9837 4290, fax (08) 9837 4291
Email fisherybeach@westnet.com.au

This is a good quality park in a quiet bush setting about 3 km from Bremer Bay. The park has very good amenities and a range of facilities including a boat park and tennis court. $$

❑ Tent sites, powered sites, drive-thru sites, ensuite sites, fits big motorhomes, on-site vans.

❑ Toilets, showers (disabled access), laundry, sewer dump-point, telephone, kiosk/shop, LP gas refills, ice, camp kitchen, pool, playground, TV cables, pets.

❑ Credit cards. Discounts: weekly.

BRIMBAGO (SA)

See Keith.

BRISBANE (QLD) p. 41

Aspley Acres Caravan Park
1420 Gympie Rd, Aspley 4034
Ph (07) 3263 2668, fax (07) 3263 4629

A large, quality tourist park with good facilities, including a camp kitchen and TV room. The park is easily accessible on the northern approach to Brisbane. A supermarket adjoins this park. $$$

❑ Tent sites, powered sites, drive-thru sites, fits big motorhomes, cabins, on-site vans.

❑ Toilets and showers (disabled access), laundry, sewer dump-point, telephone, LP gas refills, camp kitchen, playground, no pets.

❑ Credit cards. Discounts: weekly, Top Tourist.

Boat Harbour Caravan Park
Reef Point Esplanade, Scarborough 4020
Ph (07) 3203 8868, fax (07) 3203 8868
Email boatharbour@bigpond.com

A basic park in a pretty location. Located on the shores of Deception Bay, it adjoins the marina and a nice waterfront parkland. The park has a limited number of tourist sites; however this is a convenient park for those seeking to stay on the Redcliffe Peninsula. Small pets are sometimes allowed in this park. $$$

❑ Tent sites, powered sites, drive-thru sites, fits big motorhomes, on-site vans.

❑ Toilets and showers (disabled access), laundry, telephone, kiosk/shop, LP gas refills, ice, boat ramp, no pets.

❑ Credit cards. Discounts: pensioners, seniors, weekly

Caravan Village Brisbane
763 Zillmere Rd, Aspley 4034
Ph (07) 3263 4040 or 1800 060 797, fax (07) 3263 7702
Email holiday@caravanvillage.com.au
Website www.caravanvillage.com.au

A good quality park close to the northern approach to Brisbane. Facilities include an internet terminal, a pool and camp kitchen. This park is a good base from which to explore the northern suburbs of Brisbane. $$$$

❑ Tent sites, powered sites, drive-thru sites, ensuite sites, cabins.

❑ Toilets and showers, laundry, sewer dump-point, telephone, kiosk/shop, LP gas refills, ice, camp kitchen, pool, playground, internet terminal, no pets.

❑ Bookings required, credit cards. Discounts: weekly, Big4.

Dress Circle Holiday Village
10 Holmead Rd, Eight Mile Plains 4113
Ph (07) 3341 6133, fax (07) 3341 0274
Email sales@dresscircle.com.au
Website www.dresscircle.com.au

A large, quality park on the south side of the city. This park has a great range of facilities including a tennis court, convenience store, cafe, camp kitchen and lovely grassy sites. For the children there is a novelty swimming pool and a new playground. The park is a good base for exploring Brisbane. $$$$

❑ Tent sites, powered sites, fits big motorhomes, cabins.

❑ Toilets and showers, laundry, sewer dump-point, telephone, kiosk/shop, LP gas refills, ice, camp kitchen, pool, playground, pets.

❑ Credit cards. Discounts: weekly.

Gateway Village
200 School Rd, Rochedale 4123
Ph (07) 3341 6333 or 1800 442 444, fax (07) 3341 8022
Email bookings@gatewayvillage.com.au
Website www.gatewayvillage.com.au

A good quality park with easy access to all the major highways, including the Pacific Motorway, and 16 km from the city centre. Facilities include a resort-style pool, a good playground, tennis courts and free gas barbecues. $$$$

❑ Tent sites, powered sites, cabins.

❑ Toilets and showers, laundry, telephone, camp kitchen, pool, playground, internet terminal, no pets.

❑ Bookings required, credit cards. Discounts: weekly, Big4.

Newmarket Gardens Caravan Park
199 Ashgrove Ave, Ashgrove 4060
Ph (07) 3356 1458, fax (07) 3352 7273
Email caravan@powerup.com.au

The closest caravan park to Brisbane's city centre, this older park has good basic facilities. It is popular with backpackers

and travellers in campervans, with the city less than 4 km away. $$$

❑ Tent sites, powered sites, drive-thru sites, fits big motorhomes, cabins, on-site vans.

❑ Toilets and showers, laundry, sewer dump-point, telephone, kiosk/shop, LP gas refills, ice, internet terminal, no pets.

❑ Credit cards. Discount: seniors, weekly, FPA.

BROKEN HEAD NATURE RESERVE (NSW)

See Suffolk Park.

BROKEN HILL (NSW) p. 244

⊛ Broken Hill Caravan Park
Rakow Street (Adelaide Road), Broken Hill 2880
Ph (08) 8087 3841 or 1800 803 842, fax (08) 8087 3841
Email bhttp@bigpond.com

With its heated pool, covered barbecues and well-stocked kiosk, this large park is our pick of the Broken Hill parks and we regularly stay here. It is easily accessible from the Barrier Highway and is a good base in Broken Hill. $$$

❑ Tent sites, powered sites, drive-thru sites, ensuite sites, fits big motorhomes, cabins, on-site vans.

❑ Toilets and showers (disabled access), laundry, sewer dump-point, telephone, kiosk/shop, LP gas refills, ice, camp kitchen, pool, playground, pets.

❑ Bookings required, credit cards. Discounts: Top Tourist.

BROOME (WA) p. 90

Cable Beach Caravan Park
Millington Road, Cable Beach 6725
Ph (08) 9192 2066, fax (08) 9192 1997

This is a very large park about 5.5 km from central Broome and close to Cable Beach. The park has been recently extended and only the older section has large shady trees. We have visited this park over many years and enjoy it. $$$

❑ Tent sites, powered sites, drive-thru sites, fits big motorhomes, cabins, on-site vans.

❑ Toilets and showers (disabled access), laundry, sewer dump-point, telephone, kiosk/shop, LP gas refills, ice, camp kitchen, pool, playground, no pets.

❑ Credit cards, holiday loading. Discounts: weekly, Big4.

Palm Grove Holiday Resort
Corner Murray and Cable Beach Roads, Cable Beach 6725
Ph (08) 9192 3336 or 1800 803 336, fax (08) 9192 3306
Email reservations@palmgrove.com.au
Website www.palmgrove.com.au

This is a very well laid out tourist park about 5 km from the centre of town and close to Cable Beach. The park has excellent amenities and a good range of facilities. This is a newer park and the shade trees are still growing. $$$

❑ Tent sites, powered sites, drive-thru sites, fits big motorhomes, cabins.

❑ Toilets and showers (disabled access), laundry, sewer dump-point, telephone, kiosk/shop, LP gas refills, ice, camp kitchen, pool, internet terminal, no pets.

❑ Bookings required, credit cards, holiday loading. Discounts: Top Tourist.

BROOMS HEAD (NSW) p. 32

Brooms Head Caravan Park
Ocean Road, Brooms Head 2463
Ph (02) 6646 7144, fax (02) 6646 7144
Email bhcp@msc.nsw.gov.au
Website www.msc.nsw.gov.au

In an out-of-the-way place, this park spreads along more than 1.5 km of beachfront, surrounded by national park. This is a popular beachside holiday destination and bookings are necessary in peak holiday times. $$

❑ Tent sites, powered sites, drive-thru sites, fits big motorhomes, cabins.

❑ Toilets and showers (disabled access), laundry, telephone, LP gas refills, ice, playground, no pets.

❑ Credit cards, holiday loading. Discounts: pensioners, seniors, weekly.

BROULEE (NSW) p. 12

Broulee Beach Van Park
6 Lyttle Street, Broulee 2537
Ph (02) 4471 6247 or 1800 633 590, fax (02) 4471 5157
Email info@brouleebeach.com
Website www.brouleebeach.com

This is a quality caravan park located on a picturesque patrolled beach. There is a resort-style pool to relax in and undercover barbecues. Minimum bookings apply during the busy Christmas and Easter holidays. $$$

❑ Tent sites, powered sites, drive-thru sites, cabins.

❑ Toilets and showers, laundry, telephone, pool, playground, no pets.

❑ Credit cards, holiday loading. Discounts: weekly, Big4.

BRUNSWICK HEADS (NSW) p. 34

Ferry Reserve Caravan Park
Pacific Highway, Brunswick Heads 2483
Ph (02) 6685 1872, fax (02) 6685 0135
Email ferry@bshp.com.au
Website www.bshp.com.au/ferry

This park has very easy access to the Pacific Highway, from the roundabout at the front gate. It is also situated on a picturesque estuary, popular for fishing. The grounds and amenities are very neat and well maintained and the park is ideal for a holiday or a convenient overnight stop. $$$

❑ Tent sites, powered sites, fits big motorhomes, cabins.

❑ Toilets and showers (disabled access), laundry, sewer dump-point, telephone, kiosk/shop, LP gas refills, ice, boat ramp, no pets.

❑ Credit cards, holiday loading. Discounts: weekly, FPA.

Massey Greene Holiday Park
1 Old Pacific Highway, Brunswick Heads 2483
Ph (02) 6685 1329, fax (02) 6685 0139
Email massey@bshp.com.au
Website www.bshp.com.au/massey

This neat, riverfront park is located adjacent to the boat harbour and a short walk from town. The Brunswick Heads Fishermen's Cooperative is next door and they always have a good range of fresh or cooked fish. The park has good estuary frontage and those who enjoy fishing will enjoy this park. $$$

❑ Tent sites, powered sites, fits big motorhomes, cabins.

❑ Toilets and showers (disabled access), laundry, telephone, LP gas refills, ice, playground, no pets.

❑ Bookings required, credit cards, holiday loading. Discounts: weekly.

BUDGEWOI (NSW) p. 26

Budgewoi Tourist Park
Weemala Street, Budgewoi 2262
Ph (02) 4390 9019, fax (02) 4399 1904

This large council-operated park has good facilities and is well suited for a beachside family holiday. Those wanting to fish can make use of the nearby boat ramp. $$

❑ Tent sites, powered sites, drive-thru sites, fits big motorhomes, cabins.

❑ Toilets and showers (disabled access), laundry, telephone, kiosk/shop, LP gas refills, ice, playground, boat ramp, pets.

❑ Credit cards, holiday loading. Discounts: weekly.

BULAHDELAH (NSW) p. 28

Alum Mountain Caravan Park
Pacific Highway, Bulahdelah 2423
Ph (02) 4997 4565, fax (02) 4997 4565

Located on the edge of town alongside the Pacific Highway, this is an older park with basic facilities. It is very convenient for an overnight stop or as a base to explore the local lakes and forests. $$

❑ Tent sites, powered sites, drive-thru sites, fits big motorhomes, on-site vans.

❑ Toilets and showers (disabled access), laundry, telephone, kiosk/shop, LP gas refills, camp kitchen, pool, pets.

❑ Credit cards, holiday loading. Discounts: weekly.

BULLI (NSW)

See Wollongong.

BUNBURY (WA) pp. 110, 112

Bunbury Village Holiday Park
Corner Bussell Highway and Washington Avenue, Bunbury 6230
Ph (08) 9795 7100 or 1800 007 100, fax (08) 9795 7107
Email bunbury@resortparks.com.au
Website www.resortparks.com.au

This is a very good quality park on the highway, 6 km from the city centre. It has some great features including three tennis courts, mini-golf, a shop and a restaurant. The park is an excellent base for a holiday in Bunbury. $$$

❑ Tent sites, powered sites, drive-thru sites, ensuite sites, fits big motorhomes, cabins.

❑ Toilets and showers (disabled access), laundry, telephone, kiosk/shop, LP gas refills, ice, camp kitchen, pool, playground, no pets.

❑ Credit cards, holiday loading. Discounts: weekly, Top Tourist.

Glade Caravan Park
Corner Bussell Highway and Timperley Road, Bunbury 6230
Ph (08) 9721 3800 or 1800 113 800, fax (08) 9721 3848
Email info@glade.com.au
Website www.glade.com.au

A good quality park just 3 km south of the city centre. The park has well-maintained grounds, good amenities and a range of quality facilities. It is easily accessible from the Bussell Highway. $$$

❑ Tent sites, powered sites, drive-thru sites, fits big motorhomes, cabins.

❑ Toilets and showers, laundry, telephone, kiosk/shop, LP gas refills, ice, pool, playground, no pets.

❑ Credit cards. Discounts: weekly, Big4.

BUNDABERG (QLD) p. 46

Cane Village Holiday Park
94 Twyford Street, Bundaberg 4670
Ph (07) 4155 1022 or 1800 242 387, fax (07) 4155 3326
Email canevillage@bigpond.com

This is a very good quality park on the western approach to town. It is in a convenient location for an overnight stay or a good base for a longer holiday. There are shops close by. $$$

❑ Tent sites, powered sites, fits big motorhomes, cabins.

❑ Toilets and showers, laundry, telephone, kiosk/shop, LP gas refills, ice, camp kitchen, pool, playground, no pets.

❑ Bookings required, credit cards. Discounts: weekly, Big4.

Glenlodge Caravan Park
321 Goodwood Road, Bundaberg 4670
Ph (07) 4153 1515, fax (07) 4153 2990
Email glenlodge@bigpond.com

This newer, owner-operated park is 6 km south of the town centre and is ideal for an overnight stay or as a base for a few days exploring the region. The park has good amenities. $$$

❑ Tent sites, powered sites, drive-thru sites, fits big motorhomes, cabins.

❑ Toilets and showers (disabled access), laundry, sewer dump-point, telephone, kiosk/shop, LP gas refills, ice, pool, no pets.

❑ Credit cards. Discounts: weekly, Top Tourist.

BURKE AND WILLS ROADHOUSE (QLD) p. 178

Burke and Wills Roadhouse Caravan Park
Burke Developmental Road (Matilda Highway), via Cloncurry 4823
Ph (07) 4742 5909, fax (07) 4742 5958

This basic park is attached to the Burke and Wills Roadhouse 180 km north of Cloncurry at the junction of the Burke Developmental Road and the Wills Developmental Road. The roadhouse has extensive facilities including a range of accommodation, a licensed restaurant and a selection of takeaway food. Travellers often leave their vans here and pack the tent for a trip to Lawn Hill National Park. $$

❑ Tent sites, powered sites, drive-thru sites, fits big motorhomes, cabins.

❑ Toilets and showers, laundry, telephone, kiosk/shop, LP gas refills, ice, pets.

❑ Credit cards.

BURKETOWN (QLD) p. 68

Escott Barramundi Lodge Caravan Park
via Burketown 4830
Ph (07) 4748 5577, fax (07) 4748 4649
Email escottbarralodg@austarnet.com.au

Located about 17 km from Burketown on the Nicholson River (the turn-off is about 5 km from Burketown) this is a popular park on a working station. The park is accessible only via unsealed roads but is popular with travellers and those who enjoy fishing. It has a nice grassed camping area and a range of facilities. $$$

❑ Tent sites, powered sites, drive-thru sites, fits big motorhomes, cabins.

❑ Toilets and showers, laundry, telephone, kiosk/shop, ice, pool, playground, boat ramp, pets.

❑ Credit cards. Discounts: weekly.

BURLEIGH HEADS (QLD)

See Gold Coast.

BURNIE (TAS) p. 288

Treasure Island Caravan Park
253 Bass Highway, Cooee 7320
Ph (03) 6431 1925, fax (03) 6431 1753

This is a good basic park on the Bass Highway west of Burnie. It has good amenities but basic facilities. Bookings are necessary in holiday periods. $$

❑ Tent sites, powered sites, ensuite sites, fits big motorhomes, cabins, on-site vans.

❑ Toilets and showers, laundry, telephone, kiosk/shop, LP gas refills, camp kitchen, pool, no pets.

❑ Credit cards. Discounts: weekly.

BURONGA (NSW) p. 220

Buronga Riverside Tourist Park
West Road, off Sturt Highway, Buronga 2739
Ph (03) 5023 3040, fax (03) 5023 3040
Email brtp@ruralnet.net.au
Website www.ruralnet.net.au/brtp

Located on the banks of the river close to the bridge and opposite Mildura Wharf, this park has plenty of space for larger rigs. Large shady river red gums and a pool help to ensure this will be an enjoyable stay. Minimum bookings apply during holiday periods. $$

❑ Tent sites, powered sites, drive-thru sites, fits big motorhomes, cabins.

❑ Toilets and showers (disabled access), laundry, sewer dump-point, telephone, kiosk/shop, LP gas refills, ice, pool, playground, pets.

❑ Credit cards. Discounts: pensioners, weekly.

BURRA (SA) p. 246

⊛ **Burra Caravan and Camping Park**
12 Bridge Terrace, Burra 5417
Ph (08) 8892 2442, fax (08) 8892 2442
Email burracvp@chariot.net.au

This picturesque park is situated along a creek just two minutes walk from the centre of Burra – a historic mining town. The park has good basic facilities and plenty of large shady trees. It is an excellent base from which to explore the town. Minimum bookings are required at Easter and on long weekends. $$

❑ Tent sites, powered sites, fits big motorhomes, on-site vans.

❑ Toilets and showers, laundry, telephone, kiosk/shop, pets.

❑ Credit cards. Discounts: weekly.

BUSSELTON (WA) p. 112

Busselton Villas and Caravan Park
163 Bussell Highway, Busselton 6280
Ph (08) 9752 1175, fax (08) 9752 1175

Just a kilometre from town, this small beachfront park is well operated with good facilities. There is a minimum stay during peak periods, and pets are only allowed in the off-season. $$$

❑ Tent sites, powered sites, drive-thru sites, cabins, on-site vans.

❑ Toilets and showers (disabled access), laundry, telephone, kiosk/shop, LP gas refills, ice, pool, playground, pets.

❑ Credit cards, holiday loading. Discounts: weekly.

Kookaburra Caravan Park
66 Marine Terrace, Busselton 6280
Ph (08) 9752 1516, fax (08) 9752 1516
Email kookpark@compwest.net.au

This is a very good council-owned park, close to the centre of town and just a short walk from the famous Busselton jetty. Camping sites are spacious and amenities are good. No pets are allowed during Christmas and Easter holiday periods. $$$

❑ Tent sites, powered sites, drive-thru sites, fits big motorhomes, cabins, on-site vans.

❏ Toilets and showers (disabled access), laundry, sewer dump-point, telephone, kiosk/shop, camp kitchen, playground, pool, TV cables, pets.

❏ Credit cards, holiday loading. Discounts: pensioners, seniors.

⊛ Mandalay Holiday Resort

652 Geographe Bay Road, Busselton 6280
Ph (08) 9752 1328 or 1800 248 231,
fax (08) 9752 2835
Email info@mandalayresort.com.au
Website www.mandalayresort.com.au

This is an excellent quality caravan park for tourists, one of the best in Australia. It is just across the road from the beach and about 4 km from the town centre. There is a popular resort-style pool, large grassed playing areas and a convenient boat park. Holiday periods are extremely busy, when booking is essential. **$$$$**

❏ Tent sites, powered sites, drive-thru sites, cabins.

❏ Toilets and showers (disabled access), laundry, sewer dump-point, telephone, kiosk/shop, ice, camp kitchen, pool, playground, internet terminal, no pets.

❏ Credit cards, holiday loading. Discounts: Top Tourist.

BYRON BAY (NSW) p. 34

First Sun Caravan Park

Lawson Street, Byron Bay 2481
Ph (02) 6685 6544, fax (02) 6685 7046
Email first@bshp.com.au
Website www.bshp.com.au/first

Every now and then we discover a park in a fabulous position. This park is on the beach at Byron Bay, within walking distance of the town centre, the restaurants and the nightlife. The park is busy year-round and is popular with backpackers. There are a limited number of beachfront sites and bookings in peak periods are essential. **$$$**

❏ Tent sites, powered sites, fits big motorhomes, cabins.

❏ Toilets and showers (disabled access), laundry, telephone, ice, camp kitchen, playground, no pets.

❏ Credit cards, holiday loading. Discounts: weekly.

Glen Villa Resort

Butler Street, Byron Bay 2481
Ph (02) 6685 7382, fax (02) 6685 7382
Email glenvilla@bryonbayresorts.com
Website www.byronbayresorts.com

This is a high quality park about 400 m from the town centre. It uniquely caters for couples: all the park cabins and sites are designed for just two persons. The park has modern facilities and is within walking distance of the town and the beach. **$$$$**

❏ Tent sites, powered sites, drive-thru sites, fits big motorhomes, cabins.

❏ Toilets and showers (disabled access), laundry, sewer dump-point, telephone, camp kitchen, pool, no pets.

❏ Credit cards, holiday loading. Discounts: weekly.

CABLE BEACH (WA)

See Broome.

CAIRNS (QLD) pp. 56, 60

See also Lake Placid.

⊛ Cairns Coconut Caravan Resort

Corner Bruce Highway and Anderson Road, Woree 4868
Ph (07) 4054 6644 or 1800 363 622,
fax (07) 4054 7591
Email coco@coconut.com.au
Website www.coconut.com.au

Enjoy the excellent facilities of this five-star park, on the southern approach to the city 7 km from the centre of Cairns. There is a cafe, a kids club in school holidays, free mini-golf, tennis and aqua aerobics, and the list continues. Yes, we have stayed here often and we like it a lot. **$$$$**

❏ Tent sites, powered sites, ensuite sites, fits big motorhomes, cabins.

❏ Toilets and showers (disabled access), laundry, sewer dump-point, telephone, kiosk/shop, LP gas refills, ice, camp kitchen, pool, playground, internet terminal, no pets.

❏ Bookings required, credit cards, holiday loading. Discounts: weekly, Big4.

Cairns Villa and Leisure Park

28 Pease Street, Manunda 4870
Ph (07) 4053 7133 or 1800 644 861,
fax (07) 4053 5914
Email info@cairnsvilla.com.au
Website www.cairnsvilla.com.au

The park is 4 km from the centre of Cairns, set in a quiet area with beautiful tropical surrounds. The park has very good facilities including a mini-mart and a TV room with cable TV. It is an ideal park for a holiday. **$$$**

❏ Tent sites, powered sites, fits big motorhomes, cabins.

❏ Toilets and showers (disabled access), laundry, sewer dump-point, telephone, kiosk/shop, LP gas refills, ice, camp kitchen, pool, playground, no pets.

❏ Bookings required, credit cards, holiday loading. Discounts: pensioners, seniors, weekly.

CALEN (QLD) p. 53

St Helens Gardens Caravan Park

Bruce Highway, Kolijo, via Calen 4798
Ph (07) 4958 8152, fax (07) 4958 8152

A basic park with good facilities situated on the Kolijo creek, 1 km south of the Calen PO. This is a good overnight stop. **$$**

❏ Tent sites, powered sites, drive-thru sites, fits big motorhomes, cabins, on-site vans.

❏ Toilets and showers, laundry, telephone, LP gas refills, ice, pool, playground, pets.

❏ Credit cards. Discounts: 2nd night.

CALIGUEL LAGOONS (QLD)

See Condamine.

CALLIOPE (QLD) p. 48

Calliope River Camping Area

Off Bruce Highway, near old Calliope Village 4860

This is a lovely grassed area on the banks of the Calliope River. It is a popular free overnight stop. Turn off on the north bank of the river and follow the old road south over the old crossing. The area has a 48-hour camping limit. ⊛

❏ Tent sites, drive-thru sites, fits big motorhomes.

❏ Toilets, boat ramp, pets.

CALOUNDRA (QLD) p. 44

Dicky Beach Family Holiday Park

4 Beerburrum Street, Caloundra 4551
Ph (07) 5491 3342, fax (07) 5491 3342

This is a popular beachside holiday park adjoining a busy patrolled swimming beach. The park is across the road from a small shopping strip and a few minutes from the centre of Caloundra. There is a tennis court and covered barbecues. For us, this is a great beachside base at the southern end of this fabulous strip of coast. **$$$**

❏ Tent sites, powered sites, drive-thru sites, fits big motorhomes, cabins.

❏ Toilets and showers (disabled access), laundry, sewer dump-point, telephone, kiosk/shop, LP gas refills, camp kitchen, pool, playground, no pets.

❏ Bookings required, credit cards, holiday loading. Discounts: weekly.

CAMOOWEAL (QLD) p. 260

Camooweal Van Park

Barkly Highway, Camooweal 4828
Ph (07) 4748 2155, fax (07) 4748 2132

This caravan park is located in Camooweal at the rear of the Shell roadhouse. The park has basic facilities, a motel adjacent, and is well located for an overnight stay. **$$**

❏ Tent sites, powered sites, drive-thru sites, fits big motorhomes, basic cabins.

❏ Toilets and showers (disabled access), laundry, telephone, kiosk/shop, LP gas refills, ice, pets.

❏ Credit cards. Discounts: weekly.

CAMPERDOWN (VIC) p. 137

Camperdown Caravan Park

220 Park Road, Camperdown 3260
Ph (03) 5593 1253

This park has an incredible outlook perched on the rim of a crater lake, 3 km from town. The park has basic facilities at a budget price. **$$**

❏ Tent sites, powered sites, drive-thru sites, fits big motorhomes, cabins.

❏ Toilets and showers, laundry, telephone, ice, kiosk/shop, playground, pets.

❏ Credit cards. Discounts: weekly.

CANBERRA (ACT) pp. 210, 215

See also Queanbeyan and Sutton.

Canberra Motor Village

Kunzea Street, O'Connor 2601
Ph (02) 6247 5466 or 1800 026 199,
fax (02) 6249 6138
Email tourpark@tourapark.com.au
Website www.canberravillage.com

Located in a quiet bushland setting 3 km from the centre of Canberra, this park has a dining hall, a TV room, a licensed restaurant and a tennis court. It makes a good base for exploring Canberra, with just a short drive to the city and most of the attractions. **$$$$**

❏ Tent sites, powered sites, drive-thru sites, fits big motorhomes, cabins.

❏ Toilets and showers (disabled access), laundry, telephone, kiosk/shop, LP gas refills, ice, camp kitchen, pool, no pets.

❏ Credit cards, holiday loading. Discounts: pensioners, seniors, weekly.

CANNONVALE (QLD)

See Airlie Beach and Shute Harbour.

CAPE CONRAN (VIC) p. 8

See also Marlo.

Cape Conran Coastal Park

Yeerung Road, Cape Conran 3888
Ph (03) 5154 8438, fax (03) 5154 8496

This national park beachside camping area has a large selection of unpowered sites and cabins. The camping sites are located in bushland areas just a short walk from the beach. This is a quiet, out-of-the-way area, but it is popular during peak holiday periods. **$$**

❏ Tent sites, drive-thru sites, fits big motorhomes, cabins.

❏ Toilets and showers, telephone, ice, no pets.

❏ Credit cards, holiday loading. Discounts: weekly.

CAPE CRAWFORD (NT)

See Heartbreak Hotel.

CAPE HILLSBOROUGH (QLD) p. 53

Fmalleys Beach Camping Area

Cape Hillsborough 4740

This is a small beachside park inside the Cape Hillsborough National Park. Its basic facilities come at a basic price. To get to Fmalleys Beach, turn left off Cape Hillsborough Road. The park is about 45 km from Mackay. **$**

❏ Tent sites, drive-thru sites, fits big motorhomes.

❏ Toilets, no pets.

❏ No credit cards.

CAPE JAFFA (SA) p. 132

Cape Jaffa Caravan Park
18 King Drive, Cape Jaffa 5275
Ph (08) 8768 5056, fax (08) 8768 5056
Email cjcp@capejaffacp.com.au
Website www.capejaffacp.com.au

The small coastal community of Cape Jaffa is a popular holiday destination renowned for its good fishing and local wineries. This owner-operated park is very good quality, close to the beach and within walking distance of the town's limited services. It offers a licensed bottleshop, a dive shop, a TV room, fuel and basic takeaway. $$

❑ Tent sites, powered sites, drive-thru sites, fits big motorhomes, cabins.

❑ Toilets and showers, laundry, telephone, kiosk/shop, LP gas refills, ice, camp kitchen, TV cables, pets.

❑ Credit cards, holiday loading. Discounts: weekly, Top Tourist.

CAPEL (WA) p. 112

Peppermint Grove Holiday Park
Peppermint Grove Beach, Capel 6271
Ph (08) 9727 2351, fax (08) 9727 2959

This is a basic, reasonably priced beachside holiday park. It has a well-stocked store, TV room, tennis courts and mini-golf. $$$

❑ Tent sites, powered sites, fits big motorhomes, cabins, on-site vans.

❑ Toilets and showers, laundry, telephone, kiosk/shop, LP gas refills, ice, camp kitchen, playground, pool, pets.

❑ Credit cards. Discounts: pensioners, seniors, weekly.

CARDWELL (QLD) p. 54

Sunrise Village
43A Marine Parade, Cardwell 4849
Ph (07) 4066 8550, fax (07) 4066 8941

The park is centrally located just a short distance from the centre of town and across the road from the beach (good for fishing). The park has good facilities and a licensed restaurant/cafe in the attached motel. $$$

❑ Tent sites, powered sites, drive-thru sites, fits big motorhomes, cabins.

❑ Toilets and showers (disabled access), laundry, telephone, kiosk/shop, LP gas refills, ice, camp kitchen, pool, no pets.

❑ Credit cards, holiday loading. Discounts: weekly.

CARMILA BEACH (QLD) p. 50

Carmila Beach
Carmila 4739

This is a free camping area on the beachfront. It is 6.5 km from Carmila, of which the last 1.5 km are unsealed. There is a maximum stay of three days. There are no facilities. ⓢ

❑ Tent sites, fits big motorhomes.

CARNARVON (WA) p. 98

Capricorn Holiday Park
North West Coastal Highway, Carnarvon 6701
Ph (08) 9941 8153, fax (08) 9941 8057

Capricorn is conveniently located at the junction of Highway One and Robinson Street, the main access road to town. This is a convenient park for an overnight stop or an extended stay to explore the area. $$$

❑ Tent sites, powered sites, cabins.

❑ Toilets and showers, laundry, telephone, kiosk/shop, LP gas refills, ice, camp kitchen, pool, no pets.

❑ Credit cards. Discounts: weekly, FPA.

Marloo Retiree/Senior Tourist Caravan Park
Wise Street, Carnarvon 6701
Ph (08) 9941 1439, fax (08) 9941 3634

This is a unique caravan park that specifically caters for retirees and seniors, without any facilities for children. There are lawn camping sites, a camp kitchen and some very good amenities. Activities on offer include table-tennis and badminton. This is a good choice for the travelling retiree. $$$

❑ Tent sites, powered sites, drive-thru sites, fits big motorhomes.

❑ Toilets and showers, laundry, telephone, LP gas refills, camp kitchen, pool, no pets.

❑ Bookings required, no credit cards. Discounts: pensioners, seniors, weekly.

Wintersun Caravan Park
546 Robinson Street, Carnarvon 6701
Ph (08) 9941 8150 or 1300 555 585, fax (08) 9941 8150
Email wintersuncpk@wn.com.au

Wintersun is a quality park with good amenities and a wide range of facilities, including mini-golf and lawn bowls. It is a convenient base for exploring the greater Carnarvon region or simply to relax. $$$

❑ Tent sites, powered sites, fits big motorhomes, cabins, on-site vans.

❑ Toilets and showers (disabled access), laundry, telephone, kiosk/shop, LP gas refills, ice, camp kitchen, pool, playground, no pets.

❑ Credit cards. Discount: seniors, weekly, Top Tourist.

CAVES BEACH (NSW) p. 26

The Breakers Holiday Park
7 Mawson Close, Caves Beach 2281
Ph (02) 4971 4610, fax (02) 4971 4610

Situated on a rise overlooking the beach, this park has a great outlook. There is a range of accommodation and the amenities are bright and modern. This is a great park for a weekend away. $$$

❑ Tent sites, powered sites, drive-thru sites, fits big motorhomes, cabins.

❑ Toilets and showers (disabled access), laundry, sewer dump-point, telephone, kiosk/shop, pool, no pets.

❑ Credit cards, holiday loading. Discounts: weekly.

CEDUNA (SA) p. 121

Ceduna Foreshore Caravan Park
South Terrace, Ceduna 5690
Ph (08) 8625 2290, fax (08) 8625 2290

This is a tidy park, very centrally located and just across the road from the beach. It has good basic amenities and is within walking distance of many shops and services. We enjoy staying here. $$$

❑ Tent sites, powered sites, drive-thru sites, fits big motorhomes, cabins.

❑ Toilets and showers, laundry, telephone, kiosk/shop, LP gas refills, ice, playground, pets.

❑ Credit cards. Discounts: weekly, Top Tourist.

Ceduna Shelly Beach Caravan Park
Lot 178 Decres Bay Road, Ceduna 5690
Ph (08) 8625 2012, fax (08) 8625 2012
Email shellycp@tpg.com.au

This is a small park in a quiet area 3 km from the town centre. Situated on the beach, there is good swimming, snorkelling and fishing. Facilities are good. $$$

❑ Tent sites, powered sites, drive-thru sites, fits big motorhomes, cabins.

❑ Toilets and showers (disabled access), laundry, kiosk/shop, camp kitchen, playground, pets.

❑ No credit cards. Discounts: pensioners, seniors, weekly, FPA.

CERVANTES (WA) p. 102

Cervantes Pinnacles Caravan Park
Aragon Street, Cervantes 6511
Ph (08) 9652 7060, fax (08) 9652 7112
Email cerpinnpark@wn.com.au

This is a popular beachside holiday park near the Pinnacles and just a short walk to the centre of town. With the opening of the sealed Lancelin to Cervantes road the park is sure to increase in popularity. The fishing and windsurfing are great along this section of coast. $$$

❑ Tent sites, powered sites, drive-thru sites, fits big motorhomes, cabins, on-site vans.

❑ Toilets and showers, laundry, telephone, kiosk/shop, ice, camp kitchen, playground, pets.

❑ Credit cards, holiday loading. Discounts: weekly.

CHAIN OF LAGOONS (TAS)

See Lagoons Beach.

CHARLEVILLE (QLD) p. 170

✪ **Bailey Bar Caravan Park**
196 King Street, Charleville 4470
Ph (07) 4654 1744 or 1800 065 311, fax (07) 4654 3740
Email bailey@growzone.com.au

We regularly stay at this very good owner-operated park. Set in a quiet, off-highway location about 1.5 km from the town centre, the park has great lawns, clean amenities and good facilities. It offers a range of accommodation and runs bush poetry events during the middle months of the year. $$$

❑ Tent sites, powered sites, drive-thru sites, fits big motorhomes, cabins, on-site vans.

❑ Toilets and showers, laundry, telephone, kiosk/shop, LP gas refills, ice, pets.

❑ Credit cards. Discounts: weekly, Top Tourist.

CHARTERS TOWERS (QLD) p. 265

Aussie Outback Oasis Cabin and Van Village
61–77 East Flinders Highway, Charters Towers 4820
Ph (07) 4787 8722, fax (07) 4787 8722

This new owner-operated park is conveniently located on the main highway east of town. The park has excellent facilities in a nice bush setting. $$$

❑ Tent sites, powered sites, drive-thru sites, fits big motorhomes, cabins.

❑ Toilets and showers (disabled access), laundry, sewer dump-point, telephone, LP gas refills, ice, camp kitchen, pool, playground, pets.

❑ Credit cards. Discounts: weekly.

Dalrymple Tourist Van Park
Lynd Highway, Charters Towers 4820
Ph (07) 4787 1121, fax (07) 4787 8848

This is a well-established park about 2 km north of the city. The park has good facilities including a pool, sauna and kiosk. It makes a good base for exploring this historic mining area. $$

❑ Tent sites, powered sites, drive-thru sites, fits big motorhomes, cabins, on-site vans.

❑ Toilets and showers (disabled access), laundry, telephone, kiosk/shop, LP gas refills, ice, pool, pets.

❑ Credit cards. Discounts: seniors, weekly.

CHEYNE BEACH (WA) p. 116

Cheyne Beach Caravan Park
Cheyne Road, via Manypeaks 6328
Ph (08) 9846 1247, fax (08) 9846 1311

Cheyne Beach is an extremely picturesque coastal village. The large caravan park is a short walk to the beach and well protected from the elements. It is very popular and bookings are required in holiday periods. $$$

❑ Tent sites, powered sites, drive-thru sites, fits big motorhomes, cabins.

❑ Toilets and showers (disabled access), laundry, telephone, kiosk/shop, LP gas refills, ice, camp kitchen, playground, no pets.

❑ Credit cards. Discounts: weekly.

CHINCHILLA WEIR (QLD) p. 253

Chinchilla Weir
Tara Road, Chinchilla 4413

Located 9 km south of town alongside the Tara Road, this is a popular rest area in dry weather. Rains can make the park inaccessible. There is a maximum two-night stay and camping, powered or unpowered, is free. Pets are welcome at this picturesque site on the shores of the weir. Facilities are limited to a toilet. ⓢ

❑ Tent sites, powered sites, drive-thru sites, fits big motorhomes.

❑ Toilets, boat ramp, pets.

CHINDERAH (NSW) p. 34

Hacienda Caravan Village
300/37 Chinderah Bay Drive, Chinderah 2487
Ph (02) 6674 1245 or 1800 350 707,
fax (02) 6674 4836
Email info@haciendacv.com.au
Website www.haciendacv.com.au

At the southern end of the fabulous Gold Coast, this park is in a popular year-round holiday region. It has good facilities, good access to the highway and is right on the banks of the Tweed River. $$$

❑ Tent sites, powered sites, drive-thru sites, ensuite sites, cabins.

❑ Toilets and showers, laundry, telephone, kiosk/shop, LP gas refills, ice, camp kitchen, pool, playground, boat ramp, no pets.

❑ Credit cards, holiday loading. Discounts: pensioners, seniors, weekly.

CLIFTON BEACH (QLD) p. 60

Billabong Caravan Park
Cook Highway, Clifton Beach 4879.
Ph (07) 4055 3737, fax (07) 4059 1165
Email billabongpark@bigpond.com

This neatly groomed park is on the Cook Highway. It has good basic facilities and is conveniently located for either an overnight stop or a few days. $$$$

❑ Tent sites, powered sites, drive-thru sites, fits big motorhomes, units, on-site vans.

❑ Toilets and showers (disabled access), laundry, telephone, kiosk/shop, LP gas refills, ice, pool, playground, TV cables, pets.

❑ Credit cards. Discounts: pensioners, seniors, weekly.

CLONCURRY (QLD) pp. 176, 266

⊛ Gilbert Park Tourist Village
McIlwraith Street (via Flinders Highway), Cloncurry 4824
Ph (07) 4742 2300 or 1800 422 300, fax (07) 4742 2303
Email gilpark@bigpond.com

We regularly stay at this quality family-operated park, located on the main highway 2 km east of the town centre. Relax in the pool and spa or enjoy a meal in the covered barbecue area. With clean amenities and a range of facilities, the park also adjoins a small rocky hill known as Sunset Hill, the perfect place to sit and enjoy the sunset. $$$

❑ Tent sites, powered sites, drive-thru sites, fits big motorhomes, cabins.

❑ Toilets and showers (disabled access), laundry, sewer dump-point, telephone, kiosk/shop, LP gas refills, ice, pool, no pets.

❑ Bookings required, credit cards. Discounts: weekly, Big4.

COBAR (NSW) pp. 166, 242

Cobar Caravan Park
101 Barrier Highway, Cobar 2835
Ph (02) 6836 2425, fax (02) 6836 2425

This park appeals to us whenever we have stayed here. The neat, well-maintained park is located on the Barrier Highway about 1 km west of the shopping centre. There are good amenities and the park is an ideal overnight stop for travellers or a good base for exploring the local area. $$

❑ Tent sites, powered sites, drive-thru sites, fits big motorhomes, cabins, on-site vans.

❑ Toilets and showers (disabled access), laundry, telephone, kiosk/shop, LP gas refills, ice, pets.

❑ Bookings required, credit cards. Discounts: weekly.

COBDOGLA (SA) p. 225

Cobdogla Station Caravan Park
14 Shueard Road, Cobdogla 5346
Ph (08) 8588 7164, fax (08) 8588 7221
Email cobby@riverland.net.au
Website www.cobdoglacaravanpark.com.au

This is a good quality waterfront park in the heart of the Riverland, with expanses of lawn and shady trees. The park is easily accessed from the highway and has appeal for those looking for a quiet holiday on the river. Minimum bookings apply during long weekends and holiday periods. $$$

❑ Tent sites, powered sites, drive-thru sites, fits big motorhomes, cabins.

❑ Toilets and showers, laundry, telephone, LP gas refills, pool, playground, boat ramp, pets.

❑ Credit cards. Discounts: pensioners, seniors, weekly, Top Tourist.

COBRAM (VIC) pp. 154, 218

See also Barooga.

Cobram East Caravan Park
Murray Valley Highway, Cobram 3644
Ph (03) 5872 1207, fax (03) 5871 2459

This good quality park is 4 km east of town alongside the Murray Valley Highway, among some of the region's vast orchards. The park has facilities including a solar-heated pool and shady sites, and will be busy during the summer fruit-picking season. $$$

❑ Tent sites, powered sites, fits big motorhomes, cabins.

❑ Toilets and showers, laundry, telephone, kiosk/shop, LP gas refills, ice, camp kitchen, pool, playground, pets.

❑ Credit cards. Discounts: weekly.

Oasis Caravan Park
Corner Koonoomoo and Racecourse roads, Cobram 3644
Ph (03) 5871 2010, fax (03) 5871 2873
Email oasis@cml.com.au
Website www.oasishomes.com.au

This new park opened in the summer of 2000 with uniquely designed facilities and will develop into an outstanding park. The individual multi-sided amenity blocks are a feature of the park, which is about 4 km west of the Cobram town centre. We like the concept. $$

❑ Tent sites, powered sites, drive-thru sites, ensuite sites, fits big motorhomes, cabins.

❑ Toilets and showers (disabled access), laundry, sewer dump-point, camp kitchen, pool, TV cables, pets.

❑ Credit cards. Discounts: weekly.

COFFS HARBOUR (NSW) p. 30

Park Beach Holiday Park
Ocean Parade, Coffs Harbour 2450
Ph (02) 6648 4888 or 1800 200 111, fax (02) 6651 2465
Email pbcpark@chcc.nsw.gov.au
Website www.parkbeachcaravanpark.com.au

This is a large beachfront council park 4 km from the centre of town and close to the popular jetty precinct. The park boasts a wide range of facilities and is very popular during peak holiday periods. $$$

❑ Tent sites, powered sites, drive-thru sites, ensuite sites, fits big motorhomes, cabins.

❑ Toilets and showers (disabled access), laundry, sewer dump-point, telephone, kiosk/shop, LP gas refills, ice, camp kitchen, pool, internet terminal, no pets.

❑ Bookings required, credit cards, holiday loading. Discounts: weekly, Top Tourist.

Tourist Caravan Park
123 Pacific Highway, Coffs Harbour 2450
Ph (02) 6652 1694, fax (02) 6651 3632

This basic park adjoins the showgrounds and is just a short stroll to the centre of town. It is budget-priced and in a convenient highway position, with sports fields, a walking track and a shopping centre nearby. $$

❑ Tent sites, powered sites, drive-thru sites, fits big motorhomes, cabins, on-site vans.

❑ Toilets and showers (disabled access), laundry, sewer dump-point, telephone, kiosk/shop, LP gas refills, camp kitchen, playground, pets.

❑ Credit cards, holiday loading. Discounts: weekly.

CONDAMINE (QLD) p. 160

Caliguel Lagoons
Meandarra Road, Condamine 4416

This free camping ground is in a picturesque area alongside Caliguel Lagoons, 7 km from Condamine off the Meandarra Road. The basic camping area has no showers but is otherwise ideal for those seeking out a cheap night or two. Take a rest alongside this small stretch of water. ⊛

❑ Tent sites, drive-thru sites, fits big motorhomes.

❑ Toilets, boat ramp, pets.

Condamine River Caravan Park
Wambo Street, Condamine 4416
Ph (07) 4627 7179, fax (07) 4627 7179

This is a small, pretty park located in the centre of the small township and within easy walking distance of the hotel. The park has a range of accommodation, clean basic amenities and is a great overnight stop. $$

❑ Tent sites, powered sites, drive-thru sites, fits big motorhomes, cabins.

❑ Toilets and showers (disabled access), laundry, telephone, pets.

❑ No credit cards. Discounts: weekly.

COOBER PEDY (SA) p. 182

Coober Pedy Oasis Caravan Park
Hutchison Street, Coober Pedy 5723
Ph (08) 8672 5169 or 1800 650 541, fax (08) 8672 5165
Email cooberpedybig4@ozemail.com.au

Located at the eastern end of the main street, this is a well-established, good quality park with a range of features, including an indoor pool. The park owners also offer opal mine tours. Water is a scarce commodity in Coober Pedy so the caravan parks don't have lawns. Nor do they have water hook-ups; each has coin-in-the-slot points for filling tanks. $$$

❑ Tent sites, powered sites, drive-thru sites, ensuite sites, fits big motorhomes, cabins, on-site vans.

❑ Toilets and showers, laundry, telephone, kiosk/shop, LP gas refills, ice, camp kitchen, pool, no pets.

❑ Bookings required, credit cards, holiday loading. Discounts: pensioners, weekly, Big4.

Opal Inn Caravan Park
Hutchison Street, Coober Pedy 5723
Ph (08) 8672 5054, fax (08) 8672 5501
Email reservations@opalinn.com.au
Website www.opalinn.com.au

This is a comfortable park, centrally located in town and part of the hotel complex. Coober Pedy is a dusty town but the amenities at this park are clean and the facilities are good. $$$

❑ Tent sites, powered sites, drive-thru sites, fits big motorhomes, on-site vans.

❑ Toilets and showers, laundry, telephone, internet terminal, ice, kiosk/shop, pets.

❑ Credit cards. Discounts: pensioners, seniors, Top Tourist.

⊛ Stuart Range Caravan Park
Corner Hutchison Street and Stuart Highway, Coober Pedy 5723
Ph (08) 8672 5179, fax (08) 8672 5148

Located close to the Stuart Highway, this park has good facilities including an extensive range of accommodation, a pool and barbecues. Stop for dinner at the park's very popular pizza shop. $$$

❑ Tent sites, powered sites, drive-thru sites, fits big motorhomes, cabins.

❑ Toilets and showers (disabled access), laundry, telephone, kiosk/shop, LP gas refills, ice, camp kitchen, pool, playground, pets.

❑ Bookings required, credit cards. Discounts: weekly.

COOINDA (NT)

See Kakadu National Park.

COOLUM BEACH (QLD) p. 44

Coolum Beach Caravan Park
David Low Way, Coolum 4573
Ph (07) 5446 1474 or 1800 461 474, fax (07) 5446 1474
Email coolum@maroochypark.com
Website www.maroochypark.qld.gov.au

This is a popular beachfront holiday park just across the road from the centre of Coolum.

Walk to the shops and restaurants, swim at the patrolled beach or soak up the sunshine, or do all three! The park gets busy in peak holiday periods. $$$

❏ Tent sites, powered sites, drive-thru sites, fits big motorhomes.

❏ Toilets and showers (disabled access), laundry, sewer dump-point, telephone, LP gas refills, ice, camp kitchen, internet terminal, no pets.

❏ Credit cards, holiday loading. Discounts: weekly, FPA.

COOMA (NSW) p. 217

Snowtels Caravan Park
Snowy Mountains Highway, Cooma 2630
Ph (02) 6452 1828, fax (02) 6452 7192
Email info@snowtels.net.au
Website www.snowtels.com.au

This park is located on the south side of town and is easily accessible from the Monaro Highway. It is popular during the winter months with tourists visiting the Snowy Mountains. There are very good amenities and facilities include mini-golf, a tennis court and recreation room. This is a good base for exploring the region and we stay here when visiting Cooma. $$$

❏ Tent sites, powered sites, drive-thru sites, fits big motorhomes, cabins, on-site vans.

❏ Toilets and showers, laundry, sewer dump-point, telephone, kiosk/shop, LP gas refills, ice, camp kitchen, playground, internet terminal, pets.

❏ Credit cards. Discounts: pensioners, seniors, weekly.

COONABARABRAN (NSW) p. 158

Warrumbungles Holiday Camp
Timor Road, Coonabarabran 2357
Ph (02) 6842 3400, fax (02) 6842 3401
Email warcamp@bigpond.com

For those looking for something different, this park may appeal. It is a large rural expanse in a quiet off-road area, 11 km from town along the road to the Warrumbungle Ranges. This is a very good base from which to explore the Warrumbungles. The park has a range of accommodation, a heated pool and a volleyball court; however, there are a limited number of powered sites. $$

❏ Tent sites, powered sites, drive-thru sites, fits big motorhomes, cabins.

❏ Toilets and showers (disabled access), laundry, telephone, camp kitchen, pool, pets.

❏ Bookings required, credit cards. Discounts: weekly.

Wayfarer Caravan Park
Newell Highway, Coonabarabran 2357
Ph (02) 6842 1773, fax (02) 6842 1773

This is a budget-priced park on the southern approaches to town. It has good basic facilities and is an ideal stopover on the Newell Highway. It is also a convenient park to leave the van at and explore the Warrumbungles or the nearby observatories. Caravan parks in Coonabarabran become very busy in the winter tourist season. $$$

❏ Tent sites, powered sites, drive-thru sites, fits big motorhomes, cabins.

❏ Toilets and showers, laundry, sewer dump-point, telephone, kiosk/shop, LP gas refills, pool, playground, pets.

❏ Credit cards. Discounts: weekly.

COPPER HILLS (SA) p. 184

Copper Hills Homestead
(32 km east of Cadney Homestead)
Ph (08) 8670 7995

This is a small, private camping area alongside a small waterhole on Cadney Park Station. Access is along 32 km of unsealed road. The park is an ideal base to explore the Painted Desert or just a relaxing spot to camp in the shade and watch the birds. The amenities are a short walk away, close to the homestead. $$

❏ Tent sites, powered sites.

❏ Toilets and showers, no pets.

❏ No credit cards.

CORAL BAY (WA) p. 98

⊛ **Peoples Park Caravan Village**
Coral Bay, 6701
Ph (08) 9942 5933, fax (08) 9942 5866

This park is a great holiday spot, set in a wonderful location across the road from the fabulous beach and close to the coral reef. Diving and fishing are very popular along with coral viewing in glass-bottom boats. Coral Bay is very busy during holidays and booking is essential. The park adjoins a cafe and a well-stocked general store. $$$

❏ Tent sites, powered sites, drive-thru sites, fits big motorhomes, cabins.

❏ Toilets and showers, laundry, sewer dump-point, telephone, kiosk/shop, LP gas refills, ice, boat ramp, no pets.

❏ Bookings required, credit cards.

COROWA (NSW) p. 218

Ball Park Caravan Park
Bridge Road, Corowa 2646
Ph (02) 6033 1426, fax (02) 6033 4282
Email ballpark@corowa.albury.net.au

This large council park fronts the Murray River and is just a short walk from the town centre. It adjoins the large bowling club complex. This is a popular riverside holiday park and pets are permitted outside the Christmas, January and Easter holiday periods. The park has good facilities and is a good central base in the town. $$

❏ Tent sites, powered sites, drive-thru sites, fits big motorhomes, cabins.

❏ Toilets and showers (disabled access), laundry, telephone, kiosk/shop, LP gas refills, ice, pool, playground, boat ramp, pets.

❏ Credit cards, holiday loading. Discounts: weekly.

Corowa Caravan Park
84 Federation Avenue, Corowa 2646
Ph (02) 6033 1944, fax (02) 6033 0075
Email corowacv@cln.com.au

The park is 2 km east of town with frontage to the Murray River. It is the closest park to the popular golf course and has boats and bikes for hire. The park has large shady river red gums and is great for a break. $$

❏ Tent sites, powered sites, drive-thru sites, fits big motorhomes, cabins.

❏ Toilets and showers, laundry, telephone, kiosk/shop, LP gas refills, ice, camp kitchen, pool, playground, boat ramp, no pets.

❏ Credit cards, holiday loading. Discounts: pensioners, seniors, weekly.

CORRIMAL (NSW)

See Wollongong.

CORRYONG (VIC) p. 216

Corryong Creek Caravan Park
Murray Valley Highway, Corryong 3707
Ph (02) 6076 1520, fax (02) 6076 1520

We like this spacious park that is 7 km west of town, under large shady trees and alongside a popular trout-fishing stream. The budget-priced park in *The Man from Snowy River* territory has basic amenities and is ideal for a few days' stay or even just overnight. $$

❏ Tent sites, powered sites, drive-thru sites, fits big motorhomes, cabins, on-site vans.

❏ Toilets and showers, laundry, telephone, kiosk/shop, LP gas refills, ice, playground, pets.

❏ Bookings required, credit cards. Discounts: weekly.

COWARAMUP (WA) p. 112

See also Gracetown.

⊛ **Taunton Farm Caravan Park**
Bussell Highway, Cowaramup 6284
Ph (08) 9755 5334 or 1800 248 777,
fax (08) 9755 5597
Email enquiries@tauntonfarm.com.au
Website www.tauntonfarm.com.au

We think this is possibly the best base for exploring the wonderful Margaret River region and its many wineries. It is a quality park in a great farm setting and we always enjoy our stays here. $$$

❏ Tent sites, powered sites, drive-thru sites, fits big motorhomes, cabins, on-site vans.

❏ Toilets and showers (disabled access), laundry, sewer dump-point, telephone, kiosk/shop, LP gas refills, ice, camp kitchen, playground, no pets.

❏ Credit cards. Discounts: pensioners, seniors, weekly, Big4.

CRADLE MOUNTAIN (TAS) p. 290

⊛ **Cradle Mountain Tourist Park**
Cradle Valley, Cradle Mountain 7306
Ph (03) 6492 1395 or 1800 068 574,
fax (03) 6492 1438
Email cradle@cosycabins.com
Website www.cosycabins.com/cradle

Set in bushland just outside the World Heritage-listed Tasmanian wilderness area, this quality park has good facilities including a large recreation building with open fireplaces. It is a popular camping site for walkers from around the world who come to walk the renowned Overland Track in the Cradle Mountain–Lake St Clair National Park. $$$

❏ Tent sites, powered sites, drive-thru sites, fits big motorhomes, cabins.

❏ Toilets and showers, laundry, telephone, kiosk/shop, LP gas refills, ice, camp kitchen, pool, playground, boat ramp, no pets.

❏ Credit cards, holiday loading. Discounts: pensioners, seniors, weekly.

CRAYFISH CREEK (TAS) p. 288

Caradale Caravan Park
Bass Highway, Crayfish Creek 7321
Ph (03) 6443 4228, fax (03) 6443 4228
Email caradale@aur.net.au

In a unique bushland setting, this park is tucked away on the banks of Crayfish Creek, a short way in from the coast. It is a popular park during holiday periods, when the weather is warmer for swimming and camping. $$

❏ Tent sites, powered sites, drive-thru sites, fits big motorhomes, cabins, on-site vans.

❏ Toilets and showers, laundry, telephone, kiosk/shop, ice, camp kitchen, playground, TV cables, pets.

❏ Credit cards. Discounts: seniors, weekly.

CRESCENT HEAD (NSW) p. 30

Crescent Head Holiday Park
Pacific Street, Crescent Head, 2440.
Ph (02) 6566 0261 or 1800 006 600,
fax (02) 6566 0251.
Email 4shore@tsn.cc

This is a large beachside caravan park close to the town centre. Crescent Head is small, making it easy to walk to the shops, the bowling club or the golf club. $$

❏ Tent sites, powered sites, drive-thru sites, fits big motorhomes, cabins.

❏ Toilets and showers (disabled access), laundry, sewer dump-point, telephone, shop/kiosk, LP gas refills, ice, playground, internet terminal, no pets.

❏ Credit cards, holiday loading. Discounts: pensioners, seniors, weekly.

CROKI (NSW) p. 28

⊛ **Riverside Caravan Park**
Reid Street, Croki 2430
Ph (02) 6556 3274

Set on the banks of the Manning River in a quiet off-highway location, this small, well-designed owner-operated park is a perfect base from which to explore the attractions of Ellenborough Falls and Crowdy Bay National Park. The park has drive-through sites ideally suited for an overnight stop; however, if there is time, stay two nights so you can have a chance to see the local area. $$

❏ Tent sites, powered sites, drive-thru sites, cabins, onsite vans.

❏ Toilets and showers, laundry, sewer dump-point, kiosk/shop, LP gas refills, ice, no pets.

❏ No credit cards. Discounts: pensioners, seniors, weekly.

CROOKHAVEN HEADS (NSW) p. 14

Crookhaven Heads Tourist Park
Prince Edward Avenue, Culburra Beach 2540
Ph (02) 4447 2849 or 1300 733 026,
fax (02) 4447 2849
Email crookhaven@shoalhaven.nsw.gov.au
Website www.holidayhaven.com.au

This is a large council holiday park located on the southern headland of the Crookhaven River. It has ocean views, good facilities and is close to deep-water and estuarine fishing spots. $$$

❏ Tent sites, powered sites, drive-thru sites, fits big motorhomes, cabins.

❏ Toilets and showers (disabled access), laundry, sewer dump-point, telephone, kiosk/shop, LP gas refills, ice, playground, boat ramp, no pets.

❏ Bookings required, credit cards, holiday loading. Discounts: pensioners, seniors, weekly.

CROYDON (QLD) p. 66

Croydon Caravan Park
Corner Brown and Alldridge streets,
Croydon 4871
Ph (07) 4745 6238

This well-maintained council-owned park is close to the centre of town. It has lots of green grass, large shady trees and cable TV. The park is within walking distance of everything in town. $$

❏ Tent sites, powered sites, drive-thru sites, fits big motorhomes.

❏ Toilets and showers (disabled access), laundry, telephone, kiosk/shop, pool, TV cables, pets.

❏ No credit cards. Discounts: weekly.

CRYSTAL BROOK (SA) p. 124

The Brook Caravan Park
Eyre Road, Crystal Brook 5523
Ph (08) 8636 2640, fax (08) 8636 3149

This is a small, neat council-owned park just on the edge of town. It is a very pretty park with large red gums, a creek alongside, and lawn sites. We find this park good value. $

❏ Tent sites, powered sites, fits big motorhomes, cabins.

❏ Toilets and showers, laundry, pets.

❏ Credit cards. Discounts: weekly.

CUDMIRRAH (NSW) p. 14

Swan Lake Tourist Village
4 Goonawarra Drive, Cudmirrah 2540
Ph (02) 4441 2219 or 1300 555 517,
fax (02) 4441 2219
Email swanlake@shoalhaven.nsw.gov.au
Website www.holidayhaven.com.au

This is a popular holiday park located across the road from Swan Lake and just a short distance to the beach. Minimum bookings apply over Christmas, Easter and long weekends. $$$

❏ Tent sites, powered sites, cabins.

❏ Toilets and showers (disabled access), laundry, sewer dump-point, telephone, kiosk/shop, ice, camp kitchen, playground, no pets.

❏ Credit cards, holiday loading. Discounts: pensioners, seniors, weekly.

CULLULLERAINE (VIC) p. 222

Lake Cullulleraine RSL Holiday Park
Riverside Drive, Cullulleraine 3496
Ph (03) 5028 2226

This is a council-owned park on the banks of Lake Cullulleraine. There are green lawns, shady trees and a kiosk that opens only during busy holiday periods. This is a good basic park at a budget price. $$

❏ Tent sites, powered sites, drive-thru sites, fits big motorhomes, on-site vans.

❏ Toilets and showers, laundry, telephone, playground, boat ramp, pets.

❏ No credit cards. Discounts: pensioners, seniors, weekly.

CUMBERLAND RIVER (VIC)

See Lorne.

CUNNAMULLA (QLD) p. 170

Jack Tonkin Caravan Park
Watson Street, Cunnamulla 4490
Ph (07) 4655 1421, fax (07) 4655 1421

This is a typical country-town, council caravan park with good amenities, good basic facilities and a resident manager. The park is in a quiet, off-highway location and is an ideal base for exploring the area or a good choice for an overnight stay. $$

❏ Tent sites, powered sites, drive-thru sites, fits big motorhomes, cabins.

❏ Toilets and showers (disabled access), laundry, sewer dump-point, telephone, kiosk/shop, ice, camp kitchen, pets.

❏ Credit cards. Discounts: 2nd and 3rd night, weekly.

CURRARONG (NSW) p. 14

Currarong Beachside Tourist Park
Nowra Road, Currarong 2540
Ph (02) 4448 3027 or 1300 555 515,
fax (02) 4448 3027
Email currarong@shoalhaven.nsw.gov.au
Website www.holidayhaven.com.au

This is a large caravan park on the waterfront with clean, modern amenities, a fish-cleaning and boat-washing area, two boat ramps and a half tennis court. It is a popular holiday park for fishing enthusiasts. $$$

❏ Tent sites, powered sites, drive-thru sites, fits big motorhomes, cabins.

❏ Toilets and showers (disabled access), laundry, sewer dump-point, telephone, kiosk/shop, LP gas refills, ice, camp kitchen, playground, boat ramp, no pets.

❏ Credit cards, holiday loading. Discounts: pensioners, seniors, weekly.

DALBY (QLD) p. 250

❂ **Myall Creek Caravan Park**
32 Myall Street, Dalby 4405
Ph (07) 4662 4793, fax (07) 4669 6898

Enjoy dinner at one of the local bistros, pop into the RSL club for a drink or walk to the centre of town – all possible from this conveniently located park. Owner-operated, it is a good quality park with clean, modern amenities and easy access to the highway. $$

❏ Tent sites, powered sites, drive-thru sites, ensuite sites, fits big motorhomes, cabins, on-site vans.

❏ Toilets and showers, laundry, sewer dump-point, telephone, camp kitchen, no pets.

❏ Credit cards. Discounts: 3rd night.

DALY WATERS (NT) pp. 70, 196

Daly Waters Pub Caravan Park
Daly Waters 0852
Ph (08) 8975 9927, fax (08) 8975 9982

This is an enormously popular stop where the adjoining historic pub provides its famous Beef and Barra Barbecue every night between April and September. The caravan park is little more than a grassy paddock and the amenities are extremely basic. The attraction is the overall package and an early arrival is often necessary to get a site. We like the pub and the meals but the park is basic. $$

❏ Tent sites, powered sites, drive-thru sites, fits big motorhomes, cabins.

❏ Toilets and showers (disabled access), laundry, telephone, kiosk/shop, LP gas refills, ice, pool, pets.

❏ Credit cards. Discounts: weekly.

DAMPIER (WA) p. 96

Dampier Transit Caravan Park
The Esplanade, Dampier 6713
Ph (08) 9183 1109
Email dca@starwon.com

A small park with about 20 sites, this is operated by the Dampier community and there is a 3-night maximum stay. The park is across the road from the water and within sight of Hamersley Iron's Parker Point loading facility. Pets other than dogs may be allowed. $$

❏ Tent sites, powered sites, fits big motorhomes.

❏ Toilets and showers, laundry, no pets.

❏ No credit cards.

DARLINGTON POINT (NSW) p. 166

Riverside Caravan Park
Kidman Way, Darlington Point 2706
Ph (02) 6968 4237, fax (02) 6968 4237
Email pcfrost@webfront.net.au

This park is located on the banks of the Murrumbidgee River under large, shady river red gums. An ideal place for an overnight stop or a few days watching the Murrumbidgee slip by. $$

❏ Tent sites, powered sites, drive-thru sites, fits big motorhomes, cabins.

❏ Toilets and showers, laundry, telephone, LP gas refills, ice, playground, pets.

❏ Credit cards. Discounts: weekly.

DARWIN (NT) pp. 74, 79

Malak Caravan Park
McMillans Road, Malak 0812
Ph (08) 8927 3500

Located about 14 km from Darwin City, this all-ensuite park only has sites for caravans and motorhomes. The park has basic facilities and the laundry is in the neighbouring camping ground. On Thursdays the council fun bus comes to entertain the kids. $$$$

❏ Ensuite sites.

❏ Toilets and showers, telephone, pool, playground, no pets.

❏ Credit cards. Discounts: weekly.

❂ **Palms Village Resort**
901 Stuart Highway, Palmerston, 0830
Ph (08) 8935 0888 or 1800 350 888,
fax (08) 8935 0777
Email reservations@palmsresort.com.au
Website www.palmsresort.com.au

Located on the Stuart Highway 19 km from Darwin, this is a large park with good facilities and a quality licensed restaurant. We find it a good base for exploring Darwin and the surrounding areas. $$$$

❏ Tent sites, powered sites, drive-thru sites, fits big motorhomes, cabins, on-site vans.

❏ Toilets and showers (disabled access), laundry, telephone, kiosk/shop, LP gas refills, ice, pool, internet terminal, no pets.

❏ Credit cards. Discounts: weekly.

DELORAINE (TAS) p. 278

Apex Caravan Park
51 West Parade, Deloraine 7304
Ph (03) 6362 2345

With good amenities and facilities, this park is about a one-and-a-half hour drive to Cradle Mountain and about half that to Great Lake. There are many good bushwalks around Deloraine. $$

❏ Tent sites, powered sites, fits big motorhomes.

❏ Toilets and showers (disabled access), laundry, sewer dump-point, telephone, pets.

❏ Credit cards. Discounts: weekly.

DENHAM (WA) p. 100

❂ **Denham Seaside Tourist Village**
Knight Terrace, Denham 6537
Ph (08) 9948 1242 or 1300 133 733,
fax (08) 9948 1196
Email shark.bay@wn.com.au
Website www.sharkbayfun.com

Our favourite place to stay in the area, this well-managed park is located at the end of the main street and has a fabulous panoramic view over the sparkling calm waters of Shark Bay. We recommend this park to anyone keen on fishing: there is easy access to a good boat ramp or you can join a fishing charter just a short stroll away at the town jetty. The park is uniquely paved with local shell grit. Monkey Mia Reserve is just a 20-minute drive and the rugged Francois Peron National Park is nearby. **$$$**

❑ Tent sites, powered sites, ensuite sites, fits big motorhomes, cabins.

❑ Toilets and showers, laundry, telephone, kiosk/shop, LP gas refills, ice, camp kitchen, boat ramp, pets.

❑ Credit cards. Discounts: seniors, weekly.

DENMARK (WA) p. 115

Rivermouth Caravan Park
Inlet Drive, Denmark 6333
Ph (08) 9848 1262, fax (08) 9848 1262
Website www.geocities.com/rivermouthpark

This popular park is located right on the waters, a short 1 km walk from the town. This is a basic holiday park at a competitive price. The boat ramp adjoins the park. **$$**

❑ Tent sites, powered sites, fits big motorhomes, cabins, on-site vans.

❑ Toilets and showers, laundry, sewer dump-point, telephone, kiosk/shop, LP gas refills, ice, camp kitchen, playground, boat ramp, pets.

❑ Credit cards. Discounts: weekly.

DERBY (WA) p. 90

Kimberley Entrance Caravan Park
Rowan Street, Derby 6728
Ph (08) 9193 1055, fax (08) 9193 1503

Just a 100-m walk from the centre of town, this park has good facilities and nice shady trees. An ideal base for a longer stay in the area. (Please note that at the time of publication, management was changing hands.) **$$$**

❑ Tent sites, powered sites, drive-thru sites, fits big motorhomes.

❑ Toilets and showers (disabled access), laundry, sewer dump-point, telephone, kiosk/shop, LP gas refills, ice, pets.

❑ Credit cards.

DERWENT BRIDGE (TAS)

See Lake St Clair.

DEVONPORT (TAS) pp. 278, 289

Bay View Holiday Village
2–12 North Caroline Street,
East Devonport 7310
Ph (03) 6427 0499, fax (03) 6427 0544

Close to the beach on the east side of Devonport, this quiet park is in an out-of-town area. The park has very good facilities but has no facilities for tents. It is just a short drive to the Spirit of Tasmania ferry terminal. **$$**

❑ Drive-thru sites, ensuite sites, fits big motorhomes, cabins.

❑ Toilets and showers, laundry, telephone, pets.

❑ Credit cards. Discounts: seniors, weekly, FPA.

DOOMADGEE (QLD)

See Kingfisher Camp.

DONGARA (WA)

See Port Denison.

DOUGLAS DALY TOURIST PARK (NT) p.74

⊙ **Douglas Daly Tourist Park**
Oolloo Road, Douglas Daly 0822
Ph (08) 8978 2479, fax (08) 8978 2479
Email douglasdalypark@bigpond.com

This is a picturesque park on the banks of the Douglas River. Each Thursday they serve free coffee and scones for morning tea and on Wednesday and Sunday evenings they have buffalo roasts. The park is about 40 km along a sealed road from the Stuart Highway (turn off the highway 6 km north of the Hayes Creek Roadhouse). It has good facilities, including a licensed restaurant, and is close to the Douglas Hot Springs. **$$$**

❑ Tent sites, powered sites, drive-thru sites, fits big motorhomes, cabins.

❑ Toilets and showers (disabled access), laundry, telephone, kiosk/shop, LP gas refills, ice, pool, playground, no pets.

❑ Credit cards. Discounts: weekly, Big4.

DROUIN WEST (VIC) p. 4

Glen Cromie Caravan Park
850 Main Neerim Road, Drouin West 3818
Ph (03) 5626 8212, fax (03) 5626 8214
Email glencromie@telstra.com

In a large, park-like setting on the banks of a stream, this is a popular caravan park during weekends and holiday periods. It is a great place for a family break, being just a short drive from the greater Melbourne area. **$$$**

❑ Tent sites, powered sites, fits big motorhomes, on-site vans.

❑ Toilets and showers, laundry, telephone, kiosk/shop, LP gas refills, ice, playground, pets.

❑ Credit cards, holiday loading. Discounts: weekly.

DUARINGA (QLD) p. 259

Mackenzie Park Tourism and Recreation Area
Capricorn Highway, Duaringa 4702

This is little more than a large rest area alongside the highway. At the time of publication overnight camping was free, with a two-night limit. A tourist information centre is nearby. ⊛

❑ Tent sites, drive-thru sites, fits big motorhomes.

❑ Toilets and showers (disabled access), playground, pets.

DUBBO (NSW) pp. 156, 240

Dubbo Cabin and Caravan Parklands
Whylandra Street, Dubbo 2830
Ph (02) 6884 8633 or 1800 033 072,
fax (02) 6884 8341
Email parkland@tpgi.com.au
Website www.dubboparkland.com.au

This is a very good park at the southern entrance to the city, the closest to the

Western Plains Zoo. The park has a range of accommodation and very good amenities. Caravan parks within the Dubbo area can become very busy during the winter months as travellers flee north escaping the southern winter. It is necessary to book ahead. **$$$**

❑ Tent sites, powered sites, drive-thru sites, ensuite sites, fits big motorhomes, cabins.

❑ Toilets and showers (disabled access), laundry, telephone, kiosk/shop, LP gas refills, ice, camp kitchen, pool, playground, no pets.

❑ Bookings required, credit cards, holiday loading. Discounts: weekly, Big4.

⊙ **Dubbo City Caravan Park**
Corner Whylandra and Alfred streets,
Dubbo 2830
Ph (02) 6882 4820, fax (02) 6884 2062
Email dccp@dubbo.nsw.gov.au

Enjoy the sights of Dubbo from this quality park. Conveniently located on the Newell Highway about 2 km from the city centre and just a short drive from the Western Plains Zoo, this park has a selection of accommodation, plush lawns and good facilities, including a car-washing bay. **$$$**

❑ Tent sites, powered sites, drive-thru sites, ensuite sites, fits big motorhomes, cabins.

❑ Toilets and showers (disabled access), laundry, sewer dump-point, telephone, kiosk/shop, LP gas refills, ice, camp kitchen, pool, playground, no pets.

❑ Credit cards. Discounts: Top Tourist.

DUNMARRA (NT) p. 196

Dunmarra Caravan Park
Stuart Highway, Dunmarra 0862
Ph (08) 8975 9922, fax (08) 8975 9981

The Dunmarra Caravan Park is part of a roadhouse complex, as many of the parks along this section of highway. The roadhouse has a good restaurant and a licensed bar and the park is fine for an overnight stop. **$$**

❑ Tent sites, powered sites, drive-thru sites, fits big motorhomes, cabins.

❑ Toilets and showers, telephone, kiosk/shop, LP gas refills, ice, pool, pets.

❑ Credit cards. Discounts: 2nd and 3rd nights.

DURAL (NSW)

See Sydney.

DURRAS (NSW) pp. 14, 211

Lakesea Park
Durras Lake Road, Durras 2536
Ph (02) 4478 6122, fax (02) 4478 6257
Email lakeseapark@bigpond.com
Website www.southcoast.com.au/lakesea/

Strategically located between the beach and the pristine Durras Lake, this park has a well-stocked shop and facilities that include a tennis court and canoe hire. With its fabulous location, it is no wonder that it is such a popular south-coast holiday park. **$$$**

❑ Tent sites, powered sites, drive-thru sites, cabins.

❑ Toilets and showers, laundry, telephone, kiosk/shop, LP gas refills, ice, playground, boat ramp, no pets.

❑ Bookings required, credit cards, holiday loading. Discounts: weekly.

Murramarang Resort
Banyandah Street, South Durras 2536
Ph (02) 4478 6355, fax (02) 4478 6230
Email murra@batemansbay.com
Website www.murramarangresort.com

This is a luxury caravan park with a five-star AA rating. It has exceptional facilities and extensive activities on offer, all in a great beachside location. Minimum bookings apply during peak holiday periods. **$$$**

❑ Tent sites, powered sites, ensuite sites, fits big motorhomes, cabins.

❑ Toilets and showers (disabled access), laundry, telephone, kiosk/shop, LP gas refills, ice, camp kitchen, pool, playground, boat ramp, no pets.

❑ Bookings required, credit cards, holiday loading. Discounts: weekly.

EAGLE POINT (VIC) p. 6

⊙ **Lake King Waterfront Caravan Park**
67 Bay Road, Eagle Point 3870
Ph (03) 5156 6387, fax (03) 5156 6387

Ideal for a family holiday or as a relaxing retreat, this neat and tidy park fronts onto a lake and has its own jetties and boat ramp. It is a popular recreation area and the park has good holiday camping facilities. **$$**

❑ Tent sites, powered sites, drive-thru sites, fits big motorhomes, cabins, on-site vans.

❑ Toilets and showers, laundry, sewer dump-point, telephone, kiosk/shop, LP gas refills, ice, pool, playground, boat ramp, pets.

❑ Credit cards, holiday loading. Discounts: weekly.

EBDEN (VIC) p. 216

See also Albury and Wodonga.

⊙ **Boathaven Holiday Park**
Boathaven Road, Ebden 3691
Ph (02) 6020 6130 or 1800 352 982,
fax (02) 6020 6066
Email boathaven@iprimus.com.au
Website www.boathaven.com.au

Located about 12 km east of Wodonga, this park is one of Australia's few five-star rated caravan parks. Set on 4 ha of landscaped grounds on the shores of Lake Hume, Boathaven offers a range of recreational facilities including a pool, spa, tennis court, volleyball court and canoe and bicycle hire. There is a large kiosk and a number of pleasant, shaded sites. Minimum bookings apply during Christmas, January and the Easter holiday periods. **$$$$**

❑ Tent sites, powered sites, drive-thru sites, ensuite sites, fits big motorhomes, cabins.

❑ Toilets and showers (disabled access), laundry, sewer dump-point, telephone, kiosk/shop, LP gas refills, ice, camp kitchen, pool, playground, no pets.

❑ Credit cards, holiday loading. Discounts: seniors, Big4.

ECHUCA (VIC) p. 218

See also Moama.

Echuca Caravan Park

Corner Crofton and Dickson streets,
Echuca 3564
Ph (03) 5482 2157, fax (03) 5480 1551

This is a popular, quality riverside park just a short walk from the historic port precinct of this old Murray River port town. The spacious park has a range of accommodation, modern amenities and good facilities. This is a very good base to explore the local area or just watch the paddle-steamers cruise past the park. The position is great. $$$

❏ Tent sites, powered sites, drive-thru sites, fits big motorhomes, cabins.

❏ Toilets and showers (disabled access), laundry, sewer dump-point, telephone, kiosk/shop, camp kitchen, pool, playground, boat ramp, no pets.

❏ Credit cards, holiday loading. Discounts: weekly, Top Tourist.

Rich River Caravan and Tourist Park

Crescent Street, Echuca 3564
Ph (03) 5482 3658, fax (03) 5480 2214
Email info@richriver.net
Website www.richriver.net

Located 2 km east of town this popular park has great lawns and large shady trees in a quiet off-highway location. The owner-operated park has good facilities including a pool and covered barbecues. Minimum bookings apply at Christmas, January and Easter holidays. $$$

❏ Tent sites, powered sites, drive-thru sites, ensuite sites, fits big motorhomes, cabins.

❏ Toilets and showers (disabled access), laundry, sewer dump-point, telephone, kiosk/shop, LP gas refills, ice, pool, playground, TV cables, internet terminal, no pets.

❏ Bookings required, credit cards, holiday loading. Discounts: weekly, FPA.

EDEN (NSW) p. 10

Eden Tourist Park

Ashlings Beach, Eden 2551
Ph (02) 6496 1139, fax (02) 6496 4068
Email admin@edentouristpark.com.au
Website www.edentouristpark.com.au

Situated across the road from the beach, the park is 2 km from the town centre. This popular holiday park caters predominantly for tourists, offering good amenities and facilities. This is a good base from which to explore the area. $$$

❏ Tent sites, powered sites, fits big motorhomes, cabins, on-site vans.

❏ Toilets and showers (disabled access), laundry, telephone, kiosk/shop, LP gas refills, ice, playground, no pets.

❏ Bookings required, credit cards, holiday loading. Discounts: seniors, weekly.

⊙ Garden of Eden Caravan Park

Corner Princes Highway and Barclay Street,
Eden 2551
Ph (02) 6496 1172 or 1800 224 460,
fax (02) 6496 3618
Email garden01@austarnet.com.au
Website www.acr.net.au/~garden/

Enjoy the excellent amenities, tennis court and swimming pool at this well-appointed, reasonably priced park, just 2 km from the town centre. Things are always going on at this park, like the recent construction of a new laundry block and the installation of TV cables. This is a great place for an overnight stay or for a longer holiday. Pets are allowed at the owners' discretion. $$$

❏ Tent sites, powered sites, drive-thru sites, fits big motorhomes, cabins.

❏ Toilets and showers (disabled access), laundry, sewer dump-point, telephone, kiosk/shop, LP gas refills, ice, camp kitchen, pool, playground, TV cables, pets.

❏ Credit cards. Discounts: seniors, weekly, Top Tourist.

EDITH FALLS (NT)

See Nitmiluk National Park.

EIGHTY MILE BEACH (WA) p. 92

⊙ Eighty Mile Beach Caravan Park

Eighty Mile Beach, 6725
Ph (08) 9176 5941, fax (08) 9176 5941
Email eightymilebeach@bigpond.com.au

We often stay at this quality beachside park, located 9 km off the Great Northern Highway and 45 km west of Sandfire Roadhouse. The owners have spent a lot of time developing it and we like what they have done. It is a popular fishing spot and a great place to rest and read a good book. $$$

❏ Tent sites, powered sites, drive-thru sites, fits big motorhomes, cabins.

❏ Toilets and showers (disabled access), laundry, sewer dump-point, telephone, kiosk/shop, LP gas refills, ice, camp kitchen, internet terminal, pets.

❏ Credit cards. Discounts: weekly.

ELLIS BEACH (QLD) p. 60

Ellis Beach Oceanfront Bungalows and Leisure Park

Captain Cook Highway, Ellis Beach 4879
Ph (07) 4055 3538 or 1800 637 036,
fax (07) 4055 3077
Email stay@ellisbeachbungalows.com.au
Website www.ellisbeachbungalows.com

This small, absolute beachfront park is 30 km north of Cairns. Ellis Beach was voted the cleanest beach in Queensland in 1999 and has a patrolled swimming area. $$$$

❏ Tent sites, powered sites, drive-thru sites, cabins.

❏ Toilets and showers, laundry, sewer dump-point, telephone, LP gas refills, ice, camp kitchen, pool, TV cables, no pets.

❏ Bookings required, credit cards.

EMERALD (QLD) p. 258

Lake Maraboon Holiday Village

Fairbairn Dam Access Road, via Emerald 4720
Ph (07) 4982 3677, fax (07) 4982 1932
Email lakemaraboon@bigpond.com

This park is located 18 km south-west of Emerald on the banks of Lake Maraboon, a popular spot for water sports and fishing. Red claw crayfish are one of the attractions. The park has a range of facilities including a covered barbecue, a kiosk and a pool. The park is in a pleasant location and many visitors to the area come specifically to stay at Lake Maraboon. $$$

❏ Tent sites, powered sites, drive-thru sites, fits big motorhomes, cabins.

❏ Toilets and showers (disabled access), laundry, sewer dump-point, telephone, kiosk/shop, LP gas refills, ice, camp kitchen, pool, boat ramp, no pets.

❏ Credit cards. Discounts: weekly, Top Tourist.

EMERALD BEACH (NSW) p. 32

Emerald Beach Holiday Park

Fishermans Drive, Emerald Beach 2456
Ph (02) 6656 1521 or 1800 681 521,
fax (02) 6656 1611
Email info@ebhp.com.au
Website www.emerald-beach.com

This is a quality park with comprehensive facilities and excellent amenities. The park is located in a picturesque beachside location, with good access to the Pacific Highway. Swimming, surfing and fishing are all popular here. This is a great park for a family holiday or convenient for an overnight stop. $$$

❏ Tent sites, powered sites, drive-thru sites, ensuite sites, fits big motorhomes, cabins, on-site vans.

❏ Toilets and showers (disabled access), laundry, sewer dump-point, telephone, kiosk/shop, LP gas refills, ice, camp kitchen, pool, playground, TV cables, internet terminal, no pets.

❏ Credit cards, holiday loading. Discounts: weekly, Big4.

EMU PARK (QLD) p. 50

Bell Park Caravan Park

Pattison Street, Emu Park 4702
Ph (07) 4939 6202, fax (07) 4939 6202

This is a good quality council park with large grassy areas on a picturesque coastline. Just walk over the dunes to the beach or walk to the centre of town. There is a pool and playground beside the park, in Bell Park. $$

❏ Tent sites, powered sites, drive-thru sites, fits big motorhomes, cabins.

❏ Toilets and showers (disabled access), laundry, sewer dump-point, telephone, LP gas refills, ice, no pets.

❏ Credit cards. Discounts: weekly.

ENEABBA (WA) p. 102

Western Flora Caravan Park

Brand Highway, 22 km north of Eneabba 6518
Ph (08) 9955 2030, fax (08) 9955 2003
Email westernflora.tinker@wn.com.au

Visit this park during the wildflower season when more than 300 varieties of stunning wildflowers can be viewed on the property and more than 2000 varieties within 40 km of the park. The park has very good amenities and has a small shop that sells a range of wildflower-related souvenirs. $$$

❏ Tent sites, powered sites, drive-thru sites, fits big motorhomes, cabins, on-site vans.

❏ Toilets and showers (disabled access), laundry, telephone, kiosk/shop, camp kitchen, no pets.

❏ Credit cards. Discounts: weekly.

ERLDUNDA (NT) p. 184

Desert Oaks Caravan Park

Stuart Highway, Erldunda 0871
Ph (08) 8956 0984, fax (08) 8956 0942
Email erldunda@bigpond.com

Erldunda is an important service centre strategically located at the junction of the Stuart and Lasseter highways. This is a good quality park and is an excellent overnight stop. The facilities include a pool, tennis court and licensed restaurant. The roadhouse has all normal services and an impressive range of takeaway food. We enjoy staying here. $$$$

❏ Tent sites, powered sites, drive-thru sites, fits big motorhomes.

❏ Toilets and showers (disabled access), laundry, telephone, kiosk/shop, LP gas refills, ice, pool, playground, internet terminal, pets.

❏ Credit cards. Discounts: weekly.

ESCOTT BARRAMUNDI LODGE (QLD)

See Burketown.

ESPERANCE (WA) p. 117

Croker's Park Holiday Resort

817 Harbour Road, Esperance 6450
Ph (08) 9071 4100 or 1800 001 466,
fax (08) 9071 5100
Email crokerspark@bigpond.com

This is a very good park, located 3 km from the centre of town. Its facilities include a well-stocked shop and a recreation room. Minimum bookings are required on long weekends and during holiday periods. $$$

❏ Tent sites, powered sites, drive-thru sites, ensuite sites, fits big motorhomes, cabins.

❏ Toilets and showers, laundry, sewer dump-point, telephone, kiosk/shop, LP gas refills, ice, camp kitchen, pool, playground, no pets.

❏ Bookings required, credit cards, holiday loading. Discounts: weekly, Big4.

Esperance Seafront Caravan Park
Goldfields Road, Esperance 6450
Ph (08) 9071 1251, fax (08) 9071 7003
Email espseafrontcvp@wn.com.au
Website www.esperanceseafront.com

This large park is just 2 km from the town centre and across the road from the beach – in fact it is possible to walk to town along the beach. The park has good amenities and a lovely grassed playground area that seems to host a serious 'beach' cricket match most summer afternoons. We enjoy spending a few days here. **$$$**

❏ Tent sites, powered sites, drive-thru sites, fits big motorhomes, cabins, on-site vans.

❏ Toilets and showers, laundry, telephone, kiosk/shop, LP gas refills, ice, camp kitchen, playground, no pets.

❏ Credit cards. Discounts: weekly, Top Tourist.

Pink Lake Tourist Park
Pink Lake Road, Esperance 6450
Ph (08) 9071 2424 or 1800 011 311,
fax (08) 9071 5075
Email pinklake@comswest.net.au
Website www.pinklakepark.com.au

This is a quality park at a competitive price. Located just 2 km from the centre of town, the park has a wide range of facilities and amenities including a good camp kitchen. The park is popular with campervans and campers. Bookings are necessary during holiday periods. **$$$**

❏ Tent sites, powered sites, fits big motorhomes, cabins, on-site vans.

❏ Toilets and showers, laundry, sewer dump-point, telephone, kiosk/shop, LP gas refills, ice, camp kitchen, playground, pets.

❏ Credit cards, holiday loading. Discounts: weekly, FPA.

EUCLA (SA) p. 119

Eucla Caravan Park
Eyre Highway, Eucla 6443
Ph (08) 9039 3468, fax (08) 9039 3401

We feel this is the best park between Norseman and Ceduna. It forms part of the roadhouse complex and has good amenities and basic facilities. It is a short stroll from the park to the roadhouse where there is a good takeaway-food bar or a more formal dining room. The park is laid out on white gravel atop the ridge, with an outlook over the sand dunes to the south. **$**

❏ Tent sites, powered sites, drive-thru sites, fits big motorhomes, cabins.

❏ Toilets and showers (disabled access), laundry, telephone, kiosk/shop, LP gas refills, ice, pool, playground, pets.

❏ Credit cards. Discounts: weekly.

EVANS HEAD (NSW) p. 32

Silver Sands Caravan and Camping Reserve
Park Street, Evans Head 2473
Ph (02) 6682 4212, fax (02) 6682 4212
Email silversands@richmondvalley.nsw.gov.au

This is a large beachside park with good facilities just a short walk from the centre of town. The park has many permanent holiday vans and is a very popular holiday park with people from the nearby inland towns. The town and park will be busy in peak holiday periods. **$$**

❏ Tent sites, powered sites, drive-thru sites, ensuite sites, cabins.

❏ Toilets and showers (disabled access), laundry, telephone, kiosk/shop, playground, no pets.

❏ Credit cards, holiday loading. Discounts: weekly.

EXMOUTH (WA) p. 98

Lighthouse Caravan Park
Yardie Creek Road, Vlaming Head 6706
Ph (08) 9949 1478

Located 17 km north of Exmouth beneath the lighthouse at Vlaming Head, the park is just across the road from the ocean. The park has basic facilities and a cafe during peak season. There are pleasant views from the lighthouse. **$$$**

❏ Tent sites, powered sites, cabins.

❏ Toilets and showers, laundry, telephone, kiosk/shop, LP gas refills, ice, camp kitchen, pool, no pets.

❏ Bookings required, credit cards. Discounts: weekly.

Ningaloo Caravan Holiday Resort
Murat Road, Exmouth 6707
Ph (08) 9949 2377 or 1800 652 665,
fax (08) 9949 2577
Email reception@exmouthresort.com
Website www.exmouthresort.com

Located close to the town centre, this is a convenient base from which to explore the area, including Ningaloo Reef and Cape Range National Park. The park has an extensive grassed area, good amenities and a wide range of facilities. **$$$**

❏ Tent sites, powered sites, fits big motorhomes, cabins.

❏ Toilets and showers (disabled access), laundry, telephone, kiosk/shop, LP gas refills, camp kitchen, pool, internet terminal, pets.

❏ Bookings required, credit cards, holiday loading. Discounts: Top Tourist.

FINGAL HEAD (NSW) p. 34

Fingal Holiday Park
Prince Street, Fingal Head 2487
Ph (07) 5524 2208, fax (07) 5524 7092

The lovely beach is right at your door in this quiet, out-of-the-way spot. The park has good basic facilities. It is ideal for a family holiday or a few days at the beach. The park will be very busy in peak holiday periods. **$$$**

❏ Tent sites, powered sites, drive-thru sites, cabins, on-site vans.

❏ Toilets and showers (disabled access), laundry, sewer dump-point, telephone, kiosk/shop, LP gas refills, ice, playground, no pets.

❏ Credit cards, holiday loading. Discounts: 3rd night.

FINLEY (NSW) p. 154

Lakeside Caravan Park
Newell Highway, Finley 2713
Ph (03) 5883 1170, fax (03) 5883 1770
Email shazet@bigpond.com

The park, at the northern end of Finley's main street, is on the shore of a small lake. There are good basic facilities and the park is a good place for an overnight stay. A public swimming pool is right behind the park. **$$**

❏ Tent sites, powered sites, drive-thru sites, fits big motorhomes, cabins, on-site vans.

❏ Toilets and showers, laundry, pets.

❏ Bookings required, no credit cards. Discounts: pensioners, seniors, weekly.

FITZROY CROSSING (WA) p. 88

Fitzroy River Lodge Caravan Park
Great Northern Highway, Fitzroy Crossing 6765
Ph (08) 9191 5141, fax (08) 9191 5142
Email fitzroyriverlodge@bigpond.com

The Fitzroy River Lodge is a quality accommodation complex that includes a comfortable caravan park and safari huts. The park has very good amenities, a pool and a tennis court, and is a convenient overnight stop or base from which to explore Geikie Gorge. **$$$**

❏ Tent sites, powered sites, drive-thru sites, fits big motorhomes.

❏ Toilets and showers (disabled access), laundry, sewer dump-point, telephone, kiosk/shop, LP gas refills, ice, pool, pets.

❏ Credit cards. Discounts: weekly.

FLYING FISH POINT (QLD) p. 56

 Flying Fish Point Caravan Park
39 Elizabeth Street, Flying Fish Point 4860
Ph (07) 4061 3131, fax (07) 4061 8533
Email ffpvanpark@znet.net.au

This quality owner-operated park is opposite the water in this small town about 7 km from Innisfail. The park provides patrons with a free fish barbecue for lunch each Wednesday during the tourist season and there are a limited number of fishing dinghies available for use. The park has very good facilities. **$$$**

❏ Tent sites, powered sites, drive-thru sites, fits big motorhomes, cabins.

❏ Toilets and showers, laundry, telephone, kiosk/shop, LP gas refills, ice, camp kitchen, pool, playground, TV cables, pets.

❏ Credit cards. Discounts: weekly, FPA.

FONTY'S POOL (WA) pp. 110, 113

Fonty's Pool Caravan Park
Seven Day Road, Manjimup 6258
Ph (08) 9771 2105, fax (08) 9771 2105

This is a budget-priced park in a great rural location, 10 km from Manjimup. Fonty's Pool is in fact a spring-fed swimming hole, with a rich history dating back to 1925. The park will take dogs. **$$**

❏ Tent sites, powered sites, drive-thru sites, fits big motorhomes, cabins, on-site vans.

❏ Toilets and showers, laundry, sewer dump-point, telephone, kiosk/shop, LP gas refills, ice, camp kitchen, pool, playground, pets.

❏ Credit cards. Discounts: weekly.

FORBES (NSW) p. 156

Apex Riverside Tourist Park
Reymond Street, Forbes 2871
Ph (02) 6851 1929, fax (02) 6851 1700
Email apex@touristpark.com.au
Website www.touristpark.com.au

The park is about 3 km from the town centre on a picturesque bend of the Lachlan River, which some sites overlook. The park is managed on behalf of Apex and is of good quality, with a swimming pool and free gas barbecues. The owners offer discount fuel to all visitors. **$$**

❏ Tent sites, powered sites, drive-thru sites, fits big motorhomes, cabins.

❏ Toilets and showers (disabled access), laundry, telephone, kiosk/shop, LP gas refills, ice, camp kitchen, pool, playground, TV cables, no pets.

❏ Credit cards, holiday loading. Discounts: weekly.

 Forbes River Meadows Caravan Park
Corner Newell Highway and River Road, Forbes 2871
Ph (02) 6852 2694, fax (02) 6852 2692

Located about 1.5 km south of Forbes, alongside the highway, this owner-operated park is a convenient and ideal overnight stop. It has shady trees, large expanses of lawn, spotless amenities and a pool. We like staying here. **$$**

❏ Tent sites, powered sites, drive-thru sites, fits big motorhomes, cabins, on-site vans.

❏ Toilets and showers (disabled access), laundry, sewer dump-point, telephone, kiosk/shop, LP gas refills, ice, camp kitchen, pool, playground, pets.

❏ Credit cards. Discounts: weekly.

Lachlan View Caravan Park
141 Flint Street, Forbes 2871
Ph (02) 6852 1055 or 1800 641 207,
fax (02) 6852 4095
Email lachview@westserv.net.au
Website www.lanis.com.au

This is a good owner-operated park, about 2 km from the centre of town on the Cowra road. The park caters predominantly for tourists and has good amenities and most facilities, including a service station with a convenience shop. **$$$**

❏ Tent sites, powered sites, drive-thru sites, ensuite sites, fits big motorhomes, cabins, on-site vans.

❏ Toilets and showers, laundry, sewer dump-point, telephone, kiosk/shop, LP gas refills, ice, pool, playground, TV cables, no pets.

❏ Credit cards. Discounts: weekly, Big4.

FOREST GLEN (QLD) p. 44

Forest Glen Holiday Resort
71 Owen Creek Road (Tanawha Tourist Drive), Forest Glen 4556
Ph (07) 5476 6646 or 1800 669 955, fax (07) 5445 8956
Email info@forestglenresort.com.au
Website www.forestglenresort.com.au

This award-winning park is set on over 19 ha of parkland. There is a large pool, tennis court, squash court and a licensed restaurant. The Bruce Highway is close by and the Sunshine Coast beaches are just 15 minutes away. **$$$**

❑ Tent sites, powered sites, drive-thru sites, ensuite sites, fits big motorhomes, cabins.

❑ Toilets and showers, laundry, telephone, kiosk/shop, LP gas refills, ice, camp kitchen, pool, playground, internet terminal, no pets.

❑ Credit cards, holiday loading. Discounts: weekly, Big4.

FORSTER–TUNCURRY (NSW) p. 28

Forster Beach Caravan Park
Reserve Road, Forster–Tuncurry 2428
Ph (02) 6554 6269, fax (02) 6555 2549
Email fbcp@tpgi.com.au

This council-operated park is just a 2-minute walk from the centre of town, located on the headland overlooking the estuary and town centre. There are many parks to choose from in this popular resort area, but this park is close to town and has good amenities. We regularly stay here. **$$**

❑ Tent sites, powered sites, fits big motorhomes, cabins.

❑ Toilets and showers (disabled access), laundry, sewer dump-point, telephone, camp kitchen, playground, no pets.

❑ Credit cards, holiday loading. Discounts: weekly.

Smugglers Cove Holiday Village
45 The Lakes Way, Forster–Tuncurry 2428
Ph (02) 6554 6666, fax (02) 6554 6666
Email smuggler@hardnet.com.au
Website www.smugglerscove.com.au

This is a quality, award-winning park with great holiday entertainment and a range of activities all year round. A great family park, it is set in a wonderful subtropical palm grove. **$$$**

❑ Tent sites, powered sites, drive-thru sites, fits big motorhomes, cabins.

❑ Toilets and showers (disabled access), laundry, sewer dump-point, telephone, kiosk/shop, LP gas refills, ice, camp kitchen, pool, playground, no pets.

❑ Credit cards, holiday loading. Discounts: pensioners, seniors, Big4.

GAWLER (SA) p. 246

Gawler Caravan Park
Main North Road, Gawler 5118
Ph (08) 8522 3805, fax (08) 8522 3805
Email gawlercaravanpk@adelaide.on.net

This is a good quality park close to the town centre and located on the banks of the Gawler River. It is a good base for exploring

---

the nearby Barossa Valley and has freeway access to Adelaide. The park also has good access to the Sturt and Barrier highways. **$$$**

❑ Tent sites, powered sites, fits big motorhomes, cabins, on-site vans.

❑ Toilets and showers, laundry, telephone, LP gas refills, camp kitchen, playground, no pets.

❑ Credit cards. Discounts: weekly.

GEELONG (VIC) p. 139

Barwon Caravan and Tourist Park
153 Barrabool Road, Belmont 3216
Ph (03) 5243 3842, fax (03) 5241 3149
Email barwontourist@bigpond.com

This park is located on the south side of the Barwon River, about 2 km from the city centre. The park has good facilities and is easily accessed from the Princes Highway. It has modern amenities and some nicely shaded sites, and it is just a short walk to a large shopping centre. **$$$**

❑ Tent sites, powered sites, drive-thru sites, ensuite sites, fits big motorhomes, cabins, on-site vans.

❑ Toilets and showers, laundry, telephone, kiosk/shop, LP gas refills, camp kitchen, playground, internet terminal, TV cables, no pets.

❑ Credit cards, holiday loading. Discounts: pensioners, seniors, weekly.

City Southside and Riverglen Holiday Park
75 Barrabool Road, Belmont 3216
Ph (03) 5243 5505, fax (03) 5243 4760

Two caravan parks merged in 2001 to form this large park. It has good facilities and is located just 2 km from the centre of Geelong. **$$$**

❑ Tent sites, powered sites, drive-thru sites, ensuite sites, fits big motorhomes, cabins.

❑ Toilets and showers, laundry, telephone, kiosk/shop, LP gas refills, camp kitchen, playground, TV cables, no pets.

❑ Credit cards, holiday loading. Discounts: weekly, FPA.

GEMINI DOWNS (SA)

See Salt Creek.

GEORGETOWN (QLD) p. 66

Midway Van Park
North Street, Georgetown 4871
Ph (07) 4062 1219, fax (07) 4062 1227
Email midwayss@tpg.com.au

This park is 500 m from the town centre on the main through-road. A service station completes the complex, and discounted fuel is available there for park visitors. The park has good basic facilities. **$$**

❑ Tent sites, powered sites, drive-thru sites, fits big motorhomes, cabins.

❑ Toilets and showers (disabled access), laundry, telephone, kiosk/shop, LP gas refills, ice, pool, pets.

❑ Credit cards. Discounts: weekly.

GERALDTON (WA) p. 100

See also Greenough.

Sunset Beach Holiday Park
Bosley Street, Geraldton 6530
Ph (08) 9938 1655, fax (08) 9938 1850
Email sunsetbeach@bigpond.com

Located on the beach 6 km north of the city and in a quiet location, this is a popular park with tourists. Things to do here include windsurfing, angling and beachcombing. The park is well appointed and a good base from which to explore the region or sit and watch the sun set over the sea. Geraldton is a major city on the west coast and has several caravan parks; however, this is the one that appeals to us. **$$$**

❑ Tent sites, powered sites, drive-thru sites, fits big motorhomes, cabins, on-site vans.

❑ Toilets and showers (disabled access), laundry, telephone, kiosk/shop, LP gas refills, ice, camp kitchen, playground, internet terminal, no pets.

❑ Credit cards. Discounts: weekly, Big4.

GERROA (NSW) p. 16

◉ Seven Mile Beach Holiday Park
Crooked River Road, Gerroa 2534
Ph (02) 4234 1340, fax (02) 4234 1340
Email sevenmile@kiama.net
Website www.kiama.net/holiday/sevenmile

Swim at the beach or sit back, relax and watch TV at this large, fabulous beachside park. It has great facilities, including ensuite sites with full Austar TV hook-up. It also has excellent amenities and is in a wonderful location. The park is divided into two units by the main road. Pets are not allowed in busy periods. **$$$$**

❑ Tent sites, powered sites, ensuite sites, fits big motorhomes, cabins, on-site vans.

❑ Toilets and showers (disabled access), laundry, sewer dump-point, telephone, kiosk/shop, LP gas refills, ice, camp kitchen, pool, playground, TV cables, internet terminal, pets.

❑ Credit cards, holiday loading. Discounts: pensioners, seniors, weekly.

GILGANDRA (NSW) p. 158

Rotary Caravan Park
Newell Highway, Gilgandra 2827
Ph (02) 6847 2423, fax (02) 6026 2423

Located alongside the highway on the northern side of the Castlereagh River, this budget-priced park is set on an impressive expanse of lawn with large shady trees. Enjoy the pool, cook a barbecue or take your dog for a walk. This is a convenient park for an overnight stop and we regularly stay here. **$$**

❑ Tent sites, powered sites, drive-thru sites, fits big motorhomes, cabins.

❑ Toilets and showers (disabled access), laundry, telephone, pool, playground, pets.

❑ Credit cards. Discounts: weekly.

GLADSTONE (QLD) p. 48

See also Lake Awoonga.

Barney Beach with the Seabreeze Caravan Park
10 Friend Street, Gladstone 4680
Ph (07) 4972 1366, fax (07) 4972 7549
Email barneybeachqpark@bigpond.com

This is a very good quality park with a good range of facilities and spotless amenities. It is in a quiet area away from the centre of town and just 80 m from the beach. **$$$**

❑ Tent sites, powered sites, drive-thru sites, fits big motorhomes, cabins, on-site vans.

❑ Toilets and showers, laundry, sewer dump-point, telephone, kiosk/shop, LP gas refills, ice, camp kitchen, pets.

❑ Credit cards. Discounts: weekly.

GLASS HOUSE MOUNTAINS (QLD) p. 44

Log Cabin Caravan Park
Glass House Mountains Tourist Drive, Glass House Mountains 4518
Ph (07) 5496 9338, fax (07) 5496 9338
Email logcabin@powerup.com.au

This is a basic caravan park, close to the picturesque Glass House Mountains and several hinterland attractions. The park has a cafe and a limited number of tourist sites in a treed area (although the park is currently expanding). **$$**

❑ Tent sites, powered sites, drive-thru sites, fits big motorhomes, cabins, on-site vans.

❑ Toilets and showers, laundry, sewer dump-point, telephone, kiosk/shop, LP gas refills, camp kitchen, pool, playground, pets.

❑ Credit cards. Discounts: weekly.

GLEBE WEIR (QLD) p. 162

◉ Glebe Weir
Glebe Weir Road, off Leichhardt Highway, via Taroom 4420

Fishing is the main attraction at this popular, out-of-the-way camping area, 52 km north-east of Taroom. The weir is a renowned spot for yellow-belly and saratoga. The camping ground is reached along a narrow bitumen road from the highway. Amenities are basic and the showers are cold water only, but there are a number of powered sites. This is a great park for the budget conscious and is suitable for larger motorhomes. **$**

❑ Tent sites, powered sites, drive-thru sites, fits big motorhomes.

❑ Toilets and showers, boat ramp, pets.

❑ No credit cards.

GOL GOL (NSW) p. 220

River Gardens Tourist Park
Corner Sturt Highway and Punt Road, Gol Gol 2738
Ph (03) 5024 8541 or 1800 816 326, fax (03) 5024 8723
Email rivergarden@ncable.com.au

This is a neat riverfront park on the Sturt Highway close to Mildura and just 1 km from the centre of Gol Gol. It is a good owner-operated park with a range of accommodation and good facilities. Minimum booking periods apply. **$$$**

❏ Tent sites, powered sites, drive-thru sites, ensuite sites, fits big motorhomes, cabins, on-site vans.

❏ Toilets and showers (disabled access), laundry, telephone, kiosk/shop, LP gas refills, ice, camp kitchen, pool, playground, boat ramp, pets.

❏ Credit cards, holiday loading. Discounts: Top Tourist.

GOLD COAST (QLD) pp. 36–7

See also Jacobs Well, Ormeau and Tweed Heads.

◉ Broadwater Tourist Park

Gold Coast Highway, Southport 4215
Ph (07) 5581 7733, fax (07) 5591 4059
Email bwater@gctp.com.au
Website www.gctp.com.au/bwater

Position is everything, and this spacious council-owned park fronts the Gold Coast broadwater. It has very good facilities and outstanding views across the water to Marina Mirage. The park has several restaurants within walking distance and is about 1.5 km from the Southport business and shopping centre. **$$$$**

❏ Tent sites, powered sites, ensuite sites, fits big motorhomes, cabins.

❏ Toilets and showers (disabled access), laundry, sewer dump-point, telephone, kiosk/shop, LP gas refills, ice, camp kitchen, pool, playground, boat ramp, no pets.

❏ Bookings required, credit cards, holiday loading. Discounts: weekly, Top Tourist.

Burleigh Beach Tourist Park

Goodwin Terrace, Burleigh Heads 4220
Ph (07) 5581 7755, fax (07) 5535 3127
Email burly@gctp.com.au
Website www.gctp.com.au/burly

This is one of the older council parks on the Gold Coast. The park has good basic facilities and is popular with holiday-makers, as it is across the road from a patrolled surf beach. It is a short stroll to the shops, restaurants and nightlife. The park is very busy during peak holiday periods. **$$$**

❏ Tent sites, powered sites, cabins.

❏ Toilets and showers (disabled access), laundry, telephone, LP gas refills, ice, TV cables, no pets.

❏ Bookings required, credit cards, holiday loading. Discounts: weekly.

Kirra Beach Tourist Park

Charlotte Street, Kirra 4225
Ph (07) 5581 7744, fax (07) 5599 3877
Email kirra@gctp.com.au
Website www.gctp.com.au/kirra

This is a spacious, good quality caravan park, popular with beach devotees, backpackers and international travellers. Enjoy a swim in the pool, a barbecue under the covered facilities or just relax. The popular Kirra Beach is just a couple of blocks away. **$$$**

❏ Tent sites, powered sites, fits big motorhomes, cabins.

❏ Toilets and showers (disabled access), laundry, sewer dump-point, telephone, kiosk/shop, LP gas refills, ice, camp kitchen, pool, playground, no pets.

❏ Credit cards, holiday loading. Discounts: weekly, Top Tourist.

Main Beach Tourist Park

Main Beach Parade, Main Beach 4217
Ph (07) 5581 7722, fax (07) 5532 0316
Email main@gctp.com.au
Website www.gctp.com.au/main

This is a unique park set amid the famous Gold Coast high-rise buildings. From here it is a short walk to some of the coast's best beaches and the fashionable Tedder Avenue restaurant strip. The park is neat and well maintained with good amenities. A booking is usually necessary year-round. **$$$**

❏ Tent sites, powered sites, ensuite sites, cabins.

❏ Toilets and showers (disabled access), laundry, sewer dump-point, telephone, kiosk/shop, LP gas refills, ice, camp kitchen, pool, playground, TV cables, internet terminal, no pets.

❏ Bookings required, credit cards, holiday loading. Discounts: weekly.

Ocean Beach Tourist Park

2 Hythe Street (corner Gold Coast Highway), Miami 4220
Ph (07) 5581 7711, fax (07) 5535 8210
Email ocean@gctp.com.au
Website www.gctp.com.au/ocean

This is one of several Gold Coast City Council parks that has very good basic facilities and is just across the road from the beach. Access from the Gold Coast Highway is excellent. A good park for a family holiday or a few days break on the fabulous Gold Coast. **$$$**

❏ Tent sites, powered sites, drive-thru sites.

❏ Toilets and showers (disabled access), laundry, sewer dump-point, telephone, kiosk/shop, LP gas refills, ice, TV cables, no pets.

❏ Credit cards, holiday loading. Discounts: weekly.

◉ Tallebudgera Creek Tourist Park

1544 Gold Coast Highway, Palm Beach 4221
Ph (07) 5581 7700, fax (07) 5576 4157
Email tally@gctp.com.au
Website www.gctp.com.au/tally

A favourite of ours, this popular holiday caravan park is about 5 km north of Palm Beach, towards Burleigh Heads. It fronts onto the Tallebudgera Creek and is just a short walk to the beach. This park is among the Gold Coast's best parks, centrally located with very good amenities and a wide range of facilities, including a tennis court and a heated pool. **$$$**

❏ Tent sites, powered sites, drive-thru sites, ensuite sites, fits big motorhomes, cabins.

❏ Toilets and showers (disabled access), laundry, sewer dump-point, telephone, kiosk/shop, LP gas refills, ice, camp kitchen, pool, playground, boat ramp, no pets.

❏ Credit cards, holiday loading. Discounts: weekly, FPA.

Treasure Island Holiday Park

117 Brisbane Road, Biggera Waters 4216
Ph (07) 5537 1511 or 1800 339 966, fax (07) 5537 4233
Email jollyroger@treasureisland.com.au
Website www.treasureisland.com.au

This is a good quality park with a licensed family bistro and a range of great facilities including a resort-style pool, spas, a tennis court and mini-golf. The park is a short stroll from the large Harbour Town shopping complex and a Readings multi-cinema complex. Access is very good from the Gold Coast Highway. **$$$**

❏ Tent sites, powered sites, cabins.

❏ Toilets and showers, laundry, sewer dump-point, telephone, kiosk/shop, LP gas refills, ice, camp kitchen, pool, playground, boat ramp, internet terminal, no pets.

❏ Bookings required, credit cards, holiday loading. Discounts: weekly, Big4.

GOONDIWINDI (QLD) p. 160

Gundy Star Caravan Park

Old Cunningham Highway, Goondiwindi 4390
Ph (07) 4671 2900, fax (07) 4671 2999

The park is located in a quiet, out-of-the-way location and has good basic facilities at a budget price. There are some nice grassed areas and this is our pick of the parks in town. **$$**

❏ Tent sites, powered sites, drive-thru sites, fits big motorhomes, cabins.

❏ Toilets and showers (disabled access), laundry, sewer dump-point, telephone, kiosk/shop, camp kitchen, LP gas refills, ice, playground, pets.

❏ Credit cards. Discounts: 2nd and 3rd nights, weekly.

GRACETOWN (WA) p. 112

Gracetown Caravan Park

Corner Cowaramup Bay and Caves roads, Gracetown 6284
Ph (08) 9755 5301, fax (08) 9755 5508
Email gracetowncaravanpark@bigpond.com

This is a quality park close to the Margaret River wineries, beaches and other attractions. It is conveniently located, has good amenities and a great range of facilities, including tennis courts. **$$$**

❏ Tent sites, powered sites, fits big motorhomes, cabins, on-site vans.

❏ Toilets and showers, laundry, telephone, kiosk/shop, LP gas refills, ice, camp kitchen, TV cables, no pets.

❏ Credit cards, holiday loading. Discounts: seniors, Top Tourist.

GRAFTON (NSW) p. 32

The Gateway Village

598 Summerland Way, Grafton 2460
Ph (02) 6642 4225 or 1800 012 019, fax (02) 6643 3360
Email gateway@hotkey.net.au

This is a very good quality caravan park, 3.5 km north of the town centre, along the Summerland Way. Good facilities and a lovely garden setting make this an attractive spot for those wishing to explore Grafton. **$$$**

❏ Tent sites, powered sites, drive-thru sites, ensuite sites, fits big motorhomes, cabins, on-site vans.

❏ Toilets and showers (disabled access), laundry, sewer dump-point, telephone, kiosk/shop, LP gas refills, camp kitchen, pool, no pets.

❏ Credit cards. Discounts: weekly, Big4.

GRAMPIANS NATIONAL PARK (VIC)

See Halls Gap.

GREEN HEAD (WA) p. 102

Green Head Caravan Park

Lot 228 Green Head Road, Green Head 6514
Ph (08) 9953 1131, fax (08) 9953 1151

This is a small, tidy park with basic amenities, located in the small coastal community of Green Head. Crayfish boats operate from the town during the season. Pets are allowed, though not in holiday seasons. **$$**

❏ Tent sites, powered sites, drive-thru sites, fits big motorhomes, cabins, on-site vans.

❏ Toilets and showers, laundry, telephone, kiosk/shop, LP gas refills, ice, playground, pets.

❏ Credit cards, holiday loading. Discounts: weekly.

GREENOUGH (WA) p. 102

◉ Greenough Rivermouth Caravan Park

4 Hull Street, Cape Burney, Greenough 6530
Ph (08) 9921 5845 or 1800 800 580, fax (08) 9921 5845
Email grcp@wn.com.au

Set at the mouth of the Greenough River just 10 km south of Geraldton, this large, well-shaded park is protected from the onshore winds and has very good facilities. Cook in the camp kitchen or buy takeaway food from the park's well-stocked shop. This is an enjoyable place to stay, especially for a family holiday, and we like to stay here and commute to Geraldton. **$$$**

❏ Tent sites, powered sites, drive-thru sites, fits big motorhomes, cabins, on-site vans.

❏ Toilets and showers (disabled access), laundry, sewer dump-point, telephone, kiosk/shop, LP gas refills, ice, camp kitchen, pool, playground, pets.

❏ Credit cards. Discounts: weekly, Top Tourist.

GREGORY (WA) p. 100

Port Gregory Caravan Park

131 Stanford Road, Port Gregory 6535
Ph (08) 9935 1052, fax (08) 9935 1093

The completion of the sealed road linking Northampton and Kalbarri has assured an increased traffic flow to towns in the area, including the small historic township of Gregory. Located in the centre of town, this park is neatly maintained and will appeal to those wanting to stay in a smaller, quiet park close to the beach. **$$$**

❑ Tent sites, powered sites, fits big motorhomes, cabins, on-site vans.

❑ Toilets and showers (disabled access), laundry, sewer dump-point, telephone, kiosk/shop, LP gas refills, ice, camp kitchen, playground, pets.

❑ Credit cards. Discounts: 2nd night, weekly.

GRIFFITH (NSW) p. 166

◉ Griffith Tourist Caravan Park
919 Willandra Avenue, Griffith 2680
Ph (02) 6964 2144, fax (02) 6964 1126

This owner-operated caravan park stands out because of its excellent facilities and the fact that it is a great base from which to explore the interesting Griffith area. It has a large number of ensuite sites, a pool, a spa and a tennis court. We always enjoy staying at Griffith. $$

❑ Tent sites, powered sites, drive-thru sites, ensuite sites, cabins.

❑ Toilets and showers (disabled access), laundry, telephone, kiosk/shop, LP gas refills, ice, camp kitchen, pool, playground, pets.

❑ Credit cards, holiday loading. Discounts: weekly.

GUILDERTON (WA) p. 102

Guilderton Caravan Park
2 Dewar Street, Guilderton 6041
Ph (08) 9577 1021, fax (08) 9577 1670

Located in a picturesque setting at the mouth of the Moore River, this popular beachside holiday park is on the water's edge and has good camping and caravan sites. Amenities are basic and a small shop and cafe are opposite the park. $$$

❑ Tent sites, powered sites, fits big motorhomes.

❑ Toilets and showers (disabled access), laundry, telephone, kiosk/shop, LP gas refills, ice, playground, boat ramp, no pets.

❑ Credit cards.

GUNNS PLAINS (TAS) p. 288

Wings Farm Park
137 Winduss Road, Gunns Plains 7315
Ph (03) 6429 1335, fax (03) 6429 1151
Email wfp@tassie.net.au

Staying here is a different experience. The park has good facilities and an adjoining animal park, including reptiles, trout and Tasmanian wildlife. Entry into the animal park is free for lodgers. A stay here would be a great adventure, especially for the city family with young children. $

❑ Tent sites, powered sites, fits big motorhomes, cabins.

❑ Toilets and showers (disabled access), laundry, kiosk/shop, pets.

❑ Credit cards.

HAHNDORF (SA) p. 132

◉ Hahndorf Resort
145 Main Street, Hahndorf 5245
Ph (08) 8388 7921 or 1800 350 143, fax (08) 8388 7282
Email enquiries@hahndorfresort.com.au
Website www.hahndorfresort.com.au

This is a budget-priced park with good amenities and a great location. In a rural setting, the park is just 1.5 km from the centre of Hahndorf, a very popular tourist destination. It has small lakes with ducks and other birdlife, a range of accommodation and an appealing restaurant. We regularly stop off here for a night or two. $$

❑ Tent sites, powered sites, drive-thru sites, fits big motorhomes, cabins.

❑ Toilets and showers, laundry, telephone, kiosk/shop, LP gas refills, ice, pool, no pets.

❑ Credit cards. Discounts: weekly.

HALLS CREEK (WA) p. 89

Halls Creek Caravan Park
4 Roberta Avenue, Halls Creek 6770
Ph (08) 9168 6169, fax (08) 9168 6277
Email lanus@bigpond.com

Just a short walk from the middle of town and close to the hotel, this park has a well-stocked shop, a nicely shaded lawn area for camping, a popular pool and a good amenities block. $$$

❑ Tent sites, powered sites, drive-thru sites, fits big motorhomes, cabins, on-site vans.

❑ Toilets and showers (disabled access), laundry, sewer dump-point, telephone, kiosk/shop, LP gas refills, ice, pool, pets.

❑ No credit cards.

HALLS GAP (VIC) p. 230

◉ Halls Gap Caravan and Tourist Park
Dunkeld Road, Halls Gap 3381
Ph (03) 5356 4251, fax (03) 5356 4421
Email hgcp@netconnect.com.au

We find this large park ideal for a holiday at any time of the year and regularly stay here. Located in the centre of town, it is within easy reach of most of the area's attractions and makes a good base for exploring the Grampians. A playground and pool are nearby. Minimum bookings apply during all holiday periods. $$$

❑ Tent sites, powered sites, drive-thru sites, fits big motorhomes, cabins, on-site vans.

❑ Toilets and showers (disabled access), laundry, telephone, LP gas refills, ice, no pets.

❑ Credit cards, holiday loading. Discounts: pensioners, seniors, weekly.

Halls Gap Lakeside Caravan Park
Tymna Drive, Halls Gap 3381
Ph (03) 5356 4281 or 1800 100 478, fax (03) 5356 4527
Email lakeside@netconnect.com.au
Website www.holidayparksvictoria.net.au

A good quality owner-operated park in a quiet location, 4 km from Halls Gap, close to Lake Bellfield. The park has a solar-heated pool and a range of accommodation.

Minimum bookings apply during holiday periods. $$$

❑ Tent sites, powered sites, drive-thru sites, fits big motorhomes, cabins.

❑ Toilets and showers (disabled access), laundry, telephone, kiosk/shop, LP gas refills, ice, camp kitchen, pool, playground, no pets.

❑ Credit cards, holiday loading. Discounts: pensioners, seniors, weekly, Top Tourist.

Park Gate Resort
Grampians Road, Halls Gap 3381
Ph (03) 5356 4215 or 1800 810 781, fax (03) 5356 4472
Email bookings@grampians.com
Website www.grampians.com

This is a very good quality tourist park just 1.5 km from the township of Halls Gap. The park has great recreational facilities including a tennis court and a pool. This is a popular holiday destination and a great base from which to explore the Grampians. $$$

❑ Tent sites, powered sites, drive-thru sites, ensuite sites, fits big motorhomes, cabins.

❑ Toilets and showers (disabled access), laundry, sewer dump-point, telephone, kiosk/shop, ice, camp kitchen, pool, playground, internet terminal, no pets.

❑ Credit cards, holiday loading. Discounts: Big4.

HASTINGS POINT (NSW) p. 34

◉ North Star Holiday Resort
Coast Road, Hastings Point 2489
Ph (02) 6676 1234 or 1800 645 790, fax (02) 6676 2217
Email northstar@northstar.com.au
Website www.northstar.com.au

This award-winning park has an impressive range of excellent facilities, including a fully licensed restaurant. This park is a cut above most: the amenities are excellent, the beach is a short walk across the road and the town centre is just 500 m away – we highly recommend it. $$$

❑ Tent sites, powered sites, drive-thru sites, ensuite sites, fits big motorhomes, cabins.

❑ Toilets and showers (disabled access), laundry, sewer dump-point, telephone, kiosk/shop, LP gas refills, ice, camp kitchen, pool, playground, TV cables, internet terminal, no pets.

❑ Bookings required, credit cards, holiday loading. Discounts: weekly, Big4.

HAWKS NEST (NSW) p. 28

Hawks Nest Beach Caravan Park
Booner Street, Hawks Nest 2324
Ph (02) 4997 0239, fax (02) 4997 2144
Email enquiries@hawksnestcaravan.com.au
Website www.hawksnestcaravan.com.au

Located just a short walk from a popular beach and the Hawks Nest Surf Club, this park is also only a kilometre from the centre of town. It has large expanses of lawn and is ideal for a family holiday or just a few nights on this fabulous section of coast. Minimum bookings apply over Christmas. $$

❑ Tent sites, powered sites, drive-thru sites, fits big motorhomes, cabins.

❑ Toilets and showers (disabled access), laundry, telephone, LP gas refills, ice, no pets.

❑ Credit cards, holiday loading. Discounts: weekly.

Myall River Camp
Mungo Brush Road, Hawks Nest 2324
Ph (02) 4997 0091

This unpowered bush camp is located a few kilometres north of Hawks Nest, along a road accessible by conventional vehicles. The park has limited facilities on a large grassy expanse alongside the picturesque Myall River. This is a budget-priced wilderness camp that will suit self-sufficient travellers. $

❑ Tent sites, fits big motorhomes.

❑ Toilets, no pets.

❑ No credit cards, holiday loading.

HAY POINT (QLD) p. 50

Hay Point Caravan Park
Tug Harbour Road, Hay Point 4740
Ph (07) 4956 3413, fax (07) 4956 3125

Hay Point is a major coal-loading point 35 km from Mackay. This is a popular park during winter months with tourists and those who enjoy fishing. The park is close to the beach and just a short walk from the local tavern. $$

❑ Tent sites, powered sites, drive-thru sites, ensuite sites, fits big motorhomes, cabins, on-site vans.

❑ Toilets and showers, laundry, sewer dump-point, telephone, LP gas refills, ice, pool, boat ramp, pets.

❑ No credit cards. Discounts: weekly.

HEARTBREAK HOTEL (NT) p. 70

Heartbreak Hotel Caravan Park
Corner Carpentaria and Tablelands highways, Cape Crawford 0854
Ph (08) 8975 9928, fax (08) 8975 9993

The park forms part of the Heartbreak Hotel complex. It has good basic amenities and a large grassed camping area, and the hotel serves a good range of counter meals to be enjoyed on the wide verandah. The owners also offer helicopter rides to local sights, including the Lost City. $$$

❑ Tent sites, powered sites, drive-thru sites, fits big motorhomes.

❑ Toilets and showers, laundry, telephone, kiosk/shop, ice, pool, playground, pets.

❑ Credit cards. Discounts: weekly.

HELLS GATE ROADHOUSE (QLD) p. 68

Hells Gate Roadhouse
Savannah Way, Burketown 4830
Ph (07) 4745 8258, fax (07) 4745 8225
Email hellsgateroadhouse@bigpond.com
Website www.hellsgateroadhouse.com.au

This camping area is part of the Hells Gate Roadhouse complex, in a remote location but good for an overnight stop along the Savannah Way. There are good basic amenities and the adjoining roadhouse serves meals. $$$

❑ Tent sites, powered sites, drive-thru sites, fits big motorhomes.

❑ Toilets and showers, laundry, telephone, kiosk/shop, ice, pets.

❑ Credit cards.

HERVEY BAY (QLD) p. 46

⊛ Fraser Lodge
Fraser Street, Torquay 4655
Ph (07) 4124 9999 or 1800 641 444,
fax (07) 4125 3090
Email fraserlodge@optusnet.com.au
Website www.fraserlodge.com.au

Explore Hervey Bay, go whale-watching or relax and enjoy the pool, the barbecues and the tennis court at Fraser Lodge, a quality tourist park in Torquay, a quiet area of Hervey Bay. The park is just a short walk from the beach and close to many local restaurants. $$$$

❑ Tent sites, powered sites, ensuite sites, fits big motorhomes, cabins.

❑ Toilets and showers (disabled access), laundry, sewer dump-point, telephone, kiosk/shop, camp kitchen, LP gas refills, ice, pool, playground, no pets.

❑ Credit cards. Discounts: weekly, Big4.

Harbour View Caravan Park
Jetty Road, Hervey Bay 4655
Ph (07) 4128 9374, fax (07) 4128 9374

Hervey Bay is a major tourist destination and this owner-operated waterfront park is close to the large marina complex where the whale-watching cruises depart during the season. This is a good park with basic facilities, at a competitive price. $$$

❑ Tent sites, powered sites, drive-thru sites, fits big motorhomes, cabins, on-site vans.

❑ Toilets and showers, laundry, telephone, kiosk/shop, LP gas refills, ice, camp kitchen, pool, no pets.

❑ Credit cards. Discounts: weekly, FPA.

HILLSTON (NSW) p. 166

Hillston Caravan Park
Corner High Street and Oxley Avenue,
Hillston 2675
Ph (02) 6967 2575, fax (02) 6967 1036

This is a tidy park on the northern edge of town. The park has modern amenities and good facilities, though it can be very busy in the winter months during the peak tourist season. There is also a large influx of fruit pickers and other seasonal workers at this time. $$

❑ Tent sites, powered sites, drive-thru sites, fits big motorhomes, cabins.

❑ Toilets and showers (disabled access), laundry, telephone, kiosk/shop, LP gas refills, ice, pool, playground, TV cables, pets.

❑ Credit cards. Discounts: weekly.

HOBART (TAS) p. 285

Sandy Bay Caravan Park
Peel Street, Sandy Bay 7005
Ph (03) 6225 1264, fax (03) 6225 1265

This smaller park is only 2 km from the centre of Hobart and within easy walking distance

of the Hobart Casino. The park has good facilities but often fills quickly: we strongly recommend booking ahead in busy seasons. It is especially popular with small campervans and campers. $$$

❑ Tent sites, powered sites, drive-thru sites, fits big motorhomes, cabins, on-site vans.

❑ Toilets and showers, laundry, sewer dump-point, telephone, kiosk/shop, camp kitchen, no pets.

❑ Credit cards. Discounts: weekly.

⊛ Treasure Island Caravan Park
671 Main Road, Berridale 7011
Ph (03) 6249 2379, fax (03) 6249 1420

Located about 9 km north-west of the city, this is a quiet, off-highway park on the banks of the Derwent River. The park is close to the Cadbury Factory, a popular tourist attraction, and close to shops. This park has good basic amenities and though both recommended parks in Hobart are of similar quality, we prefer to use this park when we're in the area. $$$

❑ Tent sites, powered sites, fits big motorhomes, cabins, on-site vans.

❑ Toilets and showers, laundry, telephone, sewer dump-point, LP gas refills, camp kitchen, playground, no pets.

❑ Bookings required, credit cards. Discounts: weekly.

HOPETOUN (WA) p. 116

Hopetoun Caravan Park
Spence Street, Hopetoun 6348
Ph (08) 9838 3096, fax (08) 9838 3124

This is an informal beachside park in the small coastal community of Hopetoun, with basic beachside caravan park amenities. It is situated on the coastal fringe with a path leading to the beach and is just a 400-m walk to the town centre. $$

❑ Tent sites, powered sites, drive-thru sites, fits big motorhomes, cabins, on-site vans.

❑ Toilets and showers, laundry, telephone, camp kitchen, playground, TV cables, pets.

❑ Credit cards. Discounts: weekly.

HORSHAM (VIC) p. 230

Horsham Caravan Park
190 Firebrace Street, Horsham 3400
Ph (03) 5382 3476 or 1800 032 217,
fax (03) 5381 2170
Email horshampark@telstra.com

This is a good quality, quiet park on the banks of the Wimmera River, just 1 km from the centre of town. It is budget priced but comfortable, with a range of accommodation. The park is off the main highway. $$

❑ Tent sites, powered sites, drive-thru sites, ensuite sites, fits big motorhomes, cabins, on-site vans.

❑ Toilets and showers (disabled access), laundry, telephone, kiosk/shop, LP gas refills, ice, camp kitchen, playground, boat ramp, pets.

❑ Credit cards.

Wimmera Lakes Caravan Resort
Western Highway, Horsham 3400
Ph (03) 5382 4481 or 1800 632 310,
fax (03) 5382 6556
Email info@wimmeralakes.com
Website www.wimmeralakes.com

This is a spacious park on the fringe of Horsham, 4 km south-east of the town centre on the Western Highway. The park has a range of facilities including a pool, spa, mini-golf and a tennis court. This park is a good base for exploring the local area. $$$

❑ Tent sites, powered sites, drive-thru sites, fits big motorhomes, cabins.

❑ Toilets and showers (disabled access), laundry, telephone, kiosk/shop, LP gas refills, ice, camp kitchen, pool, playground, no pets.

❑ Credit cards, holiday loading. Discounts: pensioners, seniors, weekly, Big4.

HOWARD SPRINGS (NT) pp. 74, 79

Howard Springs Caravan Park
170 Whitewood Road, Howard Springs 0835
Ph (08) 8983 1169 or 1800 831 169,
fax (08) 8983 2487
Email reservations@howardspringscaravanpark.com.au
Website www.howardspringscaravanpark.com.au

The popular park is 23 km from Darwin City, in a quiet position off the main highway. It is close to Palmerston shopping centre and an easy drive into Darwin. The park is a popular tourist destination and a good base to spend time discovering the Darwin region. $$$

❑ Tent sites, powered sites, drive-thru sites, fits big motorhomes, cabins, on-site vans.

❑ Toilets and showers (disabled access), laundry, sewer dump-point, telephone, kiosk/shop, LP gas refills, ice, camp kitchen, pool, playground, no pets.

❑ Credit cards. Discounts: pensioners, seniors, weekly, Big4.

HUGHENDEN (QLD) p. 264

Allan Terry Caravan Park
Resolution Street, Hughenden 4821
Ph (07) 4741 1190, fax (07) 4741 1190

This is a good, basic council park adjoining the town's swimming pool, about 1.5 km from the centre of Hughenden. Porcupine Gorge is nearby. $$

❑ Tent sites, powered sites, drive-thru sites, fits big motorhomes, cabins.

❑ Toilets and showers, laundry, telephone, ice, pool, pets.

❑ Credit cards. Discounts: weekly.

HUSKISSON (NSW) p. 14

Huskisson Beach Tourist Park
Beach Street, Huskisson 2540
Ph (02) 4441 5142 or 1300 733 027,
fax (02) 4441 5142
Email huskybeach@shoalhaven.nsw.gov.au
Website www.shoal.net.au/~huskybeach

Looking out over Jervis Bay and close to the centre of town, this park has great facilities including a tennis court, volleyball court and

swimming pool. It is usually necessary to make a booking because this park is such a popular holiday spot. $$$$

❑ Tent sites, powered sites, cabins.

❑ Toilets and showers (disabled access), laundry, sewer dump-point, telephone, kiosk/shop, LP gas refills, ice, pool, playground, no pets.

❑ Bookings required, credit cards, holiday loading. Discounts: pensioners, seniors, weekly.

Huskisson White Sands Tourist Park
Corner Nowra and Beach Streets,
Huskisson 2540
Ph (02) 4441 6025 or 1300 733 028,
fax (02) 4441 6025

This park is located on the beachfront overlooking Jervis Bay, just 1 km from the town centre. It has clean, new amenities and from the front of the park you can often see the dolphins playing in Jervis Bay. Minimum bookings apply during holiday periods. $$$$

❑ Tent sites, powered sites, fits big motorhomes, cabins, on-site vans.

❑ Toilets and showers (disabled access), laundry, kiosk/shop, LP gas refills, ice, playground, no pets.

❑ Credit cards, holiday loading. Discounts: pensioners, seniors, weekly.

ILFRACOMBE (QLD) p. 174

Wellshot Caravan Park
Landsborough (Matilda) Highway,
Ilfracombe 4727
Ph (07) 4658 2106, fax (07) 4658 3926

This park adjoins the Wellshot Hotel, where a nightly outdoor stockman show entertains travellers during the winter tourist season. The park has a small number of sites and good basic facilities. It is within walking distance of town where a display of historic equipment adorns the main street. $$

❑ Tent sites, powered sites, fits big motorhomes.

❑ Toilets and showers, laundry, telephone, LP gas refills, ice, pets.

❑ Credit cards. Discounts: 2nd night, weekly.

ILUKA (NSW) p. 32

See also Palmers Island.

Anchorage Holiday Park
Marandowie Drive, Iluka 2466
Ph (02) 6646 6210 or 1800 639 127,
fax (02) 6646 6844
Email info@anchorageholidaypark.com.au
Website www.anchorageholidaypark.com.au

This is a well-established, owner-operated park with very good facilities. It is situated across the road from the wide Clarence River estuary and is 2 km from the town centre. Minimum bookings apply during peak holiday periods. $$$

❑ Tent sites, powered sites, fits big motorhomes, cabins.

❑ Toilets and showers (disabled access), laundry, telephone, kiosk/shop, LP gas refills, ice, camp kitchen, pool, playground, boat ramp, pets.

❑ Credit cards, holiday loading. Discounts: weekly, Top Tourist.

Iluka Riverside Tourist Park
4 Charles Street, Iluka 2466
Ph (02) 6646 6060, fax (02) 6646 5419

This is a large riverside tourist park with good facilities. Enjoy the riverfront barbecues and picnic tables, the grassed waterfront sites or the fully equipped camp kitchen overlooking the river. **$$$**

❏ Tent sites, powered sites, drive-thru sites, cabins.

❏ Toilets and showers (disabled access), laundry, sewer dump-point, telephone, camp kitchen, playground, boat ramp, no pets.

❏ Credit cards, holiday loading. Discounts: weekly.

INDEE STATION (WA) pp. 92, 204

Indee Station
Newman Road, off Great Northern Highway, Port Hedland 6721
Ph (08) 9176 4968, fax (08) 9176 4968

Indee Station is 49 km south-west of Port Hedland and 25 km south of the North West Coastal Highway intersection. The homestead is a further 8 km from the front gate along a reasonable dirt track. Call from the front gate on UHF channel 15. This small, basic and unpowered park is alongside the station homestead. Guided tours to a commercial aircraft wreck and aboriginal art sites are on offer. **$**

❏ Tent sites, drive-thru sites, fits big motorhomes, cabins.

❏ Toilets and showers, camp kitchen, pets.

❏ No credit cards. Discounts: weekly.

INGHAM (QLD) p. 54

Palm Tree Caravan Park
Bruce Highway, Ingham 4850
Ph (07) 4776 2403, fax (07) 4776 2403

This park is 3 km south of Ingham, on the Bruce Highway. It has good facilities, including a TV room, and is conveniently located for an overnight stop. **$$$**

❏ Tent sites, powered sites, drive-thru sites, fits big motorhomes, cabins.

❏ Toilets and showers, laundry, telephone, kiosk/shop, LP gas refills, ice, camp kitchen, pool, playground, pets.

❏ No credit cards. Discounts: weekly.

INNOT HOT SPRINGS (QLD) p. 64

Hot Springs Village
Kennedy Highway, Innot Hot Springs 4872
Ph (07) 4097 0136, fax (07) 4097 0136

This park is located in the centre of the small town and has good facilities. A relaxing dip in the spring-fed spa pools in the park is most enjoyable at the end of the day. The local hotel is just a short walk away. **$$$**

❏ Tent sites, powered sites, drive-thru sites, fits big motorhomes, cabins.

❏ Toilets and showers, laundry, telephone, kiosk/shop, LP gas refills, ice, pool, pets.

❏ Bookings required, credit cards. Discounts: weekly, seniors.

ISLA GORGE NATIONAL PARK
(QLD) p. 162

Isla Gorge Camping Area
Isla Gorge National Park, via Theodore 4719

This small camping area is 1.3 km from the highway along an unsealed road, 37 km south of Theodore. It is too stony for tents but most suitable for campervans or smaller motorhomes. The camping area adjoins the lookout. ⑤

❏ Tent sites.

❏ Toilets and showers, no pets.

JABIRU (NT) p. 81

Kakadu Lodge Caravan Park
Jabiru Drive, Jabiru 0866
Ph (08) 8979 2422 or 1800 811 154,
fax (08) 8979 2254
Email klodge@aurora-resorts.com.au
Website www.aurora-resorts.com.au

This large, well-maintained park has a great central pool and bistro complex. It is an ideal base from which to explore Kakadu. **$$$$**

❏ Tent sites, powered sites, drive-thru sites, fits big motorhomes, cabins.

❏ Toilets and showers (disabled access), laundry, telephone, kiosk/shop, LP gas refills, ice, camp kitchen, pool, internet terminal, no pets.

❏ Credit cards. Discounts: weekly.

JACOBS WELL (QLD) p. 36

See also Gold Coast.

Jacobs Well Tourist Park
Pimpama–Jacobs Well Road, Jacobs Well 4208
Ph (07) 5546 2016, fax (07) 5546 1688
Email jacobs@gctp.com.au
Website www.gctp.com.au/jacobs

This is a good Gold Coast City Council park. The park is located in a quiet township on the protected waterways north of the Gold Coast. This is a very popular park with families and those who fish, and will be busy during holiday periods. **$$$**

❏ Tent sites, powered sites, drive-thru sites, fits big motorhomes, cabins.

❏ Toilets and showers (disabled access), laundry, telephone, kiosk/shop, LP gas refills, ice, playground, boat ramp, no pets.

❏ Credit cards, holiday loading. Discounts: weekly.

JERILDERIE (NSW) p. 154

Jerilderie Motel and Caravan Park
121 Newell Highway, Jerilderie 2716
Ph (03) 5886 1366, fax (03) 5886 9010
Email howzy@bigpond.com

This neat and tidy, budget-priced park is located in Jerilderie's main street. The park is an ideal overnight stop for travellers along the Newell Highway. Pets are permitted for one night only. **$$**

❏ Tent sites, powered sites, drive-thru sites, fits big motorhomes, cabins, on-site vans.

❏ Toilets and showers, laundry, telephone, playground, pets.

❏ Credit cards. Discounts: weekly.

JOURAMA FALLS (QLD) p. 54

Jourama Falls Camping Area
Paluma Range National Park,
via Bambaroo 4850

This camping area is north of Bambaroo and the access route has 2.8 km of unsealed surface; with care, it is suitable for caravans. The camping area is well shaded and just a short walk from the falls. **$**

❏ Tent sites, drive-thru sites, fits big motorhomes.

❏ Toilets and showers.

❏ No credit cards.

JULIA CREEK (QLD) p. 266

Julia Creek Caravan Park
Old Normanton Road, Julia Creek 4823
Ph (07) 4746 7108, fax (02) 4746 7108

This is a large, open, council park adjoining a swimming pool, about 1 km from the town centre in an off-highway location. The park has basic facilities and caters for travellers. It is good for an overnight stay and small pets are allowed. **$$**

❏ Tent sites, powered sites, drive-thru sites, fits big motorhomes, cabins.

❏ Toilets and showers (disabled access), laundry, telephone, ice, pool, pets.

❏ No credit cards. Discounts: weekly.

JUNCTION HILL (NSW)

See Grafton.

JURIEN BAY (WA) p. 102

Jurien Bay Caravan Park
Roberts Street, Jurien Bay 6516
Ph (08) 9652 1595, fax (08) 9652 1595

This basic beachside park is in the centre of town, adjoining the jetty. There are good facilities and the park shop has an extensive range of takeaway food. This strip of coast is a popular fishing area, and the park will take pets in quiet times only. **$$$**

❏ Tent sites, powered sites, drive-thru sites, fits big motorhomes, on-site vans.

❏ Toilets and showers (disabled access), laundry, sewer dump-point, telephone, kiosk/shop, LP gas refills, ice, camp kitchen, playground, boat ramp, pets.

❏ Credit cards, holiday loading. Discounts: pensioners, seniors, weekly.

KAKADU NATIONAL PARK
(NT) p. 81

See also Jabiru.

Gagudju Lodge Cooinda Caravan Park
Kakadu Highway, Cooinda 0886
Ph (08) 8979 0145, fax (08) 8979 0148
Email reservations@gagudjulodgecooinda.com.au
Website www.gagudju-dreaming.com

Located close to the famous Yellow Water Billabong, this park is just off the Kakadu Highway, 54 km south of Jabiru. It is a great choice, especially if you are planning a cruise on Yellow Water, as the cruise bus departs from the front gate. **$$$$**

❏ Tent sites, powered sites, drive-thru sites, fits big motorhomes.

❏ Toilets and showers (disabled access), laundry, telephone, kiosk/shop, LP gas refills, ice, camp kitchen, pool, playground, internet terminal, no pets.

❏ Credit cards. Discounts: weekly.

KALGOORLIE–BOULDER
(WA) p. 271

Goldminer Caravan Park
Great Eastern Highway, Kalgoorlie 6430
Ph (08) 9021 3713, fax (08) 9022 4545
Email hartland@emerge.net.au

This park is conveniently located on the Coolgardie Road, about 4 km west of the city centre. It has good facilities at a budget price and a range of accommodation. **$$$**

❏ Tent sites, powered sites, drive-thru sites, ensuite sites, fits big motorhomes, cabins, on-site vans.

❏ Toilets and showers, laundry, sewer dump-point, telephone, kiosk/shop, LP gas refills, ice, pets.

❏ Credit cards. Discounts: pensioners, seniors, weekly.

⊙ **Kalgoorlie Accommodation Village**
Burt Street, Boulder 6430
Ph (08) 9039 4800 or 1800 004 800,
fax (08) 9039 4888
Email resortpk@ca.com.au
Website www.resortparks.com.au

Excellent quality and convenience make this a stand-out park in our opinion, and it is a great base from which to explore the goldmining history of Kalgoorlie. Located off the main road, close to the airport and about 2 km from the centre of Boulder, it has a wide range of facilities to suit both overnight travellers or those staying longer. There is a pool, a camp kitchen and a range of accommodation. We always stay here when we pass through Kalgoorlie. **$$$**

❏ Tent sites, powered sites, drive-thru sites, ensuite sites, fits big motorhomes, cabins.

❏ Toilets and showers (disabled access), laundry, sewer dump-point, telephone, LP gas refills, camp kitchen, pool, playground, internet terminal, no pets.

❏ Credit cards, holiday loading. Discounts: seniors, weekly, Top Tourist.

KANGAROO VALLEY (NSW) p. 16

Kangaroo Valley Glenmack Caravan Park
Main Road, Kangaroo Valley 2577
Ph (02) 4465 1372, fax (02) 4465 1468
Email glenmack@shoal.net.au
Website www.glenmack.com.au

Away from the coastal strip, this large, owner-operated park has good facilities including mini-golf and a tennis court. A public pool is next door and it is just a short walk from the centre of town. $$$

❏ Tent sites, powered sites, fits big motorhomes, cabins.

❏ Toilets and showers (disabled access), laundry, telephone, kiosk/shop, LP gas refills, ice, camp kitchen, playground, no pets.

❏ Credit cards. Discounts: 5th night.

KARRATHA (WA) p. 96

Pilbara Holiday Park
Rosemary Road, Karratha 6714
Ph (08) 9185 1855, fax (08) 9144 1243
Email pilbaraholidaypark@fleetwood.com.au
Website www.fleetwoodparks.com.au

This highly recommended caravan park is a member of the generally reliable WA Fleetwood Holiday Parks chain. It is an ideal central base from which to explore the many and varied attractions of the area. The facilities are good and it is just a short drive to Dampier. $$$

❏ Tent sites, powered sites, ensuite sites, cabins, on-site vans.

❏ Toilets and showers, laundry, sewer dump-point, telephone, kiosk/shop, LP gas refills, ice, camp kitchen, pool, playground, internet terminal, no pets.

❏ Credit cards. Discounts: weekly, Big4.

KARRIDALE (WA)

See Alexandra Bridge.

KARUAH (NSW) p. 28

Karuah Jetty Village
88 Holdom Road, Karuah 2324
Ph (02) 4997 5520, fax (02) 4997 5950
Email village@bmr.com.au
Website www.portstephens.org.au

Located in a quiet position a short distance from the Pacific Highway, this park has very good amenities and looks across the northern arm of Port Stephens. There is a long jetty, good for fishing, and a limited number of tourist sites. $$$

❏ Tent sites, powered sites, drive-thru sites, fits big motorhomes, cabins.

❏ Toilets and showers, laundry, sewer dump-point, telephone, kiosk/shop, LP gas refills, camp kitchen, pool, playground, boat ramp, no pets.

❏ Bookings required, credit cards, holiday loading. Discounts: Big4.

KARUMBA (QLD) p. 178

Gulf Country Caravan Park
69 Yappar Street, Karumba 4891
Ph (07) 4745 9148, fax (07) 4745 9148

Karumba is an extremely popular winter destination, when southern tourists flock north during the cooler winter season. A reservation is necessary during this extremely busy period. This park is just 50 m from the town centre and close to the town boat ramp. The owners offer a range of activities, like fish-and-chip barbecues on Saturday nights. Great fishing is the major attraction. $$$

❏ Tent sites, powered sites, fits big motorhomes, cabins.

❏ Toilets and showers (disabled access), laundry, sewer dump-point, telephone, kiosk/shop, ice, pool, pets.

❏ Credit cards.

⊙ **Karumba Point Tourist Park**
The Point Road, Karumba 4891
Ph (07) 4745 9306, fax (07) 4745 9238

We like this popular, quality park, located 7.5 km from Karumba. It has a unique attraction: a free fish barbecue for guests each Wednesday and Saturday night during the winter tourist season. The park is always busy during the tourist season so a booking is necessary. $$$

❏ Tent sites, powered sites, drive-thru sites, fits big motorhomes, on-site vans.

❏ Toilets and showers (disabled access), laundry, telephone, kiosk/shop, ice, pool, pets.

❏ Credit cards. Discounts: weekly.

KATHERINE (NT) p. 75

See also Nitmiluk (Katherine Gorge) National Park.

Knotts Crossing Caravan Park
Corner Giles and Cameron streets, Katherine 0850
Ph (08) 8972 2511, fax (08) 8972 2628
Email reservations@knottscrossing.com.au
Website www.knottscrossing.com.au

Take the road leading to the gorge to discover this very tidy, good quality park set in lush tropical surrounds. It has a range of accommodation and good facilities, including a fully licensed restaurant. $$$

❏ Tent sites, powered sites, ensuite sites, cabins.

❏ Toilets and showers, laundry, telephone, kiosk/shop, ice, pool, no pets.

❏ Credit cards. Discounts: weekly.

⊙ **Low Level Caravan Park**
Shadforth Road, Katherine 0850
Ph (08) 8972 3962 or 1800 501 984, fax (08) 8972 2230
Email lowlevel@austarnet.com.au

This is one of the more appealing parks in Australia and we really enjoy staying here. Owner-operated, it has excellent facilities, including a relaxed licensed bistro and kiosk that operate during the winter tourist season. Bookings are absolutely essential at peak times. $$$$

❏ Tent sites, powered sites, drive-thru sites, fits big motorhomes, cabins.

❏ Toilets and showers (disabled access), laundry, sewer dump-point, telephone, kiosk/shop, LP gas refills, ice, camp kitchen, pool, no pets.

❏ Credit cards. Discounts: Big4.

KEITH (SA) p. 232

Pendleton Farm Retreat
Eckerts Road (off Dukes Highway), Keith 5267
Ph (08) 8756 7042, fax (08) 8756 7067
Email pendleton@adelaide.on.net
Website www.pendletonfarm.com

Located 12 km east of Keith, the 485-ha Pendleton Farm has great facilities. It caters for groups so there are often a lot of people around. There are farm activities on offer and facilities include a solar-heated pool. The park has a small number of tourist sites. $$

❏ Tent sites, powered sites, drive-thru sites, fits big motorhomes.

❏ Toilets and showers (disabled access), laundry, telephone, kiosk/shop, pool, playground, pets.

❏ Credit cards. Discounts: weekly.

KELSO (NSW) p. 238

⊙ **East's Bathurst Holiday Park**
Sydney Road, Kelso 2795
Ph (02) 6331 8286 or 1800 669 911, fax (02) 6332 6439
Email eastsbathurstholidaypark@bigpond.com
Website www.eastholidayparks.com.au

This park is owned by one of the East brothers, well known in the caravan park industry. It is a quality park on the Great Western Highway, 5 km east of the centre of Bathurst, and offers a range of accommodation and great facilities. Minimum bookings apply during the Easter holidays, the October long weekend and Mount Panorama race weekends. $$$

❏ Tent sites, powered sites, ensuite sites, fits big motorhomes, cabins.

❏ Toilets and showers (disabled access), laundry, sewer dump-point, telephone, kiosk/shop, LP gas refills, ice, pool, playground, TV cables, no pets.

❏ Credit cards, holiday loading. Discounts: weekly, Big4.

KELSO (TAS) p. 278

Kelso Sands Caravan Park
Paranaple Road, Kelso 7270
Ph (03) 6383 9130 or 1800 039 139, fax (03) 6383 9191
Email kelsocaravanpark@tassie.net.au

The park is set on a large expanse of grassy, maintained grounds and includes a small golf course. It has good amenities, a well-stocked store and a great outlook over the broad estuary of the River Tamar. Wombats regularly graze in the park. $$$

❏ Tent sites, powered sites, drive-thru sites, fits big motorhomes, cabins, on-site vans.

❏ Toilets and showers, laundry, telephone, kiosk/shop, LP gas refills, ice, pool, playground, no pets.

❏ Credit cards. Discounts: weekly, Big4.

KENNETT RIVER (VIC) p. 139

Kennett River Caravan Park
Great Ocean Road, Kennett River 3221
Ph (03) 5289 0272, fax (03) 5289 0237
Email info@kennettriver.com
Website www.kennettriver.com

Located midway between Lorne and Apollo Bay, this recently redeveloped park has good basic facilities. It is squeezed between the Otway Ranges and a safe surf beach. $$$

❏ Tent sites, powered sites, fits big motorhomes, cabins.

❏ Toilets and showers (disabled access), laundry, telephone, kiosk/shop, LP gas refills, ice, playground, no pets.

❏ Credit cards, holiday loading. Discounts: weekly.

KERANG (VIC) p. 220

Ibis Caravan Park
Corner Murray Valley and Loddon highways, Kerang 3579
Ph (03) 5452 2232

This park is 3 km south of Kerang, with nice shady spots and a tennis court. It is an excellent overnight stop. This is a budget-priced park with minimum booking periods during holiday seasons. $$

❏ Tent sites, powered sites, drive-thru sites, fits big motorhomes, cabins, on-site vans.

❏ Toilets and showers, laundry, sewer dump-point, telephone, kiosk/shop, LP gas refills, ice, camp kitchen, pool, playground, pets.

❏ No credit cards, holiday loading. Discounts: pensioners, seniors, weekly.

KIALLA (VIC)

See Shepparton.

KIAMA (NSW) p. 16

⊙ **Blowhole Point Holiday Park**
Lighthouse Road, Kiama 2533
Ph (02) 4232 2707, fax (02) 4232 2707
Email blowhole@kiama.net
Website www.kiama.net/holiday

With an outlook over the town and harbour, this park occupies a fabulous piece of real estate adjoining the lighthouse and the famous blowhole. Mostly protected from the south-easterly wind, the park has basic amenities, a restaurant, tennis courts and two rock pools for swimming in, but it is the spectacular views that make it so good. $$$$

❏ Tent sites, powered sites, drive-thru sites, fits big motorhomes, cabins, on-site vans.

❏ Toilets and showers, laundry, sewer dump-point, telephone, kiosk/shop, ice, pool, boat ramp, internet terminal, no pets.

❏ Credit cards, holiday loading. Discounts: pensioners, seniors, weekly.

Easts Van Park
Ocean Street, Kiama 2533
Ph (02) 4232 2124 or 1800 674 444,
fax (02) 4233 1009
Email eastpark@ozemail.com.au

This is a fabulous, large and well laid out beachfront park with very good facilities and amenities. The East families are prominent owners of many New South Wales caravan parks and this is a fine example of one of their establishments. $$$

❏ Tent sites, powered sites, drive-thru sites, ensuite sites, fits big motorhomes, cabins.

❏ Toilets and showers (disabled access), laundry, sewer dump-point, telephone, ice, camp kitchen, playground, TV cables, no pets.

❏ Credit cards, holiday loading. Discounts: weekly, Big4.

KINGFISHER CAMP (QLD) p. 68

❂ **Kingfisher Camp**
Bowthorn Station, via Doomadgee 4830
Ph (07) 4745 8212, fax (07) 4745 8212
Website www.ozemail.com.au/~bowthorn

This is a great place to spend a few quiet days under shady trees on lush lawns beside a large waterhole on the Nicholson River. There are dinghies for hire. The camp is open between April and October and is reached along unsealed roads from Savannah Way to the west of Doomadgee. It is part of Bowthorn station. $$

❏ Tent sites, drive-thru sites, fits big motorhomes.

❏ Toilets and showers, kiosk/shop, ice, boat ramp, pets.

❏ Credit cards. Discounts: weekly.

KINGS CANYON (NT) p. 186

Kings Canyon Resort
Luritja Road, Kings Canyon 0872
Ph (08) 8956 7442 or 1800 817 622,
fax (08) 8956 7410
Email reskcr@austarnet.com.au
Website www.voyages.com.au

This is a very good resort and caravan park located about 7 km from Kings Canyon. The resort has a range of accommodation, a restaurant, a well-stocked shop and a large roadhouse. The resort offers most facilities including a pool and barbecues. $$$$

❏ Tent sites, powered sites, fits big motorhomes, cabins.

❏ Toilets and showers (disabled access), laundry, telephone, kiosk/shop, LP gas refills, ice, camp kitchen, pool, internet terminal, pets.

❏ Credit cards.

❂ **Kings Creek Station**
Luritja Road, Kings Canyon 0872
Ph (08) 8956 7474, fax (08) 8956 7468
Email info@kingscreekstation.com.au
Website www.kingscreekstation.com.au

This large camping area on a cattle station is our choice of places to stay when we visit the Kings Canyon area. It caters solely for tourists and has numerous sites in bush settings. The facilities include a pool, barbecues, a restaurant and a shop. The station also offers several fabulous activities including camel rides, helicopter flights and quad (four-wheel motorbike) rides. Kings Canyon is 39 km away along a sealed road. $$$$

❏ Tent sites, powered sites, drive-thru sites, fits big motorhomes, cabins.

❏ Toilets and showers (disabled access), laundry, telephone, kiosk/shop, LP gas refills, ice, pool, playground, internet terminal, pets.

❏ Credit cards. Discounts: 4th night.

KINGSCLIFF (NSW) p. 34

Drifters Holiday Village
Wommin Bay Road, Kingscliff 2487
Ph (02) 6674 2505, fax (02) 6674 5719
Email drifters@better.net.au
Website www.bigvolcano.com.au/custom/drifters

This family-run park is a popular resort-style place to stay. The facilities are good quality and the park is a good base at the southern end of the Gold Coast, close to the Pacific Motorway. $$$

❏ Tent sites, powered sites, ensuite sites, cabins, on-site vans.

❏ Toilets and showers, laundry, telephone, kiosk/shop, LP gas refills, ice, camp kitchen, pool, playground, TV cables, no pets.

❏ Credit cards, holiday loading. Discounts: weekly, Top Tourist.

Kingscliff Beach Holiday Park
Marine Parade, Kingscliff 2487
Ph (02) 6674 1311, fax (02) 6674 0091
Email tweedparks@bigpond.com

This is a popular council park across the road from the shopping strip. The park has good basic facilities and a fabulous position on the beachfront. It gets busy on weekends and during peak holiday periods. $$$

❏ Tent sites, powered sites, fits big motorhomes, cabins, on-site vans.

❏ Toilets and showers, laundry, telephone, no pets.

❏ Credit cards, holiday loading. Discounts: 3rd night.

KINGSTON-ON-MURRAY (SA) p. 224

Kingston-on-Murray Caravan Park
River Terrace, Kingston-on-Murray 5331
Ph (08) 8583 0209, fax (08) 8583 0209
Email kompark@riverland.com.au
Website www.komcaravanpark.com.au

This is a quiet, waterfront, owner-operated park just off the highway and ideal for a few restful days on the riverbank. The park has good basic facilities and is an enjoyable base for exploring the local area, including the Banrock Station winery. Small pets are sometimes allowed. $$$

❏ Tent sites, powered sites, drive-thru sites, fits big motorhomes, cabins.

❏ Toilets and showers (disabled access), laundry, telephone, kiosk/shop, LP gas refills, ice, pool, playground, boat ramp, no pets.

❏ Credit cards. Discounts: pensioners, seniors, weekly.

KINGSTON S.E. (SA) p. 132

Kingston Caravan Park
Marine Parade, Kingston S.E. 5275
Ph (08) 8767 2050, fax (08) 8767 2440

This popular park is just across the road from the beach. Other attractions include the lighthouse and good fishing. The park is competitively priced and located 1.5 km south of the town centre. There is a well-stocked kiosk. $$$

❏ Tent sites, powered sites, drive-thru sites, fits big motorhomes, cabins, on-site vans.

❏ Toilets and showers, laundry, sewer dump-point, telephone, kiosk/shop, LP gas refills, ice, playground, boat ramp, pets.

❏ Credit cards. Discounts: pensioners, seniors.

KINKA BEACH (QLD) p. 50

Island View Caravan Park
Scenic Highway, Kinka Beach 4703
Ph (07) 4939 6284, fax (07) 4939 6434
Email islandview@cqnet.com.au
Website www.kinka.contact.com.au

This is a popular, good quality park opposite the beach, just 14 km south of Yeppoon. It is in a great holiday area and bookings are required in peak holiday periods. $$$

❏ Tent sites, powered sites, drive-thru sites, fits big motorhomes, cabins.

❏ Toilets and showers, laundry, telephone, kiosk/shop, LP gas refills, ice, camp kitchen, pool, playground, TV cables, pets.

❏ Credit cards. Discounts: weekly, Top Tourist.

KIOLOA (NSW) p. 14

See also Bawley Point.

Kioloa Beach Holiday Park
635 Murramarang Road, Kioloa 2539
Ph (02) 4457 1072, fax (02) 4457 1481
Email holidays@kioloabeach.com
Website www.kioloabeach.com

This large beachfront park has good facilities, including a shaded pool and a tennis court. It fronts onto a safe swimming beach where snorkelling is popular. There is also good fishing in the area. $$$

❏ Tent sites, powered sites, cabins.

❏ Toilets and showers (disabled access), laundry, telephone, kiosk/shop, LP gas refills, ice, pool, playground, boat ramp, pets.

❏ Credit cards, holiday loading. Discounts: weekly.

KIRRA BEACH (QLD)

See Gold Coast.

KUNUNURRA (WA) p. 86

Ivanhoe Village Caravan Resort
Corner Ivanhoe Road and Coolibah Street, Kununurra 6743
Ph (08) 9169 1995 or 1800 668 367,
fax (08) 9169 1985
Email big4kununurra@westnet.com.au

This is a high quality park just 600 m from the town centre. It has excellent amenities and a wide range of facilities, including a resort-style pool with a spa. $$$$

❏ Tent sites, powered sites, drive-thru sites, ensuite sites, fits big motorhomes, cabins.

❏ Toilets and showers (disabled access), laundry, sewer dump-point, telephone, LP gas refills, ice, camp kitchen, pool, playground, internet terminal, no pets.

❏ Credit cards, holiday loading. Discounts: Big4.

Kona Lakeside Tourist Park
Lakeview Drive, Kununurra 6743
Ph (08) 9168 1031, fax (08) 9169 1135
Email kona@wn.com.au
Website www.konalakeside.com.au

This caravan park is just 2 km west of town, on the banks of Lake Kununurra. This popular park is off the main highway in a picturesque, quiet location. There is a nicely grassed tent area, shady waterfront sites and very good amenities. The park has bicycles and canoes for hire. $$$

❏ Tent sites, powered sites, drive-thru sites, fits big motorhomes, cabins, on-site vans.

❏ Toilets and showers (disabled access), laundry, telephone, kiosk/shop, LP gas refills, ice, camp kitchen, pool, boat ramp, no pets.

❏ Credit cards. Discounts: weekly.

KURRIMINE BEACH (QLD) p. 56

King Reef Resort Hotel and Caravan Park
Jacobs Road, Kurrimine Beach 4871
Ph (07) 4065 6144, fax (07) 4065 6172
Email kingsreef@znet.net.au

This beachside caravan park is part of the hotel complex. The park has good basic facilities and is very popular during peak holiday periods. Meals and normal hotel services are available at the hotel. $$$

❏ Tent sites, powered sites, drive-thru sites, fits big motorhomes, cabins.

❏ Toilets and showers, laundry, sewer dump-point, telephone, kiosk/shop, LP gas refills, ice, camp kitchen, pool, boat ramp, no pets.

❏ Credit cards. Discounts: weekly.

LAGOONS BEACH (TAS) p. 303

Lagoons Beach
Tasman Highway, Lagoons Beach 7215

This beachside national park camping area is about 29 km north of Bicheno on the Tasman Highway, about 2 km north of the road that takes you north-west to St Marys. It has a recently upgraded toilet block and stays here are limited to a maximum of four weeks. ❂

❏ Tent sites, fits big motorhomes.

❏ Toilets (disabled access), pets.

LAKE AWOONGA (QLD) p. 48

Lake Awoonga Caravan Park
Lake Awoonga Road, Benaraby 4680
Ph (07) 4975 0155, fax (07) 4975 0090

This is a popular park on the shores of picturesque Lake Awoonga. It is 9 km from the Bruce Highway along a sealed road. The dam is stocked with barramundi. $$$

❑ Tent sites, powered sites, drive-thru sites, fits big motorhomes, cabins.

❑ Toilets and showers, laundry, telephone, kiosk/shop, LP gas refills, ice, camp kitchen, playground, boat ramp, no pets.

❑ Credit cards. Discounts: weekly.

LAKE BENNETT (NT) p. 74

Lake Bennett Wilderness Resort
Chinner Road, Lake Bennett 0822
Ph (08) 8976 0960 or 1800 999 089,
fax (08) 8976 0256
Email lakebennett@octa4.net.au
Website www.lakebennettwildernessresort.com.au

Located 7 km off the highway between Adelaide River and the outskirts of Darwin, this lakeside resort has a neat lawn camping area and powered sites. Most facilities are available including a quality, licensed restaurant. Large tour groups often stay here, so bookings are advised. $$$$

❑ Tent sites, powered sites, cabins.

❑ Toilets and showers (disabled access), laundry, telephone, kiosk/shop, LP gas refills, ice, no pets.

❑ Credit cards, holiday loading.

LAKE BOGA (VIC) p. 220

Lake Boga Caravan Park
Murray Valley Highway, Lake Boga 3584
Ph (03) 5037 2386, fax (03) 5037 2386

Squeezed between the Murray Valley Highway and the shores of Lake Boga, this is ideal for an overnight stop or a restful few days. The park has basic amenities and a great outlook at a budget price. This is a good value park where sailing, water-skiing and swimming are popular. $$

❑ Tent sites, powered sites, drive-thru sites, fits big motorhomes, on-site vans.

❑ Toilets and showers, laundry, telephone, kiosk/shop, LP gas refills, ice, boat ramp, pets.

❑ Credit cards, holiday loading.

LAKE BURBURY (TAS) p. 292

Lake Burbury Picnic Ground and Camping Area
Lake Burbury, Queenstown 7466
Ph (03) 6471 1058

Located on the shores of Lake Burbury, 15 km east of Queenstown, this is a park with basic facilities but no powered sites. It is ideal for an overnight stop or for a fishing trip. $

❑ Tent sites, drive-thru sites.

❑ Toilets, playground, boat ramp, pets.

❑ No credit cards.

LAKE BURRENDONG (NSW) p. 240

Lake Burrendong State Park
Fashions Mount Road, Mumbil 2820
Ph (02) 6846 7435, fax (02) 6846 7515
Email burrdong@well-com.net.au
Website www.stateparks.nsw.gov.au

Lake Burrendong is a major water-storage area and a mecca for water-skiers. It also has fabulous fishing. It is 26 km east of Wellington along a sealed road. The park has tennis courts, two nine-hole golf courses, good basic amenities, a good kiosk and kilometres of water. There are many permanent holiday vans at the park but also a number of tourist sites. $$

❑ Tent sites, powered sites, drive-thru sites, fits big motorhomes, cabins.

❑ Toilets and showers (disabled access), laundry, telephone, kiosk/shop, LP gas refills, ice, playground, boat ramp, pets.

❑ Credit cards. Discounts: pensioners, seniors, weekly.

LAKE CLIFTON (WA) p. 110

Lake Clifton Caravan Park
Old Coast Road, Lake Clifton 6215
Ph (08) 9739 1430, fax (08) 9739 1430

A tidy, budget-priced park on the highway south of Mandurah, this is a convenient spot for an overnight stop. It is just a short walk to the local tavern for a meal. $$

❑ Tent sites, powered sites, drive-thru sites, fits big motorhomes.

❑ Toilets and showers, laundry, telephone, kiosk/shop, ice, pets.

❑ No credit cards.

LAKE CONJOLA (NSW) p. 14

Conjola Lakeside Van Park
Norman Street, Lake Conjola 2539
Ph (02) 4456 1407 or 1800 354 243,
fax (02) 4456 1608
Email conjolalake@shoal.net.au
Website www.shoal.net.au/~conjolalake

This is a newly developed park on the shores of Lake Conjola with its own nine-hole golf course. It has good amenities and good access to the lake. $$$

❑ Tent sites, powered sites, drive-thru sites, fits big motorhomes, cabins.

❑ Toilets and showers (disabled access), laundry, sewer dump-point, LP gas refills, playground, boat ramp, no pets.

❑ Credit cards, holiday loading. Discounts: weekly.

Lake Conjola Entrance Tourist Park
Main Road, Lake Conjola 2539
Ph (02) 4456 1141 or 1300 133 395,
fax (02) 4456 1141
Email conjola@shoalhaven.nsw.gov.au

This is a large waterfront park with good facilities. Activities include tennis, basketball, volleyball and cricket, or swimming in the lake. Kangaroos and other wildlife like to wander around the park. $$$

❑ Tent sites, powered sites, drive-thru sites, fits big motorhomes, cabins.

❑ Toilets and showers (disabled access), laundry, sewer dump-point, telephone, kiosk/shop, camp kitchen, LP gas refills, ice, pool, playground, boat ramp, no pets.

❑ Credit cards, holiday loading. Discounts: pensioners, seniors, weekly.

LAKE FYANS (VIC) p. 230

Lake Fyans Holiday Park
Lake Fyans Tourist Road, Lake Fyans 3381
Ph (03) 5356 6230 or 1800 631 856,
fax (03) 5356 6330
Email fyans@motorvillage.com.au

This is a spacious waterfront park on the banks of Lake Fyans, a popular water-sports area to the south-west of Stawell. The park has a cafe and also canoes for hire. It is just a short drive to nearby Halls Gap and is an excellent destination for a break. $$$

❑ Tent sites, powered sites, ensuite sites, fits big motorhomes, cabins, on-site vans.

❑ Toilets and showers (disabled access), laundry, sewer dump-point, telephone, kiosk/shop, LP gas refills, ice, camp kitchen, playground, boat ramp, no pets.

❑ Credit cards, holiday loading. Discounts: Big4.

LAKE MONDURAN (QLD) p. 48

Lake Monduran Camping Area
Lake Monduran 4671

The camping area overlooking Lake Monduran, just 4 km from the Bruce Highway, was upgraded from a free camping spot to a basic camping ground in 2002. Facilities include a laundry, sewer dump-point and powered sites. There is also a boat ramp, though the lake has been somewhat empty in recent years. $$

❑ Tent sites, powered sites, drive-thru sites, fits big motorhomes.

❑ Toilets and showers, laundry, sewer dump-point, boat ramp, no pets.

❑ No credit cards.

LAKE MUNMORAH (NSW) p. 26

Lake Munmorah State Recreation Area
Lake Munmorah 2281
Ph (02) 4358 0400, fax (02) 4358 8336

The National Parks and Wildlife Service manage this recreation area. There are two camping areas, Fraser and Freemans, with tent sites and a limited number of unpowered caravan sites. It is just a short walk through the dunes to a popular beach. There are limited facilities here and the park is better suited to tents or campervans and small motorhomes. $

❑ Tent sites.

❑ Toilets and showers, no pets.

❑ Bookings required, credit cards, holiday loading.

LAKE PLACID (QLD) pp. 56, 60

Lake Placid Caravan Park
Lake Placid Road, Lake Placid 4878
Ph (07) 4039 2509 or 1800 807 383,
fax (07) 4039 2803
Email lkplacidtourpk@austarnet.com.au
Website www.holidaynq.com.au/Cairns/LakePlacid/LakePlacid.html

This park is about 10 km north of Cairns, on the bank of the Barron River. Enjoy the pool, the covered barbecue or cook in the camp kitchen. The Skyrail terminal, a major attraction, is nearby. $$$

❑ Tent sites, powered sites, drive-thru sites, fits big motorhomes, cabins, on-site vans.

❑ Toilets and showers (disabled access), laundry, telephone, kiosk/shop, LP gas refills, ice, camp kitchen, pool, TV cables, no pets.

❑ Credit cards. Discounts: weekly, Top Tourist.

LAKE ST CLAIR (TAS) p. 293

Lakeside St Clair Wilderness Holidays
Derwent Bridge 7140
Ph (03) 6289 1137, fax (03) 6289 1250
Email lakestclair@trump.net.au
Website www.tasmaniaadventures.com.au

This park, on the southern shores of Lake St Clair, is 5 km from Derwent Bridge. The park has basic national park-style amenities and is located next to the interpretive centre within the park boundary. A national park entry fee needs to be paid in addition to camping fees. $$

❑ Tent sites, powered sites, drive-thru sites, fits big motorhomes, cabins.

❑ Toilets and showers (disabled access), laundry, telephone, kiosk/shop, LP gas refills, ice, boat ramp, no pets.

❑ Bookings required, credit cards.

LAKE TYERS (VIC) p. 6

Lake Tyers Camp and Caravan Park
558 Lake Tyers Beach Road, Lake Tyers 3909
Ph (03) 5156 5530, fax (03) 5156 5702
Email ltc&cp@net-tech.com.au
Website www.laketyerscaravanpark.com.au

This beachfront park is owned and operated by the Uniting Church. It is a great family park, ideal for a beachside holiday. The park operates in conjunction with a school camp and the consumption of alcohol is permitted in the park but restricted to the sites and not permitted in the public areas. $$

❑ Tent sites, powered sites, drive-thru sites, fits big motorhomes, cabins.

❑ Toilets and showers, laundry, sewer dump-point, telephone, kiosk/shop, LP gas refills, playground, no pets.

❑ Credit cards, holiday loading. Discounts: pensioners, seniors.

LAKES ENTRANCE (VIC) p. 6

Idlehours Caravan Park
Corner Princes Highway and Whiters Street, Lakes Entrance 3909
Ph (03) 5155 1788

This small, unique family-owned and operated park only has individual ensuite sites and is very popular with regular customers. The water is just across the road and it is 1.5 km to the centre of town. Bookings are essential during holiday periods. $$$

❑ Ensuite sites, cabins.

❑ Toilets and showers, laundry, sewer dump-point, LP gas refills, TV cables, pets.

❑ No credit cards, holiday loading. Discounts: weekly.

LAUNCESTON (TAS) pp. 279, 302

Treasure Island Caravan Park
94 Glen Dhu Street, South Launceston 7250
Ph (03) 6344 2600, fax (03) 6343 1764

Launceston has just this one caravan park. It is about 2 km south of the city centre and is easily accessible from the freeway approaching Launceston from the south. The park has good facilities and is a good base to use when visiting the city. $$$

❑ Tent sites, powered sites, fits big motorhomes, cabins, on-site vans.

❑ Toilets and showers, laundry, telephone, LP gas refills, camp kitchen, playground, no pets.

❑ Credit cards.

LENNOX HEAD (NSW) p. 34

See also Ballina.

Lake Ainsworth Caravan Park
Pacific Parade, Lennox Head 2478
Ph (02) 6687 7249, fax (02) 6687 7249
Email lakeains@lis.net.au

Located alongside Lake Ainsworth and across the road from the beach, this is a basic park in a great position. The surf club is nearby and the popular beach is great for swimming or walking. This is a council park on an excellent piece of real estate. $$$

❑ Tent sites, powered sites, drive-thru sites, fits big motorhomes, cabins.

❑ Toilets and showers (disabled access), laundry, sewer dump-point, telephone, no pets.

❑ Credit cards, holiday loading. Discounts: weekly.

LITCHFIELD NATIONAL PARK
(NT) p. 74

Wangi Falls Camping Area
Wangi Falls, Litchfield National Park, via Batchelor 0845

Since the road from Batchelor was sealed in the 1990s, the popularity of this camping area close to the foot of the fabulous Wangi Falls has increased. There is a good swimming hole and a kiosk beside the camping area. The amenities are basic national park-style, but the area is quite pretty. $$

❑ Tent sites, fits big motorhomes.

❑ Toilets and showers (disabled access), telephone, kiosk/shop, ice, no pets.

❑ No credit cards.

LITHGOW (NSW) p. 236

Lithgow Tourist and Van Park
58 Cooerwull Road, Lithgow 2790
Ph (02) 6351 4350, fax (02) 6351 4384
Email lacey@lisp.com.au

This budget-priced park has good facilities and is an ideal location for an overnight or extended stay. It offers a selection of accommodation and shady sites in a quiet off-highway position, at the western edge of town. $$

❑ Tent sites, powered sites, drive-thru sites, fits big motorhomes, cabins.

❑ Toilets and showers (disabled access), laundry, telephone, kiosk/shop, LP gas refills, camp kitchen, playground, no pets.

❑ Credit cards. Discounts: weekly.

LOCH SPORT (VIC) p. 6

Loch Sport Caravan Park
Charles Street, Loch Sport 3851
Ph (03) 5146 0264, fax (03) 5146 0265
Email lochsportpark@telstra.com

Located on the shores of Lake Victoria, this popular holiday park enjoys a great position in this resort town. Shady trees and good amenities are a feature of the park. Bookings will be essential during peak holiday periods. $$$

❑ Tent sites, powered sites, drive-thru sites, fits big motorhomes, cabins, on-site vans.

❑ Toilets and showers, laundry, telephone, LP gas refills, ice, camp kitchen, playground, boat ramp, pets.

❑ Credit cards, holiday loading.

Ninety Mile Beach Holiday Retreat
Track 10 (off Seacombe Road), Loch Sport 3851
Ph (03) 5146 0320, fax (03) 5146 0327
Email jan@i-o.net.au
Website www.ninetymilebeach.com

This unique camping park on a private farming property is just a stroll away, over the sand dunes, from the fabulous Ninety Mile Beach. The owner-operated park is reached along a short section of unsealed access road but the trip is worthwhile. $$$

❑ Tent sites, powered sites, drive-thru sites, fits big motorhomes, cabins, on-site vans.

❑ Toilets and showers, laundry, telephone, kiosk/shop, LP gas refills, ice, camp kitchen, playground, pets.

❑ Credit cards, holiday loading. Discounts: pensioners, weekly.

LONGFORD (TAS) pp. 279, 280

Longford Riverside Caravan Park
Archer Street, Longford 7310
Ph (03) 6391 1470

The park is located on the banks of the Macquarie River. It has good amenities and is only a few hundred metres from the centre of town. $$

LONGREACH (QLD) p. 174

Gunnadoo Caravan Park
12 Thrush Street, Longreach 4730
Ph (07) 4658 1781, fax (07) 4658 0034
Email gunadoo@tpg.com.au

Longreach is a busy tourist centre during the cooler months and a booking is generally essential. This park has good facilities including a block of individual amenities that we like. We regularly stay at the park, which is within walking distance of the Australian Stockman's Hall of Fame and about 2 km from the town centre. $$$

❑ Tent sites, powered sites, drive-thru sites, fits big motorhomes, cabins.

❑ Toilets and showers (disabled access), laundry, sewer dump-point, telephone, kiosk/shop, LP gas refills, ice, pool, pets.

❑ Bookings required, credit cards. Discounts: weekly.

LORNE (VIC) p. 139

Cumberland River Holiday Park
Great Ocean Road, Cumberland River 3232
Ph (03) 5289 1790, fax (03) 5289 1790
Email cumberland@netconnect.com

Set in a picturesque spot on this scenic coastal strip, this holiday park has only unpowered sites. It is close to the beach and a good base for exploring the Otways. Minimum booking periods apply during Christmas, January and Easter holiday periods. $$

❑ Tent sites, fits big motorhomes, cabins.

❑ Toilets and showers (disabled access), laundry, telephone, kiosk/shop, LP gas refills, ice, playground, no pets.

❑ Credit cards, holiday loading.

The Lorne Foreshore Caravan Parks
2 Great Ocean Road, Lorne 3232
Ph (03) 5289 1382, fax (03) 5289 2225
Email lfcmd@bigpond.com
Website www.lorneforeshore.asn.au

This is actually a group of five parks all within Lorne, and all five parks are administered from the one office. Each of the parks is well positioned and within walking distance of the resort-style town centre. Lorne is one of Victoria's most popular beachside tourist destinations and the parks are very busy in summer. Minimum bookings apply during Christmas, January and Easter holidays. $$$

❑ Tent sites, powered sites, drive-thru sites, fits big motorhomes, cabins.

❑ Toilets and showers (disabled access), laundry, sewer dump-point, telephone, playground, no pets.

❑ Credit cards, holiday loading. Discounts: pensioners, seniors.

LOXTON (SA) p. 222

Loxton Riverfront Caravan Park
Riverfront Road, Loxton 5333
Ph (08) 8584 7862 or 1800 887 733, fax (08) 8584 7862
Email loxtoncp@hotkey.net.au

This is a neat, tidy and spacious park with good amenities and large shady trees along the banks of the river. Several new sites have recently been completed above the high flood level. Interestingly, the level of many of the great floods of past years are recorded on a tree near the park entrance. This is a good park for a quiet holiday. $$$

❑ Tent sites, powered sites, drive-thru sites, ensuite sites, fits big motorhomes, cabins.

❑ Toilets and showers (disabled access), laundry, telephone, kiosk/shop, LP gas refills, ice, camp kitchen, playground, no pets.

❑ Credit cards. Discounts: weekly, Big4.

LUCINDA (QLD) p. 54

Wanderers Holiday Village
18 Bruce Parade, Lucinda 4850
Ph (07) 4777 8213, fax (07) 4777 8131
Email stay@wanderers-lucinda.com.au
Website www.wanderers-lucinda.com.au

This park is a popular holiday destination for people keen on fishing. It is close to the centre of town and bookings are essential at Easter. There are covered barbecues and a boat parking area. $$$

❑ Tent sites, powered sites, drive-thru sites, fits big motorhomes, cabins.

❑ Toilets and showers, laundry, sewer dump-point, telephone, kiosk/shop, LP gas refills, ice, pool, playground, internet terminal, no pets.

❑ Credit cards. Discounts: pensioners, seniors, weekly.

MACKAY (QLD) p. 50

Andergrove Van Park
Beaconsfield Road, North Mackay 4740
Ph (07) 4942 4922 or 1800 424 922, fax (07) 4942 3257
Email andvanpk@mackay.net.au
Website www.andergrovepark.com.au

Sweeping lawns meet you as you enter this very good quality park. The park is in a quiet, off-highway position with good access from the Bruce Highway. It has good features at a good price and is a good base for exploring the Mackay region. $$$

❑ Tent sites, powered sites, drive-thru sites, ensuite sites, fits big motorhomes, cabins, on-site vans.

❑ Toilets and showers (disabled access), laundry, sewer dump-point, telephone, kiosk/shop, LP gas refills, ice, camp kitchen, pool, playground, no pets.

❑ Credit cards. Discounts: weekly, Top Tourist.

Beach Tourist Park
8 Petrie Street, Mackay 4740
Ph (07) 4957 4021 or 1800 645 111,
fax (07) 4951 4551
Email stay@beachtouristpark.com.au
Website www.beachtouristpark.com.au

This is a very good beachfront caravan park
with good amenities and facilities, including
a kiosk, a gym and a fully equipped camp
kitchen. The park is about 4 km from the
centre of the city and is an excellent park
for a beachside holiday. **$$$**

❏ Tent sites, powered sites, drive-thru sites,
ensuite sites, fits big motorhomes, cabins.

❏ Toilets and showers (disabled access),
laundry, sewer dump-point, telephone,
kiosk/shop, LP gas refills, ice, camp kitchen,
pool, playground, TV cables, internet terminal,
no pets.

❏ Credit cards. Discounts: weekly, Big4.

MACKSVILLE (NSW) p. 30

Nambucca River Tourist Park
999 Nursery Road, Macksville 2447
Ph (02) 6568 1850, fax (02) 6568 1546.

About 6 km north of Macksville just off the
Pacific Highway, this neat, family-owned park
is adjacent to the Nambucca River. Ideal for
an overnight stop or a couple of days. Dogs
are the only pets allowed in this park. **$$**

❏ Tent sites, powered sites, drive-thru sites,
cabins.

❏ Toilets and showers, laundry, telephone,
kiosk/shop, LP gas refills, ice, camp kitchen,
pool, playground, pets.

❏ Credit cards, holiday loading. Discounts:
weekly.

MAIN BEACH (QLD)

See Gold Coast.

MALLACOOTA (VIC) p. 9

⊛ **Mallacoota Foreshore Camp Park**
Allan Drive, Mallacoota 3892
Ph (03) 5158 0300, fax (03) 5158 0300
Email camppark@vicnet.net.au
Website www.mallacoota.com

This amazing, picturesque caravan park
sprawls along the water's edge. There are
over 600 sites in the park and the reception
building is just 150 m from the town centre.
Some waterfront sites even have their own
moorings. **$$$**

❏ Tent sites, powered sites, drive-thru sites,
fits big motorhomes, on-site vans.

❏ Toilets and showers (disabled access),
laundry, sewer dump-point, telephone,
LP gas refills, playground, boat ramp, pets.

❏ Credit cards, holiday loading. Discounts:
weekly.

MANNING POINT (NSW) p. 28

See also Croki.

Manning Point Ocean Caravan Park
Manning Street, Manning Point 2430
Ph (02) 6553 2624, fax (02) 6553 2869
Email oceanpark@tsn.cc
Website www.oceancaravanpark.com

This is a quality, award-winning caravan
park just a short walk from 14 km of unspoilt
ocean beach. The park has excellent facilities
for people with disabilities. A quiet place
where a few days could slip by very quickly.
$$

❏ Tent sites, powered sites, drive-thru sites,
fits big motorhomes, cabins, on-site vans.

❏ Toilets and showers (disabled access),
laundry, telephone, kiosk/shop, LP gas refills,
ice, camp kitchen, pool, playground, pets.

❏ Credit cards, holiday loading. Discounts:
weekly, Top Tourist.

MANYALLALUK (NT) p. 72

Manyallaluk – The Dreaming Place
Central Arnham Highway, Manyallaluk 0850
Ph (08) 8975 4727 or 1800 644 727,
fax (08) 8975 4724
Email manyallaluk@bigpond.com

This is a small camping area and a unique
Aboriginal cultural experience. Camping is
available to those taking part in an afternoon
of Aboriginal crafts. Alcohol is not permitted
in the community. Camping fees are included
in the day's activities and advance bookings
are required for this great experience. **$**

❏ Tent sites, powered sites, drive-thru sites,
fits big motorhomes.

❏ Toilets and shower (disabled access),
laundry, sewer dump-point, telephone,
kiosk/shop, pool, no pets.

❏ Bookings required, credit cards.

MARENGO (VIC) p. 138

Marengo Holiday Park
Marengo Crescent, Apollo Bay 3233
Ph (03) 5237 6162, fax (03) 5237 7744
Email marengo@vicnet.net.au
Website www.vicnet.net.au/~marengo

This park is situated on an absolute
beachfront property, 1.5 km south of the
Apollo Bay township. It is budget-priced,
especially considering the location. **$$**

❏ Tent sites, powered sites, fits big
motorhomes, cabins.

❏ Toilets and showers (disabled access),
laundry, sewer dump-point, camp kitchen,
playground, pets.

❏ Credit cards, holiday loading. Discounts:
weekly.

MARGARET RIVER (WA) p. 112

Margaret River Tourist Park
44 Station Road, Margaret River 6285
Ph (08) 9757 2180, fax (08) 9757 3159
Email info@mrtouristpark.com
Website www.mrtouristpark.com

Located 1 km from the centre of town, this
park is a convenient base to explore this

popular holiday region. The park has good
facilities including all-new amenities,
laundry, TV room and camp kitchen. **$$$**

❏ Tent sites, powered sites, drive-thru sites,
ensuite sites, fits big motorhomes, cabins,
on-site vans.

❏ Toilets and showers (disabled access),
laundry, telephone, kiosk/shop, LP gas refills,
ice, camp kitchen, pool, playground, pets.

❏ Credit cards, holiday loading. Discounts:
pensioners, seniors, weekly, FPA.

MARLO (VIC) p. 8

Burbang Adventure Caravan Park
Cape Conran Road, Marlo 3888
Ph (03) 5154 8219, fax (03) 5154 8475
Email burbang@net-tech.com.au

This park is situated on 200 acres of privately
owned bushland, 17 km east of Marlo. There
are 2 km of unsealed access road. The park
will appeal to those wanting to escape the
hustle and bustle of the busy beachside
parks. Facilities include tennis courts,
a pool and a games room. **$$**

❏ Tent sites, powered sites, drive-thru sites,
fits big motorhomes, cabins, on-site vans.

❏ Toilets and showers, laundry, telephone,
kiosk/shop, LP gas refills, ice, pool, playground,
pets.

❏ Credit cards. Discounts: pensioners, seniors,
weekly.

MAROOCHYDORE (QLD) p. 44

Maroochy Palms Holiday Village
319 Bradman Avenue, Maroochydore 4558
Ph (07) 5443 8611 or 1800 623 316,
fax (07) 5443 6199
Email enquiries@maroochypalms.com.au
Website www.maroochypalms.com.au

This is a very good quality park in a popular
holiday destination. The park has great
facilities, including a mini-mart and covered
barbecues. The owners offer courtesy
transfers and the park is just across the road
from the Maroochy River. **$$$$**

❏ Tent sites, powered sites, drive-thru sites,
ensuite sites, fits big motorhomes, cabins.

❏ Toilets and showers (disabled access),
laundry, sewer dump-point, telephone,
kiosk/shop, LP gas refills, ice, camp kitchen,
pool, playground, boat ramp, TV cables,
internet terminal, no pets.

❏ Credit cards, holiday loading. Discounts:
weekly, Big4.

MARYBOROUGH (QLD) p. 46

Wallace Caravan Park
22 Ferry Street, Maryborough 4650
Ph (07) 4121 3970, fax (07) 4123 5111
Email shamie@iprimus.com.au
Website www.wallacemotel.4mg.com

This is a good quality, older park, close to
the centre of town. It has a diverse range
of accommodation on offer. Access is easy
from the southern approach to the town. **$$**

❏ Tent sites, powered sites, drive-thru sites,
ensuite sites, fits big motorhomes, cabins,
on-site vans.

❏ Toilets and showers (disabled access),
laundry, sewer dump-point, telephone, LP gas
refills, camp kitchen, pool, pets.

❏ Credit cards. Discounts: weekly.

MATARANKA (NT) p. 73

Mataranka Homestead
Homestead Road, Mataranka 0852
Ph (08) 8975 4544, fax (08) 8975 4580
Email matarankahomestead@bigpond.com

This popular park is situated alongside the
Mataranka Thermal Pool. Many people come
here to swim in the hot, crystal-clear springs.
There are good amenities, a licensed bistro
and a well-stocked shop. An area just outside
the park is set aside for dog owners, though
pets are generally not allowed. **$$$**

❏ Tent sites, powered sites, drive-thru sites,
fits big motorhomes, cabins.

❏ Toilets and showers, laundry, telephone,
kiosk/shop, ice, no pets.

❏ Credit cards. Discounts: weekly.

Territory Manor Caravan Park
Martins Road, off Stuart Highway,
Mataranka 0852
Ph (08) 8975 4516, fax (08) 8975 4612

This is a good quality, smaller park alongside
a motel with tidy surrounds. It is close to the
centre of town and a major daily attraction is
feeding barramundi inside the grounds. **$$$**

❏ Tent sites, powered sites, drive-thru sites,
ensuite sites, fits big motorhomes.

❏ Toilets and showers (disabled access),
laundry, telephone, kiosk/shop, ice, pool,
playground, no pets.

❏ Credit cards.

MAYFIELD BAY (TAS) p. 298

Mayfield Beach Coastal Reserve
via Swansea 7190

This beachside camping reserve is 15 km
south of Swansea. Limited facilities here
but suitable for the budget traveller. ⑤

❏ Tent sites, fits big motorhomes.

❏ Toilets, pets.

MEEKATHARRA (WA) p. 202

Meekatharra Caravan Park
Main Street, Meekatharra 6622
Ph (08) 9981 1253, fax (08) 9981 1253

This is a basic caravan park with the bare
essentials, conveniently located within walking
distance of the town centre. The park office
includes a takeaway-food shop that stocks a
range of other items. Amenities are clean and
the park is located on the main highway. **$$**

❏ Tent sites, powered sites, drive-thru sites,
fits big motorhomes, cabins.

❏ Toilets and showers, laundry, telephone,
kiosk/shop, LP gas refills, ice, pets.

❏ Credit cards.

MELBOURNE (VIC) pp. 146–7

See also Pakenham.

Ashley Gardens Holiday Village
129 Ashley Street, Braybrook 3019
Ph (03) 9318 6866 or 1800 061 444,
fax (03) 9318 6661
Email holiday@ashleygardens.com.au
Website www.ashleygardens.com.au

In the western suburbs of Melbourne, this is a large, easily located park just off the Western Highway. The park has great facilities including a heated pool, heated amenities and a tennis court. It is just 9.5 km from the centre of Melbourne and could be a good choice of park for those sailing on the ferry to Tasmania. There are direct bus services from the park to the city and a supermarket is right next door. $$$$

❑ Tent sites, powered sites, drive-thru sites, ensuite sites, fits big motorhomes, cabins.

❑ Toilets and showers (disabled access), laundry, sewer dump-point, telephone, LP gas refills, camp kitchen, pool, playground, internet terminal, no pets.

❑ Bookings required, credit cards. Discounts: weekly, Big4.

Crystal Brook Holiday Centre
182 Warrandyte Road, Doncaster East 3109
Ph (03) 9844 3637, fax (03) 9844 3342
Email crystalbrook@ezweb.com.au
Website www.wheretostay.net/crystalbrook

This older, tidy park is in a quiet bush setting with large shady trees. The family-owned park has good amenities and is well located in the north-eastern suburbs. $$$

❑ Tent sites, powered sites, drive-thru sites, ensuite sites, fits big motorhomes, cabins, on-site vans.

❑ Toilets and showers (disabled access), laundry, sewer dump-point, telephone, kiosk/shop, LP gas refills, camp kitchen, pool, playground, TV cables, no pets.

❑ Bookings required, credit cards. Discounts: weekly.

⊛ Frankston Holiday Village
Corner Frankston–Flinders and
Robinson roads, Frankston 3199
Ph (03) 5971 2333 or 1800 623 491,
fax (03) 5971 2111
Email info@frankstonholidayvillage.com.au
Website www.frankstonholidayvillage.com.au

Catering specifically for tourists, this is a good quality park in the south-eastern suburbs. It is ideal for those exploring the Mornington Peninsula or connecting with the Sorrento to Queenscliff ferry. The park offers a very good range of facilities including a heated pool and tennis court. Minimum bookings apply during holiday periods. $$$

❑ Tent sites, powered sites, drive-thru sites, ensuite sites, fits big motorhomes, cabins, on-site vans.

❑ Toilets and showers, laundry, sewer dump-point, telephone, kiosk/shop, LP gas refills, ice, camp kitchen, pool, playground, no pets.

❑ Credit cards, holiday loading. Discounts: Big4.

Melbourne Big4 Holiday Park
265 Elizabeth Street, Coburg 3058
Ph (03) 9354 3533 or 1800 802 678,
fax (03) 9354 4550
Email holidaypark@big4melb.com
Website www.big4melb.com

This is a tourist park in a quiet area of Melbourne's northern suburbs, just 9 km from Melbourne's CBD. The park has relatively easy access to the Hume Highway and other northern approaches and is a popular park with international campers, motorhomes and campervans. There is a heated pool and heated amenity block and minimum booking periods apply during holidays and major Melbourne events. $$$$

❑ Tent sites, powered sites, ensuite sites, fits big motorhomes, cabins.

❑ Toilets and showers, laundry, sewer dump-point, telephone, LP gas refills, ice, camp kitchen, pool, playground, internet terminal, no pets.

❑ Credit cards. Discounts: Big4.

Twin Bridge Tourist Park
370 Frankston Road, Dandenong South 3175
Ph (03) 9706 5492 or 1800 648 346,
fax (03) 9706 5076
Email info@twinbridgetouristpark.com.au
Website www.twinbridgetouristpark.com.au

Just 6 km south of Dandenong, this is a good quality park with a limited number of tourist sites. It's a good park for those wanting to stay on the eastern side of Melbourne. Minimum bookings apply during holiday periods. $$$

❑ Tent sites, powered sites, drive-thru sites, fits big motorhomes, cabins, on-site vans.

❑ Toilets and showers, laundry, sewer dump-point, telephone, LP gas refills, camp kitchen, playground, no pets.

❑ Credit cards, holiday loading. Discounts: Big4.

Wantirna Park
203 Mountain Highway, Wantirna 3152
Ph (03) 9887 1157, fax (03) 9887 1909
Email wantirna-park@bigpond.com

This is a large park with a limited number of tourist sites. Located in the eastern suburbs, the park has good facilities including a swimming pool, tennis courts and recreation room. A good choice for those looking to stay in this part of Melbourne. $$$

❑ Powered sites, drive-thru sites, fits big motorhomes, cabins.

❑ Toilets and showers (disabled access), laundry, telephone, camp kitchen, pool, playground, no pets.

❑ Credit cards, holiday loading. Discounts: pensioners, seniors.

MENA CREEK (QLD) p. 56

Paronella Park
Japoonvale Road, Mena Creek 4871
Ph (07) 4065 3225, fax (07) 4065 3022
Email info@paronellapark.com.au
Website www.paronellapark.com.au

The park adjoins the fabulous Paronella Park Heritage Gardens. Admission to the gardens is $16 per adult at the time of publication, and accommodation fees are separate.

At night, the Mena Creek waterfall is lit up. Patrons can enjoy a quiet pre-dinner drink at the water's edge in this amazing setting. Sites in the camping ground aren't large and the park has basic facilities. $$

❑ Tent sites, powered sites, drive-thru sites, fits big motorhomes.

❑ Toilets and showers, laundry, kiosk/shop, LP gas refills, pets.

❑ Credit cards. Discounts: pensioners, seniors, weekly.

MENINGIE (SA) p. 132

Lake Albert Caravan Park
Narrung Road, Meningie 5264
Ph (08) 8575 1411, fax (08) 8575 1411
Email lacp@lm.net.au

Located on the shores of the freshwater Lake Albert, about 1 km from the town centre, this is a budget-priced park with a great expanse of lawn and shady trees. It is a well laid out and owner-operated park, with good facilities and a great outlook. $$$

❑ Tent sites, powered sites, drive-thru sites, fits big motorhomes, cabins, on-site vans.

❑ Toilets and showers (disabled access), laundry, telephone, kiosk/shop, LP gas refills, ice, boat ramp, pets.

❑ Credit cards. Discounts: Top Tourist.

MERREDIN (WA) p. 272

⊛ Merredin Caravan Park and Av-a-Rest Village
Great Eastern Highway, Merredin 6415
Ph (08) 9041 1535, fax (08) 9041 1535

This park is of a quality that is rarely found in an inland town the size of Merredin and we highly recommend it. From here it is a comfortable 260 km to Perth or 335 km to Kalgoorlie; Merredin is an excellent choice for an overnight stop. The park facilities include a pool and camp kitchen, and the adjoining roadhouse serves meals. $$$

❑ Tent sites, powered sites, drive-thru sites, fits big motorhomes, cabins, on-site vans.

❑ Toilets and showers, laundry, sewer dump-point, telephone, kiosk/shop, LP gas refills, ice, camp kitchen, pool, playground, boat ramp, pets.

❑ Credit cards. Discounts: weekly.

MIAMI (QLD)

See Gold Coast.

MIDGE POINT (QLD) p. 53

See also Proserpine.

⊛ Travellers Rest Caravan and Camping Park
29 Jackson Street, Midge Point 4799
Ph (07) 4947 6120, fax (07) 4947 6111

There are no more sandflies or midges at Midge Point than elsewhere, but there is a wonderful out-of-the-way beachside caravan park with lovely manicured lawns, large shady trees and a host of great features. We really enjoy staying here. $$

❑ Tent sites, powered sites, drive-thru sites, fits big motorhomes, cabins, on-site vans.

❑ Toilets and showers (disabled access), laundry, sewer dump-point, telephone, kiosk/shop, LP gas refills, ice, camp kitchen, pool, no pets.

❑ Credit cards. Discounts: weekly, Top Tourist.

MILDURA (VIC) p. 220

All Seasons Caravan Park
818 Fifteenth Street (Calder Highway),
Mildura 3500
Ph (03) 5023 3375, fax (03) 5021 4537
Email info@allseasonscaravanpark.com.au
Website www.allseasonscaravanpark.com.au

This is a very good quality park on the southern approaches to Mildura, about 4.5 km from the city centre and 500 m from the junction of the Calder and Sturt highways. Minimum bookings apply during holiday periods. $$$

❑ Tent sites, powered sites, drive-thru sites, ensuite sites, fits big motorhomes, cabins.

❑ Toilets and showers, laundry, telephone, kiosk/shop, LP gas refills, camp kitchen, pool, playground, no pets.

❑ Credit cards, holiday loading. Discounts: pensioners, seniors, weekly, FPA.

Calder Caravan Park
775–783 Fifteenth Street (Calder Highway),
Mildura 3500
Ph (03) 5023 1310, fax (03) 5021 1394
Email caldercp@ruralnet.net.au

This is a very good quality, centrally located park. It is close to the Mildura Centre Plaza and easily accessible. $$$

❑ Tent sites, powered sites, drive-thru sites, fits big motorhomes, cabins, on-site vans.

❑ Toilets and showers, laundry, sewer dump-point, telephone, kiosk/shop, LP gas refills, ice, camp kitchen, pool, playground, no pets.

❑ Credit cards, holiday loading. Discounts: Top Tourist.

Golden River Caravan Gardens
Flora Avenue, Mildura 3500
Ph (03) 5021 2299 or 1800 621 262,
fax (03) 5021 1364
Email big4@ruralnet.net.au
Website www.ruralnet.net.au/big4

This is a very good quality park on the banks of the Murray River, 4.5 km west of the town centre. The park has a range of accommodation and good facilities including covered barbecues, bicycles and canoes for hire, a heated pool and a boat parking area. $$$

❑ Tent sites, powered sites, ensuite sites, cabins.

❑ Toilets and showers (disabled access), laundry, telephone, kiosk/shop, LP gas refills, ice, camp kitchen, pool, playground, no pets.

❑ Credit cards, holiday loading. Discounts: pensioners, seniors, Big4.

Mildura and Deakin Holiday Park
Corner Sturt and Calder highways,
Mildura 3500
Ph (03) 5023 0486 or 1800 060 705,
fax (03) 5022 2729
Email admin@mildura-deakin.com.au
Website www.mildura-deakin.com.au

Strategically located on a highway junction, this good quality caravan park is just a short walk from the Mildura Centre Plaza and the great Hudak's bakery. This is a convenient, shady park, ideal for an overnight stay or a few days. $$$

❑ Tent sites, powered sites, drive-thru sites, ensuite sites, cabins.

❑ Toilets and showers, laundry, telephone, LP gas refills, ice, camp kitchen, pool, playground, no pets.

❑ Credit cards, holiday loading. Discounts: pensioners, seniors, weekly, Big4.

The Palms Caravan Park
Corner Cowra and Cureton Avenues, Mildura 3500
Ph (03) 5023 1774, fax (03) 5023 5714
Email palms@ncable.com.au

This is a good quality park in a quiet area on the edge of town, and will appeal to those travelling with dogs. There is a great dog exercise area and dog bath facilities. The park has a range of accommodation facilities. Minimum bookings apply during holiday periods. $$

❑ Tent sites, powered sites, drive-thru sites, ensuite sites, cabins, on-site vans.

❑ Toilets and showers (disabled access), laundry, telephone, kiosk/shop, LP gas refills, ice, camp kitchen, pool, playground, pets.

❑ Credit cards. Discounts: seniors, weekly.

⊛ **River Beach Camping Ground**
Cureton Avenue, Chaffey's Bend, Mildura 3500
Ph (03) 5023 6879, fax (03) 5021 5390
Email apex@ruralnet.net.au

The beautiful setting of this park – shady trees, green lawns and the river winding by – makes it a favourite of ours. Large and spacious, the park is located 4 km west of Mildura opposite a popular swimming beach. Sit back and enjoy the scenery with a fresh lunch from the park's takeaway shop. The park has good basic facilities and minimum bookings apply during peak periods. $$$

❑ Tent sites, powered sites, fits big motorhomes, cabins.

❑ Toilets and showers, laundry, sewer dump-point, telephone, kiosk/shop, LP gas refills, ice, camp kitchen, boat ramp, pets.

❑ Credit cards. Discounts: weekly.

MILES (QLD) pp. 160, 252

Coloumboola Country
Ryalls Road, Miles 4415
Ph (07) 4665 8293, fax (07) 4665 8293

This park is located in a quiet rural location 30 km north-east of Miles, reached by turning off the Warrego Highway 15 km east of Miles. The park has good facilities including a large camp kitchen complex and would be ideal for a few days' relaxation. $$

❑ Tent sites, powered sites, drive-thru sites, fits big motorhomes, cabins.

❑ Toilets and showers, laundry, telephone, camp kitchen, pool, pets.

❑ No credit cards.

⊛ **Possum Park Caravan and Camping Park**
Leichhardt Highway, Miles 4415
Ph (07) 4627 1651, fax (07) 4627 1651

We always enjoy staying at this unique caravan park – once a World War II munitions

dump, the underground bunkers have been converted to cabins. Owner-operated, it is a great park set in a quiet location alongside the Leichhardt Highway, 20 km north of Miles. It has clean amenities and good facilities. $$

❑ Tent sites, powered sites, drive-thru sites, ensuite sites, fits big motorhomes, cabins.

❑ Toilets and showers (disabled access), laundry, telephone, kiosk/shop, camp kitchen, no pets.

❑ Credit cards. Discounts: weekly.

MILLICENT (SA) p. 132

Millicent Lakeside Caravan Park
12 Park Terrace, Millicent 5280
Ph (08) 8733 3947, fax (08) 8733 3947

This is a spacious, neat and tidy park with good basic facilities. A convenient, well-stocked shop is adjacent, at the town's excellent swimming complex (a man-made swimming lake). A change of management, however, may mean that some aspects of the park have changed since the time of writing. $$

❑ Tent sites, powered sites, drive-thru sites, fits big motorhomes, cabins, on-site vans.

❑ Toilets and showers (disabled access), laundry, sewer dump-point, telephone, kiosk/shop, LP gas refills, playground, pets.

❑ Credit cards. Discounts: weekly, FPA.

MISSION BEACH (QLD) p. 56

See also Mission Beach South.

Mission Beach Hideaway Holiday Village
Porters Promenade, Mission Beach 4852
Ph (07) 4068 7104 or 1800 687 104,
fax (07) 4068 7492
Email hideaway@austarnet.com.au

This is an excellent park at the heart of a very popular tourist destination and just a short walk to the beach, the shops or the local restaurants. The park has all the facilities you would expect of an establishment of this quality. $$$

❑ Tent sites, powered sites, drive-thru sites, fits big motorhomes, cabins.

❑ Toilets and showers, laundry, sewer dump-point, telephone, LP gas refills, ice, camp kitchen, pool, playground, TV cables, internet terminal, no pets.

❑ Credit cards, holiday loading. Discounts: weekly, Big4.

MITCHELL (QLD) p. 254

⊛ **Major Mitchell Caravan Park**
Warrego Highway, Mitchell 4465
Ph (07) 4623 1073, fax (07) 4623 1074

Soak away your aches at the artesian spa pools or wander into the centre of town for a bit of sightseeing, both just a short walk from this, modern popular park. Its greatest attraction, however, is the unique offer of the first two nights free, on all sites. This park gets very busy during the tourist season and space is often scarce. Check in at the Great Artesian Spa complex just over the river from

the park (their phone and fax numbers are the ones listed). $

❑ Tent sites, powered sites, drive-thru sites, ensuite sites, fits big motorhomes.

❑ Toilets and showers (disabled access), sewer dump-point, pets.

❑ Credit cards.

MOAMA (NSW) p. 218

See also Echuca.

Cottonwood Holiday Park
Off Chanter Street, Moama 2731
Ph (03) 5480 9253, fax (03) 5482 1732
Email cottonwood@murrayriverholiday.com
Website www.murrayriverholiday.com

Located 2.5 km from the town centre on the banks of the Murray River, this popular holiday park is home to many annual vans and has a limited number of tourist sites. The park has good facilities including a tennis court and a pool. The park is a good base, especially for those travelling with pets. $$

❑ Tent sites, powered sites, fits big motorhomes, cabins.

❑ Toilets and showers, laundry, telephone, kiosk/shop, LP gas refills, ice, camp kitchen, pool, playground, boat ramp, pets.

❑ Credit cards, holiday loading. Discounts: weekly.

Maidens Inn Holiday Park
100 Chanter Street, Moama 2731
Ph (03) 5482 5235, fax (03) 5480 9676
Email maidensinn@murrayriverholiday.com
Website www.murrayriverholiday.com

This is a good quality park just 2 km from town, on the banks of the Murray River. The park has good facilities, including a tennis court, and makes an ideal holiday destination or a great weekend stop. $$$

❑ Tent sites, powered sites, drive-thru sites, ensuite sites, fits big motorhomes, cabins.

❑ Toilets and showers (disabled access), laundry, telephone, kiosk/shop, LP gas refills, ice, camp kitchen, pool, playground, boat ramp, TV cables, no pets.

❑ Credit cards, holiday loading. Discounts: weekly, Big4.

MON REPOS (QLD)

See Bargara.

MONKEY MIA (WA) p. 100

⊛ **Monkey Mia Dolphin Resort**
Monkey Mia Road, Monkey Mia 6537
Ph (08) 9948 1320 or 1800 653 611,
fax (08) 9948 1034
Email sales@monkeymia.com.au
Website www.monkeymia.com.au

If you are keen on wildlife watching, this large, family park, set on the shores of Shark Bay, is for you. Watch the famous Monkey Mia dolphins play at the water's edge, just metres from the park, or take a catamaran ride on the calm waters in search of dolphins and dugong. Some people come to see the dolphins while others come to soak up the

balmy winter climate and perhaps catch a few fish. Along with very good facilities and a wide range of accommodation options, the park has a fully licensed restaurant, a well-stocked general store and a cafe. $$$

❑ Tent sites, powered sites, drive-thru sites, fits big motorhomes, cabins, on-site vans.

❑ Toilet and showers, laundry, sewer dump-point, telephone, kiosk/shop, LP gas refills, ice, camp kitchen, pool, playground, boat ramp, internet terminal, pets.

❑ Bookings required, credit cards. Discounts: seniors, weekly.

MOOLOOLABA (QLD) p. 44

⊛ **Mooloolaba Beach Caravan Park**
Parkyn Parade, Mooloolaba 4564
Ph (07) 5444 1201 or 1800 441 201,
fax (07) 5444 1042
Email mooloolaba@maroochypark.com
Website www.maroochypark.qld.gov.au

This park is split into two sites. The main section is in Parkyn Parade, while the smaller section is at Mooloolaba Beach. We think the beachside section has the best outlook of any park in Australia: it overlooks the fabulous beach and is just across the road from the resort-style main street of this popular holiday town. The beachside section has sites for motorhomes, campervans and caravans but there are no tent sites. Registration is at Parkyn Parade. $$$

❑ Tent sites, powered sites, cabins.

❑ Toilets and showers, laundry, sewer dump-point, telephone, ice, no pets.

❑ Credit cards, holiday loading. Discounts: weekly, FPA.

MOONEE BEACH (NSW) p. 32

Moonee Beach Reserve
Moonee Beach Road, Moonee Beach 2450
Ph (02) 6653 6552, fax (02) 6653 6552

This popular beachfront caravan park has basic facilities, including a tennis court and open grassy sites with views out to sea. Swimming is good, as are the nature walks around the reserve. Cats are not allowed. $$

❑ Tent sites, powered sites, fits big motorhomes, cabins, on-site vans.

❑ Toilets and showers (disabled access), laundry, telephone, LP gas refills, camp kitchen, playground, pets.

❑ Bookings required, credit cards, holiday loading. Discounts: weekly.

Split Solitary Caravan Park
Split Solitary Road, Coffs Harbour 2450
Ph (02) 6653 6212, fax (02) 6656 4599
Email splitsolitarycaravanpark@bigpond.com

A lovely, shady beachside park south of Moonee Beach, 9 km north of Coffs Harbour. This park has good facilities, including a pool and a TV and games room. $$

❑ Tent sites, powered sites, cabins.

❑ Toilets and showers, laundry, sewer dump-point, telephone, kiosk/shop, LP gas refills, ice, pool, playground, no pets.

❑ Credit cards, holiday loading. Discounts: weekly.

MOREE (NSW) p. 160

Gwydir Carapark
Corner Newell Highway and Amaroo Drive,
Moree 2400
Ph (02) 6752 2723, fax (02) 6752 2723

This park is located on the southern approaches to Moree, about 3 km from the city centre. It has good amenities but its most attractive feature is the hot mineral spa and pool. A relaxing dip in a thermal pool is very welcome at the end of a long day on the road. This is an ideal park for an overnight stay. $$$

❑ Tent sites, powered sites, drive-thru sites, ensuite sites, fits big motorhomes, cabins.

❑ Toilets and showers, laundry, sewer dump-point, telephone, kiosk/shop, ice, pool, pets.

❑ Credit cards. Discounts: weekly, FPA.

MORGANS BEACH (VIC) pp. 154, 218

Morgans Beach Caravan Park
1 Wasers Road, Strathmerton 3641
Ph (03) 5868 2259, fax (03) 5868 2259

The park is 17 km north-west of town along an unsealed road. It is popular with water-sports enthusiasts and home to many annual vans. The park is close to the river and has good facilities including a licensed store, tennis court, pool and boat storage area. This is a park in a quiet out-of-the-way area but will be busy during the peak holiday periods. $$

❑ Tent sites, powered sites, on-site vans.

❑ Toilets and showers, laundry, telephone, kiosk/shop, LP gas refills, ice, pool, playground, pets.

❑ Credit cards.

MORUYA (NSW) p. 12

River Breeze Tourist Park
Princes Highway, Moruya 2537
Ph (02) 4474 2370, fax (02) 4474 4651
Email info@riverbreeze.com.au
Website www.riverbreeze.com.au

This park overlooks the Moruya River on the north bank adjoining the highway. It is a well-maintained park, popular with travellers and close to some good fishing spots. River, estuary, rock, beach and ocean fishing spots are all nearby. There are very good amenities and it is just a short walk to the centre of town. $$$

❑ Tent sites, powered sites, drive-thru sites, fits big motorhomes, cabins.

❑ Toilets and showers (disabled access), laundry, telephone, kiosk/shop, LP gas refills, ice, camp kitchen, pool, no pets.

❑ Credit cards. Discounts: weekly, Top Tourist.

MOUNT GAMBIER (SA) p. 132

Blue Lake Holiday Park
Bay Road, Mount Gambier 5290
Ph (08) 8725 9856 or 1800 676 028,
fax (08) 8725 1711
Email bookings@bluelakeholidaypark.com.au
Website www.bluelakeholidaypark.com.au

Located south of the city centre, this well-shaded quality park adjoins the golf course and is adjacent to Mount Gambier's premier attraction, the spectacular Blue Lake. This is a fabulous base for exploring the region. $$$

❑ Tent sites, powered sites, drive-thru sites, ensuite sites, fits big motorhomes, cabins.

❑ Toilets and showers (disabled access), laundry, sewer dump-point, telephone, kiosk/shop, LP gas refills, ice, camp kitchen, pool, playground, no pets.

❑ Credit cards. Discounts: weekly, Big4.

Kalganyi Holiday Park
Corner Penola and Bishop roads,
Mount Gambier 5290
Ph (08) 8723 0220 or 1800 651 746,
fax (08) 8723 0218
Email big4@kalganyi.com.au
Website www.kalganyi.com.au

This is a very good park set in a quiet, treed area on the northern outskirts of Mount Gambier. It has extensive facilities and most of the powered sites are also ensuite sites. This is a good base from which to explore the fabulous Mount Gambier region. $$$

❑ Tent sites, powered sites, drive-thru sites, ensuite sites, fits big motorhomes, cabins, on-site vans.

❑ Toilets and showers (disabled access), laundry, sewer dump-point, telephone, kiosk/shop, ice, camp kitchen, playground, no pets.

❑ Credit cards. Discounts: weekly, Big4.

MOUNT GARNET (QLD) p. 64

Mount Garnet Caravan Park
Kennedy Highway, Mount Garnet 4872
Ph (07) 4097 9249, fax (07) 4097 9018

This is a small, neat and tidy park with basic facilities 500 m from the town centre. The park is attached to a BP roadhouse that serves meals. $$

❑ Tent sites, powered sites, drive-thru sites, fits big motorhomes, motel rooms.

❑ Toilets and showers, laundry, telephone, kiosk/shop, LP gas refills, ice, pets.

❑ Credit cards. Discounts: weekly.

MOUNT ISA (QLD) p. 261

⚙ **Sunset Caravan Park**
14 Sunset Drive, Mount Isa 4825
Ph (07) 4743 7668 or 1800 786 738,
fax (07) 4743 7668
Email sunpark@austarnet.com.au

Relax by the pool or enjoy a meal in the pleasant barbecue area at this popular owner-operated park, situated 1.6 km from the centre of town and away from highway traffic. We feel that this is the best caravan park in Mount Isa and it may be necessary to book during the peak winter months. $$$

❑ Tent sites, powered sites, drive-thru sites, fits big motorhomes, cabins.

❑ Toilets and showers (disabled access), laundry, sewer dump-point, telephone, kiosk/shop, LP gas refills, ice, camp kitchen, pool, pets.

❑ Credit cards. Discounts: Top Tourist.

MOUNT MAGNET (WA) p. 200

Mount Magnet Shire Caravan Park
Hepburn Street, Mount Magnet 6638
Ph (08) 9963 4198, fax (08) 9963 4961

We sometimes stay here and this is a good quality council caravan park with all basic facilities. There are shady trees, a patch of lawn for tents and basic but clean amenities. It is a good day's drive north of Perth and a popular overnight stop. $$

❑ Tent sites, powered sites, drive-thru sites, fits big motorhomes, cabins, on-site vans.

❑ Toilets and showers (disabled access), laundry, telephone, LP gas refills, pets.

❑ No credit cards. Discounts: pensioners, weekly.

MOUNT MORGAN
(QLD) pp. 48, 162, 259

Silver Wattle Tourist Park
Burnett Highway, Mount Morgan 4714
Ph (07) 4938 1550, fax (07) 4938 1550
Email silvwatl@ozemail.com.au

This tidy, owner-operated park has good facilities at a budget price. The park is on the western edge of town and has a pool and a small shop. Mount Morgan is steeped in history and this park is a good base for exploring the area. $$

❑ Tent sites, powered sites, drive-thru sites, fits big motorhomes, cabins.

❑ Toilets and showers, laundry, sewer dump-point, telephone, kiosk/shop, LP gas refills, ice, camp kitchen, pool, pets.

❑ Credit cards. Discounts: weekly

MOUNT SURPRISE (QLD) p. 67

**Mount Surprise Tourist Park
and Motel**
23 Garland Street, Mount Surprise 4871
Ph (07) 4062 3153, fax (07) 4062 3162

The park is located in the centre of town and has grassed sites, large shady trees and a cafe/restaurant. It has basic amenities and offers patrons a fuel discount at the adjoining BP service station. $$

❑ Tent sites, powered sites, drive-thru sites, fits big motorhomes, cabins, on-site vans.

❑ Toilets and showers (disabled access), laundry, telephone, kiosk/shop, ice, pool, pets.

❑ Credit cards. Discounts: pensioners, seniors, weekly.

MULWALA (NSW) p. 218

See also Yarrawonga.

Lake Mulwala Holiday Park
Melbourne Street, Mulwala 2647
Ph (03) 5744 1050, fax (03) 5743 1876
Email holidaypark@mulwalawaterski.com.au
Website www.mulwalawaterski.com.au

Superbly located on the banks of Lake Mulwala, adjoining the Mulwala Water Ski Club, this is a popular park with a limited number of tourist sites. Minimum bookings apply during Christmas, January and Easter holiday periods. $$

❑ Tent sites, powered sites, fits big motorhomes, cabins.

❑ Toilets and showers, laundry, sewer dump-point, telephone, kiosk/shop, LP gas refills, ice, camp kitchen, playground, boat ramp, no pets.

❑ Credit cards, holiday loading. Discounts: pensioners, seniors, weekly, FPA.

MUMBIL (NSW)

See Lake Burrendong.

MUNJINA (WA)

See Auski Roadhouse.

MURRAY BRIDGE (SA) p. 132

Long Island Caravan Park
100 Roper Road, Murray Bridge 5253
Ph (08) 8532 6900, fax (08) 8532 6261

This is a newer park in a great location, away from busy roads and adjoining the marina on the shores of the Murray River. The spacious park has good amenities and is about 3 km from the town centre. The owners will not take dogs. $$

❑ Tent sites, powered sites, drive-thru sites, ensuite sites, fits big motorhomes, cabins, on-site vans.

❑ Toilets and showers (disabled access), laundry, sewer dump-point, telephone, kiosk/shop, LP gas refills, ice, boat ramp, pets.

❑ Credit cards. Discounts: weekly, FPA.

MURRAY FALLS (QLD) p. 56

Murray Falls Camping Area
Murray Falls State Forest Park, Cardwell 4849
Ph (07) 4066 8779, fax (07) 4066 2041

The camping area is in a lovely, forested area, just a short distance from the cascading falls. To reach the park, turn off the Bruce Highway 22 km north of Cardwell and travel 18 km along a good road. The amenities only have cold showers. $

❑ Tent sites, fits big motorhomes.

❑ Toilets and showers, no pets.

❑ Credit cards.

MYRTLE BANK (TAS) p. 302

Myrtle Park
Tasman Highway, Myrtle Bank 7259
Ph (03) 6399 3368

The park is midway between Launceston and Scottsdale alongside the Tasman Highway. It is a wide, spacious, unpowered park with limited but good facilities at a nominal price. Good value for the budget-minded traveller. $

❑ Tent sites, drive-thru sites, fits big motorhomes.

❑ Toilets (disabled access), kiosk/shop, playground, pets.

❑ No credit cards.

NABIAC (NSW) p. 28

Nabiac Caravan Park
Pacific Highway, Nabiac 2312
Ph (02) 6554 1213, fax (02) 6554 1213

A small, neat caravan park alongside the Pacific Highway, attached to a roadhouse. The roadhouse serves coffee and light meals while the park has basic amenities and is conveniently located for an overnight stop. $$

❏ Tent sites, powered sites, drive-thru sites, fits big motorhomes, cabins.

❏ Toilets and showers (disabled access), laundry, kiosk/shop, LP gas refills, ice, pool, pets.

❏ Credit cards. Discounts: weekly.

NAMBUCCA HEADS (NSW) p. 30

White Albatross Holiday Centre
Wellington Drive, Nambucca Heads 2448
Ph (02) 6568 6468, fax (02) 6569 4698
Email manager@white-albatross.com.au
Website www.white-albatross.com.au

This is a quality park in a prime position next to a lagoon. It boasts a very good restaurant as well as a range of other features. $$$

❏ Tent sites, powered sites, drive-thru sites, ensuite sites, fits big motorhomes, cabins, on-site vans.

❏ Toilets and showers (disabled access), laundry, sewer dump-point, telephone, kiosk/shop, LP gas refills, ice, camp kitchen, playground, pets.

❏ Credit cards, holiday loading. Discounts: weekly.

NAROOMA (NSW) p. 12

⊛ **Island View Beach Resort**
Princes Highway, Narooma 2546
Ph (02) 4476 2600 or 1800 465 432, fax (02) 4476 3466
Email bookings@islandview.com.au
Website www.islandview.com.au

Stroll to the beach or picnic on green lawns under shady trees at this quality park, located on the Princes Highway 5 km south of Narooma. With very good amenities and lots of appeal, it is ideal for a family holiday and conveniently located for an overnight stay. $$$

❏ Tent sites, powered sites, drive-thru sites, fits big motorhomes, cabins.

❏ Toilets and showers (disabled access), laundry, telephone, kiosk/shop, LP gas refills, ice, camp kitchen, pool, playground, no pets.

❏ Credit cards, holiday loading. Discounts: 3rd night, weekly.

NARRABRI (NSW) p. 158

Ninghdoo View Bush Camping and Caravan Park
Off Mount Kaputar Road, Narrabri 2390
Ph (02) 6793 5272

This is a small, private park with a difference, located 28 km from Narrabri off the Mount Kaputar Road. Located right in the foothills of the Mount Kaputar National Park, it has terrific mountain views and is a good base from which to explore the national park.

It has good basic facilities and a limited number of powered sites. $$

❏ Tent sites, powered sites, drive-thru sites, fits big motorhomes, on-site vans.

❏ Toilets and showers, laundry, ice, pets.

❏ No credit cards. Discounts: weekly.

NARRANDERA (NSW) p. 156

Lake Talbot Tourist Park
Gordon Street, Narrandera 2700
Ph (02) 6959 1302 or 1800 106 601, fax (02) 6959 1949
Email ltcp@webfront.net.au
Website www.webfront.net.au/~ltcp

This is a large lakeside park in a quiet location away from the highway, adjoining the town's popular swimming pool complex. The park has good amenities, a range of accommodation and nicely maintained lawns and trees. $$$

❏ Tent sites, powered sites, drive-thru sites, fits big motorhomes, cabins.

❏ Toilets and showers (disabled access), laundry, telephone, kiosk/shop, LP gas refills, ice, camp kitchen, pool, playground, boat ramp, pets.

❏ Credit cards, holiday loading. Discounts: weekly, Top Tourist.

NARRAWONG (VIC) p. 134

⊛ **Narrawong Holiday Park**
Caravan Park Road, Narrawong 3285
Ph (03) 5529 5282, fax (03) 5529 5507
Email nhpark@ansonic.com.au

This pretty park is in a fabulous, quiet beachside and riverfront position off the main highway. Offering a range of accommodation, it is close to Portland and has good fishing and swimming, and a range of facilities including tennis courts. Campfires are permitted. Just a short walk to the centre of the small community, this park is in a great position and is reasonably priced. $$$

❏ Tent sites, powered sites, fits big motorhomes, cabins, on-site vans.

❏ Toilets and showers, laundry, telephone, kiosk/shop, LP gas refills, ice, camp kitchen, playground, boat ramp, no pets.

❏ Credit cards, holiday loading. Discounts: seniors, weekly.

NARROMINE (NSW) pp. 156, 242

⊛ **Rose Gardens Tourist Park**
69 Mitchell Highway, Narromine 2821
Ph (02) 6889 1623, fax (02) 6889 5102
Email rosegardensnarramine@mail.com
Website www.rosegardens.contact.com.au

Within the grounds of this quality owner-operated park you will find a historic church, built in 1872. Along with this unusual feature the park offers a range of accommodation, including an ensuite railway carriage, and bicycles for hire. It is set alongside the Mitchell Highway on the eastern approach to Narromine and, in our opinion, is a great park at a very competitive price. $$$

❏ Tent sites, powered sites, drive-thru sites, fits big motorhomes, cabins.

❏ Toilets and showers, laundry, sewer dump-point, telephone, LP gas refills, ice, camp kitchen, pool, playground, no pets.

❏ Credit cards. Discounts: weekly.

NELLIGEN (NSW) pp. 14, 211

⊛ **Nelligen Park**
Kings Highway, Nelligen 2536
Ph (02) 4478 1076
Email relaxing@nelligenpark.com.au
Website www.nelligenpark.com.au

What makes this park so appealing is its lovely setting on a grassy bend of the Clyde River. The township of Nelligen, just 10 km from Batemans Bay, is a great place to stay for a few days or even just overnight. The park is only a short walk from the town centre and the local hotel, which is well known for its meals. The park has good facilities and great expanses of green grass, spacious enough for a game of cricket. $$$

❏ Tent sites, powered sites, drive-thru sites, fits big motorhomes, cabins.

❏ Toilets and showers (disabled access), laundry, telephone, kiosk/shop, LP gas refills, ice, playground, boat ramp, no pets.

❏ Credit cards, holiday loading. Discounts: seniors, weekly.

NELSON (VIC) p. 134

Kywong Caravan Park
North Nelson Road, Nelson 3292
Ph (08) 8738 4174, fax (08) 8738 4174

Located on the northern side of town, this large budget-priced park has modern amenities and good facilities. The park is about 1.5 km from the centre of the small township. $$

❏ Tent sites, powered sites, drive-thru sites, fits big motorhomes, cabins, on-site vans.

❏ Toilets and showers, laundry, telephone, playground, no pets.

❏ Credit cards. Discounts: weekly.

NELSON BAY (NSW) p. 28

Halifax Holiday Park
5 Beach Road, Nelson Bay 2315
Ph (02) 4981 1522 or 1800 600 201, fax (02) 4984 9099
Email halifax@beachsideholidays.com.au
Website www.beachsideholidays.com.au

Close to the centre of Nelson Bay, this well-maintained tourist park adjoins a busy public boat ramp on the eastern shores of Port Stephens. There are often people cleaning their catch near the boat ramp and numerous pelicans awaiting handouts. This park is a great place for a family holiday and will suit those keen on fishing. Pets are allowed outside holiday periods. $$$

❏ Tent sites, powered sites, drive-thru sites, fits big motorhomes, cabins.

❏ Toilets and showers (disabled access), laundry, sewer dump-point, telephone, kiosk/shop, LP gas refills, ice, camp kitchen, playground, boat ramp, pets.

❏ Credit cards, holiday loading. Discounts: seniors, 3rd night, weekly.

NEW NORFOLK (TAS) pp. 285, 295

New Norfolk Caravan Park
The Esplanade, New Norfolk 7140
Ph (03) 6261 1268, fax (03) 6261 5868

Across the road from the Derwent River, the park is in a picturesque location just 1.5 km from the centre of town. The owners will allow some small pets. $$

❏ Tent sites, powered sites, drive-thru sites, fits big motorhomes, cabins, on-site vans.

❏ Toilets and showers, laundry, sewer dump-point, telephone, kiosk/shop, camp kitchen, boat ramp, pets.

❏ No credit cards. Discounts: weekly.

NEWCASTLE (NSW) p. 26

See also Belmont.

Stockton Beach Tourist Park
Pitt Street, Stockton 2295
Ph (02) 4928 1393, fax (02) 4920 1301

This park is located on the beachfront, just north of the port of Newcastle. Stroll along the beach, join in with the fishing on the breakwater, or just watch the large ships come and go. The park has large grassed areas with very good amenities. $$

❏ Tent sites, powered sites, fits big motorhomes, cabins.

❏ Toilets and showers (disabled access), laundry, sewer dump-point, telephone, kiosk/shop, LP gas refills, camp kitchen, playground, no pets.

❏ Credit cards, holiday loading. Discounts: pensioners, weekly.

NEWMAN (WA) p. 202

Dearlove's Caravan Park
Cowra Drive, Newman 6753
Ph (08) 9175 2802, fax (08) 9177 8451
Email dearlovescp@benet.net.au

The caravan parks in Newman have a fluctuating population of semi-permanent residents who come and go with work contracts in the mining industry. In recent years the parks in town have slipped in quality as far as tourists are concerned. This park has good basic facilities and is a good base for tourists visiting the area. It is just a short walk to a nearby tavern that serves good meals. $$$

❏ Tent sites, powered sites, drive-thru sites, ensuite sites, fits big motorhomes, cabins.

❏ Toilets and showers (disabled access), laundry, sewer dump-point, telephone, LP gas refills, ice, camp kitchen, pool, playground, pets.

❏ Credit cards. Discount: pensioners, seniors, weekly.

NHILL (VIC) p. 233

Nhill Caravan Park
Western Highway, Nhill 3418
Ph (03) 5391 1683, fax (03) 5391 1669
Email nhillpark@telstra.com

This is a convenient park on the Western Highway, on the western outskirts of Nhill. The park has good basic amenities and is conveniently located for overnight stops midway between Melbourne and Adelaide. **$$$**

❏ Tent sites, powered sites, drive-thru sites, ensuite sites, fits big motorhomes, cabins, on-site vans.

❏ Toilets and showers, laundry, telephone, kiosk/shop, camp kitchen, pool, playground, pets.

❏ Credit cards. Discounts: weekly

NITMILUK NATIONAL PARK
(WA) p. 75

Edith Falls Camp Ground
Nitmiluk National Park, Edith Falls, via Katherine 0850
Ph (08) 8975 4869, fax (08) 8975 4869
Email edithfalls@bigpond.com

This is a good camping area within Nitmiluk National Park, jointly managed by the traditional owners. It is reached along a 19-km sealed road. Turn off the Stuart Highway 42 km north of Katherine. The base of the falls is a short walk from the camping ground. **$$**

❏ Tent sites.

❏ Toilets and showers (disabled access), laundry, telephone, kiosk/shop, ice, no pets.

❏ Credit cards. Discounts: weekly.

Nitmiluk Gorge Caravan Park
Gorge Road, Nitmiluk Gorge National Park, via Katherine 0850
Ph (08) 8972 1253, fax (08) 8971 0715
Email info@travelnorth.com.au

This is a Northern Territory National Parks camping area, adjoining the visitor centre in the Nitmiluk (Katherine Gorge) National Park. The park has lovely, shady grassed sites and is within walking distance of the remarkable gorge. **$$$**

❏ Tent sites, powered sites, fits big motorhomes.

❏ Toilets and showers (disabled access), laundry, telephone, kiosk/shop, LP gas refills, ice, camp kitchen, playground, no pets.

❏ Credit cards.

NORAH HEAD (NSW) p. 26

Norah Head Tourist Park
Victoria Street, Norah Head 2263
Ph (02) 4396 3935, fax (02) 4397 1285
Website www.wyongtouristparks.com.au

This large, council-operated beachside park is a popular holiday destination. It has good facilities and is ideal for a family holiday. **$$**

❏ Tent sites, powered sites, drive-thru sites, fits big motorhomes, cabins.

❏ Toilets and showers (disabled access), laundry, sewer dump-point, telephone, kiosk/shop, LP gas refills, ice, playground, pets.

❏ Credit cards, holiday loading. Discounts: weekly.

NORMANTON (QLD) p. 178

Normanton Caravan Park
Brown Street, Normanton 4890
Ph (07) 4745 1121, fax (07) 4745 1319

Located in the centre of town, the park has good amenities, some large, shady trees and the town's swimming pool within its bounds. The park is within walking distance of the main businesses in town. **$$$**

❏ Tent sites, powered sites, fits big motorhomes, cabins.

❏ Toilets and showers, laundry, telephone, ice, camp kitchen, pool, pets.

❏ Credit cards. Discounts: weekly.

NORSEMAN (WA) pp. 117, 271

Gateway Caravan Park
1175 Prinsep Street, Norseman 6443
Ph (08) 9039 1500, fax (08) 9039 1500

A very conveniently situated park at the western end of the Nullarbor Plain. It is close to the highway junction and about 1 km from the centre of town. The park has good amenities and most basic facilities. It is a good place for an overnight stay or as a base to spend a couple of days in the area. **$$$**

❏ Tent sites, powered sites, drive-thru sites, fits big motorhomes, cabins, on-site vans.

❏ Toilets and showers (disabled access), laundry, sewer dump-point, LP gas refills, camp kitchen, playground, pets.

❏ Credit cards. Discounts: weekly.

NORTHAM (WA) p. 272

Northam Caravan Park
150 Yilgarn Ave, Northam 6401
Ph (08) 9622 1620, fax (08) 9622 5898
Email northam_caravan@wn.com.au

On the highway 3 km east of the town centre, this park is a good overnight stop. It has good amenities and basic facilities. No cats are allowed. **$$**

❏ Tent sites, powered sites, drive-thru sites, ensuite sites, fits big motorhomes, cabins, on-site vans.

❏ Toilets and showers, laundry, telephone, kiosk/shop, ice, pets.

❏ Credit cards. Discounts: pensioners, seniors, weekly.

NOWRA (NSW) p. 14

Shoalhaven Caravan Village
Terara Road, Nowra 2541
Ph (02) 4423 0770, fax (02) 4423 2720

This is a large, owner-operated riverfront park just 1 km east of Nowra. It has a high number of permanent residents but retains several tourist sites. There are good amenities and facilities include a tennis court, boat ramp and swimming pool. **$$**

❏ Tent sites, powered sites, drive-thru sites, fits big motorhomes, cabins, on-site vans.

❏ Toilets and showers, laundry, sewer dump-point, telephone, LP gas refills, pool, playground, boat ramp, pets.

❏ No credit cards, holiday loading. Discounts: weekly.

NUBEENA (TAS)

See White Beach.

NURIOOTPA (SA) pp. 224, 246

Barossa Valley SA Tourist Park
Penrice Road, Nuriootpa 5355
Ph (08) 8562 1404 or 1800 251 634, fax (08) 8562 2615
Email barpark@bigpond.com
Website www.barossa-tourist-park.com.au

This good quality Barossa Valley caravan park has a large number of sites, a choice of accommodation and a range of facilities including tennis courts. It is within walking distance of the town centre and close to several prominent wineries. **$$$**

❏ Tent sites, powered sites, drive-thru sites, fits big motorhomes, cabins.

❏ Toilets and showers (disabled access), laundry, sewer dump-point, telephone, kiosk/shop, LP gas refills, ice, camp kitchen, playground, pets.

❏ Bookings required, credit cards. Discounts: pensioners, weekly, Top Tourist.

NYNGAN (NSW) p. 242

◎ **Riverside Caravan Park**
Barrier Highway, Nyngan 2825
Ph (02) 6832 1729, fax (02) 6832 1767

We really like it when a lot of effort has gone into a park and this is the case with Riverside. The park is set in a quiet riverfront location on the western side of Nyngan and strategically located near the junction of the Mitchell and Barrier highways. It has most of the normal park facilities and, while it has highway frontage, it is set well back in large spacious grounds. **$$**

❏ Tent sites, powered sites, drive-thru sites, ensuite sites, fits big motorhomes, cabins, on-site vans.

❏ Toilets and showers (disabled access), laundry, telephone, kiosk/shop, LP gas refills, ice, playground, boat ramp, pets.

❏ Credit cards. Discounts: weekly.

OCEAN GROVE (VIC) p. 141

Riverview Family Caravan Park
Barwon Heads Road, Ocean Grove 3226
Ph (03) 5256 1600, fax (03) 5256 2162
Email bookings@barwoncoast.com.au
Website www.barwoncoast.com.au

This is a large holiday park with a long frontage to the Barwon River. The park is popular with families during summer holidays and minimum bookings apply over Christmas and Easter holiday periods. **$$$**

❏ Tent sites, powered sites, drive-thru sites, fits big motorhomes, cabins.

❏ Toilets and showers, laundry, telephone, kiosk/shop, playground, boat ramp, no pets.

❏ Credit cards, holiday loading. Discounts: weekly.

OLD ADAMINABY (NSW) p. 216

See also Anglers Reach.

Rainbow Pines Tourist Caravan Park
Lucas Street, Old Adaminaby 2630
Ph (02) 6454 2317, fax (02) 6454 2677
Email info@rainbowpines.com.au
Website www.rainbowpines.com.au

This is a popular holiday park where trout fishing, sailing and canoeing are all available. It is on the shores of Lake Eucumbene, about 7 km from the Snowy Mountains Highway. This is a good quality park and minimum bookings apply during the Christmas, January and Easter holiday periods. It is only possible to fit big motorhomes in low season. **$$$**

❏ Tent sites, powered sites, drive-thru sites, ensuite sites, cabins, on-site vans.

❏ Toilets and showers, laundry, telephone, kiosk/shop, LP gas refills, ice, boat ramp, pets.

❏ Credit cards, holiday loading. Discounts: weekly, Top Tourist.

OLD BAR (NSW) p. 28

Old Bar Beachfront Holiday Park
Old Bar Road, Old Bar 2430
Ph (02) 6553 7274, fax (02) 6553 6913
Email richoe@tpg.com.au
Website www.beachfrontholiday.com.au

Close to the popular Old Bar beach and suitable for an overnight stay or a family holiday, this is a neatly maintained, peaceful family park with wonderful grassy sites. New additions include a fully equipped camp kitchen with TV room adjoining. **$$**

❏ Tent sites, powered sites, drive-thru sites, fits big motorhomes, cabins.

❏ Toilets and showers (disabled access), laundry, sewer dump-point, telephone, kiosk/shop, LP gas refills, ice, camp kitchen, pool, playground, no pets.

❏ Credit cards, holiday loading. Discounts: pensioners, seniors, weekly.

ONSLOW (WA) p. 96

Ocean View Caravan Park
Second Avenue, Onslow 6710
Ph (08) 9184 6053, fax (08) 9184 6274
Email oceanview@kisser.net.au

Situated on the beachfront, this park is ideal for fishing enthusiasts. It is also a good place for a rest, with clean basic facilities. In the busy season the park holds sausage sizzles and morning teas once a week. **$$$**

❏ Tent sites, powered sites, drive-thru sites, fits big motorhomes, cabins, on-site vans.

❏ Toilets and showers (disabled access), laundry, telephone, LP gas refills, ice, boat ramp, no pets.

❏ Credit cards. Discounts: weekly.

ORANGE (NSW) p. 238

Colour City Caravan Park
203 Margaret Street, Orange 2800
Ph (02) 6362 7254

This is a council park with good basic facilities in a quiet, off-highway position, about 2 km north of the city centre, adjoining the showgrounds. It is a basic park at a budget price. **$$**

❑ Tent sites, powered sites, drive-thru sites, fits big motorhomes, cabins.

❑ Toilets and showers (disabled access), laundry, telephone, no pets.

❑ Credit cards.

ORBOST (VIC) p. 7

Snowy River Orbost Camp Park
2–6 Lochiel Street, Orbost 3888
Ph (03) 5154 1097, fax (03) 5154 1032

The centre of town is only a short 500 m walk from this park. The park is off the main highway and has large shady trees and good basic facilities. It is conveniently located for an overnight stop or as a base from which to explore the local area. **$$$**

❑ Tent sites, powered sites, drive-thru sites, fits big motorhomes, on-site vans.

❑ Toilets and showers (disabled access), laundry, telephone, LP gas refills, playground, pets.

❑ No credit cards, holiday loading. Discounts: pensioners, seniors, weekly.

ORMEAU (QLD) p. 36

See also Gold Coast.

Ormeau Motel and Cabin Park
Corner Goldmine Road and Pacific Highway, Ormeau 4208
Ph (07) 5546 6285 or 1800 807 311, fax (07) 5546 6031
Email ormpark@winshop.com.au

The park is located alongside the Pacific Motorway a few kilometres north of the Gold Coast. It has basic facilities at a budget price, and it is one of the few parks in the region where pets are welcome. **$$**

❑ Tent sites, powered sites, fits big motorhomes, cabins.

❑ Toilets and showers, laundry, telephone, LP gas refills, ice, pool, playground, pets.

❑ Credit cards, holiday loading. Discounts: weekly.

PACIFIC PALMS (NSW) p. 28

Sandbar and Bushland Caravan Park
The Lakes Way, Pacific Palms 2428
Ph (02) 6554 4095, fax (02) 6554 4253
Email sandbar@paspaley.com.au

Some 20 km south of Forster, this park is tucked away in a secluded bush location on the shores of the tranquil Smiths Lake, just a short walk from Sandbar Beach. Located in over 240 ha of bushland, the park even boasts its own nine-hole golf course. **$$**

❑ Tent sites, powered sites, drive-thru sites, fits big motorhomes, cabins.

❑ Toilets and showers, laundry, telephone, kiosk/shop, LP gas refills, ice, playground, no pets.

❑ Credit cards, holiday loading. Discounts: pensioners, seniors, weekly.

PAKENHAM (VIC) p. 4

Pakenham Caravan Park
Corner Princes Highway and Racecourse Road, Pakenham 3810
Ph (03) 5941 2004

This is a small park adjoining the Princes Highway, on the eastern outskirts of the greater Melbourne metropolitan area. The park has good, basic facilities and is ideal for an overnight stay. Close to the Pakenham Racecourse. **$$$**

❑ Tent sites, powered sites, drive-thru sites, cabins, on-site vans.

❑ Toilets and showers (disabled access), laundry, telephone, playground, pets.

❑ No credit cards. Discounts: weekly.

PALM BEACH (QLD)

See Gold Coast.

PALMERS ISLAND (NSW) p. 32

Clarence River Resort
O'Keefe's Lane, Palmers Island 2463
Ph (02) 6646 0255 or 1800 460 468, fax (02) 6646 0466
Email resort@hotkey.net.au
Website www.clarencecoast.info

This neat, spacious, riverfront park 10 km from Yamba has very good facilities. The park is quiet and out of the way. It is situated on a large, sweeping bend of the Clarence River and has great appeal to those who enjoy estuary fishing or want a quiet break. **$$**

❑ Tent sites, powered sites, ensuite sites, drive-thru sites, fits big motorhomes, cabins.

❑ Toilets and showers (disabled access), laundry, telephone, kiosk/shop, LP gas refills, ice, camp kitchen, pool, playground, boat ramp, internet terminal, no pets.

❑ Credit cards, holiday loading. Discounts: weekly.

PAMBULA BEACH (NSW) p. 10

⊕ **Holiday Hub Beach Resort**
Pambula Beach Road, Pambula Beach 2549
Ph (02) 6495 6363 or 1800 677 808, fax (02) 6495 8701
Email info@holidayhub.com.au
Website www.holidayhub.com.au

This beachside park is one of our favourite parks in the popular family holiday region of the south coast of New South Wales. It has a new pool complex, a licensed restaurant and spotless amenities, and is a great family park. The resident kangaroos will be a hit with the children. A beach and a national park form the park's boundaries. **$$$$**

❑ Tent sites, powered sites, drive-thru sites, ensuite sites, fits big motorhomes, cabins.

❑ Toilets and showers (disabled access), laundry, sewer dump-point, telephone, kiosk/shop, LP gas refills, ice, camp kitchen, playground, internet terminal, no pets.

❑ Credit cards, holiday loading. Discounts: weekly, Big4.

PANDURRA (WA) p. 123

Nuttbush Retreat Caravan Holiday Park
Pandurra Station, Eyre Highway, Port Augusta 5710
Ph (08) 8643 8941, fax (08) 8643 8906
Email nuttbush@ozemail.com.au
Website www.nuttbush.com.au

This park adjoins the huge Pandurra sheep and cattle station, 40 km west of Port Augusta on the Eyre Highway. The park has very good facilities, including a licensed dining room and bar, and offers patrons a free barbecue on Tuesdays and Thursdays during the tourist season. Some of the activities on offer include four-wheel drive tours of the station and horse trail-rides. This is a park with a difference. **$$$**

❑ Tent sites, powered sites, drive-thru sites, fits big motorhomes, cabins.

❑ Toilets and showers (disabled access), laundry, telephone, ice, camp kitchen, pool, pets.

❑ Credit cards. Discounts: pensioners.

PARKES (NSW) p. 156

Spicer Caravan Park
Albert Street, Parkes 2870
Ph (02) 6862 6162, fax (02) 6862 6162

This is a council-owned park with good basic facilities, about 2 km from the town centre. It is in a quiet spot, off the main highway, about 16 km from the Parkes satellite dish. **$$**

❑ Tent sites, powered sites, drive-thru sites, fits big motorhomes, cabins.

❑ Toilets and showers (disabled access), laundry, sewer dump-point, telephone, camp kitchen, playground, pets.

❑ Credit cards. Discounts: weekly.

PEACEFUL BAY (WA) p. 114

Peaceful Bay Caravan Park
Peaceful Bay Road, Peaceful Bay 6333
Ph (08) 9840 8060, fax (08) 9840 8282

Peaceful Bay, a popular holiday area, is 50 km west of Denmark. The park is budget priced and has good amenities and a well-stocked shop. New owners mean that there are other facilities in construction. **$$**

❑ Tent sites, powered sites, drive-thru sites, fits big motorhomes, on-site vans.

❑ Toilets and showers, laundry, telephone, kiosk/shop, LP gas refills, ice, camp kitchen, boat ramp, pets.

❑ Credit cards.

PEAK HILL (NSW) p. 156

Peak Hill Caravan Park
2 Ween Street, Peak Hill 2869
Ph (02) 6869 1422, fax (02) 6869 1422
Email phcaravan@bigpond.com

This owner-operated park offers a range of accommodation and is ideal for an overnight stay. The park is small, off the main highway and just a short walk from the town centre. **$$$**

❑ Tent sites, powered sites, drive-thru sites, fits big motorhomes, cabins, on-site vans.

❑ Toilets and showers, laundry, sewer dump-point, kiosk/shop, LP gas refills, ice, playground, TV cables, pets.

❑ Credit cards. Discounts: weekly.

PEARL BEACH (NSW)

See Umina.

PEMBERTON (WA) pp. 113–14

Pemberton Caravan Park
1 Pump Hill Road, Pemberton 6260
Ph (08) 9776 1300, fax (08) 9776 1800
Email park@karriweb.com.au

This is a spacious park with lots of shade and trees, just 1 km from the town centre. The park is budget priced with basic amenities, and a natural-style pool right next door. **$$**

❑ Tent sites, powered sites, fits big motorhomes, cabins.

❑ Toilets and showers (disabled access), laundry, telephone, kiosk/shop, ice, pool, playground, no pets.

❑ Credit cards, holiday loading. Discounts: weekly.

PENGUIN (TAS) p. 288

Penguin Beachside Tourist Park
Johnsons Beach Road, Penguin 7316
Ph (03) 6437 2785, fax (03) 6437 1897

This is a good quality beachfront caravan park. It features an adjoining fully licensed restaurant and coffee shop. **$$**

❑ Tent sites, powered sites, drive-thru sites, fits big motorhomes, cabins.

❑ Toilets and showers (disabled access), laundry, sewer dump-point, LP gas refills, camp kitchen, playground, pets.

❑ Credit cards. Discounts: weekly

PENTLAND (QLD) p. 264

Pentland Caravan Park
Flinders Highway, Pentland 4816
Ph (07) 4788 1148, fax (07) 4788 1225

This tidy park in the small township of Pentland has a well-stocked shop and a small cafe. The park is great for an overnight stop. **$$**

❑ Tent sites, powered sites, drive-thru sites, fits big motorhomes, cabins, on-site vans.

❑ Toilets and showers, laundry, sewer dump-point, telephone, kiosk/shop, LP gas refills, ice, camp kitchen, pool, playground, pets.

❑ Credit cards. Discounts: weekly.

PEPPERMINT GROVE (WA)

See Bremer Bay.

PEPPERMINT GROVE BEACH (WA)

See Capel.

PERTH (WA) p. 107

Fremantle Village
Lot 1 Cockburn Road, South Fremantle 6162
Ph (08) 9430 4866 or 1800 999 938,
fax (08) 9430 8053
Email admin@fremantlevillage.com.au
Website www.fremantlevillage.com.au

Just 3 km from the centre of Fremantle, this park has a mixture of residential park homes and tourist sites, all with ensuite amenities. It makes a good base from which to explore Fremantle and Perth. $$$

❏ Tent sites, powered sites, ensuite sites, fits big motorhomes, cabins, on-site vans.

❏ Toilets and showers, laundry, sewer dump-point, telephone, LP gas refills, ice, camp kitchen, playground, no pets.

❏ Credit cards. Discounts: seniors, weekly.

Karrinyup Waters Resort
467 North Beach Road, Gwelup 6018
Ph (08) 9447 6665 or 1800 633 665,
fax (08) 9246 1466
Email kwresort@iinet.net.au
Website www.kwr.net.au

Just 14 km north of Perth and close to the Mitchell Freeway, this park is just a short distance from the beach. With very good amenities and facilities that include a heated pool, spa and barbecue area, this is a good base on the north side of Perth. $$$

❏ Tent sites, powered sites, drive-thru sites, fits big motorhomes, cabins, on-site vans.

❏ Toilets and showers (disabled access), laundry, sewer dump-point, telephone, kiosk/shop, LP gas refills, pool, playground, no pets.

❏ Credit cards. Discounts: weekly, Top Tourist.

Perth Holiday Park
91 Benara Road, Caversham 6055
Ph (08) 9279 6700 or 1800 679 992,
fax (08) 9377 4599
Email perthholiday@fleetwood.com.au
Website www.fleetwoodparks.com.au

Situated in the grape-growing area of the Upper Swan River, about 14 km from the centre of Perth, this quality park has easy access to the main routes north and east. It has grassed and concrete sites, some with good shade. $$$

❏ Tent sites, powered sites, drive-thru sites, ensuite sites, fits big motorhomes, cabins.

❏ Toilets and showers (disabled access), laundry, sewer dump-point, telephone, kiosk/shop, LP gas refills, ice, camp kitchen, pool, playground, internet terminal, no pets.

❏ Credit cards. Discounts: weekly, Big4.

⊛ Perth International Tourist Park
186 Hale Road, Forrestfield 6058
Ph (08) 9453 6677 or 1800 626 677,
fax (08) 9359 1787
Email bookings@perthinternational.com.au

This is a magnificent park with excellent amenities in the eastern suburbs, 17 km from the centre of Perth. In the high season the park runs children's activities and walking tours. It also has a secure van-storage area. $$$$

❏ Tent sites, powered sites, drive-thru sites, fits big motorhomes, cabins.

❏ Toilets and showers (disabled access), laundry, sewer dump-point, telephone, kiosk/shop, LP gas refills, ice, camp kitchen, pool, playground, internet terminal, no pets.

❏ Credit cards. Discounts: weekly, Big4.

Rockingham Holiday Village
147 Dixon Road, Rockingham 6168
Ph (08) 9527 4240, fax (08) 9592 3189

Close to the South Coast Highway and just 4 km from the centre of Rockingham, this park has good basic amenities. It is set in a quiet area and is easily accessible from the southern approaches to Perth. $$$

❏ Tent sites, powered sites, fits big motorhomes, cabins, on-site vans.

❏ Toilets and showers (disabled access), laundry, telephone, kiosk/shop, LP gas refills, ice, playground, no pets.

❏ Credit cards. Discounts: weekly.

Woodman Point Holiday Park
132 Cockburn Road, Munster 6166
Ph (08) 9434 1433 or 1800 244 133,
fax (08) 9434 1746
Email woodmanpoint@fleetwood.com.au
Website www.fleetwoodparks.com.au

Large and popular, this tourist park has walking access to the beach and is just 7 km from Fremantle. The managers run nature walks around the local area year round. $$$

❏ Tent sites, powered sites, fits big motorhomes, cabins.

❏ Toilets and showers (disabled access), laundry, sewer dump-point, telephone, kiosk/shop, LP gas refills, ice, camp kitchen, pool, playground, internet terminal, no pets.

❏ Bookings required, credit cards, holiday loading. Discounts: weekly, Big4.

PETERBOROUGH (SA) p. 246

Peterborough Caravan Park
36 Grove Street, Peterborough 5422
Ph (08) 8651 2545, fax (08) 8651 2545

This is a tidy park located off the main road in a quiet part of town. The park adjoins the town's swimming pool and has an animal enclosure with kangaroos, emus and deer. The park has modern amenities and is conveniently located for overnight stops between Broken Hill and Adelaide or Port Augusta. We regularly stop here. $$

❏ Tent sites, powered sites, drive-thru sites, fits big motorhomes, cabins.

❏ Toilets and showers (disabled access), laundry, telephone, kiosk/shop, ice, pool, playground, pets.

❏ Credit cards. Discounts: weekly.

PETERBOROUGH (VIC) p. 138

Great Ocean Road Tourist Park
Great Ocean Road, Peterborough 3270
Ph (03) 5598 5477 or 1800 200 478,
fax (03) 5598 5477
Email stay@gortp.com.au
Website www.gortp.com.au

Situated just off the Great Ocean Road at the mouth of the Curdies River, this park is popular with those keen on fishing. It is just a short walk from the centre of town and the beach and has good facilities. $$$

❏ Tent sites, powered sites, drive-thru sites, fits big motorhomes, cabins.

❏ Toilets and showers (disabled access), laundry, telephone, LP gas refills, ice, playground, boat ramp, internet terminal, no pets.

❏ Credit cards, holiday loading. Discounts: weekly, Top Tourist.

POINT SAMSON (WA) p. 96

Solveig Caravan Park
Point Samson Road, Point Samson 6720
Ph (08) 9187 1414, fax (08) 9187 1907

This is a small, neat park with just 20 sites. The beach is across the road and the adjoining fish-and-chip shop is recommended. We liked it here. $$$

❏ Tent sites, powered sites.

❏ Toilets and showers, laundry, telephone, kiosk/shop, ice, no pets.

❏ Credit cards. Discounts: weekly.

PORT ARTHUR (TAS) p. 300

See also White Beach.

⊛ Port Arthur Caravan and Cabin Park
Garden Point, Port Arthur 7182
Ph (03) 6250 2340 or 1800 620 708,
fax (03) 6250 2509
Email paccp@tassie.net.au
Website www.portarthurcaravan-cabinpark.com.au

Explore the historic Port Arthur area from this popular, quality caravan park, only 1 km from the Port Arthur Historic Site and high above sheltered waters. It offers a good range of facilities and lots of shady trees. Bookings are recommended during busy holiday periods. $$$

❏ Tent sites, powered sites, drive-thru sites, ensuite sites, fits big motorhomes, cabins.

❏ Toilets and showers (disabled access), laundry, sewer dump-point, telephone, kiosk/shop, LP gas refills, ice, camp kitchen, playground, no pets.

❏ Credit cards. Discounts: weekly, Big4.

PORT AUGUSTA (SA) pp. 123, 183

See also Pandurra and Stirling North.

Port Augusta Big4 Holiday Park
Corner Stokes Terrace and Eyre Highway, Port Augusta 5700
Ph (08) 8642 2974 or 1800 833 444,
fax (08) 8642 6455
Email holiday@portaugustabig4.com.au
Website www.portaugustabig4.com.au

The Port Augusta Big4 Holiday Park has very good facilities and is easily accessible on the Eyre Highway. The town centre is at walking distance. It can get quite busy here, even in the low season. $$$

❏ Tent sites, powered sites, drive-thru sites, ensuite sites, fits big motorhomes, cabins, on-site vans.

❏ Toilets and showers, laundry, sewer dump-point, telephone, kiosk/shop, LP gas refills, ice, camp kitchen, pool, playground, internet terminal, no pets.

❏ Bookings required, credit cards. Discounts: weekly, Big4.

Shoreline Caravan Park
Gardiner Avenue, Port Augusta 5700
Ph (08) 8642 2965 or 1800 422 965,
fax (08) 8642 2965
Email shorelinecp@centralonline.com.au

This park has good facilities in a quiet off-the-highway location. It has sea frontage and views of the Flinders Ranges. $$$

❏ Tent sites, powered sites, drive-thru sites, fits big motorhomes, cabins, on-site vans.

❏ Toilets and showers (disabled access), laundry, sewer dump-point, telephone, kiosk/shop, LP gas refills, ice, camp kitchen, pool, playground, pets.

❏ Credit cards. Discounts: weekly, Top Tourist.

PORT CAMPBELL (VIC) p. 138

Port Campbell National Park Cabin and Camping Park
Morris Street, Port Campbell 3269
Ph (03) 5598 6492, fax (03) 5598 6493
Email campinport@datafast.net.au

This park is in a scenic location close to the centre of town and adjoining a beach. The park is privately managed but forms part of the national park. This is a fabulous location and will be busy during holiday periods. $$$

❏ Tent sites, powered sites, fits big motorhomes, cabins.

❏ Toilets and showers (disabled access), laundry, sewer dump-point, camp kitchen, no pets.

❏ Credit cards, holiday loading. Discounts: pensioners, seniors, weekly.

PORT DENISON (WA) p. 102

Dongara Denison Beach Holiday Park
250 Ocean Drive, Port Denison 6525
Ph (08) 9927 1131 or 1800 600 776,
fax (08) 9927 1902
Email skyoffice@bigpond.com

This smaller park is ideally located on an estuary beach and was totally refitted in 2001. It has very good amenities and big motorhomes can fit here, though not on the ensuite sites. The park is busy in holiday periods and bookings will be necessary. Enjoy the short stroll to the busy boat harbour. $$$

❏ Tent sites, powered sites, drive-thru sites, ensuite sites, fits big motorhomes, cabins, on-site vans.

❏ Toilets and showers (disabled access), laundry, sewer dump-point, telephone, kiosk/shop, LP gas refills, ice, camp kitchen, playground, boat ramp, TV cables, no pets.

❏ Credit cards, holiday loading. Discounts: pensioners, seniors, weekly, Big4.

Dongara Denison Tourist Park
8 George Street, Port Denison 6525
Ph (08) 9927 1210, fax (08) 9927 2001
Email touristpark@wn.com.au

Set on the beach at Port Denison, this is a spacious tourist park with a small number of great informal grassed sites on the sand dunes looking out to sea. The park has good amenities and basic facilities. Bookings will be required in peak holiday periods. $$

❏ Tent sites, powered sites, drive-thru sites, fits big motorhomes, on-site vans.

❏ Toilets and showers, laundry, telephone, kiosk/shop, LP gas refills, ice, camp kitchen, playground, pets.

❏ Credit cards. Discounts: weekly.

PORT DOUGLAS (QLD) p. 61

Pandanus Van Park
107 Davidson Street, Port Douglas 4871
Ph (07) 4099 5944, fax (07) 4099 4034
Email pandanus@austarnet.com.au

This park is just 2 km from the centre of Port Douglas, on the main road into town. The park is busy in holiday periods and a booking will be necessary. $$$

❏ Tent sites, powered sites, fits big motorhomes, cabins, on-site vans.

❏ Toilets and showers, laundry, telephone, kiosk/shop, LP gas refills, camp kitchen, pool, no pets.

❏ Credit cards.

PORT FAIRY (VIC) p. 135

Anchorage Holiday Park
115 Princes Highway, Port Fairy 3284
Ph (03) 5568 1145 or 1800 063 346,
fax (03) 5568 1145
Email anchorage@standard.net.au

This quality owner-operated park has large shade trees and informal grassy sites, and is conveniently located alongside the Princes Highway just 1.5 km from the town centre. The park has a range of facilities including mini-golf and a recreation room. $$$

❏ Tent sites, powered sites, cabins, on-site vans.

❏ Toilets and showers, laundry, telephone, kiosk/shop, LP gas refills, camp kitchen, pool, playground, no pets.

❏ Credit cards, holiday loading. Discounts: weekly, Big4.

Belfast Cove Caravan Park
139 Princes Highway, Port Fairy 3284
Ph (03) 5568 1816, fax (03) 5568 1816
Email belcove@standard.net.au

Conveniently located alongside the Princes Highway, just 1.8 km from the centre of town, the park offers a range of quality accommodation. Facilities include a boat parking area, a tennis court and covered barbecues. Minimum bookings apply during the Christmas and Easter holiday periods. $$$

❏ Tent sites, powered sites, drive-thru sites, fits big motorhomes, cabins.

❏ Toilets and showers, laundry, sewer dump-point, telephone, kiosk/shop, LP gas refills, playground, pets.

❏ Credit cards, holiday loading. Discounts: weekly, Top Tourist.

Port Fairy Gardens Caravan Park
111 Griffiths Street, Port Fairy 3284
Ph (03) 5568 1060, fax (03) 5568 2576
Email portfairygardens@telstra.com.au

A large council-owned park about 5 minutes' walk from the town centre and just 200 m from the beach. There are level grassed sites, modern amenities and a range of facilities including a tennis court. The park also

incorporates the seasonal Gardens Reserve Caravan Park. $$$

❏ Tent sites, powered sites, fits big motorhomes, cabins.

❏ Toilets and showers (disabled access), laundry, sewer dump-point, telephone, LP gas refills, ice, camp kitchen, playground, pets.

❏ Credit cards, holiday loading. Discounts: weekly.

PORT HEDLAND (WA) pp. 92, 204

See also South Hedland.

Cooke Point Holiday Park
Corner Athol and Taylor roads,
Port Hedland 6721
Ph (08) 9173 1271 or 1800 459 999,
fax (08) 9173 3671
Email cookepoint@fleetwood.com.au
Website www.fleetwoodparks.com.au

This park is located on the beach in an off highway position at the quiet end of Port Hedland. It is part of the Fleetwood Holiday Parks chain, a group we have generally found to be of high quality. This park overlooks the Pretty Pool Inlet, a popular town beach, and is a great base for tourists visiting the town. $$$

❏ Tent sites, powered sites, cabins.

❏ Toilets and showers (disabled access), laundry, sewer dump-point, telephone, kiosk/shop, LP gas refills, ice, camp kitchen, pool, playground, internet terminal, no pets.

❏ Credit cards, holiday loading. Discounts: Big4.

PORT MACDONNELL (SA) p. 134

Woolwash Caravan Park
Sea Parade, Port MacDonnell 5291
Ph (08) 8738 2095, fax (08) 8738 2094

A good value, budget-priced park situated on the beachfront, about 1.5 km from the centre of Port MacDonnell. The park has good quality basic facilities and is an ideal location to spend a few days and explore this historic region. $$

❏ Tent sites, powered sites, drive-thru sites, fits big motorhomes, on-site vans.

❏ Toilets and showers, laundry, telephone, kiosk/shop, LP gas refills, ice, camp kitchen, playground, boat ramp, pets.

❏ No credit cards. Discounts: weekly.

PORT MACQUARIE (NSW) p. 30

Sundowner Breakwall Tourist Park
1 Munster St, Port Macquarie 2444
Phone (02) 6583 2755, fax (02) 6584 0123
Email admin@sundowner.net.au
Website www.sundowner.net.au

Only a few minutes walk from the centre of Coffs Harbour, this is a large, quality park right on the waterfront. Recent additions include a pool and a playground, and free internet access is available at reception.

❏ Tent sites, powered sites, drive-thru sites, fits big motorhomes, cabins.

❏ Toilets and showers (disabled access), laundry, sewer dump-point, telephone, kiosk/shop, LP gas refills, ice, camp kitchen, pool, playground, internet terminal, no pets.

❏ Credit cards, holiday loading. Discounts: weekly, Big4.

PORT PIRIE (SA) p. 124

Port Pirie Beach Caravan Park
Beach Road, Port Pirie 5540
Ph (08) 8632 4275 or 1800 819 323,
fax (08) 8633 2446

This beachfront caravan park is just 1.5 km from the town centre. There are good quality basic amenities and a limited range of facilities. We feel this is the best park in the town. $$

❏ Tent sites, powered sites, drive-thru sites, fits big motorhomes, cabins.

❏ Toilets and showers (disabled access), laundry, sewer dump-point, telephone, no pets.

❏ Credit cards. Discounts: weekly, Big4.

PORT SMITH (WA) p. 93

Port Smith Caravan Park
Port Smith 6725
Ph (08) 9192 4983, fax (08) 9192 4983

This park is located 140 km south of Broome and 23 km from the Great Northern Highway in a secluded but popular fishing area. Port Smith also has a bird park with a large collection of birds from around the world. $$$

❏ Tent sites, powered sites, drive-thru sites, fits big motorhomes, cabins.

❏ Toilets and showers (disabled access), laundry, telephone, kiosk/shop, LP gas refills, ice, pets.

❏ Credit cards.

PORT SORELL (TAS) p. 278

ⓦ **Port Sorell Lions Caravan Park**
Meredith Street, Port Sorell 7307
Ph (03) 6428 7267, fax (03) 6428 7269
Email ptsrlcaravanpark@bigpond.com

This popular beachfront park is owned and operated by the Lions Club. It is close to the centre of town, adjacent to the boat ramp and ideal for family holidays. It is an easy drive to the Devonport ferry terminal from here. Bookings are required in holiday periods. $$

❏ Tent sites, powered sites, drive-thru sites, fits big motorhomes, cabins, on-site vans.

❏ Toilets and showers (disabled access), laundry, sewer dump-point, telephone, kiosk/shop, LP gas refills, ice, camp kitchen, playground, boat ramp, TV cables, no pets.

❏ Credit cards. Discounts: weekly.

PORTARLINGTON (VIC) p. 141

Portarlington Seaside Resort
Sproat Street, Portarlington 3223
Ph (03) 5259 2764, fax (03) 5259 2272
Email info@portarlingtonresort.com.au

This beachfront park is enormous with more than 1200 powered sites, one of the country's larger parks. It is a very popular summer-holiday park on a safe, bayside beach, with loads of appeal to the family. The park has extensive facilities including

two kiosks (in season) and is just 1.25 km from the centre of town. $$$

❏ Tent sites, powered sites, drive-thru sites, ensuite sites, fits big motorhomes, cabins.

❏ Toilets and showers (disabled access), laundry, telephone, kiosk/shop, ice, playground, boat ramp, no pets.

❏ Credit cards, holiday loading. Discounts: Big4.

PORTLAND (VIC) p. 134

Centenary Caravan Park
184 Betinck Street, Portland 3305
Ph (03) 5523 1487, fax (03) 5523 1487

Well protected from the elements, this budget-priced park is located on the northern approaches just 1 km from the centre of town. The park has a range of accommodation and many features, including a nearby shop. $$

❏ Tent sites, powered sites, drive-thru sites, fits big motorhomes, cabins.

❏ Toilets and showers (disabled access), laundry, sewer dump-point, telephone, kiosk/shop, ice, playground, no pets.

❏ Credit cards. Discounts: pensioners, seniors.

Henty Bay Beachfront Van and Cabin Park
Dutton Way, Portland 3305
Ph (03) 5523 3716, fax (03) 5523 3186
Email hentybay@hotkey.net.au

This large, spacious park is located on the beachfront 6 km north-east of the centre of town. The park boasts a licensed dining room and a well-stocked shop with takeaway food and a good selection of fishing tackle and bait. $$$

❏ Tent sites, powered sites, drive-thru sites, fits big motorhomes, cabins, on-site vans.

❏ Toilets and showers, laundry, telephone, kiosk/shop, LP gas refills, ice, camp kitchen, playground, boat ramp, pets.

❏ Credit cards, holiday loading. Discounts: FPA.

Portland Haven Village Caravan Park
74A–76A Garden Street, Portland 3305
Ph (03) 5523 5673, fax (03) 5523 6633

A budget-priced park set in a residential area of town, about 1.6 km from the town centre. This owner-operated park has good facilities and a corner store is conveniently located opposite the park. $$

❏ Tent sites, powered sites, drive-thru sites, ensuite sites, fits big motorhomes, cabins.

❏ Toilets and showers, laundry, telephone, no pets.

❏ Credit cards, holiday loading.

POSSUM PARK (QLD)

See Miles.

POTTSVILLE (NSW) p. 34

Pottsville Beach Holiday Park South
Coast Road, Pottsville Beach 2489
Ph (02) 6676 1050, fax (02) 6676 3015

This riverfront park is a popular holiday destination with good basic facilities. The sites are shallow and big rigs do not fit easily. The park has good facilities and is just a short walk to the shops. $$$

❏ Tent sites, powered sites, cabins, on-site vans.

❏ Toilets and showers (disabled access), laundry, telephone, camp kitchen, boat ramp, no pets.

❏ Credit cards, holiday loading. Discounts: weekly.

Pottsville Beach North Holiday Park
27 Coast Road, Pottsville 2489
Ph (02) 6676 1221, fax (02) 6676 3013

A quiet and spacious council park with good basic facilities. The park is just a short walk from the beach and facilities include volleyball and basketball courts and a swimming pool. $$$

❏ Tent sites, powered sites, drive-thru sites, fits big motorhomes, cabins.

❏ Toilets and showers (disabled access), laundry, sewer dump-point, telephone, ice, pool, no pets.

❏ Credit cards, holiday loading. Discounts: 3rd night.

PROSERPINE (QLD) p. 53

Whitsunday Tourist Park
O'Connell River, Bruce Highway, Proserpine 4800
Ph (07) 4947 5148, fax (07) 4947 5294

A developing park with good facilities located alongside the highway, 22 km south of Proserpine. This is an ideal park for an overnight stop. $

❏ Tent sites, powered sites, drive-thru sites, fits big motorhomes, cabins, on-site vans.

❏ Toilets and showers (disabled access), laundry, telephone, kiosk/shop, LP gas refills, ice, camp kitchen, pool, pets.

❏ Credit cards. Discounts: weekly.

QUEANBEYAN (NSW) pp. 210, 215

Queanbeyan Riverside Tourist Park
41A Morrisett Street, Queanbeyan 2620
Ph (02) 6297 4749, fax (02) 6299 2677

This park is set in a lovely location on the banks of the Queanbeyan River, just a short stroll from the heart of town. It has a large number of cabins, many tourist-van sites, good basic amenities and is easily accessible from the main thoroughfare. A park and playground area is right next door. $$

❏ Tent sites, powered sites, fits big motorhomes, cabins.

❏ Toilets and showers, laundry, sewer dump-point, pets.

❏ Credit cards. Discounts: weekly.

QUEENSCLIFF (VIC) p. 141

⊛ Beacon Resort
78 Bellarine Highway, Queenscliff 3225
Ph (03) 5258 1133 or 1800 351 152, fax (03) 5258 1152
Email book@beaconresort.com.au
Website www.beaconresort.com.au

This is one of Victoria's few five-star caravan parks. The award-winning establishment has all the trimmings you would expect from a five-star park, including very good recreational facilities – an indoor heated swimming pool and tennis courts. In addition to all this, it is just a short walk to the beach. $$$$

❏ Tent sites, powered sites, drive-thru sites, ensuite sites, fits big motorhomes, cabins.

❏ Toilets and showers (disabled access), telephone, laundry, sewer dump-point, LP gas refills, camp kitchen, pool, playground, internet terminal, no pets.

❏ Credit cards, holiday loading. Discounts: Big4.

QUEENSTOWN (TAS) p. 292

See also Lake Burbury.

Queenstown Cabin and Tourist Park
17 Grafton Street, Queenstown 7467
Ph (03) 6471 1332, fax (03) 6471 1125

This is a good basic park with a range of facilities. It is a convenient base for exploring the local area. $$

❏ Tent sites, powered sites, drive-thru sites, fits big motorhomes, cabins, on-site vans.

❏ Toilets and showers, laundry, camp kitchen, playground, pets.

❏ Credit cards, holiday loading. Discounts: weekly.

RAINBOW BEACH (QLD) p. 46

Rainbow Waters Holiday Park
Carlo Road, Rainbow Beach 4581
Ph (07) 5486 3200, fax (07) 5486 3572

This is a grassy, spacious park out of the town area, with good facilities. The park is popular with fishing enthusiasts and is located at the southern approach to Fraser Island. $$$

❏ Tent sites, powered sites, drive-thru sites, fits big motorhomes, cabins, on-site vans.

❏ Toilets and showers (disabled access), laundry, sewer dump-point, telephone, kiosk/shop, LP gas refills, ice, playground, boat ramp, TV cables, pets.

❏ Credit cards, holiday loading.

RAINBOW VALLEY (NT) p. 189

Rainbow Valley Conservation Reserve
Off Stuart Highway (77 km south of Alice Springs, 0870)

The Rainbow Valley Conservation Reserve is 23 km from the Stuart Highway along an unsealed road, suitable for four-wheel drives only. The spectacular valley is a popular destination for photographers. The park has a small number of unpowered sites and free gas barbecues. Payment is by the national park self-registration system. $

❏ Tent sites.

❏ Toilets, no pets.

❏ No credit cards.

RAWSON (VIC) p. 4

Rawson Caravan Park and Camping Area
Depot Road, Rawson 3825
Ph (03) 5165 3439

Close to Walhalla, Thomson Dam, the forests and the mountains, this not very well-known park is an excellent base for exploring the local area. The park has good facilities, including a new bistro, and offers discounts to retirees. All sites have ensuites. We enjoy camping here under the tall trees. $$$$

❏ Drive-thru sites, ensuite sites, fits big motorhomes, cabins.

❏ Toilets and showers, laundry, sewer dump-point, kiosk/shop, camp kitchen, pool, pets.

❏ Credit cards. Discounts: pensioners, seniors.

RAYMOND TERRACE (NSW) p. 28

Bellhaven Caravan Park
206 Pacific Highway, Raymond Terrace 2324
Ph (02) 4987 2423, fax (02) 4987 2423
Email bellhaven@bigpond.com

Set next to the Pacific Highway, this park is ideal as a base for exploring the area or simply as an overnight stop. The town centre is only a few minutes away. $$

❏ Tent sites, powered sites, drive-thru sites, cabins.

❏ Toilets and showers, laundry, telephone, kiosk/shop, LP gas refills, ice, pool, playground, no pets.

❏ Credit cards, holiday loading. Discounts: weekly.

Pacific Gardens Caravan Park
260 Pacific Highway, Raymond Terrace 2324
Ph (02) 4987 2224, fax (02) 4987 2432

Located alongside the Pacific Highway, this park is an ideal overnight stop for those travelling through Raymond Terrace. The town centre is now bypassed and is only a short drive away. A Seven-Eleven is just across the highway. $$

❏ Tent sites, powered sites, drive-thru sites, fits big motorhomes, cabins, on-site vans.

❏ Toilets and showers, laundry, sewer dump-point, telephone, LP gas refills, pool, playground, pets.

❏ Credit cards. Discounts: pensioners, seniors, weekly.

RENMARK (SA) p. 222

⊛ Renmark Riverfront Caravan Park
Sturt Highway, Renmark 5341
Ph (08) 8586 6315, fax (08) 8586 5200
Email renrivcarapark@riverland.net.au
Website www.homestead.com/renrivcarapk/title.html

This park makes a perfect holiday destination and we have stayed here many times. It is an ideal base from which to explore the area. Set on the Murray River about 2 km from the town centre, it has shady grassed areas – great for relaxing picnics – and good facilities. Minimum bookings are required during long weekends and holiday periods. $$

❏ Tent sites, powered sites, drive-thru sites, fits big motorhomes, cabins, on-site vans.

❏ Toilets and showers (disabled access), laundry, sewer dump-point, telephone, kiosk/shop, LP gas refills, ice, camp kitchen, playground, boat ramp, no pets.

❏ Credit cards. Discounts: weekly.

Riverbend Caravan Park
Sturt Highway, Renmark 5341
Ph (08) 8595 5131, fax (08) 8595 5431

Large, shady river red gums, green grass and absolute river frontage are the main attractions of this park. This is a good park in a great location 3 km east of the town centre. Facilities include a volleyball court and canoe hire. The entrance is at the immediate western edge of a bridge over the river and while access is simple from the highway, the entrance can be easily missed. $$

❏ Tent sites, powered sites, drive-thru sites, fits big motorhomes, cabins.

❏ Toilets and showers (disabled access), laundry, sewer dump-point, telephone, kiosk/shop, LP gas refills, ice, playground, no pets.

❏ Credit cards. Discounts: Top Tourist.

RENNER SPRINGS (NT) p. 196

Renner Springs Desert Inn
Stuart Highway, Renner Springs 0862
Ph (08) 8964 4505, fax (08) 8964 4525
Email rennersprings@bigpond.com
Website www.rennersprings.com

Renner Springs is an owner-operated roadhouse complex complete with a motel and caravan park. The park has good basic facilities and is ideal as an overnight stop when travelling along the Stuart Highway. Facilities include a convenient takeaway-food shop and a restaurant. Renner Springs is one of several parks in Australia that, with great logistical difficulties, work to provide good facilities; we like to support them when we pass this way. $$$

❏ Tent sites, powered sites, drive-thru sites, fits big motorhomes.

❏ Toilets and showers, laundry, telephone, kiosk/shop, LP gas refills, ice, camp kitchen, internet terminal, pets.

❏ Credit cards. Discounts: weekly.

RIANA (TAS) p. 288

Pioneer Park
Pine Road, Riana 7316
Ph (03) 6437 6137, fax (03) 6437 6137

This park is just a small grassed area in a rural setting. It is run by a team of volunteers and the overnight tariff is one of the lowest in the country. It has basic facilities and is suitable for an overnight stop. $

❏ Tent sites, powered sites, drive-thru sites, fits big motorhomes.

❏ Toilets and showers (disabled access), playground, pets.

❏ No credit cards.

ROBE (SA) p. 132

Lakeside Tourist Park
24 Main Road, Robe 5276
Ph (08) 8768 2193, fax (08) 8768 2722
Email lakeside@seol.net.au

This spacious lakeside park is located about 1 km from the centre of this popular coastal town. There is plenty of green grass and good facilities at a budget price. Pets are allowed only in the off-season. $$$

❑ Tent sites, powered sites, fits big motorhomes, cabins, on-site vans.

❑ Toilets and showers, laundry, telephone, kiosk/shop, LP gas refills, ice, playground, pets.

❑ Credit cards, holiday loading. Discounts: Top Tourist.

Robe Long Beach Tourist Park
The Esplanade, Robe 5276
Ph (08) 8768 2237 or 1800 106 106,
fax (08) 8768 2730
Email robelongbeachpark@bigpond.com
Website www.robelongbeach.com.au

This good quality park is just a short walk across the road from a popular beach, about 2 km from the centre of the coastal resort town. This is a good park at a reasonable price. $$$

❑ Tent sites, powered sites, drive-thru sites, fits big motorhomes, cabins.

❑ Toilets and showers, laundry, sewer dump-point, telephone, kiosk/shop, LP gas refills, ice, camp kitchen, playground, no pets.

❑ Credit cards, holiday loading. Discounts: weekly, Big4.

Seavu Caravan Park
1 Squire Drive, Robe 5276
Ph (08) 8768 2273, fax (08) 8768 2277
Email robeseavu@bigpond.com
Website www.robeseavu.com

This park is a short walk to the beach and just 1 km from Robe. Areas of this park are elevated with views out to sea. Pets are not allowed in peak periods. $$$

❑ Tent sites, powered sites, fits big motorhomes, cabins, on-site vans.

❑ Toilets and showers (disabled access), laundry, telephone, kiosk/shop, LP gas refills, ice, camp kitchen, playground, pets.

❑ Credit cards, holiday loading. Discounts: pensioners, seniors, weekly, FPA.

ROBINVALE (VIC) p. 220

Riverside Caravan Park
Riverside Drive, Robinvale 3549
Ph (03) 5026 4646, fax (03) 5026 4640
Email river@ruralnet.net.au

The park is on the banks of the Murray River, just 1 km from the town centre. There is a large expanse of green lawn and shady river red gums at a budget price. Great for a couple of days or an overnight stay. $$

❑ Tent sites, powered sites, drive-thru sites, ensuite sites, fits big motorhomes, cabins, on-site vans.

❑ Toilets and showers (disabled access), laundry, telephone, kiosk/shop, LP gas refills, ice, playground, boat ramp, pets.

❑ Credit cards, holiday loading. Discounts: pensioners, seniors, weekly.

ROCKHAMPTON (QLD)
pp. 48, 162, 259

Riverside Tourist Park
2 Reaney Street, Rockhampton 4701
Ph (07) 4922 3779, fax (07) 4922 3779

This is a council park on the riverfront, a short walk over the bridge from the city centre. It is a park that will suit those looking for a cheaper, no-frills stay. $$$

❑ Tent sites, powered sites, drive-thru sites, fits big motorhomes, cabins, on-site vans.

❑ Toilets and showers, laundry, sewer dump-point, telephone, no pets.

❑ Credit cards. Discounts: weekly.

Southside Holiday Village
Lower Dawson Road (Bruce Highway), Rockhampton 4700
Ph (07) 4927 3013, fax (07) 4927 7750
Email book@sshv.com.au
Website www.sshv.com.au

This is a good-quality park on the southern approaches to Rockhampton, 3.5 km from the city centre. Enjoy the heated swimming pool and the camp kitchen here. This is a good base for a stay in Rockhampton. $$$

❑ Tent sites, powered sites, drive-thru sites, ensuite sites, fits big motorhomes, cabins, on-site vans.

❑ Toilets and showers, laundry, sewer dump-point, telephone, kiosk/shop, LP gas refills, ice, camp kitchen, pool, playground, no pets.

❑ Credit cards. Discounts: pensioners, seniors, weekly, Top Tourist.

Tropical Wanderer Resort
394 Yaamba Road (Bruce Highway),
North Rockhampton 4701
Ph (07) 4926 3822 or 1800 815 563,
fax (07) 4928 8510
Email resort@tropicalwanderer.com.au
Website www.tropicalwanderer.com.au

This is a very good quality park on the north side of Rockhampton, easily accessible from the highway. The park has many of the features you would expect in a park of this quality, including a licensed restaurant, half tennis court, mini-golf course, pool and coffee shop. This is a great base in Rockhampton. $$$$

❑ Tent sites, powered sites, fits big motorhomes, cabins

❑ Toilets and showers, laundry, telephone, kiosk/shop, LP gas refills, ice, camp kitchen, pool, playground, no pets.

❑ Credit cards. Discounts: weekly, Big4.

ROLLINGSTONE (QLD) p. 54

Bushy Parker Park
Rollingstone 4816

This is a grassy, creek-side camping area with shady trees close to the centre of town. Camping is free for 48 hours. The area is easily accessible from the highway and ideal for an overnight stop. Facilities include toilets and an outdoor shower. Ⓢ

❑ Tent sites, drive-thru sites, fits big motorhomes.

❑ Toilets and showers, pets.

ROMA (QLD) p. 252

Ⓢ **Villa Holiday Park**
Northern Road (Injune Road), Roma 4455
Ph (07) 4622 1309, fax (07) 4622 1319
Email villapk@hwy54.com.au

This is our choice of places to stay in Roma. A winery and shop adjoin the park, and there are large grassed areas, modern facilities and a large selection of cabins. The park is well maintained and located about 2 km from the town centre. The quality of this park means it gets very busy during the tourist season and space is often scarce. We recommend you to book. $$$

❑ Tent sites, powered sites, drive-thru sites, ensuite sites, fits big motorhomes, cabins.

❑ Toilets and showers, laundry, sewer dump-point, telephone, kiosk/shop, LP gas refills, ice, camp kitchen, pool, playground, no pets.

❑ Credit cards. Discounts: weekly, Big4.

ROSEBERY (TAS) p. 290

Rosebery Caravan and Cabin Park
Park Road, Rosebery 7470
Ph (03) 6473 1366, fax (03) 6473 1366

This is a basic park with basic facilities, but ideal for those planning an overnight stop in town. A public swimming pool is a five-minute walk down the road. $$

❑ Tent sites, powered sites, fits big motorhomes, cabins, on-site vans.

❑ Toilets and showers, laundry, LP gas refills, playground, pets.

❑ No credit cards. Discounts: weekly.

ROSS (TAS) p. 280

Ross Caravan Park and Cabins
Bridge Street, Ross 7209
Ph (03) 6381 5224

Close to the centre of town, on the banks of the Macquarie River and adjoining historic buildings, this small, appealing park is one of the better parks in the midlands. Bookings and enquiries should be directed to the Ross post office (their number is listed). $$

❑ Tent sites, powered sites, drive-thru sites, fits big motorhomes, cabins.

❑ Toilets and showers (disabled access), laundry, playground, pets.

❑ No credit cards. Discounts: weekly.

ROSS RIVER (NT) p. 193

Ross River Resort
Ross Highway, via Alice Springs 0871
Ph (08) 8956 9711 or 1800 241 711,
fax (08) 8956 9823
Email rrr@rossriverresort.com.au
Website www.rossriverresort.com.au

Ross River Resort is located 80 km from Alice Springs in the east Macdonnell Ranges. There is a very good caravan park here with a large expanse of shaded grass. The resort has numerous features including a historic homestead, a restaurant and several activities including camel rides. The park is reached along a fully sealed road and can get busy with school groups. $$$$

❑ Tent sites, powered sites, drive-thru sites, fits big motorhomes, cabins.

❑ Toilets and showers, laundry, telephone, kiosk/shop, LP gas refills, ice, pool, boat ramp, pets.

❑ Bookings required, credit cards. Discounts: weekly.

ST HELENS (TAS) p. 303

St Helens Caravan Park
2 Penelope Street, St Helens 7216
Ph (03) 6376 1290, fax (03) 6376 1514

This is a good quality campground 1.5 km south of this pretty east-coast town. The park is a popular holiday destination and a reservation is essential in holiday periods. $$

❑ Tent sites, powered sites, drive-thru sites, ensuite sites, fits big motorhomes, cabins, on-site vans.

❑ Toilets and showers, laundry, sewer dump-point, telephone, kiosk/shop, LP gas refills, ice, camp kitchen, playground, pets.

❑ Credit cards, holiday loading. Discounts: pensioners, seniors, weekly, FPA.

ST LAWRENCE (QLD) p. 50

St Lawrence Recreation Reserve
St Lawrence 4707

The park is 6 km off the Bruce Highway and is a free overnight stop, with a good amenities block but not a lot of shade. Hot showers are available at a small fee, and the barbecues are free. Ⓢ

❑ Tent sites, drive-thru sites, fits big motorhomes.

❑ Toilets and showers (disabled access), pets.

SALE (VIC) p. 5

Sale Motor Village
Princes Highway, Sale 3850
Ph (03) 5144 1366, fax (03) 5143 2785
Email sale@motorvillage.com.au

This is a good quality caravan park alongside the highway, just 1 km west of the town centre. It is a very good base for exploring the area or a convenient overnight stop. Minimum bookings apply during holiday periods. $$$

❑ Tent sites, powered sites, drive-thru sites, fits big motorhomes, cabins, on-site vans.

❑ Toilets and showers (disabled access), laundry, telephone, kiosk/shop, LP gas refills, ice, pool, playground, no pets.

❑ Credit cards, holiday loading. Discounts: weekly, Big4.

SALT CREEK (SA) p. 132

Gemini Downs Coorong Holiday Centre
Highway One, Salt Creek 5264
Ph (08) 8575 7013, fax (08) 8575 7081

This is an unusual style park consisting of a camping ground on a farming property just 3 km north of Salt Creek. There is a selection of camping areas with a limited number of powered sites. A great rural location close to the Coorong. **$$**

❑ Tent sites, powered sites, fits big motorhomes, cabins.

❑ Toilets and showers, laundry, telephone, pool, playground, pets.

❑ Credit cards. Discounts: weekly.

SAPPHIRE (QLD) p. 258

◉ **Blue Gem Caravan and Tourist Park**
Main Road, Sapphire 4702
Ph (07) 4985 4162, fax (07) 4985 4162

For those interested in trying their luck in the gemfields, this award-winning park is a good base. It forms part of a shop and service station complex and is centrally located in Sapphire on the banks of Retreat Creek, where sapphires were first discovered in 1875. Facilities at this park are excellent for the price. **$$**

❑ Tent sites, powered sites, drive-thru sites, fits big motorhomes, on-site vans.

❑ Toilets and showers (disabled access), laundry, sewer dump-point, telephone, kiosk/shop, LP gas refills, ice, camp kitchen, pool, playground, internet terminal, pets.

❑ Credit cards. Discounts: weekly.

SAWTELL (NSW) p. 30

Sawtell Beach Caravan Park
Lyons Road, Sawtell 2452
Phone (02) 6653 1379, fax (02) 6653 3910
Email sbcp@bigpond.com
Website www.sawtellbeachcaravanpark.com.au

This large, spacious park has a wonderful outlook over the ocean and is just a short walk from Sawtell shopping centre. The owners have been busy renovating recently, and new additions include a camp kitchen and new cabins. A pool is just across the road. **$$$**

❑ Tent sites, powered sites, drive-thru sites, fits big motorhomes, cabins, on-site vans.

❑ Toilets and showers (disabled access), laundry, sewer dump-point, telephone, kiosk/shop, LP gas refills, ice, camp kitchen, pool, playground, no pets.

❑ Credit cards, holiday loading. Discounts: weekly.

SCAMANDER (TAS) p. 303

◉ **Scamander Forest Campground**
via Scamander 7215

Enjoy the peace and quiet at this Forestry Tasmania camping area, set in a forested area on the banks of the upper Scamander River. Access is along 10 km of unsealed roads; just follow the signs. It is ideal for motorhomes and camper-trailers and camping is free. Ⓢ

❑ Tent sites, drive-thru sites, fits big motorhomes.

❑ Toilets (disabled access), boat ramp, pets.

SCOTTSDALE (TAS) p. 302

North East Park Camping Ground
Ringarooma Road, Scottsdale 7260
Ph (03) 6352 2017

This small, picturesque roadside camping ground has just a handful of sites in a park-like setting. It is a good spot for an overnight stay, 1 km from the centre of town. **$**

❑ Tent sites, powered sites, fits big motorhomes.

❑ Toilets and showers, laundry, playground, pets.

❑ No credit cards. Discounts: weekly.

SEACOMBE (VIC) p. 6

See also Loch Sport.

Seacombe Landing Recreation Reserve
Seacombe Road, Seacombe 3851

This is a small national park camping area popular with anglers as it has good access to Lake Wellington and Lake Victoria. There is an open, grassed area and a convenient overnight campsite for motorhomes and campervans. No facilities are on site other than a barbecue and a toilet block. Ⓢ

❑ Tent sites, drive-thru sites, fits big motorhomes.

❑ Toilets, pets.

SEAFORTH (QLD) p. 53

Seaforth Camping Area
Seaforth 4741

A popular open camping area right on the beachfront in the heart of the small town. Camping fees are payable at the general store. A good park for a few days. **$**

❑ Tent sites, drive-thru sites, fits big motorhomes.

❑ Toilets and showers (disabled access), laundry, telephone, kiosk/shop, LP gas refills, ice, no pets.

❑ No credit cards. Discounts: weekly.

SEAL ROCKS (NSW) p. 28

Seal Rocks Camping Reserve
Kinka Road, Seal Rocks 2423
Ph (02) 4997 6164, fax (02) 4997 6250

The Seal Rocks Camping Reserve is located in an idyllic position overlooking a popular beach. The park's new powered sites have proven very popular and bookings for them are advised. It is reached along 10 km of unsealed road that may be corrugated at times. The basic services available at Seal Rocks are just a short walk away. **$$$**

❑ Tent sites, powered sites, drive-thru sites, fits big motorhomes, cabins, on-site vans.

❑ Toilets and showers (disabled access), laundry, telephone, LP gas refills, ice, camp kitchen, no pets.

❑ Bookings required, credit cards. Discounts: weekly.

SEVENTEEN SEVENTY (QLD) p. 48

◉ **Seventeen Seventy Camping Ground**
Captain Cook Drive, Seventeen Seventy 4677
Ph (07) 4974 9286, fax (07) 4974 9583

It is hard to resist the excellent, absolute beachfront location of this council-owned park. At this subtropical hideaway it is almost possible to tie the dinghy up to the caravan. The park has good basic amenities, with a playground next door. Beachfront sites are unpowered yet very popular. Minimum bookings apply in holiday season. **$$$**

❑ Tent sites, powered sites, drive-thru sites, fits big motorhomes.

❑ Toilets and showers (disabled access), laundry, telephone, kiosk/shop, LP gas refills, ice, camp kitchen, playground, no pets.

❑ Bookings required, credit cards. Discounts: weekly.

SEYMOUR (VIC) p. 152

Goulburn River Caravan Park
Progress Street, Seymour 3660
Ph (03) 5792 1530, fax (03) 5799 1032
Email grcpark@eck.net.au

This budget-priced park is on the banks of the Goulburn River, about 1 km from the town centre. The park has basic facilities but is clean and well maintained in a quiet, off-highway location. **$$**

❑ Tent sites, powered sites, drive-thru sites, fits big motorhomes, cabins, on-site vans.

❑ Toilets and showers (disabled access), laundry, telephone, kiosk/shop, LP gas refills, ice, playground, boat ramp, no pets.

❑ Credit cards. Discounts: weekly.

SHELLHARBOUR (NSW)

See Wollongong.

SHEPPARTON (VIC) p. 152

Pine Lodge Caravan Park
Corner Orrvale Road and Midland Highway, Shepparton 3630
Ph (03) 5829 2396 or 1800 022 345, fax (03) 5829 2662
Email pinepark@mcmedia.com.au

On the Midland Highway 5 km to the east of Shepparton, this quality park in a rural setting has great amenities and facilities including a tennis court. As with many caravan parks in the Shepparton area, it can become busy with seasonal workers during the fruit-picking season. **$$$**

❑ Tent sites, powered sites, drive-thru sites, ensuite sites, fits big motorhomes, cabins.

❑ Toilets and showers, laundry, telephone, kiosk/shop, LP gas refills, ice, camp kitchen, pool, playground, no pets.

❑ Credit cards, holiday loading. Discounts: weekly, Big4.

Shepparton Parklands Motor Village
7835 Goulburn Valley Highway, Kialla 3631
Ph (03) 5823 1576, fax (03) 5823 2087

The park is 5 km south of Shepparton, opposite the airport on the southern approaches to the city. It is a large, quality owner-operated park with both permanent and tourist sites. It has a range of accommodation and is well maintained, with good amenities and facilities. **$$**

❑ Tent sites, powered sites, drive-thru sites, ensuite sites, fits big motorhomes, cabins.

❑ Toilets and showers, laundry, sewer dump-point, telephone, kiosk/shop, LP gas refills, ice, pool, playground, pets.

❑ Credit cards. Discounts: weekly.

◉ **Victoria Lake Holiday Park**
Wyndham Street (Goulburn Valley Highway), Shepparton 3630
Ph (03) 5821 5431 or 1800 880 070, fax (03) 5821 5431
Email info@viclakeholidaypark.com.au
Website www.viclakeholidaypark.com.au

Set on the shores of Victoria Park Lake, this picturesque park is centrally located on the main highway 1 km south of the city centre (although there are plans to construct a bypass around Shepparton). With good facilities and great waterfront sites, it is the park we like to stay at when in Shepparton. **$$$**

❑ Tent sites, powered sites, drive-thru sites, ensuite sites, fits big motorhomes, cabins.

❑ Toilets and showers, laundry, telephone, kiosk/shop, LP gas refills, camp kitchen, pool, playground, TV cables, pets.

❑ Credit cards, holiday loading. Discount: weekly, Top Tourist.

SHOAL BAY (NSW)

See Nelson Bay.

SHOALHAVEN HEADS (NSW) p. 16

Mountain View Caravan and Mobile Home Village
14 Shoalhaven Heads Road, Shoalhaven Heads 2535
Ph (02) 4448 7281, fax (02) 4448 8200
Email info@mtview.com.au
Website www.mtview.com.au

This is a large, quality park with a limited number of tourist sites. It has very good facilities including tennis courts and a mini-golf course and good amenities. Ask about the courtesy bus that runs from the park to the Shoalhaven Heads Bowls Club. **$$$**

❑ Tent sites, powered sites, drive-thru sites, ensuite sites, cabins.

❑ Toilets and showers, laundry, sewer dump-point, telephone, camp kitchen, pool, playground, no pets.

❑ Credit cards, holiday loading. Discounts: weekly, Top Tourist.

Shoalhaven Heads Tourist Park
Shoalhaven Heads Road,
Shoalhaven Heads 2535
Ph (02) 4448 7178 or 1300 782 222,
fax (02) 4448 7178
Email shoheads@shoalhaven.nsw.gov.au
Website www.holidayhaven.com.au

The Holiday Haven family tourist parks are very good establishments, owned and operated by the Shoalhaven Council. This large, award-winning riverfront park has very good facilities. It is just a short walk through to the beach and a great spot for a family holiday. **$$$**

❑ Tent sites, powered sites, fits big motorhomes, cabins.

❑ Toilets and showers (disabled access), laundry, sewer dump-point, telephone, LP gas refills, ice, camp kitchen, playground, boat ramp, no pets.

❑ Credit cards, holiday loading. Discounts: pensioners, seniors, weekly.

SHUTE HARBOUR (QLD) p. 53

Flame Tree Tourist Village
Shute Harbour Road, Shute Harbour 4802
Ph (07) 4946 9388 or 1800 069 388,
fax (07) 4946 9501
Email flametree@whitsunday.net.au
Website www.flametreevillage.com.au

This is a well-known, good quality park in the heart of a popular holiday destination. Enjoy the heated pool, the covered barbecues and the other great features. A good park for a holiday in this great tourist region. **$$$**

❑ Tent sites, powered sites, drive-thru sites, fits big motorhomes, cabins, on-site vans.

❑ Toilets and showers (disabled access), laundry, sewer dump-point telephone, kiosk/shop, LP gas refills, ice, camp kitchen, pool, playground, internet terminal, pets.

❑ Credit cards. Discounts: weekly, Top Tourist.

SILVERTON (NSW) p. 244

Penrose Park
Silverton 2880
Ph (08) 8088 5307

This camping area covers some 40 ha and is a good base for exploring the historic town. The park is within a large recreational area, with lots of play equipment and domestic animals on site. Facilities include a large camp kitchen, which may incur an additional fee. There is plenty of space here for large rigs. **$**

❑ Tent sites, powered sites, drive-thru sites, fits big motorhomes, cabins.

❑ Toilets and showers, laundry, LP gas refills, ice, camp kitchen, playground, pets.

❑ No credit cards. Discounts: weekly.

SOUTH HEDLAND (WA) pp. 92, 204

See also Indee Station and Port Hedland.

Blackrock Caravan Park
Corner North Circular and Stanley streets,
South Hedland 6722
Ph (08) 9172 3444, fax (08) 9140 2228

This is a new caravan park built in 1999. It has been well laid out with good facilities

and, in time, will develop into a quality park. It is close to the highway. **$$$**

❑ Tent sites, powered sites, drive-thru sites, ensuite sites, fits big motorhomes.

❑ Toilets and showers (disabled access), laundry, sewer dump-point, telephone, kiosk/shop, camp kitchen, pool, playground, TV cables, internet terminal, pets.

❑ Credit cards. Discounts: weekly.

SOUTH MISSION BEACH
(QLD) p. 56

See also Mission Beach.

⊛ Beachcomber Coconut Caravan Village
Kennedy Esplanade, South Mission Beach 4852
Ph (07) 4068 8129 or 1800 008 129,
fax (07) 4068 8671
Email big4bccv@bigpond.com

Mission Beach is a dream holiday destination and this park is a perfect place to stay. It is set in a fabulous location just across the road from the beach. Walk to the shops, play on the half-size tennis court or enjoy a barbecue. The park also has a resort-style swimming pool. **$$$**

❑ Tent sites, powered sites, drive-thru sites, cabins.

❑ Toilets and showers (disabled access), laundry, telephone, kiosk/shop, LP gas refills, ice, camp kitchen, pool, playground, boat ramp, no pets.

❑ Credit cards, holiday loading. Discounts: weekly, Big4.

SOUTH WEST ROCKS (NSW) p. 30

Arakoon State Recreation Area
Trial Bay Gaol, South West Rocks 2431
Ph (02) 6566 6168, fax (02) 6566 6507

This is a national park camping area located adjacent to the historic Trial Bay Gaol. It is virtually on the beach and is a lovely spot to stay for a few days. Large motorhomes can fit, though not on powered sites. **$$$**

❑ Tent sites, powered sites, drive-thru sites, fits big motorhomes.

❑ Toilets and showers (disabled access), laundry, telephone, kiosk/shop, ice, playground, no pets.

❑ Credit cards, holiday loading.

SOUTHPORT (QLD)

See Gold Coast.

STANLEY (TAS) p. 288

⊛ Stanley Cabin and Tourist Park
Wharf Road, Stanley 7331
Ph (03) 6458 1266 or 1800 444 818,
fax (03) 6458 1266
Email enquiries@stanleycabinpark.com.au
Website www.stanleycabinpark.com.au

This park, on the water's edge, is a 200-m stroll from the centre of town – a perfect base for exploring historic Stanley. The spectacular geological feature, The Nut, which is the remains of an old volcano,

forms a towering backdrop behind the town. The park has very good amenities and nicely grassed sites, and booking is necessary in holiday periods. **$$$**

❑ Tent sites, powered sites, drive-thru sites, ensuite sites, fits big motorhomes, cabins, on-site vans.

❑ Toilets and showers (disabled access), laundry, telephone, camp kitchen, playground, boat ramp, no pets.

❑ Credit cards. Discounts: weekly, Big4.

STIRLING NORTH (SA) pp. 123, 183

Port Augusta Caravan Park
9 Brook Street, Stirling North 5710
Ph (08) 8643 6357, fax (08) 8643 6759

This is a neat and tidy park just 6 km from Port Augusta. The park is very popular with tourists during the cooler months and is an ideal base to head to the Flinders Ranges. **$$**

❑ Tent sites, powered sites, drive-thru sites, fits big motorhomes, cabins, on-site vans.

❑ Toilets and showers (disabled access), laundry, telephone, kiosk/shop, LP gas refills, ice, playground, pets.

❑ Credit cards. Discounts: weekly.

STOCKTON (NSW)

See Newcastle.

STRAHAN (TAS) p. 292

⊛ Strahan Caravan and Tourist Park
Corner Andrews and Innes streets,
Strahan 7468
Ph (03) 6471 7239, fax (03) 6471 7692

Explore the fabulous western coastal region from this popular resort-style park, only 1.5 km west of the centre of Strahan. It has basic but good amenities. We stay here when we visit Strahan. **$$$**

❑ Tent sites, powered sites, cabins, on-site vans.

❑ Toilets and showers, laundry, kiosk/shop, camp kitchen, playground, no pets.

❑ Bookings required, holiday loading, credit cards. Discounts: weekly.

STRATFORD (VIC) p. 6

Stratford Top Tourist Park
McMillan Street, Stratford 3862
Ph (03) 5145 6588, fax (03) 5145 6588

This is a good quality park with a range of accommodation, just a short 600 m walk from the centre of the small town. There are good amenities and facilities and it is a suitable park for overnight or longer stays. **$$$**

❑ Tent sites, powered sites, drive-thru sites, ensuite sites, fits big motorhomes, cabins, on-site vans.

❑ Toilets and showers, laundry, sewer dump-point, telephone, LP gas refills, camp kitchen, pool, playground, pets.

❑ Credit cards, holiday loading. Discounts: weekly, Top Tourist.

STRATHMERTON (VIC)

See Morgans Beach.

SUFFOLK PARK (NSW) p. 34

Broken Head Holiday Park
Beach Road, Broken Head 2481
Ph (02) 6685 3245, fax (02) 6685 4810
Email broken@bshp.com.au
Website www.bshp.com.au/broken

This stretch of coast is a busy holiday area. Broken Head Caravan Park is located on the beach and has good facilities, and Byron Bay is 7 km north. **$$$**

❑ Tent sites, powered sites, fits big motorhomes, cabins.

❑ Toilets and showers (disabled access), laundry, sewer dump-point, telephone, kiosk/shop, LP gas refills, ice, no pets.

❑ Credit cards, holiday loading. Discounts: weekly.

Suffolk Park Holiday Park
Alcorn Street, Suffolk Park 2480
Ph (02) 6685 3353, fax (02) 6685 3180
Email suffolk@bshp.com.au
Website www.bshp.com.au/suffolk

A popular beachside holiday park that is busy year-round. The park has good facilities and is 6 km south of Byron Bay. It is close to some popular surfing and swimming beaches. **$$$**

❑ Tent sites, powered sites, drive-thru sites, fits big motorhomes, cabins.

❑ Toilets and showers, laundry, sewer dump-point, telephone, LP gas refills, ice, camp kitchen, no pets.

❑ Credit cards, holiday loading. Discounts: weekly.

SUTTON (NSW) pp. 210, 215

⊛ White Ibis Holiday Village
47 Bidges Road, Sutton 2620
Ph (02) 6230 3433 or 1800 664 269,
fax (02) 6230 3483
Email whiteibis@iprimus.com.au
Website www.sydneycaravanparks.com.au

Take the time to sit by the lake, relax and feed the ducks at White Ibis, one of our favourite parks. Located in a spacious rural setting around a lake, it is just 14 km north of Canberra and easily accessible from the Federal Highway. This is a good base for exploring Canberra and the park's facilities include a range of accommodation, a well-stocked shop and a tennis court. We enjoy staying here. **$$**

❑ Tent sites, powered sites, drive-thru sites, fits big motorhomes, cabins.

❑ Toilets and showers (disabled access), laundry, sewer dump-point, telephone, kiosk/shop, LP gas refills, ice, camp kitchen, pool, playground, TV cables, internet terminal, no pets.

❑ Credit cards, holiday loading. Discounts: FPA.

SWAN HILL (VIC) p. 220

Pioneer City Caravan Park
186 Murray Valley Highway, Swan Hill 3585
Ph (03) 5032 4372, fax (03) 5032 1513
Email pioneer@swanhill.net.au
Website www.murray-river.net

On the northern edge of town, this is a very good quality park that will satisfy the most fastidious traveller. The owner-operated park has a range of accommodation and good facilities including covered barbecues, a six-hole golf course and a tennis court. Minimum bookings apply during holiday periods. $$$

❑ Tent sites, powered sites, drive-thru sites, ensuite sites, fits big motorhomes, cabins, on-site vans.

❑ Toilets and showers, laundry, telephone, kiosk/shop, LP gas refills, ice, camp kitchen, pool, playground, pets.

❑ Credit cards, holiday loading. Discounts: weekly, FPA.

Swan Hill Riverside Caravan Park
Monash Drive, Swan Hill 3585
Ph (03) 5032 1494, fax (03) 5032 3025
Email cammpark@swanhill.net.au
Website www.swanhillriverside.com.au

This park is walking distance to the centre of town, with large expanses of green lawn and a long frontage to the Murray River. The park has a heated pool, undercover barbecues and a very well-stocked shop. In holiday periods minimum bookings apply and pets are not allowed. $$$

❑ Tent sites, powered sites, fits big motorhomes, cabins, on-site vans.

❑ Toilets and showers (disabled access), laundry, sewer dump-point, telephone, kiosk/shop, LP gas refills, ice, camp kitchen, pool, playground, pets.

❑ Credit cards, holiday loading. Discounts: weekly, Top Tourist.

SWANSEA (NSW) p. 26

Swansea Gardens Lakeside Holiday Park
Wallarah Street, Swansea 2281
Ph (02) 4971 2869, fax (02) 4971 1160

This large, council-operated waterfront park is located in a quiet area on the shores of Lake Macquarie. It is a popular holiday park and a booking is essential in busy periods. Facilities are good and include tennis courts and a kiosk open in the summer months. $$

❑ Tent sites, powered sites, fits big motorhomes, cabins, on-site vans.

❑ Toilets and showers (disabled access), laundry, sewer dump-point, telephone, kiosk/shop, ice, pool, playground, boat ramp, pets.

❑ Credit cards, holiday loading. Discounts: pensioners, seniors, weekly.

SWANSEA (TAS) p. 298

See also Mayfield Bay.

Swansea Holiday Park
Shaw Street, Swansea 7190
Ph (03) 6257 8177, fax (03) 6257 8511
Email enquiries@swansea-holiday.com.au
Website www.swansea-holiday.com.au

The park is just 500 m from town and has absolute beachfront sites. The views over Great Oyster Bay and Freycinet National Park are breathtaking. Facilities here are good, including a new amenities block. $$

❑ Tent sites, powered sites, fits big motorhomes, cabins.

❑ Toilets and showers (disabled access), laundry, telephone, kiosk/shop, LP gas refills, camp kitchen, pool, playground, internet terminal, pets.

❑ Credit cards, holiday loading. Discounts: weekly, FPA.

SYDNEY (NSW) p. 23

Dural Village Caravan Park
269 New Line Road, Dural 2158
Ph (02) 9651 2555 or 1300 135 296, fax (02) 9651 2070
Email info@duralvillage.com.au
Website www.duralvillage.com.au

This is a quality park in the north-western suburbs of Sydney and can be easily accessed from Route 7. The well-designed park has a very good shop and is in a nice area. It is ideal for a holiday base in this part of Sydney. $$$$

❑ Tent sites, powered sites, ensuite sites, cabins.

❑ Toilets and showers, laundry, sewer dump-point, telephone, kiosk/shop, camp kitchen, pool, playground, no pets.

❑ Credit cards, holiday loading. Discounts: weekly, Top Tourist.

La Mancha Carapark
901 Pacific Highway, Berowra 2081
Ph (02) 9456 1766 or 1800 456 176, fax (02) 9456 2067
Email admin@lamanchasydney.com.au
Website www.lamanchasydney.com.au

This is a good quality park on the northern fringe of Sydney, with excellent access to the Sydney–Newcastle freeway. The park is on the old highway. A direct train service to the city from the nearby railway station is an added convenience. $$$$

❑ Tent sites, powered sites, ensuite sites, fits big motorhomes, cabins, on-site vans.

❑ Toilets and showers, laundry, sewer dump-point, telephone, kiosk/shop, LP gas refills, ice, camp kitchen, pool, playground, internet terminal, no pets.

❑ Credit cards. Discounts: pensioners, weekly, Big4.

Lane Cove River Tourist Park
Plassey Road, North Ryde 2113
Ph (02) 9888 9133, fax (02) 9888 9322
Email lccp@npws.nsw.gov.au
Website www.lanecoveriver.com

This is the closest caravan park to Sydney – just 10 km away, and yet in a bush setting. Adjoining the Lane Cove River, the popular park has lovely treed areas and very good facilities. A regular bus service operates to the city. The park is well run by the NSW National Parks and Wildlife Service and is an excellent base for exploring Sydney. Access to the park is good from all directions. $$$$

❑ Tent sites, powered sites, fits big motorhomes, cabins.

❑ Toilets and showers (disabled access), laundry, sewer dump-point, telephone, kiosk/shop, LP gas refills, camp kitchen, pool, playground, no pets.

❑ Credit cards, holiday loading. Discounts: weekly.

⊕ **Sydney Lakeside Narabeen**
Lake Park Road, North Narrabeen 2101
Ph (02) 9913 7845, fax (02) 9970 6385
Email info@sydneylakeside.com.au
Website www.sydneylakeside.com.au

This is our pick of Sydney's caravan parks. It is a large, well-grassed park on the banks of Narrabeen Lake and just a short stroll from the beach. It is located in a quiet area, away from the city humdrum on the north shore. The excellent amenities complete the picture. This is a good base for exploring Sydney. $$$$

❑ Tent sites, powered sites, fits big motorhomes, cabins.

❑ Toilets and showers (disabled access), laundry, sewer dump-point, telephone, kiosk/shop, ice, camp kitchen, playground, boat ramp, internet terminal, no pets.

❑ Credit cards, holiday loading. Discounts: weekly.

Woronora Caravan Park
1 Menai Road, Woronora 2232
Ph (02) 9521 2291, fax (02) 9545 0794

This is an older, basic park in a quiet location on the Woronora River. There is just a small number of tourist sites in the park, and it is easily reached from the Princes Highway. This is a good location for those seeking a place to stay on the south side of the city. $$$

❑ Tent sites, powered sites, cabins.

❑ Toilets and showers, laundry, LP gas refills, no pets.

❑ Credit cards, holiday loading.

TABOURIE LAKE (NSW) p. 14

Lake Tabourie Tourist Park
Princes Highway, Tabourie Lake 2539
Ph (02) 4457 3011 or 1300 559 966, fax (02) 4457 3011
Email tabourie@shoalhaven.nsw.gov.au
Website www.holidayhaven.com.au

This is a large waterfront park with a wide range of facilities including a tennis court and canoes for hire. It has good amenities and wide, spacious grassy areas. This is a well-operated council park. $$$

❑ Tent sites, powered sites, drive-thru sites, fits big motorhomes, cabins.

❑ Toilets and showers (disabled access), laundry, sewer dump-point, telephone, kiosk/shop, LP gas refills, ice, camp kitchen, pool, playground, boat ramp, no pets.

❑ Credit cards, holiday loading. Discounts: pensioners, seniors, weekly.

TAILEM BEND (SA) pp. 132, 232

Westbrook Park River Resort
Princes Highway, Tailem Bend 5260
Ph (08) 8572 3794, fax (08) 8572 4121

This owner-operated park has grassy sites snuggled alongside the banks of the Murray River, just 6 km north-west of town. Within easy driving distance of Adelaide, it is good for an overnight stop or suitable for a longer stay, where you can rest in the shade and watch the river glide by. $$

❑ Tent sites, powered sites, fits big motorhomes, cabins.

❑ Toilets and showers (disabled access), laundry, kiosk/shop, LP gas refills, ice, camp kitchen, playground, boat ramp, no pets.

❑ Credit cards. Discounts: pensioners, seniors, weekly.

TANNUM SANDS (QLD) p. 48

See also Boyne Island.

Tannum Beach Caravan Village
The Esplanade, Tannum Sands 4680
Ph (07) 4973 7201 or 1800 684 003, fax (07) 4973 7777
Email tannumvillage@bigpond.com

This is a spotless park with good facilities. Close to Gladstone and only a short distance from the beach, this park is ideal for a few days or convenient for an overnight stay. $$

❑ Tent sites, powered sites, drive-thru sites, fits big motorhomes, cabins.

❑ Toilets and showers (disabled access), laundry, sewer dump-point, telephone, kiosk/shop, LP gas refills, ice, camp kitchen, pool, playground, TV cables, no pets.

❑ Credit cards. Discounts: weekly.

TANUNDA (SA) pp. 224, 246

⊕ **Tanunda Caravan and Tourist Park**
Barossa Valley Way, Tanunda 5352
Ph (08) 8563 2784, fax (08) 8563 3711
Email enquiries@tanundacaravantouristpark.com.au
Website www.tanundacaravantouristpark.com.au

Enjoy the Barossa Valley experience from this popular park. Situated right in the heart of the Barossa Valley, it is a great base for exploring this fabulous wine-producing region. Located 1.5 km from the town centre, with easy access, it offers patrons a good range of accommodation and facilities, including bicycle hire. $$$

❑ Tent sites, powered sites, drive-thru sites, fits big motorhomes, cabins, on-site vans.

❑ Toilets and showers (disabled access), laundry, sewer dump-point, telephone, kiosk/shop, LP gas refills, ice, camp kitchen, playground, pets.

❑ Bookings required, credit cards. Discounts: weekly, FPA.

TAREE (NSW) p. 28

See also Croki.

Taree Caravan Park
7 Cowper Street (on the old Pacific Highway), Taree North 2430
Ph (02) 6552 1751

The Pacific Highway now bypasses the town of Taree, but many travellers make the deviation into the town centre. Those visiting the town have a couple of parks to choose from but this good basic park is one that we would choose. **$$**

❑ Tent sites, powered sites, drive-thru sites, fits big motorhomes.

❑ Toilets and showers (disabled access), laundry, telephone, pets.

❑ Credit cards. Discounts: weekly.

TARGA (TAS)

See Myrtle Bank.

TAROOM (QLD) p. 162

See also Glebe Weir.

Taroom Caravan Park
1 Short Street, Taroom 4420
Ph (07) 4627 3218

This is a council park with good basic amenities and limited facilities at a budget price. It is within walking distance of the town centre. **$**

❑ Tent sites, powered sites, drive-thru sites, fits big motorhomes.

❑ Toilets and showers, pets.

❑ No credit cards. Discounts: 2nd night, weekly.

TATHRA (NSW) p. 10

Tathra Beach Tourist Park
Andy Poole Drive, Tathra 2550
Ph (02) 6494 1302, fax (02) 6494 1025

This good quality, absolute beachfront park is surrounded by national park. Just stroll onto the beach from your site or take a short walk to the town centre, restaurants or clubs. Tathra is a popular holiday town and a booking at the park will be necessary in peak periods. Pets are allowed only in the low season. **$$$**

❑ Tent sites, powered sites, drive-thru sites, fits big motorhomes, cabins, on-site vans.

❑ Toilets and showers (disabled access), laundry, telephone, LP gas refills, ice, playground, TV cables, pets.

❑ Credit cards, holiday loading. Discounts: weekly.

TENNANT CREEK (NT) pp. 194, 260

⊛ **Outback Caravan Park**
Peko Road, Tennant Creek 0860
Ph (08) 8962 2459, fax (08) 8962 1278
Email outback@swtch.com.au

This large, well-appointed park is just 1 km from the town centre and off the highway. We find it an ideal base for a few days exploring this interesting area. Facilities include a pool, spa and a new entertainment area, for bush cooking and poetry recitals. **$$$**

❑ Tent sites, powered sites, drive-thru sites, fits big motorhomes, cabins, on-site vans.

❑ Toilets and showers, laundry, sewer dump-point, telephone, kiosk/shop, LP gas refills, ice, camp kitchen, pool, no pets.

❑ Credit cards. Discounts: weekly.

TEWANTIN (QLD) p. 44

Bougainvillia Caravan Park
141 Cooroy–Noosa Road, Tewantin 4565
Ph (07) 5447 1712 or 1800 041 444, fax (07) 5474 0596
Email jsjs@optusnet.com.au

This is a good quality park opposite the Noosa golf course. There are good facilities and the park is very popular year-round. The range of facilities includes a pool and a basketball and volleyball court. This is a great base for spending a holiday in the Noosa area. **$$$$**

❑ Tent sites, powered sites, ensuite sites, fits big motorhomes, cabins.

❑ Toilets and showers (disabled access), laundry, sewer dump-point, telephone, kiosk/shop, LP gas refills, ice, camp kitchen, pool, internet terminal, no pets.

❑ Credit cards. Discounts: weekly, Big4.

Noosa North Shore Retreat and Caravan Park
Beach Road, North Shore, Tewantin 4565
Ph (07) 5447 1706, fax (07) 5442 4452
Email info@noosaretreat.com.au
Website www.noosaretreat.com.au

The large park is north of the Noosa River, away from the rush of the holiday centre. From here there is good access to the northern beach and it is possible to drive four-wheel-drive vehicles the 57 km along the beach to Rainbow Beach. The park has a range of accommodation and facilities include a gym, a tennis court and mini-golf. There are lots of activities on offer, from camel riding to canoeing. **$$**

❑ Tent sites, powered sites, drive-thru sites, fits big motorhomes, cabins.

❑ Toilets and showers (disabled access), laundry, telephone, kiosk/shop, LP gas refills, ice, playground, pool, internet terminal, pets.

❑ Bookings required, credit cards, holiday loading.

THE CAVES (QLD) pp. 50, 259

Capricorn Caverns Tourist Park
30 Olsen's Caves Road, The Caves 4702
Ph (07) 4934 2883, fax (07) 4934 2936
Email capcave@cqnet.com.au
Website www.capricorncaves.com.au

This good-quality owner-operated park forms part of the fabulous Olsen's Caverns complex. The park is just walking distance to the caves and there are many features including a cafe. Visit the caves and stay overnight. We enjoyed our visit. **$$$**

❑ Tent sites, powered sites, drive-thru sites, fits big motorhomes, cabins.

❑ Toilets and showers (disabled access), laundry, telephone, kiosk/shop, LP gas refills, ice, camp kitchen, pool, no pets.

❑ Credit cards.

THE ENTRANCE (NSW) p. 26

Dunleith Caravan Park
Hutton Road, North Entrance 2261
Ph (02) 4332 2172, fax (02) 4333 3609

This park is situated on the foreshore where Tuggerah Lake meets the sea. It has good tourist facilities and is a short walk into town. Pelican feeding occurs nearby at 3.30 pm every day. Pets are allowed at the park, though not in holiday periods. **$$$**

❑ Tent sites, powered sites, drive-thru sites, ensuite sites, cabins, on-site vans.

❑ Toilets and showers, laundry, telephone, kiosk/shop, LP gas refills, ice, playground, boat ramp, pets.

❑ Credit cards, holiday loading. Discounts: weekly, Top Tourist.

THEODORE (QLD)

See Isla Gorge National Park.

TI TREE (NT) p. 194

Ti Tree Roadhouse Caravan Park
Stuart Highway, Ti Tree 0872
Ph (08) 8956 9741, fax (08) 8956 9780

The Ti Tree area supports large commercial orchards and vegetable crops. This is a great place to stop if travelling on the Stuart Highway. The complex, which includes motel rooms and backpacker accommodation, can get unexpectedly busy with events in neighbouring towns. **$$**

❑ Tent sites, powered sites, drive-thru sites, fits big motorhomes.

❑ Toilets and showers, laundry, telephone, kiosk/shop, ice, pool, pets.

❑ Credit cards.

TIMBER CREEK (NT) p. 87

Big Horse Creek Camping Area
Gregory National Park, Victoria Highway, Timber Creek 0852

This national park camping area is adjacent to the highway on the banks of the Victoria River, 11 km west of Timber Creek. There are no showers but the area is a convenient overnight stop for the self-sufficient traveller. **$**

❑ Tent sites, drive-thru sites, fits big motorhomes.

❑ Toilets, boat ramp, no pets.

❑ No credit cards.

Timber Creek Gunamu Tourist Park
(also known as Circle F)
Victoria Highway, Timber Creek 0852
Ph (08) 8975 0722, fax (08) 8975 0772
Email stoneynt@bigpond.com

With only a couple of parks to choose from in this area, this one is our selection. The caravan park is part of a roadhouse complex in the centre of the Timber Creek township. It is a convenient overnight stop and a good place to stay for a few days while exploring the surrounding area. The park has shaded sites, good basic amenities, a spa and a pool. **$$$**

❑ Tent sites, powered sites, drive-thru sites, fits big motorhomes, cabins, on-site vans.

❑ Toilets and showers, laundry, telephone, kiosk/shop, LP gas refills, ice, pool, playground, pets.

❑ Credit cards. Discounts: weekly.

TINAROO FALLS (QLD) p. 64

Lake Tinaroo Holiday Park
Dam Road, Lake Tinaroo 4872
Ph (07) 4095 8232, fax (07) 4095 8808

This park is located on Tinaroo Dam, 17 km from Atherton. It is popular with fishermen who come year-round to catch barramundi from the stocked reservoir. The park has good basic facilities. **$$$**

❑ Tent sites, powered sites, drive-thru sites, fits big motorhomes, cabins.

❑ Toilets and showers (disabled access), laundry, sewer dump-point, telephone, kiosk/shop, LP gas refills, ice, boat ramp, pets.

❑ Credit cards. Discounts: pensioners, seniors, weekly.

TOCUMWAL (NSW) p. 154

⊛ **Boomerang Way Tourist Park**
65 Murray Street, Tocumwal 2714
Ph (03) 5874 2313, fax (03) 5874 2313
Email wboon@cobram.net.au

This well-cared-for, owner-operated park is 500 m from the centre of Tocumwal and away from the highway's noise. The park has a large swimming pool as well as a covered barbecue area and is ideal both for an overnight stay or an entire holiday. Minimum bookings apply during the Christmas, January and Easter holiday periods. **$$**

❑ Tent sites, powered sites, drive-thru sites, ensuite sites, fits big motorhomes, cabins.

❑ Toilets and showers (disabled access), laundry, telephone, kiosk/shop, LP gas refills, ice, camp kitchen, pool, no pets.

❑ Credit cards, holiday loading. Discounts: weekly, Top Tourist.

TOOWOOMBA (QLD) p. 250

Garden City Caravan Park
34A Eiser Street, Toowoomba 4350
Ph (07) 4635 1747 or 1800 333 667, fax (07) 4635 7690
Email gardenc@icr.com.au

This is a very good quality park in a quiet location, about 3 km south of the city centre. The park has good amenities and is a great base to use when exploring the local area. It offers a selection of accommodation and its facilities include a pool and barbecues. **$$$**

❑ Tent sites, powered sites, drive-thru sites, ensuite sites, cabins, on-site vans.

❑ Toilets and showers, laundry, telephone, LP gas refills, camp kitchen, pool, playground, no pets.

❑ Credit cards. Discounts: weekly, Big4.

**Toowoomba Motor Village
Caravan Park**
821 Ruthven Street (New England Highway),
Toowoomba 4350
Ph (07) 4635 8186 or 1800 675 105,
fax (07) 4636 1825

The park is located on the New England
Highway, on the southern approach to
Toowoomba. It is an older park but has good
facilities and amenities and is an ideal base
for exploring Toowoomba and the
surrounding area. $$$

❏ Tent sites, powered sites, fits big
motorhomes, cabins, on-site vans.

❏ Toilets and showers, laundry, sewer dump-
point, telephone, kiosk/shop, LP gas refills,
playground, no pets.

❏ Credit cards. Discounts: seniors, weekly,
Top Tourist.

TOOWOON BAY (NSW) p. 26

Toowoon Bay Tourist Park
Koongara Street, Toowoon Bay 2261
Ph (02) 4332 2834, fax (02) 4334 2575

This is a large council-operated park on the
waterfront. The facilities are good and some
of the attractions in the area include pelican
feeding and fishing. $$

❏ Tent sites, powered sites, fits big
motorhomes, cabins.

❏ Toilets and showers (disabled access),
laundry, telephone, LP gas refills, ice,
playground, pets.

❏ Credit cards, holiday loading. Discounts:
weekly.

TORQUAY (QLD)

See Hervey Bay.

TORQUAY (VIC) p. 139

Bernell Holiday Park
55 Surfcoast Highway, Torquay 3228
Ph (03) 5261 2493, fax (03) 5261 4689

The park is located on the highway about
400 m from the centre of town. This is a very
good quality park and facilities include tennis
courts, putting greens and private bathrooms
with spas. $$$

❏ Tent sites, powered sites, drive-thru sites,
cabins.

❏ Toilets and showers, laundry, telephone,
kiosk/shop, LP gas refills, ice, pool, playground,
no pets.

❏ Credit cards, holiday loading. Discounts:
weekly.

⊗ **Zeally Bay Caravan Park**
Corner Darian Road and The Esplanade,
Torquay 3228
Ph (03) 5261 2400, fax (03) 5261 2696

Great for a family holiday and just across
the road from the beach, this quality
caravan park caters especially for tourists
and families. Facilities include a tennis court
and a cafe, and the park is only 1.2 km north
of the town centre. $$$$

❏ Tent sites, powered sites, drive-thru sites,
cabins.

❏ Toilets and showers (disabled access),
laundry, telephone, kiosk/shop, LP gas refills,
ice, playground, no pets.

❏ Credit cards, holiday loading. Discounts:
weekly.

TORRENS CREEK (QLD) p. 264

⊗ **Exchange Hotel Van and
Camping Park**
Flinders Highway, Torrens Creek 4816
Ph (07) 4741 7342, fax (07) 4741 7342

This park has an unusual appeal and
we like it. It is small, well maintained and
conveniently located next to the Exchange
Hotel. It is good value, being budget priced
but with plenty of green grass, although
there are only a small number of powered
sites. $$

❏ Tent sites, powered sites, fits big
motorhomes, on-site vans.

❏ Toilets and showers, laundry, telephone,
kiosk/shop, ice, pool, pets.

❏ Credit cards.

TOUKLEY (NSW) p. 26

Canton Beach Tourist Park
Oleander Street, Canton Beach 2263
Ph (02) 4396 3252 or 1800 241 342,
fax (02) 4397 1290

On the shores of Tuggerah Lake, this is a
large council-operated park with good
facilities. It is a great spot for a family holiday
on the protected waterway and ideal for
water-sports enthusiasts. $$

❏ Tent sites, powered sites, fits big
motorhomes, cabins.

❏ Toilets and showers, laundry, telephone,
kiosk/shop, LP gas refills, ice, playground,
boat ramp, pets.

❏ Credit cards, holiday loading. Discounts:
3rd night, weekly.

TOWNSVILLE (QLD) pp. 52, 265

Rowes Bay Caravan Park
Heatley Parade, Rowes Bay 4810
Ph (07) 4771 3576, fax (07) 4724 2017

This good-quality owner-operated park is in
a quiet off-highway location and close to the
beach. An ideal park for a longer stay. $$$

❏ Tent sites, powered sites, cabins.

❏ Toilets and showers (disabled access),
laundry, telephone, kiosk/shop, LP gas refills,
ice, pool, playground, no pets.

❏ Credit cards. Discounts: weekly.

Walkabout Palms Caravan Park
Corner Bruce and Flinders highways,
Townsville 4811
Ph (07) 4778 2480 or 1800 633 562,
fax (07) 4778 2640
Email walkab@austarnet.com.au
Website www.walkaboutpalms.com.au

This is a good quality park with very good
facilities. It is easy to find, behind the
roadhouse. There are a couple of dining
opportunities within walking distance. The
park is about 5 km from the city centre. $$$

❏ Tent sites, powered sites, drive-thru sites,
ensuite sites, fits big motorhomes, cabins.

❏ Toilets and showers (disabled access),
laundry, sewer dump-point, telephone,
kiosk/shop, LP gas refills, ice, camp kitchen,
pool, playground, internet terminal, no pets.

❏ Credit cards. Discounts: seniors, weekly,
Big4.

⊗ **Woodlands Holiday Village**
548 Bruce Highway, Deeragun 4818
Ph (07) 4751 6955 or 1800 251 485,
fax (07) 4751 6140

This is an interesting park located about
15 km north of the city alongside the Bruce
Highway. The park has a good range of
facilities and each site has private ensuite
amenities. We find it a convenient place to
stop overnight, and often stay here. $$$$

❏ Tent sites, powered sites, ensuite sites,
fits big motorhomes, cabins.

❏ Toilets and showers, laundry, sewer dump-
point, telephone, kiosk/shop, LP gas refills, ice,
camp kitchen, pool, playground, internet
terminal, no pets.

❏ Credit cards. Discounts: seniors, weekly,
Big4.

TRANGIE (NSW) p. 243

Tandara Caravan Park
55 John Street, Trangie 2623
Ph (02) 6888 7330, fax (02) 6888 7330

This owner-operated park is located in a
quiet off-highway location. Seasonal workers
in the cotton industry often use the park. It
has good amenities, limited facilities and a
well-stocked shop. This is a good, budget-
priced park, and one of its more unusual
features is the renovated old train carriages
which people can stay in. $$

❏ Tent sites, powered sites, drive-thru sites,
fits big motorhomes, cabins.

❏ Toilets and showers, laundry, sewer dump-
point, telephone, kiosk/shop, camp kitchen,
pool, playground, no pets.

❏ No credit cards.

TRARALGON (VIC) p. 4

**Parklane Mobile Home and
Caravan Park**
26–28 Park Lane, Traralgon 3844
Ph (03) 5174 6749, fax (03) 5174 6749
Email hellings@austarnet.com.au

This is a very good quality owner-operated
park with gleaming amenities and excellent
facilities. The park is about 2 km east of
town, not far from the highway and easily
accessible. It is a good base from which to
explore the Latrobe Valley and surrounding
areas. $$$

❏ Tent sites, powered sites, drive-thru sites,
ensuite sites, fits big motorhomes, cabins.

❏ Toilets and showers, laundry, sewer dump-
point, telephone, kiosk/shop, LP gas refills,
camp kitchen, pool, playground, pets.

❏ Credit cards. Discounts: weekly, Top Tourist.

TRIAL BAY GAOL (NSW)

See South West Rocks.

TULLY (QLD) p. 56

Green Way Caravan Park
Murray Street, Tully 4854
Ph (07) 4068 2055, fax (07) 4068 0681
Email mclagan@znet.net.au

This is a good basic park with a range of
facilities. The park is just a brief walk to the
town centre and close to the Bruce Highway.
$$

❏ Tent sites, powered sites, drive-thru sites,
fits big motorhomes, cabins.

❏ Toilets and showers, laundry, sewer dump-
point, telephone, kiosk/shop, LP gas refills, ice,
camp kitchen, pets.

❏ No credit cards. Discounts: weekly.

TULLY HEADS (QLD) p. 56

Googarra Beach Caravan Park
Tully Heads Road, Tully Heads 4854
Ph (07) 4066 9325, fax (07) 4066 9966

The park, close to Tully Heads, has a cafe and
a very well-stocked shop and also sells fuel.
This is a convenient overnight stop or a good
base to explore the area. $$

❏ Tent sites, powered sites, fits big
motorhomes, cabins, on-site vans.

❏ Toilets and showers (disabled access),
laundry, telephone, kiosk/shop, LP gas refills,
ice, camp kitchen, pool, playground, pets.

❏ Credit cards. Discounts: weekly.

TURKEY CREEK (NT) p. 89

Turkey Creek Roadhouse
Great Northern Highway, Turkey Creek 6743
Ph (08) 9168 7882, fax (08) 9168 7925
Email turkeycreekroadhouse@bigpond.com

This park is part of the roadhouse complex,
very close to the Bungle Bungles. The park
has recently expanded across the road and
now includes a visitors centre with an
internet kiosk. Caravan storage is available
for people visiting the Bungle Bungles,
and helicopter flights also operate from
alongside the roadhouse. A convenient
overnight stop. $$$

❏ Tent sites, powered sites, fits big
motorhomes, cabins.

❏ Toilets and showers (disabled access), laundry,
telephone, kiosk/shop, LP gas refills, ice, pool, pets.

❏ Credit cards.

TUROSS HEAD (NSW) p. 12

Tuross Lakeside Tourist Park
211 Hector McWilliam Drive, Tuross Head 2537
Ph (02) 4473 8181, fax (02) 4473 8181

This is a neat owner-operated caravan park
situated on the shores of Tuross Lake. It is
a relaxing holiday park with good, basic
amenities and free barbecues. Fishing, sailing
and windsurfing are all popular recreational
activities. $$$

❏ Tent sites, powered sites, fits big motorhomes, cabins.

❏ Toilets and showers, laundry, telephone, LP gas refills, no pets.

❏ Credit cards, holiday loading. Discounts: weekly.

TWEED HEADS (NSW) p. 34

Boyds Bay Holiday Park
Corner Pacific Highway and Dry Dock Road, Tweed Heads South 2486
Ph (07) 5524 3306, fax (07) 5524 8052

A large riverfront park, with easy access to the highway. This park has new facilities in planning, including a playground. $$$

❏ Tent sites, powered sites, fits big motorhomes, cabins.

❏ Toilets and showers, laundry, sewer dump-point, telephone, kiosk/shop, ice, boat ramp, TV cables, no pets.

❏ Credit cards, holiday loading, Discounts: 3rd night.

Pyramid Caravan Park
145 Kennedy Drive, Tweed Heads 2485
Ph (07) 5536 3666, fax (07) 5536 3761
Email holiday@pyramidpark.com.au
Website www.pyramidpark.com.au

This is a good quality park on the southern end of the Gold Coast. The budget-priced park will suit those chasing the winter warmth and who do not wish to be right beside the beach. The park is well presented and offers a range of accommodation. $$$

❏ Tent sites, powered sites, ensuite sites, fits big motorhomes, cabins.

❏ Toilets and showers, laundry, sewer dump-point, telephone, kiosk/shop, LP gas refills, ice, pool, playground, TV cables, no pets.

❏ Credit cards, holiday loading. Discounts: weekly, FPA.

Tweed Billabong Holiday Park
Holden Street, Tweed Heads South 2486
Ph (07) 5524 2444 or 1800 650 405, fax (07) 5524 9669
Email bookings@tweedbillabong.com.au
Website www.tweedbillabong.com.au

Tweed Billabong Holiday Park is a very good quality, award-winning holiday park boasting its own large and popular tidal billabong. This is a great park for the family as it offers a kids club during school holidays and many other great recreational features including a tennis court, basketball court and a resort-style heated pool. $$$$

❏ Tent sites, powered sites, drive-thru sites, ensuite sites, fits big motorhomes, cabins.

❏ Toilets and showers (disabled access), laundry, sewer dump-point, telephone, LP gas refills, ice, camp kitchen, pool, playground, TV cables, no pets.

❏ Credit cards, holiday loading. Discounts: weekly, Big4.

ULLADULLA (NSW) p. 14

Beach Haven Holiday Resort
Princes Highway, Ulladulla 2539
Ph (02) 4455 2110, fax (02) 4454 0367
Email reception@beachhaven.com.au
Website www.beachhaven.com.au

This park is conveniently located on the Princes Highway, just 2 km south of Ulladulla and only a short walk over the dunes to the beach. It has very good quality facilities including a heated pool, spa, sauna and tennis court. Minimum bookings apply over Christmas, Easter and long weekends. $$$$

❏ Tent sites, powered sites, drive-thru sites, ensuite sites, fits big motorhomes, cabins.

❏ Toilets and showers (disabled access), laundry, sewer dump-point, telephone, LP gas refills, camp kitchen, pool, playground, TV cables, internet terminal, no pets.

❏ Credit cards, holiday loading. Discounts: seniors, weekly, Big4.

Ulladulla Headland Tourist Park
South Street, Ulladulla 2539
Ph (02) 4455 2457 or 1300 733 021, fax (02) 4455 2457
Email aticone@scoastnet.com.au
Website www.holidayhaven.com.au

This park overlooks the sea from a headland vantage point. It is a good quality council-managed park, just 1 km from the centre of town. The park has minimum booking periods over Christmas, Easter and long weekends. $$$

❏ Tent sites, powered sites, drive-thru sites, ensuite sites, fits big motorhomes, cabins.

❏ Toilets and showers (disabled access), laundry, sewer dump-point, telephone, LP gas refills, camp kitchen, pool, playground, no pets.

❏ Credit cards, holiday loading. Discounts: pensioners, seniors, 4th night.

ULVERSTONE (TAS) p. 289

Ulverstone Caravan Park
57 Water Street, Ulverstone 7315
Ph (03) 6425 2624 or 1800 008 028, fax (03) 6425 4654

This is a good quality park with a range of facilities, about 1 km from the town centre. The park is almost adjacent to the surf club on the East Beach. $$

❏ Tent sites, powered sites, fits big motorhomes, cabins, on-site vans.

❏ Toilets and showers (disabled access), laundry, telephone, LP gas refills, camp kitchen, playground, no pets.

❏ Credit cards. Discounts: weekly, Big4.

UMINA (NSW) p. 26

◎ Ocean Beach Holiday Park
Sydney Avenue, Umina 2257
Ph (02) 4341 1522 or 1800 611 522, fax (02) 4341 4855
Email oceanbeachholidaypark@bigpond.com
Website www.oceanbeachholidaypark.com.au

Just 2 km from the centre of Umina and set in a fabulous beachfront position, this quality park is a favourite of ours. There is a wide range of facilities, and kids' activities are

held most weekends and during the school holidays. It is only about an hour from Sydney. Minimum bookings sometimes apply. $$$$

❏ Tent sites, powered sites, fits big motorhomes, cabins.

❏ Toilets and showers (disabled access), laundry, sewer dump-point, telephone, kiosk/shop, LP gas refills, pool, playground, TV cables, internet terminal, no pets.

❏ Credit cards, holiday loading. Discounts: Big4.

UNDARA VOLCANIC NATIONAL PARK (QLD) p. 67

Undara Lava Lodge
via Mount Surprise 4871
Ph (07) 4097 1411 or 1800 990 992, fax (07) 4097 1450
Email res@undara.com.au
Website www.undara.com.au

This camping area is part of the Undara Experience complex, 40 km from Mount Surprise. The final 15 km access is by a well-maintained gravel, all-weather road. The complex has a range of accommodation, a licensed restaurant and a well-stocked gift shop, and the owners run guided tours to the nearby lava tubes. There is only limited power available. $$$

❏ Tent sites, powered sites, drive-thru sites, fits big motorhomes, cabins.

❏ Toilets and showers (disabled access), laundry, telephone, kiosk/shop, LP gas refills, ice, camp kitchen, pool, internet terminal, no pets.

❏ Bookings required, credit cards.

URUNGA (NSW) p. 30

Urunga Heads Holiday Park
2 Morgo Street, Urunga 2455
Ph (02) 6655 6355, fax (02) 6655 3455

On the river estuary at Urunga, this park is an excellent overnight stop. It is far enough off the highway to be quiet and has an excellent outlook. A shopping centre is nearby and the park will be busy in holidays. $$

❏ Tent sites, powered sites, cabins.

❏ Toilets and showers (disabled access), laundry, sewer dump-point, telephone, kiosk/shop, LP gas refills, camp kitchen, playground, no pets.

❏ Credit cards, holiday loading. Discounts: weekly.

VICTORIA RIVER ROADHOUSE (NT) p. 84

Victoria River Roadhouse
Victoria Highway, Victoria River 0852
Ph (08) 8975 0744, fax (08) 8975 0819
Email vicrivernt@bigpond.com

Victoria River Crossing is a key landmark on the Victoria Highway and this park is part of the roadhouse and accommodation complex on the banks of the Victoria River. It has shady sites, good basic amenities and is ideal for an overnight stop or longer. Things to do nearby include bushwalks and boat cruises. $$$

❏ Tent sites, powered sites, drive-thru sites, fits big motorhomes.

❏ Toilets and showers, laundry, telephone, kiosk/shop, LP gas refills, ice, pets.

❏ Credit cards. Discounts: weekly.

WAIKERIE (SA) p. 224

Waikerie Caravan Park
Ramco Road, Waikerie 5330
Ph (08) 8541 2651, fax (08) 8541 2651

A large council park close to the river on the edge of town. The park is in a pretty setting, easily located, with good amenities and a range of facilities including covered barbecues and a camp kitchen. Minimum bookings apply during long weekends and holidays. Good value here. $$

❏ Tent sites, powered sites, drive-thru sites, fits big motorhomes, cabins.

❏ Toilets and showers (disabled access), laundry, telephone, kiosk/shop, camp kitchen, playground, TV cables, pets.

❏ Credit cards. Discounts: seniors, weekly.

WALHALLA (VIC) p. 4

North Gardens Campground
Walhalla 3825

This is a small camping area at the north end of Walhalla. It is one of the few pieces of flat ground in the area and will suit overnight campers, caravans and motorhomes. In summer, however, it can very full, making it difficult to manoeuvre large vehicles. ⑤

❏ Tent sites, fits big motorhomes.

❏ Toilets, pets.

WALLAGARAUGH (VIC) p. 10

Wallagaraugh River Retreat
Wallagaraugh Road, via Genoa 3891
Ph (03) 5158 8211, fax (03) 5158 8211

This park is located along 8 km of good, unsealed road and the turn-off is well signposted on the Princes Highway, to the east of Genoa. The quiet, out-of-the-way park is located on the banks of the Wallagaraugh River. There are good amenities and wide spaces, but just a limited number of sites with generator power. It is a secluded location for fishing, canoeing and general peace and quiet. $$

❏ Tent sites, powered sites, drive-thru sites, fits big motorhomes, cabins.

❏ Toilets and showers, LP gas refills, pets.

❏ No credit cards. Discounts: weekly.

WALPOLE (WA) p. 114

Coalmine Beach Caravan Park
Knoll Drive, Walpole 6398
Ph (08) 9840 1026, fax (08) 9840 1346
Email coalmine@agn.net.au

This is a large tourist park, situated near an inlet, with good amenities and a range of facilities. The Valley of the Giants is nearby, as are some good fishing spots. $$$

❏ Tent sites, powered sites, drive-thru sites, fits big motorhomes, cabins.

❏ Toilets and showers (disabled access), laundry, telephone, kiosk/shop, LP gas refills, ice, camp kitchen, playground, boat ramp, internet terminal, no pets.

❏ Credit cards. Discounts: weekly, Top Tourist.

Rest Point Holiday Village
Rest Point Road, Walpole 6398
Ph (08) 9840 1032, fax (08) 9840 1302
Email restpoint@wn.com.au

This is an ideal holiday park in an informal setting, located on the water's edge just 5 km from the town. The park has good quality amenities and facilities, at a reasonable price. There is a minimum booking during holiday periods. $$$

❏ Tent sites, powered sites, fits big motorhomes, cabins.

❏ Toilets and showers, laundry, telephone, kiosk/shop, LP gas refills, ice, boat ramp, pets.

❏ Credit cards. Discounts: weekly.

WANGI FALLS (NT)

See Litchfield National Park.

WARMUN (NT)

See Turkey Creek.

WARRAGUL (VIC) p. 4

Warragul Gardens Caravan Park
44 Burke Street, Warragul 3820
Ph (03) 5623 2707, fax (03) 5622 2229
Email enquiries@warragulcaravanpark.com.au
Website www.warragulcaravanpark.com.au

This is a neat and tidy, owner-operated park. Spacious grassed sites, good facilities and good amenities make this an enjoyable place to stay. Pets are allowed, though not during the easter holidays. We have stopped overnight here on several occasions. $$$

❏ Tent sites, powered sites, drive-thru sites, fits big motorhomes, cabins.

❏ Toilets and showers (disabled access), laundry, telephone, LP gas refills, camp kitchen, pool, playground, pets.

❏ Credit cards. Discounts: weekly.

WARRNAMBOOL (VIC) p. 136

Fig Tree Holiday Village
33 Lava Street, Warrnambool 3280
Ph (03) 5561 1233 or 1800 611 233,
fax (03) 5561 3068
Email reservations@figtreepark.com
Website www.figtreepark.com

Centrally located about 600 m from the centre of town, this is a very good quality and good value park in a quiet off-highway position. The park has a heated indoor pool, covered barbecues and a tennis court. We like it. $$$

❏ Tent sites, powered sites, drive-thru sites, ensuite sites, fits big motorhomes, cabins.

❏ Toilets and showers, laundry, telephone, kiosk/shop, camp kitchen, pool, playground, no pets.

❏ Credit cards, holiday loading. Discounts: weekly, Top Tourist.

⊘ **Ocean Beach Holiday Village**
Pertobe Road, Warrnambool 3280
Ph (03) 5561 4222 or 1800 808 130,
fax (03) 5562 0392
Email oceanbeach@ansonic.com.au
Website www.oceanbeachvillage.com.au

Across the road from the beach, this well-kept, owner-operated park is ideal for a holiday or just a few days away. With its excellent facilities, including a popular undercover camp kitchen and a new movie room, the park can be busy; it is a good idea to book in holiday periods. (Minimum bookings apply during the Christmas and Easter holidays.) We always enjoy staying here. $$$

❏ Tent sites, powered sites, drive-thru sites, ensuite sites, cabins.

❏ Toilets and showers (disabled access), laundry, telephone, kiosk/shop, camp kitchen, pool, playground, internet terminal, no pets.

❏ Credit cards, holiday loading. Discounts: Big4.

Warrnambool Surfside Holiday Park
Pertobe Road, Warrnambool 3280
Ph (03) 5561 2611, fax (03) 5562 7109
Email alewis@warrnambool.vic.gov.au

This is a very large, good quality council-owned park right on the beachfront. Great for a family beachside holiday, the park has good facilities including a seasonal kiosk and is just 1 km from the city centre. The park has an eastern section that only operates during holiday periods. Minimum bookings apply during Christmas and January, and the park permits pets only outside holiday periods. $$$

❏ Tent sites, powered sites, fits big motorhomes, cabins.

❏ Toilets and showers (disabled access), laundry, telephone, kiosk/shop, ice, playground, pets.

❏ Credit cards, holiday loading. Discounts: pensioners, seniors.

WATARRKA NATIONAL PARK (NT)

See Kings Canyon.

WAUCHOPE (NSW) p. 30

Broadaxe Caravan Park
230 High Street (Oxley Highway),
Wauchope 2446
Phone (02) 6585 1355 or 1800 501 879,
fax (02) 6585 3776

Located adjacent to the Timbertown theme park, this is a convenient park not too far off the Pacific Highway. Facilities include a half-court tennis court and a swimming pool. $$

❏ Tent sites, powered sites, drive-thru sites, cabins.

❏ Toilets and showers, laundry, sewer dump-point, telephone, kiosk/shop, LP gas refills, camp kitchen, pool, TV cables, no pets.

❏ Credit cards. Discounts: pensioners, seniors, weekly.

WAYATINAH (TAS) p. 294

Wayatinah Camping Ground and Caravan Park
Wayatinah 7140
Ph (03) 6289 3317, fax (03) 6289 3317
Email peterwayatinah@bigpond.com

This is a basic park but popular with fishing enthusiasts, who flock to the region. There are many permanent sites and the park is in a bush setting with lake frontage. Tourists visit mainly in the warmer months. $

❏ Tent sites, powered sites, drive-thru sites, fits big motorhomes.

❏ Toilets and showers, laundry, sewer dump-point, pool, pets.

❏ No credit cards. Discounts: weekly.

WAYCHINICUP NATIONAL PARK (WA)

See Cheyne Beach.

WELLINGTON (NSW) p. 240

⊘ **Caves Caravan Park**
Caves Road, Wellington 2820
Ph (02) 6845 2970, fax (02) 6845 3188

Relax and let a few days slip by at this spacious park, located 6 km south of the town centre alongside the Wellington Caves, a popular tourist attraction. It is a quality park and makes an ideal stopover. $$

❏ Tent sites, powered sites, drive-thru sites, fits big motorhomes, cabins.

❏ Toilets and showers, laundry, telephone, kiosk/shop, LP gas refills, ice, pool, playground, pets.

❏ Credit cards. Discounts: weekly.

Wellington Riverside Caravan Park
Federal Street, Wellington 2820
Ph (02) 6845 1370, fax (02) 6845 1370

This is a well-maintained park on the banks of the Macquarie River, close to the highway and just a short walk to the centre of town. The park has good basic facilities at a budget price. $$

❏ Tent sites, powered sites, drive-thru sites, fits big motorhomes, cabins, on-site vans.

❏ Toilets and showers, laundry, telephone, kiosk/shop, LP gas refills, pets.

❏ Credit cards. Discounts: weekly.

WEST WYALONG (NSW) p. 156

Ace Caravan Park
Corner Newell and Mid Western highways,
West Wyalong 2671
Ph (02) 6972 3061, fax (02) 6972 4425
Email plymberg@westserv.net.au

An owner-operated park with a good choice of accommodation. The park is just 500 m from the town centre and easily accessed from the major highways. Facilities include a pool and barbecues. $$

❏ Tent sites, powered sites, drive-thru sites, ensuite sites, fits big motorhomes, cabins, on-site vans.

❏ Toilets and showers, laundry, sewer dump-point, telephone, kiosk/shop, LP gas refills, ice, camp kitchen, pool, TV cables, pets.

❏ Credit cards. Discounts: FPA.

WESTERN FLORA CARAVAN PARK (WA)

See Eneabba.

WHITE BEACH (TAS) p. 300

White Beach Caravan and Cabin Park
White Beach Road, Nubeena 7184
Ph (03) 6250 2142, fax (03) 6250 2575
Email wbcp@southcom.com.au

This is a high-quality park with good facilities, close to the beach. The area is popular for surfing, fishing and bushwalking, and the park is a good base to explore the region. $$

❏ Tent sites, powered sites, drive-thru sites, fits big motorhomes, cabins, on-site vans.

❏ Toilets and showers, laundry, sewer dump-point, telephone, kiosk/shop, LP gas refills, ice, camp kitchen, playground, TV cables, no pets.

❏ Credit cards, holiday loading. Discounts: weekly.

WINDANG (NSW)

See Wollongong.

WINGS FARM (TAS)

See Gunns Plains.

WINTON (QLD) p. 174

Matilda Country Tourist Park
43 Chirnside Street, Winton 4735
Ph (07) 4657 1607 or 1800 001 383,
fax (07) 4657 1607
Email tmatpark@tpg.com.au

Winton is a popular tourist town and visitor numbers peak during the cooler winter months. This tourist park has good amenities, basic facilities and is an ideal base from which to explore the area. The park is about 1 km from the town centre, conveniently located on the highway. $$$

❏ Tent sites, powered sites, drive-thru sites, fits big motorhomes, cabins.

❏ Toilets and showers, laundry, sewer dump-point, telephone, kiosk/shop, LP gas refills, ice, pool, pets.

❏ Credit cards. Discounts: Top Tourist.

WODONGA (VIC) p. 216

See also Albury.

Borderland Caravan Park
13 McKoy Street, Wodonga 3690
Ph (02) 6024 3906, fax (02) 6056 5501
Email borderland@primus.com.au

The park is on the western edge of town, conveniently located in a quiet off-the-highway location. The park has good facilities and is our choice of parks in the town area. $$$

❏ Tent sites, powered sites, drive-thru sites, ensuite sites, fits big motorhomes, cabins, on-site vans.

❏ Toilets and showers, laundry, sewer dump-point, telephone, kiosk/shop, LP gas refills, camp kitchen, pool, playground, no pets.

❏ Credit cards. Discounts: Big4.

WOLLONGONG (NSW) p. 16

Bulli Beach Tourist Park
1 Farrel Road, Bulli 2516
Ph (02) 4285 5677, fax (02) 4285 5062
Email bullitp@wollongong.nsw.gov.au

This popular, council-owned holiday park adjoins a patrolled beach with beach pools. In a quiet area, this park will appeal to families or those just spending a few peaceful days out of the holiday season. $$$

❏ Tent sites, powered sites, drive-thru sites, ensuite sites, fits big motorhomes, cabins.

❏ Toilets and showers (disabled access), laundry, sewer dump-point, telephone, kiosk/shop, ice, camp kitchen, pool, playground, no pets.

❏ Credit cards, holiday loading. Discounts: pensioners, seniors, weekly.

Corrimal Beach Tourist Park
Lake Parade, Corrimal 2518
Ph (02) 4285 5688, fax (02) 4285 5079
Email corrimaltp@wollongong.nsw.gov.au

This is a council-owned beachside park on the north side of Wollongong. The park has good amenities and is a popular holiday destination. $$$

❏ Tent sites, powered sites, drive-thru sites, ensuite sites, fits big motorhomes, cabins.

❏ Toilets and showers (disabled access), laundry, sewer dump-point, telephone, kiosk/shop, ice, camp kitchen, playground, no pets.

❏ Credit cards, holiday loading. Discounts: seniors, weekly.

Shellharbour Beachside Tourist Park
John Street, Shellharbour 2529
Ph (02) 4295 1123, fax (02) 4297 1799
Email touristpark@ozemail.com.au

This caravan park is in a quiet location on the beachfront, adjoining the beachside baths. The shops, including some eateries, are just a short stroll away. This is a popular coastal holiday region. $$$

❏ Tent sites, powered sites, drive-thru sites, fits big motorhomes, cabins.

❏ Toilets and showers (disabled access), laundry, sewer dump-point, kiosk/shop, pool, playground, pets.

❏ Credit cards, holiday loading. Discounts: weekly.

Windang Beach Tourist Park
Fern Street, Windang 2528
Ph (02) 4297 3166, fax (02) 4296 9589
Email windangtp@wollongong.nsw.gov.au

This is a council-owned, popular beachside holiday park located on the south side of Wollongong, next to Lake Illawarra. Facilities here include a new pool and playground. $$$

❏ Tent sites, powered sites, drive-thru sites, fits big motorhomes, cabins.

❏ Toilets and showers (disabled access), laundry, sewer dump-point, telephone, ice, pool, playground, boat ramp, no pets.

❏ Credit cards, holiday loading. Discounts: seniors, weekly.

WONGA (QLD) p. 61

Pinnacle Village Holiday Park
Vixies Road, Wonga Beach via Mossman 4873
Ph (07) 4098 7566 or 1800 222 728, fax (07) 4098 7813
Email pinnvill@bigpond.com

This absolute beachfront park is 22 km north of Mossman. There are plenty of shady trees and a great expanse of green lawn. A good base for exploring the local region. $$$

❏ Tent sites, powered sites, drive-thru sites, fits big motorhomes, cabins.

❏ Toilets and showers, laundry, sewer dump-point, telephone, kiosk/shop, LP gas refills, ice, camp kitchen, pool, playground, boat ramp, internet terminal, no pets.

❏ Credit cards. Discounts: weekly, Top Tourist.

WOODGATE (QLD) p. 46

Barkala Caravan Park
88 The Esplanade, Woodgate 4660
Ph (07) 4126 8802, fax (07) 4126 8699
Email barkala@isis01.com.au

This is a convenient park in the centre of the small town and just across the road from a wonderful beach. The park has good basic facilities. Minimum bookings are required during holiday periods. $$

❏ Tent sites, powered sites, fits big motorhomes, cabins, on-site vans.

❏ Toilets and showers (disabled access), laundry, sewer dump-point, telephone, kiosk/shop, LP gas refills, ice, camp kitchen, pets.

❏ Credit cards, holiday loading. Discounts: weekly.

WOOLGOOLGA (NSW) p. 32

Lakeside Caravan Park
Lake Road, Woolgoolga 2456
Ph (02) 6654 1210, fax (02) 6654 1210

This beachside park is in a quiet location about 1 km from the town centre. It is a good basic park with lake and beach access and has recently been taken over by council, who hope to modernise the facilities. $$

❏ Tent sites, powered sites, fits big motorhomes, cabins, on-site vans.

❏ Toilets and showers, laundry, telephone, ice, playground, boat ramp, no pets.

❏ Credit cards, holiday loading. Discounts: weekly.

Woolgoolga Beach Caravan Park
Beach Street, Woolgoolga 2456
Ph (02) 6654 1373, fax (02) 6654 1373

This popular beachfront park is 100 m from the centre of town, next to the surf club and looking out to sea. In this case position is everything. There are good amenities but no unpowered sites. A reserve with a playground is right next door, and this park is busy for most of the year. $$$

❏ Powered sites, cabins.

❏ Toilets and showers, laundry, telephone, playground, TV cables, no pets.

❏ Bookings required, credit cards, holiday loading. Discounts: weekly.

WYCLIFFE WELL ROADHOUSE (NT) p. 194

Wycliffe Well Holiday Park
Stuart Highway, Wycliffe Well 0862
Ph (08) 8964 1966 or 1800 222 195, fax (08) 8964 1961
Email info@wycliffe.com.au
Website www.wycliffe.com.au

This park is 130 km south of Tennant Creek and would be a good choice if you plan to stop north of Alice Springs. Nearby activities include fishing on the lake or birdwatching. $$$

❏ Tent sites, powered sites, drive-thru sites, fits big motorhomes, cabins, on-site vans.

❏ Toilets and showers (disabled access), laundry, telephone, kiosk/shop, LP gas refills, ice, camp kitchen, pool, playground, internet terminal, no pets.

❏ Credit cards. Discounts: Big4.

WYE RIVER (VIC) p. 139

Wye River Valley Tourist Park
Great Ocean Road, Wye River 3221
Ph (03) 5289 0241, fax (03) 5289 0200
Email info@wyerivervalleypark.com.au
Website www.wyerivervalleypark.com.au

This is a pleasant owner-operated park with good facilities, located in a popular coastal resort strip. The park has a range of accommodation and good facilities, and minimum booking periods apply during Christmas and Easter holiday periods. $$$$

❏ Tent sites, powered sites, drive-thru sites, fits big motorhomes, cabins.

❏ Toilets and showers, laundry, sewer dump-point, telephone, kiosk/shop, LP gas refills, camp kitchen, playground, no pets.

❏ Credit cards, holiday loading. Discounts: Big4.

WYNYARD (TAS) p. 288

Beach Retreat Tourist Park
30B Old Bass Highway, Wynyard 7325
Ph (03) 6442 1998

Located at the mouth of the Inglis River and on the beachfront, this park is within walking distance of the town centre. The park has good basic amenities and is ideal for an overnight stay or a longer holiday. $$

❏ Tent sites, powered sites, fits big motorhomes, cabins, on-site vans.

❏ Toilets and showers, laundry, telephone, kiosk/shop, camp kitchen, playground, pets.

❏ Credit cards. Discounts: weekly.

YALLINGUP (WA) p. 112

Canal Rocks Beach Resort
Smiths Beach Road, Yallingup 6282
Ph (08) 9755 2116, fax (08) 9754 1663
Email bookings@canalrocks.com.au
Website www.canalrocks.com.au

The Yallingup area is an extremely popular beach-holiday spot. The park is just a stroll from the beach and close to the Leeuwin–Naturaliste National Park. Facilities include a cafe and bottle shop, and bookings are essential during holiday periods. $$$

❏ Tent sites, powered sites, cabins, on-site vans.

❏ Toilets and showers, laundry, telephone, kiosk/shop, LP gas refills, ice, playground, no pets.

❏ Credit cards, holiday loading. Discounts: seniors, weekly.

Yallingup Beach Holiday Park
Valley Road, Yallingup 6282
Ph (08) 9755 2164 or 1800 220 002, fax (08) 9755 2164
Email yalbeach@wn.com.au
Website www.yallingupbeach.com.au

This park is in the centre of Yallingup and a short walk to everything. The popular surfing beach is just metres away and the resort-style holiday centre is just a brief stroll from the gate. The park is very well maintained and has particularly good holiday park facilities. $$$

❏ Tent sites, powered sites, drive-thru sites, cabins, on-site vans.

❏ Toilets and showers (disabled access), laundry, telephone, kiosk/shop, LP gas refills, ice, playground, no pets.

❏ Bookings required, credit cards, holiday loading. Discounts: Top Tourist.

YAMBA (NSW) p. 32

See also Palmers Island.

✪ Blue Dolphin Holiday Resort
Yamba Road, Yamba 2464
Ph (02) 6646 2194, fax (02) 6646 2274
Email enquiry@bluedolphin.com.au
Website www.bluedolphin.com.au

This riverfront, award-winning park is on the Clarence River estuary. It is an excellent park, with everything you would expect of a five-star establishment, including a cafe. Yamba is a popular holiday town and minimum bookings apply during holiday periods. $$$

❏ Tent sites, powered sites, drive-thru sites, ensuite sites, fits big motorhomes, cabins.

❏ Toilets and showers (disabled access), laundry, sewer dump-point, telephone, kiosk/shop, LP gas refills, ice, camp kitchen, pool, playground, boat ramp, internet terminal, no pets.

❏ Credit cards, holiday loading. Discounts: pensioners, weekly.

East's Calypso Holiday Park
Harbour Street, Yamba 2464
Ph (02) 6646 2468 or 1800 462 468,
fax (02) 6646 1978
Email eastscalypsohp@bigpond.com
Website www.eastholidayparks.com.au

This older-style park has a great position on the waterfront. It is a short stroll to the centre of town and just a brief walk to the beach. $$$

❏ Tent sites, powered sites, drive-thru sites, cabins.

❏ Toilets and showers (disabled access), laundry, sewer dump-point, telephone, ice, pool, playground, internet terminal, no pets.

❏ Credit cards, holiday loading. Discounts: weekly, Big4.

Yamba Waters Caravan Park
Golding Street, Yamba 2464
Ph (02) 6646 2930, fax (02) 6646 2905
Email enquiry@yambawaters.com.au
Website www.yambawaters.com.au

This is a quality park about 2.5 km from the centre of this popular tourist destination. Enjoy the swimming pools or the large saltwater lagoon. $$$

❏ Tent sites, powered sites, drive-thru sites, ensuite sites, fits big motorhomes, cabins.

❏ Toilets and showers (disabled access), laundry, sewer dump-point, telephone, kiosk/shop, LP gas refills, ice, camp kitchen, pool, playground, pets.

❏ Credit cards, holiday loading. Discounts: weekly, Top Tourist.

YARRAWONGA (VIC) p. 218

See also Mulwala.

Cool Waters Caratel
Corner Hume and Hunt Streets, Yarrawonga 3730
Ph (03) 5744 3768, fax (03) 5744 2816
Email hilton@ozemail.com.au

This small, owner-operated, all ensuite-site park, is immediately opposite the Lake Mulwala foreshore and just a short walk from the main shopping strip, hotels and restaurant. Minimum bookings apply during Christmas, January and Easter holiday periods. $$$

❏ Ensuite sites, drive-thru sites, cabins.

❏ Laundry, pool, playground, boat ramp, no pets.

❏ Credit cards, holiday loading. Discounts: weekly.

Yarrawonga Caravan Park
Piper Street Extension, Yarrawonga 3730
Ph (03) 5744 3420, fax (03) 5744 2938
Email ycp@cnl.com.au

This is a very large, popular council-owned park on the banks of the Murray River, just below the Yarrawonga Weir. The park is situated around some of the towns sporting facilities, including the public swimming pool, and experiences major influxes during the holiday periods when bookings are essential. $$

❏ Tent sites, powered sites, drive-thru sites, fits big motorhomes, cabins.

❏ Toilets and showers (disabled access), laundry, sewer dump-point, telephone, pool, playground, boat ramp, no pets.

❏ Credit cards, holiday loading. Discounts: weekly.

YEPPOON (QLD) p. 50

Beachside Caravan Park
Farnborough Road, Yeppoon 4703
Ph (07) 4939 3738, fax (07) 4939 3738

This is a popular beachside park with good basic facilities, located on the shores of Keppel Bay. It is necessary to book a site in holiday periods. $$

❏ Tent sites, powered sites, fits big motorhomes.

❏ Toilets and showers, laundry, telephone, kiosk/shop, ice, no pets.

❏ Bookings required, credit cards. Discounts: weekly.

YORK (WA) p. 272

Mount Bakewell Caravan Park
Eighth Road, York 6302
Ph (08) 9641 1421, fax (08) 9641 1129

The park is on the outskirts of the historic town of York. It has the basics and is suitable for a night or two for those planning a visit to the historic town. A TV room with a microwave and fridge is on offer. $$$

❏ Tent sites, powered sites, drive-thru sites, fits big motorhomes, on-site vans.

❏ Toilets and showers, laundry, telephone, no pets.

❏ No credit cards. Discounts: weekly.

YULARA (NT) p. 186

Ayers Rock Campground
Yulara Drive, Yulara 0872
Ph (08) 8957 7001 or 1300 139 889,
fax (08) 8957 7004
Email camp.ground@ayersrockresort.com.au
Website www.voyages.com.au

This is a large campground with a beautiful lawn area for campers and a separate caravan section. The park has clean, modern amenities, a great camp kitchen and a pool, and is within walking distance of most of Yulara's resort-style facilities. Dogs are the only pets allowed. $$$$

❏ Tent sites, powered sites, fits big motorhomes, cabins.

❏ Toilets and showers (disabled access), laundry, telephone, kiosk/shop, LP gas refills, ice, camp kitchen, pool, playground, internet terminal, pets.

❏ Credit cards. Discounts: weekly.

ZEEHAN (TAS) p. 292

Treasure Island West Coast Caravan Park
Hurst Street, Zeehan 7469
Ph (03) 6471 6633, fax (03) 6471 6615

This park is in a lovely rural setting with lots of trees. Facilities here include mini-golf and a camp kitchen. $$

❏ Tent sites, powered sites, drive-thru sites, fits big motorhomes, cabins, on-site vans.

❏ Toilets and showers, laundry, telephone, LP gas refills, camp kitchen, playground, pets.

❏ Credit cards, holiday loading.

INDEX

This index contains all towns and road-houses that appear in the touring and road atlas sections of this book. Also included are museums, national parks, markets, reserves and other places of interest. For those with more specialised interests, there are separate categories listed alphabetically including Aboriginal heritage, caves, fossicking, historic sites and towns, natural wonders, railways, tours, walks, waterfalls, wildflowers, wildlife and wine regions.

Place names are followed by one of two kinds of page references, or both. One reference is to the text page (or pages) it appears on in the book. The other is to the page it appears on in the road atlas, with the appropriate grid reference. For example:

Fraser Island Qld 47, 339 L6
Fraser Island: place name
Qld: state
47: page number
339 L6: road atlas page number and grid reference

The alphabetical order followed in the index is that of 'word by word', where all entries under one word are grouped together. Where a place name consists of more than one word, the order is governed by the first and then the second word. For example:

Green Hills
Green Island

Greenbank
Greenmount

Place names beginning with abbreviations like St (Saint) are listed in the order they would be if spelt out. For example:

Safety Bay
St Albans
St Andrews

State and Territory abbreviations are standard, with the lesser-known abbreviation of JBT standing for Jervis Bay Territory, east of the Australian Capital Territory.

ACKNOWLEDGEMENTS

Authors' acknowledgements

We would like to thank all those people who have helped with the preparation of *Explore Australia by Caravan* and sincerely thank the staff at Explore Australia Publishing for their great support with this project. We have been energised by the great working relationship, the expertise, the understanding, and the development of rewarding friendships.

We have had a long and valuable relationship with Yokohama Tyres (Australia) Pty Ltd and we thank them for their ongoing support. Yokohama Tyres have played a crucial part in our life on the road for more than a decade and their continued reliability is extremely comforting.

And thank you to all those wonderful people in tourism who have knowingly or unknowingly helped with this book and to all those great people from tourist attractions and caravan parks who have given so generously of their time to talk with us.

Publisher's acknowledgements

Managing editor
Alexandra Payne

Design
Cover design
John Canty, and Peter Dyson, P.A.G.E. Pty Ltd

Internal design
Tony Palmer

Layout, additional design and pagination
Peter Dyson, P.A.G.E. Pty Ltd

Cartography
Bruce McGurty, Paul de Leur, Colin Critchell

Map checking and research
Mike Archer, Paul de Leur, Bruce McGurty, Simon Hrabe

Editors
Clare Coney, Liz McCormack, Nan McNab, Ingrid Ohlsson, Helen Duffy, Astrid Browne, Rachel Pitts, Saskia Adams, Susan McLeish, Heidi Marfurt

Photographic research
Simon James, Heidi Marfurt

Index
Fay Donlevy

Production
Sue Van Velsen, Astrid Browne

Aboriginal lands and parks and reserves
The maps in this book were produced with data from the following organisations:
New South Wales National Parks and Wildlife Service
Australian Capital Territory Land Information Centre
National Parks and Wildlife South Australia, Department of Environment and Heritage
Primary Industries and Resources South Australia
Department of Conservation and Land Management Western Australia
Aboriginal Affairs Department Western Australia
Parks and Wildlife Commission Northern Territory, Strategic Planning and Development Unit
Northern Territory Department of Lands, Planning and Environment (also supplied data for Alice Springs–Darwin railway)
Environmental Protection Agency (QLD)
Queensland Department of Natural Resources
Forestry Tasmania

Explore Australia Publishing indemnifies the above government authorities, which remain custodians and retain copyright of their data used in this publication. Data on Aboriginal lands and parks and reserves is current to 2000.

Assistance with cartographic research
Roads and Traffic Authority (NSW)
VicRoads
Transport SA
Main Roads Western Australia
Department of Transport and Infrastructure (NT)
Department of Main Roads (Qld)
Department of Infrastructure, Energy and Resources (Tas.)
Bureau of Meteorology
Australian Bureau of Statistics

Photo credits
Note: Where more than one photo appears on a page, the order they are credited in follows a clockwise direction from the top.

Abbreviations
AUS Auscape International
BB Bill Belson
BD Brett Dennis
DH Dennis Harding
DS Dennis Sarson
DSK Don Skirrow
EA Explore Australia Publishing
GA George Apostolidis
GL Gary Lewis
GM Geoff Murray
GMH Graeme & Margaret Herald
JEB J. P. & E. S. Baker
JF Jean-Paul Ferrero
JJT John and Jan Tait
JK John Krutop
JL Jiri Lochman
JLR Jean-Marc La Roque
JM John Meier
KS Ken Stepnell
LCH Lochman Transparencies
LN Lance Nelson
ML Marie Lochman
NR Nick Rains
PL Peter Lik
SATC South Australian Tourism Commission
SP Stock Photos
SS Steve Strike
TNSW Tourism New South Wales
TQ Tourism Queensland
TT Tourism Tasmania

Chapter openings
Ch. 1 Driving past Rex's Lookout between Cairns and Port Douglas/TQ; Ch. 2 Driving near the Hamersley Range, Western Australia/SP (DSK); Ch. 3 Field at Capella, west of Rockhampton/TQ; Ch. 4 The Nut at Stanley/AUS (Geoffrey Lea); Ch. 5 Driving through the west MacDonnell Ranges/EA (DSK).

City features
Sydney pp. 18–19 SP (David Scaletti), p. 20 SP (LN); Brisbane TQ; Cairns TQ; Darwin AUS (Tim Acker); Perth EA (NR); Adelaide EA (JEB); Melbourne pp. 142–3 & 144 SP (Roger du Buisson); Alice Springs SS; Canberra JEB; Hobart Geoff Murray.

Pages
xi Aaron Tait; xii (a) Aaron Tait, (b) EA (JEB); xiii Holiday Hub Beach Resort; xiv (a) One Mile Beach Holiday Park, (b) Ocean Beach Holiday Park; xv (a) EA (JEB), (b) Kings Creek Station, (c) McDonnell Range Holiday Park; xvii TQ; xviii Cradle Mountain Tourist Park; xix (a) Hall Gap Caravan and Tourist Park, (b) Boathaven Holiday Park; xx Denham Seaside Tourist Village; xxi (a) Esperance Seafront Caravan Park, (b) Perth International Tourist Park; 2 AG; 3 (EA) JJT; 4 EA (JEB); 5 Brian Tucker; 6 AUS (JLR); 7 EA (KS); 8 AUS (JLR); 9 AUS (John Shaw); 11 (a) TNSW, (b) SP (Roy Bisson); 12 AUS (JF); 13 (JJT); 14 AUS (Graham Robertson); 15 EA (NR); 16 JEB; 17 EA (NR); 24 EA (JEB); 25 TQ; 26 TNSW; 27 EA (JJT); 29 (a) JEB, (b) JEB; 30 & 31 EA (JJT); 32 AUS (Jaime Plaza Van Roon); 33 Thursday Plantation; 34 AUS (JF); 35 AG; 36 EA (NR); 37 (a) TQ, (b) TQ (PL); 42 (a) TQ, (b) TQ, (main) AG; 44 JEB; 45 TQ; 47 (a) TQ (PL), (b) TQ; 48 TQ (PL); 49 TQ (Ian Quatermass); 50 TQ (Doug Steley); 51 TQ (PL); 52 TQ; 53 TQ; 54 Hinchinbrook Visitor Centre; 55, 56 & 57 TQ (PL); 62 EA (GL); 63 JM; 64 TQ; 65 & 66 EA (JJT); 67 TQ; 68 (a) Bureau of Meteorology (Russel White), (b) SS; 70 (a) & (b) SS; 72 (a) AUS (S. Wilby & C. Ciantar), (b) SS; 74 EA (NR); 75 SS; 80 (a) & (b) SS; 82 LCH (JL); 83 EA (GMH); 84 (a) & (b) EA (NR); 85 (a) Bernice Carter, (b) EA (DSK); 88 (a) EA (JJT), (b) EA (GMH); 90 (a) EA (JJT), (b) LCH (DS), (c) LCH (Wade Hughes); 92 EA (KS); 93 LCH (DS); 94 LCH (Jay Sarson); 95 (a) LCH (JL), (b) LCH (ML); 96 & 97 LCH (JL); 98 LCH (BB); 99 EA (NR); 100 EA (DSK); 101 (EA) GMH); 102 EA (JEB); 103 LCH (ML); 108 EA (JJT); 109 LCH (BB); 110 LCH (DS); 111 EA (JJT); 112 LCH (BD); 113 LCH (JL); 114 LCH (DS); 115 EA (JJT); 116 LCH (DS); 117 EA (JJT); 118 (a) LCH (Peter Marsack), (b) LCH (ML), (c) LCH (Raoul Slater); 119 EA (JJT); 120 (a) NR, (b) LCH (BD); 121 EA (JJT); 122 (a) Wadlata Outback Centre, (b) EA (Chris Groenhout); 123 LCH (JL); 124 (a) & (b) SATC; 125 LCH (ML); 130 KS; 131 JM; 132 SATC; 133 EA (NR); 134 KS; 135 & 136 EA (JJT); 137 EA (JEB); 138 JM; 139 EA (JJT); 140 (a) EA (GL), (b) EA (JJT); 150 EA (JJT); 151 EA (JEB); 152 SP (David Simmonds); 153 EA (JJT); 154 EA (Michael Archer); 155 National Library of Australia; 156 David Malin; 157 EA (JJT); 158 David Malin; 159 AUS (Jaime Plaza Van Roon; 160 & 161 TQ; 162 AUS (Ian Beattie); 163 TQ; 165 (a) SP (LN), (b) TQ; 166 NSW Department of Mineral Resources; 167 EA (JJT); 168 (a) The Fred Hollows Foundation (Michael Amendolia), (b) NR; 169 SP (LN); 170 TQ; 171, 172 & 173 EA (JJT); 174 TQ (John Elliot); 175 TQ; 176 (a) NR, (b) TQ; 177 TQ; 178 EA (JJT); 179 TQ; 180 (a) EA (NR), (b) EA (JEB); 182 (a) EA (JJT), (b) SATC; 183 & 184 EA (KS); 185 AUS (JLR); 186 & 187 JM; 188 SS; 189 AUS (JLR); 194 SS; 195 AUS (Daniel Zupanc); 196 & 197 SS; 199 (a) LCH (JL), (b) LCH (ML); 200 EA JJT; 201 LCH (DS); 202 (a) EA (JJT), (b) EA (KS); 203 EA (JJT); 204 EA (DSK); 205 LCH (John Kleczkowski); 208 EA (JEB); 209 JM; 210 EA (JJT); 211 EA (JEB); 216 (a) EA (JJT), (b) Phillip Weigall; 218 EA (JEB); 219 LCH (Len Stewart); 220 JM; 221 Tourism Victoria; 222 EA, (b) AUS (Nicholas Birks); 224 (a) JJT, (b) SATC; 226 LCH (JL); 227 EA (GL); 228 (a) EA (KS), (b) EA (JEB); 230 (a) AUS (JLR), (b) EA (JJT); 232 EA (GL); 233 LCH (JL); 234 Bathurst Visitor Information Centre; 235 AUS (JLR); 236 JM; 237 TNSW; 238 JM; 239 (a) JJT, (b) Sport The Library (Robb Cox); 240 (both) & 241 JJT; 242 AUS (Andrew Henley); EA (JK); 244 TNSW; 245 (AUS) Norman Plant; 246 & 247 SATC; 248 EA (JK); 249 TQ; 250 (both) EA (NR); 252 NR; 253 (a) EA, (b) Jimbour House; 254 (both) AUS (Wayne Lawler); 255 EA (JJT); 256 EA (JK); 256–7 TQ; 258 (a) TQ, (b) EA, (c) TQ; 260 EA; 261 TQ; 262 JM; 262–3 TQ; 264 & 265 EA (JJT); 266 TQ; 266–7 EA (JJT); 268 EA; 269 EA (NR); 270 (a) LCH (DS), (b) NR; 272 (a) LCH (BD), (b) EA (JJT); 276 AUS (DH); 277 TT (Ray Joyce); 278 (a) AUS (John Fairhall), (b) AUS (David Parer & Elizabeth Parer-Cook); 280 & 281 TT (Ray Joyce); 286 & 288 (a) TT (GA), 288 (b) TT (DH); 290 TT (GM); 291 TT (JEB); 292 TT (DH); 293 TT; 294 GM; 295 TT (GA); 296 TT (John de la Roche); 297 & 298 TT; 299 TT (GA); 301 (a) GM, (b) SP (Paul Steel); 302 (a) TT (GM), (b) Nick Morey; 306 (all) Jayco; 307 (1 & 4) Heaslip Camper Trailers, (2) Trakka, (3) Swagman Motorhomes; 308 Jayco; 310 EA (NR); 312 EA (DSK); 313 EA (NR); 315 SP (Bill Bachman); 317 EA (JJT); 321 KS; 324 EA (NR); 325 EA (DSK); 329 EA (NR); 330 Maui; 331 JM; 333 TQ.

The publisher would also like to acknowledge Australia Post for permission to reproduce the stamp that appears on the 'best time to go' postcard appearing throughout the book.

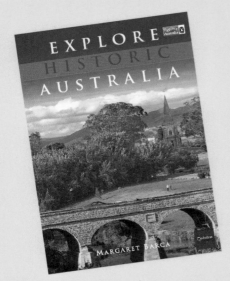

Discover Australia's past

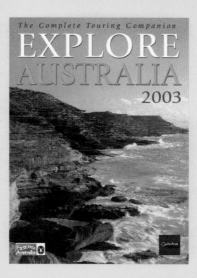

Australia's premier travel book

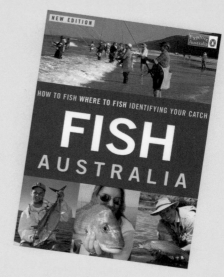

The ultimate guide to fishing

Touring companions for
Victoria, Tasmania, Queensland and
New South Wales

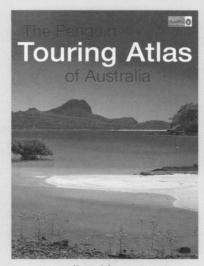

Australia-wide coverage
in large format

Coastal and inland fishing in
New South Wales, Victoria and
Queensland

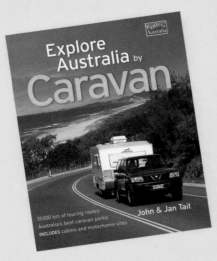

Exciting new publication

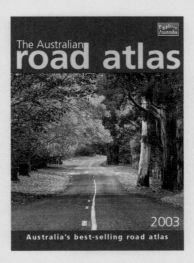

Updated annually

Sheet maps for all states,
territories and capital cities

Explore Australia GUIDES MAPS ATLASES

Accident Action – Feel Confident with St John First Aid

It is reassuring to know that you have the simple skills to preserve life if, at any moment, you are confronted with an emergency.

Priorities at an Accident Site

In dealing with the casualties of an accident, the St John DRABC Action Plan remains the first priority. However, an accident brings in other factors that have to be considered. The following guidelines will help:

Hazards:

- Make sure everyone at accident site is protected, by safely parking your car and putting hazard lights on
- Light up a night accident scene with headlights
- Assess scene for other dangers and remove if possible
- Move casualty from danger if this is more appropriate (e.g. if there is a fire).

Assessment:

Make a rapid assessment of:
- How many casualties
- Severity of injuries
- Any dangerous circumstances to report
- Whether anyone is trapped

Ensure all occupants of cars are accounted for.

Help:

- Call 000 for an ambulance and police
- Consider need to call other services (e.g. fire brigade, electricity authority).

Follow the remainder of the St John DRABC Action Plan to manage casualties.

St John DRABC Action Plan

This Action Plan is a vital aid to the first aider in assessing whether the casualty has any life-threatening conditions and if any immediate first aid is necessary.

D - check for Danger

- to you
- to others
- to casualty

R - check Response

- is casualty conscious?
- is casualty unconscious?
  If not responsive, turn casualty into the recovery position and **ring 000 for an ambulance.**

A - check Airway

- is airway clear of objects?
- is airway open?

B - check for Breathing

- is chest rising and falling?
- can you hear casualty's breathing?
- can you feel the breath on your cheek?

C - check for signs of Circulation

- can you see any movement including swallowing or breathing?
- can you see any obvious signs of life?
- can you feel a pulse?

In any life-threatening situation, ring 000 for an ambulance. If possible, ask someone to do this for you so that you can stay with the casualty.

Learn St John First Aid